FARM HOLIDAY
BUREAU

Stay on a farm

GW00721909

JARROLD
PUBLISHING

Northern Ireland
Tourist Board

SCOTLAND

English Tourism Council

BWRDD CROESO CYMRU
WALES TOURIST BOARD

1/99
Published by Jarrold Publishing, Whitefriars,
Norwich NR3 1TR
in association with the Farm Holiday Bureau (UK) Ltd,
the English Tourism Council and the National Tourist
Boards of Scotland, Wales and Northern Ireland
© Farm Holiday Bureau (UK) Ltd 1999
National Agricultural Centre, Stoneleigh Park,
Warwickshire CV8 2LZ

ISBN 0 7117 1092 9

The information contained in this Guide has been
published in good faith on the basis of the details
submitted by the proprietors of the premises listed. These
proprietors are current members or associates of the
Farm Holiday Bureau (UK) Ltd and have paid for their
entries in this Guide. Whilst every effort has been made
to ensure accuracy in this publication, neither the
publisher, the Farm Holiday Bureau (UK) Ltd, the English
Tourist Board, the National Tourist Boards of Scotland,
Wales and Northern Ireland nor their agents can
guarantee the accuracy of the information in this Guide
and accept no responsibility for any error or
misrepresentation. All liability for loss, disappointment,
negligence or other damage caused by reliance on the
information contained in this Guide, or in the event of
bankruptcy, or liquidation, or cessation of trade of any
company, individual or firm mentioned is hereby
excluded.

The Farm Holiday Bureau (UK) Ltd gratefully
acknowledges the continuing assistance and advice
offered by the English Tourism Council and the National
Tourist Boards, the Farming and Rural Conservation
Agency (FRCA) of the Ministry of Agriculture, the
Scottish Agricultural Organisations Society Ltd, and all
those who seek to maintain a balance in the rural
community.

Produced for the English Tourism Council and the
National Tourist Boards by The Pen & Ink Book
Company Limited, Huntingdon, Cambridgeshire.

Front cover photograph by David Hobart Photography

Printed and bound in Great Britain.

Contents

elcome to the Farm Holiday Bureau

nk you for choosing to stay on a farm. The m Holiday Bureau is a network of over ,000 farming families, throughout the United Kingdom, that provide value for money, good food and a warm welcome in quality assured bed and breakfast and self-catering accommodation. All the farms are of a high standard and have been quality assessed under national grading schemes.

Staying on a farm does not mean *working* there (as it does in some countries), though you may be able to help out on some farms if you wish. Many farms also offer activities for all ages, from waymarked walks to riding and fishing, and most farms now also cater for business people and small meetings. By staying on a farm you can be assured of an extra-special welcome to the countryside from the people who know it best.

Enjoy your stay on a farm – the best welcome to the British countryside

For overseas visitors

Overseas visitors can book directly with the farm or through our appointed agent, *Host and Guest Service*. As well as being an easy and convenient way of booking, they can offer itineraries linking several farms. Contact:

Host and Guest Service, 103 Dawes Road, London SW6 7DU
Tel: 020 7385 9922 Fax: 020 7386 7575
E-mail: farm@host-guest.co.uk
Internet: http//www.host-guest.co.uk

If you are telephoning from outside the UK, precede all telephone numbers with 44 and delete the first 0 – for example 020 7385 9922 becomes 44 20 7385 9922.

Bienvenue au Farm Holiday Bureau

Merci d'avoir choisi de faire un séjour à la ferme. Le Farm Holiday Bureau est un réseau de plus de 1000 familles d'agriculteurs, partout au Royaume-Uni, qui proposent des formules économiques, une bonne table et un accueil chaleureux, soit en chambre d'hôtes soit en locations de vacances de qualité assurée. Toutes les fermes sont de grande qualité, car elles ont été inspectées et classées dans le cadre de programmes nationaux.

Faire un séjour à la ferme ne signifie pas que vous allez *travailler* à la ferme (comme c'est le cas dans certains pays), mais si vous le voulez, vous pourrez peut-être aider certains agriculteurs. Beaucoup de fermes proposent aussi des activités pour tous les âges, qu'il s'agisse de circuits fléchés, d'équitation ou de pêche. La plupart des fermes accueillent aussi désormais les hommes et femmes d'affaires et peuvent organiser de petites réunions. En faisant un séjour à la ferme, vous savez que vous pouvez compter sur un accueil particulièrement chaleureux dans la campagne britannique, assuré par ceux qui la connaissent le mieux.

Appréciez votre séjour à la ferme – le meilleur accueil dans la campagne britannique

Touristes étrangers

Les touristes étrangers peuvent réserver directement à la ferme ou par l'intermédiaire de notre agence agréée, *Host and Guest Service*. C'est un moyen pratique de réserver, et cette agence vous proposera aussi des itinéraires qui combinent un séjour dans plusieurs fermes. Contacter:

Host and Guest Service, 103 Dawes Road, London SW6 7DU
Tél: 020 7385 9922 Fax: 020 7386 7575
E-mail: farm@host-guest.co.uk
Internet: http//www.host-guest.co.uk

Si vous téléphonez depuis un pays autre que le Royaume-Uni, ajoutez le 44 devant le numéro et supprimez le premier 0. Par exemple, pour obtenir le 020 7385 9922, composez le 44 20 7385 9922.

Willkommen beim Farm Holiday Bureau

Wir freuen uns, daß Sie sich für Ferien auf dem Bauernhof entschieden haben. Dem Farm Holiday Bureau sind über 1000 Bauernfamilien in ganz Großbritannien angeschlossen, die Ihnen gutes Essen, eine herzliche Aufnahme und Übernachtung und Frühstück sowie Unterkünfte für Selbstversorger bieten, wobei Ihnen Qualität sicher ist und das Preis-Leistungsverhältnis stimmt. Alle Bauernhöfe entsprechen einem hohen Niveau und wurden gemäß nationaler Einstufungskriterien nach Qualität beurteilt.

Ferien auf dem Bauernhof bedeuten keine *Arbeit* (wie das in manchen Ländern der Fall ist), allerdings können Sie auf einigen Bauernhöfen durchaus mitanpacken, wenn Sie das möchten. Viele Bauernhöfe bieten außerdem Unternehmungen für alle Altersstufen an, angefangen von beschilderten Wanderwegen bis hin zum Reiten und Angeln. Die meisten Bauernhöfe weisen inzwischen auch Einrichtungen für Geschäftsleute und kleine Konferenzen auf. Wenn Sie sich für den Aufenthalt auf einem Bauernhof entscheiden, können Sie sich sicher sein, daß Sie auf dem Land von den Menschen, die es am besten kennen, besonders herzlich aufgenommen werden.

Genießen Sie Ihren Aufenthalt auf einem Bauernhof – so lernen Sie die britische Landschaft am besten kennen

Für Besucher aus dem Ausland

Besucher aus dem Ausland können ihren Aufenthalt direkt beim betreffenden Bauernhof oder über unseren Partner *Host and Guest Service* buchen. Dort bietet man Ihnen nicht nur einen reibungslosen Reservierungsdienst, sondern stellt Ihnen auch gerne Reiserouten zu mehreren Bauernhöfen zusammen. Ansprechpartner:

Host and Guest Service, 103 Dawes Road, London SW6 7DU
Tel: 020 7385 9922 Fax: 020 7386 7575
E-Mail: farm@host-guest.co.uk
Im Internet: http//www.host-guest.co.uk

Wenn Sie von außerhalb Großbritanniens anrufen, müssen Sie die Vorwahl 44 wählen und die erste 0 weglassen. Zum Beispiel: anstatt 020 7385 9922 wählen Sie 44 20 7385 9922.

Farm Holiday Bureau (UK) Ltd
National Agricultural Centre
Stoneleigh Park
Warwickshire
CV8 2LZ

☎ 024 7669 6909
Fax: 024 7669 6630
E-mail: admin@fhbaccom.demon.co.uk
http://www.webscape.co.uk/farmaccom/

w to use this guide

farm listings

the farms in *Stay on a farm* are members or associates of the Farm Holiday Bureau (FHB). They are easy to find, listed under counties or tourism areas within one of seven main sections covering Scotland, England, Wales and Northern Ireland. This year, some farms have also paid for full colour advertisements which can be found on pages 31–48.

Browse the comprehensive UK maps (pages 15–30) for ideas of places to visit, then turn to the Where to go maps on pages 8–10 to find the key to the appropriate section.

Each of the seven main sections is introduced with a key map and index directing you to those counties/tourism areas that contain farm entries. County/tourism area sections open with a description of the area covered and an outline map showing the location of each farm. Farms are then listed alphabetically by type of accommodation: Bed and Breakfast, Self-Catering, Camping & Caravanning and/or Bunkhouses/Camping Barns. Each illustrated farm entry clearly sets out the information about the farm, its accommodation and facilities (see example entry below).

FHB Group contacts
All the farms listed here belong to one of 91 FHB Groups. The local FHB Group contacts listed on pages 392–395 will be pleased to help you find a vacancy in your chosen area.

Index to farms
The comprehensive index on pages 399–428 lists all the farms in this guide under the appropriate country and county/tourism area. As well as giving the page number for each farm, it indicates those farms that:

- offer access to disabled visitors (see page 13 for explanation of symbol)
- offer camping/caravanning facilities
- are working farms (and also those that welcome safe participation by guests)
- offer stabling/grazing for guests' horses
- offer en suite facilities
- welcome business people (with meeting room capacity where provided)
- accept *Stay on a farm* gift tokens (see opposite).

Making your booking

All you have to do is telephone or write to the farm of your choice and remember:

- First, please mention this guide.
- State your planned arrival and departure dates.
- State the exact number in your party or family, including children.
- State the accommodation needed and any particular requirements, eg twin beds, family room, private bath, ground floor, cot.

EXAMPLE ONLY

❶ **Honeybrook Farm**, Ramswood, Nr Swindon, Wiltshire SN12 3RT

❷ *Mrs Jill Whitehead*
❸ ☎/Fax 01552 224553
❹ BB From £22–£25
❺ Sleeps 6
❻ ☺ ♿ 🐎 ✂ 🌲 💼 ◎
❼ ♦♦♦♦ Silver Award

❽ Honeybrook Farm is a Grade II listed building in an idyllic rural setting just one mile from the pretty village of Ramswood. Small, family-run farm with dairy cows and sheep. All bedrooms en suite with colour TV and hospitality tray. We offer a warm, friendly welcome and delicious breakfasts using local produce, served in our conservatory. Open Mar-Dec. See colour ad on
❾ page 00.

Key
❶ Farm name and address
❷ Contact name
❸ Telephone and fax number
❹ Prices
❺ Number of bed spaces
❻ Facilities symbols (see pages 13–14)
❼ Accommodation symbol/award (see pages 11–13)
❽ Description (provided by owner)
❾ Cross-reference to colour advertisement

- Specify the terms required, eg B&B, evening meal, etc and check meal times.
- State special requirements, eg special diets, facilities for disabled people, arrangements for children, dogs, horses.
- Check prices and what they include and also any reductions that may be offered.
- When booking self-catering accommodation, it is advisable to find out whether linen or gas, electricity and telephone charges are included.
- Check the required method and date of payment.
- Check whether a deposit is payable and, if so, what charges will apply if the booking is cancelled (see 'Cancellations').
- Check whether B&B access is restricted through the day. (If there is free access to the farm, please ensure that children are always well supervised.)
- Check the best time to arrive and what time you must leave by.
- Ask for directions to the farm.
- Give your name, address and telephone number.

NB We recommend that, time permitting, all telephone bookings are confirmed in writing, specifying exactly what you have booked and the price you expect to pay.

Cancellations
Once a booking has been agreed, on the telephone or letter, a legally binding contract has been made with the host. If you cancel a reservation, fail to take up the accommodation or leave prematurely (regardless of the reasons), the host may be entitled to compensation if it cannot be relet for all or a good part of the booked period. If a deposit has been paid it is likely to be forfeited and an additional payment may be demanded.

Insurance
Travel and holiday insurance protection policies can be taken out to safeguard visitors in the event of cancellation or curtailment. Insurance of personal property can also be sought. Hosts cannot accept liability for any loss or damage to visitors' property, however caused. Do make sure that your valuables are covered by your household insurance before you take them away.

Compliments and complaints

Many visitors write to the FHB saying how much they have enjoyed their stay. If you feel that something or someone deserves acknowledgement, please write to the Farm Holiday Bureau (UK) Ltd, National Agricultural Centre, Stoneleigh Park, Warwickshire CV8 2LZ, or ring 024 7669 6909.

If you are dissatisfied, please make your complaint to the host there and then. Please write to the FHB if the host fails to resolve the problem – we shall be happy to help.

here to go

e outline maps show how the guide is divided into seven
n sections covering the countries of Scotland, England,
ales and Northern Ireland. Each section is picked out in a
colour and divided into counties (for England and Northern
Ireland) and tourism areas (for Scotland and Wales).

Counties/tourism areas containing farm entries are listed
alphabetically by section in the coloured panels alongside the
maps. Page numbers are given for easy reference.

For more detail, see the comprehensive UK map section on
pages 15–30.

Shetland Isles

Scotland

Orkney Isles

Western Isles

Highlands

Aberdeen &
Grampian

Angus
& City of
Dundee

Perthshire

Argyll, the
Isles, Loch Lomond,
Stirling & Trossachs

Kingdom
of Fife

Edinburgh &
Lothians

Greater
Glasgow &
Clyde Valley

Scottish
Borders

Ayrshire
& Arran

Dumfries &
Galloway

England

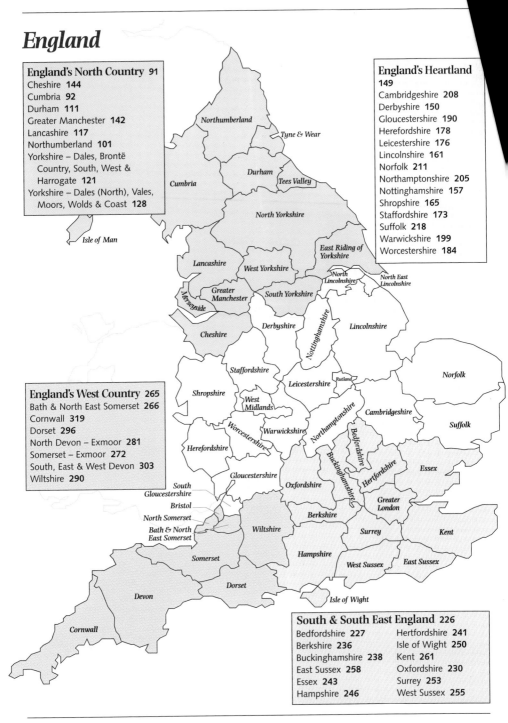

England's North Country 91
Cheshire **144**
Cumbria **92**
Durham **111**
Greater Manchester **142**
Lancashire **117**
Northumberland **101**
Yorkshire – Dales, Brontë
   Country, South, West &
   Harrogate **121**
Yorkshire – Dales (North), Vales,
   Moors, Wolds & Coast **128**

England's Heartland
149
Cambridgeshire **208**
Derbyshire **150**
Gloucestershire **190**
Herefordshire **178**
Leicestershire **176**
Lincolnshire **161**
Norfolk **211**
Northamptonshire **205**
Nottinghamshire **157**
Shropshire **165**
Staffordshire **173**
Suffolk **218**
Warwickshire **199**
Worcestershire **184**

England's West Country 265
Bath & North East Somerset **266**
Cornwall **319**
Dorset **296**
North Devon – Exmoor **281**
Somerset – Exmoor **272**
South, East & West Devon **303**
Wiltshire **290**

South & South East England 226
Bedfordshire **227**   Hertfordshire **241**
Berkshire **236**   Isle of Wight **250**
Buckinghamshire **238**   Kent **261**
East Sussex **258**   Oxfordshire **230**
Essex **243**   Surrey **253**
Hampshire **246**   West Sussex **255**

ales

Northern Ireland

Quality assured accommodation

FHB standards

Farm Holiday Bureau members are inspected by their appropriate group to ensure that a high standard of cleanliness, courtesy and service is maintained. All members must also be inspected by their National Tourist Organisation and agree to meet its Minimum Standards and observe its Code of Conduct.

FHB members and associates

Most of the farms listed in this guide are full **members** of the Farm Holiday Bureau. They belong to local groups that share information and best practice and help to raise quality standards to the highest level. **Associates** are not members of local groups and may only recently have joined the Bureau. They are identified by the word 'Associate' in their guide entry and may become full members in due course.

Accommodation symbols and awards

Each National Tourist Organisation operates its own classification/assessment/grading schemes for serviced accommodation and self-catering properties. Different symbols are used for different schemes, and these are explained in the following pages. This year the English Tourism Council is launching a new Diamond Scheme for guest accommodation.

Accommodation symbols and awards are shown in each farm entry. Any farm that is awaiting inspection by its National Tourist Organisation at the time of going to press will have the word 'Applied' in place of a symbol or award.

Scotland

Serviced and self-catering accommodation
The Scottish Tourist Board has introduced a new Star Scheme for both serviced and self-catering accommodation where the Star award is determined by quality, not by the size of the accommodation or the range of facilities.

For self-catering accommodation, the quality standard of the fabric, furnishings, decor, equipment and ambience of the property result in the Star awards. For serviced accommodation, the award also takes account of the welcome and service, the food and the hospitality. Awards range from **1–5 Stars**:

★	Fair and acceptable
★★	Good
★★★	Very good
★★★★	Excellent
★★★★★	Exceptional, world-class

In ★★★★ and ★★★★★ self-catering properties you will be guaranteed a wider range of equipment.

England

Serviced accommodation
The English Tourism Council has introduced a new Diamond Scheme for guest accommodation. Establishments are rated from **1–5 Diamonds**. The more Diamonds, the higher the quality and the greater the level of customer care.

Some establishments may also have a **Gold** or **Silver Award**. These are also new and are exclusive to the English Tourism Council. The awards are given to establishments that not only achieve the overall quality required for their Diamond rating, but also reach the highest levels of quality in the areas that guests identify as being really important. They will reflect the quality of comfort and cleanliness in the bedrooms and bathrooms and the quality of service to be found throughout the stay.

Farms marked '*Awaiting new rating*' were awaiting a new Quality Assured Diamond rating at the time of going to press. These properties were awarded Crowns under the old English Tourist Board's classification scheme.

Self-catering
Self-catering accommodation is currently classified by the English Tourism Council, according to the range of facilities provided, in a range from **1–5 Keys**:

Holiday homes are also quality graded '**Approved**', '**Commended**', '**Highly Commended**' or '**De Luxe**' alongside the classification symbol.

Unless stated, English farms in this guide are all quality assessed by the English Tourism Council. Under the new harmonised inspection scheme, some Diamond ratings may have been awarded by other organisations, such as the AA. This is shown alongside appropriate ratings.

Wales

Serviced accommodation
The Wales Tourist Board operates a **1–5 Star** grading scheme which is based on quality. Places that score highly will have an especially welcoming atmosphere and pleasing ambience, and high levels of comfort and guest care. All establishments have been visited and checked by the Wales Tourist Board. The Star grades are:

★	Fair to good
★★	Good
★★★	Very good
★★★★	Excellent
★★★★★	Exceptional

It is important to bear in mind that the Star grade takes into account the nature of the property and the expectation of the guests – so a farmhouse is just as entitled to five Stars as a country hotel, as long as what it offers is of the highest quality.

Self-catering
As in previous years, quality standards of holiday homes are graded on a scale of **1–5 Dragons**:

Northern Ireland

All visitor accommodation is inspected annually by the Northern Ireland Tourist Board under a statutory system, and all the farms listed offer a high standard.

Holiday caravan, camping and chalet parks

The National Tourist Organisations operate a common grading scheme, the **British Graded Holiday Parks Scheme**. Parks are visited annually by trained, impartial assessors. A rating of from **1–5 Stars** is awarded, based on the quality of what is provided in terms of service, cleanliness, environment and facilities:

★	Fair and acceptable
★★	Good
★★★	Very good
★★★★	Excellent
★★★★★	Exceptional, world-class

In ★★★★ and ★★★★★ self-catering properties you will be guaranteed a wider range of equipment.

Wheelchair accessibility

All the places that display one of the symbols shown here have been checked by an English Tourism Council, National Tourist Board or Holiday Care Service inspector against standard criteria that reflect the practical needs of wheelchair users. There are three categories of accessibility:

 Category 1:
Accessible to all wheelchair users including those travelling independently

 Category 2:
Accessible to a wheelchair user travelling with a helper

 Category 3:
Accessible to a wheelchair user able to walk short distances and up three steps

Please check at the time of booking if you have special needs.

Inspected accessible schemes have been developed throughout the UK by the English Tourism Council, National Tourist Boards and Tourism for All Consortium in conjunction with the Holiday Care Service. They are designed to provide disabled travellers with reliable information on standards and facilities. Additional help and guidance on finding suitable holiday accommodation for those with special needs can be obtained from the Holiday Care Service on 01293 774535.

Welcome Host

The English Tourism Council and the National Tourist Boards operate a Welcome Host scheme and training programme which places the emphasis on warm hospitality and first-class service. Recipients of the Welcome Host certificate or badge are part of a fine tradition – a tradition of friendliness.

Look for these symbols to find those farm entries participating in the Welcome Host scheme.

 Scotland

 England

 Wales

 Northern Ireland

Wales Farmhouse Award

The Farmhouse Award is given to proprietors who have successfully completed an approved course in farm-based tourism or guest house management, together with the Welcome Host Manager course. A higher level of customer care can be expected.

Key to facilities symbols

Symbol	Explanation	French	German
𝅉	Wheelchair accessibility category (see page 13)	Symbole d'accessibilité aux fauteuils roulants	Zeichen der Zugänglichkeit für Rollstuhlfahrer
⏃(3)	Children welcome (minimum age)	Enfants bienvenus (âge minimum)	Kinder willkommen (Mindestalter)
🐕	Dogs by arrangement	Chiens autorisés sous réserve d'accord préalable	Hunde nach Vereinbarung
⚲	No smoking	Non fumeurs de préférence	Nichtraucher bevorzugt
💳	Credit cards accepted	Cartes de crédit acceptées	Kreditkarten werden akzeptiert
💼	Business people welcome	Facilités pour hommes et femmes d'affaires	Geschäftsreisende willkommen
🌲	Waymarked walks on farm	Itinéraires fléchés sur la propriété de la ferme	Wanderwege gezeichnet
🗣	Foreign language(s) spoken	Langue(s) étrangère(s) parlée(s)	Hier werden Fremdsprachen gesprochen
🐎	Riding on farm	Randonnée à poney ou équitation à la ferme	Reiten auf Ponys oder Pferden
🎣	Fishing on farm	Pêche à la ferme	Angeln
ⓒⓗ	Country house, not a working farm	Manoir (non pas ferme en exploitation)	Landhaus, kein aktiver Bauernhof
⛺	Camping facilities	Camping	Camping – Einrichtungen
🚐	Caravanning facilities	Caravaning	Caravan – Einrichtungen
◉	Welcome Host certificate holder (see page 13)	Détenteur du certificat 'Welcome Host'	Absolventen der 'Welcome Host'

Symbol	Prices	Prix	Preise
BB	Price per person per night for bed and breakfast	Prix par personne par nuit pour chambre + petit déjeuner	Preis pro Person pro Nacht für Bett und Frühstück
EM	Price per person for evening meal	Prix par personne pour repas du soir	Preis pro Person für Abendessen
SC	Price per unit per week self-catering	Prix par location par semaine	Preis pro Einheit pro Woche bei Selbstversorgung
Tents	Price per tent pitch per night	Prix par emplacement de tente par nuit	Preis pro Zeltaufstellung pro Nacht
Caravans	Price per caravan pitch per night	Prix par emplacement de caravane par nuit	Preis pro Caravanaufstellung pro Nacht
Bunkhouses/ Camping Barns	Price per person per night	Gîtes d'étape/Refuges – Prix par personne par nuit	Übernachtungs-/ Camping-Hütte – Preis pro Person pro Nacht

All prices include VAT and service charge if any.

TVA et service compris dans le prix

Alle Preise inklusive MWSt und Bedienungsgeld, wenn überhaupt

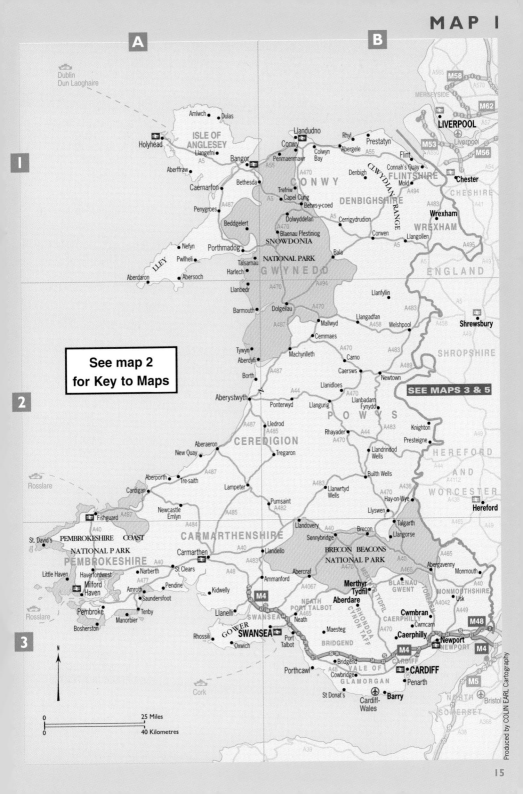

MAP I

See map 2
for Key to Maps

SEE MAPS 3 & 5

Produced by COLIN EARL Cartography

MAP 2

A **B**

1

2

3

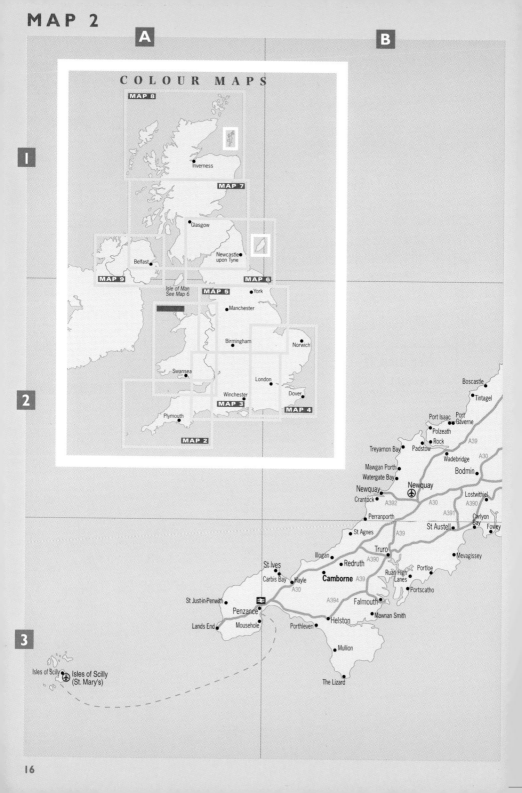

COLOUR MAPS

MAP 8

Inverness

MAP 7

Glasgow

Newcastle
upon Tyne

Belfast

MAP 9

Isle of Man
See Map 6

MAP 6

MAP 5

York

Manchester

Birmingham

Norwich

Swansea

London

Winchester

Dover

MAP 3

MAP 4

Plymouth

MAP 2

Boscastle

Tintagel

Port Isaac Port
Gaverne

Polzeath

Treyarnon Bay Rock
Padstow

A39

Mawgan Porth Wadebridge

A30

Watergate Bay

Bodmin

Newquay Newquay

Crantock

Lostwithiel

A392 A30 A390

Perranporth

A391 Carlyon
Bay

St Agnes

St Austell Fowey

Truro

Mevagissey

Illogan A390

St Ives Redruth

Portloe

Ruan High
Carbis Bay Hayle Camborne A39 Lanes

Portscatho

A30

St Just-in-Penwith A394 Falmouth

Penzance Helston Mawnan Smith

Lands End Mousehole Porthleven

Mullion

Isles of Scilly Isles of Scilly
(St. Mary's)

The Lizard

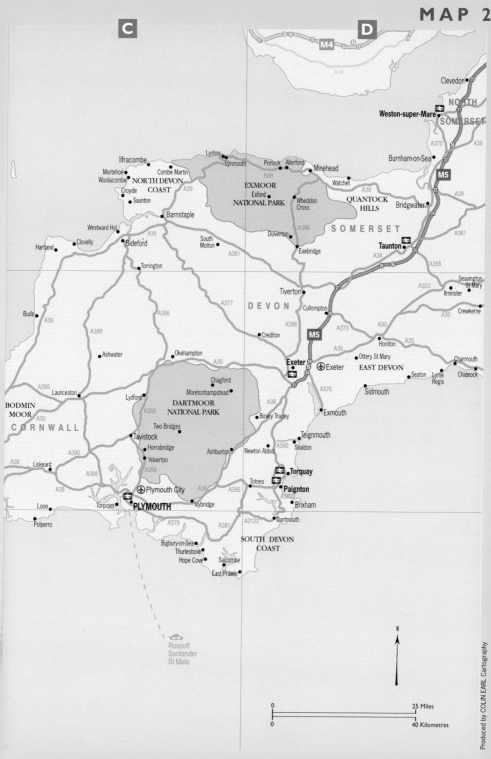

MAP 2

C D

M4

Clevedon

NORTH
Weston-super-Mare SOMERSET

Burnham-on-Sea

M5

Lynton
Lynmouth Porlock Allerford
Ilfracombe Minehead
Combe Martin Watchet
Mortehoe NORTH DEVON Wheddon A39
Woolacombe COAST Exford Cross QUANTOCK
Croyde EXMOOR HILLS Bridgwater
Saunton NATIONAL PARK
A39 Dulverton SOMERSET
Barnstaple Exebridge A361
Westward Ho! A39 South A396 Taunton
Hartland Clovelly Molton A358
Bideford A361 A38 Seavington
Torrington St Mary
Tiverton DEVON A303 Ilminster
Bude Cullompton A30 Crewkerne
A39 A386 A396 A30
A388 Crediton M5 A373 Honiton A35
Ashwater Okehampton A30 Charmouth
Launceston A30 Exeter Ottery St Mary Seaton Lyme Chideock
Chagford EAST DEVON Regis
BODMIN Lydford Moretonhampstead Exeter A376 Sidmouth
MOOR DARTMOOR A38
CORNWALL A30 NATIONAL PARK Bovey Tracey Exmouth
Two Bridges Teignmouth
A390 Tavistock A380 Shaldon
A38 Liskeard Horrabridge Ashburton Newton Abbot
Yelverton Torquay
A386 Totnes Paignton
Looe Plymouth City A38 A385 A3022 Brixham
PLYMOUTH Ivybridge Dartmouth
Torpoint
Polperro A379 A381 A3122
Bigbury-on-Sea SOUTH DEVON
Thurlestone COAST
Hope Cove Salcombe
East Prawle

Roscoff
Santander
St Malo

N

0 25 Miles
0 40 Kilometres

Produced by COLIN EARL Cartography

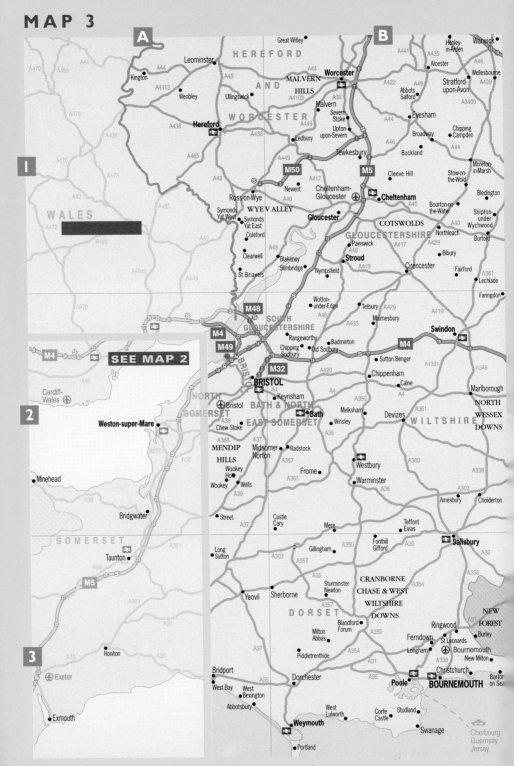

MAP 3

A   B

1

WALES

SEE MAP 2

2

3

18

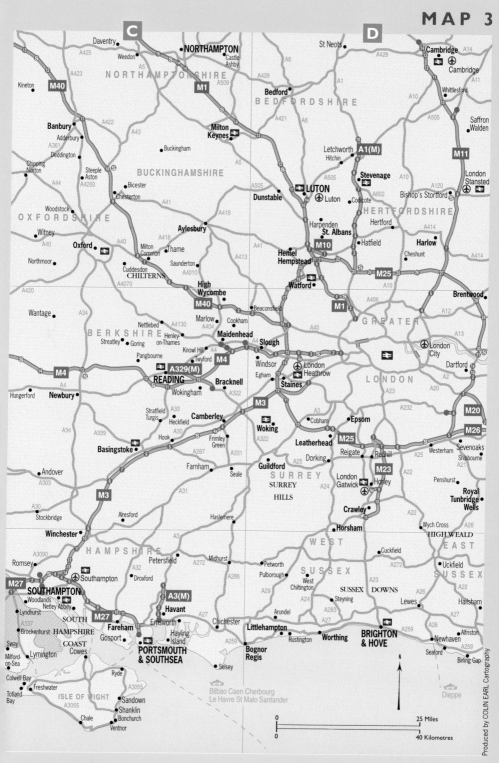

MAP 3

C   D

Daventry
Weedon
Castle Ashby
St Neots
Cambridge
Cambridge
A14
NORTHAMPTON
A425
A423
A5
A509
M1
A6
A428
A11
Whittlesford
M40
NORTHAMPTONSHIRE
A428
A1
A10
Saffron Walden
Kineton
Bedford
A505
BEDFORDSHIRE
M11
Banbury
A422
A421
A6
London Stansted
Adderbury
Milton Keynes
A361
Letchworth
A1(M)
Deddington
Buckingham
Hitchin
Stevenage
Bishop's Stortford
Chipping Norton
Steeple Aston
Bicester
A5
Dunstable
Luton
Codicote
A602
HERTFORDSHIRE
A44
A4260
Chesterton
BUCKINGHAMSHIRE
A505
LUTON
Luton
A505
Harlow
Woodstock
A41
A418
St. Albans
Hertford
A414
Cheshunt
Witney
Aylesbury
Milton Common
Thame
A413
Harpenden
Hatfield
A414
A40
Oxford
A40
Saunderton
Hemel Hempstead
M10
Northmoor
Cuddesdon
A4010
CHILTERNS
A41
Watford
M25
A420
A4070
High Wycombe
Beaconsfield
A10
Brentwood
Wantage
A34
M40
Marlow
Cookham
A406
GREATER
A12
Nettlebed
A404
Maidenhead
A40
A13
BERKSHIRE
Henley-on-Thames
Knowl Hill
Slough
London City
Streatley
Goring
Twyford
M4
Windsor
London Heathrow
Dartford
Pangbourne
A329(M)
Bracknell
Egham
A2
M4
A4
READING
Wokingham
Staines
LONDON
A20
Hungerford
Newbury
A322
M3
A23
Stratfield Turgis
Camberley
Cobham
Epsom
M20
Heckfield
Woking
A232
A30
Leatherhead
M25
M26
Hook
Frimley Green
A322
Dorking
Reigate
Redhill
Westerham
Sevenoaks
Basingstoke
A287
A331
Guildford
A25
M23
A22
Shipbourne
A21
Andover
Farnham
Seale
SURREY
A24
London Gatwick
Horley
Penshurst
A303
A31
SURREY HILLS
Royal Tunbridge Wells
M3
Alresford
Haslemere
Crawley
A22
A26
Stockbridge
Horsham
Wych Cross
HIGH WEALD
Winchester
HAMPSHIRE
Petersfield
Midhurst
WEST
Cuckfield
Uckfield
EAST
Romsey
A3090
A32
A272
Petworth
A286
SUSSEX
A272
SUSSEX
A287
Droxford
Pulborough
West Chiltington
A23
SOUTHAMPTON
Southampton
A29
SUSSEX DOWNS
Lewes
A22
Woodlands
Netley Abbey
A3(M)
Steyning
A26
Hailsham
Lyndhurst
M27
Havant
A27
Arundel
A24
A283
A27
Sway
Brockenhurst
Fareham
Emsworth
Chichester
Littlehampton
Alfriston
Milford-on-Sea
Lymington
Gosport
Hayling Island
A259
Rustington
Worthing
BRIGHTON & HOVE
A259
Newhaven
Colwell Bay
Cowes
PORTSMOUTH & SOUTHSEA
A259
Bognor Regis
Seaford
Birling Gap
Totland Bay
Freshwater
Ryde
Selsey
Dieppe
Chale
ISLE OF WIGHT
A3055
Sandown
Bilbao Caen Cherbourg
Le Havre St Malo Santander
N
Shanklin
Bonchurch
Ventnor

0   25 Miles
0   40 Kilometres

Produced by COLIN EARL Cartography

MAP 4

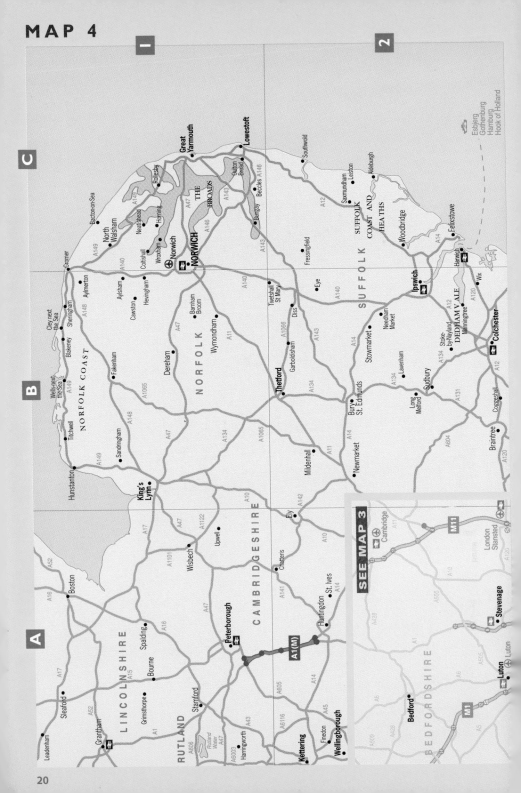

1   **2**

C   **B**   **A**

Great Yarmouth
Lowestoft
Southwold
Hemsby
Rollesby
Gorton Broad
Beccles
A146
THE BROADS
A143
Aldeburgh
Leiston
Saxmundham
A12
SUFFOLK COAST AND HEATHS
Bacton-on-Sea
North Walsham
A149
A140
Neatishead
Horning
A47
A146
Bungay
Fressingfield
Woodbridge
A14
Felixstowe
Cromer
Cottshall
Wroxham
Norwich
NORWICH
A143
SUFFOLK
Harwich
Wix
A120
Aylmerton
A148
Aylsham
Hevingham
A140
A47
Barnham Broom
Tivetshall St Mary
Diss
Eye
A140
Ipswich
A12
DEDHAM VALE
Manningtree
Colchester
A12
Cley next the Sea
Sheringham
Cawston
A47
Wymondham
A11
A143
A14
Stoke-by-Nayland
A134
Wellsnext-the-Sea
Blakeney
A149
Fakenham
Dereham
NORFOLK
Garboldisham
A1066
Stowmarket
Needham Market
Laver ham
A134
Sudbury
A131
Coggeshall
NORFOLK COAST
A1065
A148
A134
Thetford
A134
Bury St. Edmunds
A14
Long Melford
A804
Braintree
A120
Titchwell
Sandringham
A47
A1065
Mildenhall
A11
Newmarket
A14
Hunstanton
A149
A134
King's Lynn
A10
Ely
A142
CAMBRIDGESHIRE
A17
A1122
Upwell
Chatteris
A10
Huntingdon
St. Ives
A14
Boston
A16
Wisbech
A1101
A47
Spalding
A16
A141
Peterborough
A1(M)
LINCOLNSHIRE
A15
Bourne
A6121
A605
A45
Finedon
Wellingborough
A52
Sleaford
Grimsthorpe
Stamford
RUTLAND
Rutland Water A47
A6003
Harringworth
A43
Kettering
Leadenham
Grantham
A1

SEE MAP 3
Cambridge
M11
A11
London Stansted
A10
A505
Stevenage
A1
A428
BEDFORDSHIRE
Bedford
A6
M1
A5
Luton
A505
A6
A509
A428

20

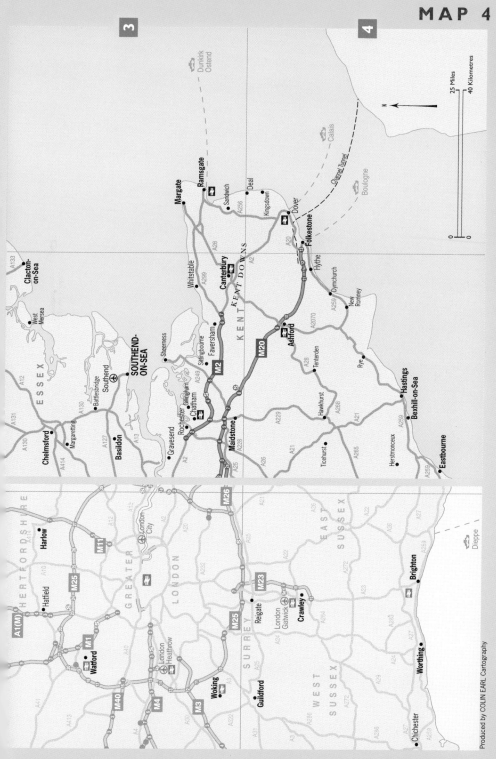

MAP 4

3

4

25 Miles

40 Kilometres

N

Dunkirk
Ostend

Ramsgate

Margate

Sandwich

Deal

A256

Kingsdown

Dover

Calais

Channel Tunnel

Boulogne

Folkestone

A20

Hythe

A2

K E N T   D O W N S

Canterbury

Whitstable

A299

Dymchurch

A259

New Romney

A2070

Ashford

A28

Tenterden

Rye

A28

M20

Faversham

Sittingbourne

A249

Sheerness

SOUTHEND-
ON-SEA

Southend

West
Mersea

Clacton-
on-Sea

A133

E S S E X

A12

A130

Battlesbridge

Basildon

A127

A13

Gravesend

A2

Rochester

Chatham

Gillingham

M2

Maidstone

M20

A228

Margaretting

A131

A414

Chelmsford

A130

A12

Hawkhurst

A268

A229

A21

Hastings

Bexhill-on-Sea

A259

Eastbourne

A259

Herstmonceux

A271

Ticehurst

A265

A21

A26

M26

M25

Harlow

M11

A1(M)

Hatfield

H E R T F O R D S H I R E

A10

London
City

A12

A127

M25

M1

Watford

M40

M4

M3

Woking

Guildford

London
Heathrow

G R E A T E R

L O N D O N

A3

A22

A23

M23

M25

Reigate

Crawley

London
Gatwick

A264

S U R R E Y

W E S T
S U S S E X

E A S T
S U S S E X

Brighton

Worthing

Chichester

Dieppe

A27

A259

A272

A29

A286

A24

A281

A3

Produced by COLIN EARL Cartography

21

MAP 5

MAP 5

C
D

25 Miles
40 Kilometres

N

A19
A64
York York
A59
YORK
A166
Driffield
EAST RIDING
OF
YORKSHIRE
Brandesburton
Hornsea
A614
A1079
Beverley
A64
A19
A614
A1079
A165
KINGSTON
UPON HULL
HULL
A1
Selby
A63
Monk Fryston
A1041 Howden **M62**
A63
A645
Goole
A15
Pontefract
Goole
A614
A1
NORTH
LINCOLNSHIRE
A180
A638
A18
Scunthorpe
A635
Doncaster
M180
Humberside
A1173
Grimsby
NORTH EAST
LINCOLNSHIRE
Rotterdam
Zeebrugge
A614
A46
A18
YORKSHIRE
A630
A1(M)
A159
A631
A631
A15
A16
LINCOLNSHIRE
WOLDS
Louth
A631
Blyth
Gainsborough
A57
A1
A156
A46
Worksop
A60
A614
A57
A158
Horncastle
A60
A1
Lincoln
A158
A46
A15
LINCOLNSHIRE
Skegness
M1
Redditch
Mansfield
A38
Woodhall Spa
A16
A52
NOTTINGHAMSHIRE
South Normanton
A60
A617
A6097
Newark
A52
A16
Boston
SEE MAP 4
A17
A52
NOTTINGHAM
Beeston
Redmile
A52
Grantham
A149
Langar
A453
A606
A15
A17
A46
King's Lynn
stle Donington
Kegworth
A16
East Midlands
A46
Melton
Mowbray
A607
A1
A1104
A47
A10
Loughborough
A6
Quorn
RUTLAND
Stamford
A134
LEICESTERSHIRE
Markfield
Oakham
A47
LEICESTER
Uppingham
Peterborough
M69
A6
Medbourne
A43
CAMBRIDGESHIRE
M1
A6116
A605
M6
A5
Theddingworth
A6
A141
Ely
A142
A1065
A1(M)
gby
Kettering
M45
A4304
NORTHAMPTONSHIRE
A508
A43
A45
A14
Huntingdon
A10

Produced by COLIN EARL Cartography

23

MAP 6

A **B**

1

SCOTLAND

SEE MAP 7

M74

A74(M)

A74(M)

Berwick-upon-Tweed

Holy Island

Crookham

Belford

Wooler

NORTHUMBERLAND

NATIONAL PARK

Rothbury

Otterburn

NORTHUMBERLAND

Kielder Water

Bellingham

Wark

Barrasford

Haltwhistle

Haydon Bridge

Hexham

Corbridge

Langley-on-Tyne

Shotley Bridge

Blanchland

Consett

2

SOLWAY COAST

Carlisle

Carlisle

Brampton

M6

NORTH PENNINES

DURHAM

Ireby

Cockermouth

Bassenthwaite

Bassenthwaite Lake

Mungrisdale

Troutbeck

Penrith

Middleton-in-Teesdale

Workington

Whitehaven

Braithwaite

Keswick

Helton

Ullswater

Shap

Appleby-in-Westmorland

Barnard Castle

Ennerdale

Buttermere

Borrowdale

Cleator

Egremont

CUMBRIA

Grasmere

Orton

Ravenstonedale

Arkengarthdale

3

LAKE DISTRICT

NATIONAL PARK

Langdale

Eskdale

Coniston

Hawkshead

Ambleside

Troutbeck

Windermere

Sawrey

Thwaite

Reeth

Leyburn

Broughton in Furness

Newby Bridge

Crosthwaite

Oxenholme

Kendal

M6

Endmoor

Dent

Hawes

Askrigg

Bainbridge

West Witton

Witherslack

Heversham

Lupton

Sandside

Kirkby Lonsdale

YORKSHIRE DALES

NATIONAL PARK

Ulverston

Cartmel

Grange-over-Sands

ARNSIDE & SILVERDALE

Kettlewell

Barrow-in-Furness

Barrow-in-Furness

Ingleton

Austwick

Grassington

Morecambe

Settle

Malham

Burnsall

Lancaster

24

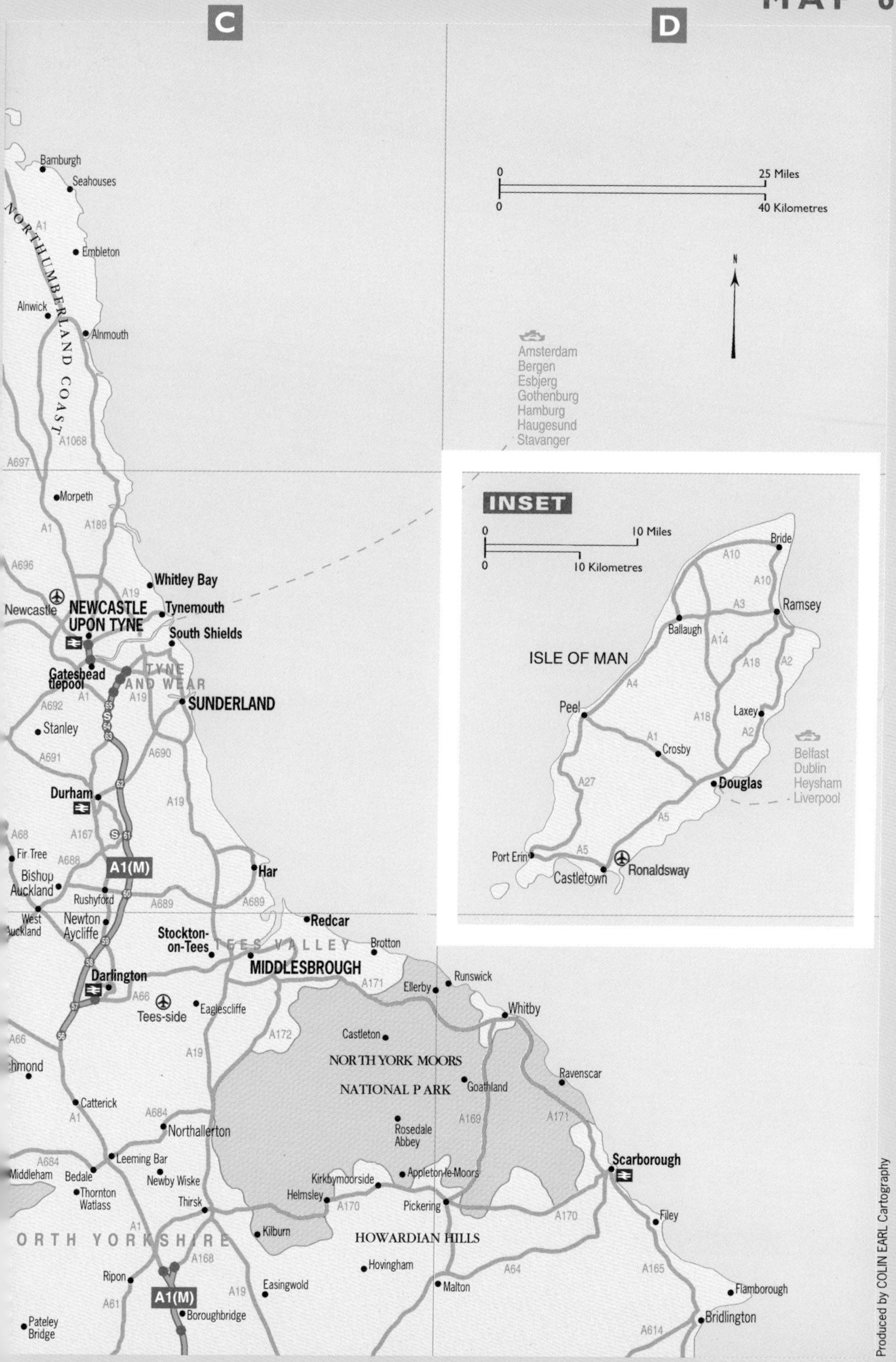

MAP 6

C D

25 Miles
40 Kilometres

N

Amsterdam
Bergen
Esbjerg
Gothenburg
Hamburg
Haugesund
Stavanger

INSET

10 Miles
10 Kilometres

Bamburgh
Seahouses
Embleton
NORTHUMBERLAND COAST
Alnwick
Alnmouth
A1
A1068
A697
Morpeth
A1
A189
A696
Whitley Bay
A19
Newcastle
NEWCASTLE UPON TYNE
Tynemouth
South Shields
Gateshead
tlepool
TYNE AND WEAR
SUNDERLAND
A692
Stanley
A691
A690
Durham
A19
A68
A167
Fir Tree
A688
Bishop Auckland
A1(M)
Rushyford
West Auckland
Newton Aycliffe
A689
A689
Har
Stockton-on-Tees
Redcar
Brotton
TEES VALLEY
MIDDLESBROUGH
Darlington
A66
Tees-side
Eaglescliffe
A171
Ellerby
Runswick
Whitby
A172
Castleton
A66
chmond
A19
NORTH YORK MOORS
NATIONAL PARK
Goathland
Ravenscar
Catterick
A1
A684
Northallerton
A169
A171
A684
Leeming Bar
Middleham
Bedale
Newby Wiske
Rosedale Abbey
Appleton-le-Moors
Thornton Watlass
Kirkbymoorside
Scarborough
Thirsk
Helmsley
A170
Pickering
A170
Filey
Kilburn
A1
HOWARDIAN HILLS
ORTH YORKSHIRE
A168
Hovingham
A64
A165
Ripon
Easingwold
Malton
Flamborough
A61
A1(M)
A19
Bridlington
Pateley Bridge
Boroughbridge
A614

ISLE OF MAN
Bride
A10
A10
Ramsey
A3
Ballaugh
A14
A18
A2
Peel
A4
A18
Laxey
A2
A1
Crosby
A27
A2
Douglas
Belfast
Dublin
Heysham
Liverpool
Port Erin
A5
A5
Castletown
Ronaldsway

Produced by COLIN EARL Cartography

25

MAP 7

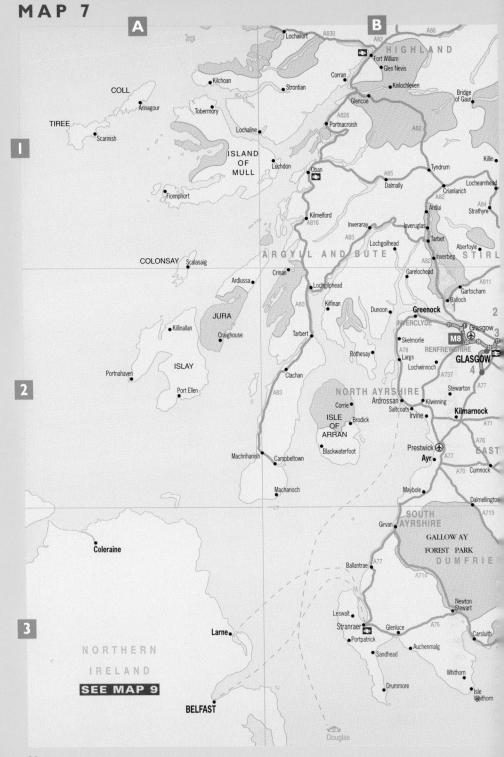

A

B

A830
A82
A86

HIGHLAND

Lochailort

Fort William
Glen Nevis

Kilchoan
Corran
Kinlochleven

Strontian

Bridge
of Gaur

Glencoe

A828

Tobermory

Portnacroish
A82

COLL
Arinagour

Lochaline

TIREE

Scarinish

**ISLAND
OF
MULL**

Lochdon

Killin

A85
Tyndrum

Oban
Dalmally
Lochearnhead

Fionnphort

A82
Crianlarich

Kilmelford
A816
Ardlui
Strathyre
A84

Inveraray
Inveruglas

COLONSAY
Scalasaig

A83
Lochgoilhead
Tarbet

A R G Y L L   A N D   B U T E
Inverbeg
Aberfoyle

Garelochhead
S T I R L

Ardlussa
Crinan
A82

Lochgilphead
A811
Gartocharn

Kilfinan
Balloch

JURA
A83
Dunoon
Greenock
INVERCLYDE
Glasgow

Kilnallan
Tarbert
Skelmorlie
M8
GLASGOW

Craighouse
Rothesay
A78
Largs
RENFREWSHIRE

Clachan
Lochwinnoch

ISLAY
A83
A737

Port Ellen
Stewarton
A77

Portnahaven
NORTH AYRSHIRE

Corrie
Ardrossan
Kilwinning

**ISLE
OF
ARRAN**
Brodick
Saltcoats
Irvine
Kilmarnock

EAST
A71

Blackwaterfoot
A76

Machrihanish
Campbeltown
Prestwick
Ayr
A77

Macharioch
A70
Cumnock

Maybole
Dalmellington

A713

**SOUTH
AYRSHIRE**
Girvan
GALLOWAY

FOREST   PARK

Coleraine
DUMFRIE

Ballantrae
A77
A714

Newton
Stewart

Leswalt
Carsluith

Larne
Stranraer
Glenluce
A75

Portpatrick
Auchenmalg

N O R T H E R N
Sandhead

I R E L A N D
Whithorn

SEE MAP 9
Drummore
Isle
Whithorn

BELFAST

Douglas

I

2

3

MAP 7

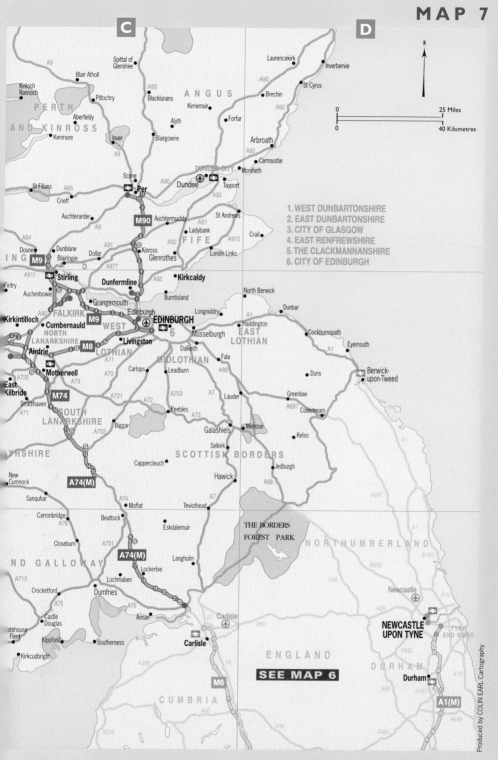

C   D

N

0 ———————— 25 Miles
0 ———————— 40 Kilometres

1. WEST DUNBARTONSHIRE
2. EAST DUNBARTONSHIRE
3. CITY OF GLASGOW
4. EAST RENFREWSHIRE
5. THE CLACKMANNANSHIRE
6. CITY OF EDINBURGH

Spittal of Glenshee
Laurencekirk
Inverbervie
Blair Atholl
Kinloch Rannoch
A9
St Cyrus
Brechin
A90
Pitlochry
Blacklunans
A93
ANGUS
Kirriemuir
Aberfeldy
Alyth
Forfar
A92
PERTH
Kenmore
Inver
Blairgowrie
AND KINROSS
Arbroath
A9
A92
Carnoustie
St Fillans
Scone
Monifieth
Crieff
A85
Per
DUNDEE CITY
Dundee
Tayport
A90
A92
Auchterarder
M90
Auchtermuchty
St Andrews
A91
Ladybank
A84
A9
FIFE
Crail
Doune
A91
A915
Dunblane
Dollar
Kinross
Lundin Links
M9
Blairlogie
Glenrothes
ING
A977
Kirkcaldy
Stirling
A92
AB11
Dunfermline
Burntisland
North Berwick
Fintry
Auchenbowie
Grangemouth
Longniddry
Dunbar
FALKIRK
Edinburgh
A1
A80
M9
EDINBURGH
Haddington
Cockburnspath
Kirkintilloch
WEST
Musselburgh
EAST
Eyemouth
Cumbernauld
6
LOTHIAN
NORTH
M8
Livingston
LOTHIAN
LANARKSHIRE
Dalkeith
Berwick-upon-Tweed
Airdrie
LOTHIAN
Fala
A71
MIDLOTHIAN
Motherwell
A70
Carlops
Leadburn
A86
Duns
A73
East Kilbride
A725
A721
A7
Lauder
A72
Greenlaw
Strathaven
A703
Peebles
A697
Coldstream
M74
SOUTH
A72
A71
LANARKSHIRE
Galashiels
Melrose
Kelso
Biggar
A702
Selkirk
SCOTTISH BORDERS
A1
New Cumnock
Cappercleuch
A74(M)
Jedburgh
AYRSHIRE
Hawick
A68
Sanquhar
Moffat
Teviothead
A7
A897
Carronbridge
Beattock
A76
THE BORDERS
Eskdalemuir
FOREST PARK
NORTHUMBERLAND
A1
Closeburn
A701
A189
ND GALLOWAY
Langholm
A696
A74(M)
Lockerbie
A66
A713
Lochmaben
Crocketford
Dumfries
Newcastle
A19
A75
Annan
A69
Castle Douglas
A75
Carlisle
NEWCASTLE
A7
A69
ENGLAND
UPON TYNE
atehouse Fleet
Kippford
Carlisle
TYNE AND WEAR
Kirkcudbright
Southerness
A392
DURHAM
SEE MAP 6
M6
Durham
A193
A1(M)
CUMBRIA
A66
A167
A66
A596
A69
A688

Produced by COLIN EARL Cartography

MAP 8

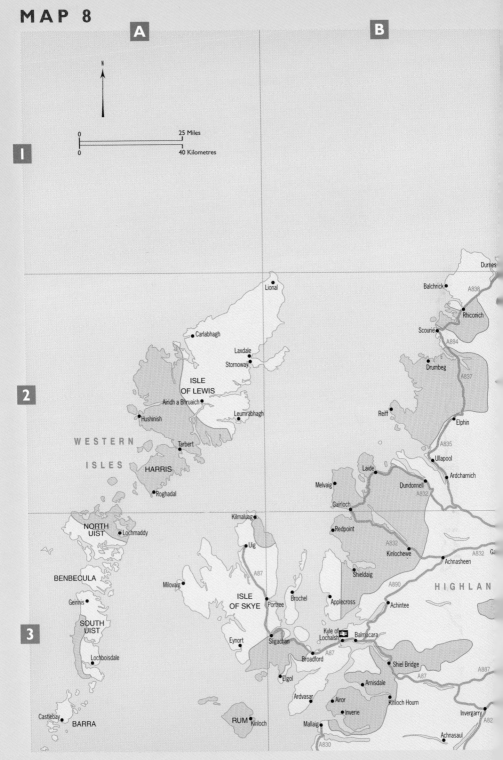

A

B

1

N

| 0 | 25 Miles |
| 0 | 40 Kilometres |

2

3

Durnes

Balchrick

A838

Rhiconich

Scourie

A894

Drumbeg

A837

Lional

Carlabhagh

Laxdale

Stornoway

ISLE
OF LEWIS

Airidh a Bhruaich

Leumrabhagh

Reiff

Elphin

Hushinish

A835

Ullapool

WESTERN

Tarbert

Laide

Ardcharnich

ISLES

HARRIS

Melvaig

Dundonnell

A832

Roghadal

Gairloch

NORTH
UIST

Kilmaluag

Lochmaddy

Redpoint

A832

Kinlochewe

Achnasheen

A832   Ga

Uig

Milovaig

A87

Shieldaig

A890

HIGHLAN

BENBECULA

Geirinis

ISLE
OF SKYE

Brochel

Applecross

Achintee

SOUTH
UIST

Portree

Kyle of
Lochalsh

Balmacara

Eynort

Sligachan

A87

Lochboisdale

Broadford

Shiel Bridge

A87

A887

Elgol

Arnisdale

Ardvasar

Airor

Kinloch Hourn

Inverie

Castlebay

BARRA

RUM

Kinloch

Mallaig

Invergarry

A82

Achnasaul

A830

28

MAP 8

C   D

Pierowall

Broughtown

Brinyan

Twatt

Aith

Sandgarth

ORKNEY

Stromness

Kirkwall

ISLANDS

Rackwick

Hurliness

Burwick

John o'Groats

Portskerra

Thurso   Dunnet

A9

Bettyhill

A836

Halkirk

A838

Tongue

A882

Eriboll

Watten

Wick

Ulbster

A9

A99

Altnaharra

Kinbrace

Latheron

A836

A9

Helmsdale

Lairg

Rogart

Brora

Bonar Bridge

Dornoch

Portmahomack

Tain

Boath

A9   Nigg

Burghead

Evanton   Invergordon

Cromarty

Elgin

Dingwall

Fochabers

Cullen   Portsoy   Rosehearty   Fraserburgh

Contin

Tore

Forres

A96

Banff   A98

A35

Inverness

Nairn

A96

Keith   New Byth

A90

Crimond

Rothes

A941

A95

A952

Mintlaw   Peterhead

Inverness

Aberlour

Huntly

A96

Kirkton of
Culsalmond

A90   Cruden Bay

A82

M O R A Y

A95

Inverurie

Foveran

Drumnadrochit

A9

Tomatin

Grantown-
on-Spey

Kildrummy

Aberdeen

Foyers

A95

Tomintoul

A939

A B E R D E E N S H I R E

CITY OF
ABERDEEN

Invermoriston

Aviemore

Tarland

Aberdeen

Kingussie

Kincraig

A86

Laggan

A9

Braemar

A93

Ballater   Aboyne   A93   Banchory   A90

Muchalls

INSET

SHETLAND

ISLANDS

Baltasound

Tresta

Hillswick

Ulsta

Brae

Walls

Lerwick

0   10 Miles

0   15 Kilometres

Sumburgh

Produced by COLIN EARL Cartography

MAP 9

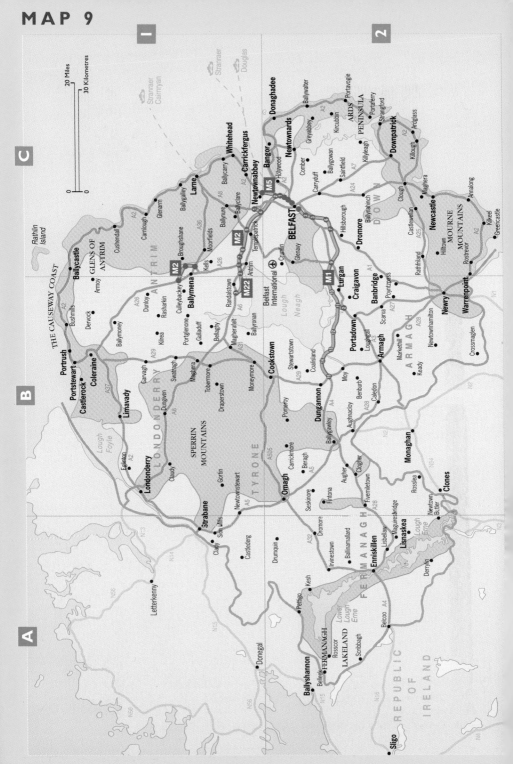

Tarnside Cottages, Cumbria. *See page 100.*

Cornhills, Northumberland. *See page 102.*

Rock Midstead Farmhouse, Northumberland. *See page 105.*

Outchester and Ross Farm Cottages, Northumberland. *See page 110.*

Titlington Hall Farm, Northumberland. *See page 110.*

Romaldkirk Cottages, Durham. *See page 115.*

Laskill Farm Country House, Yorkshire. *See page 133.*

Sunset Cottages, Yorkshire. *See page 140.*

Beeches Farmhouse, Derbyshire. *See page 151.*

Dannah Farm Country House, Derbyshire. *See page 152.*

Shallow Grange, Derbyshire. *See page 153.*

Burton Manor Farm Cottages, Derbyshire. *See page 154.*

Moor Court Farm, Herefordshire. *See page 180*.

Lowerfield Farm, Gloucestershire. *See page 194*.

Colveston Manor, Norfolk. *See page 212.*

Salamanca Farm Guest House, Norfolk. *See page 214.*

Hall Farm, Suffolk. *See page 221.*

Rectory Farm and Rectory Farm Cottages, Oxfordshire. *See pages 233 and 234.*

Burnt House Farm and Leigh Holt, Somerset. *See pages 273 and 279.*

New House Farm, Somerset. *See page 276.*

Wood Advent Farm, Somerset. *See page 277.*

Oxenleaze Farm Caravans, Somerset. *See page 280.*

Combas Farm, North Devon. *See page 282.*

Denham Farm, Barley Cottage and Old Granary, North Devon. *See pages 282 and 285.*

Nethercott Manor Farm, North Devon. *See page 287.*

Buddens Farm, Dorset. *See page 300.*

Hartgrove Farm Cottages, Dorset. *See page 301.*

Pinn Barton Farm, East Devon. *See page 311.*

Tregaddra Farm, Cornwall. *See page 324.*

Tregondale Farm, Cornwall. *See page 325.*

Tresulgan Farm, Cornwall. *See page 326.*

Katie's Cottage, Cornwall. *See page 328.*

Plas y Nant Cottages, Snowdonia. *See page 347.*

Lochmeyler Farm, Pembrokeshire. *See page 366.*

Farm listings

Scotland

Farm entries in this section are listed under those tourism areas shown in green on the key map opposite. The index below gives appropriate page numbers. You will see that we have listed the tourism areas geographically so that you can turn more easily to find farms in neighbouring areas.

At the start of each tourism area section is a detailed map with numbered symbols indicating the location of each farm. Different symbols denote different types of accommodation; see the key below each tourism area map. Farm entries are listed alphabetically under type of accommodation. Some farms offer more than one type of accommodation and therefore have more than one entry.

❶ Shetland Isles
❷ Orkney Isles
❸ Western Isles
❹ Highlands
❺ Aberdeen & Grampian
❻ Argyll, Isles, Loch Lomond, Stirling & Trossachs
❼ Perthshire
❽ Angus & City of Dundee

❾ Kingdom of Fife
❿ Greater Glasgow & Clyde Valley
⓫ Edinburgh & Lothians
⓬ Ayrshire & Arran
⓭ Dumfries & Galloway
⓮ Scottish Borders

KEY MAP TO SCOTLAND

51

Highlands

John O'Groats, Moray Firth, Glen Affric, Loch Ness, Cairngorms, Strathspey & Ben Nevis

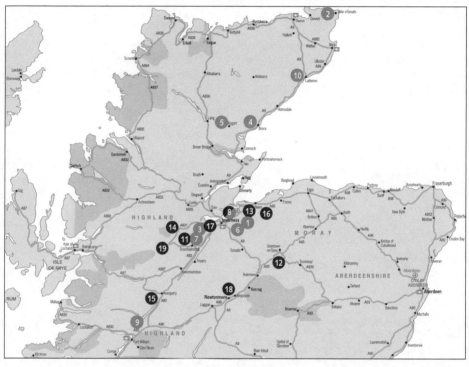

Key

🔵 **1** Bed & Breakfast

🔵 **1** Self-Catering

🔵 **1** B&B and SC

🟦 **1** Camping Barns

🔺 **1** Camping & Caravanning

'Ceud mìle fàilte' – a hundred thousand welcomes – to the Highlands and Islands, nearly 15,000 square miles of unsurpassed scenic beauty in mountains, glens, lochs, lonely sandy beaches and rugged, unspoilt coastline. There is something for everyone here. Enthusiasts of boating, fishing, golf, walking, birdwatching and geology are well catered for. In the land where deer and eagle roam free, wildlife lovers can also observe seals, osprey and otters in their natural habitat. Old castles, battlefield monuments and folk museums testify to a past rich in history, culture and folklore. The traditional Highland welcome is famed throughout the world. Come and try it.

If you would like help in finding suitable farm accommodation, turn to the full listing of FHB Groups on pages 392 to 395 to find appropriate contact details for this area.

Bed and Breakfast
(and evening meal)

Balaggan Farm, Culloden Moor, By Inverness, Inverness-shire IVO2 5EL ①

Mrs Phyllis Alexander
☎/Fax 01463 790213
[BB] From £17
EM From £11
Sleeps 5
⅏(3) ♈ 丸 ▄ W
★★★
BED & BREAKFAST

We offer friendly hospitality at our comfortable traditional-style farmhouse. Enjoy delicious home cooking and log fires in sitting and dining rooms. Tea/coffee-making facilities and electric blankets in bedrooms. Our upland farm is an ideal base for touring with Culloden battlefield and Cawdor Castle close by. Situated 8 miles from Inverness, the Highland capital. Open April–Nov.

Bencorragh House, Upper Gills, Canisbay, By John O'Graots, Caithness KW1 4YB ②

Mrs Sandy Barton
☎/Fax 01955 611449
[BB] From £19–£20
Sleeps 11
⅏(3) ♈ 🄳 W
★★★
BED & BREAKFAST

A warm welcome awaits you at our croft. We have Highland cattle, Jacob sheep, horses, pony and trap, ducks and geese. Panoramic views over the island of Stroma to the Orkney Islands. The garden room is used as a bright and sunny dining room and there is a comfortable TV lounge.

Cherry Trees, Kiltarlity, Beauly, Inverness-shire IV4 7JQ ③

Mrs J Matheson
☎ 01463 741368
[BB] From £15–£19
Sleeps 4
⅍
★★★
BED & BREAKFAST

A warm welcome awaits you on our small stock rearing farm. Choice of breakfasts. Tea and coffee served in the lounge on request. Log fires in lounge and breakfast room. Central heating and electric blankets. Near Loch Ness, fishing and golf. Easy access to the North and West. Open Mar–Nov.

Clynelish Farm, Brora, Sutherland KW9 6LR ④

Mrs J Ballantyne
☎/Fax 01408 621265
[BB] From £20–£25
Sleeps 6
⅏ ♈ ▄ ⅍ W
★★
BED & BREAKFAST

Family-run coastal stock rearing farm of 300-acres with listed house (1865). Secluded location in scenic area with abundant wildlife, including seals and sandy beaches. Distillery, woollen mill, 18-hole links golf course and sea and river fishing. Dunrobin castle, swimming pool, bowls and heritage centres in the locality. Station 1 mile, A9 ½ mile. Open Mar–Nov.

Dalbhioran, 177 Muie, Rogart, Sutherland IV28 3UB ⑤

Mrs A Nicolson
☎ 01408 641345
[BB] From £16–£18
Sleeps 6–7
⅏ ♈ ▄
★
BED & BREAKFAST

Small working croft in the lovely valley of Strathfleet on main A839 road. Good for hill walking, rabbit shooting on croft. Highland cattle nearby. Within easy reach of swimming pool and golf course. Visitors made very welcome. Open June–Oct.

---

6 **Daviot Mains Farm,** Daviot, Nr Inverness, Inverness-shire IV2 5ER

Margaret & Alex Hutcheson
☎ 01463 772215
Fax 01463 772099
BB From £21–£26
EM From £13.50
Sleeps 6
🐴(3) 🐇 ✗ 🖸 🛁 W
★★★★
BED & BREAKFAST

Comfortable early 19th century listed farmhouse in quiet situation near Inverness. Relax in the warm atmosphere of this friendly home where delicious meals are thoughtfully prepared for you (residents' licence). Log fires in sitting and dining rooms. En suite/private facilities. The perfect base for exploring the Scottish Highlands. Selected by "Taste of Scotland", recommended by Elizabeth Gundrey's S.O.T.B.T. and Fodor. Closed Christmas. E-mail: farmhols@globalnet.co.uk

7 **Drumbuie Farm,** Drumbuie, Loch Ness, Drumnadrochit, Inverness-shire IV3 6XP

Mrs Caroline Urquhart
☎ 01456 450634
Fax 01456 450595
BB From £18–£23
Sleeps 6
🐴(12) ✗ 🛏 🖸 🛁 W
★★★★
BED & BREAKFAST

Custom-built farmhouse with en suite accomodation (including four-poster bed) overlooking Loch Ness and surrounding hills. Farm is mostly cattle including several Highland (hairy) cows and calves. Drumnadrochit is the perfect base when visiting the Highlands. Skye, Ullapool and the North all within easy reach. You are assured of a Scottish welcome at Drumbuie. Open all year.

8 **Easter Dalziel Farm,** Dalcross, Inverness, Inverness-shire IV2 7JL

Bob & Margaret Pottie
☎/Fax 01667 462213
BB From £17–£20
EM From £12
Sleeps 6
🐴 🐇 🖸 🕷 🛁 W
★★★★
BED & BREAKFAST

Relax in the traditional style of our lovely early Victorian home. This friendly Scottish farming family offers comfortable guest rooms and delicious home cooking. Set amid farmland with panoramic views, this is the ideal Highland touring base. Locally are Culloden, Cawdor and Fort George. Recommendations include *The Good Guide to Britain*, *The Best Bed and Breakfast* and Fodor. Open all year except Christmas & New Year.

9 **Strone Farm,** By Banavie, Fort William PH33 7PB

Eileen Cameron
☎/Fax 01397 712773
BB From £18–£25
EM From £10
Sleeps 6
🐴(7) 🖸 🛁
★★★
BED & BREAKFAST

A friendly welcome awaits you in our beautiful farmhouse which sits in a rural setting with magnificent panoramic views of Ben Nevis and Caledonian Canal. All double bedrooms tastefully decorated with en suite facilities and hostess tray. Large lounge with woodburning stove. Fresh food well presented. Open Feb–Nov.

10 **Upper Latheron Farm,** Latheron, Caithness KW5 6DT

Mrs Camilla Sinclair
☎ 01593 741224
BB From £17–£19
Sleeps 6
🐴 🐇 ✗ 🛁 🕷 W
★★★★
BED & BREAKFAST

Relax in the romantic Highlands amidst tranquil surroundings and enjoy magnificent coastal scenery from your bedroom windows. Beautifully renovated farmhouse offers high standard of food, comfort and cleanliness. For the energetic there is a wide range of outdoor activities. Enjoy a day trip to Orkney and John O'Groats. Perfect centre for exploring the far North and discovering its exceptional attractions. Open May–Sept.

FARM HOLIDAY BUREAU

Please mention *Stay on a Farm* when booking

Self-Catering

Achmony Holidays, Drumnadrochit, By Loch Ness IV63 6UX

Mrs Elizabeth Mackintosh
☎ **01456 450357**
Fax 01456 450830
SC **From £190–£530**
Sleeps 6
★★★★
SELF CATERING

Enjoy your holiday in an idyllic location above Loch Ness. Each 3 bedroomed chalet bungalow is situated to afford maximum privacy in over 40 acres of silver birch-studded hillside. Central for touring (car essential), Drumnadrochit has several hotels, restaurants, shops, exhibition centres, pony trekking, fishing and boat trips on Loch Ness. Open all year. E-mail: info@achmony.freeserve.co.uk

---

Auchernack Farm, Grantown on Spey, Morayshire PH26 3NH

Mrs E A Smith
☎/Fax **01479 872093**
SC **From £250–£350**
Sleeps 6
★★★
SELF CATERING

Enjoy a relaxing holiday on our dairy farm and stay in our very comfortable farmhouse which is tastefully furnished to a high standard. Ideally situated for touring, visiting famous distilleries, Wild Life Park, RSPB Reserve close by. Landmark Carr Bridge and the famous River Spey for salmon and sea trout fishing is 5 mins' walk from our farrm. Open Mar–Nov.

Balblair Cottages, Balblair, Croy, Inverness IV2 5PH

Mrs Agnes Strachan
☎/Fax **01667 493407**
SC **From £100–£420**
Sleep 2–8
★★★
SELF CATERING

Converted from stone steading to three comfortable cottages, Balblair is an ideal base from which to explore the Highlands. Cawdor Castle, Fort George, Culloden battlefield and Nairn's beaches are all within 6 miles. Each cottage has its own south-facing patio and wood-burning stove. Linen and towels provided. Open all year. E-mail: b.strachan@virgin.net

---

Culligran Cottages, Glen Strathfarrar, Struy, Nr Beauly, Inverness-shire IV4 7JX

Frank & Juliet Spencer-Nairn
☎/Fax **01463 761285**
SC **From £109–£419**
Sleeps 5–7
★★ *up to* ★★★
SELF CATERING

A regular? You soon could be. So don't delay – send for a brochure! This is your opportunity to stay on a deer farm within the beautiful Strathfarrar Nature Reserve. Watch the wild deer from your window and feed the farm deer during a conducted tour. Choice of chalet or cottage. Bikes for hire. Salmon and trout fishing. Hotel and inn nearby. Open late Mar–mid Nov.

Easter Dalziel Farm, Dalcross, Inverness, Inverness-shire IV2 7JL

Bob & Margaret Pottie
☎/Fax **01667 462213**
SC **From £130–£415**
Sleeps 4/6
★★★ *up to* ★★★★
SELF CATERING

Enjoy a relaxing holiday in our cosy, traditional stonebuilt cottages. Between Inverness and Nairn on our stock/arable farm. A truly central location from which to explore the Highlands. The local area offers a wide range of activities to suit the sports-minded, tourer or walker alike. Look out for dolphins, badgers and buzzards, visit Cawdor, Culloden, Fort George and Loch Ness. Short breaks or long stays welcome all year. Brochure. Open all year.

---

15 **Faichemard Farm,** Invergarry, Inverness-shire PH35 4HG

Joan & Duncan Grant
☎ **01809 501314**
[SC] **From £160–£285**
Sleeps 5
☽ ☗
★★
SELF CATERING

Four chalets, all out of sight from each other, on a quiet corner of a working hill farm. A good centre for touring, walking or fishing, or simply relaxing and admiring the magnificent views. Local shop, pubs and restaurant. Please ring for a brochure. Open Apr–Oct.

16 **Laikenbuie Holidays,** Grantown Road, Nairn, Moray Firth IV12 5QN

Thérèse Muskus
☎ **01667 454630**
[SC] **From £100–£472**
Sleeps 6
☖ ☽ ☗ ✕ ☜ [W]
★★★★
SELF CATERING

Watch roe deer and osprey among the abundant wildlife on tranquil organic croft (cows, sheep, hens) with beautiful outlook over trout loch amid natural birch woods. Large warm chalet (quality unbeaten) or residential caravan provide luxury accommodation. Excellent holiday centre, safe for children, low rainfall, plentiful sunshine, sandy beaches and dolphins. Near Loch Ness, Cairngorms, Cawdor Castle. Colour brochure. No smoking inside. Open all year. E-mail: muskus@bigfoot.com

17 **Mains of Aigas,** By Beauly, Inverness-shire IV4 7AD

Mrs Jessie Masheter
☎/Fax **01463 782423**
[SC] **From £160–£425**
Sleep 4/6
☽ ⊞ ☜ ⌂ [W]
Guide dogs only
★★★ *up to* ★★★★
SELF CATERING

Absorb the peace and quiet of this beautiful, unspoilt area. Enjoy special guest rates on our own challenging 9-hole golf course, tour the Highland beauty spots, study the abundant wildlife or simply "stay at home", relax and unwind. Comfortable attractive courtyard house and self-contained apartments. Open Mar–Nov.
E-mail: aigas@cali.co.uk

18 **Strone Cottage,** Croft Holidays, Newtonmore, Inverness-shire PH20 1BA

Mary Mackenzie
☎/Fax **01540 673504**
[SC] **From £180**
Sleeps 6
☽ ☗ ☼ ⌂ [W]
★★★
SELF CATERING

You'll be very welcome at our croft on the outskirts of our lovely Highland village. Cosy renovated cottage has open fire, double glazing and CH. Downstairs en suite bedroom, upstairs 2 bedrooms, bathroom and small drying room. Electricity & coal incl. Enjoy peace and scenery, visit local attractions or take part in varied activities. Central for touring. Edinburgh 2 hours, Loch Ness 1 hour, Aviemore 15 mins. Brochure/special offers. Open all year.
E mail: mmackenzie@sprite.co.uk

19 **Tomich Holidays,** Guisachan Farm, Tomich, by Beauly, Inverness-shire IV4 7LY

Mr & Mrs D J Fraser
☎ **01456 415332**
Fax 01456 415499
[SC] **From £160–£500**
Sleeps 4–6
☽ ☗ ⌂ ☜ ☼ ⊞ [W]
★★★ *up to* ★★★★
SELF CATERING

Our magnificent farm steading houses three luxury cottages and a heated indoor swimming pool. Other accommodation is in spacious chalets set in woodland and a Victorian dairy. All have central heating, hot water and electricity included in the price. Tomich, in the depths of the Highlands near Glen Affric, is an ideal base for walking, touring or just relaxing. Open all year.
E-mail: tomicholidays@zetnet.co.uk

NO ANSWER?
Farmers are mostly out and about during the day.
Try to telephone before 9.30am or after 4pm.

Aberdeen & Grampian

Moray Firth, Spey & Don Valleys, Royal Deeside, Gardenstown & Pennan

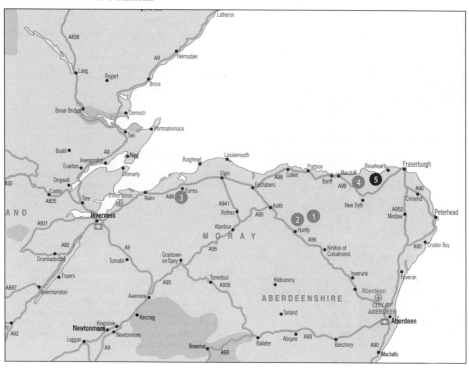

Key

1	Bed & Breakfast
1	Self-Catering
1	B&B and SC
1	Camping Barns
1	Camping & Caravanning

The eagle soaring in the sky over a vastness of magnificent scenery sets the stage for this beautiful part of Scotland. On your travels take in the heather-clad mountains, home of the red deer; the unspoilt north-east where farming and fishing go hand in hand; the long winding rivers of the Spey and Dee; sophisticated Aberdeen, the 'Granite City', and picturesque fishing villages and harbours. Agricultural shows and Highland Games are held throughout the summer. Explore Royal Deeside and follow a Castle, Whisky, Coastal or Victorian Heritage 'Trail', or try one of the many championship golf courses. Come and enjoy a holiday to remember.

If you would like help in finding suitable farm accommodation, turn to the full listing of FHB Groups on pages 392 to 395 to find appropriate contact details for this area.

Bed and Breakfast
(and evening meal)

---

① **Bandora,** Yonder Bognie, Forgue, By Huntly, Aberdeenshire AB54 6BR

Paula Ross
☎ 01466 730375
BB From £16–£18
EM From £8
Sleeps 4
★★★
BED & BREAKFAST

Comfortable accommodation near Huntly on castle and whisky trails. Central heating throughout, residents' lounge with colour TV. En suite bedrooms have electric blankets, colour TV, tea/coffee-making facilities and hairdryers. Food hygiene certificate held. French and Italian spoken. Warm welcome assured. Open all year.

---

② **Haddoch Farm,** By Huntly, Aberdeenshire AB54 4SL

Mrs Alice Jane Morrison
☎ 01466 711217
BB From £14–£16
EM From £10
Sleeps 6
☺(5) ⚕ ▪
★★★
BED & BREAKFAST

Family-run farm situated 15 miles from Moray coast. The town of Huntly has a castle, leisure centre, swimming pool and golf course with forest walks nearby. Enjoy well cooked Scottish fayre in a peaceful location. Excellent view from our 19th century farmhouse.Tastefully decorated, spacious bedrooms in a friendly atmosphere. Ideal touring base. Open Apr–Oct.

---

③ **Milton of Grange Farmhouse,** By Forres, Morayshire IV36 2TR

Mrs Hilda Massie
☎/Fax 01309 676360
BB From £18.50–£25
Sleeps 6
☺ ⚕ ▪ W
★★★★
BED & BREAKFAST

Enjoy a warm welcome with home baking on arrival. Our en suite bedrooms are tastefully furnished to a high standard. Close to Forres and Kinloss, the farm adjoins Findhorn Nature Reserve, popular with bird watchers, while nearby is the Findhorn Foundation eco-village which offers free tours of its facilities. Excellent base for golf, castles, whisky trails, watersports and dolphin spotting along Moray Firth. Open all year.

---

④ **The Palace Farm,** Gamrie, Banff, Aberdeenshire AB45 3HS

Mrs Pat Duncan
☎ 01261 851261
Fax 01261 851401
BB £20
Sleeps 6
☺ ▪ ⚔ ❋ W
★★★
BED & BREAKFAST

Enjoy a warm Scottish welcome on our mixed arable farm. Late 18th century farmhouse set in wooded garden amidst rolling farm landscapes. Beautiful, quaint fishing villages of Gardenstown and Pennan only 5 minutes away, waiting to be explored. Fresh farm produce and seafood from along the Moray Firth shores. Certificate of Excellence and Scotland's Best. Open Mar–Oct.

Our farms offer a range of facilities that are illustrated by symbols in each entry.
Turn to page 14 for an explanation of the symbols.

Self-Catering

Upper Crichie, Stuartfield, Peterhead, Aberdeenshire AB42 5DX ❺

P Ferguson
☎/Fax 01771 624206
SC From £250–£400
Sleeps 8
★★
SELF CATERING

Old world farm cottage, 3 miles from Pennan and film sets for 'Local Hero' and TV series. Beautiful, peaceful rugged coast, cliffs and beaches. Near Whiskey Trail and many golf courses. Fishing in locality for rainbow trout, shooting. Quiet and very private. Very comfortable, fully equipped, inglenook fireplace. Ideal for family holiday.

CONFIRM BOOKINGS

Disappointments can arise from misunderstandings over the telephone. Please write to confirm your booking.

FARM HOLIDAY BUREAU

Our Internet address is
http://www.webscape.co.uk/farmaccom/

FOLLOW THE COUNTRY CODE

Leave nothing but footprints,
Take nothing but photographs,
Kill nothing but time!

Argyll, Isles, Loch Lomond, Stirling & Trossachs

Stirling, Oban & the Mull of Kintyre

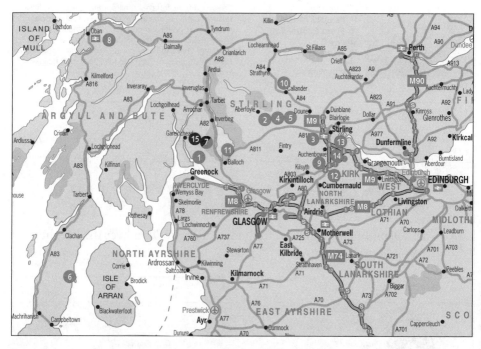

Key

- ⓵ Bed & Breakfast
- ⓵ Self-Catering
- ⓵ B&B and SC
- ⓵ Camping Barns
- 🔺 Camping & Caravanning

Here, at the gateway to the Highlands, climb the Munros, walk the West Highland Way or the Ochil Ridge overlooking Stirling Castle and the Wallace Monument. Wind your way round the dramatic sea lochs to Oban, the port to the Isles, or explore the quiet softness of the Mull of Kintyre.

Visit numerous castles, museums and stately homes including Inveraray, the Burrell Collection in Glasgow, Rennie Mackintosh's Hillhouse and Hopetoun House. Children will love the award-winning Farmlife Centre. Sample the 'water of life' at Glen Turret distillery, cruise Loch Lomond and Loch Awe. Enjoy watersports, fishing and golf and a wealth of culture and Highland games culminating in Edinburgh's famous Military Tattoo. Access is easy by road, rail or air – we welcome you.

If you would like help in finding suitable farm accommodation, turn to the full listing of FHB Groups on pages 392 to 395 to find appropriate contact details for this area.

Bed and Breakfast
(and evening meal)

Drumfork Farm, Helensburgh, Argyll, Bute G84 7JY ①

Elizabeth Howie
☎ 01436 672329
BB From £18–£25
Sleeps 6
★★★
BED & BREAKFAST

Traditional sandstone farmhouse, extensively refurbished, all rooms en suite, some with sea view. Organic food served and we offer packed lunches, afternoon teas, high teas and babysitting for children. The Victorian seaside town of Helensburgh, with its wide streets and stylish architecture, is port of call for paddle steamer 'Waverley' and home to Hill House by Charles Rennie Mackintosh. Open all year. E-mail: drumforkfarm@aol.com.uk

---

Inchie Farm, Port of Menteith, Stirling FK8 3JZ ②

Mrs Norma Erskine
☎/Fax 01877 385233
Mobile 0402 364614
BB From £16–£17
EM From £10
Sleeps 5
★★★
BED & BREAKFAST

Family farm on the shores of Lake of Menteith where ospreys nest between April and Sept. Featured in 'Wish You Were Here' TV programme. Comfortable twin/family rooms both with washbasins and tea-making facilities, also guests' own bathroom and lounge with colour TV. Central heating throughout. Ideal for trout fishing or hill walking in nearby Trossachs. Open Mar–Oct.

Lochend Farm, Carronbridge, Denny, Stirlingshire FK6 5JJ ③

Jean Morton
☎ 01324 822778
BB From £20
Sleeps 4
★★★★
BED & BREAKFAST

Peace, panoramic view and good wholesome food. Delightfully situated overlooking Loch Coulter in unspoiled countryside, yet only 5 miles from M9/M80 (jct 9). A perfect base for exploring this beautiful part of Scotland. Farmhouse centrally heated, traditionally furnished. 2 double bedrooms with washbasin, TV, radio, tea-making facilities; also guests' own bathroom, dining room and lounge with colour TV. Selected by '*Which*' Good Bed & Breakfast Guide. Open Easter–Oct or by arrangement.

Lochend Farm, Port of Menteith, Stirling FK8 3JZ ④

Mrs Rhona Millar
☎ 01877 385235
BB From £20–£22
EM From £10
Sleeps 4
★★★
BED & BREAKFAST

Enjoy a peaceful stay at Lochend, a mixed arable stock farm next to Scotland's only Lake in the heart of the Trossachs. Farmhouse dates back to 1726 being the former dower house of the estate. Spacious accommodation with en suite bedrooms. A warm friendly atmosphere and good home cooking await. Open April–Oct. E-mail: lochend@easynet.co.uk

---

Lower Tarr Farm, Ruskie, Port of Menteith, Stirling FK8 3LG ⑤

Mrs Effie Bain
☎/Fax 01786 850202
BB From £18–£20
EM From £10
Sleeps 6 + cot
★★★
BED & BREAKFAST

On our mixed farm guests can dine in our conservatory and enjoy the peaceful situation, panoramic views and pretty garden, with Ruskie burn flowing past. Good home cooking and baking are served, ensuring an enjoyable stay. Cattle, sheep and hens plus interesting wildlife can be seen. Central for touring the Trossachs, Loch Lomond, Stirling and Edinburgh. En suite room. Open Feb–Nov.

---

6 Mains Farm, Carradale, Campbeltown, Argyll PA28 6QG

Mrs Dorothy MacCormick
☎ **01583 431216**
🅱 **From £17–£18**
EM from £7
Sleeps 6
★★
BED & BREAKFAST

Comfortable accommodation in traditional farmhouse five minutes' walk from mile-long safe beach, forest walks. Golf and river fishing. Scenic views of Isle of Arran over the Kilbrannon Sound and picturesque fishing harbour. Good home cooking and warm hospitality with coal fires and heating in rooms. Not suitable for disabled visitors. Open Apr–Oct.

7 Shantron Farm, Luss, Alexandria, Dumbartonshire G83 8RH

Anne M Lennox
☎/Fax **01389 850231**
Mobile 0468 378400
🅱 **From £20–£25**
Sleeps 11
★★★
BED & BREAKFAST

Enjoy a relaxing break in a spacious bungalow with outstanding views of Loch Lomond. The farm is Morag's croft in 'High Road' and other scenes. Four miles south of Luss. Ideal for touring, hillwalking, fishing, watersports and golf on the new Loch Lomond Golf Course. En suite available. Open Mar–Nov.
E mail: rjlennox@shantron.u-net.com

8 Thistle-Doo, Kilchrenan, by Taynuilt, Oban, Argyll PA35 1HF

K Lambie
☎ **01866 833339**
🅱 **From £20**
Sleeps 6
★★★
BED & BREAKFAST

Awe-inspiring view of Loch Awe from our friendly family-run establishment. Ideal for all outdoor activities. Very peaceful and relaxing. 20 miles east of Oban, taking the B845 off the A85 at Taynuilt to the shore of Loch Awe. Open all year.

9 The Topps Farm, Fintry Road, Denny, Stirlingshire FK6 5JF

Mrs Jennifer Steel
☎ **01324 822471**
Fax 01324 823099
🅱 **From £20–£24**
EM From £12
Sleeps 14
★★
GUEST HOUSE

A modern farmhouse guesthouse in a beautiful hillside location with stunning, panoramic views. Family, double or twin-bedded rooms available, all en suite with tea/coffee, shortbread, TV, radio, telephone. Food a speciality ("Taste of Scotland" listed). Restaurant open to non-residents. A la carte menu only. Easy access to all major tourist attractions. Your enjoyment is our aim and pleasure! Open all year.

10 Trean Farm, Leny Feus, Callander, Perthshire FK17 8AS

Janette Donald
☎/Fax **01877 331160**
🅱 **From £18–£21**
Sleeps 6
★★★
BED & BREAKFAST

A working farm situated in open parkland beside Callander with a 15 minute walk to shops. Outstanding views of Ben Ledi. An ideal base for touring and hill walking. 2 en suite rooms with TV and 1 with washbasin. Tea/coffee facilities. Residents' lounge. Open May–Oct.

11 West Auchencarroch Farm, Balloch, By Loch Lomond, Dunbartonshire G83 9LU

Margaret Kay
☎ **01389 710998**
🅱 **From £17–£25**
Sleeps 6
★★★
BED & BREAKFAST

A warm welcome awaits you at our family-run dairy farm where you can relax and enjoy the picturesque views of the hills of Loch Lomondside in peaceful surroundings. Comfortable en suite bedrooms, all with colour TV and tea/coffee-making facilities. Log fire in lounge. Ideal for touring Loch Lomond, Trossachs, Stirling, Glasgow and Edinburgh. Open all year.

Wester Carmuirs Farm, Larbert, By Falkirk, Stirlingshire FK5 3NW

Mrs Sheila Taylor
☎ 01324 812459
BB From £19
Sleeps 6
⛱ 🐾 ⚓ W
★★★
BED & BREAKFAST

Relax and enjoy friendly hospitality and good food in our comfortable home on mixed farm on A803 near Falkirk (M9/A80). Comfortable twin/double/family rooms all with washbasins and tea/coffee. Guests' own bathroom, shower room, dining room and TV room with log fire. Ideal centre to visit local attractions, eg. Mariner Centre with swimming pool; also Trossachs, Loch Lomond, Stirling, Glasgow and Edinburgh. Open Jan–Nov.

West Plean, Denny Road, Stirling FK7 8HA

Mrs Moira Johnston
☎ 01786 812208
Fax 01786 480550
BB From £22–£26
Sleeps 6
⛱ 🐎 ✂ ⛳ Å ❤ 🚲 ⚓ 🐾 W
★★★
BED & BREAKFAST

Enjoy warm Scottish farming hospitality in a historic setting, with sweeping lawns, walled garden, extensive woodland walks, surrounded by our mixed farm. We offer quality food, spacious comfort, bedrooms en suite, hot drink facilities and attentive hosts. Riding and fishing can be arranged locally. Located on the A872 Denny road, 2 minutes from M9/M80 (jct9). Open Feb–Nov.
E-mail: west.plean@virgin.net

Woodcockfaulds Farm, Thorneydyke Road, Via Denny, Stirlingshire FK6 6RH

Mrs Mary Galloway
☎ 01786 811985
Fax 01786 814858
BB From £20–£25
Sleeps 6
⛱ ⚓
★★
BED & BREAKFAST

Spacious country farmhouse situated in idyllic rural location with breathtaking views of the Ochil Hills and Forth Road Bridges. Short drive from main Glasgow, Edinburgh and Perth to Stirling motorways makes it an ideal touring base. One large double, one family and one twin bedroom, all en suite with tea/coffee-making facilities and TV. Hearty Scottish breakfast. Warm atmosphere and a friendly welcome. Ample car parking.

Self-Catering

Edenbrook Cottage, Edentaggart Farm, Luss, Alexandria, Dumbartonshire G83 8PB

FARM HOLIDAY
BUREAU

Mrs Clare Rankin
☎ 01436 860226
SC From £200–£280
Sleeps 4
⛱ 🐾
★★★
SELF CATERING

Very comfortable cottage on sheep farm in peaceful picturesque setting in hills above Loch Lomond. Good hill walking. Ideally situated for sightseeing to Oban, Glasgow, Stirling and Inverary areas. Modern appliances. Children welcome. Open May–Oct.

Shemore Farm Cottage, Shantron Farm, Luss, Alexandria, Dumbartonshire G83 8RH

Mrs Anne M Lennox
☎/Fax 01389 850231
Mobile 0468 378400
SC From £150–£375
Sleeps 6
⛱ 🏠 🐾 ⚓ W
★★★
SELF CATERING

Regulars often return to this traditional stone cottage attractively situated on a hill sheep farm, 300 ft above Loch Lomond, over which the cottage has magnificent views. The farm has often been filmed for 'High Road' TV series. Four miles south of picturesque village of Luss. Edinburgh, Oban, Fort William, Ayr – 1½ hours. Ideal for hillwalking, fishing, watersports. Children love to feed lambs. Short breaks available. Open all year.
E mail: rjlennox@shantron.u-net.com

Perthshire

Highland Perthshire, glens & lochs, Strathearn & Tay Valley

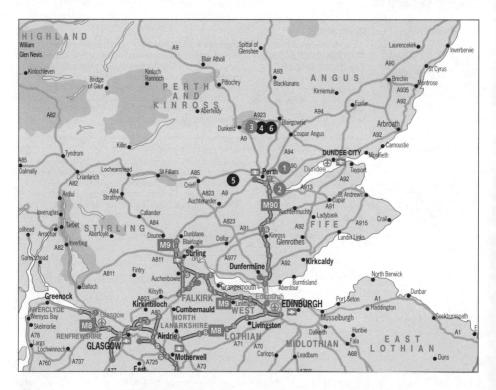

Key

- 🅱 Bed & Breakfast
- 🆂 Self-Catering
- 🅱🆂 B&B and SC
- ▢ Camping Barns
- ▲ Camping & Caravanning

Perthshire lies at the very centre of Scotland so it is the ideal base for your holiday. Here you'll find the grandeur of mountains and glens, the glimmer of lochs and the River Tay, an angler's paradise. See Perthshire at work producing top-quality glass, pottery, hand-knitted woollens, leather goods, hornware and the 'water of life' in its four malt whisky distilleries. There's something for everyone – historic castles, houses and gardens, the world's highest beech hedge, Europe's oldest living tree, Perth's ultra-modern leisure pool, 25 golf courses, a range of watersports, theatres and numerous highland nights and ceilidhs.

If you would like help in finding suitable farm accommodation, turn to the full listing of FHB Groups on pages 392 to 395 to find appropriate contact details for this area.

Bed and Breakfast
(and evening meal)

Blackcraigs Farm, Scone, Perthshire PH2 7PJ

Irene Millar
☎/Fax 01821 640254
[BB] From £17–£20
Sleeps 6

★★★
BED & BREAKFAST

18th century farmhouse set in a well maintained garden where a warm welcome awaits you. Relax and enjoy the quiet, peaceful surroundings. Comfortable bedrooms all with colour TV and tea/coffee-making facilities. Elegant residents' lounge with an open fire. The Fair City of Perth has lots of charm and amenities and is an ideal touring area. From Perth take the A94 and travel 4 miles to find your perfect holiday. Open all year.

Fingask Farm, Rhynd, Perth PH2 8QF

Mrs E Stirrat
☎ 01738 812220
Fax 01738 813325
[BB] From £18–£21
EM From £8
Sleeps 6
☻(12) ♨
★★★★
BED & BREAKFAST

We offer spacious accommodation in our well appointed farmhouse in peaceful central Perthshire, where a warm welcome is assured. Play croquet or relax in our beautifully landscaped walled garden. Afternoon tea may be served on the terrace. One large twin room with private bathroom, double and single room with shared bathroom. Log fire in cosy residents' lounge. Evening meals by arrangement. Easy access from motorway. Open Apr–Nov. E-mail: liBBy@agstirrat.sol.co.uk

Letter Farm, Loch of the Lowes, By Dunkeld, Perthshire PH8 0HH

Jo Andrew
☎ 01350 724254
Fax 01350 724341
[BB] From £20–£27
Sleeps 6
☻ ♨
★★★★
BED & BREAKFAST

Enjoy our recently renovated farmhouse, kingsize beds in en suite rooms, log fire in guest lounge and good home baking. Our family-run stock farm nestles next to the Loch of Lowes Wildlife Reserve, home to ospreys, otters and others. It exudes peace and tranquillity – come see for yourselves, you'll be warmly welcomed. Open mid Jan–mid Dec. E-mail: letterlowe@aol.com

Self-Catering

Laighwood Holidays, Laighwood, Butterstone, Dunkeld, Perthshire PH8 0HB

Fiona Bruges
☎ 01350 724241/724208
Fax 01350 724259
[SC] From £130–£570
Sleeps 3–8
☻ ♨
★★★ *up to* ★★★★
SELF CATERING

Queen Victoria used to holiday in these parts – Why don't you? A former hunting ground of the Dukes of Atholl, Laighwood is now a family-run hill farm offering a variety of self-catering holiday accommodation, thoughtfully prepared for your comfort. Enjoy spectacular views over the surrounding hills and lochs. Central for touring and golf courses. Please send for brochure, stating numbers in party. Open all year.

5   **Strathearn Holidays,** Bachilton Farm, Methven, Perth PH1 3QX

Howard England
☎ 01738 633322
☎ 01738 840263 (eves)
Fax 01738 621177
⃞SC From £266–£385
Sleeps 2–6

⛄ 🏠 🐕 ⊞ 🎿 🎣 ⛷ 🎿 🅆
★★★★
SELF CATERING

Enjoy our home from home holidays in fully equipped and beautifully furnished south-facing properties on our 710-acre farm in the very heart of Scotland. The ideal base for sporting or touring holidays. Each property has colour TV, microwave, dishwasher, etc. Price includes linen and electricity. Ring for brochure. Open all year.
E-mail: scotland-holidays.com

6   **West Cottage,** Craigie, Blairgowrie, c/o Kirktonley, Essendy, Blairgowrie, Perthshire PH10 6RE

Janet Cope
☎ 01250 884228
Fax 01250 884376
⃞SC From £150–£350
Sleeps 4

⛄ 🏠 🐕 ⛺
★★
SELF CATERING

The perfect base for touring, fishing, golf, walking and birdwatching. We are 30 miles from ski area, 6 miles from shops, 1½ hours from Edinburgh and Glasgow and 16 miles from Perth Races and bull sales. Plenty of lochs and castles in the area. Open all year.

STAY ON A FARM GIFT TOKENS

FARM HOLIDAY BUREAU

If you have enjoyed your Stay on a Farm, why not treat your friends and relatives to *Stay on a Farm* gift tokens? Available from the Bureau office (tel: 024 7669 6909), they can be redeemed against accommodation and are accepted by the majority of farms (see Index). Please check when booking to avoid disappointment.

FOLLOW THE COUNTRY CODE

Leave nothing but footprints,
Take nothing but photographs,
Kill nothing but time!

THE 1000+ BUREAU MEMBERS OFFER A UNIQUE LINK TO CUSTOMERS ACROSS THE UK

FARM HOLIDAY BUREAU

All Bureau members belong to a local Group. Each member can refer you to an equally high quality member within the Group... or across the UK: England, Northern Ireland, Scotland, Wales.

Angus & City of Dundee

Angus Glens, Pictish trails, castles & sandy beaches

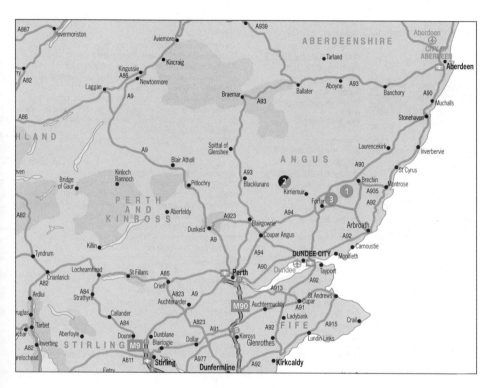

Key

🔵 1 Bed & Breakfast

⚫ 1 Self-Catering

🟡 1 B&B and SC

⬜ 1 Camping Barns

🔺 1 Camping & Caravanning

Whatever you seek in Scotland you'll find in Angus, where the braes meet the valley of Strathmore, from the glens with their gushing waterfalls to the numerous sandy beaches and bays along the east coast. Visit Glamis Castle, former home of the Queen Mother, and Dunnottar and Edzell Castles. At Kirriemuir visit the birthplace of J.M. Barrie (*Peter Pan*). Sports include hillwalking, cycling, birdwatching, riding, watersports and, in winter, curling and skiing. You can fish on river, loch and sea, or take your pick of glorious golf courses. The Heritage Trail is a must for the visitor taking in Arbroath Abbey, Brechin Cathedral and Restenneth Priory, or follow the Pictish Trail from the new Pitacavia Centre. Angus is an ideal base for a day visit to Perth, St Andrews, Stirling or Edinburgh, or north to Aberdeen, Pitlochry, Royal Deeside and Inverness.

If you would like help in finding suitable farm accommodation, turn to the full listing of FHB Groups on pages 392 to 395 to find appropriate contact details for this area.

Bed and Breakfast
(and evening meal)

---

① **Blibberhill Farm,** By Brechin, Angus, Tayside DD9 6TH

Mrs Wendy Stewart
☎/Fax **01307 830323**
🛏 From **£17–£20**
EM From **£10**
Sleeps **6**
❄ ✂ 🔥 🅦
★★★
BED & BREAKFAST

Peacefully situated between the Angus glens and coast, Glamis and Edzell Castles nearby. Under 1 hour's drive from Aberdeen, Royal Deeside, St Andrews and Perth. Central to many golf courses, fishing and hillwalking. Tastefully decorated and furnished en suite rooms. Centrally heated with open fires and electric blankets to keep you cosy in winter. All home cooking. Beautiful large garden. Excellent children's facilities. Evening meal optional. Open all year.

---

② **Purgavie Farm,** Lintrathen, Kirriemuir DD8 5HZ

Mrs Moira Clark
☎/Fax **01575 560213**
🛏 From **£20–£25**
EM From **£12**
Sleeps **6**
❄ 🔥 🐕 Å ⚙ 🔥 🅦
★★★★
BED & BREAKFAST

A warm welcome in homely accommodation on our farm set in peaceful countryside with excellent views. All rooms have en suite bathroom, TV and tea-making facilities. Good home cooking providing traditional Scottish fayre. Fishing on Lintrathen loch, pony trekking and hill-walking in Glen Isla. Glamis Castle 10 miles. Located 7 miles from Kirriemuir, follow the B951 to Glen Isla; farm signposted at roadside. Open all year.
E-mail: purgavie@aol.com

---

③ **Wemyss Farm,** Montrose Road, Forfar, Angus DD8 2TB

Mrs Deanna Lindsay
☎/Fax **01307 462887**
🛏 From **£16.50**
EM From **£11**
Sleeps **6**
❄ 🐕 🔥 💷 🅦
★★★
BED & BREAKFAST

190-acre mixed farm situated on the B9113 with a wide variety of animals. Ideal for touring Angus Glens, St Andrews, Royal Deeside, Aberdeen, Edinburgh, east coast resorts. Castles nearby. Shooting, fishing, golf, swimming, all in the area. Bedrooms overlook beautiful countryside. Children made welcome, reduced rates. Evening dinner optional, packed lunches. Separate dining room, lounge with log fire, TV in rooms. Quiet and peaceful, yet within easy reach of all amenities. Open all year.

Self-Catering

---

② **Purgavie Farm,** Lintrathen, Kirriemuir DD8 5HZ

Mrs Moira Clark
☎/Fax **01575 560213**
🆂🅲 From **£200–£400**
EM From **£12**
Sleeps **4/6**
🧍 ❄ 🐕 Å ⚙ 🔥 🅦
★★★ *up to* ★★★★
SELF CATERING

Escape the stress and relax in our Swedish log house or bungalow and enjoy the panoramic views of the lovely countryside. Explore the hills and see the widlife or fish in Lintrathen loch. Properties furnished to a high standard with dishwasher, shower, fridge freezer, washer dryer, payphone and microwave. Open fire in bungalow. Located 7 miles from Kirriemuir, follow B951 signposted at roadside. Open all year. E-mail: purgavie@aol.com

---

Kingdom of Fife

Firth of Forth, East Neuk & Tay estuary

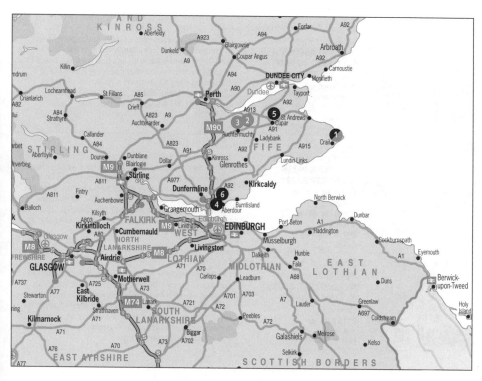

Key

🄋 Bed & Breakfast

🄋 Self-Catering

🄋 B&B and SC

🄵 Camping Barns

🄰 Camping & Caravanning

Fife is situated between the Forth and Tay rivers and has miles of clean, sandy beaches and quaint fishing villages. A visit to the Fisheries Museum at Anstruther is a must and the Secret Bunker will fascinate all ages. Fife has a wealth of historical buildings including Dunfermline Abbey, Falkland Palace and Kellie Castle. The ancient town of St Andrews not only has ancient buildings but is a mecca for all golfers. There are many fine golf courses around Fife.

Animal lovers will enjoy a visit to the Sea Life Centre at St Andrews to watch the seals being fed, the Scottish Deer Centre near Cupar, the Fife Animal Park and, not to be missed, the famous Deep Sea World at North Queensferry. Fife is also an ideal base from which to visit Edinburgh, Perth and Dundee. A warm welcome is assured.

If you would like help in finding suitable farm accommodation, turn to the full listing of FHB Groups on pages 392 to 395 to find appropriate contact details for this area.

Bed and Breakfast

(and evening meal)

1 **Cambo House,** Kingsbarns, St Andrews, Fife KY16 8QD

Mr & Mrs Peter Erskine
☎ 01333 450054/450313
Fax 01333 450987
BB From £38–£45
EM From £25
Sleeps 4
★★★★
BED & BREAKFAST

Come and lose yourself in a glorious four-poster bed in our magnificent Victorian family home hardly touched by time, set in parkland and woods that meander down to an unspoilt coastline with a fine sweeping beach. Only 10 minutes from St. Andrews. Open all year except Christmas and New Year.
E-mail: 100130,1660@compuserve.com

2 **Easter Clunie Farmhouse,** Easter Clunie, Newburgh, Fife KY14 6EJ

Mrs Kathleen Baird
☎ 01337 840218
Fax 01337 842226
BB From £17–£20
Sleeps 6
(3)
★★★
BED & BREAKFAST

David and Kathleen Baird warmly welcome you to their 18th century centrally heated home on a working farm. Comfortable bedrooms with en suite or private facilities. Home baking and tea on arrival. Relax in walled garden, enjoy panoramic views of the River Tay. Surrounding countryside provides a wealth of scenic walks. Ideal touring base for Fife and Perthshire. Situated on A913. Open Mar–Nov. E-mail: cluniefarm@aol.com

3 **Ninewells Farm,** Woodriffe Road, Newburgh, Fife KY14 6EY

Mrs Barbara Baird
☎/Fax 01337 840307
BB From £18–£25
Sleeps 6
(9)
★★★★
BED & BREAKFAST

The Bairds welcome guests to the traditional stonebuilt farmhouse on their stock/arable farm. Situated on an elevated site with magnificent panoramic views of the Tay Valley to mountains far beyond Perth. Ideal situation for touring/golfing holiday combined with quiet, comfortable accommodation with excellent breakfast. Open Mar–Oct.
E-mail: nwfarm@premier.co.uk

Self-Catering

1 **Cambo House,** Kingsbarns, St Andrews, Fife KY16 8QD

Mr & Mrs Peter Erskine
☎ 01333 450054/450313
Fax 01333 450987
SC From £190–£750
Sleeps 2/8
★★ *up to* ★★★
SELF CATERING

Come and lose yourself on an enchanting wooded coastal estate hardly touched by time. Only 10 minutes from St Andrews, the home of golf. Cottages and apartments in a magnificent country house. Ideal for families and groups of up to 32. Open all year.
E-mail: 100130,1660@compuserve.com

The Chaumer, Barns Farm, Aberdour, Fife KY3 0RY ④

Mrs Sandra Milne
☎/Fax 01383 823872
[SC] **From £150–£180**
Sleeps 2
⌣ ♠ ⌂ 🅦
★★★
SELF CATERING

The Chaumer is a recently modernised former farm bothy adjacent to the farmhouse on a working arable farm on the outskirts of Dalgety Bay. Only 10 minutes from the Forth Bridge, it is an ideal base for touring with Edinburgh, Stirling, Perth and Dundee all within easy reach. Bed linen, towels, electricity and fuel included. Open all year.
E-mail: smilne@farmersweekly.net

Kinloss Farm Holiday Cottages, Kinloss, Cupar, Fife KY15 4ND ⑤

Mr CB Addison-Scott
☎ 01334 654169
[SC] **From £250–£475**
Sleeps 4/6
⛄ ♠
★★★★
SELF CATERING

Clinkmill and Garden Cottages offer a superb selection of modernised and fully equipped farm cottages on a small working arable and stock farm with a herd of Highland cattle. The farm is a short distance from Cupar and 10 miles from St Andrews with its many golf courses.

Parkend Cottage, Parkend Farm, Crossgates, Cowdenbeath KY4 8EX ⑥

June Weatherup
☎/Fax 01383 860277
[SC] **From £225–£500**
Sleeps 5/6
⛄ ♠ ⌘ 🅦
★★★★★
SELF CATERING

Luxury traditionally refurbished 3-bedroom cottage enjoying beautiful and peaceful location on working dairy farm, 2 miles from Aberdour, with panoramic views to Firth of Forth and famous bridges. A true family 'home from home' with a warm welcome assured. Fully equipped to highest standard. Ideal base for touring Fife, Perthshire, Stirling and Edinburgh. Open all year.

USE THE INDEX

FARM HOLIDAY BUREAU

The comprehensive Index shows which farms offer access to disabled visitors; caravanning/camping facilities; the chance to participate on a working farm; stabling/grazing for visiting horses; en suite rooms; a welcome to business people; acceptance of *Stay on a Farm* gift tokens.

Greater Glasgow & Clyde Valley

Paisley, Renfrew, Glasgow, Cumbernauld, Lanark & Biggar

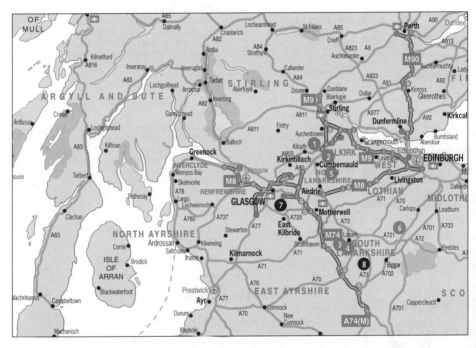

Key

1 Bed & Breakfast

1 Self-Catering

1 B&B and SC

1 Camping Barns

1 Camping & Caravanning

Welcome to the many different worlds of Greater Glasgow and Clyde Valley, where city life blends with country life. This is an ideal touring base for central Scotland. Glasgow, city of architecture and design and a paradise for shoppers, has many fascinating buildings and museums including the famous Burrell Collection and the Art Nouveau designs of Charles Rennie Mackintosh. From Biggar to Gourock enjoy the famous River Clyde: the area is steeped in history. Both city and town are complemented by the spectacular scenery and the hidden picturesque villages, such as New Lanark World Heritage Village and Carmichael Visitor Centre. Numerous golf courses, country parks, canals, castles and museums – experience them all. Whenever you arrive, both far and wide, a traditional warm Scottish welcome awaits you.

If you would like help in finding suitable farm accommodation, turn to the full listing of FHB Groups on pages 392 to 395 to find appropriate contact details for this area.

Bed and Breakfast
(and evening meal)

Allanfauld Farm, Kilsyth, Glasgow G65 9DF

Libby MacGregor
☎/Fax 01236 822155
[BB] From £18
Sleeps 4
☺ 🐾 ⅍ ♨
★★
BED & BREAKFAST

A working family farm situated close to the town of Kilsyth at the foot of the Kilsyth Hills, a great base to explore central Scotland. Located near A803 with easy access to M8 and M9. Golf, fishing, hill walking and a swimming pool are all within half a mile. Glasgow, Stirling 20 minutes. 1 twin/family room, 1 single room, both with TV and tea/coffee facilities. Open all year.

Bandominie Farm, Walton Road, Castlecary, Bonnybridge FK4 2HP

Jean Forrester
☎ 01324 840284
[BB] From £16–£17
Sleeps 5
☺ 🐾 ⅍ ♨ 📺
★★
BED & BREAKFAST

A working farm located 2 miles from the A80 at Castlecary (B816). Easy access from Glasgow and Edinburgh. Lovely view with a homely atmosphere. Central heating, TV lounge. Ample parking. Open all year except Christmas & New Year.

Clarkston Farm, Kirkfieldbank, Lanark ML11 9UN

Mrs Jean Findlay
☎ 01555 663751
[BB] From £18–£20
Sleeps 5
☺ ⅍ ♨ 🌲
★★★
BED & BREAKFAST

Clarkston Farm is a dairy farm situated in the heart of the Clyde Valley with a panoramic view second to none. A very warm welcome awaits all our guests, rooms are one double and one family with TV. Tea/coffee-making facilities and home baking served. TV lounge. Open all year.

Corehouse Farm, Kirkfieldbank, Lanark ML11 9TQ

Mrs Faye Hamilton
☎/Fax 01555 661377
[BB] From £18–£22
Sleeps 6
☺ 🐾 ⅍ ♨ 🐎 🐕 🌲 📺
★★★
BED & BREAKFAST

A warm family welcome awaits you on our traditional farm with beef cattle, sheep and horses. Located centrally between Glasgow and Edinburgh in the Clyde Valley beside the 'Falls of Clyde' Nature Reserve and New Lanark Visitor Centre. Ground level en suite rooms. Guests' TV lounge and breakfast conservatory with views of garden and countryside. Open all year.

Easter Glentore Farm, Slamannan Road, Greengairs, Airdrie, Lanarkshire ML6 7TJ

Elsie Hunter
☎/Fax 01236 830243
Mobile 0370 746950
[BB] From £22–£25
Sleeps 6
⅍ 🌐 ♨ 🌲 📺
★★★★
BED & BREAKFAST

Enjoy a warm, homely atmosphere with Scottish hosts in our 18th century ground floor farmhouse. Panoramic views. Quality accommodation, en suite or private bathroom, radio/alarms, tea/coffee facilities with home baking, lounge with TV. Evening tea tray. Excellent touring base, Glasgow and Stirling 15 miles, Edinburgh 28 miles. Near central Scotland's canals. Selected by 'Which' Good Bed and Breakfast Guide. Open all year except Christmas. E-mail: hunter@glentore.freeserve.co.uk

6 **Walston Mansion Farmhouse,** Walston, Carnwath, Lanark ML11 8NF

Mrs Margaret Kirby
☎/Fax 01899 810338
🅱🅱 £15.50–£17.50
EM From £8
Sleeps 6
🐾 🐕 🗲 Ⓦ
★★
BED & BREAKFAST

A very pleasant family home situated 5 miles from Biggar. A friendly and relaxed atmosphere; children most welcome. Good home cooking with home-produced meat, eggs and organic vegetables. Two en suite rooms, guests' lounge with log fire, TV/video and children's games. An ideal base for touring Strathclyde, Lothian and the Borders; Lanark, Edinburgh and Glasgow only a short drive away. Recommended by *Which? Good Bed & Breakfast Guide.* Open all year.

Self-Catering

7 **The Barn & The Roundhouse,** Greenleeshill Farm, Cambuslang, Glasgow G72 8YL

Anne M Leggat
☎/Fax 0141 641 3239
🆂🅲 From £195–£375
Sleeps 2/5
🐾 🍴 🗲 Ⓦ
★★★★
SELF CATERING

Unique apartments within 18th century building. Relaxed setting yet close to wide variety of sports facilities, restaurants, shops, parks, museums, etc. Glasgow city centre 5 miles. Views to Campsie Hills and Ben Lomond. Well positioned for touring Edinburgh, Clyde Valley, Ayrshire, Loch Lomond and the Trossachs. Both properties well equipped. Rates include electricity, heating, towels and linen. Open all year.
E mail: aml@greenleeshill.prestel.co.uk

8 **Carmichael Country Cottages,** Estate Office, West Mains, Carmichael, Biggar, Lanarkshire ML12 6PG

Patricia Carmichael of Carmichael
☎ 01899 308336
Fax 01899 308481
🆂🅲 From £180–£470
EM From £7.50
Sleeps 2–7
🐾 🐟 🎣 🎿 ⛱ 🗲 🎾 Ⓦ
★★ *up to* ★★★★
SELF CATERING

Fifteen 200-year-old stone cottages nestle among the woods and fields of our 700-year-old family estate. Enjoy our private tennis court and fishing loch. We guarantee comfort, warmth and a friendly welcome in an accessible, unique rural and historic time capsule. We farm deer, cattle and sheep and sell meats and tartan – Carmichael, of course. Breakfast and evening meal available. Visitor centre. Open all year. E mail: chiefcarm@aol.com.

CONFIRM BOOKINGS

Disappointments can arise from misunderstandings over the telephone.
Please write to confirm your booking.

Edinburgh & Lothians

Firth of Forth, Pentland, Moorfoot & Lammermuir Hills

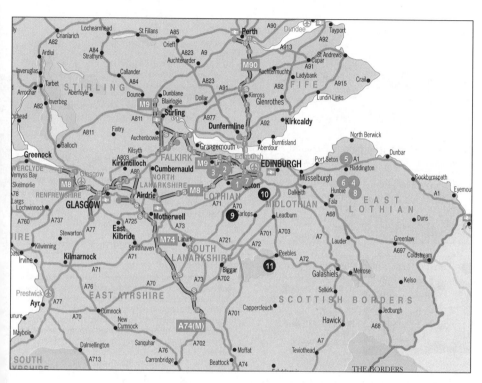

Key

- **1** Bed & Breakfast
- **1** Self-Catering
- **1** B&B and SC
- **1** Camping Barns
- **1** Camping & Caravanning

Edinburgh generates excitement. Visual drama, arresting skylines, historic buildings, elegant architecture, a guardian castle... this is Edinburgh, endlessly appealing. On its doorstep lie 40 miles of beautiful sandy beaches, rocky shores and a rolling landscape chequered with castles. Romance, history, splendour... Marvel at Linlithgow Palace, birthplace of Mary Queen of Scots. Admire the elegant grandeur of Adam's Hopetoun House, the tantalising carvings of gothic Rosslyn Chapel or spectacular Bass Rock sea-bird colony. Cruise canals or escape under the dramatic Forth Bridges to lovely Inchcolm Island or awe-inspiring Deep Sea World. Sample Scotland's golden water of life at Glenkinchie distillery... or attempt par on a world-renowned golf-link. And for youngsters? A tree-top adventure, a butterfly walk in Dalkeith? Linger in the Lothians: it's no lottery... everyone wins.

If you would like help in finding suitable farm accommodation, turn to the full listing of FHB Groups on pages 392 to 395 to find appropriate contact details for this area.

Bed and Breakfast
(and evening meal)

---

① Ashcroft Farmhouse, East Calder, Nr Edinburgh EH53 0ET

Elizabeth Scott
☎ **01506 881810**
Fax 01506 884327
BB **From £26–£30**
Sleeps 12
🐕(3) ✕ ⊞ ♨ W
★★★★
GUEST HOUSE

New farmhouse set in beautifully landscaped gardens enjoying lovely views over surrounding farmland. Only 10 miles city centre, 5 miles airport, city by-pass, M8/M9. Good parking. Bedrooms, including four-poster, attractively furnished in antique pine with co-ordinating fabrics. Choice of breakfasts including home made sausage, salmon, kippers, etc. AA 5 Diamonds. No smoking. Open all year. E-mail: ashcroftfa@aol.com

---

② Bankhead Farm, Dechmont, Broxburn, West Lothian EH52 6NB

Heather Warnock
☎ **01506 811209**
Fax 07970 691318
BB **From £20–£30**
Sleeps 5
🐕 🐴 ⊞ ✕ ♨ W
★★★
BED & BREAKFAST

This livestock farm in the Bathgate Hills has three modern en suite bedrooms and private kitchen. Panoramic views of Edinburgh, West Lothian and over the Forth to Fife belie the fact that we are close to three historic towns, and only 20 minutes from Scotland's capital city. Open all year. E-mail: bankheadbb@aol.com

---

③ Belsyde Farm, Lanark Road, Linlithgow, West Lothian EH49 6QE

Mrs Nan Hay
☎/Fax **01506 842098**
BB **From £17–£25**
Sleeps 6
🐕 🐴 ✕ ⊞ ♨ W
★★★
BED & BREAKFAST

18th century farmhouse located in large, secluded gardens with panoramic views over the Forth estuary. Golfing and fishing available locally. All bedrooms have washbasin (hot & cold), tea/coffee-making facilities, colour TV, central heating, 1 bedroom en suite. AA listed. Located close to M8, M9 and M90 and to Edinburgh airport. Follow A706 south-west from Linlithgow (1½ miles); first entrance on left after crossing Union Canal. Open all year except Christmas. E-mail: belsyde.guesthouse@virgin.net

---

④ Carfrae Farmhouse, Carfrae, Nr Garvald, Haddington, East Lothian EH41 4LP

Mrs Dorothy Gibson
☎ **01620 830242**
Fax 01620 830320
BB **From £18.50–£27**
Sleeps 6
🐕 ✕ 🐴
★★★★
BED & BREAKFAST

Set on 800-acre mixed farm, beautifully furnished farmhouse overlooking walled garden with uninterrupted views of the Lammermuir Hills. Close to many golf courses, own fishing loch. Edinburgh 35 minutes. Open Apr–Oct. E-mail: DgCarfrae@aol.com

---

⑤ Coates Farm, Longniddry, East Lothian EH32 0PL

Zoë Peace
☎/Fax **01620 822131**
BB **From £25**
Sleeps 4
🐕(12) 🦌 ✕ ♨ ✂
★★★★
BED & BREAKFAST

Spacious Georgian farmhouse tastefully decorated and furnished throughout. Ideally situated for exploring countryside, coastline or visiting Edinburgh. Train station nearby. Comfortable bedrooms with private facilities. Separate lounge and dining room for guests. Large, well tended, interesting garden. Excellent local pubs and restaurants. Coates is 1¾ miles from the A1. Open Apr–Sept.

Eaglescairnie Mains, Gifford, Haddington, East Lothian EH41 4HN

Mrs Barbara Williams
☎/Fax 01620 810491
[BB] **From £20–£27**
Sleeps 6
🐎🐕⌂🛏🎣♘🗴 Ⓦ
★★★
BED & BREAKFAST

Join us at Eaglescairnie Mains, a beautifully furnished Georgian house on our 350-acre arable/sheep farm which recently won a National Conservation Award. Near A1, ideal for the coast, golf courses, the Borders or Edinburgh. Double, twin and single rooms – some en suite, full CH, basins, tea/coffee trays. Conservatory, log fires and tennis court. Open all year (closed Christmas and New Year). E-mail: williams.eagles@btinternet.com

Overshiel Farm, East Calder, West Lothian EH53 0HT

Mrs Jan Dick
☎ 01506 880469
Fax 01506 883006
[BB] **From £16–£28**
Sleeps 6
🐎🗴🛏
★★★
BED & BREAKFAST

A traditional stonebuilt farmhouse on a working farm. The en suite bedrooms look onto a large, attractive garden and acres of farmland. Peaceful country setting yet easy access into Edingburgh city centre by car, bus or train. Several good pubs and restaurants nearby. Near airport. Safe parking. Open all year.

Rowan Park, Longnewton Farm, Gifford, East Lothian EH41 4JW

Mrs Margaret Whiteford
☎/Fax 01620 810327
[BB] **From £18**
Sleeps 6
🐎(5)🎣♘🛏
★★★★
BED & BREAKFAST

Our family farm of 450 acres consists of cattle, cereals and ponies. Situated at the foot of the Lammermuir Hills, with magnificent views to the Forth. Only 30 minutes from Edinburgh and near to the Border Country with its stately homes. Golf, fishing, tennis, swimming and pony trekking nearby. Furnished to a high standard, CH, guests' lounge, dining room and ground floor bedrooms, also welcome tray. A warm welcome awaits you. Open Mar–Nov.

Self-Catering

Crosswoodhill Farm, By West Calder, West Lothian EH55 8LP

Mrs Geraldine Hamilton
☎ 01501 785205
Fax 01501 785308
[SC] **From £230–£550**
Sleeps 5/6
🐎🐕🛏 Ⓦ
★★★ *up to* ★★★★
SELF CATERING

Imagine the best of both worlds… historic Edinburgh just ½ hour by car… rural tranquillity on our hill livestock farm with 1700 acres to roam. Ideal for exploring the Borders, Fife, Glasgow, Rob Roy and Braveheart Country. Choose between a gem of a cottage on the Pentland Hills, the wing of our handsome 18th century farmhouse or imaginatively designed Steading Cottage. All well equipped. Cosy peat fires, relaxing atmosphere. CH. Own phones. Car essential. Brochure. Open all year. E-mail: crosswd@globalnet.co.uk

Eastside Farm, Penicuik, Midlothian EH26 9LN

Susan Cowan
☎/Fax 01968 677842
[SC] **From £220–£470**
Sleeps 4
🐎🛏♘🗴
★★ *up to* ★★★★
SELF CATERING

Relax in this beautifully converted 18th century farm-steading located on a working family sheep farm in the scenic Pentland Hills Regional Park. Historic Edinburgh is only an eight mile drive away while New Lanark and the Border towns are a few miles further. Horseriding, fishing and golf nearby. Open all year. E-mail: alicowan46@aol.com

11 **Glenrath Holiday Cottages,** Glenrath Farm, Kirkton Manor, Peebles EH45 9JW

Mrs Catherine Campbell
☎ **01721 740221/740226**
Fax **01721 740314**
[SC] From **£176.50–£650**
Sleeps **6–8**
🐕 🐎 🐾 🗱 🎣 🌳 W
★★★ – ★★★★
SELF CATERING

Five very attractive properties ranging from a luxury farmhouse to a two-bedroomed cottage on working hill farms in very different locations in the county of Tweeddale. 25–50 mins by car from Edinburgh city or airport, Peebles 12 mins. Children's paradise, dogs welcome. Excellent hill walking, fishing, pony trekking and golf. Dishwashers, washer/dryers, microwaves, CH. Linen provided. Open all year.
E-mail: jacqui@easterhapprew.freeserve.co.uk

Ayrshire & Arran

North Arran, Goat Fell & Ayrshire coast

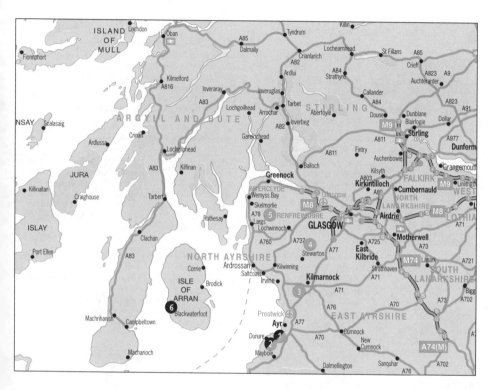

Key

- 🔵 Bed & Breakfast
- 🔴 Self-Catering
- 🟡 B&B and SC
- 🟥 Camping Barns
- 🔺 Camping & Caravanning

Wherever you travel in Ayrshire, you experience a sense of other ages, and the area's many museums and visitor centres bring them to life. The coast is lined with ancient castles such as Turnberry and the vast Culzean Castle with its lovely country park and gardens. No stay in Ayrshire is complete without a visit to Burns' Cottage, birthplace of Scotland's national poet, and the Burns experience in Alloway. From Ardrossan take the ferry to the mystical island of Arran, Scotland in miniature with rugged mountains in the north sloping to green pasture in the south. Brodick Castle is a must, as is Goat Fell, Arran's tallest mountain, for its superb views over south-west Scotland and Ireland.

If you would like help in finding suitable farm accommodation, turn to the full listing of FHB Groups on pages 392 to 395 to find appropriate contact details for this area.

Bed and Breakfast
(and evening meal)

---

1 **Dunduff Farm,** Dunure, Ayr KA7 4LH

Agnes Gemmell
☎ 01292 500225
Fax 01292 500222
🅱 From £23–£35
Sleeps 6
☺(12) ⚡ ⊞ ♿ ☕ 🎿 🆆
★★★★
BED & BREAKFAST

Dunduff Farm is a 650-acre beef and sheep farm overlooking the Firth of Clyde to the Holy Isle and Arran. Culzean Castle, Burns Cottage, Turnberry and many more are nearby. All rooms have en suite facilities or private bathroom and sea view. So come and enjoy the ambience of the Ayrshire coastline where a cheerful, warmhearted welcome awaits you. AA Selected QQQQ. Open Feb–Nov.

---

2 **Fisherton Farm,** Dunure, Ayr KA7 4LF

Mrs Lesley Wilcox
☎/Fax 01292 500223
🅱 From £18.50–£20
Sleeps 4
☺ 🎿 ♿ 🆆
★★★
BED & BREAKFAST

Delightful traditional Scottish farmhouse in coastal location on working farm. Convenient for Turnberry, Prestwick Airport, Troon and many golf courses, also agate picking, fishing, walking, touring Burns Country and Culzean Castle. Ground floor en suite bedrooms with tea/coffee-making facilities and colour TV. TV lounge. Open all year except Christmas.

---

3 **Muirhouse Farm,** Gatehead, Kilmarnock KA2 0BT

Mrs Martha S Love
☎ 01563 523975
🅱 From £17–£21
Sleeps 6
☺ 🎿 ♿ 🆆
★★
BED & BREAKFAST

A warm welcome is assured on our family-run dairy farm. In our traditional stone-built farmhouse all rooms have private or en suite bathrooms, TV and tea-making facilities. Near to Troon, we are ideally situated for golfers. Easy access to Glasgow also Arran ferry. Choice of excellent eating places nearby. Open all year.

---

4 **Shotts Farm,** Barrmill, Beith, Ayrshire KA15 1LB

Jane Gillan
☎ 01505 502273
🅱 From £13–£15
EM From £7
Sleeps 6
☺ ♿ 🆆
★★★
BED & BREAKFAST

Comfortable, friendly accommodation is offered on this 200-acre working dairy farm, south of Glasgow, accessible from A737 or A736. Well placed for visiting Loch Lomond, Arran and golf courses. Traditional breakfast which includes free range eggs and home made bread, served in a beautiful dining room with picture window. Open all year.

---

5 **South Whittlieburn Farm,** Brisbane Glen Road, Largs, Ayrshire KA30 8SN

Mrs Mary Watson
☎ 01475 675881
Fax 01475 675080
🅱 From £20
Sleeps 6
☺ ♿ 🎿 ☕ 🎿 🆆
★★★★
BED & BREAKFAST

Why not try our superb farmhouse accommodation? Situated on our working sheep farm with ample parking. Only 5 mins' drive from Largs and ferries to the islands. Warm friendly hospitality, enormous delicious breakfasts, all rooms en suite. *Which? Best Bed & Breakfast*, AA 4 Diamonds, RAC. We offer a warm welcome and a great holiday. Open all year.

Self-Catering

Bothy Cottage, Dunduff Farm, Dunure, Ayr KA7 4LH

Agnes Gemmell
☎ 01292 500225
Fax 01292 500222
[SC] From £180–£250
Sleeps 4
🐕 🐓 ♿ 🛋 🍴 ☕ ✂ [W]
★★★
SELF CATERING

Bothy Cottage is situated five miles south of Ayr at the coastal village of Dunure on a working farm. Overlooking Firth of Clyde to Arran. It has two double rooms, one is en suite, lounge and kitchen. Ideal for Culzean Castle and Parks, Burns Cottage, Galloway Forest, Farm Parks and many more. Capture this country coastal farm atmosphere at its best. Open all year.

Fisherton Farm, Dunure, Ayr KA7 4LF

Mrs Lesley Wilcox
☎/Fax 01292 500223
[SC] From £170–£350
Sleeps 6
🐕 🐓 🛋 [W]
★★★
SELF CATERING

Delightful, spacious, modern bungalow with panoramic views of Firth of Clyde, Holy Island and Isle of Arran. Adequate parking, CH plus electric heaters, linen provided. Ideally situated for Troon, Turnberry and many golf courses. Also agate picking, fishing, walking. Convenient for Culzean Castle, Prestwick Airport, touring Burns Country and Galloway Forest. Open all year.

Mill Cottage, Drumaghinier, Blackwaterfoot, Isle of Arran KA27 8EX      6

Mr Hugh Stewart
☎/Fax 01770 860308
[SC] From £200
Sleeps 6
🐕 🐓 🛋
★★ *up to* ★★★★
SELF CATERING

Recently renovated and fully equipped to the highest standards of comfort and convenience, Mill Cottage is situated approximately one mile from Blackwaterfoot on the west coast of the Isle of Arran. Set in this idyllic location, it affords a unique combination of peace, tranquillity and panoramic scenery, yet is close to all local amenities and leisure facilities. Open all year.

NO ANSWER?

Farmers are mostly out and about during the day.
Try to telephone before 9.30am or after 4pm.

FARM HOLIDAY
BUREAU

Our Internet address is
http://www.webscape.co.uk/farmaccom/

Dumfries & Galloway

Moffat & Annandale Valley, Southern Upland Way, Castle Douglas, Kirkcudbright, Solway Coast & Galloway Forest Park

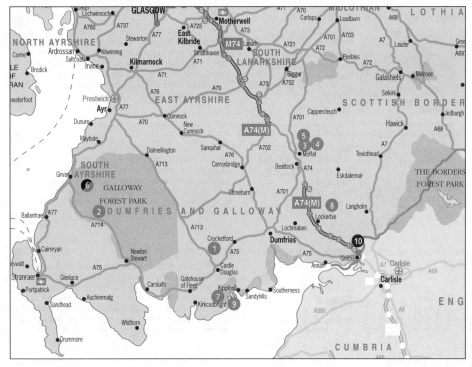

Key

1 Bed & Breakfast

1 Self-Catering

1 B&B and SC

1 Camping Barns

⚠ Camping & Caravanning

Come and discover the South-West of Scotland and you will find a variety of scenic landscapes – hillsides, valleys, moorlands, rolling farmlands, forest, and the Solway coastline with its sandy beaches and nature reserves. There's Moffat's spectacular 'Grey Mare's Tail' and 'Devil's Beef Tub', the former haunts of the Border Reivers, numerous towns and villages with interesting shops and crafts, wonderful golf courses, excellent fishing rivers and lochs, forest trails, country parks, castles, gardens and museums. In Dumfries and Galloway there is something for everyone. Do come and enjoy your holiday in our easily accessible part of Scotland. With its mild climate and warm hospitality, what more could you ask?

If you would like help in finding suitable farm accommodation, turn to the full listing of FHB Groups on pages 392 to 395 to find appropriate contact details for this area.

Bed and Breakfast

(and evening meal)

Airds Farm, Crossmichael, Castle Douglas, Kirkcudbrightshire DG7 3BG 1

Tricia Keith
☎/Fax 01556 670418
BB From £18–£23
Sleeps 10
★★★
GUEST HOUSE

Airds farmhouse overlooks lovely Loch Ken, 4 miles from Castle Douglas on the A713. All bedrooms tastefully decorated, heated, with wash handbasins, colour TV and tea and coffee facilities. Family and twin rooms are en suite. Private lounge with colour TV. Fire certificate held. Non-Smoking only. Pleasant walks within grounds. A warm welcome and comfortable stay are assured. Open all year.

Blair Farm, Barrhill, Girvan, Ayrshire KA26 0RD 2

Mrs Elizabeth Hughes
☎ 01465 821247
BB From £17–£20
EM From £9
Sleeps 6
★★★★
BED & BREAKFAST

We warmly invite you to enjoy peace, comfort and good home cooking at Blair, situated 1 mile south of Barrhill on A714, close to Glentrool in the Galloway Forest Park. Spacious accommodation, tastefully furnished and decorated throughout. Cosy double and twin rooms with en suite/private facilities and tea trays. Visitors' lounge, CH, log fires, TV etc. Convenient for Culzean Castle and Irish Ferries. Fishing available. Brochure. Open Easter–Nov.

Burnside, Well Road, Moffat, Dumfriesshire DG10 9BW 3

Mrs Kate Miller
☎/Fax 01683 221900
BB From £20–£22
Sleeps 4
(12)
★★★★
BED & BREAKFAST

Welcome to 'Burnside', a delightful and unique house set in one acre of grounds on the outskirts of Moffat. Luxurious en suite accommodation offering one double room with kingsize bed and one ground floor room, both with colour TV and tea/coffee-making facilities. Excellent base for touring, walking and golf. Lovely guided walks to our nearby land. Delicious choice breakfasts. Safe private parking. Send for brochure. Open Mar–Oct.

Coxhill Farm, Old Carlisle Road, Moffat, Dumfriesshire DG10 9QN 4

Mrs Sandra Long
☎ 01683 220471
BB From £18
Sleeps 4
★★★★
BED & BREAKFAST

A very attractive farmhouse in 70 acres of unspoilt countryside with outstanding views, beautiful rose gardens and ample parking. 2 double, 1 twin bedrooms, all with washbasins, tea/coffee-making facilities and central heating. Situated 1 mile south of the charming town of Moffat, and 1½ miles from Southern Upland Way. Excellent base for golf, tennis, fishing and touring SW Scotland. Open all year.

Ericstane, Moffat, Dumfriesshire DG10 9LT 5

Robert Jackson
☎ 01683 220127
BB From £19–£24
Sleeps 4
★★★
BED & BREAKFAST

Ericstane offers peace and quiet in attractive surroundings on a working hill farm 4 miles from Moffat. Period farmhouse with twin and double-bedded rooms with en suite facilities, TV, tea/coffee-making facilities. Central heating. In *Staying Off the Beaten Track* and *The Which Good Bed and Breakfast Guide*. Open all year.

6 **Glengennet Farm,** Barr, Girvan, Ayrshire KA26 9TY

Vera Dunlop
☎/Fax 01465 861220
BB **From £19.50–£22**
Sleeps 4
🛏 ✂ ☕ ☕ 🖥 W
★★★★
BED & BREAKFAST

Original Victorian shooting lodge with lovely views over the Stinchar valley and neighbouring Galloway Forest Park. One double and one twin, both en-suite with tea trays. Guests' lounge/dining room with colour TV. Two miles from Barr village where good meals are available. Good base for forest walking/ cycling, golf, Ayrshire coast, Burns country, Culzean Castle and Glentrool National Park.

---

7 **Mains of Collin,** Auchencairn, Castle Douglas, Kirkcudbrightshire DG7 1QN

Fiona Wallace
☎/Fax 640211
BB **From £17–£21**
Sleeps 4+cot
🛏 ☕ 🐾 ✂ ☕ ✖ ☕ ☕ 🖥 W
★★★
BED & BREAKFAST

An old stone-built farmhouse, nestling in the valley and surrounded by the green rolling hills of Galloway. Quietness, solitude and tranquillity, good food, caring, attentive hosts, and charming, comfortable accommodation. Colour TV and hospitality tray. Excellent base for touring. Pub meals available in Auchencairn (2 miles). Brochure and weekly terms on request.
E-mail: fionawallace@mainsofcollin.freeserve.co.uk

---

8 **Nether Boreland,** Boreland, Lockerbie, Dumfriesshire DG11 2LL

Amanda Saville
☎/Fax 01576 610248
BB **From £22.50–£25**
Sleeps 6
🛏 ☕ 🐾 ✂ ☕ 🐾 ✖
★★★
BED & BREAKFAST

Charming old farmhouse, comfortable and spacious. One double, one twin, both ensuite and one double with private bathroom. Rooms are tastefully furnished and have TV, electric blankets, clock radio, hairdrier and tea/coffee tray. Free range eggs, an open fire and a country welcome. The farm is part of a carriage driving and equestrian centre. Enjoy riding activities and scenic carriage drives. Golf, walking, fishing, ice skating etc available locally. Short breaks. Open all year. E-mail: amanda.chariots@virgin.net

---

9 **Rascarrel Cottage,** Rascarrel Farm, Auchencairn, Castle Douglas, Kirkcudbrightshire DG7 1RJ

Ellice Hendry
☎ 01556 640214
BB **From £20–£22**
Sleeps 4
☕ ☕ ✖ W
★★★★
BED & BREAKFAST

You will find peace, comfort and wonderful views at our attractive, well-appointed cottage. Situated on an 18th century smuggling route overlooking our 400 acre farm and the Solway Firth, it is 500 yards from the sea and 2 miles from village where good meals are available. 1 double en suite on ground floor, 1 twin en suite on first floor. Tea trays, CH, bright spacious lounge with colour TV, sunroom/dining room. Open Mar–Oct.

Self-Catering

---

10 **Aldermanseat Cottage,** Gretna, Dumfriesshire DG16 5HR

Carol Harrison
☎/Fax 01387 372242
SC **From £180–£300**
Sleeps 4 + cot
🛏 ✂
Applied

We would love to welcome you to our cosy, traditional stone cottage. It is hard to believe, with its wonderful countryside views and tranquil setting, that Gretna Green is only 2 miles and the M74 3 miles. Modernised and fully equipped with colour TV, washing machine, microwave, etc. Linen, electricity and central heating included. Open all year.

Upper Barr Farm, Glengennet, Barr, Girvan, Ayrshire KA26 9TY

Vera Dunlop
☎/Fax 01465 861220
🆂🅲 From £150–£490
Sleeps 2/8
🐕 🏠 🛏 🍴 📺
★★ *up to* ★★★★
SELF CATERING

Choose between detached period black and white farmhouse, recently modernised to provide centrally heated accommodation for 8 in 4 bedrooms (one en suite) or farmhouse wing with ground floor accommodation for 2. On working hill farm in peaceful Stinchar Valley, lovely views to Galloway Forest Park. Short breaks offseason, brochure. Open all year.

USE THE INDEX

FARM HOLIDAY BUREAU

The comprehensive Index shows which farms offer access to disabled visitors; caravanning/camping facilities; the chance to participate on a working farm; stabling/grazing for visiting horses; en suite rooms; a welcome to business people; acceptance of *Stay on a Farm* gift tokens.

STAY ON A FARM GIFT TOKENS

FARM HOLIDAY BUREAU

If you have enjoyed your Stay on a Farm, why not treat your friends and relatives to *Stay on a Farm* gift tokens? Available from the Bureau office (tel: 024 7669 6909), they can be redeemed against accommodation and are accepted by the majority of farms (see Index). Please check when booking to avoid disappointment.

Most farms are full Members of FHB. Some are shown as Associates – see page 11.

FOLLOW THE COUNTRY CODE

Leave nothing but footprints,
Take nothing but photographs,
Kill nothing but time!

Scottish Borders

Cheviot Hills, Berwickshire coast, Tweed River Valley
& Eildon Hills

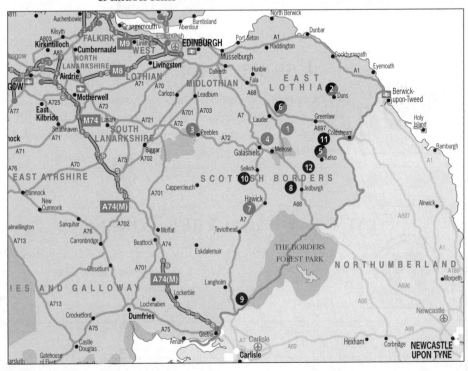

Key

- (1) Bed & Breakfast
- (1) Self-Catering
- (1) B&B and SC
- [1] Camping Barns
- (1) Camping & Caravanning

In this tranquil landscape that once bore witness to raids and battles, you'll travel quiet roads through rolling farmlands to discover bustling towns and tiny hamlets. There are historic houses and gardens of all periods, from Scott's Abbotsford to Mellerstain, the finest complete Adam house in Scotland, while the ruined abbeys of Kelso, Jedburgh, Melrose and Dryburgh stand testament to more troubled times. Everyone has their favourite view in this lovely area – the sun-dappled River Tweed, the majestic Eildon Hills, the broad sweep of the Merse. Come and discover yours in the beautiful Scottish Borders.

If you would like help in finding suitable farm accommodation, turn to the full listing of FHB Groups on pages 392 to 395 to find appropriate contact details for this area.

Bed and Breakfast
(and evening meal)

Birkenside Farm, Earlston, Berwickshire TD4 6AR ①

Sheila Hogg
☎ 01896 849224
🅱 From £16–£18
Sleeps 4
⛺ 🛁 🎍 🚾
★★★
BED & BREAKFAST

Traditional family farmhouse situated just off the A68 between Earlston and Lauder. Ideally located for touring the beautiful Borders countryside and visiting Edinburgh. Relaxing atmosphere in spacious rooms.

Cockburn Mill, Duns, Berwickshire TD11 3TL ②

Mrs A M Prentice
☎ 01361 882811
🅱 From £19–£21
EM £13
Sleeps 4
⛺ ✂ 🍴 🛁 🚾
★★★
BED & BREAKFAST

Riverside farmhouse offering 2 luxurious twin en suite bedrooms with electric blankets and tea/coffee-making facilities. Within sight and sound of River Whiteadder. Home baking and farm produce. Water from hillside spring. Trout fishing included. Abundant plant and bird life. Ideal for hill-walking, birdwatching, cycling or just relaxing. Hens, ducks, donkeys and pet lambs. Brochure and colour photo available. Open Mar–Nov.

Lyne Farm, Peebles EH45 8NR ③

Mrs Arran Waddell
☎/Fax 01721 740255
🅱 From £17–£20
Sleeps 6
⛺ 🐓 🛁 🍴 🎍 🚾
★★
BED & BREAKFAST

Spacious Georgian farmhouse situated on 1300 acre arable/stock farm with outstanding panoramic views. Tastefully decorated rooms, tea/coffee-making facilities. Walled garden. Hillwalking and picnic areas to enjoy. Excellent pubs and restaurants in picturesque town of Peebles. Ideal base for castles, historic houses, museums and outdoor pursuits. A warm welcome awaits you. Peebles 6 miles, Edinburgh 20 miles. Open all year.

Over Langshaw Farm, Langshaw, Galashiels, Selkirkshire TD1 2PE ④

Sheila Bergius
☎ 01896 860244
🅱 From £20–£24
Sleeps 4
⛺ 🐓 ✂ 🛁 🎍 🚾
★★
BED & BREAKFAST

Our beautifully situated rambling farmhouse extends a warm welcome and provides delicious food from the kitchen. Near Galashiels and Melrose, Edinburgh 34 miles. The specially large family bedroom has a dressing room and private bathroom. Very attractive double room with en suite shower room. Cot available. Our farm has dairy and beef cows, Scottish Mule and Blackface Ewes. Southern Upland Way nearby. Open all year.

Plum Braes Barn, Cliftonhill, Ednam, Kelso, Roxburghshire TD5 7QE ⑤

Maggie Stewart
☎ 01573 225028
Fax 01573 226416
🅱 From £22–£24
Sleeps 4
⛺ 🛁 🦆 🍴 🎍
Applied

Plum Braes Barn was converted in 1999 to include Garden Bank Cottage for charming B&B accommodation. This offers two ground floor bedrooms ideal for disabled guests, one twin en suite and one double with private bathroom. There is a sitting/dining room with a south-facing patio window and wood-burning stove. River walks and wild flower meadow, ideal for birdwatching. Open all year. E-mail: archie@sol.co.uk

6 Thirlestane, Thirlestane, Lauder, Berwickshire TD2 6SF

Mrs Caroline Barr
☎ 01578 722216
Fax 01578 722847
🅱 From £20–£22
Sleeps 6
🐕 ⚶ ♨ ♨ 🆆
Applied

Beautifully situated farmhouse on family-run stock farm. Spacious, tastefully decorated rooms with private facilities. Separate sitting room and dining room for guests, log fires, large attractive garden. Ideal base for walking, fishing, golf, several stately homes and castles nearby. Easy access to all Border towns and only 28 miles to Edinburgh. Open all year.

7 Wiltonburn Farm, Hawick, Roxburghshire TD9 7LL

Mrs Sheila Shell
☎ 01450 372414
Fax 01450 378098
🅱 From £18
EM From £10
Sleeps 6
🐕 ⌂ ⌂ ♨ ♨ 🆆
★★★
BED & BREAKFAST

You will be warmly welcomed and cared for as you unwind on our friendly, working mixed farm. Enjoy our rolling green hills and idyllic valley, 2 miles from Hawick, the centre of Scottish textiles. Your base for walking, riding, fishing, golf, castles and stately homes. Log fires, cosy rooms and our showroom containing designer cashmere knitwear, paintings, jewellery and small gifts will make your stay more pleasurable. Closed Christmas.
E-mail: shell@wiltonburnfarm.u-net.com

Self-Catering

8 Ashieburn Lodge, Ashieburn, Ancrum, Jedburgh, Roxburghshire TD8 6UN

Mrs Hazel Clarke
☎/Fax 01835 830358
🆂 From £150–£300
Sleeps 4
🕴 🐕 🐈 ⌂ ♨ ♨ 🆆
★★
SELF CATERING

Situated on a small pedigree stock-rearing farm, Ashieburn Lodge is quiet, cosy, comfortable and well appointed. Log fire (free logs), enclosed private garden with furniture. Easy access to Edinburgh. Ideal walking, golf and touring base. Open all year.
E-mail: mdclarke@buccleuch.com

9 Bailey Mill, Newcastleton, Roxburghshire TD9 0TR

Mrs Pamela Copeland
☎/Fax 01697 748617
🆂 From £98–£468
EM From £8
Sleeps 2–9
🐕 🐈 🐎 ♨ ⌂ ♨ 🆆
🐾🐾🐾 *Commended*

Bailey Mill is a small, friendly holiday complex and pony trekking centre situated in the beautiful Scottish Borders countryside and offering self-catering courtyard apartments. Ride, cycle or walk through the miles of forest and quiet country lanes. Return to relax in our leisure suite then have a meal or drink in our bar. Open all year.

2 Cockburn Mill, Duns, Berwickshire TD11 3TL

Ann Prentice
☎ 01361 882811
🆂 From £145–£310
Sleeps 4/5 + cot
🐕 🐈 ⌂ ♨ 🆆
★★
SELF CATERING

Stone-built cottage within sight and sound of River Whiteadder. Children welcome. Barbecue, colour TV. Bedlinen and overnight storage heating included. Trout fishing. Water from hillside spring. Abundant plant and bird life. Chicks, donkeys, ducklings and pet lambs. Coast, beaches, Edinburgh, Border keeps and abbeys within easy reach on quiet roads. Pets by arrangement. Brochure and colour photo available. Open all year.

Hutlerburn Cottage, Hutlerburn Farm, Ettrick, Selkirk TD7 5HL

Mrs Lindsay Wilson
☎ **01750 52254**
sc **From £140–£290**
Sleeps 6
� ▪ W
★★★
SELF CATERING

Delightful character cottage, tastefully furnished and fully modernised, with double glazing, oil central heating and open log fire. Pretty established garden with furniture. Superb location in the picturesque Ettrick Valley, central to all Border towns and places of interest. Selkirk 5 miles, Ettrickbridge 1 mile (food and pub). Linen included in price. Open all year.

Plum Braes Barn, Cliftonhill, Ednam, Kelso, Roxburghshire TD5 7QE

Maggie Stewart
☎ **01573 225028**
Fax 01573 226416
sc **From £190–£400**
Sleeps 2–6
ð ▪ ʀ ë ʀ
Applied

Plum Braes Barn was converted in1999 to include two charming self-catering cottages. Plum Braes has a spiral stair to a double bedroom with a balcony, while Cockle Kitty has two bedrooms. Both have a sitting room with wood burning fire and patio windows to private gardens. Bathroom. Rayburn cooker in kitchen. River walks and wild flower meadow, ideal for birdwatching. Open all year.
E-mail: archie@sol.co.uk

Rowan Tree Cottage, Karingal, Lochton, Coldstream, Berwickshire TD12 4NH

Mrs Rosalind Aitchison
☎ **01890 830205**
Fax 01890 830210
sc **From £200–£350**
Sleeps 2–6
ð ë ʀ ▪ W
★★★
SELF CATERING

Enjoy all-year-round comfort at Rowan Tree Cottage with superb views over beautiful Borders countryside. Delightful lounge with wood burner, cosy kitchen/dining area, downstairs cloakroom, 3 charming bedrooms, bath/power shower. Garden patio. Great base to explore historic Borders, Edinburgh 1 hour. Trout fish on River Tweed. Enjoy our space. Short breaks available. Open all year. E-mail: lochton@btinternet.com.

Roxburgh Newtown Farm, Kelso, Roxburghshire TD5 8NN

Mrs Pauline Twemlow
☎/Fax **01573 450250**
sc **From £120–£320**
Sleeps 2/6
ÿ ð ʀ ▪ W
★★★
SELF CATERING

In a picturesque rural location 5 miles west of Kelso, Swallow and Jimmy's Cottages have been modernised and offer spacious, comfortably furnished accommodation. Jimmy's sleeps 6 and Swallow 2. Colour TV, microwave, dishwasher, central heating, electricity and linen included. Large play area. Ample parking. Open all year.
E-mail: pauline.twemlow@which.net

Thirlestane Farm Cottages, Thirlestane, Lauder, Berwickshire TD2 6SF

Mrs Caroline Barr
☎ **01578 722216**
Fax 01578 722847
sc **From £180–£300**
Sleeps 6
ð ʀ ▪ ʀ W
★★★
SELF CATERING

Renovated to retain their original charm and character, these cottages each provide 3 bedrooms (to sleep 6), large sitting room with open fire and panoramic view, pine kitchen/dining area. Rent includes bedlinen and fuel. Ideal for touring, walking, fishing, riding, easy access to all border towns, only 28 miles from Edinburgh. Pets by arrangement. Open all year.

Our farms offer a range of facilities that are illustrated by symbols in each entry.
Turn to page 14 for an explanation of the symbols.

Established 1957

Host & Guest Service

Central reservation service for

The Farm Holiday Bureau

For overseas visitors

Easy and convenient method to book your farm holiday accommodation

Directions and maps supplied with your booking
Itineraries arranged if you require more than one location

103 Dawes Road London SW6 7DU
Tel: 020 7385 9922 Fax 020 7386 7575
E-mail: farm@host-guest.co.uk
Web: http:www.host-guest.co.uk

The British Incoming Tour Operators Association

England's North Country

Farm entries in this section are listed under those counties shown in green on the key map. The index below the map gives the appropriate page numbers. You will see that we have listed the counties geographically so that you can turn more easily to find farms in neighbouring counties.

At the start of each county section is a detailed map with numbered symbols indicating the location of each farm. Different symbols denote different types of accommodation; see the key below each county map. Farm entries are listed alphabetically under type of accommodation. Some farms offer more than one type of accommodation and therefore have more than one entry.

❶ Cumbria
❷ Northumberland
❸ *Tyne & Wear*
❹ Durham
❺ Tees Valley
❻ Lancashire
❼ Yorkshire
❽ Greater Manchester
❾ Merseyside
❿ Cheshire

KEY MAP TO ENGLAND'S NORTH COUNTRY

Cumbria

Lake District National Park, Solway Coast, Eden Valley
& North Pennines

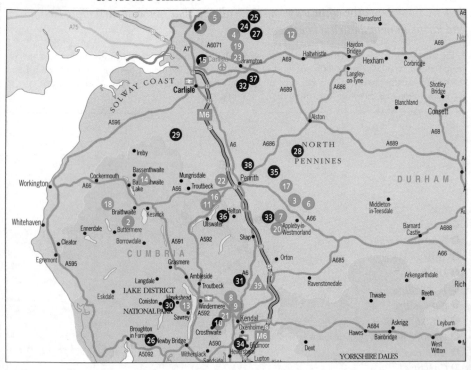

Key

- (1) Bed & Breakfast
- (1) Self-Catering
- (1) B&B and SC
- [1] Camping Barns
- (1) Camping & Caravanning

Find complete peace in Cumbria. To the north lie the Solway Coast and historic Carlisle, while charming market towns such as Alston and Appleby nestle among the hills of the North Pennines. Follow the River Eden to Penrith, gateway to the Lakes. The Carlisle-Settle railway runs right through the lush Eden Valley or try the miniature steam railway at Ravenglass. The Lake District, inspiration of Wordsworth and Beatrix Potter, is one of the best-loved parts of England with its mountains, woods and lakes. Visit the centres of Windermere, Keswick and Kendal and venture out to Wasdale, Buttermere and Longsleddale, great for fell walking. See local shows, crafts, Cumberland and Westmorland wrestling, fell running and hound trailing. It's all here in Cumbria.

If you would like help in finding suitable farm accommodation, turn to the full listing of FHB Groups on pages 392 to 395 to find appropriate contact details for this area.

Bed and Breakfast
(and evening meal)

Bessiestown Farm Country Guest House, Catlowdy, Longtown, Carlisle, Cumbria CA6 5QP

Margaret Sisson
☎ 01228 577219/577019
Fax 01228 577219
BB From £23–£30
EM £12.50
Sleeps 8
🧍 ⛷ ✂ 🏠 ♨ ☂ ◉
♦♦♦♦ Silver Award

Cumbria for Excellence and AA Best Bed & Breakfast for England award winner. Friendly, relaxing atmosphere assured. Warm, pretty en suite bedrooms with colour TV, radio and tea/ coffee. Delicious home cooking using traditional recipes. Residential drinks licence. Indoor heated swimming pool (May–Sept). Beautiful new honeymoon suite. Stop off Scotland and Northern Ireland. M6 J44, A7 to Longtown, then follow signs to Catlowdy. Open all year.

Birkrigg Farm, Newlands, Keswick, Cumbria CA12 5TS

Mrs M M Beaty
☎ 017687 78278
BB From £16–£18
Sleeps 12
⛷ ✂ 🐈 ♨
♦♦

Birkrigg is a dairy and sheep farm very pleasantly situated with excellent outlook in the peaceful Newlands Valley, 5 miles from Keswick. Surrounded by mountains, this is an ideal place to walk and climb. Central for touring. Clean, comfortable accommodation. The breakfasts are good too! Meals available at inns nearby. Packed lunches provided. Open Mar–Dec.

Bridge End Farm, Kirkby Thore, Penrith, Cumbria CA10 1UZ

Mrs Yvonne Dent
☎ 01768 361362
BB From £21–£23
EM From £10
Sleeps 6
⛷(12) ✂ 🐕 ♨
♦♦♦♦♦ Silver Award

Delightful 18th century farmhouse on a dairy farm in the Eden Valley near Appleby. Lovely, spacious, antique-furnished en suite rooms featuring patchwork quilts. Delicious homemade breakfast and dinner served in dining room. All food is freshly prepared and you will never forget Yvonne's sticky toffee pudding. Finish with a stroll along the River Eden. Open all year except Christmas.

Cracrop Farm, Kirkcambeck, Brampton, Cumbria CA8 2BW

Marjorie Stobart
☎ 016977 48245
Fax 016977 48333
BB From £25
EM From £17
Sleeps 6
⛷(12) 🏠 ✂ 🐕 ☂
♦♦♦♦♦ (AA Inspected)

Looking for somewhere special? Then try our superbly appointed large (1847) farmhouse. Set in peaceful countryside with super views, excellent for birdwatching and walking. Spacious en suite bedrooms, hostess tray, colour TV, fresh flowers. Relax in spa bath or sauna. Exercise room. Near Roman Wall, Borders, 1 mile from B6318. Excellent pubs nearby. AA QQQQQ Premier Selected . Every effort has been made to ensure a memorable stay. Open all year.

Craigburn Farm, Catlowdy, Longtown, Carlisle, Cumbria CA6 5QP

Louise Lawson
☎ 01228 577214
Fax 01228 577014
BB From £22–£23
EM From £12
Sleeps 12
⛷ ☂ ✂ 🏠 ♨ ◉
♦♦♦

A warm welcome awaits you at our family run guest house. Delicious homemade meals, sweets our speciality. Residential licence. Stopover to and from Scotland and Northern Ireland. We look forward to meeting you. Open all year.

6 **Dufton Hall Farm,** Dufton, Appleby in Westmorland, Cumbria CA16 6DD

Mrs EM Howe
☎/Fax 01768 351573
🅱 From £18–£20
Sleeps 6
🐾 ⚥ ♿
♦♦♦

Spacious Grade II listed farmhouse in the centre of the beautiful Pennine village of Dufton. 3½ miles from Appleby in Westmorland. En suite rooms with TV, tea/coffee facilities. Guests' lounge. No smoking or pets please. Off road parking. Village pub 200 yards. Superb walking area. Open Mar–Nov.

---

7 **Eden Grove House,** Bolton, Appleby in Westmorland, Cumbria CA16 6AX

Jeanette Atkinson
☎ 01768 362321
🅱 From £22–£24
EM From £12
Sleeps 4
🕭 🐾(12) ⚥ ♿ ⊛
♦♦♦♦ Silver Award

Eden Grove is my semi-retirement home after 25 years at Augill House Farm – same high standards and hospitality apply. En suite bedrooms with colour TV and hospitality tray. Good food cooked in the Aga, conservatory dining room overlooking the garden with views to the Lakes and Pennines. Bolton is a quiet Eden Valley village with church, pub and lovely walks. Ideal for Lakes, Dales and Pennines. Many recreations in the area. Open all year.

---

8 **Garnett House Farm,** Burneside, Kendal, Cumbria LA9 5SF

Mrs Sylvia Beaty
☎/Fax 01539 724542
🅱 From £16–£21
EM From £9.50
Sleeps 10
🐾 🐎 ♿ ⊛
♦♦♦ (AA Inspected)

Lovely 15th century farmhouse, ½ mile from A591 and 10 mins from Windermere. Come and see our oak panelling and 4ft thick walls. Most bedrooms are en suite (one with bathrooom and shower room nearby), all with colour TV and tea/coffee facilities. Short walk to village, inn and public transport. Golf and fishing 1 mile. Good parking. Nov–Mar 3 night breaks £48, en suite £54. Open all year.

---

9 **Gateside Farm,** Windermere Road, Kendal, Cumbria LA9 5SE

Mrs June Ellis
☎/Fax 01539 722036
🅱 From £17.50–£22
EM £9
Sleeps 10
🐾 🐎 ♿ 🌿 ⊛
♦♦♦

Traditional Lakeland working farm, 2 miles north of Kendal on A591. Easily accessible from M6 (jct36). Ideal for touring Lakes and Yorkshire Dales. 16th century farmhouse, all bedrooms have colour TV, tea/coffee facilities, most en suite. Short or weekly stays welcome. Good home cooked breakfasts and evening meals. Lovely walks from the farm with maps provided. Golf and fishing 2 miles. AA QQQ. Open all year.

---

10 **High Gregg Hall,** Underbarrow, Kendal, Cumbria LA8 8BL

Mrs Ciceley Simpson
☎ 015395 68318
🅱 From £16–£18
Sleeps 4
🐾 🐎 ♿ 🌿
♦♦

100-acre dairy/sheep farm in the Lake District National Park within easy reach of M6 jct36. Guests' sitting room, colour TV, tea-making facilities. Bath/shower room. 1 double, 1 twin with washbasins, shaver points. Pub within walking distance. Golf, swimming, horse riding 2–4 miles, Kendal 4 miles, Windermere 6 miles. Open Apr–Nov.

---

11 **Hole House Farm,** Pooley Bridge, Penrith, Cumbria CA10 2NG

Mrs Annette Coulston
☎ 017684 86325
🅱 From £18.50–£21.50
Sleeps 4
🐾(6) 🍴 ♿ 🐾 🌿
Applied

17th century farmhouse stylishly decorated and furnished. Bedrooms have TV and tea/coffee-making facilities. Situated next to the river (free fishing) in a quiet location yet only 15 minutes' walk to the inns and shops in Pooley Bridge from where Lake Ullswater starts and access to the beautiful scenery and fell walks begins. Open Easter–September.

Howard House Farm, Gilsland, Carlisle, Cumbria CA6 7AN

Elizabeth Woodmass
☎ 016977 47285
🅱🅱 From £19–£22
EM From £10
Sleeps 6
🐾(5) ☎ 🛄 ⊛
♦♦♦♦

A warm welcome and comfortable accommodation await you on beef/sheep farm. Situated on an elevated site enjoying magnificent views over 2 counties in the heart of Roman wall country. Guests lounge, colour TV, tea/coffee-making facilities. Dinner by arrangement or bar meals nearby. Discount on 3 night stay. Open all year, except Christmas.

Howe Farm, Hawkshead, Nr Ambleside, Cumbria LA22 0QB

Lisa Woodhouse
☎/Fax 015394 36345
🅱🅱 From £16–£17
Sleeps 6
🐾 ✂ 🖽 🛄 🏛
♦♦

Dating back to 1698, Howe Farm is a traditional stone-built Lakeland farmhouse overlooking Esthwaite Lake. Tastefully decorated with many original features including oak panelling, staircase and log fires. A warm welcome awaits and an excellent breakfast greets you in the morning. Open all year except Christmas and New Year.

Keskadale Farm, Newlands, Keswick, Cumbria CA12 5TS

Mrs M Harryman
☎/Fax 017687 78544
🅱🅱 From £20–£22
Sleeps 6
🐾 ✂ 🖾 🏛 🛄 ⊛
♦♦♦

Traditional Lakeland hill farm in the magnificent setting of the unspoilt Newlands Valley. Ideal for walking or touring the lakes and mountain valleys. Two rooms en suite, one with standard facilities, all with CH, tea/coffee, hairdrier and radio. On chilly evenings relax by a real open fire in the lounge with book or TV. Packed lunches available. A warm welcome awaits one and all. Open Mar–Dec.

New Pallyards, Hethersgill, Carlisle, Cumbria CA6 6HZ

Mrs Georgina Elwen
☎/Fax 01228 577308
🅱🅱 From £18–£23
EM From £13
Sleeps 6
🐾 🛉 🖾 🏇 ☎ 🏛 🛄 ⊛
♦♦♦♦

Friendly hospitality, warmth and comfort await you in this modernised 18th century farmhouse. Situated in the peaceful countryside, surrounded by nature yet easily accessible from M6, A7, M74. All bedrooms en suite, tea/coffee facilities, disabled people welcome. A wide range of leisure and recreational activities are within a few minutes' drive from the farm. National Gold Award. Open all year.

Park House Farm, Dalemain, Penrith, Cumbria CA11 0HB

Mrs Mary Milburn
☎/Fax 017684 86212
🅱🅱 From £18–£21
Sleeps 6
🐾 🏛 🛄 ⊛
♦♦♦

Peace and tranquillity in our valley – you can relax and enjoy stunning views of Lakeland fells. 3 miles from Lake Ullswater or M6 (J40) on A592 entering via Dalemain Mansion (historic house) ignoring the 'no cars' sign. Cumbrian hospitality assured, home baking and generous breakfast. Evening meals available locally. 2 family en suite bedrooms, electric blanket, heater, tea/coffee facilities. Bathroom and shower room. TV lounge with open fire. Open Apr–Oct.

Slakes Farm, Milburn, Appleby in Westmorland, Cumbria CA16 6DP

Mrs C Braithwaite
☎ 017683 61385
🅱🅱 £20
EM From £10
Sleeps 6
🐾 🛉
♦♦♦

Slakes Farm was built in 1734 and is situated between the villages of Milburn and Knock 6 miles from Appleby, in the beautiful Eden Valley. Ideal area for walking and touring. Two en suite bedrooms with tea and coffee-making facilities. Good home cooking, guests' own lounge/dining room with open fire. A very warm welcome. Open Easter–Nov.

18 Swinside End Farm, Scales, High Lorton, Nr Cockermouth, Cumbria CA13 9VA

Karen Nicholson
☎ 01900 85134
BB From £15–£20
Sleeps 6
⊃(5) ♁ ● ☎
Applied

Working farm situated in a peaceful part of Lorton Valley, the perfect base for your Lakeland holiday. Ideal for hill walking and touring around the Lake District. All rooms have CH, H&C, tea/coffee-making facilities and hairdrier. TV lounge with open fire. Magnificent views. Packed lunches available. A warm welcome awaits you. Open all year.

19 Town Head Farm, Walton, Brampton, Cumbria CA8 2DJ

Mrs Una Armstrong
☎ 016977 2730
BB From £15–£16
EM From £9
Sleeps 4
⊃♁☞⤬ ☎ ●
◆◆◆

Relax in the friendly atmosphere of our beef/sheep farm. Our cosy farmhouse overlooks the village green with play area and small nature trail. Scenic views of Pennines and Lakeland Hills. Also near Scottish Borders and Northumbria with Hadrian's Wall nearby. Ideal base for walking, cycling and touring. Delicious home cooking. Evening meals by arrangement or at local pub (400yds). Reduced rate for 3 days or more. Closed Christmas and New Year.

20 Trainlands, Maulds Meaburn, Penrith, Cumbria CA10 3HX

Carol Bousfield
☎ 017683 51249
Fax 017683 53983
BB From £15
EM From £8
Sleeps 5
⊃(12) ♁ ®
◆◆

17th/18th century farmhouse and working farm, situated away from busy roads. We offer a friendly welcome with guests' TV lounge/dining room and a real fire. Tea/coffee available in bedrooms. Evening meals by arrangement. 5 miles west of Appleby, 13 miles south of Penrith. Easy reach of M6, Lakes and Dales. Open April–Nov.
E- mail: bousfield@trainlands.u-net.com

21 Tranthwaite Hall, Underbarrow, Nr Kendal, Cumbria LA8 8HG

Mrs D Swindlehurst
☎ 015395 68285
BB From £21–£23
Sleeps 4
⊃⤬☞ ☎ ● ☜
◆◆◆◆

Magnificent old farmhouse dating back to 11th century. Beautiful oak beams, doors and rare antique fire range. Tastefully modernised with full CH, pretty en suite bedrooms with tea/coffee, radio and hairdrier. Colour TV lounge, separate dining room. This dairy/sheep farm is set in a small, picturesque village between Kendal and Windermere. Walking, golf, pony trekking. Many good pubs and inns nearby. SAE for brochure. Closed Christmas.
E-mail: B&B@tranthwaitehall.freeserve.co.uk

22 Tymparon Hall, Newbiggin, Stainton, Penrith, Cumbria CA11 0HS

Mrs Margaret Taylor
☎/Fax 017684 83236
BB From £20–£25
EM From £12
Sleeps 8
⊃♁☞⤻ ●
◆◆◆

A spacious farmhouse and colourful summer garden situated on a 150 acre sheep farm in a peaceful rural area. Good home cooking. Tea/coffee-making facilities, electric blankets in bedrooms. Open fire in lounge. Lake Ullswater 10 minutes away. Reduction for under 12s; no charge for cot. 4 miles from M6 (jct.40). Open Feb–Nov.
E-mail: margaret@peeearson.freeserve.co.uk

23 Walton High Rigg, Walton, Brampton, Cumbria CA8 2AZ

Margaret Mounsey
☎ 016977 2117
BB From £16–£18
EM From £9
Sleeps 4
⊃⤬☞ ☎ ☜ ● ®
◆◆◆

Enjoy peace, comfort and warm hospitality at this 18th century listed working dairy/sheep farm with spectacular views of the Lakes and Pennines. Explore Scotland, Hadrian's wall or the Lakes. Many lovely walks, golf, fishing, riding available nearby. Children can help to feed the animals, follow the farm trail to the waterfall or relax in the garden. Excellent home cooking. Evening meal by arrangement. Closed Christmas and New Year.

Self-Catering

Arch View and Riggfoot Cottages, Midtodhills Farm, Roadhead, Carlisle, Cumbria CA6 6PF

Jean James
☎/Fax 016977 48213
SC From £130
Sleeps 2/8
&⛄🐎🏇⚙📷☎🎪◎
🐾🐾🐾🐾🐾 Up to Highly
Commended

Arch View and Riggfoot Cottages are on a 320-acre working farm close to Cumbria/Scotland/Northumbria/ borders. Ideal for touring Hadrian's Wall, Gretna Green, Kielder, Carlisle and Lakes. The barn conversion has 5 bedrooms, 2 bathrooms, kitchen/diner, lounge. The 2-bedroomed cottages have four-poster beds, dishwasher, washer, microwave, payphone, video, garden, barbecue. Good walking, trekking, fishing. Open all year.

Bailey Mill, Bailey, Newcastleton, Roxburghshire TD9 0TR

Pamela Copeland
☎/Fax 01697 748617
SC From £98–£468
EM From £8
Sleeps 2/9
&⛄🐎🏇🎪🏇☎🎪 ◎
🐾🐾🐾 Commended

Bailey Mill is a small, friendly holiday complex and pony trekking centre situated in the beautiful Scottish Borders countryside and offering self-contained courtyard apartments. Ride, cycle or walk through miles of forest and quiet country lanes. Return to relax in our leisure suite, then have a meal or drink in our bar. Open all year.

Bessiestown Farm, Catlowdy, Longtown, Carlisle, Cumbria CA6 5QP

Margaret Sisson
☎ 01228 577219/577019
Fax 01228 577219
SC From £75–£340
EM From £12.50
Sleeps 4–5
🐎☷🏊🎪◎
🐾🐾🐾 Commended

Three tastefully converted two bedroomed courtyard cottages enjoying extensive views over Border country. Well furnished, spacious, warm and welcoming. Swim in the pool, meander through the meadows, picnic by the stream, dine in the main house – simply unwind. Indoor heated swimming pool (mid May–mid Sept). Special winter breaks. Phone for colour brochure. Open all year.

Birchbank Cottage, Birchbank, Blawith, Ulverston, Cumbria LA12 8EW

Mrs Linda Nicholson
☎ 01229 885277
SC From £125–£265
Sleeps 4 + cot
⛄🐎🏇⚙🎪🏊◎
🐾🐾🐾🐾 Commended

Relax and unwind in this lovely beamed cottage on a Lakeland sheep farm only 5 miles from Coniston Water. Enjoy marvellous views of the Duddon estuary and Coniston Old Man while walking on the fells around the farm. One double, 1 twin, linen and electricity included. Children welcome. Short winter breaks. Open all year.

Burn Cottage & Meadow View, New Pallyards, Hethersgill, Carlisle, Cumbria CA6 6HZ

Georgina Elwen
☎/Fax 01228 577308
SC From £90–£420
EM From £13
Sleep 5/8
🐎🐎☷🏇☎🏊 ◎
🐾🐾🐾 – 🐾🐾🐾🐾
Up to Highly Commended

Set amidst beautiful countryside close to the Scottish Borders, our fully centrally heated cottages offer a high standard of accommodation with all modern-day facilities. A wide range of leisure and recreational activities are within a few minutes' drive from the farm. Our on-site dining room will make your stay more enjoyable. Discount promotions. Open all year.

27 **Collin Bank,** Bewcastle, Carlisle, Cumbria CA6 6PU

Mrs J Moscrop
☎/Fax 01697 748408
SC From £230–£390
Sleeps 6
🦮 ⛅ 🎣 ⊚
🐎🐎🐎🐎 *Approved*

High on the fells of Bewcastle is Collin Bank Farm with wonderful views of the surrounding countryside. The area is ideal for walking (Hadrian's Wall is not far away), riding and birdwatching. Our chalet is well equipped and comfortable. You can enjoy a swim in our indoor heated pool. Open all year.

28 **Ghyll Burn Cottage,** Hartside Nursery Garden, Nr Alston, Cumbria CA9 3BL

Mrs Susan Huntley
☎ 01434 381372/381428
Fax 01434 381372
SC From £150–£345
Sleeps 4/6 + cot
🦮🐎 ⊞ 🕱 🍴 🎣 ⊚
🐎🐎🐎 *Commended*

Recently renovated farm buildings dating back to 1630 offer spacious and comfortable accommodation for 4/6 people. Kitchen/diner, large lounge with oak beams and wood burning stove on first floor. Attractive twin and double bedrooms, bathroom, are downstairs. Full gas central heating. The cottage is set in a secluded valley with small nursery garden. Ideal for bird wildlife and gardening enthusiasts. Open all year.

29 **Green View Lodges & Well Cottage,** Green View, Welton, Nr Dalston, Carlisle, Cumbria CA5 7ES

Anne Ivinson
☎ 016974 76230
Fax 016974 76523
SC From £155–£530
Sleeps 2/7
🕯🐎 ⊚ 🐎 ⊞ 🍴 🎣 ⊚
🐎🐎🐎🐎 – 🐎🐎🐎🐎🐎
Highly Commended

Superb Scandinavian lodges in peaceful garden setting. 17th century oak-beamed cottages oozing character, one with open fire. Also for non-smokers only, a tastefully converted Wesleyan chapel (regret no pets). Own gardens. In tiny, picturesque hamlet with unspoilt views to Caldbeck Fells 3 miles. Every home comfort provided for a relaxing country holiday. CH, telephones. ½ hr's drive from Keswick, Lake Ullswater, Gretna Green. Free hotel leisure facilities. Open all year. E-mail: grnvlodges@aol.com

30 **Hatter's Cottage,** Hawkshead Hill, Nr Hawkshead, Cumbria LA22 0PW

Mr & Mrs J Gunner
☎ 01539 436203
SC From £130–£325
Sleeps 6
🦮(12) 🍴 🎣
🐎🐎🐎 *Commended*

Detached stone cottage in secluded setting away from roads, surrounded by gardens and fields with mountain views. Situated on 5-acre smallholding at Hawkshead Hill, a picturesque hamlet near the hilltop between Hawkshead (1 mile) and Coniston (2 miles). Walking and cycling from the door. Beamed living room, separate kitchen, 3 bedrooms (1 double, 2 twin), garden. Open all year. E-mail: madhatter@newscientist.net

10 **High Gregg Hall Cottage,** Underbarrow, Kendal, Cumbria LA8 8BL

Mrs Cicely Simpson
☎ 01539 568318
SC From £200–£350
Sleeps 4
🦮 🐎 🎣 🕱
🐎🐎🐎 *Commended*

Set in quiet village near Windermere, our cottage offers beautiful views and walks. 1 double, 1 twin bedrooms, bathroom and shower room. Lounge with TV and video. Kitchen with microwave, washer, fridge, cooker. Full CH. Garden and parking area. Pub within walking distance (10mins). Easy reach of M6 J36. Electricity, bed linen and towels included. Short breaks available. Open all year.

31 **High Swinklebank Farm,** Longsleddale, Nr Kendal, Cumbria LA8 9BD

Mrs Olive Simpson
☎ 01539 823682
SC From £120–£220
Sleeps 4
🦮 🐎 🎣
🐎🐎🐎 *Commended*

High Swinklebank is near the head of the beautiful Longsleddale Valley with lovely views and walking. A recent conversion which is well appointed and includes fitted carpets throughout. Comprising lounge with electric fire, bed settee, TV, lovely kitchen, shower room, 2 bedrooms – double and bunk. Children welcome. Linen provided. Weekends available. Cleanliness and personal attention assured. Open all year.

Long Byres, Talkin Head Farm, Talkin, Brampton, Cumbria CA8 1LT   ㉜

Mrs Harriet Sykes
☎ 016977 3435
Fax 016977 2228
From £99–£303
Sleeps 2–5
Commended

Seven specially designed, fully equipped, warm holiday cottages on North Pennine hill farm. Freshly home-cooked meal service. Enjoy walking (access direct to fells); cycling (green and quiet roads); bird watching (RSPB reserve next door); touring centre for Scottish Borders, Hadrian's Wall, Lake District. Golf, boating, fishing and good pubs close by. Open all year. Email: harriet@talkinhead.demon.co.uk

Lyvennet Cottages, Keld Farm, Kings Meaburn, Penrith, Cumbria CA10 3BS   ㉝

Mrs D M Addison
☎ 01931 714226
Fax 01931 714598
From £160–£420
Sleeps 3–6 + cot
Up to Highly Commended

Four different cottages in and around a small farming village in beautiful, unspoilt Lyvennet Valley. Ideal touring centre for the Lakes or Dales. Attractively furnished with either electric storage heaters, oil CH or log and coal fires in winter inclusive. Also free fly fishing. Children and pets welcome. Open all year.

Preston Patrick Hall Cottage, Preston Patrick, Crooklands, Milnthorpe, Cumbria LA7 7NY   ㉞

Mrs Jennifer Armitage
☎/Fax 015395 67200
From £110–£310
Sleeps 2/6
Commended

Green fields with sheep and cows will be your first sight as you open your bedroom curtains. Our cottage is a self-contained, fully equipped wing of a magnificent medieval manor house. You may spend your time walking the quiet lanes, swimming in our pool or perhaps take advantage of the easy access to the Lakes, Dales and Morecambe Bay. Brochure available. Open all year.

Skirwith Hall Cottage, Skirwith Hall, Skirwith, Penrith, Cumbria CA10 1RH   ㉟

Mrs Laura Wilson
☎/Fax 01768 88241
From £160–£380
Sleeps 9
Commended

Spacious wing of Georgian farmhouse in landscaped riverside garden. Exposed beams and open fire, optional fourth ground floor en suite bedroom. All comforts of home, CH. Ideal base for touring Lakes, North Pennines and Borders or simply unwinding in the idyllic 'Garden of Eden'. Well behaved children and dogs welcome. Short breaks in low season. Brochure. Open all year. E-mail: idawilson@aol.com

Smithy Cottage, c/o Skirwith Hall, Skirwith, Penrith, Cumbria CA10 1RH   ㉟

Mrs Laura Wilson
☎/Fax 01768 88241
From £125–£280
Sleeps 4 + cot
Commended

Originally the home of the village blacksmith. Situated on the outskirts of an unspoilt village in the shadow of Crossfell. Tastefully and comfortably furnished with 1 twin and 1 double room. Nightstore heaters and open fires in sitting and dining rooms. Colour TV, telephone, cot, high chair. Private garden by stream. Good pubs, Carlisle-Settle railway, golf, riding, fishing nearby. Ideal for walking or touring Lakes, Pennine Dales or Borders. Open all year. E-mail: idawilson@aol.com

Swarthbeck Farm, Howtown-on-Ullswater, Penrith, Cumbria CA10 2ND   ㊱

Mr & Mrs WH Parkin
☎ 01768 486432
From £195–£1,164
Sleep 6–14
Up to Commended

Individual 18th century properties overlooking Ullswater, with own lake frontage, boat launching and direct access to fell. Boats and bikes for hire. Bring your own horses – miles of open bridleways. Ideal for active group/family holidays, also for peace and quiet (couples and small parties equally welcome). Open all year.

37 Tarnside Cottages, Tarnside, Farlam, Brampton, Cumbria CA8 1LA

Vicky Reed
☎ **01697 746675**
Fax **01697 746157**
SC From **£200–£360**
Sleep **1/4 + cot**
🌅 🐾 🏠
🐾🐾🐾🐾 *Highly Commended*

Two excellently equipped cottages, each with lounge, dining/kitchen, bathroom and twin bedroom downstairs and spiral staircase to double bedroom. Electricity and heating included, initial supply of logs. Located near Eden Valley, Lake District, Hadrians Wall and the Borders. Tarnside is an excellent base for exploring the area. Open all year. See colour ad on page 31.
E-mail: creed10110@aol.com

---

38 West View Cottages, West View Farm, Winskill, Penrith, Cumbria CA10 1PD

Alan and Susan Grave
☎/Fax **01768 881356**
SC From **£170–£350**
Sleeps **2–6**
🌅 🐾 £ 🏠
🐾🐾🐾🐾 *Commended*

A roomy cottage and two barn conversions on a mixed working farm. Units fully centrally heated, modern kitchen, TV, laundry, towels and linen provided. Scenic views all round from Pennines to Lake Hills. Ideal for touring, walking or restful break. Children and pets welcome. Short breaks. Open all year.

Camping and Caravanning

39 Fellview, Poppy Farm, Selside, Kendal, Cumbria LA8 9ED

Hazel Thompson
☎ **01539 823206**
SC From **£150–£220**
Sleeps **6**
🌅 🐾 🚐 🏠
Inspected

Set amidst beautiful countryside on Lakeland beef and sheep farm, a modern six-berth fully equipped caravan. Kitchen, lounge, two bedrooms, bath/shower, colour TV. Gas and linen included. Excellent views and walking in unspoilt landscape. Ideal base to explore Lakes or Dales. Handy for M6. A lovely place to stay. Open Mar–Nov.

NO ANSWER?
Farmers are mostly out and about during the day.
Try to telephone before 9.30am or after 4pm.

CONFIRM BOOKINGS
Disappointments can arise from misunderstandings over the telephone.
Please write to confirm your booking.

Northumberland

Cheviot Hills, Northumberland National Park,
Northumberland Coast, Kielder Forest & Hadrian's Wall

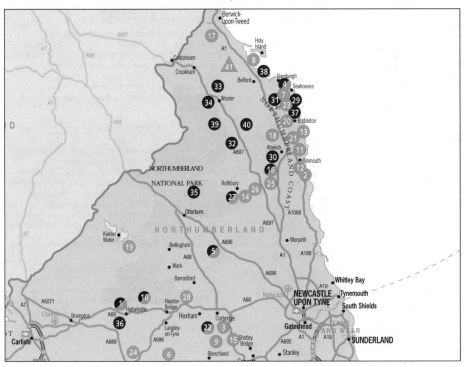

Key

🔵 1 Bed & Breakfast

🔵 1 Self-Catering

🔵 1 B&B and SC

⬜ 1 Camping Barns

🔺 1 Camping & Caravanning

This is an exciting county for the heritage enthusiast with Hadrian's Wall and many other Roman sites, the Border abbeys, the heritage coastline with castles such as Lindisfarne, Bamburgh and Dunstanburgh and, inland, Hexham Abbey and the historic homes of Alnwick Castle, Wallington Hall and Cragside. The Northumberland National Park is a haven of peace and solitude while Kielder Water offers many water activities, birdwatching and magnificent forest surroundings. We have quiet roads, charming country inns, bustling market towns, such as Berwick-upon-Tweed and Alnwick, and friendly people. When are you coming?

If you would like help in finding suitable farm accommodation, turn to the full listing of FHB Groups on pages 392 to 395 to find appropriate contact details for this area.

Bed and Breakfast
(and evening meal)

---

① **Ald White Craig Farm,** Nr. Hadrian's Wall, Haltwhistle, Northumberland NE49 9NW

Isobel Laidlow
☎/Fax 01434 320565
⌨ From £23–£26
Sleeps 4
☌ ⚘ 🍴 ⚒ ⚔ ◎
♦♦♦♦

Peaceful, award-winning en suite B&B in scenic countryside only 2 minutes from A69. Quality furnishings and friendly attention to detail ensure a relaxing holiday. Large garden with summerhouse and panoramic views. Recommended by 'Which' Good B&B Guide. No gimmicks, just genuine North Country hospitality! Good pubs nearby. Plenty to do yet space for solitude. Open Apr–Oct.

---

② **Bilton Barns,** Alnmouth, Alnwick, Northumberland NE66 2TB

Dorothy Jackson
☎ 01665 830427
Fax 01665 830063
⌨ From £22–£25
EM From £11.50
Sleeps 6
☌ ⚔ 🍴
♦♦♦♦ Silver Award

Spacious farmhouse in lovely countryside with magnificent views over Alnmouth and Warkworth bays. Many splendid walks, beaches and castles nearby. Full central heating, guests' lounge and dining room. All with en suite bedrooms, TV and tea/coffee-making facilities. Brian is pleased to take interested guests on a farm walk. Recommended in *Best Bed and Breakfast in the World* and *Which? Good B&B Guide*. Open Easter–mid Oct.

---

③ **Bromley Fell Farm,** Riding Mill, Northumberland NE44 6AY

Carol Davies
☎/Fax 01434 682682
⌨ From £17.50–£20
EM From £7.50
Sleeps 5 + cot
☌ 🍴 🍴
♦♦

Cosy, warm accommodation in separate guest annex within the farmhouse. Dining room and lounge with open beams and log fire. Ideal for families. Evening meals by arrangement using fresh local produce. Open all year.

---

④ **Burton Hall,** Bamburgh, Northumberland NE69 7AR

Eve Humphreys
☎ 01668 214213/214458
Fax 01668 214538
⌨ From £18–£30
Sleeps 19
☌(4) ⚔ 🍴 ◎
♦♦♦

A traditional farmhouse offering a friendly atmosphere with a high standard of service only 1½ miles from Bamburgh Castle. All bedrooms are spacious with tea/coffee facilities and colour TV. Ground floor bedrooms available as well as an elegant residents' lounge and dining room where delicious breakfasts are served. Open Apr–Nov.

---

⑤ **Cornhills,** Kirkwhelpington, Northumberland NE19 2RE

Lorna Thornton
☎ 01830 540232
Fax 01830 540388
⌨ From £20–£25
Sleeps 6
☌ ⚔ ⚘ ⚒ 🍴
♦♦♦♦

A large Victorian farmhouse complete with mosaic tiled hall, spacious beautifully decorated and furnished bedrooms (two en suite), all with outstanding views. Our stock farm is in the centre of Northumberland, ideal for visiting Cragside, Wallington and Belsay Hall. Recommended by the *Which* report *The Good Bed & Breakfast* guide. Newcastle 30 minutes away, 1 mile from the A696. Self-catering available. Closed April & Christmas. See colour ad on page 32. E-mail: cornhills@farming.co.uk

Dukesfield Hall Farm, Hexham, Northumberland NE46 1SH **6**

Mrs Catherine Swallow
☎ 01434 673634
[BB] From £20
Sleeps 4
🐕 🎋 ✁ ▥
♦♦♦

A comfortable Grade II listed farmhouse with log fires and walled garden, on a working farm. Surrounded by beautiful countryside, ideal for walking and touring. This is a peaceful place to stay, with residents' lounge and warm, spacious bedrooms. TV and tea/coffee-making facilities. Children's play area. Country pub with good food 1½ miles away. Open all year.

Elford Farmhouse, Elford, Seahouses, Northumberland NE68 7UT **7**

Mrs M Robinson
☎/Fax 01665 720244
[BB] From £17.50–£20
Sleeps 6
🐕(12) 🎏 ⚒ ▥ 🎾
♦♦♦♦

An old stone farmhouse of great character on an arable farm near the villages of Bamburgh and Seahouses, 1½ miles from the sea. Nearby are beautiful beaches, castles, golf, riding and boat trips to the Farnes and Holy Island. Good local restaurants. Comfortable bedrooms with central heating, colour TV, hair dryers and tea/coffee facilities. Elegant dining room. Some use of outdoor heated swimming pool and lawn tennis court in summer. Open Mar–Oct.

Fenham-le-Moor Farmhouse, Belford, Northumberland NE70 7PN **8**

Mrs K Burn
☎/Fax 01668 213247
[BB] From £18–£24
Sleeps 3
✁ 🎏 ▥ ◉
♦♦♦♦

A comfortable stone-built farmhouse in a peaceful situation with magnificent views overlooking farmland and the bay of Lindisfarne Nature Reserve. An area of outstanding natural beauty and excellent centre for birdwatching, golf, good beaches and visiting many castles. One twin room en suite, one single. Open Easter–Oct.

Flothers Farm, Slaley, Hexham, Northumberland NE47 0BJ **9**

Susan Dart
☎ 01434 673240/673587
Fax 01434 673240
Mobile 0585 038432
[BB] From £17.50–£25
Sleeps 5
🐕 🎋 ▥ ◉
♦♦♦

We are a typical Northumbrian dairy farm, set in beautiful countryside. Accommodation in self-contained area. Easy reach of Ikea, Metro Centre, and Beamish Museum. Full central heating, all rooms en suite, tea/coffee and colour TV. Country pubs within walking distance. Excellent breakfasts provided and packed lunches, if required. Open all year except Christmas.

Gibbs Hill Farm, Bardon Mill, Hexham, Northumberland NE47 7AP **10**

Mrs Valerie Gibson
☎/Fax 01434 344030
[BB] From £17.50–£23
Sleeps 4
🐕(12) ✁ ▥ ⬥ 🎏 ◉
♦♦♦

Spacious farmhouse accommodation of highest standard on traditional 700-acre hill farm/nature reserve in National Park. Beautifully furnished rooms, 1 twin, 1 double (both en suite) with tea/coffee and colour TV and spectacular views. Excellent breakfasts in huge farmhouse kitchen, guests' lounge. Private fishing on own small lake, walking, riding, birdwatching from bird hide overlooking Greenlee Lough. Five minutes to Roman Wall and main Roman sites. Open Apr–Oct.

Hawkhill Farmhouse, Hawkhill, Lesbury, Alnwick, Northumberland NE66 3PG **11**

Mrs Margery Vickers
☎/Fax 01665 830380
[BB] From £22.50–£30
Sleeps 6
🐕(12) ▥
♦♦♦♦

Large traditional farmhouse set in extensive, secluded grounds with magnificent views of the Aln valley and surrounding countryside. Midway Alnwick/Alnmouth, ideal for good beaches, castles and places of interest. One double and 2 twin rooms, all en suite with TV, tea/coffee. Very spacious guests' sitting room and dining room. Full CH and private parking. Open April–Oct.

12 **Hipsburn Farm,** Lesbury, Alnmouth, Northumberland NE66 3PY

Hilda Tulip
☎ 01665 830206
🅱🅱 From £20–£30
Sleeps 6
☞(11) ⅍ ▪ ☆
♦♦♦♦

A spacious farmhouse situated ½ mile from Alnmouth, overlooking the Aln estuary. Rooms comfortably furnished, two double en suite, one twin or double en suite. TV, tea/ coffee-making facilities in all bedrooms. All rooms are centrally heated, dining room-lounge. Ideal area for golfers, walkers and birdwatchers. Private, spacious parking. Open Easter–Oct.

13 **Howick Scar Farmhouse,** Craster, Alnwick, Northumberland NE66 3SU

Mrs Celia Curry
☎/Fax 01665 576665
🅱🅱 From £16
Sleeps 4
☞(5) ☆ ▪
♦♦♦

Comfortable farmhouse accommodation on mixed farm situated on the coast between the villages of Craster and Howick. Ideal base for walking or exploring the coast, moors and historic castles. Guests have their own television lounge/dining room, double bedrooms with washbasins and full central heating. Open May–Nov.

14 **The Lee Farm,** nr Rothbury, Longframlington, Morpeth, Northumberland NE65 8JQ

Mrs Susan Aynsley
☎ 01665 570257
🅱🅱 From £18–£21
Sleeps 5
☞ ╅ ▪ ☆
♦♦♦♦

Relax and enjoy the friendly atmosphere of this large, comfortable farmhouse only 5 mins from Rothbury. Furnished to a high standard with central heating throughout. All bedrooms have washbasin, hospitality trays and hairdrier, one en suite. Guests have exclusive use of lounge (with log fire), dining room and conservatory. Ideal base for touring Northumberland. Pets by arrangement. Private parking. Open Mar–Nov.

15 **Low Fotherley Farm,** Riding Mill, Northumberland NE44 6BB

Mrs Lesley Adamson
☎ 01434 682277
🅱🅱 From £20
Sleeps 4
☞ ╅ ⅍ ▪ ☆
♦♦♦♦

A warm family welcome awaits you in our superb Victorian farmhouse recently refurbished and redecorated to a high standard. Our bright and spacious en suite bedroom has full central heating, colour TV and tea/coffee-making facilities. Well situated for Hexham, Corbridge, Hadrian's Wall Country and the Scottish Borders. Open all year except Christmas.

16 **Lumbylaw Farm,** Edlingham, Alnwick, Northumberland NE66 2BW

Mrs Sally Lee
☎/Fax 01665 574277
🅱🅱 From £22
Sleeps 6
☞(12) ⅍ ▪ ☆ ⚘
♦♦♦♦

Friendly hospitality in a comfortable stone farmhouse on a beef and sheep farm. 6 miles between Alnwick and Rothbury. Outstanding views of the 13th century Edlingham Castle and Victorian disused railway viaduct in farm grounds. Two twin bedrooms, one double (all with washbasin; one with en suite shower). Guest's bathroom, CH throughout. Excellent local eating places available. Open May–Oct. E-mail: holidays@lumbylaw.co.uk

17 **Middle Ord Manor House,** Middle Ord Farm, Berwick-on-Tweed TD15 2XQ

Joan Gray
☎ 01289 306323
Mobile 01410 295004
Fax 01289 308423
🅱🅱 From £27
Sleeps 6
⅍ ▪ ⚘ ☆ ◎
♦♦♦♦♦ Gold Award

Feeling stressed, want to unwind, or are you just wanting to indulge yourself? Either way, why not visit our elegant home and experience the warmth and quality of gracious living in a secluded, tranquil setting. Relax in our spacious en suite rooms (four poster if desired). Holder of Pride of Northumbria Best B&B and England for Excellence Awards. Sorry no children or pets. Open Easter–Oct.
E-mail: joan@middleord.freeserve.co.uk

North Charlton Farmhouse, Chathill, Alnwick, Northumberland NE67 5HP

Mrs Sylvia Armstrong
☎/Fax 01665 579443
[BB] From £25
Sleeps 6
⛄ ♨ 🏵
♦♦♦♦♦ Silver Award

Come and visit us in our homely yet luxurious and spacious farmhouse furnished to a high standard. Two en suites, one private bathroom. One twin with private bathroom. Tea/coffee and TV in our large bedrooms with fantastic views to the sea. Home cooking, tea on arrival with a very warm welcome. Open all year.
E-mail: glenc99@aol.com

Ridge End Farm, Falstone, Kielder Water, Hexham, Northumberland NE48 1DE

Mrs Karen Hodgson
☎ 01434 240395
[BB] From £20–£27
Sleeps 5
⛄ 🐕 🍴 ♨ ☕ 🏵
♦♦♦♦

Working hill farm within Northumberland National Park, next to Kielder Water and Forest Park. This 16th century Bastle house, former home of Border Reivers, has 5ft thick walls. Roaring log fire in winter. Surrounded by magnificent scenery, close to Hadrian's Wall, Scottish Borders, watersports, mountain bike trails and wildlife. Walker's paradise. Pub nearby. Open all year except Christmas & New Year.

Rock Farmhouse, Rock Village, Alnwick, Northumberland NE66 3SB

Audrey & Douglas Turnbull
☎ 01665 579235
Fax 01665 579215
[BB] From £21–£25
EM From £12
Sleeps 6
⛄ 🐕 🍴 🖃 🧍 ♨ 🐾 ☕ 🏵
♦♦♦

Listed 16th century farmhouse with mature walled garden and tennis court, three miles from the coastal path at Dunstanburgh Castle. Award-winning beaches at Newton Bay and the Cheviot hills are nearby. Ten miles of woodland and nature trails. Home cooking with free range eggs and home made bread. Open all year except Christmas & New Year.
E-mail: 100701.2640@compuserve.com.uk

Rock Midstead Farmhouse, Rock Midstead, Alnwick, Northumberland NE66 2TH

Beth Simpson
☎ 01665 579225
Fax 01665 579326
[BB] From £16–£26
EM From £12.50
Sleeps 6
⛄ 🐕 ♨ 🏵
♦♦♦

Comfortable, spacious farmhouse on peaceful dairy farm with extensive views of surrounding countryside. Ideal for walking or cycling, exploring coastline, castles and stately homes. En suite rooms with colour TV and radio. Excellent home cooking, fresh baked bread daily. Log fires, afternoon tea on the lawn. Open all year. See colour ad on page 32. E-mail: ian@rockmidstead.freeserve.co.uk

---

Rye Hill Farm, Slaley, Nr Hexham, Northumberland NE47 0AH

Elizabeth Courage
☎/Fax 01434 673259
[BB] From £20–£25
EM From £12
Sleeps 15
⛄ 🐕 🖃 🧍 🚐 ♨ 🏵
♦♦♦♦

The bedrooms at this small hill farm have many personal touches and are bright and well equipped, all en suite. The lounge has comfy chairs and large O/S wall map. Meals are taken around pine tables in the dining room with log fires in winter, overlooking the garden. Wonderful panoramic views from the ¼ mile driveway. Laundry facilities and bike shed available. Open all year.
Email: enquiries@consult-courage.co.uk

Slate Hall Riding Centre, 174 Main Street, Seahouses, Northumberland NE68 7UA

Mrs M. Nicol
☎ 01665 720320
[BB] From £18–£25
Sleeps 6
⛄ 🐕 🍴 🐴 ♨
♦♦♦♦

Situated on the outskirts of Seahouses, we provide comfortable accommodation and delicious breakfasts. Lots to do including boat trips to Farne Islands, castles and beautiful beaches. Within walking distance of a selection of bars and cafes. Private parking. Beach rides and novice treks from the centre. Open all year. *Associate.*

24 Struthers Farm, Catton, Allendale, Hexham, Northumberland NE47 9LP

Mrs Ruby Keenleyside
☎ 01434 683580
🛏 From £18–£22
EM From £10
Sleeps 5
🐕 🐎 🧳 🛗
♦♦♦

A small working livestock farm situated in a designated area of natural beauty. Quiet country walks, ample safe parking. Children and pets by arrangement. We offer spacious double/twin en suite rooms, Guests' lounge/dining/TV room. Fresh home cooking. Come and enjoy our countryside. Open all year.

25 Swarland Old Hall, Swarland, Morpeth, Northumberland NE65 9HU

Dianne Proctor
☎ 01670 787642
🛏 From £17.50–£20
Sleeps 5
🐕(3) 🧳 🐎
♦♦♦♦

Grade II listed Georgian farmhouse situated on the banks of the River Coquet with breathtaking views. Well furnished en suite bedrooms with tea/coffee-making facilities and TV. Central heating throughout. Guests' lounge with log fire. Excellent location for coast, castles and Scottish Borders. Golf, fishing and shooting available within 1 mile. Open May–Dec.

26 Thistleyhaugh Farm, Longhorsley, Morpeth, Northumberland NE65 8RG

Enid Nelless
☎/Fax 01665 570629
🛏 From £21–£23
EM From £12
Sleeps 6
🐕 🐎 🗡 🧳 🐎
♦♦♦♦

Thistleyhaugh Farm is a spacious farmhouse situated on the banks of the River Coquet. Furnished to a high standard, all rooms are en suite, one with a private bathroom. Evening meals include wine and are followed by coffee in the lounge, with large open fires, exclusive to guests. We are a working farm with a wide variety of animals. Open all year except Christmas.

27 Tosson Tower Farm, Great Tosson, Rothbury, Morpeth, Northumberland NE65 7NW

Mrs Ann Foggin
☎/Fax 01669 620228
🛏 From £18.50–£20
Sleeps 6
🐕 🐎 🛗 🛎 🐎 ◉
♦♦♦♦

Breathtaking views over Coquet Valley and Cheviots combined with traditional farmhouse comforts in this former coaching inn nestling in peaceful hamlet. Border history starts on doorstep with ruined 15th century Tosson Pele Tower. Surrounding hills and forests provide invigorating challenges for serious walkers or a peaceful return to nature for ramblers. Private fishing. Cosy en suite bedrooms, hairdryers, electric blankets, beverages at anytime. CH, real log fires. Closed Christmas & New Year.

28 West Wharmley, Hexham, Northumberland NE46 2PL

Ros Johnson
☎ 01434 674227
🛏 From £20–£22
Sleeps 5
🐕 🐎 🗡 🛗
♦♦

Set on a 400-acre working farm, we offer a warm welcome to our well-appointed accommodation with outstanding views. Private lounge and spacious bedrooms in a self-contained wing of the 18th century farmhouse. Ideal for families. Close to Hadrian's Wall and very accessible to Northumberland's many attractions. Open all year.

LET THE TELEPHONE RING!
Some farmhouses are big places. Let the telephone ring
long enough to give the owner time to answer it.

Self-Catering

Ald White Craig Farm Cottages, Nr. Hadrian's Wall, Haltwhistle, Northumberland NE49 9NW

Isobel Laidlow
☎/Fax 01434 320565
[SC] From £150–£420
Sleeps 2–6 + cot
🐴 🛏 🐕 🖼 🍴 🎯 ⊚
Highly Commended

Warm and comfortable, these farm cottages offer you award-winning accommodation. Nearby are country inns, restaurants and varied attractions including Hadrian's Wall with its stunning scenery and peaceful moorland. On the edge of Northumberland National Park overlooking North Pennine Fells. Open all year.

Annstead Farm Cottages, Beadnell, Chathill, Northumberland NE67 5BT

Mrs Susan Mellor
☎ 01665 720387
Fax 01665 721494
[SC] From £190–£500
Sleep 4–6 + cot
🐴 🛏 🧍 🐕 🖼 🍴 🎯
Highly Commended

Three delightful country cottages situated on working farm ½ mile from Beadnell village in one of the most beautiful coastal areas in Northumberland. Equipped to high standard – heating, lighting and linen included. Ideal for walking, fishing, golfing and birdwatching or as a base to explore the surrounding area – 500yards from beautiful sandy beach. Mobile 07977 269403. Brochure available. Open all year. *Associate.*

Bilton Barns Cottage, Bilton Barns, Alnmouth, Alnwick, Northumberland NE66 2TB

Mrs Dorothy Jackson
☎ 01665 830427
Fax 01665 830063
[SC] From £170–£400
Sleeps 7
🐴 🛏
Highly Commended

Ideally situated for exploring the beautiful Northumbrian coastline with its castles and magnificent walks. Our farm cottage has been recently modernised to a very high standard with a new and fully equipped kitchen, central heating and an open fire with fuel provided. Bed linen is also included in rental. Open all year.

Broome Hill Farm Cottages, Alnwick, Northumberland NE66 2BA

Mrs Margaret McGregor
☎/Fax 01665 574460
[SC] From £200–£490
Sleeps 4/6 + cot
🐴 ⚲ 🍴 ⊚
Highly Commended

Our two cottages have recently been completely renovated to a very high standard with landscaped gardens and secure private heated storage for personal leisure equipment. They are ideally situated for the coast and hills. Open log fires, CH and solid pine furniture. All fuel, electricity and linen inclusive. Sorry no pets or smoking. Open all year.

Doxford Farm Cottage, Doxford Farm, Chathill, Northumberland NE67 5DY

Sarah Shell
☎ 01665 579348
Fax 01665 579331
[SC] From £225–£475
Sleeps 4
🐴 🛏 🖼 ☕ 🍴
Highly Commended

A delightful 17th century stone cottage with well maintained garden ideally situated midway between the Cheviot foothills and the heritage coastline. Tastefully modernised, the open beams have been retained and a woodburning stove installed in the huge stone fireplace. The cottage is very comfortable and well furnished, heated and equipped to a high standard. All fuel power and bed linen provided. Pets are welcome. Open all year.

4 East Burton Farm Holiday Cottages, Burton Hall, Bamburgh, Northumberland NE69 7AR

Eve Humphreys
☎ 01668 214213/214458
Fax 01668 214538
SC **From £250–£500**
Sleeps 4–6
🐶 🏇 🛄 ⊚
🎠🎠🎠🎠 *Up to Highly Commended*

Six comfortable cottages on a working farm 1½ miles from Bamburgh, all well equipped and furnished. Heat, light, sheets and towels included in rent. Ideal base for birdwatching, golf, sightseeing or relaxing. Open all year.

32 The Farmhouse, Northfield Farm, Glanton, Alnwick, Northumberland NE66 4AG

Jackie Stothard
☎ 01665 578203
SC **From £200–£420**
Sleeps 4 + cot
🐶 🛄
🎠🎠🎠🎠 *Highly Commended*

Traditional 18th century farmhouse, with many original features, on our 15-acre smallholding with a variety of livestock. We are in a peaceful yet central location with panoramic views. 2 miles from National Park. Ideal centre for exploring the delights of Northumberland. Comfortable, well equipped accommodation with all mod cons. Open all year.

33 Fenton Hill Farm Cottages, Fenton Hill, Wooler, Northumberland NE71 6JJ

Mrs Margaret Logan
☎/Fax 01668 216228
SC **From £140–£350**
Sleeps 4–6
🐶 🏇 ✂ 🛄 🔥
🎠🎠🎠🎠 *Highly Commended*

Three delightful cottages with superb views of the Cheviot Hills. Centrally situated for lovely beaches, Scottish Borders, hills, historic houses and picturesque valleys. Ideal for walking, family holidays or just to get away and enjoy the peace in a beautiful place. Out of season breaks. Open fires. Home from home comfort. Open all year.
E-mail: hlogan3437@aol.com

34 Firwood & Humphreys, Wooler, c/o North Charlton Farm, Chathill, Alnwick, Northumberland NE67 5HP

Mrs Sylvia Armstrong
☎/Fax 01665 579443
SC **From £200–£650**
Sleeps 6/10
🐶 🏇 🛄 ✂ 🔥
🎠🎠🎠 – 🎠🎠🎠🎠
Highly Commended

Firwood Bungalow and Humphreys House, a choice of two beautiful homes offering a unique and private situation. Standing in 1.5 acres of well maintained gardens within the National Park at the foot of the Cheviots. Ideal for walking and wildlife throughout the year. Every comfort, open fires, central heating. Aga in Firwood. Pride of Northumbria award 1997. Open all year.
E-mail: glenc99@aol.com

10 Gibbs Hill Farm Cottages, Bardon Mill, Hexham, Northumberland NE47 7AP

Mrs Valerie Gibson
☎/Fax 01434 344030
SC **From £120–£450**
Sleep 2–12 + cot
🧍 🐶 🏇 🛄 ✂ 🔥 ⊚
🎠🎠🎠🎠 *Up to De Luxe*

Superb stone cottages on 700-acre traditional hill farm nature reserve in National Park. Central heating, log fires. Outstanding views, walking, riding, trout fishing in own small lake. Birdwatching from bird hide. 5 minutes to Roman Wall and main Roman forts. Centrally placed for north east coast, Tynedale and Lakes. Brochure available. Short breaks. Open all year.

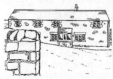

35 The Granary, Charity Hall Farm, Sharperton, Morpeth, Northumberland NE65 7AG

Mandy Lance
☎ 01669 650219
SC **From £300–£650**
Sleeps 6–8 + cot
🐶
🎠🎠🎠🎠🎠
Highly Commended

Recently converted, our farm's old mill and barn is now a well-appointed home. Many beautiful features including a large stone inglenook fireplace, exposed beams and picture window with panoramic view of the Simonside and Cheviot Hills. Fully equipped and tastefully furnished. All-inclusive rent. Perfect setting for a peaceful and relaxing holiday. *Associate.*
E-mail: charityfarm@compuserve.com

The Herdsman Cottage, Cornhills, Kirkwhelpington, Northumberland NE19 2RE

Lorna Thornton
☎ 01830 540232
Fax 01830 540388
⌗ From £200–£350
Sleeps 5
🐎 ⅍ 👫
🐾🐾🐾 *Commended*

A beamed 19th century farm cottage, provides comfortable accommodation for 5 people (double, twin, single). The fully fitted kitchen is equipped with fridge, microwave, washing machine, night storage heaters, open fire. All fuel included in price. Bed linen provided. Enjoy the peace on our stock farm, in the centre of Northumberland. B&B available, see colour ad on page 32. Open all year. E-mail: cornhills@farming.co.uk

---

Keepers Cottages, Tosson Tower Farm, Great Tosson, Rothbury, Northumberland NE65 7NW

Mrs Ann Foggin
☎/Fax 01669 620228
⌗ From £180–£480
Sleeps 4–6
🐎 ⅍ 👫 👫
🐾🐾🐾 – 🐾🐾🐾🐾
Up to Highly Commended

Four delightful cottages situated in the Coquet Valley enjoying panoramic views of the Cheviot Hills. Cosy, comfortable, centrally heated, well equipped and all with enclosed gardens. Set in National Park with many forest and moorland walks clearly marked. Private fishing. 2 miles from Rothbury and the NT property of Cragside. Very central for touring all Northumberland. Bedlinen provided. Log fires during winter. Open all year.

Kellah Cottages, Kellah Farm, Haltwhistle, Northumberland NE49 0JL

Mrs L Teasdale
☎ 01434 320816
⌗ From £110–£220
Sleeps 5
🐎 ⅍ ♣ 👫
🐾🐾🐾 *Commended*

Kellah Cottages are situated on a 280-acre working hill farm, 4 miles from Hadrian's Wall. It is an ideal base for touring and walking. Lake District, Scottish Borders, Metro Centre within an hour's drive. Children can have a hands-on experience of farm life. Central heating and open fires with fuel included. Open all year. E-mail: teasdale@ukonline.co.uk

---

Link House Farm Cottages, Newton-by-the-Sea, Alnwick, Northumberland NE66 3DF

Jayne Hellmann
☎/Fax 01665 576820
⌗ From £180–£700
Sleeps 6–10
🐎 🛋 👫
🐾🐾🐾🐾 *Up to Highly Commended*

Five individual converted cottages/houses on working farm between popular fishing villages of Craster and Beadnell. Yards from NT sand dunes, superb beach, spectacular scenic coastal paths. Units completely self contained, decorated and equipped to high standard. Communal tumble dryer. Excellent bird watching. Farm boasts fine collection of peacocks. Playground. Open all year.

Lumbylaw and Garden Cottages, Lumbylaw Farm, Edlingham, Alnwick, Northumberland NE66 2BW

Mrs Sally Lee
☎/Fax 01665 574277
⌗ From £145–£458
Sleeps 2/6 + cot
🐎 ⅍ ♣ 👫 🐕
🐾🐾🐾 – 🐾🐾🐾🐾
Highly Commended

The two cottages are situated in a beautiful valley with extensive hill views, rich in wildlife with a 13th century castle ruin and a Victorian viaduct providing easy walking along the disused railway line. Centrally heated, prettily decorated, furnished and equipped to a high standard. Own garden. All fuel, power, bedlinen, towels included in rent. Sorry no pets or smokers. Open all year. E-mail: holidays@lumbylaw.co.uk

---

Old Byre, Slaley, Nr Hexham, Northumberland NE47 0AH

Elizabeth Courage
☎/Fax 01434 673259
⌗ From £350–£650
EM From £12
Sleeps 9
🐎 ⅍ 🔲 🧍 🛋 ♣ ⊚
🐾🐾🐾🐾🐾 *Highly Commended*

Superb conversion of 17th century barns on a small hill farm with wonderful panoramic views and ¼ mile driveway. Ground floor has large two–three bedded en suite room and lounge/dining room/kitchen in semi-open plan area with long dining table and wood burner stove. Upstairs there is one double en suite, bathroom, one bunk and one twin room. Evening meals available. Open all year. Email: enquiries@consult-courage.co.uk

---

38   **Outchester & Ross Farm Cottages,** Ross Farm, Belford, Northumberland NE70 7EN

Mr J B Sutherland
☎ 01668 213336
Fax 01668 213174
⟦sc⟧ From £150–£450
Sleep 4–6
🐕 ⚓ 🎇 🍷 ⊛
🔑🔑🔑🔑 *Up to Highly Commended*

A unique secluded coastal location between the historic Holy Island of Lindisfarne and Bamburgh. Choice of warm, attractive cottages at Ross, which is a no-through-road farm from which a footpath leads to a fine sandy beach, and Outchester Farm nearby. Each has own parking and garden. Open all year. See colour ad on page 33. *Associate.*

---

39   **Shepherd's Cottage,** Ingram Farm, Powburn, Alnwick, Northumberland NE66 4LT

Sarah Wilson
☎/Fax 01665 578243
⟦sc⟧ From £245–£450
Sleeps 7
🐕 🐕 🎇 ⚓ 🍷 🎇 🍷
🔑🔑🔑🔑 *Commended*

On a working family farm in the beautiful Breamish Valley, the cottage has superb scenery on the doorstep. Explore the unspoilt Cheviot Hills or the coast and castles. Most mod cons are provided and there are no extras – fuel, linen and towels all included. Central heating from open fire. Night storage heating. Extra 'Z' bed available. Open all year except Christmas and New Year.

---

40   **Titlington Hall Farm,** Alnwick, Northumberland NE66 2EB

Mrs Vera Purvis
☎/Fax 01665 578253
⟦sc⟧ From £175–£315
Sleep 2–10
🐕 🎇 ⚓ 🍷
🔑🔑🔑🔑 *Commended*

Two lovely country cottages available for holiday lets all year round. They are situated in a beautiful area with many interesting places close by. Facilities include central heating, TV, fridge, washing machine, microwave, tumble dryer and all linen. Children and pets welcome. Can sleep families of up to 10. Open all year. See colour ad on page 34.

Camping and Caravanning

---

41   **Barmoor South Moor,** Lowick, Berwick-upon-Tweed TD15 2QF

Mrs Ann Gold
☎ 01289 388205
⟦sc⟧ From £115–£220
Sleep 6
🐕 🎇
★★★★

We have two six-berth caravans situated on a peaceful site of five caravans adjacent to the farmyard of our working farm. Both have mains services including shower, toilet, TV, fridge, a double and bunk bedroom. Ideal location for exploring the beautiful Northumberland coastline, Cheviot Hills and Scottish Borders. Open Easter–Oct.

Please mention **Stay on a Farm** when booking

110

Durham

North Pennines, Weardale, Teesdale & High Force

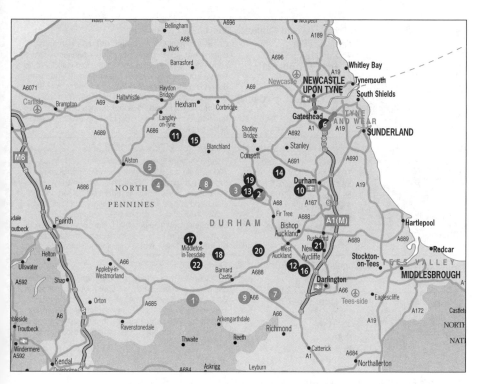

Key

1 Bed & Breakfast

1 Self-Catering

1 B&B and SC

1 Camping Barns

1 Camping & Caravanning

Come and discover for yourself the tremendous variety of County Durham, from the high, wild fells of Weardale and Teesdale in the west, designated 'England's Last Wilderness' and home to unique wild flowers and birds, the spectacular river scenery on the Tees, acres of unspoilt countryside dotted with market towns, pretty villages, castles and fortified farmhouses, and the university city with its cathedral, castle and medieval streets, to the as yet undiscovered North Sea coast in the east, now reclaimed from its industrial past.

Quiet roads make motoring a pleasure still, and there are unrivalled opportunities for walking, cycling and outdoor activities. We have wonderful museums which interpret the rich social, industrial and Christian heritage of the county and display the cultural life of the area. Add to that the proximity of vibrant Tyneside and Teesside and our famous Northern hospitalityand you have it all.

If you would like help in finding suitable farm accommodation, turn to the full listing of FHB Groups on pages 392 to 395 to find appropriate contact details for this area.

Bed and Breakfast
(and evening meal)

---

1 **East Mellwaters Farm,** Bowes, Barnard Castle, Co Durham DL12 9RH

Patricia Milner
☎/Fax 01833 628269
BB From £17.50–£20
EM From £10
Sleeps 7
🐕🐈🦃⚓👤🐏🎣🖂🏕 ⊛
♦♦♦

Come and meet Dolly, our highland cow, watch the dippers and golden plovers or glimpse badgers. Learn about the Bronze Age on our waymarked walks. Fish for brown trout, we'll show you the best pools. Visit Beamish, Bowes Museum, ancient castles, market towns or the Metro Centre for shopping (Christmas?). Then relax with a cup of tea, log fire and delicious food in best farmhouse tradition. Holidays and special break rates. Open mid Feb–mid Dec.

---

2 **Greenwell Farm,** Nr Wolsingham, Tow Law, Bishop Auckland, Co Durham DL13 4PH

Mike & Linda Vickers
☎ 01388 527248
Fax 01388 526735
BB From £20–£25
EM From £8.50
Sleeps 12
🐕🦃🖂✂🐏⚓👤🎣 ⊛
♦♦♦

There is something special about Greenwell Farm and its 300 year-old stone barn, now converted into accommodation. That speciality is homeliness, the unique atmosphere that our visitors come for. We offer warmth and comfort with blend of pine and dark oak antique furniture. High quality food using home produced, naturally reared meat and vegetables where possible. Enjoy our working mixed farm with nature trails and beautiful countryside. Closed Christmas and New Year. E-mail:greenwell@farming.co.uk

---

3 **Holywell Farm,** Wolsingham, Bishop Auckland, Co Durham DL13 3HB

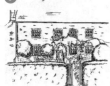

Mrs Marjorie Love
☎ 01388 527249
BB From £15–£20
Sleeps 6
🐕🦃🐾
♦♦

200-acre mixed dairy farm pleasantly situated near village and places of interest such as Beamish Museum, Hadrian's Wall, Durham City, etc. You will find a friendly warm atmosphere in this Grade II listed farmhouse with many original features. Central heating throughout with colour TV, tea/coffee-making facilities in both bedrooms. Open Mar–Nov.

---

4 **Lands Farm,** Westgate-in-Weardale, Bishop Auckland, Co Durham DL13 1SN

Mrs Barbara Reed
☎ 01388 517210
BB From £22
Sleeps 5
🐾🖂🎣
♦♦♦♦

A friendly welcome awaits you on our 280-acre beef and sheep farm peacefully situated in beautiful Weardale. All bedrooms have luxury en suite facilities, TV and tea/coffee. Conveniently located for Durham City, Beamish Museum, Hadrian's Wall, High Force and walking in the North Pennines. Open Mar–Nov.

---

5 **Low Cornrigg Farm,** Cowshill-in-Weardale, Bishop Auckland, Co Durham DL13 1AQ

Mrs Janet Ellis
☎/Fax 01388 537600
BB From £19–£22
EM From £9.80
Sleeps 6
🐕(5)🦃🖂🐾🎣🖂 ⊛
♦♦♦♦(AA Inspected)

Luxury 200-year-old farmhouse with panoramic views over High Pennines. Very central for touring Lakes, Durham, Hexham, Darlington, Newcastle. All rooms en suite with TV, tea trays, full CH. Take breakfast in conservatory, enjoy wonderful home-cooked food in licensed dining room. TV lounge. We are an Approved Riding School offering lessons and treks. Drystone walling courses. Good walking, Green Tourism Award Winner. Open all year except Christmas Day.

Low Urpeth Farm, Ouston, Chester Le Street, Co Durham DH2 1BD   6

Hilary Johnson
☎ 0191 410 2901
Fax 0191 410 0081
BB From £20–£25
Sleeps 6
✁(6) ✄ ■ ☂ ⊚
♦♦♦♦

Traditional stone farmhouse with spacious and tastefully furnished rooms. TV/beverage facilities, easy chairs, one double with washbasin, 2 twin en suite. Within easy reach of Beamish Museum, Durham and castles and coast of Northumberland. Directions – leave A1(M) at Chester Le Street, follow A693, at 2nd roundabout fork right to Ouston, continue 1½ miles down hill, over roundabout, turn left at 'Trees Please' sign. Closed Christmas and New Year. E-mail: treesplease@btinternet.com

Rokeby Close Farm, Hutton Magna, Richmond, North Yorkshire DL11 7HN   7

Don & Julie Wilkinson
☎ 01833 627171
Fax 01833 627662
BB From £20
Sleeps 6
✁(12) ✝ ■ ⊚
♦♦♦♦

Unique old farmhouse recently restored to a high standard, all rooms fully en suite. Ideal base for exploring Durham and North Yorkshire's Dales, market towns, museums, abbeys, forts, houses, wildlife trusts or miles and miles of remote moors. Breakfast in our large conservatory with stunning views. Log-fired drawing room available. Internet access and office if required. E-mail: Don.Wilkinson@farmline.com

Rose Hill Farm, Eastgate-in-Weardale, Bishop Auckland, Co Durham DL13 2LB   8

June Wearmouth
☎ 01388 517209
BB From £20
EM From £10
Sleeps 12
✁ ✝ ✄ ✆ ■
Applied

Barn conversion adjoining farmhouse on working hill farm. Attractive hilltop position with superb views. Ideal touring, walking and cycling country. Private fishing. Spacious en suite bedrooms, including ground floor rooms, offering high standards of comfort and furnishing. Situated on north side of the A689, one mile west of Eastgate. Open all year.

Wilson House, Barningham, Richmond, North Yorkshire DL11 7EB   9

Mrs Helen Lowes
☎ 01833 621218
BB From £18.50–£25
EM From £10
Sleeps 6
✁ ✝ ✄ ☂ ■
♦♦♦♦

Relax and unwind in a traditional country retreat. Set amidst magnificent scenery, Wilson House offers a high standard of accommodation, a relaxing atmosphere and friendly welcome. (FHG Diploma.) Tour the Dales by car or take one of the many beautiful walks then return to the open fire and smell of home cooking. Varied menus using fresh local/home produce and tailored to your tastes. Open all year except Christmas.

Self-Catering

Arbour House Bungalow & Cottage, Arbour House Farm, Crossgate Moor, Durham DH1 4TQ   10

Rena & John Hunter
☎ 0191 384 2418
Fax 0191 386 0738
SC From £130–£325
Sleeps 6
✁ ⊞ Å ⟐ ■ ⊚
⌁⌁⌁⌁ *Commended*

Peacefully situated on a working family farm skirting Durham City with spectacular views of extensive countryside. The secluded area is the perfect location for a quiet break or active holiday. Durham City's beautiful cathedral, castle and riverside walks are a short distance away. Metro Centre, Beamish Museum and Gateshead Angel are also close. Holy Island, the Roman Wall and Kielder Reservoir within easy reach. Open all year. E-mail: arbourhouse@btinternet.com

11 **Bail Hill,** Allenshields, Blanchland, Consett, Co Durham DH8 9PP

Jennifer Graham
☎ 01434 675274
[sc] From £150–£250
Sleeps 5
⮎ 🖾 🏠 ♨
🐾🐾🐾 *Commended*

Centrally heated, 2-bedroomed farmhouse with breathtaking views to Derwent Reservoir near Blanchland. Enjoy the peaceful surroundings of a typical hill farm or use as a central location for Tynedale, Durham and N E Coast. Blanchland is one of the most picturesque of Northumbrian historic villages with Abbey, pub and post office. Open fire and well-equipped kitchen. Enclosed garden and parking outside the house. Open all year.

12 **Brackenbury Leases Farm,** c/o Brackenbury House, Bildershaw, West Auckland, Co Durham DL14 9PL

Mrs R P Pickering
☎ 01388 832484
[sc] From £140–£250
Sleeps 7
⮎ 🐴 🏠 ♨
🐾🐾🐾 *Commended*

This modernised farmhouse offers bright, cheerful rooms with attractive rural views. CH, double glazing, open fire, well equipped kitchen with dining area and garden make this ideal for family holidays. Central for touring Teesdale, Weardale and Northumbria. The old towns of Barnard Castle, Richmond and Durham are within easy driving distance. Open all year. Email:brackenbury@clara.net

13 **Bradley Burn Cottages,** Bradley Burn Farm, Wolsingham, Weardale, Co Durham DL13 3JH

Mrs Judith Stephenson
☎/Fax 01388 527285
[sc] From £140–£330
Sleep 2–5
🏃 ⮎ 🐴 🧗 ♨ 🏠 ♨ 🖾
🐾🐾🐾🐾
Up to Highly Commended

Explore our fields and woods, observe modern farming, watch for owls and herons. Stay in one of four comfortable, well equipped cottages adjoining the farmhouse at Bradley Burn, at the gateway to Weardale and the North Pennines. Excellent sightseeing and walking base, or just unwind. Granary Cottage is ideal for families, Stable and Harvest Cottages perfect for couples. Our brochure has full details. Short breaks available. Open all year. Email: stay@bradleyburn.demon.co.uk

14 **Browney Cottage,** c/o Hall Hill Farm, Lanchester, Durham DH7 0TA

Mrs Pat Gibson
☎/Fax 01388 730300
[sc] From £150–£275
Sleeps 4
⮎ 🏠 ♨ 🖾
🐾🐾🐾🐾 *Up to*
Commended

Browney Cottages are one mile from our family-run open farm. During your stay visitors can bottle feed the lambs, see fluffy chicks and lots more. Both cottages have 1 double and 1 twin. Kitchen with fridge/freezer, microwave, washer and tumble dryer. Bedlinen included. Ample parking. Open all year except Christmas. E-mail: hallhill@globalnet.co.uk

15 **Buckshott Farm Cottage,** Blanchland, Consett, Co Durham DH8 9PL

Lorraine Bainbridge
☎ 01434 675227
[sc] From £130–£245
Sleeps 6
⮎ 🧗 ⤢ ♨
🐾🐾🐾 *Commended*

Attractive 2-bedroom cottage which adjoins the farmhouse and overlooks the beautiful Derwent Valley. Central heating, fitted kitchen, private garden, ample parking. Blanchlands historic village has a shop, post office, pub and a 12th century abbey. Hexham, Durham, Beamish Open Air Museum, Gateshead Metro Centre and the Northumberland coast are all within an easy day's outing. Open Mar–Nov.

2 **Greenwell Hill Stables & Byre,** c/o Greenwell Farm, Nr Wolsingham, Tow Law, Co Durham DL13 4PH

Linda & Mike Vickers
☎ 01388 527248
Fax 01388 526735
[sc] From £175–£385
Sleeps 4–6
⮎ 🐴 🍴 🧗 ♨ 🦌 🖾
🐾🐾🐾🐾 *Highly*
Commended

Enjoy a relaxing stay in a quality cottage with character on this traditional farm in peaceful countryside. Pleasant walks and nature trail. Both cottages are well equipped with gas CH, woodburning stove, microwave, etc. Natural beams and fitted carpets. The Stables has a four-poster, en suite bathrooms and dishwasher. We are ideally located for Beamish, Durham City and touring the Dales and Northumberland. Open all year. E-mail: greenwell@farming.co.uk

High House Farm Cottages, High House Farm, Houghton Le Side, Darlington, Co Durham DL2 2UU ⑯

Harry & Peggy Wood
☎/**Fax 01388 834879**
ⓈⒸ **From £140–£340**
Sleeps 2–6
🎠 🐴 🐕 ⛺ 🛢
🔑🔑🔑🔑 *Highly Commended*

Gateway to Northumbria with panoramic views across Teesdale to North Yorks Moors. Near A1(M), A68 scenic route and Dere Street Roman Road. Home of 'Fairisle' Shetland sheep and 'Aymara' alpacas. Smithy, Granary and Coach House conversions, sensitively combining four-poster, beams and log burning stove with night storage heaters, power showers, TVs and other modern amenities. Open all year.

Katie's Cottage, c/o Low Urpeth Farm, Ouston, Chester Le Street, Co.Durham DH2 1BD ⑥

Hilary Johnson
☎ **0191 410 2901**
Fax 0191 410 0081
ⓈⒸ **From £210–£285**
Sleeps 4
🎠 ⚱ 🛢 ⛺ ⊚
🔑🔑🔑🔑

Highly Commended

Katie's Cottage is furnished to a high standard and offers excellent accommodation. The ground floor has two en suite bedrooms and a delightful living area with timber beams. All linen, towels, electricity and CH are included. Easy access to Durham, Beamish Museum, heritage sites and sightseeing in Northumberland. Open all year.

North Wythes Hill, Wythes Hill Farm, Lunedale, Middleton-in-Teesdale, Co Durham DL12 0NX ⑰

Mrs June Dent
☎ **01833 640349**
ⓈⒸ **From £160–£350**
Sleeps 7
🎠 🐴 🛢 ⛺
🔑🔑🔑🔑 *Commended*

Cosy, three bedroomed cottage with full central heating. Peaceful situation on a working hill farm where children can feed pet lambs (in season), ducks and see plenty of wildlife. Actually on Pennine Way route. Circular walks from the door. Large garden. Prices include bedlinen and towels. Open all year.

Romaldkirk Cottages, Kleine Cottage, Romaldkirk, Barnard Castle, Co Durham DL12 9ED ⑱

Gwen Wall
☎/**Fax 01833 650794**
ⓈⒸ **From £150–£995**
Sleeps 6–17
🎠 🐴 🛢 ⛺ ⊚
🔑🔑🔑🔑 *Up to Highly Commended*

Nestling between the village green and a 120-acre farm are 3 detached stone-built cottages offering 2–7 bedrooms. Each cottage is well equipped and has ample parking and an enclosed area around it. Romaldkirk lies in the heart of Teesdale, an Area of Outstanding Natural Beauty, with endless walks, most sporting activities and many places of interest to visit. There is something for everyone in this quiet, unspoilt dale. Open all year. See colour ad on page 34.

Sandycarr Farm Cottage, c/o Holywell Farm, Wolsingham, Bishop Auckland, Co Durham DL13 3HB ⑲

Mrs Marjorie Love
☎ **01388 527249**
ⓈⒸ **From £130–£300**
Sleeps 5–6
🎠 🐴 🐦
Applied

Newly converted barn set in beautiful countryside, ideal for relaxing, touring, walking or visiting places of local interest. Tastefully decorated in keeping with character. One ground floor double bedroom, one double and one single first floor bedroom with handbasins, lounge and kitchen with dining area. Fully equipped, all linen, towels, electricity and oil CH included. Open all year.

Stonecroft, Low Lands Farm, Low Lands, Cockfield, Bishop Auckland DL13 5AW ⑳

Mr K & Mrs A Tallentire
☎/**Fax 01388 718251**
ⓈⒸ **From £150–£295**
Sleeps 4 + cot
🎠 🐴 🛢
🔑🔑🔑 *Highly Commended*

Charming old farmworker's cottage recently renovated and decorated to retain its traditional style and character. On the borders of wonderfully unspoilt Teesdale, Weardale and Durham Dales. Set in an area full of historic towns and sights. Ideally suited for walkers, families and professionals wanting a quiet restful break. Open all year.

21 West Cottage, Carrsides Farm, Rushyford, Ferryhill, Co Durham DL17 0NJ

Mrs E Wilkinson
☎/Fax 01388 720252
[SC] From £220–£350
Sleeps 4
🐕🐓✄👤🚲🛥⛺ 🏵
🎐🎐🎐🎐 *Highly Commended*

A warm welcome awaits you at Carrsides Farm. West Cottage overlooks the orchard and guests can relax in the enclosed garden. The low-beamed ceilings add atmosphere to this very well-equipped two-bedroomed cottage. Evening meals can be arranged. You can explore the whole area from this very central base.

22 Westfield Cottage, Laithkirk, Middleton-in-Teesdale, Barnard Castle, Co Durham DL12 0PN

Doreen Scott
☎ 01833 640942
[SC] From £200–£450
Sleeps 6
🐕🐓🛥☕⛺ 🏵
🎐🎐🎐🎐 *Highly Commended*

Westfield Cottage is a Grade II listed building very recently renovated and furnished to a high standard. Situated on a working farm in beautiful Teesdale. Excellent touring, cycling and walking country with the Pennine and Teesdale Ways close by. The Cumbrian border is about 6 miles away. Ample parking area, free fishing and local village only ½ mile away. Open all year.

USE THE INDEX

FARM HOLIDAY BUREAU

The comprehensive Index shows which farms offer access to disabled visitors; caravanning/camping facilities; the chance to participate on a working farm; stabling/grazing for visiting horses; en suite rooms; a welcome to business people; acceptance of *Stay on a Farm* gift tokens.

STAY ON A FARM GIFT TOKENS

FARM HOLIDAY BUREAU

If you have enjoyed your Stay on a Farm, why not treat your friends and relatives to *Stay on a Farm* gift tokens? Available from the Bureau office (tel: 024 7669 6909), they can be redeemed against accommodation and are accepted by the majority of farms (see Index). Please check when booking to avoid disappointment.

FOLLOW THE COUNTRY CODE

Leave nothing but footprints,
Take nothing but photographs,
Kill nothing but time!

Lancashire

Arnside & Silverdale, Morecambe Bay, Vale of Lune, Pennine Way, Forest of Bowland, Ribble Valley & Pendle

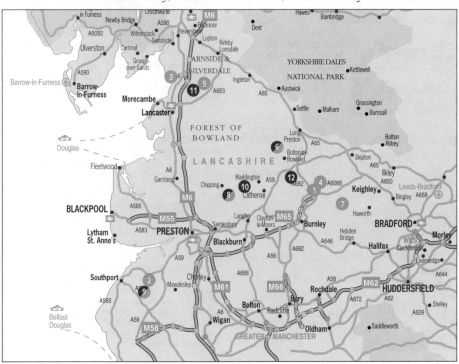

Key

1 Bed & Breakfast

1 Self-Catering

1 B&B and SC

1 Camping Barns

1 Camping & Caravanning

Lancashire is a truly beautiful county, areas of which still await discovery by many visitors – a treat lies in store for them. The bracing, northern coastline encompasses the resorts of Morecambe, Arnside and Silverdale, lively Blackpool with its famous illuminations and elegant Southport. The scenic countryside of Forest of Bowland, Ribble Valley and Pendle are rich in wildlife and offer excellent walking, while market towns like Clitheroe with its castle and such unspoilt villages as Barley, Downham (where 'Whistle Down the Wind' was filmed) and Wycoller offer havens away from the hustle and bustle. The area is also known for its 'Hetty Wainthrop' connections; and for bargain hunters, we have some of the best mill shops in the country.

If you would like help in finding suitable farm accommodation, turn to the full listing of FHB Groups on pages 392 to 395 to find appropriate contact details for this area.

Bed and Breakfast
(and evening meal)

---

1 Blakey Hall Farm, Red Lane, Colne, Lancashire BB8 9TD

Mrs R Boothman
☎ 01282 863121
BB From £18–£23
EM From £10
Sleeps 6
♠ ⛄ ⅄ ⚘ ❦ ⚒ ♦
♦♦♦

Delightful old Grade II listed working dairy farm. Oliver Cromwell is reputed to have stayed here. Ideally situated to provide the holidaymaker with a good base to visit the Yorkshire Dales/Brontë Country and Lake District. Full English breakfast. Comfortable accommodation, guests' own TV lounge. 3 bedrooms, 1 en suite, tea/coffee facilities. Open all year.

---

2 Brandreth Barn, Brandreth Farm, Tarlscough Lane, Burscough, Nr Ormskirk, Lancashire L40 0RJ

Mrs M Wilson
☎ 01704 893510
BB From £22.50–£30
Sleeps 20
♿ ⛄ ⚘ ⅄ ❦ ⚒ ♦
Awaiting new rating

Situated alongside the wildfowl trust Martin Mere, an 18th century brick-built barn conversion dated 1774. 5 minutes from A59, 15 mins from M6. All rooms fully centrally heated, with tea/coffee-making facilities. All rooms en suite plus colour TV. Licensed restaurant using fresh homegrown produce. Evening meal by arrangement. Also disabled facilities. Arable farm. Open all year except Christmas.

---

3 Galley Hall Farm, Shore Road, Carnforth, Lancashire LA5 9HZ

Vera Casson
☎ 01524 732544
BB From £16–£18
EM From £10
Sleeps 5
⛄(4) ♞ ⅄ ⚘ ⚒ ❦
♦

Galley Hall is situated on the coast within easy reach of the Lake District, the Dales and historic Lancaster. We offer a warm and friendly welcome to all at our working farm and 17th century farmhouse with views of Lakeland hills and Morecambe Bay. Share the comforts of our large lounge with TV and log fires. Bedrooms have washbasins, tea-making facilities and TV on request. 5 minutes from M6 J35. Open Jan–Nov.

---

4 Higher Wanless Farm, Red Lane, Colne, Lancashire BB8 7JP

Carole Mitson
☎ 01282 865301
Fax 01282 865823
BB From £20–£24
EM From £11
Sleeps 4
⛄(3) ⚒ ❦ ⚘ ⚞
♦♦♦♦

Ideally situated for visiting 'Pendle Witch' country, Haworth or Yorkshire Dales – the farm nestles peacefully alongside the Leeds/Liverpool Canal. Shire horses and sheep are reared on the farm, where the warmest of welcomes awaits you. Spacious and luxurious bedrooms (1 en suite) offer every comfort for our guests. Several country inns nearby offering wide range of meal facilities. AA Selected establishment. Open mid Jan–mid Dec.

---

5 Low House Farm, Claughton, Lancaster LA2 9LA

Mrs Shirley Harvey
☎ 01524 221260
BB From £18
Sleeps 6
⛄ ♞ ⅄ ⚒ ❦ ⚘ ◎
Applied

Enjoy a warm welcome on our working mixed dairy farm in the heart of the picturesque Lune Valley. All rooms have tea/coffee-making facilities and TV. Guests' TV lounge and large garden. Fishing, golf, waymarked walks and cycleways locally. Close to village pub serving traditional food. Ideal base for Lakes, Yorkshire Dales and coast. M6 J34 6 miles. Open all year.
E-mail: shirley@lunevalley.freeserve.co.uk

Middle Flass Lodge, Settle Road, Bolton-by-Bowland, Nr Clitheroe, Lancashire BB7 4NY ⑥

Joan M Simpson
☎ 01200 447259
Fax 01200 447300
BB From £20–£27.50
EM From £14
Sleeps 11
♿(2) ⌇ ✕ ⊞ ▪ ⌦
♦♦♦♦(AA Inspected)

Our tastefully converted barn/cow byre, based on the family farm, has idyllic views of the surrounding countryside. An ideal touring base, being situated on Lancashire and Yorkshire border. Full en suite facilities, tea/coffee, CH, TV, etc. Comfortable lounge with stove. Cosy dining room with chef prepared cuisine. Licensed. Open all year.

Parson Lee Farm, Wycoller, Colne, Lancashire BB8 8SU ⑦

Patricia Hodgson
☎ 01282 864747
BB From £15–£17
EM £7
Sleeps 6
⌇ ⌦ ⌦ ▪ ⓢ
♦♦♦

There's a warm welcome at our 110-acre sheep farm on the edge of beautiful Wycoller Country Park. The 250-year old farmhouse, with exposed beams and mullion windows, is peacefully located and perfect for walking, being on the Brontë and Pendle Ways. Easy access to Lancashire or Yorkshire. Pendle Way walking breaks with transport. En suite bedrooms, furnished in country style, have tea/coffee-making facilities. Open all year except Christmas & New Year. E-mail: pathodgson@hotmail.com

Rakefoot Farm, Chaigley, Nr Clitheroe, Lancashire BB7 3LY ⑧

Mrs Pat Gifford
☎ 01995 61332
BB From £14–£20
EM From £10
Sleeps 6
⌇ ⌦ ⌦ ▪ ⌦ ⓢ
Applied

A warm welcome awaits whether you are on holiday or business. Peaceful 100-acre family farm in beautiful Forest of Bowland with 17th century farmhouse and traditional stone barn conversion. Refreshments on arrival, superb home cooking. Evening meals by arrangement only. Excellent accommodation, panoramic views, original features, log fires. CH, games room, babysitting, laundry. Ground floor rooms available. 3 miles Chipping village, 8 miles M6 J31A. Open all year.

Sandy Brook Farm, Wyke Cop Road, Scarisbrick, Southport, Lancashire PR8 5LR ⑨

Mrs W E Core
☎/Fax 01704 880337
BB From £17
Sleeps 15
♿ ⌦ ▪ ⌦
♦♦♦

This small, comfortable arable farm is situated in the rural area of Scarisbrick, midway between the seaside town of Southport and the ancient town of Ormskirk. A570 ½ mile. The converted farm buildings are attractively furnished, and all bedrooms have en suite facilities, colour TV and tea/coffee facilities. Silver winners NWTB Place to Stay, 'Commended' award Holiday Care Service. Open all year except Christmas.

Self-Catering

The Coach House, Clough Bottom Farm, Bashall Eaves, Clitheroe, Lancashire BB7 3NA ⑩

Jane Backhouse
☎ 01254 826285
Fax 01254 826015
SC From £180–£250
Sleeps 4
⌦ ⌦ ⌦ ▪ ⌦ ⓢ
Applied

Newly converted Grade II listed coach house retaining its original character. Own private drive. Adjoins the orchard by the stream. Complete with own outdoor seating area. Full gas cental heating. Set on organic and conservation-minded hill farm 5 miles from market town of Clitheroe. Ideal base for Lakes/Dales. Homemade meals available for purchase on site. Open Dec 1999 onwards. E-mail: focus.training@btinternet.com

(11) Garden Cottage, High Snab, Gressingham, Lancaster LA2 8LS

Mrs Margaret Burrow
☎ 015242 21347
⑤ç From £210–£280
Sleeps 4 + cot
🛏 🎠 ⊛
⚘⚘⚘⚘ *Commended*

Garden Cottage, with its own private drive and garden, adjoins our farmhouse on a working dairy and sheep farm in a quiet location. Ideal for touring lakes, dales and coast. Award winner. Conservatory and utility room with washer and drier. Well equipped kitchen/oak beamed lounge. Two bedrooms, 1 double, 1 twin, snooker table, bathroom with shower. CH from farmhouse, cot/high chair available. Electric and linen included. 5 miles M6 J35. Brochure. Open Mar–Nov.

(12) Higher Gills Farm, Rimington, Clitheroe, Lancashire BB7 4DA

Freda M Pilkington
☎ 01200 445370
⑤ç From £180–£280
Sleeps 6
🦽🎠🐴⚘🎋🛏⊛
⚘⚘⚘ *Commended*

A traditional stable converted into two holiday apartments with spectacular views of the Ribble Valley, situated on a family working hill farm. Footpaths leading to open moorland. 4 miles from Gisburn. 'Granary' on first floor has exposed beams. 'Lower Laithe' on ground floor has Grade 2 wheelchair access. Both share large patio and safe grassed area. Open all year.

(6) Middle Flass Lodge, Settle Road, Bolton-by-Bowland, Nr Clitheroe, Lancashire BB7 4NY

Joan M Simpson
☎ 01200 447259
Fax 01200 447300
⑤ç From £95–£380
Sleeps 8
🛏🎠🕮🛏🎋
Applied

Traditional stone barn newly converted into two dwellings on three levels. Situated on family farm in prime countryside location on Lancs/Yorks border. Dates back to 1700's. Well maintained with exposed beams and open fires, cental heating. Linen included. One-bedroom apartment and three-bedroom house can be interlinked to sleep 8. Open all year.

(8) Rakefoot Barn, Rakefoot Farm, Chaigley, Nr Clitheroe, Lancashire BB7 3LY

Mrs Pat Gifford
☎ 01995 61332
⑤ç From £70–£399
Sleeps 2–8
🛏🎠🐴🛏🎋🎋⊛
⚘⚘⚘⚘ – ⚘⚘⚘⚘⚘
Up to Highly Commended

A warm welcome awaits holiday makers and business guests on peaceful 100-acre family farm in Forest of Bowland. Traditional stone barn conversion, original features, superbly furnished. Fully fitted kitchens, CH, woodburners, en suite bedrooms (some ground floor). Meals service, laundry, games room, play areas, patios, gardens, panoramic views. Babysitting. 3 miles Chipping village, 8 miles M6 J31A. 4 properties, 3 can be internally interlinked to sleep 16. Open all year.

(9) Sandy Brook Farm, Wyke Cop Road, Scarisbrick, Southport PR8 5LR

Mr W H Core
☎/Fax 01704 880337
⑤ç From £100–£270
Sleeps 2/6
🦽🎠⚘🛏🎋
⚘⚘⚘ *Commended*

Our newly converted 18th century barn, which stands in peaceful countryside, offers five superbly equipped and traditionally furnished holiday apartments. We are 3½ miles from the seaside town of Southport and close to many other places of interest. The apartments sleep 2/6 and 'The Dairy' is especially equipped for disabled guests. Open all year.

Most farms are full Members of FHB. Some are shown as Associates – see page 11.

Yorkshire

Dales, Brontë Country, South, West & Harrogate

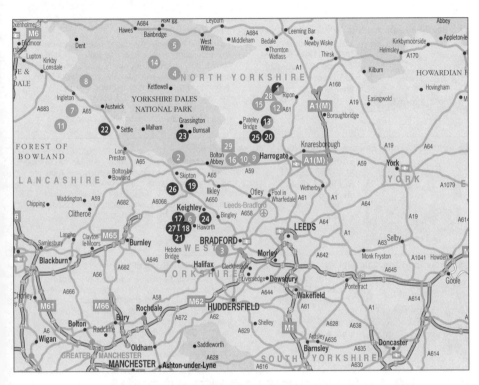

Key

- ❶ Bed & Breakfast
- ❶ Self-Catering
- ❸ B&B and SC
- ⬛ Camping Barns
- ▲ Camping & Caravanning

Mention the Yorkshire Dales and you evoke lush, green valleys, dry stone walls and fields dotted with stone barns, clear tumbling streams, quaint villages and warm, friendly people. 'Brontë Country' conjures up images of windswept moors, heather, romance, deep valleys, woollen mills and industrial heritage. For history and heritage visit Haworth and the Brontë Parsonage, Bolton Abbey, Skipton Castle and the Bradford Industrial Museum. Elegant Harrogate is famed for its wide open spaces and gardens, while 'Last of the Summer Wine Country' can be found around Holmfirth. Shop til you drop in mill shops and open-air markets or take a ride on one of our steam railways. It's all here!

If you would like help in finding suitable farm accommodation, turn to the full listing of FHB Groups on pages 392 to 395 to find appropriate contact details for this area.

Bed and Breakfast

(and evening meal)

---

1 **Bay Tree Farm,** Aldfield, Nr Fountains Abbey, Ripon, North Yorkshire HG4 3BE

Valerie Leeming
☎/Fax 01765 620394
BB From £22.50–£25
EM From £12
Sleeps 12
🐕 🐎 🌾 ⚙ 🍴 🏺 🌟 ⊛
◆◆◆◆

As featured in Which B&B, this 17th century converted stone hay barn combines character with comfort in quiet hamlet. Beautiful Fountains Abbey, ½ mile. York, Harrogate and Dales all in easy reach. Lovely circular walks from our door returning to open fires and super cooking (HE trained). All rooms en suite, CH, beverages, TV. Kettle always on the boil. Ideal for 'get togethers' or just a peaceful few days. Colour brochure. Open all year.

---

2 **Bondcroft Farm,** Embsay, Skipton, North Yorkshire BD23 6SF

Christine Clarkson
☎ 01756 793371
BB From £20–£25
Sleeps 6
🐕 🐎 🌾 ⚙ 🏺 🌾
◆◆◆◆

Stay at Bondcroft Farm and enjoy good farmhouse food. Also watch the sheep dogs – the farm is well known for breeding them – being trained for sheep dog trials. The en suite rooms have TV and tea/coffee-making facilities. The guests' lounge has a good collection of interesting books. Open Mar–Nov. E-mail: bondcroft@yorks.net

---

3 **Brow Top Farm,** Baldwin Lane, Clayton, Bradford, West Yorkshire BD14 6PS

Margaret Priestley
☎/Fax 01274 882178
BB From £20–£25
Sleeps 4
🐎 🏺 ⊛
◆◆◆◆

Visitors are most welcome to our family beef farm. The farmhouse has recently been modernised to a very high standard with central heating throughout. 1 double, 1 twin and 1 family room all with private bathroom, colour TV, fridge and tea/coffee-making facilities. Conveniently situated for visiting the Dales and Brontë Country. Plenty of good eating places in the area. Open all year (closed Christmas).

---

4 **Bushey Lodge Farm,** Starbotton, Upper Wharfedale, Skipton, North Yorkshire BD23 5HY

Rosie Lister
☎/Fax 01756 760424
BB From £22.50
Sleeps 4
🐎 🌾 🐎 🍴 🏺 🌾 ⊛
◆◆◆◆

Traditional working hill farm of over 2,000 acres set in the heart of the Yorkshire Dales. The lovely old farmhouse nestles on the edge of Starbotton village and has been sympathetically restored to create a haven of peace and tranquillity. The en suite bedrooms have TV, hairdryer and tea/coffee-making facilities. Featured in the Which? Good Bed & Breakfast guide. Open all year except Christmas.

---

5 **Church Farm,** Hubberholme, Upper Wharfedale, Nr Skipton, North Yorkshire BD23 5JE

Mrs Gill Huck
☎ 01756 760240
BB From £17.50–£20
Sleeps 4
🐾(6) 🌾
◆◆◆◆

A traditional 16th century Dales farmhouse on a working hill farm in the Upper Wharfedale village of Hubberholme. Ideally situated for walking and touring. Two bedrooms, one en suite, one with private bathroom, both with colour TV, hairdryer and tea/coffee-making facilities. Open all year.

Far Laithe Farm, Laycock, Keighley, West Yorkshire BD22 0PU   6

Sylvia Lee
☎ 01535 661993
BB From £19.50–£21.50
EM From £12.50
Sleeps 4
⛱(12) ⊞ ▪
♦♦♦♦

Traditional 17th century Yorkshire farm close to Haworth, Skipton and the Dales, set in the heart of open countryside. Tea-making facilities and colour TV in all bedrooms. Luxury en suite facilities. Enjoy dinner in our licensed oak-furnished dining room. We pride ourselves on the quality of our food and hospitality and look forward to welcoming you to our home. Open all year.

Fowgill Park Farm, High Bentham, Nr Lancaster, North Yorkshire LA2 7AH   7

Shirley Metcalfe
☎ 01524 261630
BB From £17
EM From £10
Sleeps 4
⛱ 🐾 ⤢ ▪ ⊛
♦♦♦♦

Welcome to Fowgill, a Georgian farmhouse, ideal for those who wish to stay where it is quiet. Guests enjoy panoramic views of the Dales and Fells. A good centre for visiting the Lakes, Dales, coast, waterfalls and caves. Beamed bedrooms have washbasins, shaver points and tea/coffee-making facilities; two bedrooms en suite. Comfortable beamed lounge with television. Separate dining room. Bedtime drink included. Open Easter–Oct.

Gatehouse Farm, Far Westhouse, Ingleton, North Yorkshire LA6 3NR   8

Nancy Lund
☎ 015242 41458/41307
BB From £20–£22
EM From £10
Sleeps 6
⛱ 🐾 ⤢ ▪ ↩ ⊛
♦♦♦

Bryan and Nancy welcome you to our dairy and sheep farm built in 1740, rooms with old oak beams in elevated position enjoying panoramic views over open countryside in the YORKSHIRE DALES NATIONAL PARK. Guests' dining room, and lounge with colour TV. Bedroom with private facilities and tea trays. Welcome drink on arrival. 15 miles J34 M6, also J36 1½ miles west of Ingleton just off A65. Open all year (closed Christmas and New Year).

Graystone View Farm, Graystone Plain Lane, Hampsthwaite, Harrogate, North Yorkshire HG3 2LY   9

Gloria Metcalfe
☎ 01423 770324
Fax 01423 772536
BB From £20–£25
Sleeps 6
⛱ 🐾 ⤢ ▪ ⚜ ⊛
♦♦♦♦

18th century farmhouse in tranquil setting with comfortable rooms to come back to after a lovely day seeing the wonderful sights that Yorkshire has to offer. Bedrooms have tea/coffee-making facilities. We are a family run farm set in 100 acres and located ¼ mile from the A59 west of Harrogate. Open all year except Christmas and New Year.
E-mail: mg@graystonefm.freeserve.co.uk

Knabbs Ash, Skipton Road, Kettlesing, Felliscliffe, Nr Harrogate, North Yorkshire HG3 2LT   10

Sheila Smith
☎ 01423 771040
Fax 01423 771515
BB From £22.50
Sleeps 6
⛱(10) ⤢ 🐾 ▪ ⊛
♦♦♦♦ Gold Award

White Rose Award-winning B&B. Recommended by *Which? Good Bed and Breakfast Guide.* Smallholding 6 miles west of Harrogate off the A59 in a tranquil position with delightful views over the countryside. En suite rooms enhanced by quality furnishings, colour TV, hair dryer, tea/coffee-making facilities, CH. Private guest sitting and dining room with separate tables. Ideal area for walking and touring. Good local inns. Open all year except Christmas.

Lane House Farm, High Bentham, Lancaster, North Yorkshire LA2 7DJ   11

Betty Clapham
☎ 015242 61479
BB From £17–£18.50
Sleeps 6
⛱ 🐾 ⤢ ⚜ ▪ ⊛
♦♦♦♦

Enjoy a relaxing break at our 17th century beamed farmhouse, within ½ mile of the Forest of Bowland, with beautiful views of the Yorkshire Dales. 1 mile from the market town of High Bentham, ½ hour from M6. Ideal for caves, waterfalls, touring the Lakes. Bedrooms have washbasins and tea-making trays. En suite facilities. Guests' lounge with colour TV. Separate dining room. Open Mar–Nov.

---

12 **Mallard Grange,** Aldfield, Nr Fountains Abbey, Ripon, North Yorkshire HG4 3BE

Mrs Maggie Johnson
☎ **01765 620242**
⬛ From £22.50–£25
EM From £12
Sleeps 8
⌂(12) ✂ 🐾 ⑳
♦♦♦♦Silver Award

Rambling 16th century working farm, full of character and charm, in a glorious rural setting close to Fountains Abbey. Welcoming, spacious and offering exceptional quality and comfort. All rooms en suite. Delicious breakfasts and, by arrangement, dinner. Ideal touring base as Yorkshire Dales, historic properties, gardens, York and Harrogate are within easy reach. Open all year.

---

13 **North Pasture Farm,** Brimham Rocks, Summerbridge, Harrogate, North Yorkshire HG3 4DW

Eileen Payne
☎ **01423 711470**
⬛ From £22.50
EM From £13.50
Sleeps 3
✂ 🕱 🐾
♦♦♦♦

North Pasture Farm, a 14th century listed farmhouse, beamed and mullioned and oozing with character, awaits discerning guests. Warm and cosy with central heating throughout, together with en suite bedrooms and separate dining room and separate TV lounge. Peaceful and quiet, sheltered by Brimham Rocks. Within easy reach of Harrogate, Ripon, Skipton, York and Fountains Abbey. Open Mar–Nov.

---

14 **Redmire Farm,** Buckden, Upper Wharfedale, Nr Skipton, North Yorkshire BD23 5JD

Mrs Julia Horner
☎ **01756 760253**
Fax 01756 760360
⬛ From £20–£25
EM £12.50
Sleeps 6
✂ ☕ 🕱 ⑳
♦♦♦♦

Family-run, traditional working hill farm set in heart of Yorkshire Dales. 1,600 acres of stunning woodland, moorland and farmed parkland bound by 2½ mile stretch of the River Wharfe. Former shooting lodge, now sympathetically restored and very comfortably refurbished, with 1 twin and 2 double rooms, all en suite with controllable CH, colour TV and beverages. House accessible all day, cosy lounge. A welcoming family providing a wholesome table of mainly home-reared and locally produced food. Closed Christmas.

---

15 **St George's Court,** Old Home Farm, High Grantley, Ripon, North Yorkshire HG4 3EU

Mrs Sandra Gordon
☎/Fax 01765 620618
⬛ From £22.50
Sleeps 12
⌂(2) 🐾 🖭 🐾 🕱 ⑳
♦♦♦

Beautifully situated accommodation in renovated farm buildings. Comfortable ground floor en suite rooms with colour TV and tea/coffee facilities, all with views of open countryside. Breakfast in our beautiful listed farmhouse and enjoy the view from our conservatory dining room. Peace and tranquillity are our passwords. Open all year.

---

16 **Scaife Hall Farm,** Blubberhouses, Otley, West Yorkshire LS21 2PL

Christine Ryder
☎ **01943 880354**
Fax 01943 880374
⬛ From £22.50
Sleeps 6
🐾 ✂ 🕱 🐾 ⑳
♦♦♦♦

Scaife Hall is a working farm set in a tranquil, rural location. Recommended by *Which? Good Bed and Breakfast Guide*, our 19th century farmhouse offers two double and one twin bedded rooms, each tastefully decorated. All en suite with beverage tray, clock radio, hairdryer, CH. Private guests' lounge with colour TV, dining room for hearty breakfasts. Local inns provide excellent meals. Open all year except Christmas and New Year.
E-mail: christine.a.ryder@btinternet.com

LET THE TELEPHONE RING!
Some farmhouses are big places. Let the telephone ring
long enough to give the owner time to answer it.

Self-Catering

Bottoms Farm Cottages, Bottoms Farm, Laycock, nr Keighley, West Yorkshire BD22 0QD

Mrs J Parr
☎/Fax 01535 607720
[SC] From £150–£320
Sleep 2/4
🐎 🗕 🏛 @
🐾🐾🐾🐾 *Highly*
Commended

Bottoms Farm is a rural 35-acre sheep farm situated on the south side of a beautiful valley with spectacular views. Howarth 4 miles, Skipton 7 miles. These luxury cottages have been recently converted to the highest standard from 200 year old mistal/barn. Fully equipped. Heating and linen included. Sorry no pets. Open all year.

Brontë Country Cottages, c/o West Field Farm, Tim Lane, Haworth, West Yorkshire BD22 7SA

Clare Pickles
☎ 01535 644568
Fax 01535 646686
[SC] From £120–£390
Sleeps 2/6 + cot
🐎🐓🖾🌳🏛🐈🐾 @
🐾🐾🐾 – 🐾🐾🐾🐾🐾
Highly Commended

Beautiful cottages in a stunning, peaceful location overlooking Haworth's famous Brontë Parsonage. Sheep and calves to feed, eggs to collect. Large play area. Picnics by the river, nature trail, ½ mile from Steam Railway and famous 'Railway Children' walk. Day trips to Eureka!, Skipton and the Dales, York, Saltaire, Photographic Museum, Royal Armouries and more. Open all year.

Cawder Hall Cottages, c/o Cawder Hall, Cawder Lane, Skipton, North Yorkshire BD23 2QQ

Anne Pearson
☎ 01756 791579
Fax 01756 797036
[SC] From £150–£360
Sleep 2–5
🧍 🐎 🖾 🏛 🐾 @
🐾🐾🐾 – 🐾🐾🐾🐾
Up to Highly Commended

Enjoy the peace and quiet of our warm, welcoming cottages which, while being surrounded by fields of animals are only 1 mile from Skipton with its thriving street market, medieval castle and church. Each cottage is well equipped (colour TV, video, microwave) and is suitable for disabled guests. There is a lawned garden, barbecue, phone, laundry room and children's play area. Linen, gas and electricity included as are cots and high chairs. Open all year.

Dukes Place, Fountains Abbey Road, Bishop Thornton, Harrogate, North Yorkshire HG3 3JY

Jaki Moorhouse
☎ 01765 620229
Fax 01765 620454
[SC] From £145–£375
Sleeps 2–6
🐎🐓🦢🧍🖾🏛🐎🐾 @
🐾🐾🐾 – 🐾🐾🐾🐾 *Up to*
Highly Commended

Situated in the heart of Nidderdale yet close to Harrogate, Dukes Place is a well-maintained property comprising the owners' 18th century farmhouse and cottage-style apartments developed from the original farm buildings. Working stables from which riding can be arranged. We have horses, ducks, geese, hens and Jacob sheep. Pets welcome. Open all year.

Heather & Bilberry Cottages, Hole Farm, Dimples Lane, Haworth, Keighley, West Yorkshire BD22 8QT

Mrs Janet Milner
☎/Fax 01535 644755
[SC] From £200–£500
Sleep 4/8 + cot
🐎 🗕 🏛
🐾🐾🐾🐾🐾 *Highly*
Commended

The old barn has been carefully converted to make two cottages with most bedrooms en suite. We are a small working farm, the sort that appears in children's Ladybird books. Gloria the sow, Gilbert the turkey, foals and calves. Ideal for children. A short walk to the village to see the Brontë Museum or a walk on the moors 2 minutes from our door. Sorry no pets. Open all year.

---

22 Layhead Farm Cottages, Field House, Rathmell, Settle, North Yorkshire BD24 OLD

Rosemary Hyslop
☎ 01729 840234
Fax 01729 840775
🆂 From £200–£350
Sleeps 7
🐾🏌️🏡♿🎋🐾 ⊛
🐾🐾🐾🐾 *Highly Commended*

Layhead Farm Cottages are located on a working farm on the edge of the Dales village of Rathmell, quiet and peaceful yet only 4 miles from the market town of Settle. The conversion of an old stone barn has resulted in two cottages, modern and comfortable yet full of charm and character. Open all year. E-mail: rosehyslop@easynet.co.uk

---

23 Maypole Cottage, Blackburn House Farm, Thorpe, Skipton, North Yorkshire BD23 6BJ

Liz Gamble
☎ 01756 720609
🆂 From £190–£340
Sleeps 4
🐾🏌️🏡♿🎋 ⊛
🐾🐾🐾🐾 *Highly Commended*

An 18th century stable converted to a particularly high standard in the tiny hamlet of Thorpe near Burnsall. This well equipped cottage has full central heating, exposed beams and stonework open fire. Colour TV, microwave, washer/dryer. Bathroom with shower. Linen provided. Large walled garden, ample parking. Open all year.

---

24 Meadow, Field & Daisy Cottages, Coach House, Spring Head, Tim Lane, Haworth, W Yorks BD22 7RX

David and Hilary Freeman
☎ 01535 644140
🆂 From £90–£270
Sleeps 2–4
🐾🏌️♿
🐾🐾🐾 – 🐾🐾🐾🐾
Highly Commended

A warm Yorkshire welcome is assured at our three cosy cottages, converted from a 200-year-old barn, ½ mile from the Brontë sisters' Haworth and within easy reach of the Yorkshire Dales. We pride ourselves on our high standard of cleanliness and comfort. Each cottage has full CH, with colour TV, cooker, fridge, microwave, washer, dryer. Gas, electricity, linen and towels, cot, highchair inclusive. Pets by arrangement. Open all year.

---

25 Old Spring Wood Lodges, Helme Pasture, Hartwith Bank, Summerbridge, Harrogate, N Yorks HG3 4DR

Rosemary Helme
☎ 01423 780279
Fax 01423 780994
🆂 From £165–£650
Sleep 2–12
🧍🐾🏌️♿🎋♿🐾🎋 ⊛
🐾🐾🐾 – 🐾🐾🐾🐾
Up to Highly Commended

Exclusive Scandinavian lodges in woodland setting overlooking the Nidd Valley. Also converted Dales farmhouse – mind your head on the beams! Excellently equipped, with CH. Colour TV, payphone, laundry, easy parking. Extensive woodland tracks, magnificent views. Ideal centre for Harrogate, York, Dales, coast and Herriot Country. Warm personal welcome. Pets also welcome! Open all year. E-mail: info@oldspringwoodlodges.co.uk

---

26 Street Head Farm, Lothersdale, c/o Tow Top Farm, Cononley, Skipton, N Yorks BD20 8HY

Mrs J Gooch
☎ 01535 632535
🆂 From £250–£590
Sleep 10
🐾🏌️🎋♿🎋
🐾🐾🐾🐾🐾 *Highly Commended*

Traditional Dales farmhouse set in open farmland with stunning views. Renovated to retain its original charm with oak beams, stone fireplaces and flagged floors yet excellently equipped with CH, colour TVs, dishwasher, laundry, fridge, freezer, microwave, linen, etc. Five bedrooms, one en suite, one ground floor with shower room, bathroom, two sitting rooms, open fire. Ideal for families. A warm welcome all year.

---

1 Trip's Cottage, Bay Tree Farm, Aldfield, Nr Fountains Abbey, Ripon, North Yorkshire HG4 3BE

Valerie Leeming
☎/Fax 01765 620394
🆂 From £145–£195
Sleeps 2
🏌️🐾🏡♿🎋 ⊛
🐾🐾🐾 *Commended*

Converted stable which sleeps 2, shown to the left of the farmhouse. Fine panoramic views over Fountains Abbey. Tasteful conversion consists of lobby, shower, toilet, fitted kitchen (microwave/electric cooker), lounge/ diner (with colour TV). Double bedroom, bed linen and storage heaters included in the rent. Pay–phone available. Shops at Ripon (3 miles), eating 2 miles. Private parking and gardens. Ideal for touring Dales, Moors and York. Local walks. Open all year.

Two Hoots Cottage, North Pasture Farm, Brimham Rocks, Summerbridge, N Yorkshire HG3 4DW

Eileen Payne
☎ **01423 711470**
⓼ **From £225–£450**
EM From £13.50
Sleeps 3
🚲 🎠 🛢
🐾 🐾 🐾 *De Luxe*

Warm, cosy centrally heated cottage. Use of indoor heated swimming pool. Peaceful and quiet, sheltered by Brimham Rocks. Within easy reach of Harrogate, Ripon, Skipton, York and Fountains Abbey. National Trust waymarked walks straight from cottage door. Open all year.

Well Head Cottage, Hanging Gate Lane, Oxenhope, Keighley, West Yorkshire BD22 9RJ

Mrs Nicola Binns
☎ **01535 647966**
⓼ **From £200–£400**
Sleeps 4
🐕 🚲 🎠
🐾 🐾 🐾 🐾 *Highly Commended*

Delightful, well equipped stone-built cottage, full of character and old oak beams. Recently renovated and refurbished to a high standard. Enjoy the magnificent view and peaceful, rural setting while only a short walk from the centre of Haworth. Non-smokers preferred. Open all year.

Camping and Caravanning

Woodhouse Farm Caravan Park, Winksley, Nr Ripon, North Yorkshire HG4 3PG

Alison Hitchen
☎ **01765 658309**
Fax **01765 658882**
⓼ **From £160–£200**
🐕 🐎 🛢 🎠 ⊛
★★★★

Woodhouse Farm and Country Park is set amidst 56 acres of natural woodland and meadows with its own 2½ acre coarse fishing lake, children's play area and games room. Close by are Fountains Abbey and Brimham Rocks with Ripon, Britain's smallest city and famous for its cathedral, just 6 miles away. Open Easter–Oct.

Bunkhouse/Camping Barn

West End Outdoor Centre, Whitmoor Farm, West End, Summerbridge, Harrogate, North Yorkshire HG3 4BA

Margaret Verity
☎/Fax **01943 880207**
⓼ **Sole use of centre £800 per week**
From £5 pppn
Sleeps 30
🐕 🐎 🛢 🎠 ⊛
Inspected

Set amidst stunning scenery overlooking Thruscross reservoir in a Designated Area of Outstanding Natural Beauty adjoining the Dales National Park. The Centre offers excellent facilities for 30 people in 9 bedrooms. No meters, AGA cooker, private parking. 12 miles Harrogate and Skipton, 30 miles York. Ideal venue for the larger family. Open all year.

Yorkshire

Dales (North), Vales, Moors, Wolds & Coast

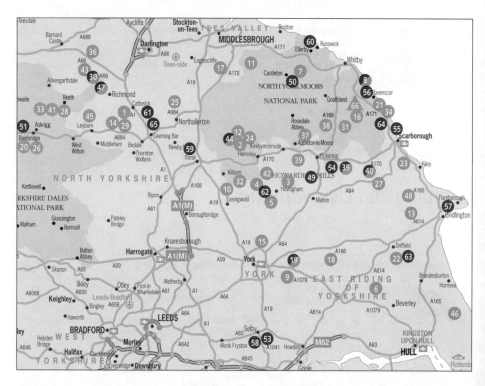

Key

(1) Bed & Breakfast

(1) Self-Catering

(1) B&B and SC

1 Camping Barns

⚠ Camping & Caravanning

From the historic city of York, with its spectacular Minster, city walls and medieval streets, to the busy harbours and endless sandy beaches of the Yorkshire coast, the wide open spaces of this part of England's largest county boast a variety of holiday options for all ages.

From Herriot Country, the North York Moors and Dales, to the rolling chalklands and quiet country walks of the Yorkshire Wolds, the ruined abbeys and stately homes, mellow villages and traditional market towns, all add up to a peaceful but varied holiday experience.

You'll not be able to see it all in one trip, so you'll just have to come back again!

If you would like help in finding suitable farm accommodation, turn to the full listing of FHB Groups on pages 392 to 395 to find appropriate contact details for this area.

Bed and Breakfast
(and evening meal)

Ainderby Myers Farm, Nr Hackforth, Bedale, North Yorkshire DL8 1PF　①

Mrs Valerie Anderson
☎ 01609 748668/748424
Fax 01609 748424
⒝⒝ From £18.50–£20
EM From £10
Sleeps 6
🐕 ⅍ 🏛 ⚓ ✿ ⊛
◆◆

Historical manor house set amidst moors and dales with origins going back to the 10th century. Terrific atmosphere. Once farmed by the monks of Jervaulx Abbey. Sheep, crops, pastures and a stream. Walk the fields and discover the wildlife. Visit castles and abbeys. Excellent base for walkers. Pony trekking and fishing by arrangement. Traditional Yorkshire breakfasts. Picnic facilities. Mobile 07803 868674. Open all year.

Barn Close Farm, Rievaulx, Helmsley, North Yorkshire YO62 5LH　②

Joan Milburn
☎ 01439 798321
⒝⒝ From £22–£25
EM From £13
Sleeps 5
🐕 🐎 🐴 🏛 ⚓
◆◆◆

Comfortable, relaxed atmosphere at Barn Close Farm set in an idyllic wooded valley of outstanding beauty close to Rievaulx Abbey and Old Byland. Aga-cooked farmhouse fayre recommended by the Daily Telegraph. Home-produced natural spring water. Riding, walking from farmyard. Central for touring countryside, 1 hour from York or coast. 1 en suite, 1 family with private bathroom, tea/coffee-making facilities. Open all year.

Beech Tree House Farm, South Holme, Slingsby, York YO62 4BA　③

Mrs Carol Farnell
☎ 01653 628257
⒝⒝ £18
EM £8
Sleeps 10
🐕 ⚓ 🏛 ✿ ⊛
◆◆◆

Large Victorian farmhouse on 260-acre arable farm with sheep, pigs, poultry. In peaceful valley close to Castle Howard, central for York, moors, dales, coast and Flamingoland. 1 family, 2 doubles, 1 twin room, 3 guest bathrooms. Lounge with log fire, TV. Snooker/games room. Large garden with safe play area, toys and cycles available. Children welcome at reduced rates. Babysitting. Open all year except Christmas.

Carr House Farm, Shallowdale, Ampleforth, York, North Yorkshire YO62 4ED　④

Anna Lupton
☎ 01347 868526
Mobile 07977 113197
⒝⒝ From £17.50
EM From £10
Sleeps 6
🐕(7) ⅄ 🚗 ⅍ ✿ 🏛 ⚓ ⊛
◆◆◆

16th century farmhouse filled with memorabilia. Part of 400-acre family farm for 5 generations. Internationally recommended, 'fresh air fiend's dream! Good food, walking, warm welcome'. Romantic four-poster bedroom en suite. Relaxing, peaceful, informal – 'Heartbeat Country'. ½ hour York. Make your holiday memorable – own spring water, north country sheep, ponds, orchards, green fields, wild flowers. Open all year.

Church Farm, Scackleton, York, North Yorkshire YO62 4NB　⑤

Mrs Cynthia Firby
☎/Fax 01653 628403
⒝⒝ From £17–£20
EM From £10
Sleeps 6
🐕 ⅍ 🐴 ⚓ ✿
◆◆◆◆

A spacious, comfortable stone farmhouse on our sheep and arable farm in a quiet hamlet in the Howardian Hills designated Area of Outstanding Natural Beauty. 1 double en suite, 1 family en suite. Tea/coffee-making facilities in all bedrooms. Central heating, good home cooking, wonderful views. Ideal base for walking or visiting York, the moors and coast. Open all year except Christmas and New Year.

---

6 **Clematis House,** 1 Eastgate, Lund, Nr Driffield, East Yorkshire YO25 9TQ

Mrs Gill Lamb
☎/Fax 01377 217204
BB From £19.50–£20.50
EM From £10
Sleeps 4
⏃ ⿻ ♨ ⊛
♦♦♦♦

Family-run 389-acre arable and livestock farm in pretty rural village. Farmhouse with character, spacious yet cosy. En suite rooms with TV and tea/coffee-making facilities. Lounge with log fire. Secluded south-facing walled garden and off-road parking. Ideal for visiting York, Hull, Beverley, the coast and North Yorkshire Moors. Open all year except Christmas.

---

7 **Crag Farm,** Danby, Whitby, North Yorkshire YO21 2LQ

Sally Smith
☎/Fax 01287 660279
BB From £17–£20
Sleeps 2/3
⏃ ⿻ ⿔ ♨
♦♦♦

Michael and Sally welcome you to their 18th century working farm. We offer a high standard of accommodation with period decoration, inglenooks and en suite facilities. Looking outward to Danby Castle, take in wonderful views in this quiet, glorious area. Walking, fishing and horse riding are all available within 2 miles of the farm. Open Mar–Nov.

---

8 **Croft Farm,** Church Lane, Fylingthorpe, Whitby, North Yorkshire YO22 4PW

Pauline Featherstone
☎/Fax 01947 880231
BB From £20–£23
Sleeps 6
⏃(5) ⿻ ♨ ♨ ⊛
♦♦♦♦

18th century farmhouse in lawned garden on small working farm overlooking Robin Hood's Bay. Tastefully furnished in the 'olde worlde' charm with open beams, staircase and fireplaces. Two double en suite rooms, one double or single with private bathroom, all with tea/coffee-making facilities and panoramic views of the sea, moors and countryside. Ideal base for coastal resorts, walking and touring the beauty spots of North Yorkshire. Our speciality is a good hearty breakfast. Open Easter–mid-Oct.

---

9 **Cuckoo Nest Farm,** Wilberfoss, York YO41 5NL

Joan Liversidge
☎ 01759 380365
BB From £18–£25
Sleeps 6
⏃ ⿔ ♨ ⊛
♦♦♦

Situated 7 miles east of York off A1079 Hull road, 200-year-old traditional red-brick farmhouse on cattle/dairy/arable farm. Oak-beamed rooms, pleasant sitting room and separate dining room. One en suite bedroom; one double and one twin, both H&C. Good country pubs nearby. Easy drive to coast, dales and moors. A warm welcome awaits you here. Open all year except Christmas.

---

10 **Dimple Wells,** Thormanby, Easingwold, North Yorkshire YO61 4NL

Lorna & Neville Huxtable
☎/Fax 01845 501068
BB £25
Sleeps 4
⏃(7) ⿻ ♨ ⿔
♦♦♦♦

Our country house is easily found, set within extensive grounds, with the backdrop of the Hambleton Hills and White Horse of Kilburn. En suite rooms have colour TV and tea/coffee tray. Aga–cooked breakfasts. York, Thirsk and Easingwold are nearby. A relaxing home from home. Open all year except Christmas and New Year.

---

11 **Dromonby Hall Farm,** Busby Lane, Kirkby-in-Cleveland, Stokesley, Middlesbrough TS9 7AP

Mrs Patricia Weighell
☎/Fax 01642 712312
BB From £18–£20
Sleeps 6
⏃(2) ⿔ ⿻ ⿹ ♨ ♨ ⿔
♦♦♦

Modern farmhouse on 170-acre working farm with superb views of Cleveland Hills. Ideal for walking, cycling, mountain biking or touring by car. Easy access from A19 and B1257, 8 miles south of Middlesbrough. ½ hr drive from coast and from Teesside. A warm welcome and good food. Horse riding available locally. Guided walks on the moors available, or bring your horse for a holiday! Enjoy the peace and beautiful surroundings. Open all year.
E-mail: PATWEIGHELL@dromonby.swinternet.co.uk

Easterside Farm, Hawnby, Helmsley, North Yorkshire YO62 5QT ⑫

Mrs Sarah Wood
☎/Fax 01439 798277
🅑🅑 From £23
EM From £12
Sleeps 12
🐴 ⬛ ♨ 🎯 ⊚
♦♦♦

A large 18th century Grade II listed farmhouse, nestling on Easterside Hill and enjoying panoramic views. Ideal base for walking, touring, the coast and the city of York. Enjoy good food and a warm welcome in comfortable surroundings. All rooms have en suite facilities. Open all year (closed Christmas).

Eastgate Farm Cottage, Rudstone, East Yorkshire YO25 4UX ⑬

Elizabeth Bowden
☎/Fax 01262 420150
🅑🅑 From £18–£22
EM From £12
Sleeps 4
🐴 🐏 💫 ♨ ♨ ⬛ ♨ 🎯

♦♦♦

Friendly 18th century cottage with superb views nestling on the edge of a medieval village with its own monolith. Ideally located for moor and coastal exploration. Freshwater or sea fishing nearby. Rural walks in beautiful countryside. Horse trekking available locally. En suite bedrooms with central heating and delightful brass and iron beds. Aga-cooked dinners available. Open all year.

Elmfield Country House, Arrathorne, Bedale, North Yorkshire DL8 1NE ⑭

Edith & Jim Lillie
☎ 01677 450558
Fax 01677 450557
🅑🅑 From £25–£35
EM From £12
Sleeps 18
🐴 ⊚ 🖭 ⬛ ♨ 🎯 ⊚
♦♦♦♦♦ (AA Inspected)

Situated between Richmond and Bedale. Superb views of surrounding countryside, relaxed friendly atmosphere in luxurious country house. 9 spacious bedrooms (all en suite) including a four-poster bed, twin and family rooms. 2 bedrooms equipped for disabled. All with colour TV (satellite channel), radio, phone, tea/coffee, CH. Lounge and bar (residential licence), dining room, games room, conservatory and solarium. Excellent home cooking. Open all year. E-mail: bed@elmfieldhouse.freeserve.co.uk

Goose Farm, Eastmoor, Sutton-on-the-Forest, York YO61 1ET ⑮

Susan Rowson
☎/Fax 01347 810577
🅑🅑 From £18–£22
Sleeps 6
🐴 🐏 💫 ⬛
♦♦♦

150-year old brick farmhouse situated 5 miles from York Minster in open countryside just off the B1363 and within easy access of Herriot Country and the Yorkshire coast. Large rooms, all en suite with TV and tea/coffee-making facilities. Central heating throughout and as warm as the welcome to yourselves. Open all year.

The Grainary, Keasbeck Hill Farm, Harwood Dale, Scarborough, North Yorkshire YO13 0DT ⑯

John & Lynda Simpson
☎/Fax 01723 870026
🅑🅑 From £20–£25
EM From £9
Sleeps 35
♿ 🐴 🐏 🖭 Å ⬛ 💫 ♨ 🎯 ⊚
♦♦♦

Midway between Scarborough and Whitby, set in 200 acres of National Park countryside, we are a mixed farm with lots of friendly animals. Close to Heartbeat Country, coast and moors, six specially created conservation areas and wildlife trails. All rooms en suite. Relax in our licensed country tea rooms. Out of season special breaks available. Open all year.

Harker Hill Farm, Harker Hill, Seamer, Stokesley, Nr Middlesbrough, North Yorkshire TS9 5NF ⑰

Pam & John Fanthorpe
☎/Fax 01642 710431
🅑🅑 From £18–£19
EM From £9
Sleeps 6
🐴 🐏 ✂ 🎯 ⬛
♦♦♦

Harker Hill is a two hundred year old farm offering warmth and comfort. The cosy accommodation includes full central heating, log fires, lounge and television. Home cooked food is served at times to suit you so businessmen visiting Teesside can enjoy early cooked breakfasts and late evening meals. Open all year except Christmas.

18 High Belthorpe, Bishop Wilton, York, YO42 1SB

Meg Abu Hamdan
☎ 01759 368238
Mobile 07802 270970
[BB] From £17.65
EM From £7.50
Sleeps 6
ᛒ ⼊ Å ⟆ ⅋ ▪ ⾕
♦♦♦

Set on an ancient moated site in the Yorkshire Wolds, this Victorian farmhouse has large comfortable bedrooms with uninterrupted panoramic views. The centre of a working livery yard, the house has own private fishing lake and access to fabulous country walks. Croquet, small snooker table available. York 12 miles, coast 20 miles. Open all year except Christmas.

---

19 High Catton Grange, High Catton, near Stamford Bridge, York YO41 1EP

Sheila Foster
☎/Fax 01759 371374
[BB] From £17–£23
Sleeps 6
ᛒ ⼊ ▪ ⅋ ◎
♦♦♦♦

Only 8 miles east of York, this 300-acre mixed farm in peaceful, rural setting has a comfortable 18th century farmhouse. A welcoming and relaxed atmosphere awaits you. Prettily furnished bedrooms – some en suite. Centrally heated throughout, tea/coffee facilities and good breakfasts. Within 2 miles local country inns providing excellent meals. Ample parking. Open all year except Christmas and New Year.

---

20 High Force Farm, Bainbridge, Leyburn, North Yorkshire DL8 3DL

Margaret Iveson
☎ 01969 650379
[BB] From £18–£22
Sleeps 6
ᛒ(4) ⼇ ▪ ⟆ ◎
♦♦♦

Working hill farm used in James Herriot TV programme. Ideal centre for exploring the Dales offering guests a warm welcome in a relaxed atmosphere. A non-smoking establishment. Open Feb–Nov.

---

21 Island Farm, Staintondale, Scarborough, North Yorkshire YO13 0EB

Mary Clarke
☎ 01723 870249
[BB] From £18–£20
Sleeps 6
ᛒ ⼇ ⼊ ▪ ◎
♦♦♦♦

Relax in our spacious and comfortable farmhouse and garden. All bedrooms have en suite facilities. Being close to coast and in open countryside, it is ideal for walking or visiting many places of interest. Visitors appreciate our large games room with toys, full size snooker table and tennis court. Brochure on request. Open Easter–Nov.

---

22 Kelleythorpe Farm, Kelleythorpe, Great Driffield, East Yorkshire YO25 9DW

Mrs Tiffy Hopper
☎ 01377 252297
[BB] From £17
EM From £10
Sleeps 6
ᛒ ⼊ ▪ ⅋ ◎
♦♦♦

Imagine peacocks strutting, ducks swimming and trout rising. Enjoy tea on the sun terrace overlooking a crystal clear shallow river, the friendly atmosphere of our lovely Georgian farmhouse with its mellow antique furniture, pretty chintz and new bathrooms, 1 en suite, is sure to captivate you. Delicious country cooking. Children very welcome. Ideally placed for touring. Open all year (closed Christmas & New Year). E-mail: kelleythorpe@mcmail.com

---

23 Killerby Cottage Farm, Killerby Lane, Cayton, Scarborough, North Yorkshire YO11 3TP

Valerie Green
☎ 01723 581236
Fax 01723 585465
[BB] From £18–£25
Sleeps 6
⊞ ▪
♦♦♦♦

Simon and Val Green welcome you to Killerby Cottage Farm in the pleasant countryside between Scarborough and Filey. The farmhouse has many charming features and our double and twin bedded rooms all have en suite facilities. Guests' lounge with log fires, sun room, lovely garden, good food – all for you to enjoy. Open all year. E-mail: val@green–glass.demon.co.uk

Laskill Farm Country House, Hawnby, Nr Helmsley, North Yorkshire YO62 5NB

Sue Smith
☎/Fax 01439 798268
BB From £25–£28
EM From £12.50
Sleeps 8
🌜🛏 🖳🏕🛌🐕🎋🛎 ⓢ
♦♦♦

Amidst beautiful North Yorkshire Moors, in heart of James Herriot and Heartbeat Country. Attractive farmhouse with own lake/large walled garden. Own natural spring water. High standard of food and comfort. Rooms have en suite, colour TV, beverage tray. Ideal for nearby places of interest and scenic beauty, or simply enjoy tranquil surroundings. Recommended in the *Sunday Times* and the BBC *Holiday Programme*. Open all year except Christmas Day. See colour ad on page 35.

Lovesome Hill Farm, Lovesome Hill, Northallerton, North Yorkshire DL6 2PB

Mrs Mary Pearson
☎ 01609 772311
BB From £19.50–£25
EM From £12
Sleeps 9
🧒🌜🛌🛎 ⓢ
♦♦♦♦

Come and experience life on our working farm just north of Northallerton. Relax in our individually furnished en suite rooms (two on the ground floor). CLA commendation for conversion. For that little extra Gate Cottage offers a romantic feel, with half-tester bed, corner bath and own patio. A warm welcome of tea and homemade biscuits and meals awaits you. You'll 'love' it. Brochure available. Open Mar–Nov.

Low Gill Farm, Aysgarth, Leyburn, North Yorkshire DL8 3AL

Mrs Val Dinsdale
☎ 01969 663554
BB From £17–£20
Sleeps 6
🌜✂🛎
♦♦♦

A warm welcome to our family-run dairy/sheep farm set in the heart of the Yorkshire Dales in peaceful location 1 mile from Aysgarth. One double room with superb views of Wensleydale, one family/twin overlooking garden, stream and hills beyond. Rooms are en suite with beverage tray. Guests' lounge/dining room with colour TV. Ideal for touring/walking. Open Feb–Oct.

Manor Farm, East Heslerton, Malton, North Yorkshire YO17 8RN

David & Elizabeth Lumley
☎/Fax 01944 728268
BB From £17.50–£20
Sleeps 6
🌜🐕✂🖳🛵🐕🎋🛎
♦♦♦

Comfortable, relaxing atmosphere in our Victorian farmhouse set in large gardens with rose garden and orchard. Very spacious centrally heated bedrooms are en suite with tea, coffee and biscuits. Our 400-acre mixed farm with farm walks and private fishing is centrally located for coast, moors, forestry and York. Open Easter–Oct. E-mail: d.c.lumley@farming.co.uk

---

Manor House Farm, Healaugh, Richmond, North Yorkshire DL11 6UA   28

Margaret Alderson
☎ 01748 884318
BB From £20–£22
Sleeps 6
🌜🛎🎋 ⓢ
♦♦♦

Manor House Farm is a small working sheep farm situated in the picturesque village of Healaugh in the heart of beautiful Swaledale. One mile from Reeth. Good walking country, ideal for touring. Rooms have en suite facilities, colour TV, tea/coffee-making facilities and hairdryer. A warm welcome assured. Open Mar–Nov.

Mill Close Farm, Patrick Brompton, Bedale, North Yorkshire DL8 1JY   29

Mrs Patricia Knox
☎ 01677 450257
Fax 01677 450585
BB From £20–£25
Sleeps 4
🌜🐕🌜🌾 ⓢ
♦♦♦♦ Silver Award

17th century working farm surrounded by beautiful rolling countryside at foothills of Yorkshire Dales. 2 miles from A1. Charming bedrooms, super king-size bed and many extras. En suite bathrooms, one with jacuzzi. Dining and sitting room with log fires. Highland cattle, sheep, calves, pony, wild flowers and woodland. A relaxing, peaceful atmosphere. Romantic walled garden with pond and summerhouse. Sumptuous breakfasts in our conservatory dining room. Colour brochure. Open Mar–Nov.

30 Mount Pleasant Farm, Whashton, Richmond, North Yorkshire DL11 7JP

Alison Pittaway
☎/Fax 01748 822784
BB From £20–£25
EM From £10
Sleeps 12
♠ ⚞ ⚲ ⚘ ▣ ⚶ ⊚
◆◆◆

A very warm welcome to our comfortable farmhouse set in beautiful, peaceful countryside with lovely views. Three miles from Richmond and ideally situated for exploring the North Yorkshire Dales. Renovated farm buildings offer cosy cottage-style en suite rooms, each with own front door, colour TV and beverage tray. All home cooking using fresh local produce. Table licence and friendly atmosphere. This really is a pleasant place to stay for your special holiday or short break. Open all year except Christmas.

31 Newgate Foot Farm, Saltersgate, Pickering, North Yorkshire YO18 7NR

Mrs Alison Johnson
☎/Fax 01751 460215
BB From £18–£24
EM From £13
Sleeps 5
⚞(5) ⊞ ⚖ ⚘ ⚶ ▣ ⚶ ⊚
◆◆◆◆

Just 1 mile off the A169, but in a world of its own in the middle of the moors with no neighbours in sight! Enjoy walking on the moors, through the forest, or trout fishing in our own lake. See the ewes and lambs and thorough-bred mares and foals. Whitby 14 miles, York 35 miles, "Aidensfield" 6 miles. One en suite bedroom, 1 twin/3 bedded, 1 single. Open all year except Christmas.

32 Oldstead Grange, Oldstead, Coxwold, York YO61 4BJ

Anne Banks
☎/Fax 01347 868634
BB From £25
Sleeps 4
⚞(5) ⚖ ⊞ ⚶ ▣ ⊚
◆◆◆◆◆

Beautiful quiet situation amidst our fields, woods and valleys near Byland Abbey in the NYM National Park. Oldstead Grange blends traditional 17th century features with superb luxury en suite bedrooms including large comfortable beds, colour TV, warm towels and robes, fresh flowers and refreshment tray with chocolates and home made biscuits. Delicious breakfasts. Light suppers on request or good evening meals locally. Brochure. Open all year. E-mail: oldstead.grange@yorkshireuk.com

33 Oxnop Hall, Low Oxnop, Gunnerside, Richmond, North Yorkshire DL11 6JJ

Annie Porter
☎/Fax 01748 886253
BB From £24–£30
EM From £15
Sleeps 16
⚞(5) ⚶ ⚖ ▣ ⊚
◆◆◆

Stay with us on our working hill farm with beef cattle and Swaledale sheep. Oxnop Hall is of historical interest and has recently been extended with all en suite rooms. Ideal walking and touring. We are in the Yorkshire Dales National Park, Herriot Country, an Environmentally Sensitive Area which is renowned for its stone walls, barns and flora. Good farmhouse food. Tea/coffee-making facilities. Open all year except Christmas.

34 Plane Tree Cottage Farm, Staintondale, Scarborough, North Yorkshire YO13 0EY

Mrs Marjorie Edmondson
☎ 01723 870796
BB From £20
EM From £10
Sleeps 4
⚖ ▣ ⚶ ⊚
◆◆◆

Plane Tree Cottage is situated on the coast, about halfway between Scarborough and Whitby. We have beautiful open views of the sea and lovely countryside. This is a small working farm with sheep, pigs, free range hens, and a very friendly cat called Danny. This small cottage is homely and cosy, and offers meals to a very high standard. Home grown produce as available. One twin, one double en suite, both with tea tray, electric blankets and radio. Guests' lounge. Often recommended. Open Mar–Nov.

35 Rains Farm, Allerston, Pickering, North Yorkshire YO18 7PQ

Jean or Lorraine Allanson
☎/Fax 01723 859333
BB From £20–£25
EM From £15
Sleeps 9
⚖ ⊞ ▣ ⊚
◆◆◆◆

Very peacefully set in Ryedale's beautiful open countryside. Relax and unwind in our recently refurbished farmhouse. Quality en suite accommodation and delicious farmhouse fayre. Five pretty en suite rooms (one ground floor), all with CH TV, hospitality tray, hairdriers. Centrally situated for moors, Dales, coast, attractions. Private parking. Totally non-smoking. Closed Christmas and New Year. E-mail: allan@rainsfarm.freeserve.co.uk

Rokeby Close Farm, Hutton Magna, Richmond, North Yorkshire DL11 7HN ③⑥

Don & Julie Wilkinson
☎ 01833 627171
Fax 01833 627662
BB From £20
Sleeps 6
☩(12) 🐾 🛆 ⊕
♦♦♦♦

Unique old farmhouse recently restored to a high standard, all rooms fully en suite. Ideal base for exploring Durham and North Yorkshire's Dales, market towns, museums, abbeys, forts, houses, wildlife trusts or miles and miles of remote moors. Breakfast in our large conservatory with stunning views. Log-fired drawing room available. Internet access and office if required.
E-mail: Don.Wilkinson@farmline.com

Rose Cottage Farm, Cropton, Nr Pickering, North Yorkshire YO18 8HL ③⑦

Mrs Joan Wood
☎ 01751 417302
BB £20
EM From £10
Sleeps 4
☩(8) ⊁
♦♦♦♦

A warm welcome awaits you at Rose Cottage Farm, with its cruck beams and many original features. Spacious, tastefully decorated en suite rooms with colour TV and tea/coffee-making facilities. Pay phone for guests' use. The unspoilt village of Cropton lies at the edge of the North York Moors. Easy access to moors, coast and York. If you enjoy walking the choice is unlimited. Open all year.

Seavy Slack, Stape, Pickering, North Yorkshire YO18 8HZ ③⑧

Anne Barrett
☎ 01751 473131
BB From £20
EM From £12
Sleeps 6
☩(5) 🐾 🛆 🐎 ⊕
♦♦♦

Relaxed, friendly atmosphere and good farmhouse cooking awaits you on this stock and arable farm situated on the edge of the North Yorkshire Moors just 7 miles from Pickering. An ideal base for walking (from farmyard) or exploring the many varied attractions. All rooms en suite with CH and tea-making facilities. Guests' lounge/ dining room with colour TV. Open all year except Christmas.

Sinnington Manor, Sinnington, York YO62 6SN ③⑨

Mrs J M Wilson
☎/Fax 01751 433296
BB From £20–£25
Sleeps 5
☩(2) ⊁ 🐾 🛆 ⊕
♦♦♦♦

Welcome to our Georgian manor house, recently restored into a warm and comfortable family home, but still retaining its original charm and elegance. En suite facilities. Relax outside in beautiful gardens or walk in 275 acres with conservation areas, woodland and beck. Farm animals include stud of coloured horses. Peaceful country-side, yet close to moors, coast, York, etc. Children, dogs and horses welcome. Open Apr–Sept.

Studley House, 67 Main Street, Ebberston, Scarborough, North Yorkshire YO13 9NR ④⓪

Ernie & Jane Hodgson
☎/Fax 01723 859285
BB From £20–£24
Sleeps 6
☩(10) ⊁ 🖅 🚗 🛆 🐎 ⊕
♦♦♦

Studley House offers superb, quality accommodation in a peaceful, picturesque setting. All bedrooms are light and spacious, fully en suite with tea tray, colour TV, own key, CH and many more little luxuries. Enjoy a hearty breakfast before exploring the moors, coastal resorts and surround-ing villages and attractions. York 45 mins. Private parking. Colour brochure. Open all year except Christmas and New Year.

Summer Lodge Farm, Low Row, Richmond, North Yorkshire DL11 6NP ④①

Carol Porter
☎ 01748 886504
BB From £20–£25
Sleeps 5
☩ ⊁ 🛆 ⊕
♦♦♦

Set in the Yorkshire Dales National Park and the heart of Herriot Country. Working hill farm pleasantly situated in its own little valley near Low Row in Swaledale, renowned for buildings, flora, fauna and wildlife in an environmentally sensitive area. Ideal walking area. One family room en suite, one double with private bathroom, both with CH, tea/coffee and colour TV. Large south-facing garden. A warm welcome is assured. Open Mar–Nov.

42 Sunley Court, Nunnington, York, North Yorkshire YO62 5XQ

Mrs Joan Brown
☎/Fax 01439 748233
BB From £17.50
EM £10
Sleeps 6
♨ ♁ ⌂ ♨ ⊕
♦♦♦

Sunley Court is a comfortable modern farmhouse with open views in a quiet secluded area. The farm is arable with sheep and horses. All bedrooms have tea/coffee-making facilities, washbasins, electric blankets, 2 have shower/toilet en suite, 2 single bedrooms. Good home cooking. Central for York, moors and coast. Open all year except Christmas.

43 Throstle Gill Farm, Dalton, Richmond, North Yorkshire DL11 7HZ

Peter Guy
☎/Fax 01833 621363
BB From £18–£20
Sleeps 4
♨(12) ♁ ⌂ ♨
♦♦♦♦

Nestling in a secluded hollow under the lee of surrounding hills beside a stream, Throstle Gill provides peace and tranquillity. Ideal for stop over between London and Scotland. The historic town of Richmond is 7 miles away and there are many pleasant walks from the farm. Superb location for touring. Open Apr–Oct

44 Valley View Farm, Old Byland, Helmsley, York, North Yorkshire YO62 5LG

Sally Robinson
☎ 01439 798221
Fax 01439 798477
BB From £25–£30
EM From £12
Sleeps 10
♨ ♁ ⌂ ⅄ ♨
♦♦♦♦

Enjoy the delights of traditional Yorkshire hospitality, hearty country breakfasts and delicious farmhouse fayre. Relax in the beautiful countryside of the North York Moors National Park or see the many places of interest and visit historic towns. Rooms are tastefully furnished and en suite. Guests' lounge with open fire. Licensed. Way marked walks from the farmyard.
E-mail: sally@valleyviewfarm.com

45 Walburn Hall, Downholme, Richmond, North Yorkshire DL11 6AF

Diana Greenwood
☎/Fax 01748 822152
BB From £23–£26
Sleeps 5
♨ ⅄ ⌂ ♨ ⊕
♦♦♦♦

Walburn Hall is one of the few remaining working farms with a fortified farmhouse, an enclosed cobbled courtyard and terraced garden. For guests' comfort there is a separate lounge and dining room with beamed ceilings, stone fireplaces and log fires (when required). Centrally heated. Double/twin rooms (en suite) with tea/coffee-making facilities. Ideally situated between Richmond and Leyburn for exploring the Dales. Open Mar–Nov.

46 West Carlton, Carlton Lane, Aldbrough, Hull HU11 4RB

Caroline Maltas
☎/Fax 01964 527724
Mobile 0467 830868
BB From £18–£22.50
Sleeps 6
♨ ⅄ ♁ ⅄ ⊿ ♨ ♨ ⊕
♦♦♦♦

Lovely south-facing Georgian farmhouse on 330-acre mixed farm. Ideally situated in a very quiet rural location yet convenient for Beverley, Hull, York and all East coast attractions. 4 miles from a sandy beach, 6 miles from Hornsea. Beautiful coordinated en suite rooms. Guests' own lounge and dining room. Ring for a brochure – you won't be disappointed. Open all year.

47 Whashton Springs Farm, Richmond, North Yorkshire DL11 7JS

Fairlie Turnbull
☎ 01748 822884
Fax 01748 826285
BB From £22–£24
Sleeps 16
♨(5) ♨ ⅄ ♨ ⊕
♦♦♦♦

400-acre beef/sheep, family working farm in heart of Herriot Country. Delightful Georgian farmhouse, featured on 'Wish You Were Here', 1988 AA 'Farmhouse of the North' Award, unusual bay windows, overlooking lawns sloping to a sparkling stream. Real Yorkshire breakfast. Home cooking using local produce. All 8 bedrooms have en suite baths/showers, TV, phone. One 4-poster bedroom. Historic Richmond 3 miles away. Open all year except Christmas & Jan.

The Wold Cottage, Wold Newton, Driffield, East Yorkshire YO25 3HL (48)

Mrs Katrina Gray
☎/Fax 01262 470696
🅱 From £20
EM From £12
Sleeps 6
🖰 ⅄ 🖾 🧍 ⟁ 🍴 ⓐ
♦♦♦♦ Silver Award

"Just what you always hope to find." Georgian farmhouse set in own grounds overlooking new and mature woodlands and continuous wold land. Come and relax and forget the pressures of everyday life. Stroll around our field margins and observe the wildlife and history. Spacious four-poster room with spa bath. All rooms en suite. Lambing breaks Jan–Mar. Open all year.
E-mail: woldcott@wold-newtonfreeserve.co.uk

Self-Catering

Bellafax Holiday Cottage, Bellafax Grange, Marishes, Malton, North Yorkshire YO17 6UG (49)

David Beal
☎ 01653 668231
🆂 From £210–£360
Sleeps 4
🖰 ⌣
🔑🔑🔑🔑 *Commended*

This is a well-equipped cottage on a working farm. It has two bedrooms, one double, one twin, with cot available. Bathroom with shower over bath. Lounge with open fire (fuel supplied). Dining room and well-equipped kitchen (microwave, dishwasher, auto washer and fridge freezer, etc. Heating by electric storage heaters (electricity included). All linen supplied. Open all year.
E-mail: davidbeal@farming.co.uk

Blackmires Farm, Danby Head, Danby, Whitby, North Yorkshire YO21 2NN (50)

Gillian & Lewis Rhys
☎ 01287 660352
🆂 From £225–£375
Sleeps 6
🖰 🐎 🍴 ⓐ
🔑🔑🔑🔑 *Commended*

Stone cottage for six. Two bedrooms and bathroom on ground floor, twin bedroom upstairs. Garden, swing and sandpit. Quiet situation adjacent to moors in an area of outstanding natural beauty. Our small farm is in Danby Dale, 3 miles from Danby, Castleton and the North York Moors National Park Information Centre. Open all year.

Clematis, Well & Shepherd's Cottages, c/o Mile House Farm, Hawes, Wensleydale, North Yorks DL8 3PT (51)

Anne Fawcett
☎ 01969 667481
🆂 From £175–£500
Sleeps 4–8
🖰 🐎 🔌 ⌣ 🛄 ⓐ
🔑🔑🔑🔑
Highly Commended

Three lovely old Dales stone cottages of character with open fires, exposed beams and Laura Ashley prints. All cottages are peacefully situated with spectacular views over Wensleydale. Fully renovated to a high standard, these cottages provide charming, spacious accommodation with delightful, old fashioned walled gardens. Free trout fishing on farm. Private parking. Open all year.

The Coach House, Whashton Springs Farm, Richmond, North Yorkshire DL11 7JS (47)

Fairlie Turnbull
☎ 01748 822884
Fax 01748 826285
🆂 From £170–£290
Sleeps 4–5
🖰 🛄 🍴 ⓐ
🔑🔑🔑🔑
Highly Commended

The Coach House offers luxury accommodation on our 400-acre working family farm near Richmond, gateway to the Dales. This warm spacious house sleeps 4–5 in double and twin bedrooms. Beamed lounge and well equipped kitchen with washer, freezer, microwave, etc. Heating and bed linen included in tariff. Good local hospitality. Open all year.

19 **The Cottage,** High Catton Grange, High Catton, near Stamford Bridge, York YO41 1EP

Sheila Foster
☎/Fax 01759 371374
SC From £160–£295
Sleeps 4–6
🛏 🐕 📻 🌾 ⊛
↝↝↝↝ Commended

This former gig shed and stable has been converted to a high standard yet retains many original features. Comfortable and tastefully furnished with colour TV, electric cooker, automatic washer/dryer, fridge, microwave, storage heaters,etc. Patio doors onto large private patio and garden furniture. Glorious views across green meadows. Working farm in peaceful, rural setting, ideally situated for York or touring. Linen/fuel included. Open all year.

40 **Cow Pasture Cottage,** c/o 67 Main Street, Ebberston, Scarborough, North Yorkshire YO13 9NR

Ernie & Jane Hodgson
☎/Fax 01723 859285
SC From £185–£320
Sleeps 4 + cot
🛏 ✂ ⊞ 🛋 📻 🌾 ⊛
↝↝↝↝ Highly Commended

Come and wind down in this luxury cottage in the countryside. Superbly equipped and designed for comfort, all one level, suit partially disabled. Situated amongst spectacular scenery, central for moors, coast, forests and York. One double, one twin, bed linen inclusive. Private parking. Sorry no pets. Colour brochure. Open all year.

8 **Croft Farm Cottage,** Croft Farm, Church Lane, Fylingthorpe, Whitby, North Yorkshire YO22 4PW

Pauline Featherstone
☎/Fax 01947 880231
SC From £155–£290
Sleeps 4
🛏 📻 🌾 ⊛
↝↝↝ Commended

Forget the pressures of everyday living! Come and relax in the cottage attached to our 18th century farmhouse on a working farm, offering spectacular views, home comforts, peace and tranquillity. Overlooking Robin Hood's Bay, within easy reach of coastal resorts, Moors Railway and termination of well-known walks. 2 bedrooms, 1 double and 1 with built-in bunk beds. Fully equipped including linen. Colour TV and sun lounge. Open all year.

53 **Dove Cottage,** Primrose Hill Farm, c/o Staynor Hall, Selby, North Yorkshire YO8 8EE

Jenny Webster
☎ 01757 708931
Fax 01757 704386
SC From £160–£350
Sleep 5+cot
🛏 ✂ 📻
↝↝↝↝ Highly Commended

A warm welcome awaits at our beautifully renovated 19th century cottage with all modern amenities. Relax in comfort and peace whilst experiencing life on a working family farm. Enjoy our animals, country walks, bird watching and abundant wildlife. Golf, fishing and horse riding nearby. Well placed for York, Dales and Moors. Children welcome. Open all year.

54 **Easthill House & Gardens,** Wilton Road, Thornton le Dale, Pickering, North Yorkshire YO18 7QP

Diane Stenton
☎ 01751 474561
SC From £155–£725
Sleep 2–8
🛏 ⊞ 📻
↝↝↝ – ↝↝↝↝
Highly Commended

Three Scandinavian pine chalets nestling in our woodland and landscaped gardens surrounding our country house (illustrated) which incorporates three luxury apartments and a cottage (individual entrances). Enjoy a tour around the sheep, feed the hens, relax on our putting green or tennis court or in the games room, or visit the beautiful Yorkshire countryside. Open all year.

55 **The Farm Cottage,** Town Farm, Cloughton, Scarborough, North Yorkshire YO13 0AE

Mr & Mrs Joe Green
☎ 01723 870278
Fax 01723 870968
SC From £175–£400
Sleeps 5/6
🛏 🐕 ✂ 📻 🌾
↝↝↝↝ Highly Commended

Delightful cottage situated on a working farm in Cloughton village. Recently refurbished to a very high standard, this luxury cottage is well equipped and very comfortable. Set between Scarborough and Whitby, on the edge of the North York Moors National Park, there is lots to see and do – an ideal base for walking and touring. Open all year. E-mail: joe.green@farmline.com

Farsyde Farm Cottages, Farsyde House Farm, Robin Hood's Bay, Whitby, North Yorkshire YO22 4UG 56

Angela Green
01947 880249
Fax 01947 880877
SC From £130–£495
Sleep 2–6
– *Up to Highly Commended*

Yorkshire stone cottages on private stud farm with land reaching the sea. Adjacent to village, close to beautiful Esk Valley and Heartbeat Country and amid spectacular coastal, country and heather moors scenery. York one hour. Riding. Private use of Chalet pool with recently-converted Mistal Cottage. Spacious parking. Open all year.

Field House, Jewison Lane, Sewerby, Bridlington, East Yorkshire YO16 6YG 57

Angela & John Foster
01262 674932
Fax 01262 608688
SC From £250–£399
Sleeps 6 + cot
Highly Commended

Our highly rated farmhouse with walled garden, tennis court and croquet lawn is an excellent base from which to explore a spectacular coastline or, within an hour's drive, some of Yorkshire's finest features. Sample life on a large dairy/arable farm. Children especially welcome. Open all year. E-mail: johnfoster@farmline.com

Lund Farm Cottage, Lund Farm, Gateforth, Selby, North Yorkshire YO8 9LE 58

Chris & Helen Middleton
/Fax 01757 228775
SC From £250–£375
EM From £7
Sleeps 6
Highly Commended

Convenient for York and the Dales, our 18th century farmyard cottage has beams, fireside range, safe patio and lawn, with barbecue, and friendly owners next door. Children most welcome. 200-acre farm with lambs, eggs to collect, Shetland pony, and bicycles. Evening meals available. Lambing breaks Dec–Mar. Prices fully inclusive. Open all year. E-mail: chris.middleton@farmline.com

Mount Pleasant Farm, Whashton, Richmond, North Yorkshire DL11 7JP 30

Alison Pittaway
/Fax 01748 822784
SC From £210–£280
Sleeps 4
Commended

Enjoy a break in one of our two newly converted cottages, set in lovely peaceful countryside with superb views. Three miles from Richmond and ideally situated for touring the North Yorkshire Dales. Each cottage comprises 1 double and 1 twin bedroom, lounge with dining area, fully equipped kitchen, shower room, colour TV, CH. Electricity, linen and heating included. Good local hospitality. Open all year.

Pasture Field House, Newsham Road, Thirsk, North Yorkshire YO7 4DE 59

Mrs J Hunter
/Fax 01845 587230
SC From £180–£220
Sleeps 4
Approved

Cottage adjoining attractive old farmhouse on small working farm with sheep, soft fruit and vegetables. Large garden, grass tennis court, snooker table. Convenient central location for North York Moors, Yorkshire Dales and York. Owner maintained.

Rains Farm, Allerston, Pickering, North Yorkshire YO18 7PQ 35

Jean or Lorraine Allanson
/Fax 01723 859333
SC From £160–£450
Sleeps 2/6
Highly Commended

Five warm and comfortable recently converted barns. Very peaceful, magnificent views. Relax, unwind and ease away the pressures of life in this idyllic rural retreat. Gaze on the ponies grazing in the paddocks. Furnished, decorated and equipped for luxury living. We are centrally situated for many attractions. Safe parking. Colour brochure. Open all year. E-mail: allan@rainsfarm.freeserve.co.uk

60 **Rhuss Cottage,** Hinderwell, Saltburn, c/o Broom House Farm, Ugthorpe, Whitby YO21 2BJ

Mrs Louise Robson
☎/Fax 01947 840454
SC From £180–£360
Sleeps 4/5+cot
🐎 ♿ ◎
♟ ♟ ♟ *Commended*

17th century beamed cottage situated in lovely village between Staithes and Runswick Bay (Whitby 6 miles). Clean, comfortable, owner maintained, with luxury oak-fitted kitchen. Linen, storage heating, real fire. Garden and private patio. Scenic walks in area of outstanding beauty. Close to good beaches. Also a chance to visit our farm and watch the cows being milked, etc. Open all year.

61 **Stanhow Farm Bungalow,** c/o Stanhow Farm, Langton-on-Swale, Northallerton, North Yorks DL7 0TJ

Lady Mary Furness
☎ 01609 748614
SC From £225–£385
Sleeps 6
🐎 🎋 🏕 ♿ 🌀 ◎
♟ ♟ ♟ ♟ *Commended*

Tailor made for you – a cosy detached bungalow with heating, CTV, video, open fire, fully equipped kitchen, washer, freezer, microwave, etc. 1 double, 2 twin bedrooms including bed linen. Lovely views of Swaledale and Herriot Country. Peacefully situated on family farm, yet close to Richmond, Thirsk and historic cities. Good local hospitality and recreations. A warm welcome assured. Open all year.

62 **Sunset Cottages,** Grimston Manor Farm, Gilling East, York YO62 4HR

Heather Kelsey
☎ 01347 888654
Fax 01347 888347
SC From £150–£350
Sleeps 3–6
🐎 ♿ ◎
♟ ♟ ♟ *Commended*

In an envied location in the middle of the Howardian Hills AONB, 17 miles north of York. Six stone-built barn and granary conversions on 175-acre sheep and arable farm. Warm and comfortable, tremendous character, thoughtfully planned. Enjoy excellent walks and our fine garden. Colour brochure. Open all year. See colour ad on page 35.

63 **Trout Inn Cottage,** Wansford, Driffield, East Yorkshire YO25 8NX

Rob & Anne Farnsworth
☎/Fax 01377 254224
SC From £150–£275
Sleeps 5 + cot
🐎 🎋 🍴 🌀 ♿ 🏕
Applied

A comfortable cottage in a quiet location with small garden. Well situated for visiting the coast 9 miles, Beverley 14 miles, York 28 miles or North Yorkshire Moors. Use of hard tennis court. Fishing is available in village. Good parking. Ring for directions. Open all year.

44 **Valley View Farm,** Old Byland, Helmsley, York, North Yorkshire YO62 5LG

Sally Robinson
☎ 01439 798221
Fax 01439 798477
SC From £210–£480
Sleeps 2–6
🐎 🎋 🅱 🧍 🏕 ♿
♟ ♟ ♟ ♟ *Highly Commended*

A beef, sheep and pig farm set on the edge of small village. Newly converted barn furnished with traditional farm theme. The cottages have TV, video, dishwasher, washer/dryer, open fires, CH. All bedrooms are en suite, beds double or twin. Delicious farmhouse meals available (see B&B listing). Phone for colour brochure. Open all year. E-mail: sally@valleyviewfarm.com

64 **Wayside Farm,** Whitby Road, Cloughton, Scarborough, North Yorkshire YO13 0DX

Mr & Mrs P Halder
☎ 01723 870519
SC From £130–£349
Sleeps 6
🐎 🎋 🅱 ♿ 🏕 ◎
♟ ♟ – ♟ ♟ ♟ *Commended*

Beautiful holiday cottages ideally situated between Scarborough and Whitby, within the North Yorkshire Moors National Park, close to the sea. Ideal for walking and visiting the picturesque villages and fishing towns close by. Full central heating. Horse stabling and grazing also available. Open all year.

Wren Cottage, Kirkby Fleetham, c/o Street House Farm, Little Holtby, Northallerton, N Yorks DL7 9LN   65

Mrs Jennifer Pybus
☎ **01609 748622**
🆂 **From £160–£285**
Sleeps 4
🐕 🐾 ⬛ ◉
🐾 🐾 🐾 🐾 *Commended*

This cosy cottage in Kirkby Fleetham overlooks the village green, with pub serving food and shop/PO nearby. Ideal centre for exploring Yorkshire Dales and North Yorkshire Moors and within easy reach of York and Durham. The cottage with its traditional oak beams and open fire in the lounge has a fully equipped kitchen with electric cooker and microwave. Also night storage heaters and telephone. Electricity included. Open all year.

Camping and Caravanning

Pond Farm, Fylingdales, Whitby, North Yorkshire YO22 4QJ   66

Grace Cromack
☎ **01947 880441**
🆂 **From £130–£220**
Sleeps 6
🐕 🐾 🚐 Å ◉

Tourist Board Inspected

We offer one 6-berth caravan, situated on 400-acre mixed stock farm edging the North Yorkshire Moors and near to Robin Hood's Bay. It is situated in a walled garden with open views and has all mains services including shower, toilet. TV, fridge, double and bunk-bedded rooms. Ideal for visiting historic towns, coastal resorts. Forest and moorland walks, pony trekking and clay pigeon shooting nearby. Short breaks out of season. Open Apr–Nov.

FINDING YOUR ACCOMMODATION

FARM HOLIDAY BUREAU

The local FHB Group contacts listed on page 392 can always help you find a vacancy in your chosen area.

FARM HOLIDAY BUREAU

Our Internet address is
http://www.webscape.co.uk/farmaccom/

Greater Manchester

South Pennines & Colne Valley

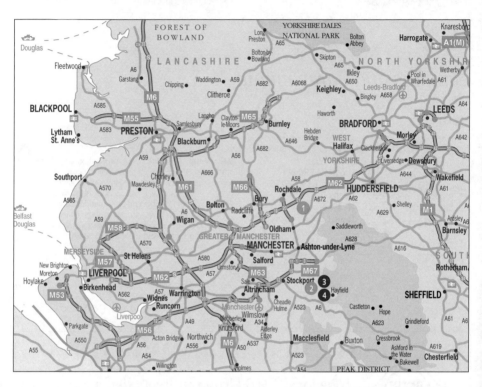

Key

 Bed & Breakfast

 Self-Catering

 B&B and SC

 Camping Barns

 Camping & Caravanning

A warm and friendly welcome awaits visitors to the dramatic South Pennines, an area still remarkably untouched by tourism. Walkers on the Pennine Way will find attractive valley towns like Delph, Uppermill, Marsden and Hebden Bridge and there are equally interesting routes over Blackstone Edge with the Roman Road, the Rossendale Way, the Calderdale Way and the Colne Valley Circular. Our textile heritage is magnificently illustrated in Golcar's Colne Valley Museum, the Helmshore Museum at Haslingden, and the Saddleworth Museum at Uppermill, and craft centres and mill shops abound. For shopping, restaurants and nightlife you can't beat cosmopolitan Manchester.

If you would like help in finding suitable farm accommodation, turn to the full listing of FHB Groups on pages 392 to 395 to find appropriate contact details for this area.

Bed and Breakfast
(and evening meal)

Boothstead Farm, Rochdale Road, Denshaw, Oldham, Greater Manchester OL3 5UE

Mrs Norma Hall
☎ 01457 878622
BB From £17.50–£20
Sleeps 4
🐴 ⛰ 🐕 ✂ 💼 🎯
♦♦♦

An 18th century hill farm catering for people in the area on business or taking a relaxing break. Ideally situated within 3½ miles of M62 Junctions 21 and 22 (A640). Cosy lounge with open fire, TV, tea/coffee-making facilities, wash basins in rooms. Good base for touring neighbouring counties and beauty spots. Close to Saddleworth leisure amenities, ie. golf, swimming, walking, sailing. Open 2 Jan–22 Dec.

Needhams Farm, Uplands Road, Werneth Low, Gee Cross, near Hyde, Cheshire SK14 3AQ

Mrs Charlotte Walsh
☎ 0161 368 4610
Fax 0161 367 9106
BB From £20–£22
EM From £7
Sleeps 14
🐴 ⛰ 🔤 💼 🎯
♦♦♦

Farmhouse accommodation dating back to the 16th century, offering 5 en suite rooms. Evening meals available each evening. Residential licence. Surrounded by lovely views. Ideal for Manchester Airport and city centre. Courtesy service from airport and Piccadilly station for a small charge. Six bedrooms in all. Open all year.
E-mail: charlotte@needhamsfarm.demon.co.uk

Self-Catering

Lake View, Ernocroft Farm, Marple Bridge, Stockport, Cheshire SK6 5NT

Monica Sidebottom
☎ 01457 866536
SC From £280–£350
Sleeps 6 + cot
🐴 ⛰ 💼
🏅 🏅 🏅 *Commended*

A new, self-catering farm bungalow, 2 miles Marple Bridge, 4 miles Glossop. Overlooking Etherow Country Park. Ideal base for exploring Peak District, Marple locks and waterways, country parks and stately homes. Peaceful location. Accommodates 6 with all mod cons. TV. Cot available. Open all year.

Shaw Farm, Shaw Marsh, New Mills, High Peak, Derbyshire SK22 4QE

Mrs Nicky Burgess
☎ 0161 427 1841
SC From £190–£360
Sleeps 8
🐴 ⛰ 💼 🎯 🔤
🏅 🏅 🏅 *Commended*

Views and cows, walks to suit, a picnic in the wood. Come to us we have it all, a real farm delight. Three bedroomed cottage, price reduced if family room not required. Full CH, south-facing garden with patio, children's play area. Pub with grub 5 mins' walk. Short breaks out of season.

Cheshire

Delamere Forest, Cheshire Plain, Shropshire Union Canal,
Alderley Edge & Peak District National Park

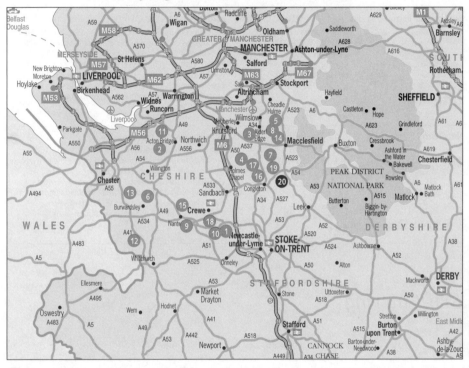

Key

- ① Bed & Breakfast
- ① Self-Catering
- ② B&B and SC
- ① Camping Barns
- ⚠ Camping & Caravanning

Cheshire is one of England's undiscovered counties. Renowned for lovely black-and-white architecture and its superb cheese, it is a county of contrasts. From the majesty of the Peak District across the Cheshire Plain to the Dee estuary, from North Wales to Manchester, from the Shropshire Hills to Liverpool, Cheshire has something for everyone. The county has a rich history, with Roman remains, a splendid cathedral and the unique 'Rows' in Chester, Elizabethan towns like Nantwich, fine castles and country mansions, and excellent museums about the Industrial Revolution. There are beautiful gardens, canals, wonderful walking, cycling and fishing. Come and discover us.

If you would like help in finding suitable farm accommodation, turn to the full listing of FHB Groups on pages 392 to 395 to find appropriate contact details for this area.

Bed and Breakfast
(and evening meal)

Adderley Green Farm, Heighley Castle Lane, Betley, Nr Crewe, Cheshire CW3 9BA ❶

Mrs Sheila Berrisford
☎ 01270 820203
Fax 01270 820542
BB From £18–£22
Sleeps 6
ゐ ⋔ 𝔁 ⚒ ▥ ⊛
◆◆◆◆

Relax in our lovely Georgian farmhouse on a 250-acre dairy farm set in large garden along a pretty country lane near an old ruined castle. Full CH. Colour TV, radio, washbasin and tea tray in all bedrooms. En suites available, draped and 4-poster beds. Beautifully decorated in the Laura Ashley style, separate tables in dining room. Ideally situated for Stapeley Water Gardens, Alton Towers and Chester. Near Keele University and Potteries, 10 mins M6 J16. Open all year except Christmas and New Year.

Ash House Farm, Chapel Lane, Acton Bridge, Northwich, Cheshire CW8 3QS ❷

Mrs Sue Schofield
☎ 01606 852717
BB From £20–£22
Sleeps 6
ゐ ⋔ 𝔁 ▥ ⊛
◆◆

A warm welcome awaits you at Ash House Farm, a mixed working farm in the heart of Cheshire in peaceful, scenic surroundings. Relax in our lovely Georgian farmhouse which is full of traditional architectural features. Guests' TV lounge and dining room with log fire. Tea/coffee facilities in bedrooms. Very rural, excellent for country walks yet only short distance from M56 J10. Secure parking. Open all year.

Astle Farm East, Chelford, Macclesfield, Cheshire SK10 4TP ❸

Gill Stubbs
☎ 01625 861270
BB From £17–£20
Sleeps 5
ゐ ⸾
Applied

This picturesque award-winning dairy and arable family farm offers you superb bed and breakfast accommodation in the heart of the Cheshire countryside. Take the A537 out of Chelford towards Macclesfield. We are on the right half mile after the roundabout. Open all year.

Bridge Farm, Bridge Lane, Blackden, Holmes Chapel, Cheshire CW4 8BX ❹

Mrs Anne Massey
☎ 01477 571202
BB From £18–£22
Sleeps 6
ゐ ⋔ ▥ ⸙ ⊛
◆◆◆

Here at Bridge Farm, only 500 yards from Jodrell Bank Telescope with its famous Visitors' Centre, we offer a warm welcome and comfortable accommodation in our 300 year old family farmhouse. Well appointed rooms and visitors' lounge overlooking 12 acres of wildflower meadows. En suite available. Situated 3 miles from M6 J18, close to Knutsford, central to Macclesfield, Chester and the Potteries. Open all year.
E-mail: pmassey648@aol.com

Carr House Farm, Mill Lane, Adlington, Macclesfield, Cheshire SK10 4LG ❺

Mrs Isobel Worthington
☎/Fax 01625 828337
BB From £16–£20
Sleeps 6
ゐ ⸾ ▥ 𝔁
◆◆◆

We extend a warm welcome to our cattle and sheep rearing farm, and offer you comfortable accommodation in our 200 year-old farmhouse in a garden setting. Tea and coffee facilities in bedrooms. Visitors' own lounge and dining room. Adlington Hall one mile, Manchester Airport approx six miles. Situated four miles north of Macclesfield just off the A523. Open Feb–Nov.

6 Ford Farm, Newton Lane, Tattenhall, Chester, Cheshire CH3 9NE

Audrey Charmley
☎ 01829 770307
▣ From £16–£17.50
Sleeps 5
⟱ ⟱ ⟱ ▦
♦♦♦

A friendly welcome to our dairy farm set in beautiful countryside with views of Beeston and Peckforton Castles. Close to ice cream farm and Cheshire workshops and many tourist attractions. Chester 7 miles, Oulton Park 8 miles. Guests' own lounge and dining room with TV. Two double rooms and one twin, tea/coffee-making facilities and TV in all rooms. Bathroom with shower. Open all year.

7 Golden Cross Farm, Siddington, Nr Macclesfield, Cheshire SK11 9JP

Hazel Rush
☎ 01260 224358
▣ From £16–£20
Sleeps 6
⟱ ⟱ ▦ ▦
♦♦♦

Small organic farm, 100 yards from the A34 on the B5392 in picturesque surroundings. Central for Macclesfield, Congleton, Holmes Chapel and Alderley Edge. Places of local interest include Capesthorne Hall, Gawsworth Hall, Tatton Hall, Styal Mill and Nether Alderley Mill. 2 double rooms, 2 single rooms, all with washbasins and tea/coffee-making facilities. Central heating, guests' lounge, colour TV. Open all year (closed Christmas & New Year).

8 Goose Green Farm, Oak Road, Mottram St Andrew, Nr Macclesfield, Cheshire SK10 4RA

Dyllis Hatch
☎/Fax 01625 828814
▣ From £20–£24
Sleeps 6
⟱(6) ⟱ ⟱ ▦ ▦
♦♦♦

Welcome to our farm set in beautiful countryside with panoramic views. Near the A538 between Wilmslow and Prestbury, in easy reach of M6, M56 and Manchester Airport. Own fishing, stabling available. Log fire, separate dining room. Pay phone. Double en suite, twin and single rooms, all with washbasin, TV, CH and tea/coffee-making facilities. Open all year.

9 Henhull Hall, Welshmans Lane, Nantwich, Cheshire CW5 6AD

Joyce & Philip Percival
☎/Fax 01270 624158
▣ From £25–£27
Sleeps 4
⟱ ⟱ ⟱ ▦ ▦ ▦
♦♦♦♦

Welcome to our spacious farmhouse,
View the garden, duckpond, cows,
Walk to Nantwich, drive to Chester,
Along the canalside you may wander.
Beds and bathrooms are luxurious
Wait no longer, come and join us.
E-mail: philip.percival@virgin.net

10 Lea Farm, Wrinehill Road, Wybunbury, Nantwich, Cheshire CW5 7NS

Allen & Jean Callwood
☎/Fax 01270 841429
▣ From £17.50
EM From £11
Sleeps 6
⟱ ⟱ ⟱ ▦ ▦ ▦
♦♦

A charming farmhouse set in landscaped gardens where peacocks roam a pedigree dairy farm. Spacious, attractive bedrooms have en suite facilities, vanity units, tea/coffee trays, colour TV. Luxurious lounge with open log fire, with dining room overlooking garden. Snooker, pool table, fishing available. Near to Stapeley Water Gardens and Bridgemere Garden World. M6 J16, Chester and Alton Towers. Open all year (closed Christmas & New Year).

11 Manor Farm, Cliff Road, Acton Bridge, Northwich, Cheshire CW8 3QP

Mrs T H Campbell
☎/Fax 01606 853181
▣ From £20–£27
Sleeps 5
⟱ ⟱ ⟱ ⟱ ▦ ▦ ▦ ▦
▦ ▦
♦♦♦♦

Set in secluded location down private drive with fields and walks beside the River Weaver. Convenient for M6, M56 (J10), Chester, Northwich and Merseyside. We give a warm welcome to our quiet country house. Comfortable bedrooms, each with private/en suite facilities. Tea/coffee, hairdrier, trouser press, drying, own TV lounge and peaceful garden. English breakfast served in elegant oak-furnished dining room. Safe car park. Open all year.

Millmoor Farm, Nomansheath, Malpas, Cheshire SY14 8ED   ⑫

Mrs Sally-Ann Chesters
☎ 01948 820304
BB From £16–£20
EM From £10
Sleeps 4

Set amongst the beautiful valleys on the South Cheshire/ Shropshire border, Millmoor Farm is a wonderful setting to escape the hurly burly of modern life. The 17th century farmhouse has recently been refurbished and boasts an exquisite en suite four-poster double bedroom. Within easy reach of Chester, North Wales and Shropshire's many attractions. Great pub meals within walking distance. Open all year.

Newton Hall, Tattenhall, Chester, Cheshire CH3 9AY   ⑬

Mrs Anne Arden
☎ 01829 770153
Fax 01829 770655
BB From £20–£25
Sleeps 5

A warm welcome to our part 16th century oak-beamed farmhouse. Set in large well kept grounds, with fine views of historic Beeston and Peckforton Castles and close to the Sandstone Trail. Six miles south of Chester off A41 and ideal for Welsh Hills. Rooms are en suite or have adjacent bathroom. TV in bedrooms. Guests' own sitting room. Full central heating.

Oldhams Hollow Farm, Manchester Road, Tytherington, Macclesfield, Cheshire SK10 2JW   ⑭

Brenda Buxton
☎ 01625 424128
Fax 01625 574280
BB From £19–£20
EM From £10
Sleeps 6

Welcome to Oldhams Hollow – a 16th century listed farmhouse one mile north of Macclesfield, close to the peaks and plains of Cheshire. Snug, warm and restful with oak beams, large lounge, open fire, spacious dining room, central heating. Comfortable bedrooms with colour TV, washbasins, tea/coffee-making facilities, electric blankets.

Poole Bank Farm, Wettenhall Road, Poole, Nantwich, Cheshire CW5 6AL   ⑮

Caroline Hocknell
☎ 01270 625169
BB From £18–£22
Sleeps 6

A charming 17th century timbered farmhouse on 200-acre dairy farm set in quiet countryside 2 miles from the historic town of Nantwich. Ideal base for discovering the beautiful Cheshire countryside. Central for Chester and the Potteries. Comfortable and attractive rooms, all with period furnishings. TV and tea/coffee making facilities. A warm welcome and an excellent breakfast are assured. Open all year.

Sandhole Farm, Hulme Walfield, Congleton, Cheshire CW12 2JH   ⑯

Veronica Worth
☎ 01260 224419
Fax 01260 224766
BB From £24.50–£49
Sleeps 36

The comfortable traditional farmhouse and delightful converted stable block are situated 2 miles north of Congleton on A34, 15 mins from M6 and 30 mins from Manchester airport. Most of our rooms have modern en suite facilities and all have the usual extras, including hairdryer, remote control teletext TV plus trouser press and direct dial telephone. Large comfortable lounge, separate newly built conservatory/dining room. Cheshire Tourism Award Winner. Now approved for Civil Marriages. Open all year.

Sandpit Farm, Messuage Lane, Marton, Macclesfield, Cheshire SK11 9HS   ⑰

Mrs I H Kennerley
☎ 01260 224254
BB From £19.50–£22
Sleeps 6

A friendly welcome to our 300 year old farmhouse surrounded by 100 acres of grassland. Traditional farmhouse with oak timber features and heated throughout. Separate dining room and TV lounge. H&C in T/S, en suite facilities in double and twin, all with tea/coffee and TV. Excellent touring centre for Peak District, Potteries, Chester. Manchester Airport 14 miles, NT properties, stately homes and Jodrell Bank Science Centre nearby. Open all year.

---

18 Snape Farm, Snape Lane, Weston, Nr Crewe, Cheshire CW2 5NB

Mrs Jean Williamson
☎/Fax 01270 820208
BB From £18–£25
EM From £10
Sleeps 6
🛌 🐓 🍴 🛄 🎯 ☺
♦♦♦

Enjoy a warm welcome to our centrally heated farmhouse on a 150-acre beef/arable farm set in rolling countryside. 3 miles from Crewe. A good centre for visiting Nantwich, Chester or the Potteries. Guests' lounge and snooker room. 1 twin (en suite), 1 twin, 1 double room, each with colour TV and tea/coffee-making facilities. 4 miles from M6 (J 16). Open all year except Christmas.

---

19 Yew Tree Farm, North Rode, Congleton, Cheshire CW12 2PF

Mrs Sheila Kidd
☎ 01260 223569
BB From £19
EM From £10
Sleeps 6
🛌 ✂ 🍴 🎯 🛄 ☺
♦♦♦♦

Discover an oasis of freedom, relaxation, wooded walks and beautiful views. Meet a whole variety of pets and farm animals on this friendly working farm. Your comfort is our priority. Good food is a speciality. Generous, scrummy breakfasts and traditional evening meals. A true taste of the countryside – just for you! Open all year.

Self-Catering

---

20 The Old Byre, Pye Ash Farm, Leek Road, Bosley, Macclesfield, Cheshire SK11 0PN

Dorothy Gilman
☎/Fax 01260 273650
SC From £200–£400
Sleeps 8 + cot
🧍 🛌 🛄 ☺
🐾🐾🐾 Commended

The Old Byre is especially designed so two families may holiday together. Cows, sheep, hens, ducks, etc make this a country paradise. Roomy enough to dine together, or good pub food is ½ mile walk away. The Peak District, Staffordshire Moorlands, Alton Towers, National Trust properties all easily reached.

LET THE TELEPHONE RING!

Some farmhouses are big places. Let the telephone ring
long enough to give the owner time to answer it.

STAY ON A FARM GIFT TOKENS

FARM HOLIDAY
BUREAU

If you have enjoyed your Stay on a Farm, why not treat your friends and relatives to *Stay on a Farm* gift tokens? Available from the Bureau office (tel: 024 7669 6909), they can be redeemed against accommodation and are accepted by the majority of farms (see Index). Please check when booking to avoid disappointment.

England's Heartland

Farm entries in this section are listed under those counties shown in green on the key map. The index below the map gives the appropriate page numbers. You will see that we have listed the counties geographically so that you can turn more easily to find farms in neighbouring counties.

At the start of each county section is a detailed map with numbered symbols indicating the location of each farm. Different symbols denote different types of accommodation; see the key below each county map. Farm entries are listed alphabetically under type of accommodation. Some farms offer more than one type of accommodation and therefore have more than one entry.

❶ *Derbyshire*
❷ *Nottinghamshire*
❸ *Lincolnshire*
❹ *Shropshire*
❺ *Staffordshire*
❻ *Leicestershire*
❼ *Herefordshire*
❽ *Worcestershire*
❾ *Gloucestershire*
❿ *West Midlands*
⓫ *Warwickshire*
⓬ *Northamptonshire*
⓭ *Cambridgeshire*
⓮ *Norfolk*
⓯ *Suffolk*

KEY MAP TO ENGLAND'S HEARTLAND

Derbyshire

Derwent Valley, Peak District National Park, Dovedale,
Manifold Valley & Heights of Abraham

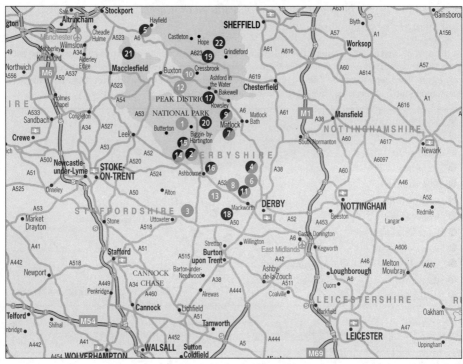

This is the home of the Peak District, Britain's first National Park. From the mellow lowlands of the south to the rugged peaks of the north, from picturesque villages to busy market towns like Ashbourne and Bakewell, from historic houses such as Chatsworth, Haddon and Hardwick to the excitement of Alton Towers and the American Adventure, a warm welcome awaits you in every corner of Derbyshire. At Matlock cable cars glide majestically across an awe-inspiring gorge, while Castleton is known for its show caves and Blue John stone. Dovedale and the Manifold Valley are justly famous for their scenery. This is ideal walking, cycling, pony trekking and fishing country, perfect for your stay on a farm.

If you would like help in finding suitable farm accommodation, turn to the full listing of FHB Groups on pages 392 to 395 to find appropriate contact details for this area.

Bed and Breakfast
(and evening meal)

Bank Top Farm, Pilsbury Road, Hartington, Buxton, Derbyshire SK17 0AD ①

Jane Pilkington
☎ 01298 84205
ⓑⓑ From £21–£30
EM From £6.50
Sleeps 6
🐴 ⅋ Å 🚗 🗢 🛄 🎾 ⊙
♦♦♦

Lying between the hills, almost off the beaten track, we entrance the imagination of those who wish to relax in a peaceful garden with English afternoon tea. Dovedale is ideal for walking, cycling and touring the area's unspoilt villages, market towns and historic houses. In our farmhouse we offer a warm hospitality and hope to fulfil your (reasonable) desires. Open all year.

Beechenhill Farm, Ilam, Ashbourne, Derbyshire DE6 2BD ②

Sue Prince
☎/Fax 01335 310274
ⓑⓑ From £22–£30
Sleeps 5
🐴 ⅋ 🛄 🎾 🐴 ⊙
♦♦♦♦

Wake up to wonderful views over a country garden, grazing cows and sheep, walkable hills and valleys. Our warm old farmhouse has two delightful en suite rooms – 1 double, 1 family – own lounge, breakfast room, all interestingly decorated by artist Sue. Carefully cooked breakfasts with famous Beechenhill porridge. Open Easter–Nov. E-mail: beechenhill@btinternet.com

---

Beeches Farmhouse, Waldley, Doveridge, Nr Ashbourne, Derbyshire DE6 5LR ③

Barbara Tunnicliffe
☎ 01889 590288
Fax 01889 590559
ⓑⓑ From £31–£48
EM From £16
🐴 🖭 🛄 ⊙
♦♦♦♦♦ *(AA Inspected)*

Relax and unwind in our rural retreat after exploring the Derbyshire Dales or the thrills of Alton Towers. Dine in our 2 AA Rosettes award-winning 18th century licensed farmhouse restaurant. Fresh English food and homemade desserts. Meet our Shetland pony, pigs, dogs, rabbits and kittens, whilst enjoying the freedom of the gardens, fields and the beautiful countryside. Closed Christmas. See colour ad on page 36. E-mail: beechesfa@aol.com

---

Chevin Green Farm, Chevin Road, Belper, Derbyshire DE56 2UN ④

Carl & Joan Postles
☎/Fax 01773 822328
ⓑⓑ From £18–£27
Sleeps 14
🐴 ⅋ 🖭 🚗 🛄 ⊙
♦♦♦

200-year-old modernised farmhouse in a quiet, peaceful setting of 38 acres of picturesque hillside scenery known as 'The Chevin'. Centrally heated en suite rooms with colour TV and tea/coffee-making facilities. Generous breakfasts using our own free range eggs. Central for all Derbyshire's attractions. Closed Christmas and New Year. E-mail: spostles@globalnet.co.uk

---

Cote Bank Farm, Buxworth, Whaley Bridge, High Peak, Derbyshire SK23 7NP ⑤

Pamela Broadhurst
☎/Fax 01663 750566
ⓑⓑ From £20–£25
Sleeps 6
🐴(10) ✖ ⅋ 🖭 🛄 ⊙
♦♦♦ Silver Award

Good old fashioned hospitality, a kettle always on the boil and a breakfast worth waking for! Treat yourself to a relaxing stay on our peaceful sheep farm with stunning views across the hills and excellent walks. A home from home for business travellers (1 mile Chinley, 3 miles A6) and a welcoming base for holidaymakers. Guests' lounge with log fire; 2 doubles, 1 twin, both en suite, with TV, radio, tea/coffee. Open Mar–Dec. E-mail: cotebank@btinternet.com

---

6 **Dannah Farm Country House,** Bowmans Lane, Shottle, Belper, Derbyshire DE56 2DR

Joan & Martin Slack
☎ 01773 550273/550630
Fax 01773 550590
[BB] From £35–£49.50
EM From £17.95
Sleeps 18
🐎 🅕 🕷 🐾 🕯 ⊚
♦♦♦♦♦ *(AA Inspected)*

Recent winners Bed & Breakfast of the Year, also top national award for farm catering. Hopefully we have it all, from stunning views to award-winning food and, above all, the warmest of welcomes! Relax and unwind in our lovely Georgian farmhouse furnished with antiques and old pine, on our mixed working farm. All rooms en suite. Colour TVs, fully licensed. Open all year except Christmas. See colour ad page 36.
E-mail: reservations@dannah.demon.co.uk

---

7 **Lydgate Farm,** Aldwark, Grange Mill, Matlock, Derbyshire DE4 4HW

Joy Lomas
☎/Fax 01629 540250
[BB] From £18–£22.50
Sleeps 6
🐎 🕯 ⊚
♦♦♦♦

A warm welcome and good food await you in our 17th century house on a 300-acre dairy and sheep farm. Lydgate is ideally situated for visiting Chatsworth, Haddon Hall and all Derbyshire has to offer. Central heating and hot drink facilities in all rooms, one family en suite, one twin en suite, one double. Guests' own dining room and sitting room. Open Feb–Nov.
E-mail: joy.lomas@btinternet.com

---

8 **Mercaston Hall,** Mercaston, Brailsford, Ashbourne, Derbyshire DE6 3BL

Angus & Vicki Haddon
☎ 01335 360263
Fax 01335 361399
[BB] From £23–£29
Sleeps 6
🐎(8) 🕷 🐿 🐾 🕷 🕯 🍴 ⊚
♦♦♦♦

Timber-framed, historic, listed building in a quiet countryside location. Situated off the A52 halfway between Derby and Ashbourne. An ideal centre for visits to the Peak District, many tourist attractions and the commercial towns and cities of the Midlands. Kedleston Hall (NT) 1 mile. Hard tennis court. Open all year except Christmas. E-mail: mercastonhall@btinternet.com

---

9 **Middlehills Farm,** Grange Mill, Matlock, Derbyshire DE4 4HY

Mrs Linda Lomas
☎/Fax 01629 650368
[BB] From £20
Sleeps 6
🐎 🕷 🐾 🐿 🕯 ⊚
♦♦♦♦

Escape the rat race – taste the fresh air, absorb the peace, feast your eyes on the beautiful scenery and magnificent views that surround our small working farm 5 miles west of Matlock on the A5012. Large walled garden, two en suite family rooms, one en suite twin, all with tea/coffee facilities. Comfortable lounge with TV and pool table. Open all year. E-mail: l.lomas@btinternet.com

---

10 **The Old Bake & Brewhouse,** Blackwell Hall, Blackwell in the Peak, Taddington, nr Buxton, Derbys SK17 9TQ

Mrs Christine Gregory
☎/Fax 01298 85271
[BB] From £19–£25
Sleeps 4
🐎 🌿 🐾 🕯 🕷 ⊚
♦♦♦

Early 18th century much loved farmhouse with its old oak, chintz and the scent of beeswax and honeysuckle, set in a peaceful, mature garden. Our home is in the Peak National Park and the farm has archaeological and conservation sites. From our door join the lovely River Wye as it meanders through spectacular Cheedale and Monsal Dale. Delicious, hearty Derbyshire breakfasts with home made preserves. Open all year except Christmas. E-mail: christine.gregory@btinternet.com

---

11 **Park View Farm,** Weston Underwood, Ashbourne, Derbyshire DE6 4PA

Mrs Linda Adams
☎/Fax 01335 360352
[BB] From £25–£38
Sleeps 6
🐎(6) 🌿 🐾 🕷 ⊚
♦♦♦♦♦ *(AA Inspected)*

Enjoy country house hospitality in our elegant farmhouse set in large gardens with lovely views overlooking the National Trust's magnificent Kedleston Park, hence the farm's name. Double en suite rooms with antique four-poster beds, twin with handbasin and bathroom. Drinks facilities. Guests' sitting room and delightful dining room. Superb English breakfasts. Country pubs and restaurants close by. AA QQQQQ Premier Selected. Closed Christmas.

Shallow Grange, Chelmorton, nr Buxton, Derbyshire SK17 9SG

Christine Holland
☎ 01298 23578
Fax 01298 78242
BB From £22–£30
Sleeps 6
⌂(5) Å ⊕ ▤ ⊼ ⊛
♦♦♦♦♦Gold Award

Spectacular views, wide open spaces and a piece of rural England all await you at Shallow Grange. Luxury accommodation includes all rooms en suite, colour TVs, etc. This working dairy farm has numerous unspoilt walks whilst Chatsworth, Buxton and Bakewell are all within a short drive. We also have 20-pitch caravan site. *Which?* recommended. Open all year. See colour ad on page 37.
E-mail: shallowgrangefarm@freeserve.co.uk

Shirley Hall, Shirley, Ashbourne, Derbyshire DE6 3AS

Mrs Sylvia Foster
☎/Fax 01335 360346
BB From £19–£26
Sleeps 6
⌂ ⅓ ⇐ ▤ ⊛
♦♦♦♦

Enjoy the tranquillity of our lovely old, part moated, timbered farmhouse, surrounded by large lawned garden and rolling dairy/arable farm just 4 miles from Ashbourne. Our English breakfasts are renowned. Village pub within walking distance for excellent evening meals. Free coarse fishing. Woodland walks. 2 double bedrooms en suite. 1 twin with handbasin and guest's bathroom. All with CH, TV and drinks facilities. Guests' sitting room. Open all year.

Throwley Hall Farm, Ilam, Ashbourne, Derbyshire DE6 2BB

Mrs MA Richardson
☎ 01538 308202
Fax 01538 308243
BB From £20–£25
Sleeps 9
⌂ ⅍ ⅓ ⊼ ⊛
♦♦♦♦

Large Georgian farmhouse on working hill farm with beef and sheep. Nestling in beautiful countryside in the Manifold Valley, close to Dovedale. Superb walking country, Alton Towers a short drive. All rooms have tea/coffee facilities, TV and washbasin, some en suite. Full English breakfast. Open all year.

Wolfscote Grange Farm, Hartington, Nr Buxton, Derbyshire SK17 0AX

Jane Gibbs
☎/Fax 01298 84342
BB From £20–£25
Sleeps 6
⌂ Å ▤ ⊼ ⊛
♦♦♦

Find an ideal 'country hideaway' on our secluded hill farm with beautiful views over the Dove Valley. Along a stone-walled road from picturesque Hartington village. Feel at home in our ancient 15th century farmhouse with all its character, original oak beams, mullion windows, spiral staircase. Spacious guests' lounge, 2 pretty bedrooms, 1 family, 1 double en suite, tea/coffee facilities. Breakfast, then explore the many footpaths leading to hidden Dales below. Open Mar–Nov. E-mail: wolfscote@btinternet.com

---

Yeldersley Old Hall Farm, Yeldersley Lane, Bradley, Ashbourne, Derbyshire DE6 1PH

Mrs Janet Hinds
☎/Fax 01335 344504
BB From £20–£25
Sleeps 6
⌂ ⅓ ▤ ⊛
♦♦♦♦

Yeldersley Old Hall Farm is a family-run dairy farm of 112 acres. The Grade II listed farmhouse is situated in pleasant and quiet rural surroundings just 3 miles from the market town of Ashbourne and within easy reach of Dovedale, Alton Towers, Matlock and many stately homes. Farmhouse breakfast provided. Lounge with log fire. All rooms en suite. Non-smokers only please. Open Mar–Nov.

Please mention *Stay on a Farm* when booking

FARM HOLIDAY BUREAU

Self-Catering

---

② Beechenhill Cottage & The Cottage by the Pond, Beechenhill Farm, Ilam, Ashbourne, Derbys, DE6 2BD

Mrs Sue Prince
☎/Fax 01335 310274
SC From £110–£500
Sleeps 2–6
♿ ♞ ⚓ ♨ ◉
♟ ♟ ♟ – ♟ ♟ ♟ ♟

Highly Commended

Beechenhill Cottage, tiny and warm in peaceful walled garden, a secluded hideaway just for two. Award-winning Cottage by the Pond for all including wheelchair users. Sleeps six in three bedrooms, two bathrooms. Both cottages have lovely views, real fires and beautiful decoration by artist Sue at organic dairy farm near Dovedale. Open all year.
E-mail: beechenhill@btinternet.com

---

⑯ Briar, Bluebell & Primrose Cottages, c/o Yeldersley Old Hall Farm, Yeldersley Lane, Bradley, Ashbourne, Derbyshire DE6 1PH

Mrs Janet Hinds
☎/Fax 01335 344504
SC From £150–£330
Sleep 5/6
♞ ♨ ◉
♟ ♟ ♟ *Commended*

Situated on a working family dairy farm in rural surroundings, our Grade II listed barn has been converted into 3 self-catering cottages. Two accommodate 5 people (maximum), one 6 people. Each has three bedrooms with bathroom containing bath and shower, fitted kitchen, colour TV. Ample parking area. Ideal spot for touring Derbyshire. Ashbourne 3 miles. Short breaks. Open all year.

---

⑰ Burton Manor Farm Cottages, Over Haddon, Bakewell, Derbyshire DE45 1JX

Mrs Ruth Shirt
☎/Fax 01298 871429
SC From £168–£594
Sleeps 3/4/8
♞ ♀ ⚓
♟ ♟ ♟ – ♟ ♟ ♟ ♟

Highly Commended

Our family-run dairy/sheep farm is an ideal base for visitors, being in the heart of the Peak District. Excellent walking in all directions with the nearby Lathkill Dale and Limestone Way. This recent barn conversion consists of four cosy cottages providing quality accommodation with excellent parking. Open all year. See colour ad on page 37.

---

⑦ Chapelgate Cottage, c/o Lydgate Farm, Aldwark, Grange Mill, Matlock, Derbyshire DE4 4HW

Joy Lomas
☎/Fax 01629 540250
SC From £200–£280
Sleeps 5 + cot
♞ ♀ ⚓ ♨ ◉
♟ ♟ ♟ ♟ *Highly Commended*

Beautiful oak beamed, stone mullioned cottage with lovely views and garden, set in the peaceful hamlet of Aldwark. Well appointed open plan kitchen/living area with log fire and colour TV. Two bedrooms and bathroom/shower room. The cottage is centrally heated, double glazed and fully carpeted throughout. Towels, fresh linen and electricity are included. Chapelgate Cottage will give you a wonderful holiday in the heart of the Peak District. Open all year. E-mail: joy.lomas@btinternet.com

---

④ Chevin Green Farm, Chevin Road, Belper, Derbyshire DE56 2UN

Carl & Joan Postles
☎/Fax 01773 822328
SC From £100–£325
Sleeps 4/6
♞ ♀ ⚓ 🖥 ⚓ ◉
♟ ♟ ♟ ♟ *Commended*

Enjoy a holiday in one of our four attractive cottages of character overlooking picturesque countryside. The cottages with original beams are fully equipped to a high standard. Lounge, fully fitted kitchen, bathroom, 2 or 3 bedrooms, one is specially adapted for the disabled. Ideally situated for all places of interest, Alton Towers, Dales, Peak District and 6 stately homes. Open all year except Christmas and New Year. E-mail: spostles@globalnet.co.uk

---

The Chop House, Windle Hill Farm, Sutton-on-the-Hill, Ashbourne, Derbyshire DE6 5JH   **18**

K E & J Lennard
☎/Fax 01283 732377
SC **From £140–£360**
Sleeps 6
☒ ☈ ☊
♟♟♟♟ *Commended*

The Chop House was originally built in 1858 as the farm corn shed. It has been carefully converted to offer cosy, well-equipped family accommodation on our small working farm. Centrally heated, fully insulated, ideal for winter or summer lets. 3 twin bedrooms, kitchen/dining room, separate living room. Sheltered garden. Set amidst tranquil countryside south of Ashbourne. Open all year.

Cote Bank Farm Cottages, Buxworth, Whaley Bridge, High Peak, Derbyshire SK23 7NP   **5**

Pamela Broadhurst
☎/Fax 01663 750566
SC **From £190–£460**
Sleeps 6 + cot
☒ ☈ ⊞ ☊ ◉
♟♟♟♟ *Highly Commended*

Two warm, welcoming cottages on peaceful sheep farm with magnificent views and excellent walks. Chinley 1 mile, Buxton 7 miles. Children can feed the hens with farmer Nic and see happy animals reared naturally. Each cottage has 3 bedrooms (double, twin, bunks), lounge with logfire, TV and video, dining room, modern kitchen, full CH. 'Amongst the best farm cottages we know' – *Good Holiday Cottage Guide 1998.* Short breaks Nov–March. Open all year. E-mail: cotebank@btinternet.com

---

Cruck & Wolfscote Cottages, Wolfscote Grange Farm, Hartington, Nr Buxton, Derbyshire SK17 0AX   **15**

Jane Gibbs
☎/Fax 01298 84342
SC **From £140–£450**
Sleeps 4–6 + cot
☒ ☈ Å ⚘ ☊ ◉
♟♟♟ *Up to Highly Commended*

Enjoy spectacular scenery from our superb cottages. Cruck Cottage 'peaceful and away from it all with no neighbours only cows and sheep!', nestling above the beautiful Dove Valley. Wolfscote Cottage in a unique position with panoramic views across open meadows, hills and dales, on a secluded working sheep farm. Cosy and welcoming 'Enjoy the views, relax in peaceful surroundings or explore the Derbyshire Dales on the cottage doorstep.' Open all year. E-mail: wolfscote@btinternet.com

---

The Hayloft, Stanley House Farm, Great Hucklow, Tideswell, Buxton, Derbyshire SK17 8RL   **19**

Margot Darley
☎ 01298 871044
SC **From £140–£295**
Sleeps 4
☒(3) ☈ Å ⚘ ☊ ◉
♟♟♟♟ *Highly Commended*

Enjoy a relaxing holiday in peaceful surroundings in our stone barn conversion which offers excellent accommodation for four people. Spacious beamed sitting room with log fire and colour TV. Quality fitted kitchen/dining room, modern bathroom/WC. The Hayloft offers an ideal centre for exploring the Peak District. All linen, towels included in price. Dogs welcome. Open all year.

Honeysuckle & Brook Cottages, c/o Park View Farm, Weston Underwood, Ashbourne, Derbys DE6 4PA   **11**

Mrs Linda Adams
☎/Fax 01335 360352
SC **From £160–£400**
Sleeps 4/6 + cot
☒ ☊ ⚘ ◉
♟♟♟ – ♟♟♟♟ *Commended*

Honeysuckle is a truly delightful country cottage set in its own secluded garden with wonderful views over the Derbyshire countryside. Full of character and charm, furnished to a very high standard, with beamed sitting room, antique furnishings and pretty four poster bed. Accommodation for 6 persons in 3 bedrooms. Brook is a welcoming village cottage with 2 bedrooms (double and twin). Short breaks. Open all year.

Honeysuckle, Jasmine & Clematis Cottages, Middlehills Farm, Grange Mill, Matlock, Derbys DE4 4HY   **9**

Linda Lomas
☎/Fax 01629 650368
SC **From £120–£450**
Sleeps 4/8
♿ ☒ ☈ Å ⊞ ☊ ◉
♟♟♟♟ *Up to Highly Commended*

Take a break from the treadmill of life. Relax on the patio beneath the sweetly scented honeysuckle and jasmine. Enjoy the peace and tranquillity at our recently converted cottages. Full of character – beams, parquet floors, rustic rose arches, yet equipped with all modern conveniences – double glazing, CH, living flame fire. Clematis Cottage, one level, newly converted for less able guests and wheelchair users. Open all year. E-mail: l.lomas@btinternet.com

5 **The Old House,** Cote Bank Farm, Buxworth, Whaley Bridge, High Peak, Derbyshire SK23 7NP

Pamela Broadhurst
☎/Fax 01663 750566
⌂ From £170–£270
Sleeps 2 + cot
⌖ ⛾ ⊞ ⚓ ⦿
⚘⚘⚘⚘ *Highly
Commended*

A honeymoon hideaway in romantic self-contained Tudor wing of farmhouse. Cleverly modernised but with original 16th century beams, mullions and oodles of character! Kitchen/diner, bathroom, large bedroom with king size bed, lounge with inglenook fireplace and log burner. Logs, coal, CH, electricity, fresh linen and towels included. Glorious views, wonderful walks, perfect peace. Chinley 1 mile. Open all year. E-mail: cotebank@btinternet.com

20 **Old House Farm Cottage,** Old House Farm, Newhaven, Hartington, Buxton, Derbyshire SK17 0DY

Sue Flower
☎/Fax 01629 636268
⌂ From £190–£350
Sleeps 6 + cot
⌖ ⛾ ⚓ ⚘ ⛾ ⦿
⚘⚘⚘⚘ *Commended*

Explore 'Peak Practice' Country from our warm well appointed cottage. Stay on a real working dairy/sheep farm where a high standard is maintained. Lambing time a must in April. We run a busy family farm, still having time to answer your questions and delighted to let you watch our farm activities. Off road cycling trails lead from our farm. Short breaks Nov–Mar. Brochure. Open all year. E-mail: s.flowerfarmaccom@btinternet.com

21 **Plattwood Farm Cottage,** Lyme Park, Disley, Cheshire SK12 2NT

Jill Emmott
☎/Fax 01625 872738
⌂ From £280–£450
Sleeps 6
⌖ ⚘ ⛾ ⚓
⚘⚘⚘⚘ *Highly
Commended*

Beautiful location within the National Trust's Lyme Park (of Pride and Prejudice fame). Excellent walks, superb views over rolling countryside, an ideal base to explore the Peak District. Cosy and welcoming, the cottage is tastefully furnished. The master bedroom has a four-poster bed and en suite facilities. Landscaped garden and colourful courtyard. Open all year. E-mail: plattwoodfarm@talk21.com

22 **Shatton Hall Farm Cottages,** Bamford, Hope Valley, nr Sheffield, Derbyshire S33 0BG

Angela Kellie
☎ 01433 620635
Fax 01433 620689
⌂ From £225–£375
Sleeps 4/6 + cot
⌖ ⛾ ⚘ ⚓ ⛾ ⚓ ⦿
⚘⚘⚘⚘ *Highly
Commended*

Our comfortable, well equipped cottages are stone barn conversions around the Elizabethan farmstead in a peaceful setting. Streamside and woodland walks. Fishing, riding, cycle hire nearby. Each cottage has terrace/garden. Ample car parking. Open plan living room, open fires, CH, colour TV, well equipped kitchen. 2 double bedrooms, linen included. Put-u-up and cot available. Laundry facilities. Hard tennis court. Open all year. E-mail: a.j.kellie@virgin.net

14 **Throwley Moor Farm & Throwley Cottage,** Ilam, Ashbourne, Derbyshire DE6 2BB

Mrs MA Richardson
☎ 01538 308202
Fax 01538 308243
⌂ From £200–£600
Sleeps 7–12
⌖ ⛾ ⦿
⚘⚘⚘⚘ *Commended*

Attractive self-catering farmhouse and cottage conveniently situated near to the beautiful Manifold Valley and Dovedale. Superb scenery and walking country, Alton Towers is a short drive away. Both well equipped with fridge, freezer, microwave, dishwasher, washing machine, TV and video. Cosy open fires. Open all year.

Most farms are full Members of FHB. Some are shown as Associates – see page 11.

Nottinghamshire

Sherwood Forest & the Dukeries

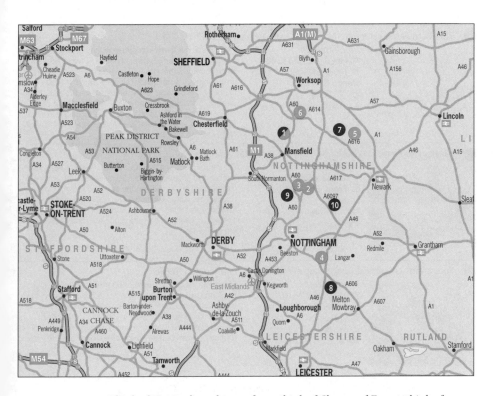

Nottinghamshire

Key

 Bed & Breakfast

 Self-Catering

 B&B and SC

 Camping Barns

 Camping & Caravanning

Think of Nottinghamshire and you think of Sherwood Forest; think of Sherwood Forest and you think of Robin Hood. He can still be found here, at the Sherwood Forest Visitor Centre near Edwinstowe and also in Nottingham, as a statue below the castle. Discover Nottingham's heritage, such as its world-famous lacemaking and the caves hidden under a modern shopping centre. Explore Nottinghamshire's countryside which has inspired writers such as Lord Byron and DH Lawrence and was home to the Pilgrim Fathers. Visit charming market towns such as Retford, Newark, renowned for its Civil War connections, and Southwell which boasts Nottinghamshire's best-kept secret – an impressive Norman cathedral.

If you would like help in finding suitable farm accommodation, turn to the full listing of FHB Groups on pages 392 to 395 to find appropriate contact details for this area.

Bed and Breakfast
(and evening meal)

---

① Blue Barn Farm, Langwith, Mansfield, Nottinghamshire NG20 9JD

June Ibbotson
☎/Fax **01623 742248**
⊞ From **£18–£22**
Sleeps 6
🐎 🎦 🛋 ⊚
♦♦♦

Welcome to our family-run 450-acre farm in peaceful surroundings on the edge of Sherwood Forest in Robin Hood country, 5 miles from M1 (J30) off A616. Many interesting places catering for all tastes only a short car journey away. Suitable for the business traveller, a place to unwind. 1 double, 1 twin en suite, 1 family, all with tea/coffee-making facilities and washbasins. Cot available. Dining room, lounge, TV. Open all year except Christmas & New Year.

---

② Far Baulker Farm, Old Rufford Road, Oxton, Nottinghamshire NG25 0RQ

Janette Esam
☎ **01623 882375**
⊞ From **£16–£25**
Sleeps 6
🐎 🅰 ⊡ 🛋
♦♦♦

Far Baulker Farm is a 300-acre arable/livestock farm set in the heart of Sherwood Forest 10 miles north of Nottingham on the A614. One double en suite, one double with washbasin, one twin, tea/coffee-making facilities and TV in all rooms. Visitors lounge with TV/video. A welcome awaits you in our family home. Open all year.

---

③ Forest Farm, Mansfield Road, Papplewick, Nottinghamshire NG15 8FL

Mrs E J Stubbs
☎ **0115 963 2310**
⊞ From **£16–£20**
Sleeps 5
🐎 ✂ 🛋
♦♦♦

Forest Farm is located on the A60 standing well back up the farm road away from traffic noise. Pleasant views from south-facing rooms, 1 double en suite, 1 single, 1 twin, all with tea-making facilities. TV in lounge/dining room. Midway between Mansfield and Nottingham, and ideal touring or business base. Open all year except Christmas.

---

④ Jerico Farm, Fosse Way, Nr Cotgrave, Nottinghamshire NG12 3HG

Mrs Sally Herrick
☎/Fax **01949 81733**
⊞ From **£20–£30**
Sleeps 6
🐎(5) ✂ ⊡ ☕ 🎦 🛋 ⁀ ⊚
♦♦♦♦ *(AA Inspected)*

A working farm with attractive accommodation surrounded by our own farmland with lovely views. Good firm beds, tea/coffee/chocolate trays and TVs in all bedrooms, (one en suite). Guests' sitting room. Good pubs nearby. Excellent location for visiting Nottingham, its universities, sports venues and tourist sites. Located down a farm drive off A46, 1 mile north of A46/A606 jct, south of Cotgrave village. Open all year (closed Christmas).
E-mail: herrick@jerico.swinternet.co.uk

---

⑤ Manor Farm, Moorhouse Road, Laxton, Newark, Nottinghamshire NG22 0NU

Mrs Pat Haigh
☎ **01777 870417**
⊞ From **£17**
Sleeps 6
🐎 🐕 🛋 🎦
♦♦

Manor Farm is a family-run dairy and arable farm of 137 acres, in the historic medieval village of Laxton, situated 10 miles north of Newark, and on the verge of the popular tourist area of Sherwood Forest in Nottinghamshire. 2 family rooms, 1 double room, tea/coffee-making facilities available. Visitors' lounge and dining room. Access to rooms at all times. Open all year (closed Christmas & New Year).

Norton Grange Farm, Norton, Cuckney, Mansfield, Nottinghamshire NG20 9LP   6

Fernie Palmer
☎ **01623 842666**
BB **From £19–£20**
Sleeps 4
🐕 🐎 💼 🛁 🎋
♦♦

Norton Grange is a Grade II listed farmhouse set in the heart of the Welbeck Estate, part of the world-famous Sherwood Forest. Ideally situated for overnight stops or touring the very beautiful countryside and the many attractions, in Nottinghamshire and Derbyshire. One double room and one twin room, both with washbasin and tea/coffee-making facilities. Open all year except Christmas & New Year.

Self-Catering

Blue Barn Cottage, c/o Blue Barn Farm, Langwith, Mansfield, Nottinghamshire NG20 9JD

June Ibbotson
☎/Fax **01623 742248**
SC **From £375–£425**
Sleeps 8 + cot
🐕 🎋 🛁 ⊚
🐾🐾🐾🐾 *Commended*

Do come and relax in peace and comfort on our family-run farm in Robin Hood country. Visit quiet villages, stately homes rich in history, ramble through country parks or hunt bargains in thriving market towns. Blue Barn is off the A616 near Cuckney. 4 bedrooms, bathroom, breakfast kitchen, dining room, lounge, TV. Utility room with shower, WC, washbasin, washing machine and tumble dryer. CH and linen included. Open all year.

Foliat Cottages, c/o Jordan Castle Farm, Wellow, Newark, Nottinghamshire NG22 0EL   7

Mrs Janet Carr
☎/Fax **01623 861088**
SC **From £200–£325**
Sleep 6 + cot
🐕 🍴 🛁 🎋
🐾🐾🐾🐾 *Commended*

Close to the heart of Sherwood Forest, our Edwardian cottages have beautiful pastoral views across our working family farm. Peaceful and cosy, with central heating, colour TV, microwave and washer/dryer. Each has 1 double and 2 twin bedrooms, bathroom and shower room. Cot and highchair available. Enclosed south-facing gardens with patios. Linen provided. Brochure available. Open all year. E-mail: janet.carr@farmline.com

Foxcote Cottage, Foxcote Hill Farm, Stanton on the Wolds, Nottinghamshire NG12 5PJ   8

Joan Hinchley
☎/Fax **0115 9374337**
SC **£300**
Sleeps 6
🐕 🐎 💼 🎋
🐾🐾🐾🐾 *Commended*

Situated seven miles south of Nottingham, on the edge of the Vale of Belvoir, within easy reach of all attractions in the Midlands. The cottage stands well back from the A606 overlooking open countryside with views of lake, and is set in a private, well-maintained garden. The cottage is fully equipped to a high standard. All bedlinen and towels included. Open all year.

The Granary, Top House Farm, Lamins Lane, Mansfield Road, Arnold, Nottingham, Notts NG5 8PH   9

Mrs Ann Lamin
☎ **0115 9268330**
SC **From £250–£295**
Sleeps 3/4
🐕 🍴 💼
🐾🐾🐾 *Commended*

Charming granary flat with beams, open fireplace, CH. Lounge has colour TV, patio doors onto garden. Kitchen has electric and microwave ovens, use of automatic washer and dryer. Within easy reach of Nottingham, Newstead Abbey, Southwell Minster, the Dukeries, Sherwood Forest, Derbyshire and the National Watersports Centre. Open all year.

The Mews, Eastwood Farm, Hagg Lane, Epperstone, Nottingham NG14 6AX

Susan Santos
☎ 0115 9663018
▣ From £150–£200
Sleeps 4 + cot
🐕 🏛 ✂ ⚘
ℱℱℱ *Approved*

Our peaceful, homely self-contained flat, with lovely views, is within easy reach of Nottingham, Southwell, Newark and Mansfield. At first floor level, adjacent to the farmhouse, it comprises 1 double, 1 twin bedroom, bathroom, living/dining room (colour TV), and well equipped kitchen. CH included in rental. Garage parking. Golf courses, Trent river and pond fishing nearby. Ideal leisure, touring or business base. Open all year.

THE 1000+ BUREAU MEMBERS OFFER A UNIQUE LINK TO CUSTOMERS ACROSS THE UK

All Bureau members belong to a local Group. Each member can refer you to an equally high quality member within the Group... or across the UK: England, Northern Ireland, Scotland, Wales.

USE THE INDEX

The comprehensive Index shows which farms offer access to disabled visitors; caravanning/camping facilities; the chance to participate on a working farm; stabling/grazing for visiting horses; en suite rooms; a welcome to business people; acceptance of *Stay on a Farm* gift tokens.

Our Internet address is
http://www.webscape.co.uk/farmaccom/

FOLLOW THE COUNTRY CODE
Leave nothing but footprints,
Take nothing but photographs,
Kill nothing but time!

Lincolnshire

Lincolnshire Wolds & Tennyson Country

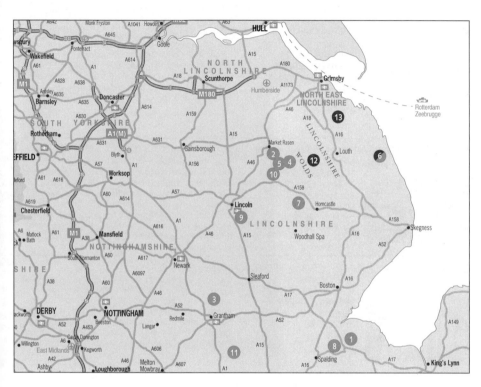

Key

 Bed & Breakfast

Self-Catering

B&B and SC

Camping Barns

Camping & Caravanning

A frequent comment of first-time visitors to Lincolnshire is: "I never realised there was so much to see and do". Don't miss Lincoln with its magnificent cathedral, castle and Museum of Lincolnshire Life; Belton House near Grantham; Stamford, a near-perfect stone town or its brick-built equivalent, Louth; and Elizabethan houses such as Doddington Hall and Burghley House. Explore the hidden lanes of Tennyson Country in the lovely Lincolnshire Wolds. Visit unspoilt market towns, walk part of the Viking Way, see Boston and its Stump, the memorial marking the spot where the Pilgrim Fathers tried to leave England... Sorry, no more space – you'll just have to come and see for yourself!

If you would like help in finding suitable farm accommodation, turn to the full listing of FHB Groups on pages 392 to 395 to find appropriate contact details for this area.

Bed and Breakfast
(and evening meal)

---

1 Cackle Hill House, Cackle Hill Lane, Holbeach, Lincolnshire PE12 8BS

Maureen Biggadike
☎ 01406 426721
Fax 01406 424659
BB From £20–£24
Sleeps 6
ᗡ(10) 🛏 ⅄ ▤ ⊚
♦♦♦♦

We welcome you to our farm situated in rural position just off the A17. Comfortable accommodation (en suites and private facilities) and traditional farmhouse fare. Farm walks, large patio and gardens. Close to the shores of the Wash with its marshes, trails and nature reserves, Spalding, Boston, Norfolk and Cambridgeshire. Open all year.

---

2 East Farm House, Middle Rasen Road, Buslingthorpe, Market Rasen, Lincolnshire LN3 5AQ

Mrs Gill Grant
☎ 01673 842283
BB From £21–£25
EM From £13
Sleeps 4
ᗡ 🛏 ⅄ ▤ ⅋
♦♦♦♦

Peace and relaxation await you in beamed 18th century listed farmhouse on 410 acre conservation award-winning farm with farm trail overlooking unspoilt countryside. Situated 4 miles SW of Market Rasen, ideal for rambling, touring beautiful Lincolnshire Wolds, coast, historic Lincoln and market towns. Wholesome farmhouse food, spacious bedrooms, TV and tea/coffee makers. 1 double en suite, 1 twin with private facilities. Guests' lounge. Open all year. E-mail: james@brailsford27.freeserve.co.uk

---

3 Gelston Grange Farm, Nr Marston, Grantham, Lincolnshire NG32 2AQ

Janet Sharman
☎/Fax 01400 250281
BB From £20–£25
Sleeps 6
ᗡ(5) ⅄ ▤
♦♦♦♦

Everyone is assured of a warm welcome at this lovely old farmhouse dating back to the 1600's. All bedrooms en suite (one four poster) and tastefully decorated. Large, pretty garden to enjoy. Ample parking. Short walk with beautiful views. Centrally situated for Grantham, Newark, Lincoln, Stamford and Nottingham. Approximately 3 miles from A1. Open all year except Christmas and New Year.

---

4 Glebe Farm, Benniworth, Market Rasen, Lincolnshire LN8 6JP

Sally Selby
☎ 01507 313231
BB From £22.50–£25
EM From £10
Sleeps 5
⅄ 🛆 ⊠ ▤ 🌾
♦♦♦♦

A hearty Lincolnshire welcome awaits in this Grade II listed farmhouse located in the peaceful, unspoilt Lincolnshire Wolds. Within easy reach of Lincoln and many quaint market towns. Excellent traditional meals using fresh local produce. Special diets catered for. En suite facilities, TV in bedrooms. Good walking country. Open all year.

---

5 The Grange, Torrington Lane, East Barkwith, Market Rasen, Lincolnshire LN8 5RY

Mrs Sarah Stamp
☎ 01673 858670
BB From £22–£28
Sleeps 4
ᗡ ⅄ ⊠ 🍴 🌾 ▤ ⊚
♦♦♦♦ Silver Award

The Stamp family gives you a warm welcome to Grange Farm, a beautiful, spacious Georgian farmhouse peacefully situated with views of Lincoln Cathedral to the west and the Wolds to the east. Two double en suite rooms with TV and tea/coffee trays. Guests' sitting room, log fires. Lawn tennis. Unwind on the award winning farm trail, stopping for a break at the secluded trout lake. England for Excellence award winner 1998. Open all year except Christmas and New Year.

Grange Farm, Maltby-Le-Marsh, Alford, Lincolnshire LN13 0JP   ⑥

Mrs Ann Graves
☎ 01507450267
Fax 01507 450180
BB From £18
Sleeps 19
👶 🐴 🐾 🏆 ⊚
♦♦

Farmhouse bed and breakfast, centrally placed between fine sandy beaches and beautiful upland Wolds area, and offering a traditional warm welcome. Choose between ground floor rooms in converted stables (pets welcome) or en suites in the farmhouse (non smoking). Private coarse fishing, poultry and livestock. Colour brochure available.

Greenfield Farm, Minting, near Horncastle, Lincolnshire LN9 5RX   ⑦

Mrs Judy Bankes Price
☎/Fax 01507 578457
Mobile 07768 368829
BB From £21
Sleeps 6
👶(10) 🍴 🏆 🏆 ⊚
♦♦♦♦ *(AA Inspected)*

Judy and Hugh welcome you to their comfortable farmhouse set in a quiet location yet central for all the major Lincolnshire attractions. Play tennis, relax by the large garden pond or enjoy the forest walks that border the farm. Modern en suite shower rooms, heated towel rails, radios, tea/coffee facilities, CH. Ample parking. Traditonal pub 1 mile. Open mid Jan–mid Dec.

Guy Wells Farm, Eastgate, Whaplode, Spalding, Lincolnshire PE12 6TZ   ⑧

Anne Thompson
☎/Fax 01406 422239
BB From £20–£23
EM From £12
Sleeps 6
👶(5) 🐾 🍴
♦♦♦

Anne and Richard welcome you to their listed Queen Anne farmhouse set in a peaceful country garden, close to the famous fenland churches, the Wash, Sandringham, the coast, Boston, Stamford and Peterborough. Guy Wells is their home offering a few guests (non-smokers) spacious en suite accommodation with full CH, flowers, log fires and TV. Open all year except Christmas and New Year.

The Manor House, Manor Farm, Sleaford Road, Bracebridge Heath, Lincoln, Lincolnshire LN4 2HW   ⑨

Mrs Jill Scoley
☎ 01522 520825
Fax 01522 542418
BB From £21–£27
Sleeps 6
👶(10) 🍴 🏆 ⊚
♦♦♦♦ Silver Award

Welcome to Lincolnshire. Stay in a lovely Georgian farmhouse situated in large walled garden. 3 miles south of Lincoln. Comfortable bedrooms two en suite, one with private facilities, all with radio, tea/coffee facilities. Large lounge with log fire for cooler evenings. Open Mar–mid Dec.

The Manor House, West Barkwith, Market Rasen, Lincoln LN8 5LF   ⑩

Mrs J A Hobbins
☎/Fax 01673 858253
BB From £22.50–£25
EM From £10
Sleeps 4
👶(12) 🍴
♦♦♦

The Manor Farm is a 400-acre arable farm. The house stands in extensive landscaped grounds overlooking lawns, ornamental pond, rock garden and lake. Screened from the road by mature trees providing an attractive setting and seclusion. All rooms enjoy an uninterrupted view of the lake. An ideal base for touring the Wolds and historic Lincoln. Closed Christmas and New Year.

Sycamore Farm, Bassingthorpe, Grantham, Lincs NG33 4ED   ⑪

Mrs Sue Robinson
☎ 01476 585274
BB From £20
EM From £10
Sleeps 6
👶(12) 🍴 🏆 ⊚
♦♦♦ Silver Award

Set in peaceful unspoilt countryside Sycamore Farm offers the perfect place to relax and unwind. Spacious, pretty bedrooms with en suite bathrooms (1 private) and lovely views, comfortable guests' lounge with guide books, board games and log fire on chilly evenings. Ideally placed for A1 (4 miles), Stamford, Lincoln, historic Belton and Burghley. Open Mar–Nov.

Self-Catering

---

(6) Grange Farm, Maltby-Le-Marsh, Alford, Lincolnshire LN13 0JP

Mrs Ann Graves
☎ 01507450267
Fax 01507 450180
SC From £260–£320
Sleeps 5
🐴 🐾 🛥 ⚙ ⊛
🐾🐾🐾 Commended

Ann and Mike welcome you to our delightful country cottage with its own patio area and gardens, adjacent to the farmhouse and grounds. We have our own fishing lake and are close to coast and the unspoilt Lincolnshire Wolds. Central heating, linen, microwave, open fire, barbecue. Brochure available. Open all year.

---

(12) Mill Lodge, Benniworth House Farm, Donington on Bain, Louth, Lincs LN11 9RD

Mrs Pamela M Cade
☎/Fax 01507 343265
SC From £250–£350
Sleeps 4
🐾(5) ⚡ 🎋 🛥
🐾🐾🐾 Commended

Ezra and Pamela Cade welcome you to a delightful cottage on a traditional farm/Nature reserve in the beautiful Bain valley. Spacious grounds with conservatory, patio, lawn, flowering shrubs and lock up garage. Lovely walks with well maintained footpaths. Many species, some rare. Children welcome. Open all year.

---

(13) Waingrove Farm Country Cottages, Fulstow, Louth, Lincolnshire LN11 0XQ

Mrs Stephanie Smith
☎/Fax 01507 363704
SC From £170–£450
Sleeps 4/6
🐾(10) 🛥 🎋 ⊛
🐾🐾🐾🐾 Highly
Commended

Award-winning country cottages – detached farmhouse and two single storey 'courtyard' cottages, beautifully presented by caring resident owners. Superbly equipped and pretty – 'your holiday begins the moment you arrive' – with fresh flowers, chilled wine and tea tray with local specialities. 'Just 2 discounts'. Colour brochure. Open all year. E-mail: macandstephanie@waingrove.demon.co.uk

---

Please mention **Stay on a Farm** when booking

FARM HOLIDAY BUREAU

FINDING YOUR ACCOMMODATION

FARM HOLIDAY BUREAU

The local FHB Group contacts listed on page 392 can always help you find a vacancy in your chosen area.

Shropshire

Shropshire Union Canal, the Wrekin, Ironbridge Gorge, Shropshire Hills, the Long Mynd, Wenlock Edge, Clun Forest & the Marches

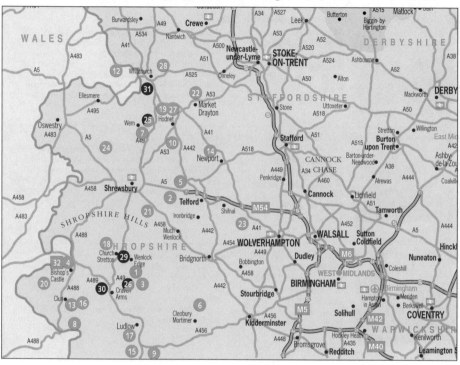

Key

- 1 Bed & Breakfast
- 1 Self-Catering
- 1 B&B and SC
- Camping Barns
- 1 Camping & Caravanning

Shropshire, with its wealth of historic houses, castles and abbeys, is England's largest landbound county. Medieval Shrewsbury, the county town, and up-to-date Telford are the principal centres together with attractive market towns such as Craven Arms, Church Stretton, Market Drayton, Newport, Whitchurch and historic Ludlow. The World Heritage Site of Ironbridge, birthplace of the Industrial Revolution, is a must with its six fascinating museums. This large county with miles of glorious country-side caters for every need, with its own lake district at Ellesmere, canals, rolling hills of South Shropshire, historic Hawkstone Park and Follies and the Severn Valley Steam Railway.

If you would like help in finding suitable farm accommodation, turn to the full listing of FHB Groups on pages 392 to 395 to find appropriate contact details for this area.

Bed and Breakfast
(and evening meal)

---

① Acton Scott Farm, Church Stretton, Shropshire SY6 6QN

Mary Jones
☎/Fax 01694 781260
BB From £18–£22
Sleeps 6
♿ 🐕 ⅍ 📷 ♨ ⊚
♦♦♦

Situated in beautiful countryside, adjacent to an historic working farm, the 17th century farmhouse of character has comfortable and spacious rooms, all with en suite facilities or private bathroom. The spectacular hills and valley of Church Stretton are nearby and we are central for visiting Shrewsbury, Ludlow and Ironbridge. We look forward to welcoming you. Open mid Feb – mid Nov.

---

② Avenue Farm, Uppington, Telford, Shropshire TF6 5HW

Mrs Mig Jones
☎ 01952 740253
Fax 01952 740401
BB From £20–£22.50
Sleeps 4
♿(5) 🐕 📷 ⅍
♦♦

Charming 18th century farmhouse situated in the quiet, unspoilt village of Uppington. Set in extensive gardens with magnificent views of the Wrekin. Conveniently situated near Shrewsbury, Ironbridge and Telford, 2 miles from M54 J7. Guests' private sitting room with TV. Open all year.

---

③ Brereton's Farm, Woolston, Church Stretton, Shropshire SY6 6QD

Joanna Brereton
☎/Fax 01694 781201
BB From £20
EM From £10
Sleeps 6
♿ ⅍ ⌁
♦♦♦

Relax, unwind and enjoy the fine views of rolling countryside from the extensive garden on our working farm. Our Victorian farmhouse offers very spacious, comfortable, en suite rooms with beverage trays and fresh milk. Lovely four-poster bed. Close to Long Mynd and Ironbridge. Open Feb–Oct.

---

④ Broughton Farm, nr Bishop's Castle, Montgomery, Powys SY15 6SZ

Mrs Kate Bason
☎ 01588 638393
BB From £17–£20
Sleeps 6
♿ 🐕 ⅍ 🗡 📷 ♨
♦♦♦

A 140-acre cattle and sheep farm located near the Welsh border. The house is oak-framed and dates back to the 15th century. Traditional country house furnishings. Central heating. Comfortable bedrooms (one en suite) have washbasins and tea/coffee trays. Stroll around the farm and meet the animals or relax in the garden and enjoy the views. Open all year.

---

⑤ Church Farm, Wrockwardine, Wellington, Telford, Shropshire TF6 5DG

Mrs Jo Savage
☎/Fax 01952 244917
BB From £20–£26
EM From £16
Sleeps 8
♿(10) 🐕 £ ♨ 📷 ⊚
♦♦♦♦

Down a lime tree avenue, in a peaceful village betwixt Shrewsbury and Telford, lies our superbly situated Georgian farmhouse. Mature gardens with medieval stonework, old roses and many unusual plants. Attractive bedrooms with TVs, tea/coffee/chocolate, some en suite with ground floor available. Inglenook fireplace in spacious guests' lounge. Delicious breakfasts helped by our free range hens! Near Ironbridge, Shrewsbury and Telford. 1 mile M54 (J7) and A5. Open all year. E-mail: jo@churchfarm.freeserve.co.uk

Cox's Barn, Bagginswood, Cleobury Mortimer, Nr Kidderminster DY14 8LS   6

Dinah Thompson
☎ 01746 718415
BB From £18–£20
EM From £10
Sleeps 6
🐴 ✄ 🐾 ▦
♦♦♦♦

Delightful converted barn on working farm set in beautiful rolling, peaceful countryside. Warm welcome assured, tea/coffee and homemade cakes on arrival. Delicious home cooking, vegetarian welcome. Full central heating. Three double en suite bedrooms (two ground floor), all with colour TV, beverage tray, radio/clock alarm and hair dryer. Non-smoking only! Open all year.

Grove Farm, Preston Brockhurst, Shrewsbury, Shropshire SY4 5QA   7

Mrs Janet Jones
☎/Fax 01939 220223
BB From £19–£25
Sleeps 6
🐴 ✄ ▦ ◉
♦♦♦♦ *(AA Inspected)*

Step into Shropshire and enjoy quality accommodation and fine home cooking using local produce. Our 322-acre farm is set in a small village 7 miles north of Shrewsbury on the A49. The 17th century house is traditionally furnished and offers warmth and comfort after the day's activities. Ideally situated for Ironbridge World Heritage Site, Shrewsbury, Chester, Potteries and Wales. Brochures available. Open mid Jan–mid Dec.

The Hall, Bucknell, Shropshire SY7 0AA   8

Mrs Christine Price
☎/Fax 01547 530249
BB From £20–£22
EM £12
Sleeps 6
🐴(7) ✄ ▦
♦♦♦

The Hall is a working farm with spacious Georgian farmhouse and peaceful garden to relax in, after a day walking or exploring the Welsh Borderland with its historic towns and castles, also the black and white villages of North Herefordshire. Guest lounge, 1 twin en suite, 2 double with washbasins, shaving points. Colour TV and tea-making facilities. Open Feb–Nov.

Haynall Villa, Little Hereford, Nr Ludlow, Shropshire SY8 4BG   9

Mrs Rachel Edwards
☎/Fax 01584 711589
BB From £17–£24
EM From £13
Sleeps 6
🐴(6) 🐾 ✄ ✿ ▦
♦♦

Farmhouse B&B as featured in the *Daily Telegraph*, nestling in Teme Valley 6m from historic Ludlow, 2m from A49. Spacious bedrooms (1 en suite) offer comfort, views to 3 counties, vanity units, tea/coffee-making facilities. Guests' bathroom. Delicious farmhouse fayre (vegetarian and special diets). Relax in lounge with TV or attractive garden. Open all year except Christmas and New Year.

Heath Farm, Hodnet, Market Drayton, Shropshire TF9 3JJ   10

Mrs Ada Drysdale
☎/Fax 01630 685570
BB From £16–£18
Sleeps 6
🐴(6) 🐾 ✄ ▦
♦♦

1866 farmhouse offering excellent breakfasts. One mile from Hodnet Hall gardens, three miles Hawkestone (golf, motorcycles, BMX), the Follies, North Shropshire shooting ground. Convenient for Chester, Potteries, Shrewsbury, Ironbridge, Bridgemere Garden World, Dorothy Clive and more. Open all year.

FARM HOLIDAY BUREAU

Please mention *Stay on a Farm* when booking

12 Horseman's Green Farm, Horseman's Green, Nr Whitchurch, Shropshire SY13 3EA

Mrs Gillian Huxley
☎ 01948 830480
Fax 01948 780552
BB From £22–£28
Sleeps 4
⬚ ⅍ ▪ ⅍ ⅏ ◉
★★
FARM

A very special Grade I listed 14th century hall house, on a working farm, with many original timbers including a rare aisle truss. Very comfortable accommodation with all private facilities and galleried sitting room. Convenient for Chester, Shrewsbury and Llangollen, the hills and coasts of North Wales within easy reach. Excellent unspoilt walking. Local and home made produce. Open all year except Christmas.

13 Hurst Mill Farm, Clun, Craven Arms, Shropshire SY7 0JA

Joyce Williams
☎ 01588 640224
BB From £19–£21
EM From £8
Sleeps 6
⬚ ⅍ ⅄ ⬚ ⅍ ⬚ ▪ ⅏ ◉
♦♦♦ *(AA Inspected)*

Winner of 'Shropshire Farm Breakfast Challenge'. A warm welcome to this working farm where the 'kettle's always on'. Well appointed bedrooms, double en suite. Riverside farmhouse and spacious gardens. Nestling in the delightful Clun Valley, between historic Clun and Clunton. Woodland and hills on either side. Two quiet riding ponies, kingfishers and herons. Pets welcome. Log fires. AA QQQ recommended. Closed Christmas.

14 Lane End Farm, Chetwynd, Newport, Shropshire TF10 8BN

Mrs Janice Park
☎/Fax 01952 550337
BB From £19–£25
EM from £11
Sleeps 6
⬚ ⅍ ▪ ◉
♦♦♦♦

Relax and feel at home in our friendly, interesting farmhouse set amidst lovely countryside. Large bedrooms with en suite facilities. Good woodland walks nearby. Located on A41 two miles North of Newport; ideal for visiting Ironbridge, Weston Park, Cosford, Potteries, Chester, etc. Working sheep farm – see the lambs in spring! Open all year.

15 Line Farm, Tunnel Lane, Orleton, Nr Ludlow, Shropshire SY8 4HY

Mrs Carol Lewis
☎ 01568 780400
BB From £22.50–£25
Sleeps 6
⅍

♦♦♦♦♦ Gold Award

Panoramic views from every room, peace, tranquillity, en suite bedrooms with tea/coffee facilities, along with good old-fashioned farmhouse hospitality, await you at Line Farm. No smoking please. Open Mar–Nov.

16 Llanhedric, Clun, Craven Arms, Shropshire SY7 8NG

Mrs Mary Jones
☎/Fax 01588 640203
BB From £18–£20
EM From £10
Sleeps 6
⬚ ⅍ ⅏ ▪ ◉
♦♦♦

Relax in traditional style in characteristic farmhouse set in the splendours of the Clun Valley. Awake to the smell of good home cooking. Enjoy the life of a modern working farm, feel the fresh breeze as you explore the beautiful countryside, then unwind in the guests' lounge by a warm inglenook fire. Comfortable bedrooms overlooking attractive gardens, double en suite, tea/coffee facilities, CH. Open Apr–Nov.

17 Longlands, Woodhouse Lane, Richards Castle, Ludlow, Shropshire SY8 4EU

Mrs Prue Kemsley
☎ 01584 831636
BB From £22.50
EM From £12.50
Sleeps 4
⬚ ⅍ ⅏ ▪ ◉
♦♦♦

Farmhouse centrally located in 35 acres within lovely rural landscape. Guests' lounge, central heating, tea/coffee-making facilities. Private suite with facilities for the elderly. Garden available with barbecue. Home-grown produce and eggs. Rare breed sheep. Convenient for historic Ludlow, NT properties, walking the Mortimer Trail and Welsh Marches. Open all year.

Malt House Farm, Lower Wood, Church Stretton, Shropshire SY6 6LF   18

Lyn Bloor
☎ 01694 751379
BB From £18.50–£20
EM From £15
Sleeps 6
✄ ⬛
◆◆◆

'The Malt House' is a working farm set in a secluded position on the lower slopes of the Long Mynd hills, an Area of Outstanding Natural beauty. Oak-beamed dining room, separate guests' lounge. All bedrooms en suite with colour TV, hairdrier and tea tray. No smoking please. Regret no children or pets. Open Feb-Nov.

Mickley House, Faulsgreen, Tern Hill, Market Drayton, Shropshire TF9 3QW   19

Mrs Pauline Williamson
☎/Fax 01630 638505
BB From £22–£32
Sleeps 6
🧍 ✄ ⬅ ♨ ⬛ ⓖ
◆◆◆◆*(AA Inspected)*

Discover peace, quiet and comfort in our home with its oak doors, beams, leaded windows and landscaped gardens. Stroll through rose-scented pergolas to pools with trickling waterfall. Restful drawing room beckons after sightseeing and meal at local restaurants/pubs. Individually styled en suite bedrooms, master bedroom with Louis XIV king-size bed. Ground floor available. All facilities. 2 miles off A41. Business visitors welcome. Closed Christmas and New Year.

New House Farm, Clun, Shropshire SY7 8NJ   20

Mrs Miriam Ellison
☎ 01588 638314
BB From £22–£25
Sleeps 5
🐱(5) 🐦 ✄ 🧍 ♨ ⬛ ⓖ
◆◆◆◆◆Gold Award

Peaceful isolated 18th century farmhouse high in Clun Hills. Near Welsh border – with Iron Age hill fort. Walks from doorstep, Offa's Dyke and Shropshire Way. Large bedrooms furnished to a high standard with scenic views. Tea/coffee facilities, colour TV. Books to browse in a large garden. Open Easter–Nov.

North Farm, Eaton Mascot, Shrewsbury, Shropshire SY5 6HF   21

Mrs Vanessa Bromley
☎ 01743 761031
Fax 01743 761854
BB From £18–£25
Sleeps 4
🐴 ✄ ♨ ⬛
◆◆◆

Traditional farmhouse situated on a 270-acre mixed arable farm within a private estate in unspoilt countryside. Easy access to Shrewsbury and M54. One double room en suite, one twin, both with hospitality tray, colour TV and central heating. Guests' sitting room and dinning room, Large garden with beautiful views, quiet and very peaceful. Guests welcome to walk local footpaths. Ample car parking. Closed Christmas.

Norton Farm, Norton-in-Hales,Market Drayton, Shropshire TF9 4AT   22

Mrs L Jane Crewe
☎/Fax 01630 653003
BB From £18–£25
Sleeps 6
🐱 🐦 ✄ 🍴 ⬅ ⬛
◆◆◆

250-acre working stock/arable farm situated 2½ miles from the A53 at Market Drayton. This 18th century centrally heated farmhouse is in the picturesque village of Norton-in-Hales. Three tastefully furnished double bedrooms – one is en suite, others have own bathroom, all have colour TV and tea/coffee-making facilities. Open all year. E-mail: info@interactive-info.co.uk

Parkside Farm, Holyhead Road, Albrighton, Nr Wolverhampton WV7 3DA   23

Margaret Shanks
☎ 01902 372310
Fax 01902 375013
BB From £22.50–£24
Sleeps 6
🐴 ✄ ⬅ ⬛ ⓖ
◆◆◆

Looking for warm and friendly welcome? Want to relax, or just need a convenient location for work or pleasure? Well look no further! Kick start your day with a farmhouse breakfast, while enjoying the view of the beautiful garden. All rooms have TV and tea/coffee facilities. Plenty of attractions to visit. Near A464 and just 2 mins' walk to a real ale pub/restaurant. Open all year.

24 Petton Hall Farm, Petton, Burlton, Shrewsbury, Shropshire SY4 5TH

Mrs Mary Kennerley
☎/Fax 01939 270601
BB From £19–£23
Sleeps 4
🐕 🐎 ⅄ ᛘ 🛄 ♨
♦♦♦♦

Petton Hall Farm is situated between historic Shrewsbury and the beautiful meres of Ellesmere, a haven for birdwatching. Our two en suite bedrooms offer comfort with character. Come and enjoy traditional home cooking from the Aga and relax in front of a real open fire on those colder evenings. Ironbridge, Hawkstone, the Potteries and the walled Roman City of Chester, a great shopping experience, all within easy reach. Open all year except Christmas.

25 Soulton Hall, near Wem, Shropshire SY4 5RS

Ann Ashton
☎ 01939 232786
Fax 01939 234097
BB From £27–£38
Sleeps 10
🐕 🐎 ⅄ 🖼 ᛐ ♨ 🛄 ❀ 🌐
♦♦♦♦ *(AA Inspected)*

Sample English country life in an Elizabethan manor house offering very relaxing holiday. Bird watching and fishing. Good food, home produce where possible, super meals. Walled garden. Licensed bar. Direct dial telephones. Plenty of parking space. We welcome you. Open all year.
E-mail: j.a.ashton@farmline.com

26 Strefford Hall Farm, Strefford, Craven Arms, Shropshire SY7 8DE

Mrs Caroline Morgan
☎/Fax 01588 672383
BB From £20–£28
EM £12
Sleeps 6
🧍 ⅄ 🌳 ᛘ 🛄 🌐
♦♦♦♦

Set in an Area of Outstanding Natural Beauty in the quiet hamlet of Strefford, against the wooded backdrop of the Wenlock Edge and with uninterrupted views of the Long Mynd and Church Stretton hills. Spacious accommodation in 2 doubles, 1 twin (all en suite) with tea/coffee and colour TV. Full English breakfast, special diets catered for. Evening meals by arrangement. Non smoking household. Closed Christmas and New Year.

27 Willow House, Shrewsbury Road, Tern Hill, Market Drayton, Shropshire TF9 3PX

Mrs Moira Roberts
☎ 01630 638326
BB From £20–£25
Sleeps 6
🐕 ⅄ 🛄 🌐
♦♦♦♦

A warm and friendly welcome awaits you at our modern farmhouse. One double with private bathroom, two twin en suite. All rooms have hot drink facilities. Guests have a separate lounge with colour TV. A good base for touring Shropshire, Cheshire, Staffordshire and local attractions of Ironbridge, Hodnet Gardens, Hawkstone Follies and the Potteries. Open all year.

28 Wood Farm, Old Woodhouses, Whitchurch, Shropshire SY13 4EJ

Mrs Val Mayer
☎ 01948 871224
BB From £19–£25
Sleeps 4
🐕 ⅄ 🛄 ᛐ ❀ 🌐
♦♦♦♦

Charming 16th century farmhouse in a traditional courtyard setting on working dairy farm in peaceful countryside. Unwind in the guests' lounge in front of an inglenook fireplace after sightseeing as we are central to Chester, Ironbridge, Shrewsbury and the Potteries. Spacious beamed bedrooms (one with traditional brass bed) and welcome baskets. Ground floor available. All facilities. 1½ miles off A41. Good food and drinking pub within walking distance. Business visitors welcome.

NO ANSWER?
Farmers are mostly out and about during the day.
Try to telephone before 9.30am or after 4pm.

Self-Catering

Botvyle Farm Cottages, All Stretton, Church Stretton, Shropshire SY6 7JN **29**

Mrs Gill Bebbington
☎ 01694 722869
SC From £140–£280
Sleeps 2–6

Commended

Situated within the beautiful Stretton Hills, the cottages are comfortably furnished and heated throughout and retain great character and charm. Quiet situation only 2 miles north of Church Stretton. Nearest shop/pub 1½ miles. Superb walking, bird watching and touring base. Ludlow, Shrewsbury and Ironbridge a short drive away. Short lets available.

Hesterworth, Hopesay, Craven Arms, Shropshire SY7 8EX **30**

Roger and Sheila Davies
☎ 01588 660487
SC From £95–£352
Sleeps 2–8

Up to Commended

A selection of comfortable country cottages and apartments surrounded by 12 acres of beautiful gardens and grounds. Large dining room ideal for families and groups. Meal service and short breaks available. Ideal for walking or visiting Shropshire's many attractions. Ludlow 10 miles. Groups welcome. Open all year.
E-mail: hesterworth@go2.co.uk

Keepers Cottage, Soulton Hall, Near Wem, Shropshire SY4 5RS **25**

Ann Ashton
☎ 01939 232786
Fax 01939 234097
SC From £200–£486
Sleeps 6

Commended

Keepers Cottage nestles on south side of 50-acres of Oak woodland offering really relaxing holidays. Woodland and riverside walks, CH, TV, fires in season. Evening meals available at Soulton Hall from £18.50, by arrangement. Shrewsbury, Chester, Ironbridge, North Wales, Potteries – all within easy reach. Open all year.
E-mail: j.a.ashton@farmline.com

The Park, Tilstock, Whitchurch, Shropshire SY13 3NL **31**

Mr & Mrs Wright
☎ 01948 880669
Fax 01270 629603
SC From £190–£350
Sleeps 4
(10)

Commended

Picturesque old farm with hay meadows, ponds and traditional countryside. Awards for farm conservation. The self-catering cottage is quiet and well equipped, an idyllic retreat for two but with space for more. Overlooks moat with interesting wildlife. Farm walks to enjoy. Important nature reserves nearby. Shrewsbury and Chester about 30 minutes' drive. Open all year. E-mail: lettings@sfc.co.uk

---

Strefford Hall Farm, Strefford, Craven Arms, Shropshire SY7 8DE **26**

Mrs Caroline Morgan
☎/Fax 01588 672383
SC From £180–£250
Sleeps 2 + cot

Commended

Set in the lovely South Shropshire countryside, surrounded by fields and close to Wenlock Edge. The coachhouse provides two luxury self-catering units, Swallows Nest on the ground floor is ideal for frail or disabled guests, Wrens Nest is on the first floor. Each has double en suite bedroom, fitted kitchen, large sitting/dining room, fitted carpets and patio area with seating. Open all year.

Bunkhouse/Camping Barn

 Broughton Bunkhouse, nr Bishop's Castle, Montgomery, Powys SY15 6SZ

Mrs Kate Bason
☎ **01588 638393**
SC **From £8.50**
Sleeps 12
🐕 🐓 🐄 ⚡ 🐝
Applied

Comfortable accommodation in converted 17th century oak-framed stable. Separate sleeping areas for men and women. Self-catering, all cooking equipment provided, or breakfasts available. Centrally heated, showers, drying facilities. Bed and breakfast in adjoining farmhouse. Transport provided to and from Shropshire Way (1mile) and Offa's Dyke (4 miles).

STAY ON A FARM GIFT TOKENS

FARM HOLIDAY BUREAU

If you have enjoyed your Stay on a Farm, why not treat your friends and relatives to *Stay on a Farm* gift tokens? Available from the Bureau office (tel: 024 7669 6909), they can be redeemed against accommodation and are accepted by the majority of farms (see Index). Please check when booking to avoid disappointment.

CONFIRM BOOKINGS

Disappointments can arise from misunderstandings over the telephone. Please write to confirm your booking.

FARM HOLIDAY BUREAU

Our Internet address is
http://www.webscape.co.uk/farmaccom/

Staffordshire

Peak District National Park, Cannock Chase, Trent Valley & the Potteries

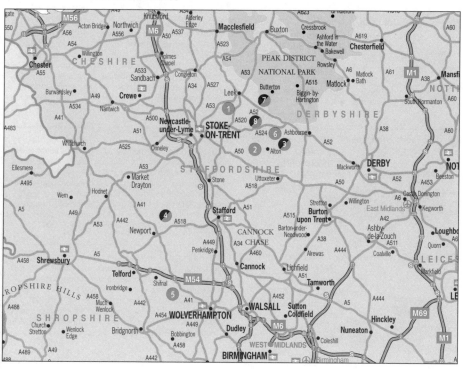

Key

1 Bed & Breakfast

1 Self-Catering

1 B&B and SC

1 Camping Barns

1 Camping & Caravanning

The varied landscape of Staffordshire ranges from that of the Peak District National Park, through the moorlands in the north to the fertile valleys of the Trent and its tributaries in the south. In the heart of the county is the extensive Cannock Chase, an Area of Outstanding Natural Beauty. The county has two excellent leisure parks: Alton Towers, famous for its exciting rides, and Drayton Manor Park. Many visitors seek out the potteries and visitor centres which offer the chance to see crafts being made and find a bargain at the factory shops. Heritage lovers should visit Stafford, Tamworth, Burton on Trent, Tutbury and the cathedral city of Lichfield, birthplace of Dr Samuel Johnson.

If you would like help in finding suitable farm accommodation, turn to the full listing of FHB Groups on pages 392 to 395 to find appropriate contact details for this area.

Bed and Breakfast
(and evening meal)

---

① Brook House Farm, Cheddleton, Leek, Staffordshire ST13 7DF

Elizabeth Winterton
☎ 01538 360296
BB From £18–£20
EM From £10
Sleeps 10
♦♦♦

A dairy farm in a picturesque and peaceful valley. Central for Peak District, Potteries, Churnet Valley steam railway, Cauldon Canal, Coombes Valley RSPB Reserve and Alton Towers. 3 spacious rooms in a tastefully converted cowshed and 2 in the farmhouse, all en suite with tea/coffee-makers and colour TV. Dine in our attractive conservatory with magnificent country views. Open all year.

---

② Ley Fields Farm, Leek Road, Cheadle, Stoke-on-Trent, Staffordshire ST10 2EF

Mrs Kathryn Clowes
☎ 01538 752875
BB From £18–£20
EM From £9.50
Sleeps 6
♦♦♦♦

Listed Georgian farmhouse amidst beautiful countryside with local walks offering abundant wildlife. Convenient for Alton Towers, Pottery museums and Peak District. Spacious, traditionally furnished accommodation includes guests' lounge and dining room. Luxury bedrooms with hot drink facilities, family suite, family en suite, double en suite. CH. Excellent home cooking and a warm welcome to our family home. Open all year except Christmas.

---

③ Manor House Farm, Prestwood, Denstone, Uttoxeter, Staffs ST14 5DD

Chris Ball
☎ 01889 590415
Fax 01335 342198
BB From £20–£25
Sleeps 6
♦♦♦♦

A beautiful Grade II listed farmhouse set amid rolling hills and rivers. Three bedrooms, all with four-poster beds, tastefully furnished with antiques and traditional features including oak-beamed ceilings and an oak panelled breakfast room. Guests may relax in the extensive gardens with grass tennis court and Victorian summer house. Alton Towers 3 miles. Open all year except Christmas.

---

④ Oulton House Farm, Norbury, Stafford, Staffordshire ST20 0PG

Mrs Judy Palmer
☎/Fax 01785 284264
BB From £22.50–£25
Sleeps 6
♦♦♦♦

A 300-acre dairy farm situated on the Shropshire/ Staffordshire border. Our large Victorian farmhouse offers warm, comfortable and well appointed en suite bedrooms, all with tea trays and TV. From your peaceful, rural base discover our many local attractions from the heritage of Ironbridge Gorge, the splendours of Shugborough to the bargains of the Potteries factory shops. Many local pubs and restaurants. Peace and quiet guaranteed. Open all year except Christmas.

---

⑤ Parkside Farm, Holyhead Road, Albrighton, Nr Wolverhampton WV7 3DA

Margaret Shanks
☎ 01902 372310
Fax 01902 375013
BB From £22.50–£24
Sleeps 6
♦♦♦

Looking for a warm and friendly welcome? Want to relax, or just need a convenient location for work or pleasure? Well look no further! Kick start your day with a farmhouse breakfast, while enjoying the view of the beautiful garden. All rooms have TV and tea/coffee facilities. Plenty of attractions to visit. Near A464 and just 2 mins' walk to a real ale pub/restaurant. Open all year.

Ribden Farm, Nr Oakamoor, Stoke-on-Trent, Staffordshire ST10 3BW   6

Christine Shaw
☎/Fax 01538 702830
[BB] From £20–£24
Sleeps 20
🐕 🍴 ♿ ♨
♦♦♦♦

Ribden Farm is an 18th Century farmhouse c1748 which is situated 1,000 ft high in the Weaver Hills yet is only 5 minutes from Alton Towers. Plenty of underused footpaths. Local inns. All rooms en suite with colour TV, coffee/tea-making facilities, some with four-poster beds. Separate TV lounge and dining room. Secure off road parking. RAC Highly Acclaimed. AA QQQQ selected. Open all year except Christmas.

Self-Catering

Keepers Cottage, Manor House Farm, Prestwood, Denstone, Uttoxeter, Staffordshire ST14 5DD   3

Chris Ball
☎ 01889 590415
Fax 01335 342198
[SC] From £150–£370
Sleeps 4 + cot
🐕 ♿ ♨
🔑🔑🔑🔑 *Highly Commended*

Beautifully converted stone cottage in the grounds of an historic Jacobean farmhouse. The cottage dates from around 1700 and has retained many original features including a four-poster bed, exposed stone walls and oak beams. Set in its own private garden, Keepers Cottage offers a delightful retreat for the discerning holidaymaker. Open all year.

Rosewood Holiday Flats, Lower Berkhamsytch Farm, Bottom House, Nr Leek, Staffordshire ST13 7QP   7

Edith & Alwyn Mycock
☎/Fax 01538 308213
[SC] From £125–£235
Sleeps 6/7
🐕 🍴 ♨ ◉
🔑🔑🔑 *Commended*

Two delightful self-contained flats on stock rearing farm each with own private entrance and within walking distance of 2 pubs serving meals. Lounge/diner with colour TV and double bed-settee. Well equipped kitchen, 1 double bedroom, 1 twin, shower room with toilet and washbasin. Ideal for Alton Towers, Potteries, Peak District and moorland beauty spots. Electricity, heating, linen included. Laundry room. Short breaks early and late season. Open all year.

Swallows Nest, Oulton House Farm, Norbury, Stafford, Staffordshire ST20 0PG   4

Mrs Judy Palmer
☎/Fax 01785 284264
[SC] From £130–£290
Sleep 2–8
🐕 ♨ ◉
🔑🔑🔑🔑
Highly Commended

Swallows Nest has been designed with the comfort of our guests in mind. We think it is special. It is self-contained, fully equipped and all inclusive. An ideal base for a relaxing holiday: patchwork quilts, pine, pot pourri, peace and quiet – perfect. See why the swallows return! Larger cottages available. Open all year.

Upper Cadlow Farm, Winkhill, Leek, Staffordshire ST13 7QX   8

Mrs S Plant
☎ 01538 266243
[SC] From £175–£350
Sleep 5
🐕 ✂ ♨ 🚶 ◉
🔑🔑🔑🔑 *Commended*

Set in a superb position with magnificent views, beautiful farm cottage overlooking large garden. Colour TV, washing machine, tumble dryer, microwave, central heating and linen included. Cot and high chair available. Near Alton Towers (4 miles), Potteries and Peak District. Short breaks available: 3 nights from £90. Open all year. Associate.

Leicestershire

Vale of Belvoir, Rutland Water & Grand Union Canal

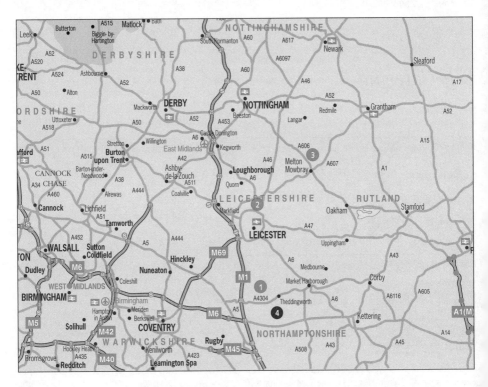

Key

🔵 **1** Bed & Breakfast

🔴 **1** Self-Catering

🟠 **1** B&B and SC

⬜ **1** Camping Barns

🔺 **1** Camping & Caravanning

Leicestershire is a land of tranquil beauty spread with reminders of a turbulent history. To find the true Leicestershire just travel over high horizons and narrow farm tracks, explore vast Rutland Water and the lazy green banks of the Grand Union Canal, take a nostalgic trip on one of our many steam railways, walk in historic Bradgate Park or 'do battle' in Bosworth Field. Explore the county's curious annual events such as Bottle Kicking and the Hare Pie Scramble between Hallaton and Medbourne, or visit our castles and museums, timber-framed cottages and grand mansions, theatres and theme parks. Find all this and more in this green and undulating county.

If you would like help in finding suitable farm accommodation, turn to the full listing of FHB Groups on pages 392 to 395 to find appropriate contact details for this area.

Bed and Breakfast
(and evening meal)

Knaptoft House Farm, Bruntingthorpe Road, Nr Shearsby, Lutterworth, Leicestershire LE17 6PR

Mrs A T Hutchinson
☎/Fax 01162 478388
[BB] From £21
Sleeps 6
🛏(5) 🍴 ⌂ ☕ 🏕 🛁 🐾 ⊚
♦♦♦♦ *(AA Inspected)*

Easy access from the motorways and Leicester (A50/5119), yet very quietly situated overlooking undulating farm land. Our accommodation is warm and welcoming, all rooms with bespoke beds ,TV, hospitality tray, en suite or adjacent facilities Furnishings are carefully chosen and co-ordinated. Interesting china, pictures, family history memorabilia/books. Secluded car parking. Excellent local pubs. Brochure. Closed Christmas and New Year.
E-mail: knight@bruntingthorpe.softnet.co.uk

Three Ways Farm, Melton Road, Queniborough, Leicester LE7 3FN

Mrs Janet S Clarke
☎ 0116 260 0472
[BB] From £19–£25
Sleeps 5
🛏 🐕 🛁 ⊚
♦♦♦

It's hard to believe you're only 6 miles north of Leicester in lovely Queniborough with its ancient church, thatched cottages and two good pubs. You'll be welcomed at the Clarkes' bungalow in peaceful fields. All bedrooms have colour TV, tea/coffee facilities. West of Melton Road, ¼ m A607 Queniborough roundabout, connects with Leicester A46 bypass. Nottingham and Birmingham NEC 40 mins. Open all year except Christmas.

White Lodge Farm, Nottingham Road, Ab Kettleby, Melton Mowbray, Leicestershire LE14 3JB

Margaret Spencer
☎ 01664 822286
[BB] From £19–£22
Sleeps 6
🛏(9) 🍴 🛁 ⊚
♦♦♦

A warm welcome and comfortable accommodation await you on our working farm at the edge of the Vale of Belvoir, 3 miles north of Melton Mowbray, home of the pork pie and Stilton cheese. Ground floor, self-contained rooms overlook the garden, all en-suite with CH, colour TV, tea coffee-making facilities and electric blankets. Open all year.

Self-Catering

Brook Meadow Holiday Chalets, Welford Road, Sibbertoft, Market Harborough, Leicestershire LE16 9UJ

Mary and Jasper Hart
☎ 01858 880886
Fax 01858 880458
[SC] From £130–£400
Sleep 4/6 + cot
🛏 🐕 ⌂ Å 🛏 ☕ 🛁 🏕
♭♭♭– ♭♭♭♭ *Up to*
Highly Commended

Stay in one of our holiday chalets in the peaceful lakeside setting at the heart of our farm. Imagine sipping a glass of wine from a complimentary bottle, relaxing in a rocking chair, whilst the sun sets over the fishing lake. Two chalets sleep 3 and one sleeps 4/6 in luxurious comfort; all are fully equipped including bed linen. Pets welcome. Colour brochure available. Open all year.
E-mail: brookmeadow@farmline.com

Herefordshire

Wye Valley & Golden Valley

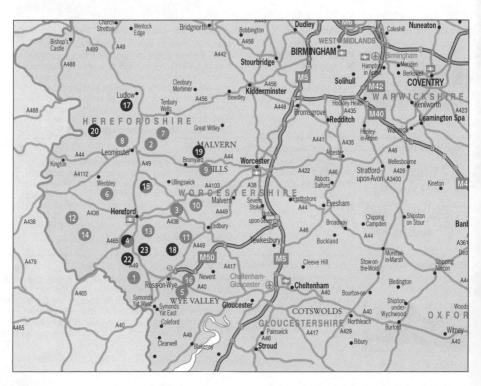

Key

1 Bed & Breakfast

1 Self-Catering

1 B&B and SC

1 Camping Barns

1 Camping & Caravanning

Herefordshire is a land of red earth, green meadows, quiet woods, streams and pretty black and white villages. In the south are the spectacular gorges of the River Wye and the lovely woodland trails of the Forest of Dean; westward lies the tranquil Golden Valley leading into Offa's Dyke. To the east, Elgar Country rises to the Malvern Hills with one of the finest ridge walks in England. The county's historic sites span every period of British history, from Iron Age hill forts, Roman remains, Norman castles and medieval manor houses to stately homes and their gardens and heritage museums. Street markets abound and Hay-on-Wye is famous for its second-hand bookshops. Come and browse.

If you would like help in finding suitable farm accommodation, turn to the full listing of FHB Groups on pages 392 to 395 to find appropriate contact details for this area.

Bed and Breakfast
(and evening meal)

Amberley, Aberhall Farm, St Owen's Cross, Hereford HR2 8LL   ①

Freda Davies
☎/Fax 01989 730256
[BB] From £19–£22
Sleeps 4
☒(10) ⚒ 🧳 ♨ ◉
♦♦♦♦

Savour the peace and tranquillity of our home with panoramic views of the rolling countryside. 132-acre working family farm offering one ground floor en suite twin/double and, upstairs, one double with private bathroom. Guests'own lounge and dining room. Tea/trays, excellent cuisine, 'home from home'. Large garden with patio. Open Mar–Nov.
E-mail: freda-davies@ereal.net

The Fieldhouse Farm, Bache Hill, Kimbolton, Leominster, Herefordshire HR6 0EP   ②

Mrs Jean Franks
☎ 01568 614789
[BB] From £18.50–£21
EM From £12
Sleeps 3
☒ 🐓 ⚒ 🧳 ♨ ◉
♦♦♦

A warm welcome awaits you on our working family farm surrounded by lush green fields and stunning panoramic views. Unwind in our guests' oak-beamed sitting room with log fires and many interesting books. We have one attractive double/twin or family bedroom with hostess tray and its own private bathroom. Delicious breakfasts are served by Jean Franks, a former home economics teacher. Open Mar–Nov.

Garford Farm, Yarkhill, Hereford HR1 3ST   ③

Helen Parker
☎ 01432 890226
Fax 01432 890707
[BB] From £18–£22
Sleeps 5
☒(2) 🐓 🧳 ♣ ♨
♦♦♦

16th century timber-framed farmhouse with scenic views. Peaceful yet within easy reach of Hereford/Worcester and the Welsh borders. Spacious bedrooms with TV and tea/coffee trays. Guests' sitting room. Pets welcome by arrangement and stabling available. Open all year.
E-mail: garfordfarm@lineone.net

Grafton Villa Farm, Grafton, Hereford, Herefordshire HR2 8ED   ④

Jennie Layton
☎/Fax 01432 268689
[BB] From £20–£25
Sleeps 4
☒ ⚒ 🙏 🖥 🧳 ♨ 🐕 ◉
♦♦♦♦ Silver Award

A farmhouse of great character and warmth set in an acre of beautiful lawns and gardens amidst the picturesque Wye Valley. Beautiful fabrics and antiques throughout. Charming, peaceful en suite bedrooms with TV and drinks tray. We offer our guests a relaxing holiday on a 'real farm', enjoying a sumptuous breakfast with farmhouse portions. Closed Christmas.

The Hill, Weston-under-Penyard, Ross-on-Wye, Herefordshire HR9 7PZ   ⑤

Gill Evans
☎/Fax 01989 750225
[BB] From £17–£20
Sleeps 4
☒ 🙏 🧳 ♨
♦♦♦

A warm welcome awaits you at our 17th century farmhouse with panoramic views over fields and woodlands. Decorated throughout in sympathy with its age and set within a peaceful garden. Adjacent to Forest of Dean and well situated for walking, touring and cycling. Good facilities for guests' horses and central to numerous racecourses. Good pubs! Open all year.

---

6 **Hill Top Farm,** Wormsley, Nr Weobley, Hereford, Herefordshire HR4 8LZ

Mr & Mrs P Jennings
☎/Fax 01981 590246
BB From £18
Sleeps 5
🐕 🍽 👤 🛢 🎄 🛢
♦♦♦

A working farm offering peace and tranquillity in our comfortable, modernised stone-built farmhouse, only 2 miles from the picturesque village of Weobley on the Black and White Trail. Stunning views surpassed only by those from Heaven! Our friendly welcome and personal attention will make your stay a delight. Open all year except Christmas.

7 **The Hills Farm,** Leysters, Leominster, Herefordshire HR6 0HP

Jane & Peter Conolly
☎ 01568 750205
Fax 01568 750306
BB From £25–£27
EM £17
Sleeps 10
🐔 🍽 ♿
♦♦♦♦♦ *(AA Inspected)*

A delightful 15th century farmhouse in an elevated position with two charming bedrooms in the main house. A further three bedrooms are in cleverly converted stone-built barns, one being ground floor. We serve scrumptious home cooked meals. Do come and join us at our award winning home for a short or long break. Open Mar-Oct. E-mail: conolly@bigwig.net

8 **Home Farm,** Bircher, Nr Leominster, Herefordshire HR6 0AX

Doreen Cadwallader
☎ 01568 780525
BB From £20–£24
Sleeps 6
🐕 🐔 🍽 👤 🛢 🛢 🎄
♦♦♦♦

We welcome you to a traditional livestock farm offering you excellent service and accommodation. Set in a peaceful, secluded area on the Welsh Border, it's 4 miles north of Leominster, 7 miles south of Ludlow, and close to Croft Castle, Berrington Hall and other attractions. All rooms have tea/coffee-making facilities. TV and washbasins. Light evening meals by request. Open all year.

9 **Linton Brook Farm,** Bringsty, Bromyard, Herefordshire WR6 5TR

Sheila & Roger Steeds
☎/Fax 01885 488875
BB From £20–£25
Sleeps 6
🐕 🐔 🍽 🛢 🎄
♦♦♦

A warm welcome awaits you at our fascinating 17th century home. This former hop farm has large en suite rooms and a comfortable sitting room with oak beams, log fires and flag and oak plank floors. Home-smoked foods provide a delicious breakfast bonus. Our rolling hills offer glorious walks; views over 8 or more counties and quite exceptional wildlife. Open all year.

10 **Moor Court Farm,** Stretton Grandison, Nr Ledbury, Herefordshire HR8 2TP

Elizabeth Godsall
☎/Fax 01531 670408
BB From £18.50
EM From £12.50
Sleeps 6
🐕 🍵 🛢 🎄 ◎
♦♦♦♦

Relax and enjoy our beautiful 15th century timber-framed farmhouse with adjoining oast houses in a peaceful location. It's a traditional working Herefordshire hop and livestock farm, in scenic countryside central to the major market towns. Easy access to the Malverns, Wye Valley and Welsh borders. Spacious bedrooms, en suite or private bathroom, tea/coffee-making facilities. Oak beamed lounge and dining room. Open all year. See colour ad on page 38.

11 **New House Farm,** Much Marcle, Ledbury, Herefordshire HR8 2PH

Mrs Anne Jordan
☎ 01531 660604/660674
BB From £17.50
EM From £12.50
Sleeps 4
🐕(6) 🛢 🏹 🎄 🎋 ◎
♦♦♦

A friendly welcome awaits you at our delightful farmhouse enjoying panoramic views over Herefordshire, Worcestershire and Gloucestershire. Relax by a log fire on chilly evenings, or enjoy a swim in our outdoor pool during summer. Horses welcome by arrangement. Open all year.

Old Court Farm, Bredwardine, Herefordshire HR3 6BT

Sue Whittall
☎ **01981 500375**
Mobile **0421 424575**
⒝⒝ From £20–£25
EM From £16
Sleeps 6
♦♦♦

Old Court (featured on BBC Food programme) is a 14th century mediaeval manor situated on the banks of the River Wye. Ideal for the Wye Valley Walk. It has been carefully restored to preserve a wealth of beams and a 15ft fireplace. Central heating. Gardens enjoy beautiful views to the river. There are 2 four-poster bedrooms, 2 en suite and four-poster family room with private bathroom, all with teamakers. Evening meals. Phone for opening times.

Sink Green Farm, Rotherwas, Hereford HR2 6LE

David & Emma Jones
☎ **01432 870223**
⒝⒝ From £20–£28
Sleeps 6
♦♦♦

Sink Green awaits you with a warm, friendly welcome to its 16th century farmhouse overlooking the River Wye and picturesque Herefordshire countryside yet only 3 miles from the cathedral city of Hereford. Comfortable bedrooms, one with four-poster bed, all en suite, tea/coffee-making facilities and colour TV. Large oak-beamed lounge and traditional farmhouse fare. Children welcome, pets by arrangement. AA listed. Open all year.
E-mail: sinkgreenfarm@classic.msn.com

Upper Gilvach Farm, St Margarets, Vowchurch, Hereford HR2 0QY

Mrs Ruth Watkins
☎/Fax **01981 510618**
⒝⒝ From £20–£30
EM From £14
Sleeps 6
♦♦♦♦

Family-run farm between Golden Valley and Black Mountains. The 300-year-old farmhouse has been in the family since the beginning of the last century and offers three spacious, attractively furnished bedrooms, all en suite with colour TV and hospitality trays. Peace and comfort in a relaxing atmosphere. Delicious evening meals and hearty farmhouse breakfasts using local wines and produce. Licensed, dinner optional. Holiday caravan available. Open all year.

The Vauld House Farm, The Vauld, Marden, Herefordshire HR1 3HA

Mrs Judith Wells
☎ **01568 797347**
Fax **01568 797366**
⒝⒝ From £20–£22.50
EM From £13.50
Sleeps 5
♦♦♦♦

Situated 6 miles north of Hereford in beautiful countryside, this 17th century farmhouse offers traditionally furnished, comfortable en suite accommodation with guests' own lounge and dining room. Open log fires. All home cooking to a very high standard using fresh local produce. Guests may enjoy relaxing in the wooded and lawned gardens with carp ponds. Open all year except Christmas and New Year.

Warren Farm, Warren Lane, Lea, Ross on Wye, Herefordshire HR9 7LT

Mrs Christine Whitehouse
☎/Fax **01989 750272**
⒝⒝ From £22–£26
Sleeps 6
♦♦♦♦

A warm welcome awaits you in our beautifully restored 16th century listed farmhouse with a multitude of exposed beams, inglenooks and antiques. Set in peaceful countryside on a mixed working farm. 1 double en suite, 1 twin en suite, 1 double with private bathroom. All have TV, tea/coffee facilities. Two 18-hole golf courses within 3 miles and ideally situated for touring the Royal Forest of Dean, Wye Valley and the Vale of Leadon. Open Mar–Oct.

Please mention *Stay on a Farm* when booking

Self-Catering

---

4 **Anvil Cottage,** Grafton Villa, Grafton, Hereford, Herefordshire HR2 8ED

Jennie Layton
☎/Fax 01432 268689
SC From £180–£350
Sleeps 4/5

Highly Commended

Beams, natural wood and beautiful fabrics make our recently converted wainhouse into a very well equipped cottage for the discerning visitor. Comfortable, spacious twin/triple and double bedded rooms, each en suite. Lovely open plan lounge leading to a sheltered patio. Suitable for disabled and wheelchair guests. Linen, electricity and CH included. Open all year.

---

17 **Brooklyn,** c/o Marlbrook Hall, Elton, Ludlow, Shropshire SY8 2HR

Mrs Valerie Morgan
☎ 01568 770230
SC From £180–£310
Sleeps 6

Commended

Situated on the Herefordshire/Shropshire border, ideal for exploring the market town of Ludlow, Mortimer Forest and Welsh Borders. Spacious accommodation consists of three bedroomed house with garden and garage. Fitted carpets and tastefully decorated. Colour TV, microwave oven, washing machine, tumble dryer, linen and towels included in price. Open all year.

---

18 **Carey Dene and Rock House,** Carey, c/o Folly Farm, Holme Lacy, Hereford HR2 6LS

Mrs Rita Price
☎/Fax 01432 870259
SC From £170–£390
Sleeps 4/8 + cot

Commended

Two oak-beamed cottages on traditional farm overlooking River Wye. Beautiful area between Hereford and Ross on Wye, for a peaceful holiday or short break. Access to the river, two minutes' walk to pub serving meals. Washing machine, microwave, colour TV, central heating. Electricity and linen included in charge. Open all year.

---

19 **Grafton Cottage,** Grafton Farm, Bockleton, Tenbury Wells, Worcestershire WR15 8PT

Mrs Sue Thomas
☎ 01568 750602
SC From £130–£300
Sleeps 8 + cot

Approved

Large semi-detached red brick cottage, well equipped and full of character, set in unspoilt countryside. Explore the 300-acre working stock farm and its wildlife. Ideal for touring with black and white village trail and Welsh border country close by. Riding lessons and trekking available on the farm. Open all year.

---

20 **Home Farm,** Lingen, Bucknell, Shropshire SY7 0DZ

Mrs Anne Thomas
☎ 01544 267271
SC From £200–£300
Sleeps 5

Commended

Situated on Herefordshire/Shropshire/Welsh borders, spacious three-bedroomed farmhouse in beautiful gardens set amidst unspoilt, picturesque countryside, ½ mile from village of Lingen. Presteigne and Knighton close by, so too is historic town of Ludlow. Ideal for walking Mortimer Trail/Offa's Dyke and touring the Wye Valley, Elan Valley, Ludlow Castle and Croft Castle.

Old Forge Cottage, Lyston Smithy, Wormelow, Nr Hereford HR2 8EL

Shirley Wheeler
☎ **01981 540625**
🅂🄲 **From £160–£314**
Sleeps 4 + cot
🛉 ⛺ 🦮 🛏 ❦
𝒫𝒫𝒫𝒫 *Commended*

The Forge cottage is all on one level and retains many original features. Large open plan living room, fully equipped kitchenette, one twin en suite, one double bedroom and bathroom. CH, telephone and TV. Linen included. 14 acres of gardens and grounds. 3 day breaks Nov–Mar. Open all year.

Poolspringe Farm Cottages, Much Birch, Hereford HR2 8JJ

David & Val Beaumont
☎/**Fax 01981 540355**
🅂🄲 **From £80–£310**
Sleeps 1–7
🛋 ⛺ 🛏 ❦ ❦
𝒫𝒫𝒫𝒫 *Approved*

Barn conversion on 17th century, 50-acre farm set in the orchards of south Herefordshire. Midway between Hereford and Ross on Wye. Indoor heated swimming pool, sauna, games room, large garden with games. Coarse fishing on farm. Dogs' walks. Pets very welcome. Reduced fees at Belmont Golf Course 7 miles away. Many excellent pubs for food. Lovely touring area within reach of Forest of Dean, Cotswolds and Wales. Open all year.

The Vauld House Farm, The Vauld, Marden, Hereford, Herefordshire HR1 3HA

Judith Wells
☎ **01568 797347**
Fax 01568 797366
🅂🄲 **From £165–£320**
EM From £13.50
Sleeps 5/2 + cot
🛋 ⚬ ❦ 🛏
𝒫𝒫𝒫𝒫 *Commended*

Set amidst beautiful countryside on family stock farm midway between Hereford and Leominster, this skilfully converted Victorian hop kiln is spacious and well-equipped. Recently renovated 17th century Cider House, retaining character and charm. Ground floor. Lawned and wooded gardens with moat and ponds extend to over an acre.

CONFIRM BOOKINGS

Disappointments can arise from misunderstandings over the telephone. Please write to confirm your booking.

FOLLOW THE COUNTRY CODE

Leave nothing but footprints,
Take nothing but photographs,
Kill nothing but time!

Worcestershire

Wyre Forest, the Severn, Teme & Avon Valleys, Abberley, Malvern, Bredon Hills & the Cotswolds

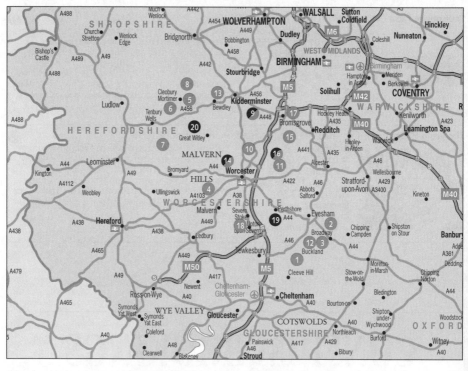

Key

- **1** Bed & Breakfast
- **1** Self-Catering
- **1** B&B and SC
- **1** Camping Barns
- **1** Camping & Caravanning

Worcestershire presents a varied landscape – beautiful wooded hills, valleys, rivers, streams, canals and pretty villages, many with their picturesque black and white thatched cottages and even a few half-timbered churches, whilst others are of mellow Cotswold stone.

The rivers Severn, Teme and Avon quietly meander through many of our smaller market towns and villages, enhancing their ancient timeless characters.

The historic county town of Worcester offers so much from riverside walks and a beautiful cathedral to a world-renowned porcelain factory. A great sense of history prevails in its gabled Tudor buildings with their Civil War connections.

The county offers great variety and you can be sure of a warm welcome.

If you would like help in finding suitable farm accommodation, turn to the full listing of FHB Groups on pages 392 to 395 to find appropriate contact details for this area.

Bed and Breakfast
(and evening meal)

Alstone Fields Farm, Teddington Hands, Stow Road, Nr Tewkesbury, Gloucestershire GL20 8NG ①

Jane Rogers
☎ 01242 620592
🅱 From £20–£30
Sleeps 12
& 🏇 ⅄ ⌂ 🏛
♦♦♦♦ Silver Award

Enjoy the friendliest welcome on our traditional family farm, surrounded by sheep, horses and dogs. Wake up in pretty en suite rooms to splendid views of rolling country-side and the delicious smell of bacon! We promise a memorably peaceful holiday and a perfect base from which to explore the picturesque Cotswolds. Open all year except Christmas.

Bowers Hill Farm, Bowers Hill, Nr Willersey, Broadway, Worcestershire WR11 5HG ②

Sarah Bent
☎ 01386 834585
Fax 01386 830234
🅱 From £22.50–£30
Sleeps 6
🏇 🛖 🏛
♦♦♦♦ (AA Inspected)

Tour the Cotswolds from here with Broadway, Chipping Campden and Stratford close by. Cosy, clean and com-fortable rooms, lovely antiques, flagstone floors, breakfast in front of log fires, homemade preserves. A beautiful, secluded spot, nature right on the doorstep with so many birds, animals and wildlife. ½ mile-long tree-lined drive from where you can view horses, cattle and sheep grazing on this 80-acre working farm. Horses welcome. Dogs in stables too! E-mail: sarah@bowershillfarm.com

---

Burhill Farm, Buckland, Nr Broadway, Worcestershire WR12 7LY ③

Mrs Pam Hutcheon
☎/Fax 01386 858171
🅱 From £20–£25
Sleeps 4
🏇 ⅄ ⌂ 🏛 ◉
♦♦♦♦ Gold Award

A warm welcome awaits our guests at our mainly grass farm lying in the folds of the Cotswolds just 2 miles south of Broadway. The Cotswold Way runs through the middle of the farm providing many lovely walks. Both guest rooms are en suite and have TV and tea/coffee facilities. Come and enjoy the peace and quiet. Open all year except Christmas.

Chirkenhill, Leigh Sinton, Malvern, Worcestershire WR13 5DE ④

Mrs Sarah Wenden
☎ 01886 832205
🅱 From £20
Sleeps 6
🏇 🛖 ⌂
♦♦♦♦

We welcome guests to Chirkenhill – or perhaps you will recognise us as 'Arkley House' in the ITV series 'Noah's Ark', shown in Autumn 1997 and 1998. Come and relax in the peace and quiet of our lovely old farmhouse amidst some of Worcestershire's most beautiful countryside. Excellent walking or drive the 'Elgar Route'. Dogs/horses housed by arrangement. Open all year.

Clay Farm, Clows Top, Nr Bewdley, Worcestershire DY14 9NN ⑤

Mike & Ella Grinnall
☎/Fax 01299 832421
🅱 From £19
Sleeps 6
🏇(6) Å 🖳 ☕ ⌂
♦♦♦♦

Fully centrally heated farmhouse with outstanding views. Friendly atmosphere, homemade cakes and tea on arrival. En suite bedrooms with tea making facilities. Full English breakfast. Spacious TV lounge, log fire, sun lounge overlooking trout and coarse fishing pools. Close to Bewdley, Ludlow, Severn Valley Railway and Witley Court. On Worcestershire and Shropshire borders on the B4202 Cleobury Mortimer Road. Open Feb–Nov.

6   **Clod Hall,** Milson, Nr Cleobury Mortimer, Worcestershire DY14 0BJ

Mrs C Morrison
☎ 01584 781421
▣ From £18–£25
Sleeps 3
🦮 🐎 🍴 🛏 ♞
◆◆

Clod Hall is a comfortable, centrally-heated house on the road between Tenbury Wells and Cleobury Mortimer commanding beautiful views over woods and farmland. Near the Clee Hills, Ludlow, Tenbury Wells and Leominster. Generous breakfasts with homemade preserves. Packed lunches available and there are good local pubs. Well placed for anglers. Open all year.

---

7   **Court Farm,** Hanley Childe, Tenbury Wells, Worcestershire WR15 8QY

Edward & Margaret Yarnold
☎ 01885 410265
▣ From £20–£25
Sleeps 4
🦮 🍴 🐎 🤝 🛏 ♞
◆◆◆◆

A warm and friendly welcome awaits you at Court Farm, a 15th century oak-beamed farmhouse, perfectly situated far from the madding crowd. A family-run farm of 200 acres with outstanding views of the Teme Valley, Clee Hills and the Welsh mountains. Near to Tenbury Wells, Ludlow and Elgar's Birthplace. Spacious en suite bedrooms, hospitality trays and guests' sitting room. Excellent meals available locally. Open Mar–Nov.

---

8   **Cox's Barn,** Bagginswood, Cleobury Mortimer, Nr Kidderminster DY14 8LS

Dinah Thompson
☎ 01746 718415
▣ From £18–£20
EM From £10
Sleeps 6
🦮 🍴 🐎 🛏
◆◆◆

Delightful converted barn on working farm set in beautiful rolling, peaceful countryside. Warm welcome assured, tea/coffee and homemade cakes on arrival. Delicious home cooking, vegetarian welcome. Full central heating. Three double en suite bedrooms (two ground floor), all with colour TV, beverage tray, radio/clock alarm and hair dryer. Non-smoking only! Open all year.

---

9   **The Durrance,** Berry Lane, Upton Warren, Bromsgrove, Worcestershire B61 9EL

Helen Hirons
☎/Fax 01562 777533
▣ From £22–£25
Sleeps 6
🦮 🍴 🛏 ♞
◆◆◆

We welcome you to our Victorian farmhouse in picturesque rural setting with large garden – ideal for children. Comfortably furnished and spacious en suite rooms, all with colour TV. Homemade tea and cakes on arrival. Enjoy total privacy as guests' accommodation is separate from family living area. One downstairs room. Convenient for NEC, 5 miles J5 M5, 7 miles J1 M42. Open all year.

---

10   **Eden Farm,** Ombersley, Nr Droitwich, Worcester WR9 0JX

Bill & Ann Yardley
☎ 01905 620244
▣ From £22–£25
Sleeps 5
🦮 🍴 🛏 🤝 ♞
◆◆◆

Come and enjoy our 17th century home with its lovely garden, fishing on the Severn and 5-acre marsh with over 100 species of flora. It's just off the A449 and the Wychavon Way, a wonderful centre for exploring the heart of England, with Worcester 7 miles, Droitwich 6 miles. Bedrooms are tastefully decorated, with bathrooms en suite, tea/coffee-making facilities and TV. Homemade produce and preserves used. Closed Christmas.

---

11   **The Green Farm,** Crowle Green, nr Worcester, Worcestershire WR7 4AB

Mrs Lucy Harris
☎/Fax 01905 381807
▣ From £22
Sleeps 3
🦮 🐎 🍴 🛏 ◉
◆◆◆

A peaceful oak-beamed Grade II listed farmhouse set in large garden and surrounding farmland. Comfortable rooms with own basin, private bathroom, tea/coffee-making facilities and CH. Guests' also have sole use of lounge with wood-burning stove and colour TV. Excellent meals within easy walking distance at local country pub. Open all year.

Laverton Meadow House, Nr Broadway, Gloucestershire WR12 7NA

Andrea Hazell
☎ 01386 584200
Fax 01386 584612
🅑🅑 From £37.50–£45
Sleeps 6
👌 🐕 ⛩
Applied

A beautiful Cotswold house with stunning views and lovely gardens. Romantic rooms with canopied beds and spacious bathrooms make this luxury accommodation. English breakfast in the kitchen by the Aga. Lavish candlelit dinners in sumptuous dining room. A log fire in the delightful sitting room offers you the perfect treat. Open all year.
E-mail: andrea@lavertonmeadows.demon.co.uk

Lightmarsh Farm, Crundalls Lane, Bewdley, Worcestershire DY12 1NE

Mrs Pauline Grainger
☎ 01299 404027
🅑🅑 From £20
Sleeps 4
👌(10) ⛩ ■ 👁
♦♦♦♦

Small, pasture farm in elevated position with fine views. Ideal for walking, wildlife and exploring Heart of England. The house is approx 200 years old, with full CH and comfortable accommodation; TV lounge with inglenook fireplace. Both rooms have private facilities. Truly rural setting, only 1 mile from Bewdley's shops and restaurants, Severn Valley Railway and West Midland Safari Park. Closed Christmas and New Year.

Little Lightwood Farm, Lightwood Lane, Cotheridge, Worcestershire WR6 5LT

Vee & Richard Rogers
☎/Fax 01905 333236
🅑🅑 From £24–£27
Sleeps 6
👌(5) ✂ 🅔 ■
♦♦♦

A friendly and warm welcome awaits you to share our family home in the heart of Worcestershire overlooking the Malvern Hills. All rooms en suite with courtesy tray, TV and CH. Also self-catering. Ours is a working dairy and cheese-making farm where you are welcome to participate. 3 miles west of Worcester, A44 to Leominster, 7 miles M5 J7. Closed Christmas.
E-mail: lightwood.holidays@virgin.net

Lower Bentley Farm, Lower Bentley Lane, Lower Bentley, Bromsgrove, Worcestershire B60 4JB

Christine Gibbs
☎ 01527 821286
Fax 01527 821193
🅑🅑 From £20–£23
Sleeps 6
👌 ■ 👁
♦♦♦ *(AA Inspected)*

Elegant Victorian farmhouse set in tranquil and picturesque countryside. Spacious bedrooms with en suite or private bathroom all with CH, colour TV and tea/coffee-making facilities. Separate guests' lounge and dinning room overlooking the large garden, where you can relax. Five miles from M5/M42, and ideal base for business or pleasure. Open all year.

Phepson Farm, Himbleton, Droitwich, Worcestershire WR9 7JZ

David & Tricia Havard
☎ 01905 391205
Fax 01905 391338
🅑🅑 From £21–£27
Sleeps 8
👌 🐕 ⚓ 🐕‍ ⛩ 👁
♦♦♦♦

In our 17th century oak beamed farmhouse we offer a warm welcome, good food and a relaxed and informal atmosphere. The recently converted Granary has two ground floor bedrooms whilst the farmhouse has double, and family accommodation. All rooms en suite with colour TV. Peaceful surroundings on family stock farm. Walking on Wychavon Way. Featured on 'Wish You Were Here'. Open all year except Christmas and New Year.
E-mail: havard@globalnet.co.uk

Stoke Cross Farm, Dusthouse Lane, Finstall, Bromsgrove, Worcestershire B60 3AE

Mrs Julie Orford
☎ 01527 876676
Fax 01527 874729
🅑🅑 From £16–£20
Sleeps 6
👌 🐕 ✂ ■ 🐎
♦♦♦

Modern, comfortable family farmhouse in rural location on quiet country lane yet Bromsgrove town centre is only 2½ miles. Convenient for M5/M42 motorways. Stratford upon Avon, NEC and airport all within easy reach. Large off-road parking area. Tea/coffee-making facilities and TV in all rooms. Dogs welcome by arrangement.

18 **Tiltridge Farm & Vineyard,** Upper Hook Road, Upton-on-Severn, Worcestershire WR8 0SA

Sandy Barker
☎ 01684 592906
Fax 01684 594142
BB From £21–£30
Sleeps 6
🛇 🛏 ⊁ ♨
♦♦♦♦

Period family farmhouse lying between the Malvern Hills and the attractive riverside town of Upton-on-Severn. Set in its own vineyard, the house is fully renovated with one double, one twin and one family room. All rooms are en suite with TV. Warm welcome and bumper breakfast with eggs from our hens and home made jams. Wine tasting encouraged in our new vineyard centre and shop. Four minutes from the Three Counties Showground. Closed Christmas and New Year. E-mail: elgarwine@aol.com

Self-Catering

9 **The Durrance,** Berry Lane, Upton Warren, Bromsgrove, Worcestershire B61 9EL

Helen Hirons
☎/Fax 01562 777533
SC From £225–£310
Sleeps 3/4
🛇 ⊁ ♨ 🕱
🐾🐾🐾🐾 *Highly Commended*

We welcome you to our newly converted single storey cottages set in peaceful surroundings and open countryside. Rooms are cosy and tastefully furnished with original oak beams. Fitted pine kitchen, dishwasher, microwave oven, full CH, colour TV. Spacious garden and patio. Ideal for children who can help collect eggs from our hens! Laundry facilities. Suitable for disabled person. Ideal for Cotswolds, Severn Valley, Malverns and NEC. Open all year.

16 **The Granary,** c/o Phepson Farm, Himbleton, Droitwich, Worcestershire WR9 7JZ

David & Tricia Havard
☎ 01905 391205
Fax 01905 391338
SC From £170–£255
Sleeps 2/3
🛇 🛏 ⊁ ♨ ☚ 🕱 ◉
🐾🐾🐾🐾 *Commended*

The recent conversion of the old granary is reached by an outside stone staircase. The light and airy flat is double-glazed and very comfortably furnished. Situated on working stock farm in peaceful surroundings. Entrance through stable door. Fitted kitchen, colour TV, double bedroom with en suite bathroom. Linen, electricity, night storage heating included. Open all year.
E-mail: havard@globalnet.co.uk

19 **The Granary,** Tibbitts Farm, Great Comberton, nr Pershore, Worcestershire WR10 3DT

Mrs Jenny Newbury
☎ 01386 710210
SC From £180–£280
Sleeps 2/3
🛇(5) ⊁ ⅄ 🐾 ♨ ⅋
🐾🐾🐾🐾 *Commended*

The Granary is attached to 16th century farmhouse and reached by external stone stairs. Wealth of exposed beams with kitchen/dining area, lounge, bedroom and bathroom for 2/3. Peaceful village location, views to open countryside and walking directly to Bredon Hill. Central for Cotswolds, Malvern Hills and Stratford. Linen and electricity included. Open all year.

14 **Little Lightwood Farm,** Lightwood Lane, Cotheridge, Worcestershire WR6 5LT

Vee & Richard Rogers
☎/Fax 01905 333236
SC From £90–£330
Sleeps 2/6
🛇 ⊁ ⊞ ♨
🐾🐾 – 🐾🐾🐾🐾
Up to Commended

A friendly and warm welcome awaits you to share our family home in the heart of Worcestershire. Self-catering in a log cabin or converted wain house. Also bed and breakfast. Ours is a working dairy and cheese-making farm where you are welcome to participate. 3 miles west of Worcester, A44 to Leominster, 7 miles M5 J7. Open all year. E-mail: lightwood.holidays@virgin.net

Old Yates Cottages, Old Yates Farm, Abberley, Nr Worcester, Worcestershire WR6 6AT   **20**

Sarah & Richard Goodman
☎ **01299 896500**
Fax 01299 896065
⟨SC⟩ From £135–£335
Sleep up to 4
↟ ⌕ ⍩ ⬛ ⊛
🎘 🎘 🎘 🎘 *Commended*

We invite you to enjoy the home comforts of our cottages, to experience their tranquil surroundings and to relax in our beautiful countryside. Games facilities and launderette on site. 1 mile from village; many restaurants, leisure and recreational facilities within easy reach. Please send for brochure. Open all year.
E-mail: rmgoodma@aol.com

CONFIRM BOOKINGS

Disappointments can arise from misunderstandings over the telephone. Please write to confirm your booking.

FARM HOLIDAY BUREAU

Our Internet address is
http://www.webscape.co.uk/farmaccom/

USE THE INDEX

FARM HOLIDAY BUREAU

The comprehensive Index shows which farms offer access to disabled visitors; caravanning/camping facilities; the chance to participate on a working farm; stabling/grazing for visiting horses; en suite rooms; a welcome to business people; acceptance of *Stay on a Farm* gift tokens.

FOLLOW THE COUNTRY CODE

Leave nothing but footprints,
Take nothing but photographs,
Kill nothing but time!

Gloucestershire

The Cotswolds, Severn Vale & Forest of Dean

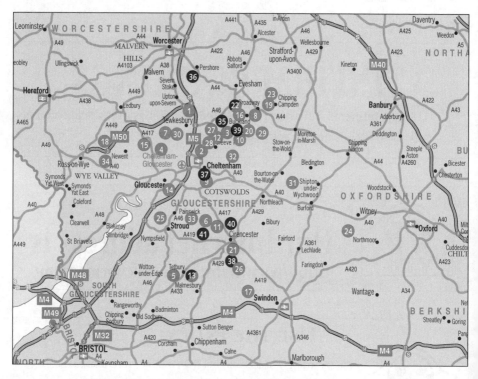

Key

1 Bed & Breakfast

1 Self-Catering

1 B&B and SC

1 Camping Barns

1 Camping & Caravanning

Gloucestershire is bisected by the River Severn which snakes down a broad, fertile vale dotted with mellow villages and farms.

To the west is the beautiful and romantic Forest of Dean, the residue of an historic royal hunting forest.

To the east are the rolling hills of the Cotswolds which rise to 2,000 feet. This area is famous for its wool towns, dry-stone walls and fine architecture, all built from the local honey-coloured limestone.

The capital, Gloucester, with parts of its Roman wall still visible, was formerly the second city of England. Nearby the leafy avenues and parks of the Regency spa town of Cheltenham make a refreshing contrast.

If you would like help in finding suitable farm accommodation, turn to the full listing of FHB Groups on pages 392 to 395 to find appropriate contact details for this area.

Bed and Breakfast
(and evening meal)

Abbots Court, Church End, Twyning, Tewkesbury, Gloucestershire GL20 6DA

Bernie Williams
☎/Fax 01684 292515
[BB] From £17–£19
Sleeps 15
🐕 🦮 ♨ 🧺
♦♦♦

Lovely, quiet farmhouse in 350 acres between Cotswolds and Malverns. All bedrooms have colour TV, most en suite, tea-making facilities. Large lounge, separate dining room, excellent home cooked food. Licensed bar. 3 games rooms with pool table, table tennis, children's TV room, grass tennis court, bowling green, children's play area on lawn. Superb touring area. River and lake fishing on the farm. Open all year (except Christmas and New Year).

Acorn Upper Farm, Brockhampton, Swindon Village, Cheltenham GL51 9RS

Carol Holder
Freephone 0800 0685684
☎/Fax 01242 525923
[BB] From £20–£22.50
Sleeps 6
🐕 ✂ 🧺
♦♦♦

17th century farmhouse decorated throughout with large beams and open fires. Very quiet situation overlooking Cleeve Hill, on the edge of Cheltenham within easy reach of the Cotswolds, Bath, Stratford upon Avon, etc. Two miles from Cheltenham Racecourse. *Associate.*

Alstone Fields Farm, Teddington Hands, Stow Road, Nr Tewkesbury, Gloucestershire GL20 8NG

Jane Rogers
☎ 01242 620592
[BB] From £20–£30
Sleeps 12
♿ 🐎 ✂ 🧺 ♨
♦♦♦♦♦ Silver Award

Enjoy the friendliest welcome on our traditional family farm, surrounded by sheep, horses and dogs. Wake up in pretty en suite rooms to splendid views of rolling countryside and the delicious smell of bacon! We promise a memorably peaceful holiday and a perfect base from which to explore the picturesque Cotswolds. Open all year except Christmas.

Ashleworth Court, Ashleworth, Gloucester GL19 4JA

Amanda Chamberlayne
☎ 01452 700241
Fax 01452 700411
[BB] From £20–£24
Sleeps 6
🐕 🐎 ✂ 🧺 ♨ 🦮 ♨
♦♦♦

On the west bank of the River Severn, Ashleworth Court sits alongside the church and tithe barn, forming a unique group of medieval buildings. One of the bedrooms boasts a Jacobean four-poster, and breakfast is served in what was part of the great hall. Two excellent pubs in the village. *Associate.* E-mail: chamberlayne@farmline.com

---

Avenue Farm, Knockdown, Tetbury, Gloucestershire GL8 8QY

Sonja King
☎ 01454 238207
Fax 01454 238033
[BB] From £20–£25
Sleeps 6
🐕 ✂ 🧺 ♨
♦♦♦

Westonbirt Arboretum adjoins our farm with many miles of walks and a large summer programme of events. We are also near the cities of Bath and Bristol and delightful villages of Lacock and Castle Combe. 'Home from home' is our motto. Open all year.

6 Bidfield Farm, The Camp, Stroud, Gloucestershire GL6 7ET

Mrs Baird
☎/Fax 01285 821263
[BB] From £17.50–£19
Sleeps 6
☺(3) ⁙ 🏠 🎄
♦♦♦

Lovely Cotswold stone 17th century farmhouse on working arable farm set in scenic Gloucester countryside on RAC scenic route (B4070). Views to open fields. Very comfortable, spacious accommodation. Easy distance to Slad valley, Painswick, Cheltenham, Cirencester and Bath. Convenient for Cheltenham Gold Cup, Gatcombe Art and Craft and Badminton Horse Trials. Open Feb-Nov.

---

7 Brawn Farm, Sandhurst, Gloucester, Gloucestershire GL2 9NR

Sally Williams
☎ 01452 731010
Fax 01452 731102
Mobile 0973 313418
[BB] From £20–£25
Sleeps 4
☺ 🐓 🦌 🎣 🎄 🏠 ◉
♦♦♦♦

Working dairy/corn farm with a 15th century listed farmhouse and large garden in an extremely quiet setting. Delightful footpaths through the farm and woods. Two very spacious bedrooms, comfortable sitting room with TV, separate dining room offering excellent breakfasts. Good local pubs. Open all year.

---

8 Burhill Farm, Buckland, Nr Broadway, Worcestershire WR12 7LY

Mrs Pam Hutcheon
☎/Fax 01386 858171
[BB] From £20–£25
Sleeps 4
☺ ⁙ 🏠 🎄 ◉
♦♦♦♦♦ Gold Award

A warm welcome awaits our guests at our mainly grass farm lying in the folds of the Cotswolds just 2 miles south of Broadway. The Cotswold Way runs through the middle of the farm providing many lovely walks. Both guest rooms are en suite and have TV and tea/coffee facilities. Come and enjoy the peace and quiet. Open all year except Christmas.

---

9 Butlers Hill Farm, Cockleford, Cowley, Cheltenham, Gloucestershire GL53 9NW

Bridget Brickell
☎/Fax 01242 870455
[BB] From £17
EM From £7
Sleeps 4
☺(6) ⁙ 🏠 ↩
♦♦♦

A warm welcome awaits you on this mixed working farm between Cheltenham and Cirencester. Relax in this modern spacious farmhouse, in a quiet part of the Churn Valley with attractive walks and an ideal centre for exploring the Cotswolds. All rooms have H&C and tea/coffee-making facilities, separate guests' sitting room with colour TV and separate dining room. Open Mar–Sept.

---

10 Cleevely, Wadfield Farm, Corndean Lane, Winchcombe, Nr Cheltenham, Gloucestershire GL54 5AL

Carole Rand
☎ 01242 602059
[BB] From £20–£25
Sleeps 4
☺ 🎄
Applied

Family-run arable/sheep farm with Cotswold Way running through. Half-timbered Cotswold stone house overlooking the Sudeley and Winchcombe Valley. Splendid views. Excellent base for touring the Cotswolds. Winter breaks – log fires. Traditional farmhouse cuisine. Twin en suite, double/family room with private bathroom, both with tea/coffee-making facilities. Parking. *Associate.*

---

11 Dix's Barn, Duntisbourne Abbots, Cirencester, Gloucestershire GL7 7JN

Mrs Rosemary Wilcox
☎ 01285 821249
[BB] From £19–£25
Sleeps 4
☺ 🐓 ⁙ 🏠
♦♦♦

Dix's Barn is situated in an Area of Outstanding Natural Beauty. It has breathtaking views of the Cotswolds and one can take lovely walks in any direction. Ideally placed for touring by car. The farm is family run, being a mixture of arable, beef and sheep. Open all year.

Elms Farm, Gretton, nr Winchcombe, Cheltenham, Gloucestershire GL54 5HQ

Rosemary Quilter
☎ 01242 620150
Fax 01242 620837
Mobile 0374 461107
BB From £18.50–£20
EM From £15
Sleeps 4
🐴 🐈 ♿
♦♦♦

Relax and enjoy the Cotswolds in our farmhouse set on the outskirts of Gretton village, with picturesque views north and south. The 120-acre arable, and sheep farm adjoins some of the many footpaths in the area. Ideal for exploring those beautiful Cotswold villages, or just sitting and enjoying the peace and quiet. En suite rooms with TV and tea/coffee. Guests' lounge with log fire. Open all year except Christmas. E-mail: rose@elmfarm.demon.co.uk

---

Folly Farm, Malmesbury Road, Tetbury, Gloucestershire GL8 8XA

Julian Benton
☎ 01666 502475
Fax 01666 502358
BB From £35–£55
Sleeps 7
🐴 🖼 🏕 ♿ ♛ ✿
♦♦

Nestled in the Cotswold countryside, a delightful Queen Anne period farmhouse, with Royal Tetbury a five minute walk away. All rooms are en suite, with colour TV and continental breakfast. Easy access to both the M4 and M5. Also, off-season cottages, weekend lets. Open all year.
E-mail: info@gtb.co.uk

Gilbert's, Gilbert's Lane, Brookthorpe, Nr Gloucester, Gloucestershire GL4 0UH

Jenny Beer
☎/Fax 01452 812364
BB From £26.50–£29.50
Sleeps 6
🐴 ✂ ♿ 🅿
♦♦♦♦

Gilbert's, which nestles beneath the Cotswolds close to Gloucester, is listed as an architectural gem. Whilst each room has modern comforts – WC, bath, shower, TV, telephone, etc. – the atmosphere is in keeping with the unpretentious nature of the house and organic smallholding. RAC Highly Acclaimed and *Which? Best Buy*. Open all year. E-mail: jenny@gilbert'sbb.demon.co.uk

---

Kilmorie Smallholding, Gloucester Road, Snigs End, Corse, Staunton, Gloucestershire GL19 3RQ

Sheila Barnfield
☎/Fax 01452 840224
BB From £16
EM From £7.50
Sleeps 11
🐴(5) 🏕 ♛ ■ 🐎 ♿
♦♦♦

Built in 1848 by the Chartists, Kilmorie is a Grade II listed smallholding keeping sheep, ponies, goats, ducks and hens. Children may help with animals. All accommodation is on ground floor, warm and cosy with CH, tea/coffee trays, colour TVs, H&C (some en suite available). Relax in large garden or walk waymarked footpaths to discover the countryside. Good home cooking, full English breakfast, 3 course dinner. Ideal for Cotswolds, Malverns, Forest of Dean. Fishing nearby. Closed Christmas & New Year.

Laverton Meadow House, Nr Broadway, Gloucestershire WR12 7NA

Andrea Hazell
☎ 01386 584200
Fax 01386 584612
BB From £37.50–£45
Sleeps 6
🐴 🐈 ♛
Applied

A beautiful Cotswold house with stunning views and lovely gardens. Romantic rooms with canopied beds and spacious bathrooms make this luxury accommodation. English breakfast in the kitchen with the Aga. Lavish candlelit dinners in sumptuous dining room. A log fire in the delightful sitting room offers you the perfect treat. Open all year.
E-mail: andrea@lavertonmeadows.demon.co.uk

Leighfield Lodge Farm, Malmesbury Road, Leigh, Swindon, Wiltshire SN6 6RH 17

Mrs Claire Read
☎/Fax 01666 860241
BB From £22.50
Sleeps 6
🐴 ✂ 🖼 ♿
♦♦♦♦

Imagine a lovely old farmhouse in a truly rural setting. Step inside and discover comfortable en suite rooms with crisp cotton bedlinen. Relax in the sitting room in front of a warm fire, after exploring the Cotswolds or Wiltshire Downs. Children will enjoy meeting the Jersey cows and may even see the wild deer! Open all year.

---

18   **Lower House Farm,** Kempley, Dymock, Gloucestershire GL18 2BS

Mrs Gill Bennett
☎/Fax 01531 890301
🅱🅱 From £18–£22
EM From £12
Sleeps 6
⌂ 🛏 🛇 ⚘ ⤳ ✿ ⚘ ◉
♦♦♦

Family dairy farm resting peacefully in180 acres, on edge of Forest of Dean. Comfortable accommodation, en suite rooms with tea/coffee. Home cooked dishes using local produce, especially our 'big breakfasts'. Easy access Wye Valley, Wales, Malverns and many local attractions. All guests welcomed with tray, tea/coffee and homemade buns. Open all year except Christmas.

---

19   **Lowerfield Farm,** Willersey, Broadway, Worcestershire WR11 5HF

Jane Hill
☎ 01386 858273
Fax 01386 854608
🅱🅱 From £22.50–£25
EM From £12.50
Sleeps 6
⌂ 🛏 ⚘ 🛇 🔥 ✿
♦♦♦♦

Lowerfield Farm is peacefully located 3 miles from Broadway and provides an ideal base for exploring the Cotswolds, Stratford on Avon, Cheltenham and beyond. Bedrooms are en suite with clock radio, TV, hairdryer and tea/coffee-making facilities. Three-course evening meal available by arrangement or good eating houses nearby. Open all year. See colour ad on page 38.
E-mail: info@lowerfield-farm.co.uk

---

20   **Lydes Farm,** Toddington, Cheltenham, Gloucestershire GL54 5DP

Mrs R Sharpley
☎/Fax 01242 621229
🅱🅱 From £18.50–£20
Sleeps 5
⌂(5) 🛏 🛇 ⚘
♦♦♦

Comfortable farmhouse between Broadway and Winchcombe with panoramic views from every room. TV in bedrooms, separate dining room, garden. Dogs taken by arrangement. A grass farm grazed by cattle and horses; visitors are welcome to walk round. Ideal centre for exploring the North Cotswolds. Golf and riding nearby. Open Jan–Nov. E-mail: lydes@sharpley.freeon-line.co.uk

---

21   **Manby's Farm,** Oaksey, Malmesbury, Wiltshire SN16 9SA

Anne Shewry-Fitzgerald
☎ 01666 577399
Fax 01666 577241
🅱🅱 From £20–£23
EM From £10
Sleeps 6
⌂ 🛇 ⊞ 🛇 ⚘ ✿
♦♦♦♦

New farmhouse ½ mile from village with beautiful views. Ideal location for visiting Cotswolds, Bath, Lacock, Oxford, etc. Golf, walking and all water sports nearby. Bright, cheerful rooms, all en suite with colour TV and tea/coffee-making facilities. Adaptable accommodation for twin beds, double or family rooms. Bicycle hire. *Associate.*
E-mail: DJHackle@compuserve.com

---

22   **Manor Farm,** Greet, Winchcombe, Cheltenham, Gloucestershire GL54 5BJ

Richard & Janet Day
☎/Fax 01242 602423
🅱🅱 From £22.50–£30
Sleeps 6
⌂ 🛇 Å 🛇 ✿ ⚘
♦♦♦♦

Luxuriously restored 16th century cotswold manor on mixed family farm, excellent views, near Sudeley Castle and steam railway. Convenient to Broadway, Cheltenham, Evesham, Tewkesbury and M5. 1½ miles from Cotswold Way and Wychavon Way. Large garden, croquet lawn, children welcome, horses can be accommodated. Self-catering cottages also available and camping space. Open Jan–Nov.

---

23   **Manor Farm,** Weston Sub-Edge, Chipping Campden, Gloucestershire GL55 6QH

Lucy King
☎ 01386 840390
Fax 08701 640638
Mobile 07889 108812
🅱🅱 From £22.50
Sleeps 6
⌂ 🛏 🛇 🔥 ✿ ⚘
♦♦♦

A warm friendly welcome and a hearty full English breakfast is assured for all guests to Manor farm, a traditional 17th century Cotswold stone oak beamed farmhouse. Excellent base for exploring the Cotswolds and Shakespeare country from our 800-acre farm with sheep, cattle and horses. Beautiful walled garden. 1½ miles from Chipping Campden. Superb local eating houses. All rooms are en suite with TV/radio, etc. Open all year. *Associate.*
E-mail: lucy@manorfarmbnb.demon.co.uk

'Morar', Weald Street, Bampton, Oxfordshire OX18 2HL

Janet Rouse
☎ 01993 850162
Fax 01993 851738
BB From £22.50–£25
EM From £14.50
Sleeps 6
♿(6) ⊞ ⊁ ▪ ☯
♦♦♦

Wake up to the smell of homemade bread, look out over rolling fields and listen to the birds welcome the new day. Relax over breakfast, make it a feast. Let us help you get the most from your stay in this most beautiful corner of England. Pet cats, sheep, goat. Doubles en suite. Open Mar–mid Dec. E-mail: morar@cwcom.net

---

Oaktree Farm, Little Haresfield, Standish, Gloucestershire GL10 3DS

Jackie Guilding
☎ 01452 883323
BB From £18–£20
EM From £12
Sleeps 4
♿ ⊁ ▪ ⚘
Applied

Enjoy that well-earned break in the friendly atmosphere of our mixed dairy farm, situated in an Area of Outstanding Natural Beauty with open views to the Malvern Hills, Forest of Dean and Cotswolds. Guests are welcome to watch the daily running of this family farm or just relax in the large garden. All rooms are en suite and equipped with the little extras to make your stay enjoyable. Open Feb–Nov.

Oakwood Farm, Upper Minety, Malmesbury, Wiltshire SN16 9PY

Mrs Katie Gallop
☎/Fax 01666 860286
Mobile 0385 916039
BB From £17
Sleeps 6
♿ ⊼ ▪
Awaiting new rating

A friendly farming couple welcome you to their working dairy farm overlooking Upper Minety church. Meander through the landscaped gardens or just relax on the croquet lawn under the old oak tree. Guests enjoy their own spacious wing with extra touches that make Oakwood Farm a special place to stay. Well situated for touring the Cotswolds, Heart of England and West Country. Open all year.

Pardon Hill Farm, Prescott, Gotherington, Cheltenham, Gloucestershire GL52 4RD

Janet Newman
☎/Fax 01242 672468
Mobile 07867 566031
BB From £22
Sleeps 5
♿ ⊼ ⅄ ▪
♦♦♦

A quiet, family-run 300-acre livestock farm, set in the beautiful Cotswold hills just 6 miles from Cheltenham and 3 miles from Winchcombe. Double, twin and single rooms, all en suite with outstanding views. A marvellous base for walking, riding and touring holidays. Open all year except Christmas. E-mail: janet@pardonhillfarm.freeserve.co.uk

---

Postlip Hall Farm, Postlip, Winchcombe, Cheltenham, Gloucestershire GL54 5AQ   28

Mrs Valerie Albutt
☎/Fax 01242 603351
BB From £21–£35
Sleeps 6
♿ ⊁ ⚘ ▪
♦♦♦♦ Gold Award

Spectacular situation, superb scenery in every direction. Set in tiny hamlet of Postlip off B4632, Winchcombe 1¾ miles. This working farm is a fantastic base for exploring Cotswolds, Warwick Castle, Blenheim Palace, Bath, Malverns. Great walking. Golf and horse riding nearby. Cosy, spacious en suite rooms, armchairs, colour TV. Beverages. Lovely welcoming atmosphere. Open all year except Christmas.

Sudeley Hill Farm, Winchcombe, Gloucestershire GL54 5JB   29

Barbara Scudamore
☎/Fax 01242 602344
BB From £22–£28
Sleeps 6
♿ ⚘ ▪
♦♦♦♦

Delightfully situated above Sudeley Castle with panoramic views across the surrounding valley, this is a 15th century listed farmhouse with a large garden on a working mixed farm of 800 acres. Ideal centre for touring the Cotswolds. Family/twin, 1 double, 1 twin, all en suite. Comfortable lounge with TV and log fires. Separate dining room. Open all year except Christmas.

30   Town Street Farm, Tirley, Gloucestershire GL19 4HG

Sue Warner
☎ 01452 780442
Fax 01452 780890
🅱 From £20–£26
Sleeps 6
🗶 🕇 🛧 ᭔ ⛱ 🏛 ᭔
◆◆◆

Town Street Farm is a typical working family farm close to the River Severn, within easy reach of M5 and M50. The farmhouse offers a high standard of accommodation with en suite facilities in bedrooms and a warm and friendly welcome. Breakfast is served overlooking the lawns, flowerbeds and tennis court which is available for use by guests. Open all year except Christmas.

31   Upper Farm, Clapton-on-the-Hill, Bourton-on-the-Water, Gloucestershire GL54 2LG

Mrs Helen Adams
☎ 01451 820453
Fax 01451 810185
🅱 From £19–£23
Sleeps 8
🗶(5) ᭔ 🏛 ⛱
◆◆◆◆◆

A mixed family farm of 140-acres in a peaceful, undiscovered village two miles from Bourton-on-the-Water. Our centrally heated period stone farmhouse has been tastefully restored and offers a warm, friendly welcome. Quality accommodation and hearty farmhouse fayre. We are centrally located for touring or walking and our hill position offers panoramic views over the surrounding Cotswold countryside. Open Mar–Nov. *Associate.*

32   Whittington Lodge Farm, Whittington, Cheltenham, Gloucestershire GL54 4HB

Mrs Cathy Boyd
☎/Fax 01242 820603
🅱 From £20–£25
Sleeps 6
🗶(12) ᭔ 🏛 ᭔ ⛱
◆◆◆◆

A friendly welcome to our 700-acre Cotswold farm, situated in the most beautiful, unspoilt village. Spacious rooms, 1 double, 2 twin. En suite available, TV and tea/coffee. Drawing room with log fire. Cotswold Way ½ mile (packed lunches available). Own tennis court. Riding nearby. Parking. 10 minute drive from Cheltenham Racecourse. Open all year except Christmas.

33   Wickridge Court Farm, Folly Lane, Stroud, Gloucestershire GL6 7JT

Gloria & Peter Watkins
☎ 01453 764357
🅱 From £20–£25
Sleeps 6
🗶 🕇 ⛱ 🏛 ◉
◆◆◆

Wickridge Court Farm is situated 1 mile from the B4070 holiday route. A farm of 250 acres with cattle and horses. The historic farmhouse is a sympathetically converted Cotswold stone barn offering all en suite rooms. It is a peaceful suntrap set in a fold of the beautiful Slad Valley offering excellent walks through National Trust woods; Stroud Leisure Centre with its heated pool is 1 mile, many places of interest within easy reach. Open all year.

34   Withyland Heights, Beavan's Hill, Kilcot, Newent, Gloucestershire GL18 1PG

Mrs Katrina Cracknell
☎ 01989 720582
Fax 01989 720238
🅱 From £16–£23
Sleeps 6
🗶 ᭔ 🏛
◆◆◆

Situated on the Herefordshire/Gloucestershire border Withyland Heights has two bedrooms which are spacious and attractively furnished with tea and coffee making facilities.The double/family room has en suite facilities and panoramic views of surrounding countryside. The twin/triple room has original beams and private bathroom. Non-smoking. Children welcome. Open all year. *Associate.*

Our farms offer a range of facilities that are illustrated by symbols in each entry. Turn to page 14 for an explanation of the symbols.

Self-Catering

Bangrove Farm, Teddington, Tewkesbury, Gloucestershire GL20 8JB ⑤⑤

Pat Hitchman
☎ 01242 620223
Fax 01242 620697
🆂 From £280–£350
Sleeps 2/8
🐎🛴🖤🎾🎾
🎗🎗🎗🎗 *Commended*

An attractive self-contained property part of 17th century oak-beamed farmhouse on arable/livestock farm in quiet rural setting near Cheltenham. Ideal for walking and touring Cotswolds. Comfortably furnished, fitted carpets throughout. 3 double bedrooms (1 with washbasin), large bathroom. Downstairs cloakroom, kitchen/diner, microwave, large lounge, TV. Linen/electricity/use of washing machine included. Children welcome. Garden, hard tennis court, barbecue. Golf/riding available. Open Mar–Oct.

Court Close Farm, Manor Road, Eckington, Pershore, Worcestershire WR10 3BH ③⑥

Eileen Fincher
☎/Fax 01386 750297
🆂 From £200–£305
Sleeps 5
🐎🍴🍷🎾🖤
🎗🎗🎗🎗 *Commended*

A self-contained wing of our lovely 18th century farmhouse and garden on village edge, bordering Gloucestershire. Outstanding views of Bredon Hill. Attractive set dairy farm with meadows sloping to the Avon. Fishing by arrangement. Central for Shakespeare, Malvern and Cotswold jaunts. Convenient kitchen/diner and comfortable sitting room with TV, storage heat and electric fire. 3 bedrooms, linen provided. Cot available. Closed Christmas.

Coxhorne Farm, London Road, Charlton Kings, Cheltenham, Gloucestershire GL52 6UY ③⑦

Mr & Mrs John Close
☎ 01242 236599
🆂 From £135–£175
Sleeps 2
🐎(2)🍴🖤
🎗🎗🎗 *Commended*

Cosy, self-contained annexe to the farmhouse on a 100-acre livestock farm on the eastern side of the Cheltenham escarpment, 3 miles from the centre of the Regency spa town. Centrally heated and fully equipped. Ideal position for walking the Cotswold Way and travelling to the lovely mellow Cotswold villages. Open all year. *Associate.*

Folly Farm Cottages, Malmesbury Road, Tetbury, Gloucestershire GL8 8XA ⑬

Julian Benton
☎ 01666 502475
Fax 01666 502358
🆂 From £180–£740
Sleep 2–8
🐎🖼🖤🎾🎾
🎗🎗🎗 – 🎗🎗🎗🎗
Commended

Close to Royal Tetbury, 11 superior 18th century cottages. Well furnished, fully equipped throughout. CH, CTV, microwave, linen provided. Some log fires. Laundry, large gardens, barbecue and play area. Fishing, golf, riding, windsurfing nearby. Pubs 4 minutes' walk. Resident host. Ideal for disabled and family reunions. Close to M4/M5. Open all year. E-mail: info@gtb.co.uk

---

Manor Farm Cottages, Greet, Winchcombe, Cheltenham, Gloucestershire GL54 5BJ ㉒

Richard & Janet Day
☎/Fax 01242 602423
🆂 From £237–£580
Sleeps 3–6
🐎🖤🔌🎾🖤
🎗🎗🎗🎗 *Highly Commended*

Beautifully restored 15th century tithe house (pictured) also 'Shuck's Cottage' and 'Bread Oven Cottage', on family farm. Central for Tewkesbury, Broadway, Evesham, Cheltenham. Sleep 3–6, cot and high-chair available. Horses accommodated. Close to Cotswold Way and Wychavon Way, in sight of steam railway. Full central heating, every modern convenience. Camping space also available. Open all year.

38 **Old Mill Farm,** nr Cirencester, c/o Ermin House Farm, Syde, Cheltenham, Gloucestershire GL53 9PN

Mrs Catherine Hazell
☎ 01285 821255
Fax 01285 821531
🆂🄲 From £150–£600
Sleep 2–7
🐕 🏠 ⚓ ☂ ⊛
🏵 🏵 🏵 🏵 *Commended*

Four superior barn conversions featuring Cotswold stone pillars and beams. Situated 4 miles from Cirencester on mixed farm beside River Thames and Cotswold Water Park for walking, birdwatching, fishing, sailing and jet skiing. Trains to London 1¼ hrs. Prices include full central heating, electricity, bed-linen, colour TV. Separate laundry room with pay-phone. Convenient for Stratford-upon-Avon, Oxford, Stonehenge, Bath and Tetbury. Open all year.

39 **The Old Stables,** Farmcote, Winchcombe, Gloucestershire GL54 5AU

Jane Eayrs
☎ 01242 603860
🆂🄲 From £200–£290
Sleeps 4
🐕 🏠 ✂ ⚓
Applied

A delightful stable conversion, set high on the Cotswold escarpment with views over the surrounding countryside. Farmcote is a tiny hamlet close to the Cotswold Way yet within striking distance of Broadway, Stratford and Chipping Campden. There are 2 bedrooms, 2 bathrooms and an open plan dining/kitchen area and sitting room. Associate.

40 **Warrens Gorse Cottages,** Home Farm, Warrens Gorse, Cirencester, Gloucestershire GL7 7JD

John & Nanette Randall
☎ 01285 831261
🆂🄲 From £140–£200
Sleeps 3–5
🐕 🏠 ✂
🏵 🏵 🏵 *Approved*

2½ miles from Cirencester between Daglingworth and Perrotts Brook, these attractive whitewashed cottages are ideally situated for touring the Cotswolds. The cottages are personally attended by the owners and are comfortably furnished and well equipped. 100-acre sheep and cattle farm. Golf club nearby. Water sports 5 miles. Open Apr–Oct.

41 **Westley Farm Cottages,** Chalford, Stroud, Gloucestershire GL6 8HP

Julian & Hege Usborne
☎/Fax 01285 760262
🆂🄲 From £150–£330
Sleep 2/6
🐕 🏠 🚶 🎠 ☂ ⚓
🏵 🏵 🏵 *Approved*

Steep meadows of wild flowers and beech woods are the setting for this old fashioned 80-acre hill farm with breathtaking panoramic views over the Golden Valley. Children especially enjoy the donkey, calves, lambs and foals. Adults may prefer the complete tranquillity and abundant wildlife. Nearby horseriding, golf, gliding, watersports. Midway Cirencester – Stroud. Four cottages, two flats. Brochure available. Open Apr–Oct.
E-mail: westleyfarm@compuserve.com

Most farms are full Members of FHB. Some are shown as Associates – see page 11.

FINDING YOUR ACCOMMODATION

FARM HOLIDAY
BUREAU

*The local FHB Group contacts listed on
page 392 can always help you find a vacancy
in your chosen area.*

Warwickshire

Shakespeare Country

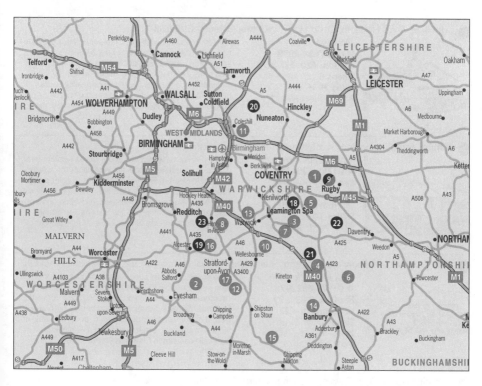

Key

🔴 **1** Bed & Breakfast

🟢 **1** Self-Catering

🔴🟢 **1** B&B and SC

🟧 **1** Camping Barns

🔺 **1** Camping & Caravanning

Birthplace of the world's greatest playwright and home to many treasures, Warwickshire is set amid a gently rolling landscape criss-crossed by rivers and canals.

The Royal Shakespeare Theatres, magnificent castles, ancient churches, historic houses and glorious gardens are among a wealth of attractions.

Explore Stratford-upon-Avon, renowned for its literary connections and superb shops; historic Warwick with its magnificent castle, beautiful church and antique shops; Royal Leamington Spa, famous for its architecture and newly-refurbished Royal Pump Rooms. Not far away is Rugby with its famous school and small towns of Kenilworth, Henley-in-Arden, Shipston-on-Stour and Alcester which all have plenty to offer.

If you would like help in finding suitable farm accommodation, turn to the full listing of FHB Groups on pages 392 to 395 to find appropriate contact details for this area.

Bed and Breakfast
(and evening meal)

1 **The Byre,** Lords Hill Farm, Coalpit Lane, Wolston, Coventry CV8 3GB

Mrs Betty Gibbs
☎ 024 7654 2098
BB From £20–£27
Sleeps 6
⌚(5) ⅍ ⅄ ▬
♦♦♦♦ Silver Award

A warm welcome awaits guests to our home, a converted barn set in a quiet country lane on a 200-acre sheep/arable farm. Attractive, spacious double/twin bedrooms, 1 en suite, 2 with washbasins. Full CH, colour TV, tea/coffee tray and many extras. Numerous village pubs nearby for evening meals. Ideally situated for visiting Stratford, NEC and NAC, 15 mins from Coventry and Rugby. Non smokers only. Closed Christmas.

2 **Church Farm,** Dorsington, Stratford-upon-Avon, Warwickshire CV37 8AX

Mrs Marian J Walters
☎ 01789 720471
and 0831 504194
Fax 01789 720830
BB From £18–£20
Sleeps 14
⅄ ⌚ ⅍ ⅊ ⅀ ▬ ◉
♦♦♦

A warm welcome awaits you at our mixed working farm with lake, equestrian course and woodlands to explore. Situated in Heart of England on outskirts of quiet pretty village yet ideal for touring Stratford, Warwick, Cotswolds, NAC, NEC, Worcester and Evesham. Most bedrooms en suite, all with tea/coffee and TV. Stabling and fishing available. Pubs and restaurants 2 miles. Open all year.

3 **The Coach House,** Snowford Hall Farm, Hunningham, Royal Leamington Spa, Warwickshire CV33 9ES

Rudi Hancock
☎ 01926 632297
Fax 01926 633599
BB From £19–£22
Sleeps 6
⌚ ▬ ⅊
♦♦♦♦

A warm welcome and peaceful surroundings in converted barn farmhouse on 200-acre working farm in rolling countryside. Near the Roman Fosse Way, ideal for visiting Stratford, Warwick, Leamington, Cotswolds, NAC and NEC. 2 double rooms en suite, 1 twin room with basin and bathroom adjacent. Singles extra. CH. Full breakfast. Open all year (closed Christmas & New Year).

4 **Crandon House,** Avon Dassett, Leamington Spa, Warwickshire CV33 0AA

Deborah Lea
☎ 01295 770652
Fax 01295 770632
Mobile 07775 626458
BB From £19.50–£28
Sleeps 10
⌚(10) ⅍ ⅊ ⅀ ▬
♦♦♦♦♦ Silver Award

We offer an exceptionally high standard of accommodation and a friendly welcome on our small farm with rare breeds. Set in peaceful countryside with beautiful views. Large garden. Full CH. 5 attractive no smoking bedrooms with en suite/private facilities, colour TV, tea/coffee tray and many extras. Extensive breakfast menu. Easy access to Stratford, Warwick, Cotswolds. Located between J11 and 12 on M40 (4 miles). Closed Christmas. E-mail: crandonhouse@talk21.com

5 **Frankton Grounds Farm,** Frankton, Nr Rugby, Warwickshire CV23 9PD

Mrs Mary Pritchard
☎ 01926 632391
BB From £20–£25
EM From £10
Sleeps 4
⌚ ⅍ ▬ ⅊
Awaitng new rating

Beautifully situated in a mixed farm of horses, sheep, pedigree and commercial cattle. A warm welcome for the visitor who enjoys peace and quiet yet with the benefit of easy access to Warwick, Leamington and Stratford. 2½ miles M45. Full CH, log fires, excellent food. 1 double with bathroom, 1 twin. Open all year.

Hill Farm, Priors Hardwick, Warwickshire CV23 8SP ⑥

Simon & Angela Darbishire
☎ 01327 260338
Mobile 0410 457262
BB From £20–£30
Sleeps 4
⌂ ⌕ ⅍ ⅄ ⚘ ■ ☕ ⚶
♦♦♦

Situated in picturesque Priors Hardwick, near the borders of Oxfordshire/Northamptonshire, we offer a warm, relaxed welcome at our mixed farm in beautiful, peaceful countryside with outstanding views. Rooms have TV and tea/coffee with guests' bathroom. Excellent walks/pubs/ nearby, and well situated for Stratford, Warwick, Oxford and the NAC. Open all year except Christmas and New Year.

Hill Farm, Lewis Road, Radford Semele, Leamington Spa, Warwickshire CV31 1UX ⑦

Mrs Rebecca Gibbs
☎ 01926 337571
BB From £18–£28
Sleeps 10
⌂ ⅍ ⚘ ■
♦♦♦♦

Hill Farm is a comfortable, friendly farmhouse situated in 350 acres of mixed farmland. Excellent breakfasts, large garden, attractive double/twin/single bedrooms, some en suite, with CH and tea/coffee-making facilities. Comfortable TV lounge, quiet room, guests' bathroom. Children welcome. AA and Farm Holiday Guide award winner. Caravanning/Camping Club certificated site. Ideal for Shakespeare Country. Open all year (closed Christmas).

Holland Park Farm, Buckley Green, Henley in Arden, Nr Solihull, Warwickshire B95 5QF ⑧

Mrs Kathleen Connolly
☎/Fax 01564 792625
BB From £20–£25
Sleeps 6
⌂ ⅍ ⚶ ■
♦♦♦

A Georgian style farmhouse, set in 300 acres of peaceful farmland, including the historic grounds of 'The Mount' and other interesting walks. Large garden with pond. Livestock includes cattle, sheep and Irish Draught horses. Ideally situated in Shakespeare's country, within easy reach of Birmingham International Airport, NEC, NAC, Stratford-upon-Avon, Warwick and the Cotswolds. Open all year.

Lawford Hill Farm, Lawford Heath Lane, Nr Rugby, Warwickshire CV23 9HG ⑨

Mrs Susan Moses
☎ 01788 542001
Fax 01788 537880
BB From £22.50–£28
Sleeps 12
⌂ ⅍ ⅄ ⚘ ■ ☕ ⚶
♦♦♦♦

You will find a warm welcome at our Grade II listed Georgian farmhouse and converted stables set in an attractive garden, on a mixed family farm. Full CH, log fire, attractive double and twin bedrooms, some en suite. Fishing available. Situated two miles from Rugby. Easy access to Stratford, NAC and NEC. Open all year except Christmas and New Year.
E-mail: lawford.hill@talk21.com

Lower Watchbury Farm, Wasperton Lane, Barford, Warwickshire CV35 8DH ⑩

Valerie Eykyn
☎/Fax 01926 624772
BB From £23.50–£25
Sleeps 5
⌂(10) ⅄ ■ ⚘ ◉
♦♦♦

In the heart of Shakespeare Country, we offer you a warm welcome in our luxurious accommodation with outstanding views over Warwickshire. 1 large twin/family en suite room with lounge area, 1 double en suite, 1 small double with own bathroom. All have colour TV, tea/coffee facilities. Excellent farmhouse breakfast. Village pubs for dinners. Large garden. Warwick, Stratford, NAC, NEC and Cotswolds nearby. Open all year except Christmas.

Packington Lane Farm, Coleshill, Warwickshire B46 3JJ ⑪

Constance Harcourt
☎/Fax 01675 462228
BB From £27–£35
Sleeps 6
⌂ ⅍ ⅄ ⚘ ■
♦♦♦♦

A warm welcome awaits you when you stay in this charming 17th century farmhouse. Tastefully furnished, comfortable rooms. Full English breakfast served on fine china. Large gardens and parking on a working farm, with pleasant views over surrounding countryside. Within 4 miles of the National Exhibition Centre and Birmingham Airport. Easy access from M6 J4 and M42 J6 & 9. Open all year.

12 **The Poplars,** Mansell Farm, Newbold on Stour, Stratford on Avon, Warwickshire CV37 8BZ

Judith Spencer
☎/Fax 01789 450540
BB From £18–£25
EM From £10.50
Sleeps 5
🐕 🐾 ⚡
♦♦♦

A warm welcome awaits you on our working dairy farm. Enjoy the views of the Cotswolds from our modern farmhouse which is in easy reach of Stratford, Warwick, Oxford and NEC. 1 family and 1 twin, both en suite. All have TV, tea tray and CH. Separate lounge and dining room with log burner in winter. Good food or walk to local hostelry. Open all year except Christmas.
E-mail: RSPENCER@farming.co.uk.

13 **Shrewley Pools Farm,** Haseley, Warwickshire CV35 7HB

Mrs Cathy Dodd
☎ 01926 484315
BB From £25–£35
EM From £7.50
Sleeps 6
🐎 🐾 🎾 🛄
♦♦♦♦

Why not sample the delights of staying in a beautiful 17th century traditional farmhouse on a working stock/arable farm? Set in an acre of landscaped garden with many interesting features, including timbered barn, huge fireplaces, and beamed ceilings. 2 bedrooms, both en suite, with tea/coffee tray. Close to Warwick, Stratford-upon-Avon, the NEC and NAC. Open all year except Christmas and New Year.

14 **Sor Brook House Farm,** Horley, Banbury, Oxfordshire OX15 6BL

Yvonne Prickett
☎ 01295 738121
BB £25
EM From £15
Sleeps 4
🐕(7) ♿ 🦌 🐎 🛄 🎾 🐎
♦♦♦♦

Tea and homemade cake await you in this charming stone farmhouse with oak beams and log fires. 1 twin and 1 double, both en suite. Full CH, colour TV, tea/coffee-making facilities. Guests' own sitting and dining rooms. Large, attractive gardens, peaceful walks. Stabling available. Closed Christmas.

15 **Tallet Barn,** Yerdley Farm, Long Compton, Shipston on Stour, Warwickshire CV36 5LH

Diana Richardson
☎ 01608 684248
BB From £19–£25
Sleeps 5
🐕(6) ⚡ 🎾
♦♦♦♦

A warm welcome and comfortable rooms await you at Yerdley Farm in the recently converted Tallet Barn annex. Both rooms have en suite shower, TV, tea/coffee. On A3400, Stratford 16 miles, Oxford 22 miles. Central for PO/stores, hotel and pub. Many Cotswold attractions nearby, wonderful walking and interesting gardens to visit. Open all year.

16 **Walcote Farm,** Walcote, Haselor, Alcester, Warwickshire B49 6LY

Prim & John Finnemore
☎/Fax 01789 488264
BB From £19–£23
Sleeps 6
🐕 ⚡ ☕ 🛄
♦♦♦♦

Come and enjoy the relaxing atmosphere at our attractive 16th century oak-beamed farmhouse with inglenook fireplaces, set in a tranquil, picturesque hamlet near Stratford-upon-Avon. En suite double and twin rooms with TV/Fastext, tea/coffee-making facilities and lovely views. Full central heating with log fires in winter. Ideal for Shakespeare's properties, Warwick Castle, NEC and the Cotswolds. Closed Christmas and New Year.
E-mail: john_finnemore@csi.com

17 **Whitchurch Farm,** Wimpstone, Stratford-upon-Avon, Warwickshire CV37 8NS

Mrs Joan James
☎/Fax 01789 450275
BB From £18–£20
EM From £10.50
Sleeps 6
🐕 ⚡ 🛄 ◎
♦♦♦

Lovely Georgian farmhouse set in park-like surroundings in peaceful Stour Valley 4½ miles from Stratford. Very convenient for Warwick Castle and Shakespeare properties. Ideal for touring the Cotswolds by car or rambling. The bedrooms are large and well furnished, all with en suite bathrooms, CH and tea/coffee-making facilities. Separate dining room and sitting room for guests. Open all year (closed Christmas Day).

Self-Catering

Furzen Hill Farm Cottages, c/o Furzen Hill Farm, Cubbington Heath, Leamington Spa, Warks CV32 6QZ

Mrs Christine Whitfield
☎/Fax 01926 424791
[SC] From £120–£320
Sleep 4/7
🐕 🐎 ♿
🎗🎗🎗 *Commended*

Furzen Hill is a mixed farm. The cottage, is part of 17th century farmhouse with a large shared garden, sleeping 7. The Barn and Dairy Cottages, both recently converted, each sleep 4. Dairy Cottage has its own small garden. The Barn shares the Cottage garden. All have the use of tennis court. Situated within easy reach of NAC, NEC, Warwick and Stratford. Open all year.

The Granary, c/o Glebe Farm, Kinwarton, Alcester, Warwickshire B49 6HB

Susan Kinnersley
☎/Fax 01789 762554
[SC] From £95–£150
Sleeps 2
🎗🎗🎗 *Commended*

Off the beaten track, yet near the small market town of Alcester, this cottage retains many interesting features of the original granary combined with modern standards of warmth and comfort. The farm is bounded by the River Alne and there are a variety of attractive country walks in the area. Linen provided, colour TV. Car space. Short breaks by arrangement. Open all year.

Hipsley Farm Cottages, Hipsley Lane, Hurley, Atherstone, Warwickshire CV9 2HS 🄴

Mrs Ann Prosser
☎/Fax 01827 872437
[SC] From £240–£360
Sleep 2/4 + cots
🎗🎗🎗 – 🎗🎗🎗🎗
Highly Commended

Hipsley Farm is situated in beautiful rolling countryside. Very peaceful and quiet yet only 3 miles from jct10, M42/A5, so easy access to all the Midlands. The barns and cowshed have been carefully converted into 6 very comfortable, individually furnished cottages. Fully equipped including gas CH, colour TV, all bed linen and towels. Laundry facilities and putting green. Ample parking on site. Open all year.

Knightcote Farm Cottages, The Bake House, Knightcote, nr Leamington Spa CV33 0SF 🄴

Fiona & Craig Walker
☎ 01295 770637
Fax 01295 770135
[SC] From £310–£520
Sleep 4/6
🎗🎗🎗🎗🎗 *Highly Commended*

Escape to the quiet and historic village of Knightcote and then relax. Three award-winning barn conversions have been lavishly equipped and furnished to ensure you are cosy and comfortable. Explore the many beautiful lanes and footpaths. One cottage wheelchair friendly. Adjacent car parking. No smoking. Open all year.
E-mail: fionawalker@cwcom.net

Lawford Hill Farm, Lawford Heath Lane, Nr Rugby, Warwickshire CV23 9HG 🄴

Susan Moses
☎ 01788 542001
Fax 01788 537880
[SC] From £250–£500
Sleeps 4/8
🐕 ♿ ☕
Applied

Attractive, newly converted barns adjacent to Georgian farmhouse and garden. Many mature trees, attractive flower/shrub borders and traditional walled vegetable garden. Farm walks, fishing, golfing and sailing facilities nearby, as are the delights of Warwick, Leamington, Stratford-upon-Avon and many wonderful National Trust properties. Open all year.
E-mail: lawford.hill@talk21.com

22 Little Biggin, c/o Broadwell House Farm, Broadwell, Rugby, Warwickshire CV23 8HF

Mrs Linda Denham
☎/Fax 01926 812347
SC From £225–£350
Sleeps 4
☺(12) ⚫ 🔥 ♨ ✿
♠♠♠♠ *Commended*

Attractive stone cottage with exposed beams, well equipped and furnished, with full central heating. Radio and colour TV. Cosy double and twin bedrooms have sloping ceilings. Bathroom has shower. Gas hob, electric oven, microwave in modern kitchen. Ample parking. Outstanding views and tranquil walks. Peacefully situated. Linen, electricity and gas included. Open all year.

23 Piggery Cottages, Grey Mill Farm, Alcester Road, Wootton Wawen, Warwickshire B95 6HL

W A Ingram
☎/Fax 01564 792582
SC From £300–£600
Sleeps 6
☺(2) 🔲 ⚫ ☕ ✿
♠♠♠ – ♠♠♠♠
Highly Commended

Piggery Cottages are set in rural Warwickshire. 5 miles north of Stratford upon Avon in the village of Wootton Wawen. Both cottages are extremely well appointed, all bedrooms en suite. There is also a covered heated swimming pool, games room and gymnasium. So for the weary traveller you need look no further. Open all year.
E-mail: tony@greymillfarm.co.uk

CONFIRM BOOKINGS

Disappointments can arise from misunderstandings over the telephone.
Please write to confirm your booking.

STAY ON A FARM GIFT TOKENS

If you have enjoyed your Stay on a Farm, why not treat your friends and relatives to *Stay on a Farm* gift tokens? Available from the Bureau office (tel: 024 7669 6909), they can be redeemed against accommodation and are accepted by the majority of farms (see Index). Please check when booking to avoid disappointment.

THE 1000+ BUREAU MEMBERS OFFER A UNIQUE LINK TO CUSTOMERS ACROSS THE UK

All Bureau members belong to a local Group. Each member can refer you to an equally high quality member within the Group... or across the UK: England, Northern Ireland, Scotland, Wales.

Northamptonshire

Rockingham Forest, Nene Valley & Grand Union Canal

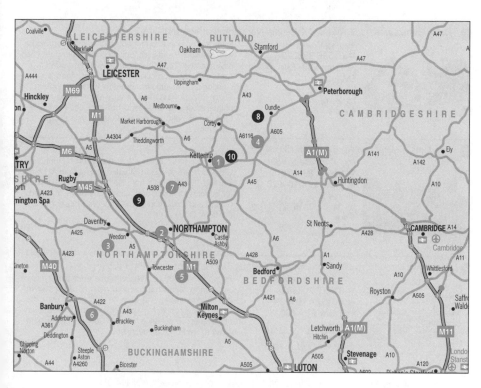

Key

1. Bed & Breakfast
1. Self-Catering
1. B&B and SC
1. Camping Barns
1. Camping & Caravanning

Northamptonshire, the county of 'squires and spires', has fine houses, monuments and churches too numerous to mention. There's Sulgrave Manor, home of George Washington's ancestors, Rockingham Castle, Boughton House, the fine Saxon church at Brixworth and, most famous of all, Althorp. The Waterways Museum at Stoke Bruerne provides a fascinating insight into the history of our canals, or take a nostalgic trip on the Nene Valley Steam Railway. The world famous motor racing circuit at Silverstone is situated in the south of the county, while a variety of gardens, antique, craft and farm shops, pubs and restaurants provide a relaxing and rewarding experience for all our visitors.

If you would like help in finding suitable farm accommodation, turn to the full listing of FHB Groups on pages 392 to 395 to find appropriate contact details for this area.

Bed and Breakfast
(and evening meal)

---

① Dairy Farm, Cranford St Andrew, Kettering, Northamptonshire NN14 4AQ

Audrey Clarke
☎ 01536 330273
🅱 From £22–£30
EM From £14
Sleeps 6
🐕 ⅙ ▣
♦♦♦♦

Enjoy a holiday in a comfortable 17th century farmhouse with oak beams and inglenook fireplaces. Four poster bed now available. Peaceful surroundings, large garden containing ancient circular dovecote. Dairy Farm is a working farm situated in a beautiful Northamptonshire village just off the A14 within easy reach of many places of interest or ideal for a restful holiday. Good farmhouse food and friendly atmosphere. Open all year except Christmas.

---

② The Elms, Kislingbury, Northampton NN7 4AH

Mrs Primrose Sanders
☎ 01604 830326
🅱 From £18.50–£20
Sleeps 5
🐕 🐾 ⅙ 🛶 ▣ 🐎
♦♦♦

A warm welcome awaits you in our Victorian farmhouse with views over the farm. Situated 2 miles from M1 junction 16 and 4 miles from Northampton. Convenient for business stopovers and touring Cotswolds, Stratford, Oxford and Cambridge. Nene Way Walk passes through the farm. Open all year.

---

③ Meadows Farm, Newnham Lane, Badby, Daventry, Northamptonshire NN11 3AA

Mrs Heather Jeffries
☎ 01327 703302
Fax 01327 703085
🅱 From £25–£30
Sleeps 4
🐕 🐾 ⅙ 🐎 ▣ 🛶
♦♦♦♦♦ Gold Award

Farmhouse recently converted from a stone barn on large arable farm commanding superb views of rolling countryside. Two bedrooms with en suite facilities and tea/coffee trays. Easy access to M1 and M40. We are 3 miles south of Daventry on the B4037, ½ mile from its junction with A361 to Banbury. Open Jan-Nov.

---

④ Pear Tree Farm, Main Street, Aldwincle, Nr Kettering, Northamptonshire NN14 3EL

Beverley Hankins
☎ 01832 720614
Fax 01832 720559
🅱 From £22
EM From £10
Sleeps 8
🐕(12) Å ⅙ 🛳 ▣ 🛶
♦♦♦♦

Pear Tree Farm is a mixed 470-acre farm consisting of cattle, sheep, poultry and arable. Comfortably furnished with relaxed family atmosphere and excellent breakfasts. Four bedrooms. Excellent for walking, birdwatching, fishing. Large garden for relaxing. Open all year except Christmas and New Year (camping Feb–Sept).

---

⑤ Spinney Lodge Farm, Forest Road, Hanslope, Milton Keynes, Buckinghamshire MK19 7DE

Mrs Christina Payne
☎ 01908 510267
🅱 From £20–£25
EM From £10
Sleeps 4
🐕(12) ⅙ 🛶 ▣
♦♦♦

Spinney Lodge is an arable, beef and sheep farm. The lovely Victorian farmhouse with its large garden and rose pergola has en suite bedrooms with colour TV and tea-making facilities. Evening meal by arrangement. M1 J15, 8 minutes, 12 minutes Northampton, 15 minutes Milton Keynes. Silverstone Circuit, Stowe Gardens and Woburn to visit in the area. Ideal base for touring. Open all year except Christmas.

Walltree House Farm, Steane, Brackley, Northamptonshire NN13 5NS   (6)

Richard & Pauline Harrison
☎ **01295 811235**
Fax **01295 811147**
Mobile **0860 913399**
BB From **£25–£30**
EM From **£15**
Sleeps 16

Our home is in the middle of nowhere but at the centre of everything. Badger woods to explore, lovely walks. Historic places to visit. Individual ground floor rooms in the courtyard now with four new additional luxury rooms, others in the adjacent licensed Victorian farmhouse. Most rooms en suite. Nearby shopping, fishing, golf, gliding, Silverstone Circuit and leisure centres. Open Feb–Nov.

Wold Farm, Old, Northampton, Northamptonshire NN6 9RJ   (7)

Anne Engler
☎ **01604 781258**
BB From **£25–£28**
Sleeps 8

♦♦♦♦ Silver Award

A friendly, informal atmosphere is offered at this 18th century farmhouse on 250-acre beef/arable farm. Main farmhouse offers attractive bedrooms. Hearty breakfast is served in oak-beamed dining room with inglenook fireplace. Relax by log fire or at snooker table. Recently converted barn provides en suite rooms overlooking pretty garden with colourful pergola. Open all year.

Self-Catering

Granary Cottage, Brook Farm, Lower Benefield, Peterborough PE8 5AE   (8)

Mrs J Singlehurst
☎ **01832 205215**
SC From **£175–£225**
Sleeps 4
🕏(4) 🜨
🐾🐾🐾 Commended

At the beginning of a gated road we offer peace and tranquillity with picturesque walks. Granary Cottage is warm, cosy and well equipped with linen provided. Close by are the historic market towns of Oundle and Stamford and the pretty village of Rockingham. Sorry no pets. Open all year.

Rye Hill Country Cottages, Rye Hill Farm, Holdenby Road, East Haddon, Northants NN6 8DH   (9)

Michael & Margaret Widdowson
☎ **01604 770990**
Fax **01604 770237**
SC From **£160–£445**
Sleeps 2/6

🐾🐾🐾🐾 Highly Commended

Children are most welcome on our delightful, peaceful smallholding. They can help feed our farm animals, collect eggs and have fun in the play area and games room. Our 5 cottages have every modern convenience combined with beams, open fires and log burning stoves. Small licensed restaurant providing good country food and cream teas. Many places of interest for all the family. Open all year. E-mail: ryehills@compuserve.com

---

Villiers Suite, Cranford Hall, Cranford, Kettering, Northamptonshire NN14 4AL   (10)

Gayle Robinson
☎ **01536 330248**
Fax **01536 330203**
SC From **£260–£300**
Sleeps 5

🐾🐾🐾 Commended

Lovely Georgian mansion in the heart of a traditional estate village which is set in parkland amidst fine gardens. Many attractive walks and drives to be taken, together with historic spots to visit and a great range of cultural activities. The Villiers Suite is a stylish, self-contained apartment within the Hall. E-mail: cranford@farmline.com

---

Cambridgeshire

The Fens & Grafham Water

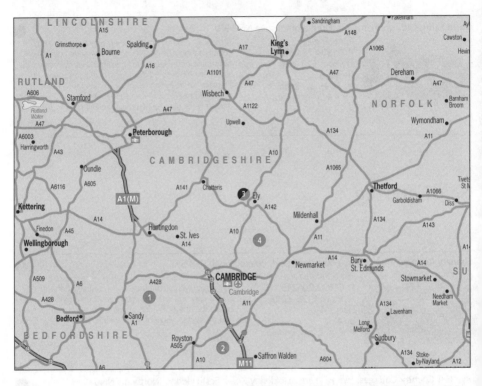

Key

 Bed & Breakfast

Self-Catering

B&B and SC

Camping Barns

Camping & Caravanning

Cambridgeshire, inspiration of Rupert Brooke, is a quintessentially English county of quiet waterways, gentle hills, lanes, pretty villages and busy towns. Best known is Cambridge itself, one of England's oldest university cities where the colleges in their architectural splendour rest near tranquil rivers overhung with willows. North of Cambridge lies the strikingly flat landscape of the Fens. For contrast there is the hustle and bustle of the modern city of Peterborough with its excellent shopping or the stately grandeur of Ely Cathedral, so-called 'Ship of the Fens'. "And is there honey still for tea?" – you never know, at our welcoming farms!

If you would like help in finding suitable farm accommodation, turn to the full listing of FHB Groups on pages 392 to 395 to find appropriate contact details for this area.

Bed and Breakfast
(and evening meal)

Gransden Lodge Farm, Little Gransden, Sandy, Bedfordshire SG19 3EB

Mrs Mary Cox
☎ 01767 677365
Fax 01767 677647
[BB] From £20–£22
Sleeps 6
☼ ⅍ 🏠 🏇
♦♦♦♦

A warm and friendly atmosphere awaits you at Gransden Lodge, where we have double, twin and single rooms with TV, clock-radio and tea/coffee-making facilities. Ample bathrooms and WCs. Dining room, also large lounge with TV. Many local pubs and restaurants for evening meals. Situated on the B1046, 10 miles west of Cambridge. London 50 miles. Also convenient for Stansted Airport (M11, J12). Open all year.

Hall Farm, Great Chishill, Nr Royston, Hertfordshire SG8 8SH

Mrs Jean Wiseman
☎/Fax 01763 838263
[BB] From £20–£30
Sleeps 6
☼ 🐾 ⅍ 🏇 🏠 ◉
Awaiting new rating

Beautiful, quiet farmhouse in secluded walled garden in a pretty hilltop village 11 miles south of Cambridge on the B1039 midway between Saffron Walden and Royston. One double en suite, one double and one twin with washbasins and share of guests' bathroom. All rooms have tea/coffee facilities, colour TV, electric blankets, hairdryers. Open all year except Christmas.

Hill House Farm, 9 Main Street, Coveney, Ely, Cambridgeshire CB6 2DJ

Hilary Nix
☎ 01353 778369
[BB] From £22–£24
Sleeps 6
☼(12) ⅍ 🏇 🏠 ◉
♦♦♦♦

Spacious Victorian farmhouse in quiet fenland village, 3 miles west of the historic cathedral city of Ely. Open views of the surrounding countryside. Easy access to Cambridge, Newmarket & Huntingdon. Wicken Fen and Welney Wildfowl Trust are nearby. 3 tastefully furnished and decorated bedrooms, all en suite (1 on ground floor). All have own entrance, colour TV, etc. Full CH. Warm welcome. Open all year except Christmas.

Spinney Abbey, Wicken, Ely, Cambridgeshire CB7 5XQ ④

Mrs Valerie Fuller
☎ 01353 720971
[BB] From £21–£22
Sleeps 6
☼(5) 🏇 🏠 ◉
♦♦♦♦

Enjoy the views across open pasture fields from our attractive Grade II listed Georgian farmhouse. Large garden with tennis court adjacent to our dairy farm which borders the National Trust nature reserve Wicken Fen. 1 double and 1 family room, both en suite and twin with private bathroom. All with TV and hospitality tray. Full CH. Guests' sitting room. Open all year except Christmas.

Please mention *Stay on a Farm* when booking

Self-Catering

Hill House Farm Cottage, 9 Main Street, Coveney, Ely, Cambs CB6 2DJ

Hill House Inn

Mrs Hilary Nix
☎ 01353 778369
⑊ From £250–£350
Sleeps 6
☼(8) ⚲ ✕ ⚓ ✿ ⊛
⚮ ⚮ ⚮ ⚮ *Highly Commended*

A tasteful barn conversion on our farm is now a comfortable cottage. Furnished and decorated to a high standard. Set in a quiet village location 3 miles west of Ely with open views of Ely Cathedral and the surrounding countryside. Ideally situated for touring Norfolk, Suffolk and Cambridgeshire. Easy access to Cambridge, Newmarket and Huntingdon. Access from A142 or A10. Regret no smoking, no pets. Open all year.

CONFIRM BOOKINGS

Disappointments can arise from misunderstandings over the telephone. Please write to confirm your booking.

USE THE INDEX

FARM HOLIDAY BUREAU

The comprehensive Index shows which farms offer access to disabled visitors; caravanning/camping facilities; the chance to participate on a working farm; stabling/grazing for visiting horses; en suite rooms; a welcome to business people; acceptance of *Stay on a Farm* gift tokens.

THE 1000+ BUREAU MEMBERS OFFER A UNIQUE LINK TO CUSTOMERS ACROSS THE UK

FARM HOLIDAY BUREAU

All Bureau members belong to a local Group. Each member can refer you to an equally high quality member within the Group... or across the UK: England, Northern Ireland, Scotland, Wales.

Norfolk

The Broads, Norfolk Coast, the Wash, Wensum Valley & Thetford Forest

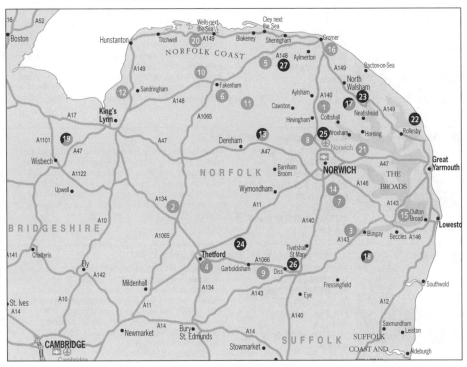

Key

① Bed & Breakfast

① Self-Catering

① B&B and SC

☐ 1 Camping Barns

▲ 1 Camping & Caravanning

Wherever you go in Norfolk, you are never far from water. There's the glorious North Norfolk coast with its nature reserves and timeless resorts such as Cromer and Wells-next-the-Sea, the picturesque flint houses of Holt and the National Trust's exquisite Blickling Hall. Further down the coast lies the traditional seaside resort of Great Yarmouth. Even inland water tends to be the theme. The famous Broads are a boating paradise of meres and rivers whose reeds are put to good use in the pretty thatched cottages of the surrounding villages. Historic Norwich lies at the confluence of the Rivers Wensum and Yare. Further west you will find royal Sandringham, Thetford, capital of forested Breckland and fascinating attractions such as the Thursford Collection and Bressingham Steam Museum.

If you would like help in finding suitable farm accommodation, turn to the full listing of FHB Groups on pages 392 to 395 to find appropriate contact details for this area.

Bed and Breakfast
(and evening meal)

---

1   **Birds Place Farm,** Back Lane, Coltishall Road, Buxton, Norwich NR10 5HD

Bill and Jenny Catchpole
☎ **01603 279585**
BB **From £19–£24**
EM From £15
Sleeps 6
⛔(8) ✝ ♿
♦♦♦♦

Small family farm in the Bure Valley in beautiful Broadland countryside. Our 17th century farmhouse is licensed and we offer excellent cuisine, much of the produce home grown. Bedrooms comprise of 1 family and 1 double room en suite, 1 single with private bathroom, all with TV and tea/coffee-making facilities. We have public footpaths and fishing nearby. Closed Christmas and New Year.

---

2   **Colveston Manor,** Mundford, Thetford, Norfolk IP26 5HU

Mrs Wendy Allingham
☎ **01842 878218**
Fax 01842 879218
BB **From £22.50–£27.50**
EM From £15
Sleeps 7
⛔(12)✝♿🗲🔥🍴♿✿◉
♦♦♦♦

Peaceful 18th century farmhouse in delightful setting in heart of Breckland. Attractive bedrooms, some en suite. We specialise in delicious cooking from the Aga, using home-grown vegetables. NT properties, cathedrals, gardens and coast within easy reach. Brochure showing location available on request. Open all year. See colour ad on page 39.

---

3   **Earsham Park Farm,** Harleston Road, Earsham, Bungay, Suffolk NR35 2AQ

Mrs Bobbie Watchorn
☎ **01986 892180**
Fax 01986 894796
BB **From £21–£35**
EM £16
Sleeps 6
⛔✝ ⊞ ♿ ✿✕✗ ◉
♦♦♦♦

Delightful, quiet and friendly farmhouse with panoramic views over the Waveney Valley. Spacious and elegantly furnished en suite rooms (one four-poster bed) with extensive facilities. CH. Guests are welcome to use the large gardens and lovely farm walks. Indulge in the delicious, home produced, huge Norfolk breakfasts. Evening meal available at certain times. Easy access coast/Norwich. Open all year.
E-mail: watchorn_s@hotmail.com

---

4   **East Farm,** Euston Road, Barnham, Thetford, Norfolk IP24 2PB

Margaret Heading
☎ **01842 890231**
Fax 01842 890457
BB **From £22–£25**
Sleeps 4
⛔✝ ♿ ◉
♦♦♦♦

Relax and enjoy the comfort and warm welcome at East Farm in the village of Barnham. We're a 1,000-acre arable farm with beef and sheep and plenty of wildlife on the edge of Breckland on Norfolk/Suffolk border between Thetford and Bury St Edmunds. A grey flint-faced house in peaceful surroundings with superb views. Spacious heated rooms with en suite bathrooms. Full English breakfast from local produce. Open all year except Jan–Feb.

---

5   **Hempstead Hall,** Holt, Norfolk NR25 6TN

Lynda-Lee Mack
☎ **01263 712224**
BB **From £20–£25**
Sleeps 6
⛔(3) ✕ ✝ ⚬ ✿
Awaiting new rating

Attractive 19th century flint farmhouse peacefully set in beautiful surroundings. 300 acre arable farm with ducks, donkey, ponies, large gardens and country walks. Close to the Georgian town of Holt and the North Norfolk coast and its many attractions including steam train rides and boat trips to Blakeney Point Seal Sanctuary. En suite family room, double with private bathroom. Colour TV. Tea/coffee-making facilities in rooms. Closed Christmas and New Year.

Highfield Farm, Great Ryburgh, Fakenham, Norfolk NR21 7AL ⑥

Mrs E Savory
☎ 01328 829249
Fax 01328 829422
BB From £20–£25
EM from £13.50
Sleeps 6
♋(12) ✗ 🎍 💼 ⛵ ◉
♦♦♦♦

Spacious, elegant and comfortable Georgian-style house 10 miles from the coast, set deep in countryside amidst 500 acres of rolling farmland. Central for historic houses and Pensthorpe. Ideal for birdwatchers. Twin room with en suite. Double and twin rooms with washbasin. Guests' sitting room and dining room, log fires, CH. Evening meals by arrangement. Grass tennis court and croquet lawn, horse riding locally. Closed Christmas & New Year.
E-mail:jegshighfield@onet.co.uk

Hillside Farm, Welbeck Road, Brooke, near Norwich, Norfolk NR15 1AU ⑦

Mrs Carolyn Holl
☎/Fax 01508 550260
BB From £18–£25
EM From £12.50
Sleeps 4
♋ 🐏 💼 ♐ 🎍 ⛵ ◉
♦♦♦♦

This is a 350-acre arable and stock farm. A beautiful 16th century thatched and timber-framed house situated in a pretty village, 7 miles south of Norwich, within easy reach of coast and Broads. One twin/family room, 1 double/family room, both with private facilities. Large games barn with snooker, pool and table tennis. Five acre private lake for coarse fishing. Relaxed family atmosphere. Open all year except Christmas.

Lower Farm, Horsford, Norwich, Norfolk NR10 3AW ⑧

Mrs Marion Jones
☎ 01603 891291
BB From £19–£30
Sleeps 6
♋ ✗ 💼

♦♦♦♦ Silver Award

Enjoy the comfort and warm welcome at Lower Farm, a mixed farm with sheep and cattle. Beautiful old farmhouse ideal for Norwich, the coast and Broads. Attractive, spacious accommodation in two en suite rooms (1 family, 1 double) with TV and beverage trays. Superb views traditional farmhouse fayre. Cot, babysitting service. Open all year.

Malting Farm, Blo Norton Road, South Lopham, Diss, Norfolk IP22 2HT ⑨

Cynthia Huggins
☎ 01379 687201
BB From £21
Sleeps 6
♋ ✗ 💼 🎍
♦♦♦

Situated on Norfolk/Suffolk border amid open countryside. A working dairy farm with some farmyard pets. Farmhouse is Elizabethan timber-framed (inside) with inglenook fireplaces. Central heating. Some four poster beds, some en suite. Easy reach Norfolk Broads, Norwich, Cambridge, Bressingham Steam Museum & Gardens. Cynthia is a keen craftswoman in patchwork, quilting, embroidery and spinning. Closed Christmas & New Year.

Manor Farm, Sculthorpe, Fakenham, Norfolk NR21 9NJ ⑩

Mrs Carol Pointer
☎ 01328 862185
Fax 01328 862033
BB From £20–£30
Sleeps 6
💼 ♐
♦♦♦♦

Manor Farm offers a warm welcome in comfortable surroundings. Two double en suite rooms, one double with private bathroom all with TV and tea/coffee-making facilities. This working mixed farm is within easy reach of coast and ideal for walking, cycling and birdwatching. Bowling green and fishing available.

Manor Farm, Hall Lane, Wood Norton, East Dereham, Norfolk NR20 5BE ⑪

Mrs Kathleen Crowe
☎ 01362 683231
BB From £20
EM From £10
Sleeps 5
♋(10) ✗ 💼
♦♦♦♦

This is a 380-acre family-run mixed farm in a rural location. Ideal centre for visiting the Norfolk coast, small market towns, Norwich and National Trust properties. The 16th century Grade II listed farmhouse has one double en suite and one twin and one single, both with private facilities. Open Mar–Dec.

12 Marsh Farm, Wolferton, King's Lynn, Norfolk PE31 6HB

Keith Larrington
☎ 01485 540265
Fax 01485 543143
BB From £20–£25
Sleeps 6
⬚ 🐎 ✂ 🅿
♦♦♦♦

You can be assured of a warm welcome at our comfortable and relaxing farmhouse, with large garden, in the quiet village of Wolferton. This working arable farm is ideally situated for walking and exploring the countryside and North Norfolk coast. RSPB reserves nearby. Open all year except Christmas and Jan.
E-mail: keith.larrington@farmline.com

13 Park Farm, Bylaugh, East Dereham, Norfolk NR20 4QE

Mrs Jenny Lake
☎ 01362 688584
BB From £17–£20
EM From £8.50
Sleeps 6
⬚ ✂ 🅿 ⊚
♦♦♦♦

Charming old family farmhouse with picturesque setting in Wensum Valley, ideally situated for exploring the Norfolk countryside and visits to Norwich, the Norfolk Broads and North Norfolk coast. One large family room, one double and one twin, all en suite. Lounge with colour TV, dining room with inglenook. Children welcome, sorry no pets. Open all year.

14 Salamanca Farm Guest House, 116–118 Norwich Road, Stoke Holy Cross, Norwich, Norfolk NR14 8QJ

Roy & Barbara Harrold
☎ 01508 492322
BB From £18–£24
Sleeps 8
⬚(6) ✂ 🅿 ⊚
♦♦♦

"Real experience of English hospitality" – "All we could have asked for" – just two comments from our visitors' book. The Harrold family have welcomed guests to their farm for 20 years. 4 miles from the cathedral city of Norwich, the valley of the River Tas, with the mill where Colmans began producing mustard, provides an attractive holiday base. All rooms have private facilities. Open 15 Jan–15 Dec. See colour ad on page 39.

15 Shrublands Farm, Burgh St Peter, nr Beccles, Suffolk NR34 0BB

Mrs Rachel Clarke
☎/Fax 01502 677241
BB From £20
Sleeps 6
⬚(10) ✂ 🅿
♦♦♦♦

Tranquillity, peaceful surroundings and a warm welcome at this attractive, homely farmhouse. Set in 550 acres of mixed working farmland in the Waveney Valley. Ideal base for touring Norfolk/Suffolk. 2 double en suite, 1 twin with private facilities, all with colour satellite TV and tea/coffee-making facilities. Excellent choice of home-cooked breakfast. Tennis court available. Swimming pool and food at River Centre nearby. Open all year except Christmas.

16 Shrublands Farm, Northrepps, Cromer, Norfolk NR27 0AA

Mrs Ann Youngman
☎/Fax 01263 579297
BB From £21–£27
EM From £11
Sleeps 6
⬚(12) 🎣 Å ⚓ ✂ ☂ 🅿 ⊚
♦♦♦♦

A warm welcome awaits you at Shrublands Farm, an arable farm set in the village of Northrepps, 2½ miles SE of Cromer and 20 miles north of Norwich. The Victorian/Edwardian house has 1 twin and 1 double room with private bathrooms and 1 twin en suite. All rooms have colour TV and tea/coffee facilities. Separate sitting room and dining room for guests. Full CH, log fires in chilly weather. Sorry, no pets. Evening meal by arrangement. Closed Christmas. E-mail: youngman@farming.co.uk

17 Sloley Farm, Sloley, Norwich, Norfolk NR12 8HJ

Mrs Ann Jones
☎ 01692 536281
Fax 01692 535162
BB From £19–£20
Sleeps 4
⬚(10) ✂ Å ⚓ 🅿 ⊚
♦♦♦♦

A warm welcome awaits you in our comfortable farmhouse, ideally situated to explore the nearby Norfolk Broads and the coast with its many attractions. One double/twin en suite, one double with private bathroom. All rooms have colour TV, tea/coffee facilities. Full central heating. Open all year except Christmas and New Year.
E-mail: sloley@farmhotel.u-net.com

South Elmham Hall, St Cross, Harleston, Norfolk IP20 0PZ

Mrs Jo Sanderson
☎ 01986 782526
Fax 01986 782203
BB From £18–£40
Sleeps 6
🐾(10) 🐴 ⊞ ✂ ☕ 🍴 ▤ ♉ 🌐
♦♦♦♦

Moated former bishop's palace with large gardens. Mixed farm, peaceful location with rare cattle and farm trails in historic landscape. Tastefully furnished comfortable rooms with tea/coffee tray. Kingsize bed, double antique brass bed and twin bedded rooms all with en suite facilities, colour TV and views of the farm and garden. Guests' lounge and dining room, full CH. Open Easter–end Dec.
E-mail: jo.sanderson@btinternet.com

Stratton Farm, West Drove North, Walton Highway, Norfolk PE14 7DP

Derek & Sue King
☎ 01945 880162
BB From £22.50–£25
Sleeps 6
♿🐾(7) ✂ 🐴 ☕ 🍴 ▤ ♉ 🌐
♦♦♦♦

We invite you to stay in our peaceful farm and meet the cows and calves or collect the bantam eggs for your breakfast. Our hedgerows abound with songbirds and our lake teams with fish. Relax in the heated (covered) swimming pool then indulge yourself with home produced sausages, bacon, eggs, bread and marmalades for breakfast. All bedrooms are ground floor with en suite facilities. 10% discount for three nights or more. Open all year (including Christmas).

Whitehall Farm, Burnham Thorpe, King's Lynn, Norfolk PE31 8HN ⑳

Valerie Southerland
☎/Fax 01328 738416
BB From £20
Sleeps 6
🐾🐴 Å ⊞ ▤
♦♦♦

Situated about 2 miles from the North Norfolk coast, Whitehall Farm is a working arable farm with a friendly family atmosphere. Comfortable rooms offering TV, tea/coffee and private bathrooms. Ample parking available and use of the garden and meadow. Valerie and Barry Southerland look forward to ensuring your stay is an enjoyable experience that you will want to repeat. Open all year.

Witton Hall Farm, Witton, Norwich, Norfolk NR13 5DN ㉑

Jane Mack
☎ 01603 714580
BB From £20–£40
Sleeps 6
🐾 ▤ 🌐
♦♦♦

This elegant Georgian farmhouse on a dairy and arable farm is set in the heart of Norfolk, 5 miles east of Norwich and 12 miles from the coast, and 3 miles from the Broads. There are two acres of mature garden. Spacious bedrooms, all with TV and en suite bathrooms. Open all year.

Self-Catering

Burnley Hall, East Somerton, Great Yarmouth NR29 4DU ㉒

Penny Beard
☎ 01493 393206
Fax 01493 393745
SC From £250–£600
Sleeps 4–8 + cot
🐾🐴 Å ▤ ♉ 🐴 🌐
🐾🐾🐾 *Up to Highly Commended*

Arable/livestock farm between Norfolk Broads and sea. We welcome families with children and well behaved dogs to our 4 holiday homes (own gardens). Equipped to a high standard with comfortable beds (linen, towels, heat, electricity included). Three-mile private beach, nature reserve, footpaths, bicycles, access to Broads. Weekend breaks. Brochure on request. Open all year.
E-mail: penny@burnleyhall.co.uk

19 Carysfort and Carysfort Too, Stratton Farm, West Drove North, Walton Highway, Norfolk PE14 7DP

Derek & Sue King
☎ 01945 880162
🅂🄲 From £165–£370
Sleeps 2/4
🏡 🐕(8) ⅟ ✎ ☇ 🎒 ⚓ 🎾 ⊚
🍃🍃🍃🍃 Highly Commended

We welcome you to our beautiful farm cottages where all 4 bedrooms have en suite bathrooms. Relax in deep comfort, peace and seclusion. You may meet the calves or walk for miles with only bird song for company. Come and catch a carp from the lake or plunge into our heated swimming pool. We can guarantee you a perfect holiday. Free secure parking for your car. Open all year including Christmas.

23 Dairy Farm Cottages, Dilham, North Walsham, Norfolk NR28 9PZ

Annabel Paterson
☎ 01692 535178
Fax 01692 536723
🅂🄲 From £200–£1100
Sleep 4–11 + cot
🏡 🐕 🐎 🄴 🎒 ⚓
🍃🍃🍃🍃 – 🍃🍃🍃🍃🍃
Highly Commended

Relax at Dairy Farm in Broadland, mixed arable and stock farm. Superb walks, acres of woodland, Victorian folly – Dilham Islands. 15 minutes to coast. Top quality accommodation, each cottage sleeps 4 to 11, all bedrooms en suite. Full kitchen facilities, laundry facilities, games room, secure play area, wheelchair access. Pets welcome. Colour brochure available. Open all year.

24 Dolphin Lodge, Roudham Farm, Roudham, East Harling, Norfolk NR16 2RJ

Mr & Mrs T Jolly
☎ 01953 717126
Fax 01953 718593
🅂🄲 From £235–£390
Sleeps 5 + cot
🐎 ⅟ ⚓ ☞ ⊚
🍃🍃🍃🍃 Highly Commended

Let us offer you a country retreat! Conveniently situated in central East Anglia, our cottages are home-from-home. Beautifully restored with beams and woodburning stoves, set in large garden by Thetford Forest. Carefully prepared for you and fully equipped, CH, Aga, washing machine, tumble drier, fridge, microwave, colour TV. Each cottage sleeps 5 in two bedrooms. Many local attractions. Ideal for relaxation or sightseeing. Open all year.
E-mail: jolly@roundhamf.demon.co.uk

18 Hall Farm Cottage, St Cross, Harleston, Norfolk IP20 0PZ

Mrs Jo Sanderson
☎ 01986 782526
Fax 01986 782203
🅂🄲 From £245–£450
Sleeps 6/8
🐎 🐓 🄴 ☞ 🎒 ⚓ 🎾
🍃🍃🍃 Commended

Pretty cottage on conservation award-winning farm. Easy reach of Southwold, Norwich and market towns with good antique shops. Free access to our historic farm walks, horse riding nearby. Large fenced garden, raised pond, conservatory, washing machine, TV/video, woodburner, Aga, CH, games. Electricity, logs and linen free. Cot available. Open all year.
E-mail: jo.sanderson@bt.internet.com

13 Meadow View, Park Farm, Bylaugh, East Dereham, Norfolk NR20 4QE

Mrs Jenny Lake
☎ 01362 688584
🅂🄲 From £110–£170
EM From £8.50
Sleeps 2/3
🐎 ⊚
🍃🍃🍃 Commended

Attached to charming old family farmhouse with picturesque setting in Wensum Valley, Meadow View is a comfortable, well equipped one bedroom bungalow with lovely countryside views. Sleeps 2 adults plus cot/child's bed and includes living room, kitchen, bathroom, colour TV and heating. Evening meals available next door served in dining room with inglenook. Children welcome, sorry no pets. Linen provided and laundry service. Open all year.

17 Piggery Cottage, Sloley Farm, Sloley, Norwich NR12 8HJ

Ann Jones
☎ 01692 536281
Fax 01692 535162
🅂🄲 From £170–£200
Sleeps 2 + cot
🐎 🐓 ⅟ 🄰 ⊕ ⚓ ⊚
🍃🍃🍃 Highly Commended

We welcome you to our beautiful farm, bungalow, ideally situated to explore the nearby Norfolk Broads and the coast with its many attractions. One double bedroom with twin/double beds, shower room/WC. Open plan kitchen/sitting/dinning room. Superbly equipped, wheelchair access. Electricity, towels, linen included. Open all year. E-mail: sloley@farmhotel.u-net.com

---

Spixworth Hall Cottages, Grange Farm, Buxton Road, Spixworth, Norwich NR10 3PR   **25**

Sheelah Cook
☎ 01603 898190
Fax 01603 897176
SC From £190–£550
Sleeps 4–8
🐴 🐎 👜 🎾
🐾 🐾 🐾 🐾 *Up to Highly Commended*

These cottages are ideal for exploring Norwich, the Broads and the coast. Situated in seclusion on the farm, they are very well equipped and furnished, with log fires, attractive gardens, games room and play area. We offer a warm welcome, farm and woodland walks, swimming, tennis and fishing, and space to relax and unwind. Brochure available. Open all year.
E-mail: hallcottages@talk21.com

Walcot Green Farm Cottage, Diss, Norfolk IP22 3SU   **26**

Nannette Catchpole
☎/Fax 01379 652806
SC From £230–£365
Sleeps 6
🐴 🖤 👜
🐾 🐾 🐾 *Commended*

Set in peaceful, idyllic countryside, central for exploring Norfolk and Suffolk's many attractions, this tastefully converted and well-equipped cottage is close to the pleasant market town of Diss. Spacious, safe garden and use of indoor swimming pool make for a relaxing holiday. Family room, one bunk, one single. Bed linen, towels, electricity and CH all included. Sorry no pets and no smoking. Colour brochure. Open Easter–Nov.

Wood Farm Cottages, Plumstead Road, Edgefield, Melton Constable, Norfolk NR24 2AQ   **27**

Diana Elsby
☎/Fax 01263 587347
SC From £150–£525
Sleeps 2–6
👜 🐴 🐎 👜
🐾 🐾 🐾 🐾 *Up to Highly Commended*

Hidden down a country lane, discover 8 converted barns and stables situated in a secluded, unspoilt 5-acre site. Many original features including beams and exposed flint walls. These clean, spacious cottages are very well equipped, tastefully furnished and impeccably maintained. Wood Farm offers quiet country walks, a superb children's play area and magnificent views. Detailed brochure. Open all year. E-mail: info@wood-farm.com

---

Our farms offer a range of facilities that are illustrated by symbols in each entry.
Turn to page 14 for an explanation of the symbols.

CONFIRM BOOKINGS

Disappointments can arise from misunderstandings over the telephone.
Please write to confirm your booking.

FARM HOLIDAY BUREAU

Our Internet address is
http://www.webscape.co.uk/farmaccom/

Suffolk

Constable Country, Waveney Valley, Suffolk Coast & Heaths

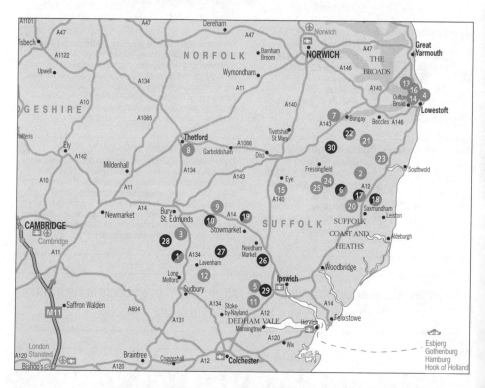

Key

- ① Bed & Breakfast
- ① Self-Catering
- ① B&B and SC
- 1 Camping Barns
- ▲ Camping & Caravanning

This beautiful, unspoilt county was the inspiration of the artists Thomas Gainsborough and John Constable who so brilliantly captured its churches, lanes, mills and farms. Suffolk is famed for its half-timbered market towns and villages – Bury St Edmunds, Sudbury, Long Melford and Lavenham, to name a few. The heritage coast and heathland are a birdwatcher's paradise and the whole county offers easy cycling and excellent walking. Oulton Broad and the Rivers Deben and Orwell are ideal for boating. For a spot of culture, take in the Aldeburgh Festival or visit stately Ickworth House and Somerleyton Hall. Suffolk has something for everyone.

If you would like help in finding suitable farm accommodation, turn to the full listing of FHB Groups on pages 392 to 395 to find appropriate contact details for this area.

Bed and Breakfast
(and evening meal)

Brighthouse Farm, Melford Road, Lawshall, near Bury St Edmunds, Suffolk IP29 4PX

Mr & Mrs Truin
☎/Fax **01284 830385**
BB From **£18–£25**
Sleeps 6
🐎 ⅃ ⅄ ⅄ 🐕 ♞ ♟ 💼 ⅄
♦♦♦♦

Timbered Georgian farmhouse, set in beautiful surroundings of the Suffolk countryside, 3 acres of picturesque gardens. We offer homely accommodation. Centrally heated throughout, log fires in TV room in winter. Two double rooms, one twin, all with en suite facilities. Historic Bury St. Edmunds/Lavenham close by. Good restaurants locally. Open all year.

Broad Oak Farm, Bramfield, Halesworth, Suffolk IP19 9AB

Mrs Patricia Kemsley
☎ **01986 784232**
BB From **£18–£24**
Sleeps 6
🐎 🐕 ♞ 💼 ⅄ ◎
♦♦♦♦

Enjoy the peace and quiet of a dairy farm, where the countryside meets the North-East Heritage Coast, only 8 miles from Southwold. Relax in our carefully modernised and spacious 16th century farmhouse, surrounded by attractive gardens and meadowland. Tennis court. One double and 2 twin rooms (2 en suite and 1 private bathroom). Separate guests' sitting room and beautiful beamed dining room. Good home cooking (EM by arrangement). Friendly, informal atmosphere. Bramfield village is on A144. Open all year.

Church Farm, Bradfield Combust, Bury St Edmunds, Suffolk IP30 0LW

Ruth Williamson
☎ **01284 386333**
BB From **£20–£25**
Sleeps 4
🐎(6) 🐕 ⅄ ♟
♦♦♦♦

Relax at our homely 18th century flint farmhouse on our 300-acre fruit farm. Guests are welcome to wander in the orchards and sample our strawberries and raspberries. Ideal base for visiting Bury St Edmunds, Lavenham, Cambridge and Newmarket. One double en suite and one twin, both comfortably furnished. Guests' lounge with log fire. Supper can be taken at the adjacent pub. Open all year.

Church Farm, Corton, Nr Lowestoft, Suffolk NR32 5HX

Elisabeth Edwards
☎ **01502 730359**
Fax **01502 733426**
BB **£20**
Sleeps 6
⅄ ⅄ 🐕 ⅄ ♟ ◎
♦♦♦♦♦

A warm welcome awaits you to relax in our comfortable Victorian farmhouse on the most easterly farm in Britain. Within easy reach of the rural beach and clifftop walks, convenient driving distance for the Norfolk Broads, the Suffolk Heritage Coast and the fine city of Norwich. Double bedded en suite rooms. Quiet garden, ample parking. Non-smoking. Selected for *'Which' Good Bed & Breakfast Guide* and mentioned in London's *Time Out* magazine. Tourist Board International Host. Open Mar–Nov.

College Farm, Hintlesham, Ipswich, Suffolk IP8 3NT

Mrs Rosemary Bryce
☎/Fax **01473 652253**
BB From **£18–£25**
Sleeps 6
🐎(12) ♟ ⅄ ♟ ◎
♦♦♦♦

Relax at our peaceful 500-year-old beamed farmhouse on 600-acre farm. Comfortable rooms, hearty breakfasts and a warm welcome. Three bedrooms (1 double en suite, 1 double/twin and 1 single) furnished to high standards with TV, CH, tea/coffee. Close to 'Constable Country' and Suffolk's coast. Country walks with golf and riding nearby. Open Jan–mid Dec. E-mail: bryce1@agripro.co.uk

6 Colston Hall, Badingham, nr Framlingham, Woodbridge, Suffolk IP13 8LB

John & Liz Bellefontaine
☎ 01728 638375
Fax 01728 638084
🅱🅱 From £20–£30
Sleeps 12
🐴 ⚡ ⚓ ⛟ 🄫
♦♦♦

We are looking forward to meeting you. Whether you choose the 'Little Maid's Room' in our Elizabethan farmhouse, or the 'Hayloft' in the stable, you will escape the rush and tear of everyday life. Our peaceful home offers you beautiful en suite bedrooms amidst a wealth of beams. We boast excellent food, ground floor rooms, fishing, indoor bowls and Easter lambs. Open all year.

7 Earsham Park Farm, Harleston Road, Earsham, Bungay, Suffolk NR35 2AQ

Mrs Bobbie Watchorn
☎ 01986 892180
Fax 01986 894796
🅱🅱 From £21–£35
EM £16
Sleeps 6
🐴 ⚡ ⚓ 🄫 🐕 🐎 🄫
♦♦♦♦

Delightful, quiet and friendly farmhouse with panoramic views over the Waveney Valley. Spacious and elegantly furnished en suite rooms (one four-poster bed) with extensive facilities. CH. Guests are welcome to use the large gardens and lovely farm walks. Indulge in the delicious, home produced, huge Norfolk breakfasts. Evening meal available at certain times. Easy access coast/Norwich. Open all year.
E-mail: watchorn_s@hotmail.com

8 East Farm, Euston Road, Barnham, Thetford, Norfolk IP24 2PB

Margaret Heading
☎ 01842 890231
Fax 01842 890457
🅱🅱 From £22–£25
Sleeps 4
🐴 ⚡ ⚓ 🄫
♦♦♦♦

Relax and enjoy the comfort and warm welcome at East Farm in the village of Barnham. We're a 1,000-acre arable farm with beef and sheep and plenty of wildlife on the edge of Breckland on Norfolk/Suffolk border between Thetford and Bury St Edmunds. A grey flint-faced house in peaceful surroundings with superb views. Spacious heated rooms with en suite bathrooms. Full English breakfast from local produce. Open all year except Jan–Feb.

9 Elmswell Hall, Elmswell, Bury St Edmunds, Suffolk IP30 9EN

Kate Over
☎/Fax 01359 240215
🅱🅱 From £20–£25
Sleeps 4
🐴 ⚓ 🐎 🄫
♦♦♦♦

A fine Georgian house set in open countryside. Large heated rooms with tea/coffee-making facilities and colour TV. Separate lounge with open log fire, hearty breakfasts, relaxed family atmosphere. Easy access A14 (Cambridge, Lavenham, Felixstowe) for touring. One family/double and 1 twin, both en suite. Open all year.

10 Grange Farm, Woolpit, Bury St Edmunds, Suffolk IP30 9RG

Kathy Parker
☎ 01359 241143
Fax 01359 244296
🅱🅱 From £21–£25
Sleeps 6
🐴 ⚡ 🄫 Å 🛋 ⛟ ⚓
♦♦♦

Grange Farm is a Grade II listed Victorian house set in the heart of Suffolk, but only 1 mile from the A14 giving easy access. Ideal centre for exploring tranquil Suffolk villages or larger historic towns of Bury St Edmunds, Sudbury, Ely and Cambridge. Two en suite rooms and one with private bath/WC, all with TV and tea/coffee facilities. Guests' lounge and dining room with period furniture. Open all year except Christmas.
E-mail: grangefarm@btinternet.com

11 Grove Farm House, Little Wenham, via Colchester, Essex CO7 6QB

Mrs Monica Collins
☎/Fax 01473 310341
🅱🅱 From £18
EM From £7.50–£12
Sleeps 5
🄫(12) 🄫 ⚡ 🄫 ⚓ 🐎 🄫
♦♦♦♦ Silver Award

Leave stress behind and enjoy warm hospitality in our 15th century farmhouse. Comfortable, centrally heated accommodation in 1 double, 1 twin and 1 single room all attractively furnished and overlooking open countryside. Cosy lounge with TV and charming dining room in which to enjoy excellent home-cooked meals. 1 mile off A12 giving easy access to Constable Country, Ipswich, Harwich. Open mid Jan–Dec.

The Hall, Milden, Nr Lavenham, Sudbury, Suffolk CO10 9NY   (12)

Juliet & Christopher Hawkins
☎/Fax 01787 247235
[BB] From £20–£30
EM From £12
Sleeps 6
ちπℋ⚒ 🛍
♦♦♦

Spacious 16th century hall farmhouse, peacefully surrounded by walled garden, flower meadows, ancient barns and hedged countryside. Explore farm nature trails around award winning woodland, castle earthworks, ponds and museum. Visit nearby historic Lavenham and 'Constable Country'. Evening meals of wild game, homegrown meat, fruit and vegetables. Relaxed family atmosphere. Open all year except Christmas.
E-mail: gjb53@dial.pipex.com

Hall Farm, Jay Lane/Church Lane, Lound, Lowestoft, Suffolk NR32 5LJ   (13)

Judith Ashley
☎ 01502 730415
[BB] From £16–£25
Sleeps 6
ちπℋ⚒ 🛍 ◉
♦♦♦♦

Share our peaceful, traditional Suffolk farmhouse 1½ miles from sea on 101-acre arable farm. Very clean, comfortable accommodation in one double and one family room, both with en suite facilities and one pretty single. All rooms have tea/coffee. Excellent breakfast with our own farm eggs. Beamed lounge, colour TV and log fire. Convenient for Broads. Open Mar–Oct. See colour ad on page 40.
E-mail: jashley@compuserve.com

Laurel Farm, Hall Lane, Oulton, Lowestoft, Suffolk NR32 5DL   (14)

Janet Hodgkin
☎/Fax 01502 568724
[BB] From £21–£26
Sleeps 6
ち(10) ⚒ 🛍 π ℋ ◉
♦♦♦♦

Spacious Georgian farmhouse set in peaceful gardens of colourful shrubs and crinkly-crankly walls. One double en suite, one double and one twin each with private bathroom. Drawing room and conservatory for guest's use. Close to sandy beaches, Oulton Broad and historic fishing port of Lowestoft. Waymarked walks. Open all year.

Moat Farm, Thorndon, Eye, Suffolk IP23 7LX   (15)

Janet & Gerald Edgecombe
☎/Fax 01379 678437
[BB] From £18–£21
Sleeps 4
ち⚒ 🛍
♦♦♦

Moat Farm is a tastefully decorated Suffolk farmhouse containing oak beams and an inglenook fire place and set in large gardens. Livestock includes pigs and horses. Village pub and local restaurants. Rooms have colour TV & tea/coffee-making facilities. The coast, Norwich, Bressingham Gardens and Thornham walks within easy driving distance. Open all year.
E-mail: geralde@clara.co.uk

Oak Farm, Market Lane, Blundeston, Lowestoft, Suffolk NR32 5AP   (16)

Julie and Keith Cooper
☎ 01502 731622
[BB] From £16–£21
Sleeps 4
ちπℋ⚒ π 🛍
♦♦♦

140-acre mixed farm set in peaceful countryside crossed by the Waveney Way footpath and 1½ miles from the sea. This Victorian house was originally farm cottages. We take a pride in our breakfast and local pubs offer other meals. Guests' stairs lead to a double and a twin room and a guests' bathroom. Tea/coffee facilities and colour TV in rooms. Children very welcome – reductions under 14. Closed Christmas & New Year.

Park Farm, Sibton, Saxmundham, Suffolk IP17 2LZ   (17)

Margaret Gray
☎ 01728 668324
Fax 01728 668564
[BB] From £19–£22
EM From £14
Sleeps 6
ち🛍 π ℋ ◉
♦♦♦♦

Enjoy friendly farmhouse hospitality at its best in our spacious 18th century house close to Heritage Coast. English breakfast and 3-course dinners imaginatively cooked from local produce. All tastes and special diets catered for. Two twins en suite, one double with private bathroom, all with tea/coffee. Ideal for birdwatching, sightseeing or relaxing. Closed Christmas.
E-mail: margaret.gray@btinternet.com

18 Priory Farm, Priory Lane, Darsham, Saxmundham, Suffolk IP17 3QD

Suzanne Bloomfield
☎ 01728 668459
Fax 01728 668744
BB From £20–£25
Sleeps 4
�(10) ⚬ 🐿 🏺 ◉
♦♦♦

Comfortable 17th century farmhouse situated in peaceful countryside. An ideal base for exploring the Suffolk coast and heathlands and other numerous local attractions. Excellent pubs and restaurants nearby. 1 double, 1 twin, each with private facilities, tea/coffee making in all bedrooms. Separate guests' dining room. Cycle hire available at the farm. Open Mar–Oct.

---

19 Red House Farm, Station Road, Haughley, Nr Stowmarket, Suffolk IP14 3QP

Mrs Mary Noy
☎ 01449 673323
Fax 01449 675413
BB From £22–£25
Sleeps 6
�(8) ⚬ 🏇 🐿 🏺 ◉
♦♦♦♦

A warm welcome and homely atmosphere awaits you at our attractive farmhouse set in the beautiful surroundings of mid Suffolk. Comfortably furnished bedrooms with en suite shower rooms, tea/coffee-making facilities. One double, one twin and two single rooms. CH. Guests' own lounge with TV and dining room. Ideal location for exploring, walking, cycling and birdwatching. No smoking or pets. Open all year except Christmas.

---

20 Rendham Hall, Rendham, Saxmundham, Suffolk IP17 2AW

Mrs Collette Strachan
☎ 01728 663440
Fax 01728 663245
BB From £20–£25
Sleeps 5/6
� ⚬ 🏺 🎋
♦♦

Escape to our green and pleasant land and enjoy our peace and warm hospitality. Meet our Shetland ponies and their foals – all characters. Explore the history and cultural pursuits of the Heritage Coast. Relax in beautiful, large south-facing rooms (double/family) overlooking the grazing for our milking herd. Large lounge and dinning room, traditionally furnished. Excellent pubs/restaurants nearby. Open all year. E-mail: strachan@anglianet.co.uk

---

21 Rumburgh Farm, Rumburgh, Halesworth, Suffolk IP19 0RU

Charlotte Binder
☎/Fax 01986 781351
BB From £19–£25
Sleeps 5
� ⚬ 🏺 ✂
♦♦♦

An attractive 17th century Suffolk farmhouse set in peaceful countryside on a working farm within easy reach of Southwold and the Heritage Coast. Comfortable accommodation comprising one double and one twin/family room, both en suite with tea/coffee-making facilities, colour TV and central heating. Well-behaved children welcome. Open all year.
E-mail: binder@rumburghfarm.freeserve.co.uk

---

22 South Elmham Hall, St Cross, Harleston, Norfolk IP20 0PZ

Mrs Jo Sanderson
☎ 01986 782526
Fax 01986 782203
BB From £18–£40
Sleeps 6
�(10) 🐓 🐝 ⚬ 🐈 🎋 🏺 ✂ ◉
♦♦♦♦

Moated former bishop's palace with large gardens. Mixed farm, peaceful location with rare cattle and farm trails in historic landscape. Tastefully furnished comfortable rooms with tea/coffee tray. Kingsize bed, double antique brass bed and twin bedded rooms all with en suite facilities, colour TV and views of the farm and garden. Guests' lounge and dining room, full CH. Open Easter–end Dec.
E-mail: jo.sanderson@btinternet.com

---

23 Uggeshall Manor Farm, Uggeshall, Nr Southwold, Suffolk NR34 8BD

Annie Davies
☎ 01502 578546
Fax 01502 578560
BB From £24.50–£29.50
Sleeps 6
�(10) 🐓 ⚬ 🏺 ◉
♦♦♦♦

Luxuriously appointed historic farmhouse in 220 acres of its own beautiful heritage countryside just 5 minutes' drive from Southwold and the coast. Explore the 6 miles of private conservation tracks offering a profusion of wildlife, birds and flowers. Two doubles and one twin room, all en suite. Guests' sitting and dining rooms. Open all year except Christmas.

Watersmeet, Chestnut Tree Farm, Framlingham Road, Laxfield, Nr Framlingham, Suffolk IP13 8HD

Mrs Margaret Jefferies
☎/**Fax 01986 798880**
BB **From £19–£22.50**
EM From £11
Sleeps 4
👶(10) ⚡ 🍴 ☕ 🐴 🌐
♦♦♦♦

Experience the warm welcome and relax at this comfortable, traditional farmhouse with log fires and wonderful food – English breakfasts, suppers and vegetarian too. One double and one twin, both with private bathrooms. Small working farm on edge of pretty village with interesting church, museum and old inns. Cycle or ramble through this part of rural Suffolk. Treat yourself to a weekend or longer stay. Open Jan–mid Dec.

Woodlands Farm, Brundish, Framlingham, Suffolk IP13 8BP

Jill Graham
☎ **01379 384444**
BB **From £20**
Sleeps 6
👶(10) 🍴 ⚡ 🌐
♦♦♦♦ *(AA Inspected)*

A friendly welcome and good home cooking assured in our comfortable, timber-framed farmhouse set in peaceful countryside near Framlingham. Within easy reach of the coast and numerous local attractions. One twin and 2 double bedrooms with en suite bathrooms, and tea/coffee facilities. Separate dining and sitting rooms with inglenooks. Centrally heated with log fires in cold weather. Evening meal by arrangement. Closed Christmas & New Year.

Self-Catering

Baylham House Farm Annexe and Flat, Mill Lane, Baylham, Ipswich, Suffolk IP6 8LG

Ann Storer
☎/**Fax 01473 830264**
SC **From £125–£300**
Sleeps 4 + cot and 2 + cot
🐴 ☕ ⚡ 🐴 🌐
🐴🐴🐴 *Commended*

Two self-contained units in old farmhouse. Small rare breeds farm on River Gipping with sheep, cattle, poultry, pigs and goats. Peaceful setting, good walks, good touring base. Fishing, garden, barbecue. Both fully equipped to high standard. Children welcome, sorry no pets. Please phone or write for further details. Open all year.
E-mail: ann@baylham-house-farm.co.uk

Bluebell, Bonny & Buttercup, Park Farm, Sibton, Saxmundham, Suffolk IP17 2LZ

Margaret Gray
☎ **01728 668324**
Fax 01728 668564
SC **From £170–£350**
Sleeps 4 + cot and 2 + cot
🐴 🍴 ⚡ 🐴 🐴 🌐
🐴🐴🐴🐴 *Highly Commended*

Bluebell, Bonny and Buttercup are three delightful single storey cottages around a flower-decked courtyard, just the place for barbecues on soft summer evenings. Equipped to a very high standard. Wide doors for wheelchairs. Games room and laundry. Close to Heritage Coast. Ideal centre for walking, cycling and birdwatching. Open all year.
E-mail: margaret.gray@btinternet.com

The Bothy, Grange Farm, Woolpit, Bury St Edmunds, Suffolk IP30 9RG

Mrs Kathy Parker
☎ **01359 241143**
Fax 01359 244296
SC **From £170–£220**
Sleeps 2
🐴 🍴 🎿 🚗 ⚡ ☕
🐴🐴🐴🐴 *Highly Commended*

The Bothy is adjacent to farmhouse in the heart of Suffolk, only one mile from A14 corridor giving easy access to East Anglia. Ideal for touring tranquil villages or visiting major towns and cities. The cottage, recently converted, consists of kitchen/diner, lounge, double bedroom, en suite shower room and balcony area. Patio with barbecue. Linen and towels provided. Open all year.
E-mail: grangefarm@btinternet.com

6 **Colston Cottage,** Colston Hall, Badingham, Woodbridge, Suffolk IP13 8LB

John & Liz Bellefontaine
☎ 01728 638375
Fax 01728 638084
[sc] From £264–£427
Sleeps 6
🐕 ✂ ▣ ☞ ⊛
🔑🔑🔑🔑🔑 *Commended*

Charming centrally heated cottage enjoying lovely views over the Alde Valley. Idyllically set in the tranquillity of the countryside, yet only minutes from the coast. ground floor bedroom. Cot and high chair available. Dishwasher, washing machine, tumble drier, freezer, colour TV telephone. Coarse fishing and indoor bowls available. Open all year.

19 **The Cottage,** Red House Farm, Station Road, Haughley, Nr Stowmarket, Suffolk IP14 3QP

⌐ *Mrs Mary Noy*
☎ 01449 673323
Fax 01449 675413
[sc] From £180–£210
Sleeps 2/4
🐕 ✂ 🛆 ⊡ ▣ ⊛
🔑🔑🔑 *Commended*

Enjoy the peace and tranquillity of Suffolk staying in our charming cottage which adjoins the farmhouse. Very well furnished and equipped. Ideal location for exploring, cycling, birdwatching and walking. All linen and towels provided. Electricity and heating included. No smoking or pets. Open all year.

1 **The Court,** Brighthouse Farm, Melford Road, Lawshall, near Bury St Edmunds, Suffolk IP29 4PX

Roberta Truin
☎/Fax 01284 830385
[sc] From £350–£450
Sleeps 5/2
🐕 ✂ 🛆 ⊡ ♞ ⚘ ▣ ▪
🔑🔑🔑🔑 *Highly*
Commended

Queen Anne cottage situated in a rural position in the glorious Suffolk countryside. Furnished and equipped to a very high standard. Set in its own garden with access to larger grounds. Local shops, pubs and restaurants, historic Bury St Edmunds, Lavenham and Constable Country nearby. Also granary suites each sleeping two. Open all year.

18 **The Granary,** Priory Fram, Darsham, Nr Saxmundham, Suffolk IP17 3QD

Suzanne Bloomfield
☎ 01728 668459
Fax 01728 668744
[sc] From £135–£340
Sleeps 4
🐕 ✂ ⊡ ▪ ⊛
🔑🔑🔑 *Commended*

17th century granary tastefully converted to provide comfortable accommodation. Situated in peaceful Suffolk countryside, an ideal base for touring Suffolk coast and heathlands and other local attractions. 1 double, 2 singles. Shower room, kitchen, dining room, sitting room. Storage heaters, colour TV, washing machine. Cycle hire. Sat–Sat. Weekend lets out of season. Open all year.

22 **Hall Farm Cottage,** St Cross, Harleston, Norfolk IP20 0PZ

Mrs Jo Sanderson
☎ 01986 782526
Fax 01986 782203
[sc] From £245–£450
Sleeps 6/8
🐕 ♞ ▣ ☞ ♨ ▪ ⚘
🔑🔑🔑 *Commended*

Pretty cottage on conservation award-winning farm. Easy reach of Southwold, Norwich and market towns with good antique shops. Free access to our historic farm walks, horse riding nearby. Large fenced garden, raised pond, conservatory, washing machine, TV/video, woodburner, Aga, CH, games. Electricity, logs and linen free. Cot available. Open all year.
E-mail: jo.sanderson@bt.internet.com

27 **Old Wetherden Hall Cottage,** Hitcham, Ipswich, Suffolk IP7 7PZ

Julie Elsden
☎ 01449 740574
[sc] From £150–£320
Sleeps 6 + cot
🐕 ⊡ ▪ ▣
🔑🔑🔑 *Commended*

15th century listed oak-beamed moated house set in large, spacious garden. Abundance of wildlife. Picturesque views from peaceful, secluded setting. Private fishing available. Open inglenook fireplace, logs supplied. Open all year.

Rowney Cottage, Rowney Farm, Whepstead, Bury St Edmunds, Suffolk IP29 4TQ   **28**

Mrs Kati Turner
☎/Fax 01284 735842
▣ From £200–£280
Sleeps 4/5
🐕 🐏 🎣 🎿 ☉
🔑🔑🔑🔑 *Commended*

Situated atop the rolling countryside of West Suffolk the 500-acre farm is ideally placed for exploring this picturesque and historically fascinating part of East Anglia. The cottage is spacious and fully equipped, with 2 bedrooms, fully fitted kitchen and bathroom and a generous lounge. The farm is safely tucked away at the end of a private drive. Bury St Edmunds 6 miles, Cambridge 32. Linen and electricity included. Children and pets welcome. Open Apr–Oct.

Stable Cottages and The Granary, Chattisham Place, Nr Ipswich, Suffolk IP8 3QD   **29**

Mrs Margaret Langton
☎/Fax 01473 652210
▣ From £145–£380
Sleeps 2/8
👪 🐏 🐎 🎿 🎣 🐕 ☉
🔑🔑🔑 – 🔑🔑🔑🔑
Highly Commended

Come and enjoy the peaceful Suffolk countryside where we have something for everyone. Making our 3 beautifully converted cottages (en suites, dishwashers) your base with all home comforts, you can relax or explore Constable Country, Lavenham and the Heritage Coast. Borrow maps for waymarked walks or bring the family to share our heated outdoor pool, tennis court, games and studio/craft room. Wheelchair users welcome. Open all year.
E-mail: margaret.langton@talk21.com

Tom, Dick and Harry, Church Farm, Withersdale, Mendham, Harleston, Norfolk IP20 0JR   **30**

Audrey & Kate Carless
☎ 01379 588091
Fax 01379 588090
▣ From £110–£250
Sleeps 2 + cot
🐕 🐏 🎿 ☉
🔑🔑🔑 *Commended*

Tom, Dick and Harry are three timber-framed converted farm buildings nestling by dewy pastures in the 'Valley of the Rams'. Walk the footpaths, watch birds, go fishing, cycle Norfolk and Suffolk's tranquil lanes, enjoy a coastal drive. Each cottage includes garden, linen/towels, electricity, open fire. Cot/high chair available, ample parking. Open Mar–Jan.

Please mention *Stay on a Farm* when booking

USE THE INDEX

FARM HOLIDAY BUREAU

The comprehensive Index shows which farms offer access to disabled visitors; caravanning/camping facilities; the chance to participate on a working farm; stabling/grazing for visiting horses; en suite rooms; a welcome to business people; acceptance of *Stay on a Farm* gift tokens.

FOLLOW THE COUNTRY CODE

Leave nothing but footprints,
Take nothing but photographs,
Kill nothing but time!

South & South East England

Farm entries in this section are listed under those counties shown in green on the key map. The index below the map gives the appropriate page numbers. You will see that we have listed the counties geographically so that you can turn more easily to find farms in neighbouring counties.

At the start of each county section is a detailed map with numbered symbols indicating the location of each farm. Different symbols denote different types of accommodation; see the key below each county map. Farm entries are listed alphabetically under type of accommodation. Some farms offer more than one type of accommodation and therefore have more than one entry.

❶ *Bedfordshire*
❷ *Oxfordshire*
❸ *Berkshire*
❹ *Buckinghamshire*
❺ *Hertfordshire*
❻ *Essex*
❼ *Greater London*
❽ *Hampshire*
❾ *Isle of Wight*
❿ *Surrey*
⓫ *West Sussex*
⓬ *East Sussex*
⓭ *Kent*

KEY MAP TO SOUTH & SOUTH EAST ENGLAND

Bedfordshire

Ivel & Ouse Valleys

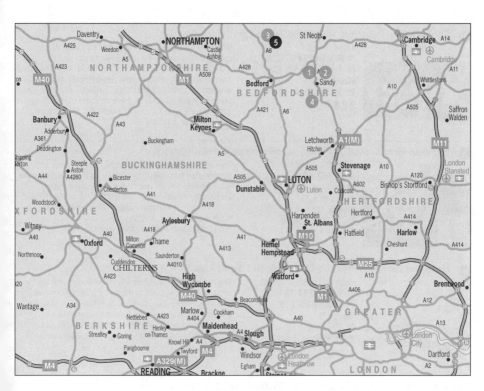

Key

🔵 Bed & Breakfast

🔵 Self-Catering

🔵 B&B and SC

🟥 Camping Barns

🔺 Camping & Caravanning

Bedfordshire is ideally situated between Oxford and Cambridge and makes perfect cycling, fishing and golfing country, while walkers will enjoy the Greensand Ridge Walk. The stately home is Woburn Abbey and there are many pretty villages with thatched cottages and beamed Tudor buildings such as Old Warden, near Bedford, which houses nearby the Shuttleworth Collection of historic aeroplanes and road vehicles. The River Ouse flows through Bedford which boasts many excellent museums and galleries. For animal lovers there is the RSPB nature reserve at Sandy, Whipsnade Zoo and Woburn's Wild Animal Kingdom.

If you would like help in finding suitable farm accommodation, turn to the full listing of FHB Groups on pages 392 to 395 to find appropriate contact details for this area.

Bed and Breakfast
(and evening meal)

---

1 **Church Farm,** High Street, Roxton, Bedford, Bedfordshire MK44 3EB

Janet Must
☎/Fax 01234 870234
BB From £22.50–£25
Sleeps 6
♨ 🐓 ⌁ ♨ 🎃 ◉
♦♦♦♦

Welcome to our historic farmhouse in a lovely village setting where we have a strong reputation for our standards of quality and service. Furnished with a pleasant mixture of family antiques, the comfortable guest rooms – all en suite – overlook the gardens. Aga cooked breakfast. Local waymarked walks in the River Ouse valley. Village inns for evening meals. Many guests return. Brochure available. Open all year.

---

2 **Highfield Farm,** Great North Road, Sandy, Bedfordshire SG19 2AQ

Margaret Codd
☎ 01767 682332
Fax 01767 692503
BB From £25
Sleeps 10
♨ 🐓 ⌁ 🖼 🎃 ◉
♦♦♦♦♦

Tom and Margaret Codd welcome guests to their comfortable farmhouse. Just 1 mile north of Sandy on the A1, Highfield Farm is excellently situated for visiting Cambridge, Shuttleworth, the RSPB, Grafham Water and for taking the Greensand Ridge Walk. Family, double and single bedrooms, most with en suite bathroom. Guests' sitting room with log fire and colour TV. Open all year.

---

3 **North End Barns,** North End Farm, Bletsoe, Bedfordshire MK44 1QT

Paul & Christine Forster
☎/Fax 01234 781320
BB From £25–£45
Sleeps 8
⌁ 🖼 🎃 ♨
♦♦♦♦ Silver Award

The old barn has been carefully converted to make 4 twin en suite rooms, situated in the quiet, peaceful surroundings of a 17th century thatched farmhouse. Farm walks and tennis on farm – riding, clay pigeon shooting and fishing can be easily arranged. Excellent local inns close by. This is a working sheep and arable farm. Open all year.

---

4 **Village Farm,** Thorncote Green, Sandy, Bedfordshire SG19 1PU

Anne Franklin
☎ 01767 627345
BB From £20
Sleeps 8
♨ ⌁ 🐓 🧍 🚗 🎃 ♨ ◉
♦♦

Family-run working mixed arable farm with a flock of 1000 free range laying hens plus turkeys and geese. One double bedroom, one twin/family room, plus bunkhouse, all en suite. Thorncote Green is a picturesque hamlet within easy reach of many interesting places to visit. Closed December.

FARM HOLIDAY BUREAU

Please mention **Stay on a Farm** when booking

Self-Catering

Scald End Farm, Scald End, Mill Road, Thurleigh, Bedford MK44 2DP

Jim Towler
☎/Fax 01234 771996
SC From £120–£220
Sleep 2–8
🌊 🏡 🛁 🌾 ⊕
↙ *Approved*

The Towler family provides self-catering accommodation in 16th century thatched cottages and modern barn conversions. The farm has cattle, horses, sheep, chickens, ducks and geese – so there is always something to see or do on the farm. The market town of Bedford is only about 15 minutes' drive away. Open all year.

USE THE INDEX

The comprehensive Index shows which farms offer access to disabled visitors; caravanning/camping facilities; the chance to participate on a working farm; stabling/grazing for visiting horses; en suite rooms; a welcome to business people; acceptance of *Stay on a Farm* gift tokens.

FARM HOLIDAY BUREAU

THE 1000+ BUREAU MEMBERS OFFER A UNIQUE LINK TO CUSTOMERS ACROSS THE UK

All Bureau members belong to a local Group. Each member can refer you to an equally high quality member within the Group... or across the UK: England, Northern Ireland, Scotland, Wales.

FARM HOLIDAY BUREAU

CONFIRM BOOKINGS

Disappointments can arise from misunderstandings over the telephone. Please write to confirm your booking.

Oxfordshire

Cotswolds, Thames Valley, Vale of the White Horse
& the Chilterns

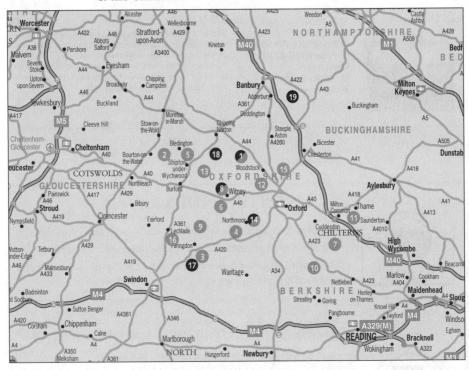

Key

- ① Bed & Breakfast
- ① Self-Catering
- ① B&B and SC
- ① Camping Barns
- ⚠ Camping & Caravanning

At the heart of historic Oxfordshire is the Thames Valley, stretching from the Chiltern Hills above Henley to the west of Oxford and the Cotswolds. Oxford itself is of great historic interest with its dreaming spires and great buildings including medieval colleges and Renaissance masterpieces such as the Sheldonian Theatre. Woodstock has many historic associations and is the site of Blenheim Palace, birthplace of Sir Winston Churchill. The county boasts many other beautiful country houses and picturesque villages with welcoming inns. There are numerous places of interest including Burford's Cotswold Wildlife Park and the Cogges Farm Museum near Witney.

If you would like help in finding suitable farm accommodation, turn to the full listing of FHB Groups on pages 392 to 395 to find appropriate contact details for this area.

Bed and Breakfast
(and evening meal)

Banbury Hill Farm, Enstone Road, Charlbury, Oxford OX7 3JH (1)

Mrs Angela Widdows
☎ 01608 810314
Fax 01608 811891
BB From £16–£25
Sleeps 30
🐎 ✝ 🖼 �A 🐚 🎋 ♨
◆◆◆◆

Natural Cotswold stone farmhouse commanding spectacular view in AONB overlooking the small township of Charlbury with the ancient Wychwood Forest nestling against the River Evenlode. Large variety of animals around the farm. Ideally centred – midway Oxford, Stratford-on-Avon, near Blenheim, Burford and Chipping Norton. Family, double (3 en suite), twin or single rooms. Ideal for families. Also self-catering cottages available. Closed Christmas & New Year.

Bould Farm, Bould, Nr Idbury, Chipping Norton, Oxfordshire OX7 6RT (2)

Mrs Lynne Meyrick
☎/Fax 01608 658850
BB From £22.50–£30
Sleeps 6
🐎 ✝ 🎋 ♨
◆◆◆

Bould Farm is a 17th century Cotswold farmhouse on a 300-acre family farm set in beautiful countryside, 10 minutes' drive from Stow-on-the-Wold and Bourton-on-the-Water and Burford. Within easy reach of Blenheim Palace and the Cotswold Wildlife Park. Children welcome. Spacious rooms with TV, tea/coffee-making facilities. Large garden. Good local pubs. Open Feb–Nov.

Bowling Green Farm, Stanford Road, Faringdon, Oxfordshire SN7 8EZ (3)

Della Barnard
☎ 01367 240229
Fax 01367 242568
BB From £22–£26
Sleeps 6
🐎 ✝ ♨ 🐾
◆◆◆

Attractive 18th century period farmhouse offering 21st century comfort situated in the Vale of the White Horse, just 1 mile south of Faringdon on the A417. Easy access to M4 for Heathrow Airport. A working farm breeding cattle and horses. Large twin/family room on ground floor en suite. All bedrooms have colour TV, electric blankets in winter, tea/coffee-making facilities and CH throughout. Open all year.

Chimney Farmhouse, Chimney on Thames, Aston, Bampton, Oxfordshire OX18 2EH (4)

Mrs Jean Kinch
☎/Fax 01367 870279
BB From £21–£25
Sleeps 5
🐎(10) ✝ ♨ ⟲ 🎋 ◉
◆◆◆◆

Enjoy the peace and quiet of Chimney Farm, on the Thames path. Our recently renovated Victorian centrally heated farmhouse offers comfortable en suite bedrooms with TV, tea/coffee facilities and guests' lounge. Enjoy local walks and golf courses. In easy reach of Oxford, Blenheim and Cotswolds. A warm welcome awaits you. Open Feb–Nov.

Crown Farm, Ascott-under-Wychwood, Oxfordshire OX7 6AB (5)

Mr & Mrs C Badger
☎ 01993 832083
BB From £20–£25
Sleeps 6
✝ �A 🐚 🎣 ♨ 🎋
◆◆◆◆

A lovely refurbished 16th century farmhouse in the wonderful Evealode Valley. En suite rooms with tea/coffee and TV. Situated halfway between Oxford and Cheltenham, the perfect peaceful spot to tour the many exciting places in the Cotswolds. Enjoy our lounge and beautiful garden. Four-mile farm walk through woods and conservation areas. Go on – pick up the phone and give yourself a treat. Open all year. *Associate.*

6 Ducklington Farm, Coursehill Lane, Ducklington, Witney, Oxon OX8 7YG

Mrs Stacey Strainge
☎ 01993 772175
BB From £19–£21
Sleeps 6
ﾊ ⅄ ｊ ⬛ 🛁 ⊛
◆◆◆

Looking forward to welcoming you to Ducklington Farmhouse. Our family-run mixed farm is situated 1½ miles from Witney on the edge of the Cotswolds. In this recently built house all rooms are en suite, have tea/coffee-making facilities and a TV. Pub meals available in village. Open all year except Christmas.

7 Fords Farm, Ewelme, Wallingford, Oxon OX10 6HU

Marlene Edwards
☎ 01491 839272
BB From £23–£35
Sleeps 4
⅄ ⬛ 🛁
◆◆◆◆

500-acre mixed farm, arable beef and sheep. Attractive farmhouse set in historic part of village with famous church almshouses and school. Peaceful surroundings with good walks and good selection of pubs nearby. Easy access to Henley, Oxford, Reading, Windsor, Heathrow and London. Friendly and comfortable atmosphere. 2 twin rooms. Open all year.

8 Hill Grove Farm, Crawley Dry Lane, Minster Lovell, Witney, Oxfordshire OX8 5NA

Mrs Katharine Brown
☎ 01993 703120
Fax 01993 700528
BB From £21–£23
Sleeps 4
ﾊ ⅄ 🛁 ⬛ 🐴
◆◆◆◆

Hill Grove is a mixed, family-run 300-acre working farm situated in an attractive rural setting overlooking the Windrush Valley. Ideally positioned for driving to Oxford, Blenheim Palace, Witney (Farm Museum) and Burford (renowned as the Gateway to the Cotswolds and for its splendid Wildlife Park). Riverside walks. Hearty breakfasts. Golf course 1 mile. 1 double/private shower, 1 twin/double en suite. Open all year (closed Christmas).

9 'Morar', Weald Street, Bampton, Oxfordshire OX18 2HL

Janet Rouse
☎ 01993 850162
Fax 01993 851738
BB From £22.50–£25
EM From £14.50
Sleeps 6
ﾊ(6) ⊞ ⅄ ⬛ ⊛
◆◆◆

Wake up to the smell of homemade bread, look out over rolling fields and listen to the birds welcome the new day. Relax over breakfast, make it a feast. Let us help you get the most from your stay in this most beautiful corner of England. Pet cats, sheep, goat. Doubles en suite. Open Mar–mid Dec. E-mail: morar@cwcom.net

10 North Farm, Shillingford Hill, Wallingford, Oxfordshire OX10 8NB

Hilary Warburton
☎ 01865 858406
Fax 01865 858519
BB From £25–£35
Sleeps 6
ﾊ(10) ⅄ ⬤ 🐴 ⬛ 🐴
◆◆◆◆

Attractive and quiet farmhouse in the middle of our 500-acre sheep and arable farm bordering the River Thames with a well-tended garden and hard tennis court. Pygmy goats and chickens. Lovely walks and private fishing available. Ideal for Oxford, Henley and the market town of Wallingford. All bedrooms have private bath/shower. Closed Christmas and New Year. E-mail: northfarm@compuserve.com

11 Oakfield, Thame Park Road, Thame, Oxfordshire OX9 3PL

Mrs C S Elton
☎/Fax 01844 213709
BB From £20–£22.50
Sleeps 6
ﾊ(8) ⅄ 🐴 ⬛
◆◆◆◆

We offer a warm welcome to our comfortable farmhouse set in 25 acres of grounds, part of our larger 400-acre mixed farm. Good food, comfortable beds and a homely atmosphere. Our sunny ground floor bedrooms overlook flower gardens and fields. All bedrooms have colour TV, hairdryer, toiletries and tea/coffee. We are out in the country but only 10 minutes walk from Thame's historic town centre. Oxford 12 miles, London 40 miles, M40 J6 5 miles. Open all year.

The Old Farmhouse, Station Hill, Long Hanborough, Oxfordshire OX8 8JZ   ⑫

Vanessa Maundrell
☎ 01993 882097
BB **From £19.50–£22.50**
Sleeps 4
ᗢ(12) ⊱ ⊕ 🏇 ⚘ ▮
◆◆◆◆

We welcome you to our former farmhouse dating from 1670 with many original features and charming bedrooms. Delicious breakfasts with freshly baked bread, homemade marmalade/jams and fresh orange juice (served in delightful cottage garden on summer mornings). Lovely country walks and good pubs within walking distance. Woodstock and Blenheim Palace nearby, Oxford a 10-minute train ride. Two doubles (1 en suite). Closed Christmas. E-mail: old.farm@virgin.net

Potters Hill Farm, Leafield, Nr Burford, Oxfordshire OX8 5QB   ⑬

Mrs Karen Stanley
☎/Fax 01993 878018
BB **From £16–£20**
Sleeps 6
ᗢ ⊱ ▮ 🏇
◆◆◆

Large family working farm set in peaceful surroundings close to the historic town of Burford. Friendly, informal atmosphere. Nearby inns serving excellent evening meals. Lots of tourist information available. Easy drive to all attractions. Open all year. E-mail: k.stanley@virgin.net

Rectory Farm, Northmoor, Witney, Oxfordshire OX8 1SX   ⑭

Mary Anne Florey
☎ 01865 300207
Fax 01865 300559
BB **From £21–£23**
Sleeps 4
⊱ ⚲ 🏇 ▮
◆◆◆◆

A pot of tea, homemade shortbread, along with a warm welcome and a peaceful, comfortable stay await you at Rectory Farm, a 16th century farmhouse retaining old charm alongside modern comforts. Both rooms have en suite facilities, CH, hot drink trays. Guests' own sitting room with woodburning stove. We are conveniently situated for Oxford (10m), the Cotswolds, Blenheim and the Thames path. Open mid Jan–mid Dec. See colour ad on page 40. E-mail: PJ.Florey@farmline.com

Vicarage Farm, Kirtlington, Woodstock, Oxfordshire OX5 3JY   ⑮

Mrs Judith Hunter
☎/Fax 01869 350254
BB **From £20–£25**
Sleeps 6
⊱ ▮ 🏇 ⊚
◆◆◆

Leave behind the bustle of everyday life and sink into the peace of the countryside. Play golf on the surrounding 18-hole course, or go on a shopping trip to the Bicester Village, or browse round the shops of nearby Woodstock and on into Blenheim Palace. Spend a day in Stratford or at Warwick Castle. Oxford only 8 miles. One twin, two doubles, one with private bathroom, all with colour TV, CH and tea/coffee-making facilities. Open Mar–Nov.

Weston Farm, Buscot Wick, Faringdon, Oxfordshire SN7 8DJ   ⑯

Mrs Jean Woof
☎/Fax 01367 252222
BB **From £23–£25**
Sleeps 6
ᗢ(10) ⊱ 🐕 ▮ ⚲ ⊚
◆◆◆◆

Come and share our idyllic 17th century Cotswold farmhouse in peaceful surroundings, as featured in *Homes and Gardens* (April 1999). Period furniture and well maintained gardens. 500-acre mixed farm. CH, tea/coffee-making facilities and own TV, one four-poster, one double and one twin room, all with private bathroom. Guests' own dining and sitting rooms, with log fires. Ideally situated to explore this beautiful area. Open all year except Christmas.

LET THE TELEPHONE RING!

Some farmhouses are big places. Let the telephone ring
long enough to give the owner time to answer it.

Self-Catering

---

① Banbury Hill Farm, Enstone Road, Charlbury, Oxford OX7 3JH

Mrs Angela Widdows
☎ 01608 810314
Fax 01608 811891
SC From £185–£295
Sleeps 2–5
🐕🐏📺🏹🚲♿💼🎋
🔑🔑🔑 – 🔑🔑🔑🔑
Highly Commended

Comfortable Cotswold farm cottages, well appointed with outstanding views in AONB between Oxford and Stratford-on-Avon. Variety of farm animals. Forest trail, play area, tennis and bike hire available. Ample parking. Open Mar–Nov.

---

⑰ Coxwell House, Little Coxwell, Faringdon, Oxfordshire SN7 7LP

Elspeth Crossley Cooke
☎ 01367 241240
Fax 01367 240911
SC From £375–£750
Sleeps 6
🐕🐏🐎♿🎋🎾♻️⊙
🔑🔑🔑🔑 *Highly Commended*

Coxwell House is the superb main 1760 part (self-contained) of a Georgian farmhouse set in an attractive, secluded walled garden. Every modern convenience. Tennis court, indoor swimming pool. Unspoilt stone walled farming village with thatched cottages and pub. Ideal for the Cotswolds, Oxford. 1½ miles Faringdon south of A420. Open all year. E mail: elspeth@coxwell.u-net.com

---

⑧ Hill Grove Cottage, Crawley Dry Lane, Minster Lovell, Witney, Oxfordshire OX8 5NA

Mrs Katharine Brown
☎ 01993 703120
Fax 01993 700528
SC From £260–£350
Sleeps 6
🐕🍴🎋♿🐎
Applied

A comfortably furnished, detached cottage situated on our 300-acre mixed working farm above the River Windrush. Ideally positioned for rural walking through the valley yet within easy driving distance of Oxford, Woodstock and Burford ('Gateway to the Cotswolds'). Golf course 1½ miles.

---

⑱ Lower Court Cottages, Lower Court Farm, Chadlington, Chipping Norton, Oxfordshire OX7 3NQ

Juliet Pauling
☎/Fax 01608 676422
SC From £195–£450
Sleeps 4/6
⊙(6) 🍴 ☕ ♿🎋
🔑🔑🔑 – 🔑🔑🔑🔑 *Up to*
Highly Commended

Alfie's Cottage is a typical, pretty Cotswold stone cottage set on this beautiful farm. Ideally situated for touring the Cotswolds and local Area of Outstanding Natural Beauty. Oxford and Sratford 18 miles, Stow-on-the-Wold, Bourton-on-the-Water, Burford 10 mile radius. Fully fitted kitchen with dishwasher, microwave, etc. Open log fire, CH. Garden with superb views, barbecue. Other cottages available. Open all year.
E-mail: juliet_lower_court@yahoo.com

---

⑭ Rectory Farm Cottages, Northmoor, Nr Witney, Oxon OX8 1SX

Mary Anne Florey
☎ 01865 300207
Fax 01865 300559
SC From £225–£375
Sleeps 4
🐕🍴♿☕🎋
🔑🔑🔑🔑 *Highly Commended*

Two delightful cottages on our farm in quiet village 10mw Oxford. South-facing enclosed gardens, field views and excellent walks. Each cottage is furnished in pine and has 1 double and 1 twin bedroom, bathroom, shower room, lounge with woodburner, TV, dining area and very well equipped kitchen. CH, ample parking, linen/towels provided. Fully inclusive price. Open all year. See colour ad on page 40. E-mail: PJ.Florey@farmline.com

Walltree House Farm, Steane, Brackley, Northamptonshire NN13 5NS   **19**

Richard & Pauline Harrison
☎ **01295 811235**
Fax 01295 811147
Mobile 0860 913399
SC **From £185–£460**
Sleeps 2–6
🛏 ⊞ ♿ ⛄ ◉
♪♪♪♪ *Highly Commended*

We have converted the granary and stables into warm, comfortable, well-equipped, quiet cottages in a courtyard adjacent to the farmhouse, overlooking lawns and garden where you are welcome to relax. Near Cotswolds, Stratford, Warwick, Blenheim, Stowe, Waddesdon and other National Trust properties. Shopping, golf and leisure centres. Every activity you can think of. A peaceful haven to return to. Open all year except Christmas and New Year.

STAY ON A FARM GIFT TOKENS

If you have enjoyed your Stay on a Farm, why not treat your friends and relatives to *Stay on a Farm* gift tokens? Available from the Bureau office (tel: 024 7669 6909), they can be redeemed against accommodation and are accepted by the majority of farms (see Index). Please check when booking to avoid disappointment.

USE THE INDEX

The comprehensive Index shows which farms offer access to disabled visitors; caravanning/camping facilities; the chance to participate on a working farm; stabling/grazing for visiting horses; en suite rooms; a welcome to business people; acceptance of *Stay on a Farm* gift tokens.

Our Internet address is
http://www.webscape.co.uk/farmaccom/

FOLLOW THE COUNTRY CODE

Leave nothing but footprints,
Take nothing but photographs,
Kill nothing but time!

Berkshire

Thames Valley, Berkshire Downs, River Kennet & Royal Windsor

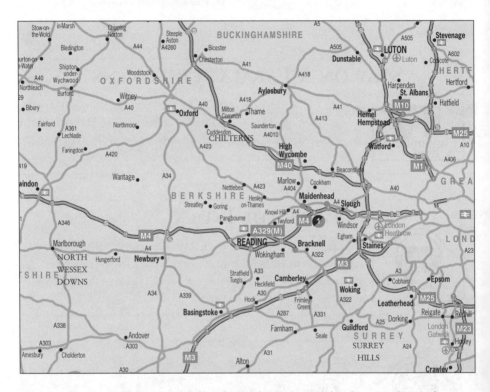

Key

🔵 **1** Bed & Breakfast

🟢 **1** Self-Catering

🟠 **1** B&B and SC

⬜ **1** Camping Barns

🔺 **1** Camping & Caravanning

Berkshire, England's only Royal County, stretches from Windsor in the east to the borders of Wiltshire in the west. The county boasts two international attractions: Windsor Castle with its recently restored Royal Apartments, and Legoland which, with its new rides, is proving as popular as ever. Away from the tourist attractions there is plenty to do and see in Berkshire. The Royal River Thames and the Kennet and Avon Canal provide the opportunity to cruise classic waterways through magnificent scenery. Near to Windsor is Eton College, the current school for the Royal princes, and the Savill Garden – a beautiful setting at any time of year. Why not visit the historic houses of Dorney Court, Mapledurham House and Stratfield Saye House? Or if it's shopping and restaurants you are after then Reading has it all along with a range of museums to satisfy every interest.

If you would like help in finding suitable farm accommodation, turn to the full listing of FHB Groups on pages 392 to 395 to find appropriate contact details for this area.

Bed and Breakfast
(and evening meal)

Moor Farm, Ascot Road, Holyport, Nr Maidenhead, Berkshire SL6 2HY ❶

Mrs Carol Bardo
☎ **01628 633761**
Fax **01628 636167**
🅱 From £40
Sleeps 4
🐴 ⚲ 🎩 ♞
◆◆◆◆

In the pretty village of Holyport, Moor Farm is 4 miles from Windsor and well placed for touring the Thames Valley and visiting London. The farmhouse is a timber-framed, 700-year-old 'listed' manor in a lovely country garden. The charming bedrooms are furnished with antiques and guests have their own sitting room. Close to Heathrow. Horses kept on farm. Excellent restaurants and pubs nearby. Open all year. E-mail: moorfm@aol.com

Self-Catering

Courtyard Cottages, Moor Farm, Ascot Road, Holyport, Nr Maidenhead, Berkshire SL6 2HY ❶

Mrs Carol Bardo
☎ **01628 633761**
Fax **01628 636167**
🆂🅲 From £280–£480
Sleeps 2/4
🐴 ⚲ 🎩 ♞
🔑🔑🔑🔑 *Highly Commended*

In the pretty village of Holyport, Courtyard Cottages are on the 700-year-old manor of Moor Farm and are conversions from a Georgian stable block and two small barns. They retain the charm of their original features and are furnished with antique pine. The 4 cottages are well placed for touring the Thames Valley and are 4 miles from Windsor and convenient for visiting London. Horses on the farm. Open all year. E-mail: moorfm@aol.com

LET THE TELEPHONE RING!
Some farmhouses are big places. Let the telephone ring
long enough to give the owner time to answer it.

CONFIRM BOOKINGS
Disappointments can arise from misunderstandings over the telephone.
Please write to confirm your booking.

Buckinghamshire

Vale of Aylesbury & the Chilterns

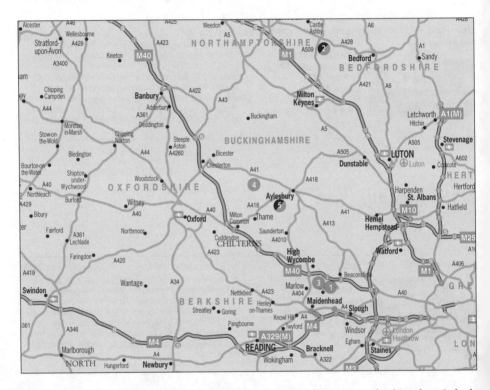

Key

1 Bed & Breakfast

1 Self-Catering

1 B&B and SC

1 Camping Barns

1 Camping & Caravanning

This is a richly agricultural county yet within easy reach of London, Oxford and Heathrow. The fertile Vale of Aylesbury takes its name from the historic county town of 'Aylesbury Duck' fame. Situated at the foot of the Chiltern Hills, this is a bustling market town offering plenty of entertainment for the visitor. Milton Keynes, Buckingham and High Wycombe are excellent for shopping or you can mess about on the River Thames at picturesque Marlow – or just while away an afternoon watching others doing the messing as they negotiate the locks! You won't be short of places to visit: Waddesdon Manor, Claydon House, Stowe Gardens and Quainton Railway Centre, to name a few.

If you would like help in finding suitable farm accommodation, turn to the full listing of FHB Groups on pages 392 to 395 to find appropriate contact details for this area.

Bed and Breakfast
(and evening meal)

Hollands Farm, Hedsor Road, Bourne End, Buckinghamshire SL8 5EE ①

Marion Lunnon
☎ 01628 520423
Fax 01628 531602
BB From £20–£30
Sleeps 6
🐎 🐓 ✗ 🜊 ❧ 🖀 ♞
♦♦♦♦

A 550-acre arable farm with Victorian farmhouse, close to the River Thames. Beautiful walks along Thames Path. Heathrow Airport 25 minutes, London 30 minutes, M4 and M40 10 minutes. Excellent location for London, Windsor, Oxford and the Chiltern Hills. Local railway station connecting to London (Paddington) 10 minutes' walk. Two en suite bedrooms, one with private bathroom, all with colour TV and tea/coffee. Open all year.

Home Farm, Warrington, Olney, Buckinghamshire MK46 4HN ②

Mr & Mrs Garry Pibworth
☎ 01234 711655
Fax 01234 711855
BB From £25–£35
Sleeps 6
🐎 ✗ ⊞ 🖀 ♞ ♈ ◉
♦♦♦♦

Our stone farmhouse offers a friendly welcome, two spacious en suite bedrooms with bath and shower, colour TV and tea/coffee-making facilities. Guests' lounge with a log burner. A peaceful arable farm 1½ miles from market town of Olney, 10 miles from Bedford, Northampton and Milton Keynes. Ideally situated for Cotswolds, Oxford, Cambridge, Stratford and London. Summer use of outdoor heated swimming pool. Open all year.
E-mail: b&b@ homefarm.force9.co.uk

Monkton Farm, Little Marlow, Buckinghamshire SL7 3RF ③

Jane & Warren Kimber
☎ 01494 521082
Fax 01494 443905
BB From £30–£40
Sleeps 6
🐎(5) ✗ 🜊 🖀
♦♦♦♦

A 150-acre working dairy farm with 14th century 'Cruck' farmhouse set in the beautiful Chiltern Hills, yet only 30 miles from London and 27 miles from Oxford. Heathrow 20 mins, 1 single, 1 double and 1 family room available. English breakfast served in the farm kitchen. Large choice of pubs and restaurants nearby. Open all year.

Poletrees Farm, Ludgershall Road, Brill, Aylesbury, Buckinghamshire HP18 9TZ ④

Anita & John Cooper
☎/Fax 01844 238276
BB From £25–£30
EM From £15
Sleeps 6
🐎(5) ✗ 🖀 ◉
♦♦♦

A 16th century working beef and sheep farm with house of architectural interest. 2 quiet bedrooms, 1 double, 1 twin, both with H&C and tea/coffee-making facilities. Guests have own lounge. En suite barn conversion in garden for couples – suppers can be ordered. Many pubs and restaurants nearby. Places of interest include Waddesdon Manor, Claydon House, Stowe Gardens and Oxford. Bicester Retail Village 6 miles. Elizabeth Gundrey recommended. Open all year.

Wallace Farm, Dinton, Nr Aylesbury, Buckinghamshire HP17 8UZ ⑤

Jackie Cook
☎ 01296 748660
Fax 01296 748851
BB From £22–£30
Sleeps 6
🐎 ⊞ ❧ ♈ ◉
♦♦♦

This 16th century listed farmhouse is situated in a quiet, rural setting in the Vale of Aylesbury, yet within easy reach of London, Oxford and Heathrow. A small family farm, rearing beef cattle and sheep, plus chickens, ducks and geese. Plenty of opportunitites for country walks, coarse fishing or browsing through our extensive library. Open all year. E-mail: jackiecook@wallacefarm.freeserve.co.uk

Self-Catering

---

2 'The Old Stone Barn', c/o Home Farm, Warrington, Olney, Buckinghamshire MK46 4HN

Mr & Mrs G Pibworth
☎ 01234 711655
Fax 01234 711855
SC From £170–£375
Sleep 1/6
🧍 🐕 ⊞ ♨ 🎿 ➿ ☺
🐾🐾🐾🐾 *Highly Commended*

A charming combination of old character and modern facilities, the Old Stone Barn is 3 ground floor and 3 first floor spacious self-contained apartments peacefully positioned on an arable farm 1½ miles north of Olney. Relax in the gardens, make use of the outdoor heated swimming pool or take day trips to Oxford, Cambridge, London or the Cotswolds. Open all year.
E-mail: accommodation@homefarm.force9.co.uk

---

5 Wallace Farm Cottages, Dinton, Nr Aylesbury, Buckinghamshire HP17 8UZ

Jackie Cook
☎ 01296 748660
Fax 01296 748851
SC From £180–£450
Sleep 2–6
🐕 🐎 ⊞ ♨ ➿ 🎿 ➿ ☺
🐾🐾🐾 *Commended*

The Old Foaling Box and Keepers Cottage are two very charming cottages set across the courtyard of a 16th century farmhouse. These adjoining cottages are on one level and comfortably giving a feeling of cosiness and welcome. This conversion of a former stable block has been kept in complete harmony with the surrounding farm. Open all year.
E-mail: jackiecook@wallacefarm.freeserve.co.uk

Please mention *Stay on a Farm* when booking

FINDING YOUR ACCOMMODATION

The local FHB Group contacts listed on page 392 can always help you find a vacancy in your chosen area.

STAY ON A FARM GIFT TOKENS

If you have enjoyed your Stay on a Farm, why not treat your friends and relatives to *Stay on a Farm* gift tokens? Available from the Bureau office (tel: 024 7669 6909), they can be redeemed against accommodation and are accepted by the majority of farms (see Index). Please check when booking to avoid disappointment.

Hertfordshire

The Chilterns

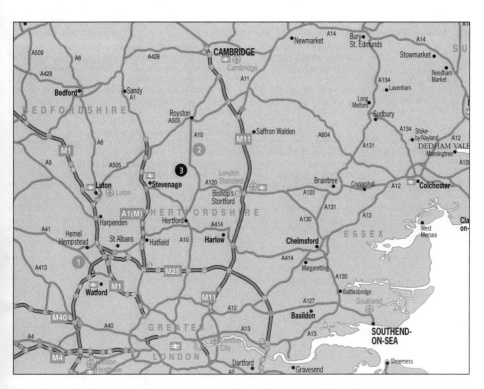

Key

- ① Bed & Breakfast
- ① Self-Catering
- ① B&B and SC
- ① Camping Barns
- ① Camping & Caravanning

Hertfordshire, a county of contrasts, is in the unique situation of being at the hub of the country's transport network whilst offering some truly unspoilt and varied rural landscapes. It has a great historical heritage with St Albans, once the Roman town Verulamium, the Old Palace and House in Hatfield Park, and Knebworth House. Come and enjoy the Chiltern landscape including many picturesque villages such as Aldbury and Frithsden and the 4,000 acres of ancient woodland of the National Trust's Ashridge Estate. We offer the business guest the chance to unwind in a homely atmosphere as little as half an hour by train from central London.

If you would like help in finding suitable farm accommodation, turn to the full listing of FHB Groups on pages 392 to 395 to find appropriate contact details for this area.

Bed and Breakfast
(and evening meal)

---

① Broadway Farm, Berkhamsted, Hertfordshire HP4 2RR

Mrs Alison Knowles
☎/Fax 01442 866541
BB From £24–£35
Sleeps 6
➳ ✕ ✂ ✿ 🛆 ◉
◆◆◆◆ Silver Award

A warm welcome is guaranteed at Broadway, a working arable farm with own fishing lake. 3 comfortable en suite rooms in converted buildings adjacent to farmhouse. Tea/coffee-making facilities, colour TV, CH. Everything for the leisure or business guest – the relaxation of farm life in an attractive rural setting, yet easy access to London, airports, motorways and mainline rail services. Open all year (closed Christmas and New Year).
E-mail: a.knowles@broadway.nildram.co.uk

---

② Buckland Bury, Buntingford, Hertfordshire SG9 0PY

Pat Hodge
☎ 01763 272958
Fax 01763 274722
BB From £20–£25
Sleeps 6
➳ 🐾 🛆
◆◆◆◆

570-acre working arable farm that has been farmed by the Hodge family for the past 50 years. The 17th century creeper-clad farmhouse offers homely accommodation with much of the original character of the house retained, especially in the dining room with its exposed beams and large open fire. All rooms have tea/coffee-making facilities, colour TV and hairdryer. No smoking in bedrooms. E-mail: buckbury@farming.co.uk

---

Self-Catering

---

③ Bluntswood Hall Cottages, Middle Farm, Throcking, Buntingford, Hertfordshire SG9 9RN

Sally Smyth
☎/Fax 01763 281204
SC From £175–£275
Sleeps 4
➳ 🛆 ✾
𝓟 𝓟 𝓟 𝓟 Commended

Stables recently converted into 2 cottages with lovely views over the countryside. Ideally situated for Cambridge, Duxford, Wimpole Hall or Knebworth Park. Each beamed cottage has double bedroom, bunk bedroom or single bed, bathroom, fitted kitchen and sitting room. R/C colour TV, CH. Linen and towels included in price. Children welcome. No pets. Open all year.

LET THE TELEPHONE RING!
Some farmhouses are big places. Let the telephone ring
long enough to give the owner time to answer it.

Essex

Dedham Vale, Essex Way & Epping Forest

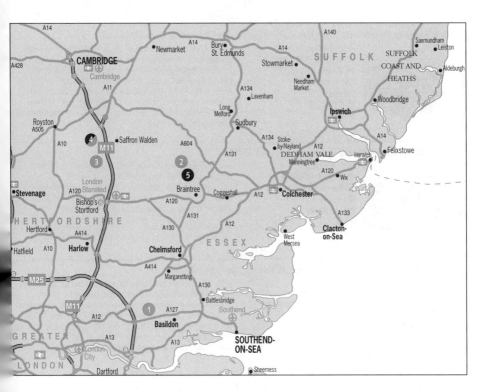

Come and discover the real Essex. Once off the beaten track you will be surprised by our pargetted cottages, unspoilt villages set in undulating countryside, stately homes, working museums and gardens like Beth Chatto's. Go back to the time of the Romans at Colchester Castle, the Saxons at unique Greenstead Church and the Second World War at Duxford Air Museum. Or walk the Essex Way from Epping, via Constable Country to the coast where you can sail and birdwatch around the creeks and estuaries. Essex can cater for all tastes and interests and we are ideally placed for travellers with the port of Harwich, Stansted Airport and easy access to London.

If you would like help in finding suitable farm accommodation, turn to the full listing of FHB Groups on pages 392 to 395 to find appropriate contact details for this area.

Bed and Breakfast
(and evening meal)

---

① Bonnydowns Farmhouse, Doesgate Lane, Bulphan, Nr Upminster, Essex RM14 3TB

Rose Newman
☎ **01268 542129**
BB **From £20–£23**
EM From £8
Sleeps 6
🛏 ⅄ ♨ 🛁
♦♦♦

Large, comfortably furnished, pleasantly situated in large garden with lovely views. Close to Langdon Hills Country Park and Basildon New Town (modern shopping centre). Convenient for London, Southend, South East England via M25, A13, A127. Sheep/cattle kept on the farm. 2 twin, 1 family bedrooms, 1 bath with toilet/shower, 1 shower room with toilet. Tea/coffee trays. Good cooking. Open all year (closed Christmas).

---

② Brook Farm, Wethersfield, Braintree, Essex CM7 4BX

Mrs A Butler
☎ **01371 850284**
BB **From £17.50–£21**
Sleeps 6
🛏 ⅄ Å ♨
♦♦♦

Beautiful listed farmhouse, parts dating back to 13th century, on a 100-acre mixed farm set on the edge of a picturesque village. Spacious and comfortable rooms, guests' lounge, safe parking. Thirty minutes from Stansted Airport. Camping also available. Open all year.

---

③ Parsonage Farm, Arkesden, nr Saffron Walden, Essex CB11 4HB

Daniele Forster
☎ **01799 550306**
BB **From £17.50–£25**
Sleeps 6
🛏(5) 🐓 ⅄ ♨ 🛁 ♞
♦♦♦♦

After a hard day's touring come and relax in our beautifully kept Victorian farmhouse, situated in the centre of an attractive small village. En suite facilities and four-poster bed available, TV and hot drinks in bedrooms. The farm is arable but a few pets are kept. Hard tennis court and picnic table in large garden. Excellent meals in local pub just 5 minutes' walk. Open all year except Christmas.

---

④ Rockells Farm, Duddenhoe End, Saffron Walden, Essex CB11 4UY

Mrs Tineke Westerhuis
☎ **01763 838053**
Fax 01763 837001
BB **From £18–£22**
Sleeps 6
🛏 ♨ 🛶 🛁 ♞
♦♦♦♦

Rockells is an arable farm in a beautiful corner of Essex. The Georgian house has a large garden with a 3-acre lake for coarse fishing. All rooms have private facilities, one room is downstairs. On the farm are several footpaths, beautiful villages in the area. Audley End, Duxford and Cambridge nearby. London is about 1 hour by car or train. Stansted Airport 30 mins. Open all year except Christmas. *Associate.*

---

⑤ Spicers Farm, Rotten End, Wethersfield, Braintree, Essex CM7 4AL

Mrs Delia Douse
☎/Fax **01371 851021**
BB **From £17**
Sleeps 6
🛏 ⅄ 🛁 ♨ ◉
♦♦♦♦

Set in a delightful, peaceful position overlooking beautiful countryside. Comfortable and welcoming atmosphere. All rooms en suite with CH, tea/coffee-making facilities, colour TV, clock radio and lovely views. Convenient for Stansted, Harwich, Cambridge and Constable Country. Ideal for touring or walking. Open all year except Christmas and New Year.

Self-Catering

The Byre, c/o Rockells Farm, Duddenhoe End, Saffron Walden, Essex CB11 4UY

Mrs Tineke Westerhuis
☎ 01763 838053
Fax 01763 837001
⟨SC⟩ From £150–£250
Sleeps 4
🧺 🛏 ⌨ 🎋 🍴
🐾 🐾 🐾 *Commended*

The Byre is part of Rockells farmyard, an arable farm in a beautiful corner of Essex. Lounge with kitchen area has original wood panelling. The cottage is fully equipped to a high standard. Garden with 3-acre lake for excellent fishing. In the area are several footpaths and beautiful villages with excellent pubs. Audley End, Duxford and Cambridge nearby. London is 1 hour by car or train, Stansted Airport 30 mins by car. Open all year. *Associate.*

USE THE INDEX

The comprehensive Index shows which farms offer access to disabled visitors; caravanning/camping facilities; the chance to participate on a working farm; stabling/grazing for visiting horses; en suite rooms; a welcome to business people; acceptance of *Stay on a Farm* gift tokens.

FINDING YOUR ACCOMMODATION

The local FHB Group contacts listed on page 392 can always help you find a vacancy in your chosen area.

FOLLOW THE COUNTRY CODE

Leave nothing but footprints,
Take nothing but photographs,
Kill nothing but time!

Hampshire

New Forest, South Hampshire Coast, the Solent & Test Valley

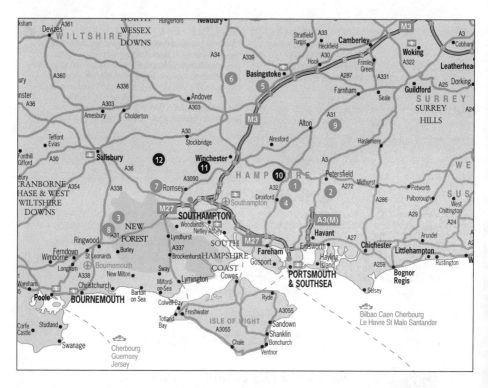

Key

🅱 Bed & Breakfast

🅢 Self-Catering

🅑 B&B and SC

⬜ Camping Barns

🔺 Camping & Caravanning

Hampshire is a beautiful county of contrasts – of creeks, harbours and beaches, grand rivers and sparkling streams, forests and lush farmland with picturesque villages and hamlets. The county has numerous links with the past. Winchester was the Saxon capital; Southampton bore witness to the Norman invasion; Portsmouth is famous for its naval heritage and as the birthplace of Charles Dickens; and Chawton was the home of Jane Austen. There are excellent walks in the lovely New Forest, along the Solent coast-line and inland along the famous Test Valley, or visit a country mansion such as Broadlands, Breamore, Stratfield Saye or Highclere Castle.

If you would like help in finding suitable farm accommodation, turn to the full listing of FHB Groups on pages 392 to 395 to find appropriate contact details for this area.

Bed and Breakfast
(and evening meal)

Brocklands Farm, West Meon, Petersfield, Hampshire GU32 1JN ①

Sue Wilson
☎/Fax 01730 829228
🅱 From £19–£21
Sleeps 6
🐕 ⅍ ⌂ ♨ ♟ ⌖
♦♦♦

Enjoy the home-baked brown bread and preserves at breakfast in the unique, traditionally furnished, modern farmhouse. Lovely views of the countryside and a sheltered sunny terrace. Mown grass walks around the farm and into West Meon, a charming village with shops and 2 friendly pubs. TV in some rooms. There are badgers on the farm. Open all year except Christmas.

Compton Farmhouse, Church Lane, Compton, Nr Chichester, West Sussex PO18 9HB ②

Mrs Melanie Bray
☎ 023 9263 1597
🅱 From £18–£20
Sleeps 6
🐕 ⅍ ♟ ♨

Listed flint farmhouse on a working mixed farm. We are 200 yards up a track from the village square, next door to the Norman church of St Mary. Large family bedroom with private bathroom. Own sitting room with TV, fridge and drink-making facilities. Within easy reach of Chichester, Portsmouth, Arundel and Goodwood. Open Jan–Nov.

Hucklesbrook Farm, South Gorley, Fordingbridge, Hampshire SP6 2PN ③

Debbie Sampson
☎ 01425 653180
🅱 From £20–£25
Sleeps 5
🐈(5) 🐕 ⅍ Å ♨ ♟
♦♦♦♦

Hucklesbrook Farm is a beautiful 17th century farmhouse set in a peaceful, secluded position by the Hucklesbrook. The charming bedrooms have wonderful views over the open farmland and the New Forest. With direct access to the New Forest, Hucklesbrook Farm makes the ideal holiday for walkers, cyclists, riders and fishermen. Open all year. E-mail: J.Sampson@virgin.net

---

Moortown Farm, Soberton, Southampton, Hampshire SO32 3QU ④

Rosemary Taylor
☎/Fax 01489 877256
🅱 From £20–£25
Sleeps 6
🐈(5) ⅍ ♨ ♟
♦♦♦

A friendly atmosphere is found at Moortown in the heart of the Meon Valley, an Area of Outstanding Natural Beauty. Crossed by the Wayfarer's Walk and South Downs Way. 1 twin en suite, 1 4-bedded with private bathroom, both with TV and tea facilities. Set in a peaceful village within easy reach of Winchester, home of King Arthur's Round Table, Portsmouth, with the Mary Rose and Nelson's flagship, Chichester and the New Forest. Open all year.

Oakdown Farm Bungalow, c/o Oakdown Farm, Dummer, Basingstoke, Hampshire RG23 7LR ⑤

Mrs Elizabeth Hutton
☎ 01256 397218
🅱 From £17.50–£20
Sleeps 6
🐈(12) ⅍ ♨ ♟ ◉
♦♦♦

Oakdown Farm Bungalow is on a secluded, private road, next to junction 7 on the M3, 1 mile south of Basingstoke and close to the village of Dummer. Excellent road communications to London, Winchester, South coast, the South-West, Oxford and the Midlands. Local historians welcome. B&B for horses. Wayfarer's Walk within 200 metres. Open all year.

6 **Peak House Farm,** Cole Henley, Whitchurch, Hampshire RG28 7QJ

Mrs Jenny Stevens
☎ 01256 892052
BB From £16–£25
Sleeps 6
🐕 💈 🏠
♦♦♦

Come and stay in our attractively furnished and decorated turn of the century farmhouse set in peaceful surroundings on working dairy farm close to Watership Down. Beautiful walks and horseriding nearby. Centrally based for New Forest, Winchester, Stonehenge, Legoland and Oxford. 1 twin en suite (ground floor, self-contained), 1 double and 1 twin with handbasin, all with colour TV, tea/coffee facilities. Lounge with log fire. Large garden, parking. Children welcome. Open all year except Christmas.

7 **Pyesmead Farm,** Plaitford, Romsey, Hampshire SO51 6EE

Mrs Christina Pybus
☎/Fax 01794 323386
BB From £17
Sleeps 6
🐕 💈 🐎 🐾 🏠
♦♦♦

A warm welcome awaits you, on the northern edge of the New Forest, at our family-run stock farm with its own coarse fishing lakes, indoor heated swimming pool and sauna. Many activities locally including horse riding, trout fishing, golf and forest walks. Within easy reach of Salisbury, Winchester, Southampton and the coast. Excellent pubs providing good food within ½ mile. Children welcome. Open all year except Christmas.

8 **Roughwood House,** Highwood, Ringwood, Hampshire BH24 3LE

Mrs Carelle Sherwood
☎ 01425 474977
Fax 01425 471005
BB From £20–£25
Sleeps 4
🐕 🐎 🐾 🧺 🏕 🎯 ⊛
♦♦♦

Roughwood is a small elegant country house in 20 acres set in a secluded valley in the heart of the New Forest. The farm has direct access to 45,000 acres of the New Forest and has the ancient rights of 'commoning' to graze cattle, ponies and pigs there. Stabling for guests' own horses. All rooms are self-contained and en suite. Stunning views and abundant wildlife. Easy access to Dorset and the coast. Open all year. E-mail: tallyho@bigfoot.com

9 **Vine Farmhouse,** Isington, Bentley, Alton, Hampshire GU34 4PW

Mrs G Sinclair
☎/Fax 01420 23262
Mobile 0467 767599
BB From £17.50–£22.50
Sleeps 5
🐕 🐾 💈 🏠 🏕 ✂
♦♦♦

Vine Farmhouse is situated halfway between Alton and Farnham in its own farmland overlooking the River Wey. Gatwick and Heathrow are 1 hour by car as is London. Local attractions are Jane Austen's house, Birdworld, steam museum and railway and numerous gardens. Pubs and restaurants nearby. Open all year except Christmas. E-mail: vinefarm@aol.com

Self-Catering

10 **Beacon Hill Farm Cottages,** Beacon Hill Lane, Exton, Southampton, Hampshire SO32 3NW

Mrs C Dunford
☎ 01730 829724
Fax 01730 829833
SC From £300–£430
Sleeps 4/5
🧍 🐕 🐾 ♿ 🏠
🐎 🐾 🐎 – 🐎 🐎 🐎
Commended

Barn conversion comprising 4 self-catering cottages. Stunning location in the Meon Valley with magnificent farmland views. Tastefully furnished with beamed ceilings and galleried landings. One suitable for disabled with carer. Close to Winchester and Portsmouth. Ideal for walkers (South Downs Way). Excellent facilities including dishwasher, microwave, barbecue, garden furniture. Open all year.

Meadow Cottage, c/o Farley Farm, Braishfield, Romsey, Hampshire SO51 0QP

Mrs Wendy Graham
☎ **01794 368265**
Fax 01794 367847
[SC] **From £190–£300**
Sleeps 5 + cot
🐕 🏇 ♿ 🏕
🌺🌺🌺🌺 *Commended*

Well equipped, semi-detached cottage on a 400-acre beef and arable farm. Outstanding views of beautiful surrounding countryside. Ideal for walking or riding, or touring historic centres of Romsey, Winchester, Salisbury, Portsmouth, New Forest and coast. Cottage has CH, log fire, colour TV, downstairs WC, washer/dryer, cot. Garden. Phone for brochure. Open Easter–Oct.

Owl Cottage, Lye Farm, West Tytherley, Romsey, Hampshire SP5 1LA ⓬

Maxine Vine
☎ **01794 341667**
[SC] **From £195–£315**
Sleeps 5
🐕 🏇 🏕 ♿ 🚶 ⚓
Applied

Owl cottage has been skillfully converted from an old barn situated in one of the most beautiful parts of Hampshire. Outstanding views, close New Forest, Salisbury, Winchester. Location perfect for touring, walking, riding in southern England. Excellently equipped cottage, central heating, electric included, washer dryer, TV, cot. Peaceful and relaxing environment. Open all year.
E-mail: maxine.vine@virgin.net

STAY ON A FARM GIFT TOKENS

FARM HOLIDAY BUREAU

If you have enjoyed your Stay on a Farm, why not treat your friends and relatives to *Stay on a Farm* gift tokens? Available from the Bureau office (tel: 024 7669 6909), they can be redeemed against accommodation and are accepted by the majority of farms (see Index). Please check when booking to avoid disappointment.

FINDING YOUR ACCOMMODATION

FARM HOLIDAY BUREAU

The local FHB Group contacts listed on page 392 can always help you find a vacancy in your chosen area.

page 392 can always help you find a vacancy

THE 1000+ BUREAU MEMBERS OFFER A UNIQUE LINK TO CUSTOMERS ACROSS THE UK

FARM HOLIDAY BUREAU

All Bureau members belong to a local Group. Each member can refer you to an equally high quality member within the Group... or across the UK: England, Northern Ireland, Scotland, Wales.

Isle of Wight

The Needles, Medina Valley, the Downs & Sandown Bay

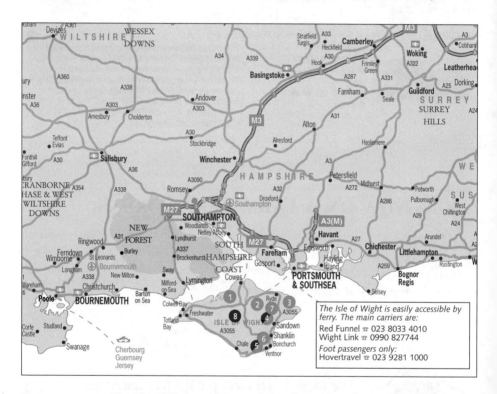

The Isle of Wight is easily accessible by ferry. The main carriers are:

Red Funnel ☎ 023 8033 4010
Wight Link ☎ 0990 827744

Foot passengers only:
Hovertravel ☎ 023 9281 1000

Key

1 Bed & Breakfast

1 Self-Catering

1 B&B and SC

1 Camping Barns

1 Camping & Caravanning

The Isle of Wight, with its sandy beaches and small, secluded coves, and the sea never more than 15 minutes from wherever you may be, has a wide variety of holiday activities and attractions. With Cowes and the Royal Yacht Squadron, an international symbol of all that is finest in yachting, the Island is famous for its seafaring activities. This is the perfect holiday retreat for ramblers on the Downs, birdwatchers, anglers, adventure sports enthusiasts and for those who merely wish to relax and drink in the glorious scenery. A climate that tops the British Isles' Sunshine League makes the Island particularly attractive in Spring or Autumn for short break holidays.

If you would like help in finding suitable farm accommodation, turn to the full listing of FHB Groups on pages 392 to 395 to find appropriate contact details for this area.

Bed and Breakfast
(and evening meal)

Auld Youngwoods Farm, Whitehouse Road, Porchfield, Newport, Isle of Wight PO30 4LJ

Judith Shanks
☎/Fax **01983 522170**
BB From **£16–£20**
Sleeps 5
🛏(8) ⅄ 🛉 ⚮ ♨ ⚘
♦♦♦

A grassland farm set in open countryside. The 18th century renovated stone farmhouse retains its original character. The guest rooms are spacious and enjoy magnificent views of the West Wight (CH throughout). Close to Newtown Nature Reserve, an ideal base for the naturalist. Wild flowers. Red squirrels, owls and butterflies locally. Cowes sailing centre 4 miles. Open all year.

Grange Farm, Staplers Raod, Wootton, Nr Ryde, Isle of Wight PO33 4RW

Rosemarie Horne
☎ **01983 882147**
BB From **£18.50–£20**
Sleeps 4
🛏(8) ♨ ⚘ ◉
♦♦♦♦

Grange Farm House offers two twin en suite rooms. It lies between Newport and Ryde on the outskirts of Wootton village down a long private drive surrounded by peaceful countryside and the beauty of the wildlife that chooses to live here too. There is a half-hourly bus service from the end of the drive. Open all year.

Harbour Farm, Embankment Road, Bembridge, Isle of Wight PO35 5NS   

Mrs D Hicks
☎ **01983 872610**
Fax **01983 874080**
BB From **£20–£25**
Sleeps 4
⅄ ♨ ⚘
♦♦♦♦

Accommodation in lovely farmhouse on large estate. Close to harbour and beaches, excellent bird watching. Ideal walking and riding country, stabling available for guests' horses. Free dinghy parking. Water sports and sea fishing nearby. Excellent local places to eat. One double en suite bedroom plus three single bedrooms. Open all year.

Kern Farm, Alverstone, Nr Sandown, Isle of Wight PO36 0EY   ④

Mrs Gaynor Oliver
☎ **01983 403721**
Fax **01983 403908**
BB From **£20**
Sleeps 5
🛏(12) ⅄ ⚮ ⚘
♦♦♦

Quiet and secluded 16th century listed stone farmhouse nestling at the foot of the Downs on a mixed farm with wonderful views. Situated on Bembridge Trail. Sandy beaches 3 miles. One double and one triple bedroom – both en suite with tea and coffee-making facilities. Colour TV. Minimum 2 nights. Open all year.

Lisle Combe, Bank End Farm, Undercliff Drive, St Lawrence, Ventnor, Isle of Wight PO38 1UW   ⑤

Hugh & Judy Noyes
☎ **01983 852582/854310**
BB From **£19.50**
Sleeps 6
🛏 ⅄ ♨
♦♦

Listed Elizabethan style farmhouse overlooking English Channel, home of the late Alfred Noyes (poet and author) and his family. 5 acre coastal garden with rare waterfowl and pheasant collection (over 100 species). Free entry to owner's rare breeds farm park. Superb sea views, coves and small beaches in Area of Outstanding Natural Beauty. Open all year.

6 **Little Span Farm,** Rew Lane, Wroxall, Ventnor, Isle of Wight PO38 3AU

Mr & Mrs Corry
☎ 01983 852419
⊞ From £17.50–£19.50
Sleeps 8
⋈ ⋔ ⋇ ⋕
♦♦♦

17th century centrally heated farmhouse in Area of Outstanding Natural Beauty on arable/stock farm close to beaches, footpaths, golf course and tourist attractions. Sky TV, tea/coffee-making facilities, log fires. Full English breakfast. Garden for guests' use, off road car parking. Cot/high chair available. Short breaks. Open all year.

7 **Little Upton Farm,** Ashey, Nr Ryde, Isle of Wight PO33 4BS

Mrs Alison Johnson
☎/Fax 01983 563236
⊞ From £18–£20
Sleeps 6
⋈(12) ⋔ ⋇ ⋕ ⋕
♦♦♦♦♦ Silver Award

Attractive, secluded 17th century listed farmhouse with beamed ceilings, inglenook fireplace, conservatory and extensive gardens. All rooms have magnificent views over outstanding landscape of ancient wooded parkland to the Downs beyond. Near Bembridge Trail, sandy beaches 2 miles. Two spacious double rooms, one twin, all en suite with CH, tea/coffee and TV. Fridge on landing. Open all year except Christmas.

Self-Catering

5 **Combe Lodge,** Bank End Farm, Undercliff Drive, St Lawrence, Ventnor, IOW PO38 1UW

Hugh & Judy Noyes
☎ 01983 852582/854310
⊞ From £260–£400
Sleeps 6 + cot
⋈ ⋇
⋆⋆⋆ Approved

Victorian-style cottage in wooded surroundings over-looking owners' rare breeds and waterfowl park to which there is free entry. Own garden within grounds of Bank End Farm. Many small coves for swimming and sunbathing. Colour TV. Everything provided except linen. Fine coastal walks within Area of Outstanding Natural Beauty. Open all year.

8 **The Stable,** Newbarn Farm, Newbarn Lane, Gatcombe, Newport, Isle of Wight PO30 3EQ

Mrs Diane Harvey
☎ 01983 721202
⊞ From £150–£450
Sleeps 6 + cot
⋈ ⋕ ⋇
⋆⋆⋆⋆ Highly Commended

Beautiful converted stable offering high standard of accommodation for up to six people. Both bedrooms have double beds, one with 3 ft bunks, other with cot. Secluded valley setting, excellent walking. Centrally situated for island attractions. Enclosed patio and parking. Linen and electricity included. Beds made up on arrival. Open all year.

4 **West Wing,** Kern Farm, Alverstone, nr Sandown, Isle of Wight PO36 0EY

Mrs Gaynor Oliver
☎ 01983 403721
Fax 01983 403908
⊞ From £275–£540
Sleeps 8
⋈(12) ⋇ ⋕ ⋕ ⋘
⋆⋆⋆ Highly Commended

Self-contained west wing of 16th century listed stone farmhouse on 250-acre mixed farm. Off beaten track, ideal for walking, painting or just relaxing. Two triple bedrooms. All linen provided. Log fire and CH. Guests' horses stay free. Regret no dogs and no children under 12. Friday bookings. Open all year.

Surrey

North Downs, Pilgrims' Way & Surrey Hills

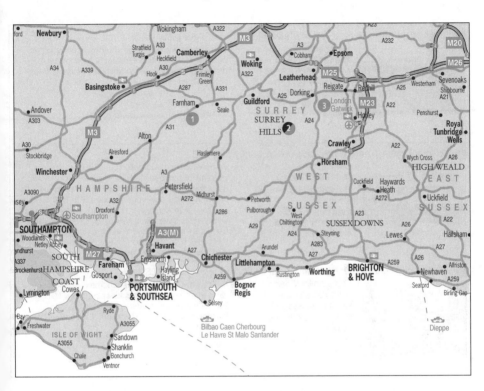

Key

🔴 Bed & Breakfast

🔴 Self-Catering

🔴 B&B and SC

🔲 Camping Barns

🔺 Camping & Caravanning

In Surrey, the North Downs provide dramatic wooded hillsides with small, attractive towns and villages nestling in the valleys. Here you can walk along the track claiming to be the Pilgrims' Way which connects Winchester to Canterbury, or clamber up famous heights like Leith Hill – just short of 1,000ft – or its neighbour Box Hill, coming down via the intriguingly named Zig Zag Hill. The charming towns of Farnham, Guildford and Dorking are excellent for shopping and there are numerous pretty villages for the lover of tea shops and antiques. The National Trust's Polesden Lacey is a jewel in a beautiful setting, yet none of this is more than an hour from London.

If you would like help in finding suitable farm accommodation, turn to the full listing of FHB Groups on pages 392 to 395 to find appropriate contact details for this area.

Bed and Breakfast

(and evening meal)

---

1 **Borderfield Farm,** Boundary Road, Rowledge, Farnham, Surrey GU10 4EP

Pam Simpson
☎ **01252 793985**
Mobile 0585 581443
BB From £19–£20
Sleeps 4

Working smallholding set in attractive countryside on outskirts of village. Two excellent pubs within walking distance. Within easy reach of London, coast and New Forest. Open all year.

---

2 **Bulmer Farm,** Holmbury St Mary, Dorking, Surrey RH5 6LG

Gill Hill
☎ **01306 730210**
BB From £21–£34
Sleeps 16
Caravans £3.50

Warm welcome guaranteed at our 30-acre farm in peaceful, picturesque Victorian village amid Surrey hills. 3 charming rooms in 17th century farmhouse; 5 en suite barn conversion, non-smoking rooms with TV around courtyard adjoining house. Homemade preserves. Large walled garden, woodland walk to award-winning lake. Good pubs nearby. Convenient for London, airports, Wisley, NT properties, sporting venues. Elizabeth Gundrey recommended. Open all year.

---

3 **Sturtwood Farm,** Partridge Lane, Newdigate, Dorking, Surrey RH5 5EE

Bridget MacKinnon
☎ **01306 631308**
Fax 01306 631908
BB From £22.50–£30
Sleeps 5

An attractive 18th century farmhouse in lovely countryside yet within 12 mins of Gatwick Airport. Many National Trust properties and gardens nearby. Also London, Brighton and several country towns. Open all year except Christmas.

Self-Catering

---

2 **'Badgersholt' and 'Foxholme',** c/o Bulmer Farm, Holmbury St Mary, Dorking, Surrey RH5 6LG

Gill Hill
☎ **01306 730210**
SC From £170–£320
Sleep 2/4

Commended

Two delightfully cosy, single-storey cottages, sympathetically converted from a Surrey barn, forming a courtyard with the farmhouse. Fully carpeted, electric CH, colour TV and linen (beds made up). Communal laundry room, use of 2-acre farmhouse garden. Situated in picturesque, quiet valley. Ideal walking country. 'Badgersholt' sleeps 2 (also suitable disabled). 'Foxholme' sleeps 4 in 2 bedrooms. Open all year.

West Sussex

Sussex Weald, Rother & Arun Valleys & Sussex Downs

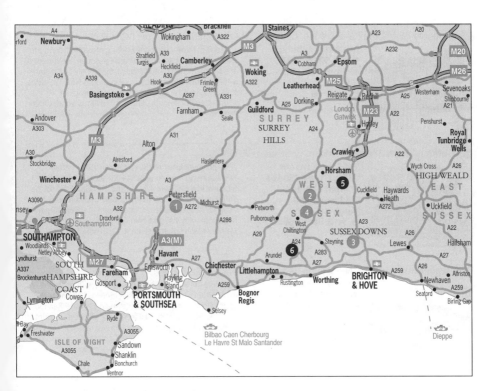

Key

 Bed & Breakfast

 Self-Catering

 B&B and SC

 Camping Barns

 Camping & Caravanning

The West Sussex coast stretches from historic Chichester and its harbour to Shoreham, taking in Bognor Regis, Littlehampton and Worthing and many picturesque smaller resorts on the way. Just inland there is the vast area of lovely downland with the South Downs Way and picturesque villages such as Storrington and Poynings waiting to be explored. West Sussex has a wealth of attractive towns: Midhurst, Horsham and East Grinstead, to name a few, and all surrounded by lush green countryside. There is history here, in Arundel's castle, Petworth House, glorious Goodwood and Fishbourne, site of the remains of a palace once ruled by a King Cogidubnus – really.

If you would like help in finding suitable farm accommodation, turn to the full listing of FHB Groups on pages 392 to 395 to find appropriate contact details for this area.

Bed and Breakfast
(and evening meal)

① Compton Farmhouse, Church Lane, Compton, Nr Chichester, West Sussex PO18 9HB

Mrs Melanie Bray
☎ 023 9263 1597
BB From £18–£20
Sleeps 5

Listed flint farmhouse on a working mixed farm. We are 200 yards up a track from the village square, next door to the Norman church of St Mary. Large family bedroom with private bathroom. Own sitting room with TV, fridge and drink-making facilities. Within easy reach of Chichester, Portsmouth, Arundel and Goodwood. Open Jan–Nov.

② Goffsland Farm, Shipley, Horsham, West Sussex RH13 7BQ

Mrs Carol Liverton
☎/Fax 01403 730434
BB From £19–£21
EM From £9.50
Sleeps 5

A friendly welcome awaits you at our 17th century farmhouse on a working farm with sheep and cattle. Situated in the Sussex Weald central to Gatwick and the South coast. Family room has double bed and bunk beds with washbasin and tea/coffee-making facilities. Own bathroom with WC and own sitting/dining room with TV. Evening meals by arrangement. Open all year.

③ Manor Farm, Poynings, Nr Brighton, West Sussex BN45 7AG

Mrs Carol Revell
☎/Fax 01273 857371
BB From £23–£25
Sleeps 6
☺(8)

260-acre family run sheep/arable farm with charming old manor house resting quietly in a green valley under the South Downs. An Area of Outstanding Natural Beauty, ideal for riders, walkers, golfers, hang gliders and country lovers. Plenty of country pubs and eating houses nearby. A23 5 mins, Hickstead 10 mins, Gatwick 30 mins, Brighton and Hove 15 mins. Open Apr–Nov.

④ New House Farm, Broadford Bridge Road, West Chiltington, Nr Pulborough, West Sussex RH20 2LA

Alma Steele
☎ 01798 812215
Fax 01798 813209
BB From £22.50–£35
Sleeps 6
☺(10)

Listed 15th century farmhouse with oak beams and inglenook fireplace, in the centre of the village, close to local inns which provide good food. An 18 hole golf course, open to non-members, is only ¼ mile away. Many places of historical interest in the area including Goodwood House, Petworth House, Parham House, Arundel Castle. Gatwick 35 minutes. En suite facilities and colour TV in bedrooms. Open all year.

FARM HOLIDAY
BUREAU

Please mention *Stay on a Farm* when booking

Self-Catering

Black Cottage, c/o Newells Farm, Newells Lane, Lower Beeding, Horsham, West Sussex RH13 6LN ⑤

Vicky Storey
☎ 01403 891326
Fax 01403 891530
⌂ From £175–£280
Sleeps 4
♿ ♞ ♟ ☂ ♠
✿ ✿ ✿ *Approved*

A delightful secluded cottage in the centre of a sheep and arable farm, with views to the South Downs. Surrounded by woods and lovely walks. Sleeps 4 in comfort. Recently modernised, it is 40 mins from Brighton, 20 mins from Gatwick, with fishing, golf and beautiful Sussex, Surrey and Kent gardens within easy reach. The ideal holiday cottage. Open all year.

Byre Cottages, c/o Sullington Manor Farm, Storrington, West Sussex RH20 4AE ⑥

Mrs G Kittle
☎/Fax 01903 745754
⌂ From £120–£350
Sleep 2–6
♿ ♞ ☂ ♠ ♟
✿ ✿ ✿ – ✿ ✿ ✿ ✿
Commended

Mixed farm with many footpaths and walks in beautiful, peaceful location on South Downs. Four spacious cottages sleeping 2, 4 or 6, converted from stables and overlooking a shared lawn and 17th century tithe barn. Outdoor swimming pool with springboard and slide, tennis court and barbecue. Beaches 30 mins. London 1 hour by regular train service. Many historic houses, castles and gardens in this lovely part of England.

NO ANSWER?

Farmers are mostly out and about during the day.
Try to telephone before 9.30am or after 4pm.

CONFIRM BOOKINGS

Disappointments can arise from misunderstandings over the telephone.
Please write to confirm your booking.

FARM HOLIDAY
BUREAU

Our Internet address is
http://www.webscape.co.uk/farmaccom/

East Sussex

Ashdown Forest, High Weald & Sussex Downs

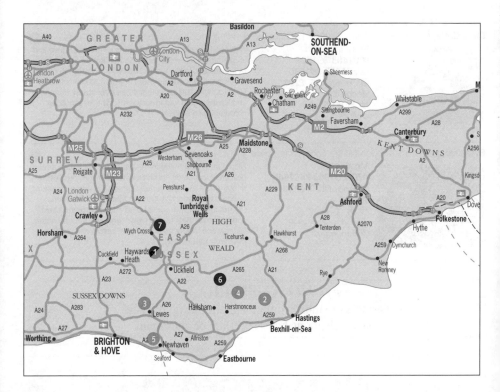

Key

🔴 1 Bed & Breakfast

🔴 1 Self-Catering

🔴 1 B&B and SC

1 Camping Barns

⚠ 1 Camping & Caravanning

'Sussex by the Sea' conjures up the famous resorts of Brighton and Eastbourne, each of which can easily fill a day out, having so much to offer. But don't forget the lesser-known delights of the East Sussex coast such as Cuckmere Haven in the Seven Sisters Country Park, or picturesque Rye, just inland. For a spot of culture you can't beat Glyndebourne, or visit exquisitely-painted Charleston, once home of the Bloomsbury set. Then there's magnificent Sheffield Park, or Battle for a bit of 1066 and all that. Give the children a turn – they'll love chugging through the glorious countryside on the Bluebell Railway or playing Pooh sticks at A.A. Milne's Hartfield in the Ashdown Forest.

If you would like help in finding suitable farm accommodation, turn to the full listing of FHB Groups on pages 392 to 395 to find appropriate contact details for this area.

Bed and Breakfast
(and evening meal)

Funnells Farm, Down Street, Nutley, East Sussex TN22 3LG

Mrs M Thomas
☎ 01825 712034
Fax 01825 713511
⒝⒝ From £20–£30
Sleep 6
�ां(10) ⅄ ▪ 🏇 🐴
♦♦♦

Traditional Sussex farmhouse quietly situated in an Area of Outstanding Natural Beauty on the edge of Ashdown Forest, which offers 6,500 acres of open country, heathland ridges and wooded valleys for walking and riding. Ideal base for touring Sussex. King size double, twin and family rooms, all en suite with colour TV and tea tray. Organic breakfasts, ample parking. Excellent pubs and restaurants nearby.

Moonshill Farm, The Green, Ninfield, Battle, East Sussex TN33 9LH

Mrs June Ive
☎/Fax 01424 892645
⒝⒝ From £17.50–£20
Sleeps 6
☰(4) 🐓 🚶 ▦ ☕ 🏇 🐴 ▪ ✝
◉
♦♦

In the heart of the '1066 Country' in the centre of Ninfield opposite pub. Farmhouse in 10 acres of garden, orchard, stables. Enjoy beautiful walks, golf and riding arranged. Comfortable rooms, 3 en suite, CH and electric fires, hospitality tray, TV, lounge, parking and garage, babysitting service. Every comfort in our safe, quiet and peaceful home. Reduced rates for weekly bookings. Open Jan–Nov.

Ousedale House, Offham, Lewes, East Sussex BN7 3QF

Roland & Brenda Gough
☎ 01273 478680
Fax 01273 486510
⒝⒝ From £25–£35
EM From £14
Sleeps 6
⅄ ⊞ ▪ ◉
♦♦♦♦ Silver Award

You are warmly welcomed to our spacious Victorian house with its garden and panoramic views of the river valley. We are retired farmers who like music (Glyndebourne nearby – speciality hampers prepared) and cooking, and are enthusiastic WI members/marketeers. Runner up 'Best B&B' in South East England Tourist Board Region. Central for touring Sussex. Courtesy car – Lewes station. Open all year.

The Stud Farm, Bodle Street Green, Nr Hailsham, East Sussex BN27 4RJ

Philippa & Richard Gentry
☎/Fax 01323 833201
⒝⒝ From £20–£25
Sleeps 6
🐴 ⅄ ▪ 🐴
♦♦♦

70 acre sheep and cattle farm situated in peaceful surround-ings and beautiful countryside, ideal for walking. 8 miles from sea, Eastbourne, Hastings, South Downs in easy reach. Upstairs, family unit of double bedded room/twin bedded room, both with handbasins, and bathroom. Downstairs twin bedded room with shower, toilet, handbasin en suite. All bedrooms with colour TV and tea/coffee-making facilities. Guests' sitting room, colour TV. Sunroom. Open all year.

Stud Farm House, Telscombe Village, Lewes, East Sussex BN7 3HZ

Tim & Nina Armour
☎/Fax 01273 302486
⒝⒝ From £20–£23.50
Sleeps 6
🐓 🐴 ☕ ▪ 🏇
♦♦♦

Family-run working 300-acre sheep farm and 17th century house in quiet hamlet on the South Downs Way in Glyndebourne and Bloomsbury area. Central for touring – Gatwick 30 mins, Brighton 15 mins, London 1 hour by train, Newhaven/Dieppe Sealink Ferries 10 mins. Guests' own 'unique' lounge. Cosy and comfortable, a relaxing break with a family atmosphere. Open Feb–Dec.

Self-Catering

6 Boring House Farm, Vines Cross, Heathfield, East Sussex TN21 9AS

Mrs Anne Reed
☎ 01435 812285
SC From £130–£200
Sleeps 6
🔆 🐎 🐕 👤 👤
🍃🍃🍃🍃 *Commended*

Peaceful farm cottage on sheep and beef farm. Marvellous views and walks, fishing available. Traditional local, good atmosphere/food in easy walking distance. Many beautiful places to visit. Beach within 15 miles. Accommodation (portion of farmhouse) comprises utility room, hall, WC, kitchen, dining room, sitting room, 3 bedrooms, 1 with shower, 1 with washbasin, bathroom and WC. Large garden. Open Mar–Nov.

7 2 High Weald Cottages, Chelwood Farm, Nutley, c/o Sheffield Park Farm, Nr Uckfield, E Sussex TN22 3QR

Mrs Nicky Howe
☎ 01825 790235/790267
Fax 01825 790151
SC From £200–£425
Sleeps 5 + cot
🔆 👤 🛏 👤
🍃🍃🍃🍃 *Commended*

Picturesque semi-detached farm cottage with garden on dairy farm adjacent Ashdown Forest. Comfortable accommodation comprises 1 double, 1 twin, 1 single room, bathroom, WC, sitting room (log fire, colour TV, phone), kitchen (fridge/freezer, auto washing machine, tumble dryer, electric cooker). Close Sheffield Park Gardens, Bluebell Railway. Easy reach Downs and coast. Cot/high chair available. Beds made up. No cot linen provided; towels on request. Open all year.

1 Stables Cottage, Funnells Farm, Down Street, Nutley, East Sussex TN22 3LG

Mrs M Thomas
☎ 01825 712034
Fax 01825 713511
SC From £250–£600
Sleeps 6
🔆(10) 🍴 🔆 🛏 👤
Applied

Tastefully converted courtyard cottage on 52-acre equestrian farm. A peaceful spot with panoramic views to the South Downs and glorious walking and riding in Ashdown Forest. One twin, 1 double, sitting room with sofa-bed/dining room, kitchen (fridge/freezer, washer, dryer, electric cooker, microwave, dishwasher) bathroom, and shower room. Sunny patio. All linen provided. Stabling and grazing available.

Please mention *Stay on a Farm* when booking

FINDING YOUR ACCOMMODATION

The local FHB Group contacts listed on page 392 can always help you find a vacancy in your chosen area.

Kent

Kent Downs, High Weald, Weald of Kent & Romney Marsh

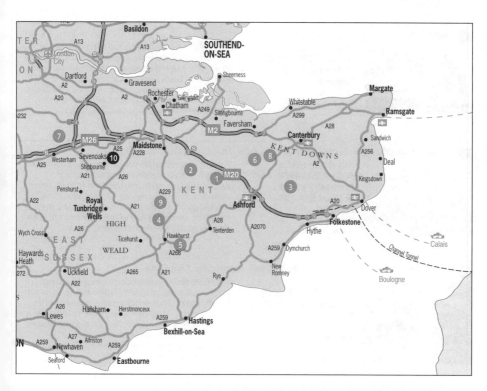

Key

- ① Bed & Breakfast
- ① Self-Catering
- ① B&B and SC
- ① Camping Barns
- ⚠ Camping & Caravanning

Kent is very much farming country, and the distinctive features are the many orchards, hop gardens and oast houses to be found in the aptly named 'Garden of England'. The lovely and varied Kent countryside is dotted with many historic towns and villages, such as the medieval port of Sandwich, Tenterden, West Malling, Cranbrook, Rochester and the hilltop village of Chilham. Kent has a wealth of attractions for the visitor, including world-famous Canterbury Cathedral, fairytale castles such as Leeds, Hever, Dover, Deal and Walmer, numerous historic houses including Churchill's Chartwell, Knole and Penshurst Place, fortifications, museums, vineyards, wildlife parks and glorious gardens.

If you would like help in finding suitable farm accommodation, turn to the full listing of FHB Groups on pages 392 to 395 to find appropriate contact details for this area.

Bed and Breakfast
(and evening meal)

---

① Barnfield, Charing, Ashford, Kent TN27 0BN

Mrs Phillada Pym
☎/Fax 01233 712421
Ⓑ From £20–£27
Sleeps 6
☼ ⚡ Å ⬛ 🛄 🕱 ⚘
◆◆◆

Charming and romantic Kent hall farmhouse built in 1420 with a wealth of character. A family home by a wildfowl lake amidst peaceful farmland. England at its very best. Excellent for Leeds Castle, Canterbury, Sissinghurst, Channel Tunnel and coastal ports. 1 family, 1 double, 1 twin and 2 singles. AA QQQ. Open all year except Christmas.

---

② Bramley Knowle Farm, Eastwood Road, Ulcombe, Maidstone, Kent ME17 1ET

Mrs Diane Leat
☎ 01622 858878
Fax 01622 851121
Ⓑ From £18–£25
Sleeps 5
☼(3) ⚡ ⬛
◆◆◆

A warm welcome awaits you at our modern farmhouse built in Kentish barn style. Set in peaceful, rural surroundings yet only 10 minutes from M20 J8. Evening meals available within walking distance. Ideal for visiting Leeds Castle, Sissinghurst Gardens, Canterbury, Rye, Knole, Chartwell and Channel ports. London 1 hour by train. Open all year except Christmas.

---

③ Great Field Farm, Misling Lane, Stelling Minnis, Canterbury, Kent CT4 6DE

Lewana Castle
☎/Fax 01227 709223
Ⓑ From £18–£22.50
Sleeps 6
☼ ⚡ ⊡ ⬛
◆◆◆◆

This comfortable, spacious farmhouse, with a wealth of old pine, sits amidst pleasant gardens and paddocks with friendly ponies. Three en suite rooms with colour TV, 1 double/family room with jacuzzi-style air bath, 2 have own lounges, 1 with kitchen. A warm welcome assured, very child friendly, all day access. Ideal location for exploring Kent, convenient for Canterbury, Chunnel and ferries. Open all year.

---

④ Hallwood Farm, Hartley, Hawkhurst Road, Cranbrook, Kent TN17 2SP

David Wickham
☎/Fax 01580 713204
Ⓑ From £20–£25
EM From £15
Sleeps 6
☼(5) 🕱 ⚡ ⬛ 🛄
◆◆◆

A lovely 15th century farmhouse with enchanting garden, surrounded by peaceful countryside. 2 miles from Cranbrook, medieval town associated with Wealden weaving and iron trades. Ideally situated for Sissinghurst Castle, other classic gardens, historic castles, NT properties. Easy access to London, Channel Tunnel. Comfortable, well furnished bedrooms, guests' lounge. Open Apr–Oct.

---

⑤ Hoads Farm, Crouch Lane, Sandhurst, Cranbrook, Kent TN18 5PA

Anne Nicholas
☎/Fax 01580 850296
Ⓑ £19
EM From £10–£14
Sleeps 6
☼ ⊡ 🛄 ⬛ ⚘
◆◆◆

Bed and breakfast available in 17th century farmhouse on hop vine and sheep farm. Comfortable furnishings, sitting room with colour TV. Good centre for the coast, Bodiam Castle, Sissinghurst Castle, Scotney Castle and other National Trust properties. Excellent train service to London from Etchingham or Staplehurst. Dinner by arrangement. Dropside cot available on request. Open all year.

Leaveland Court, Leaveland, Faversham, Kent ME13 0NP ⑥

Mrs Corrine Scutt
☎ 01233 740596
Fax 01233 740015
[BB] From £22.50–£25
Sleeps 6
🐶 ⅄ ⬛ 🎄 ▪ ◉
◆◆◆◆

Captivating 15th century timbered farmhouse on 300-acre downland farm. Easy access, 3 miles south of M2 junction 6, Faversham 5 minutes, Canterbury 20 minutes. Situated in a quiet setting with attractive garden and outdoor heated swimming pool. All rooms have en suite facilities, colour TV and tea/coffee trays. Traditional farmhouse food and warm welcome assured. Brochure available. Open Feb–Nov.

Preston Farmhouse, Shoreham, Sevenoaks, Kent TN14 7UD ⑦

Mrs Shirley Montgomerie
☎ 01959 522029
Fax 01959 524375
[BB] From £22–£24
Sleeps 4
🐶(10) ⅄ 🎄 ▪
◆◆◆

We look forward to welcoming you to our 18th century farmhouse in the beautiful Darenth Valley. We are an ideal base for visiting London, 35 minutes by train, and there are many NT properties in the area. Guests' sitting room, TV and conservatory. Open all year except Christmas.

South Wootton House, Capel Road, Petham, Canterbury, Kent CT4 5RG ⑧

Frances Mount
☎ 01227 700643
Fax 01227 700613
[BB] From £20–£25
Sleeps 4
🐶 🐴 ⅄ 🏕 🐕 🐎 🎄 ▪
◆◆◆

A beautiful farmhouse with a conservatory set in extensive garden, surrounded by fields and woodland. Fully coordinated bedroom with private bathroom. Tea/coffee facilities, colour TV. Children and dogs welcome. Canterbury 4 miles. Open all year.

Tanner House, Tanner Farm, Goudhurst Road, Marden, Tonbridge, Kent TN12 9ND ⑨

Lesley Mannington
☎ 01622 831214
Fax 01622 832472
[BB] From £20–£22.50
EM From £14
Sleeps 6
🐶(12) ⅄ ⬛ 🏕 🐕 ⟵ 🎄 ▪ ◉
◆◆◆◆

For a restful break, holiday or stop over, we are ideally placed in the beautiful Weald countryside. Our Tudor farmhouse in the centre of our working arable farm offers excellent accommodation and cuisine. All our rooms, 1 double and 2 twins, have en suite shower/WC, colour TV, radio, tea/coffee. One with a genuine four-poster bed. We specialise in a countryside welcome. Visa/Access/Switch. Open all year except Christmas. E-mail: tannerfarm@compuserve.com

---

Self-Catering

Golding Hop Farm Cottage, c/o Golding Hop Farm, Bewley Lane, Plaxtol, Nr Sevenoaks, Kent TN15 0PS ⑩

Jacqueline Vincent
☎ 01732 885432
[SC] From £180–£380
Sleeps 5 + cot
🐶 🐴 ⅄ 🎄 ▪ 🌾
🐾 🐾 🐾 🐾

Highly Commended

13-acre farm producing Kent cobnuts for London markets. Surrounded by orchards and close to attractive village of Plaxtol. Secluded cottage, but not isolated. Sleeps 5, 2 double and 1 single, CH, colour TV, washer dryer and fridge/freezer, payphone. Horse riding, golf nearby. Car essential. Covered parking. Local station 2 miles with frequent trains to London. Motorway 4 miles. Dogs by arrangement only. Agency priority mid March to October. Open all year.

Stay on a farm

Gift Tokens

FOR A PRESENT TO REMEMBER

Available from

Farm Holiday Bureau (UK) Ltd,
National Agricultural Centre, Stoneleigh Park,
Warwickshire CV8 2LZ

Telephone: 024 7669 6909
Fax: 024 7669 6630

England's West Country

Farm entries in this section are listed under those counties shown in green on the key map. The index below the map gives the appropriate page numbers. You will see that we have listed the counties geographically so that you can turn more easily to find farms in neighbouring counties.

At the start of each county section is a detailed map with numbered symbols indicating the location of each farm. Different symbols denote different types of accommodation; see the key below each county map. Farm entries are listed alphabetically under type of accommodation. Some farms offer more than one type of accommodation and therefore have more than one entry.

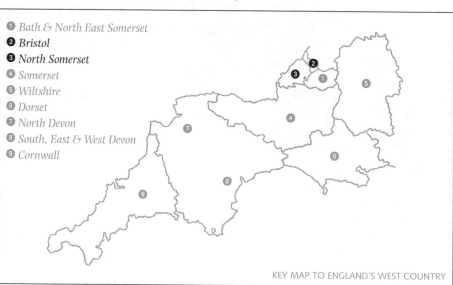

❶ *Bath & North East Somerset*
❷ *Bristol*
❸ *North Somerset*
④ *Somerset*
⑤ *Wiltshire*
⑥ *Dorset*
⑦ *North Devon*
⑧ *South, East & West Devon*
⑨ *Cornwall*

KEY MAP TO ENGLAND'S WEST COUNTRY

Bath & North East Somerset

Bristol & Kennet & Avon Canal

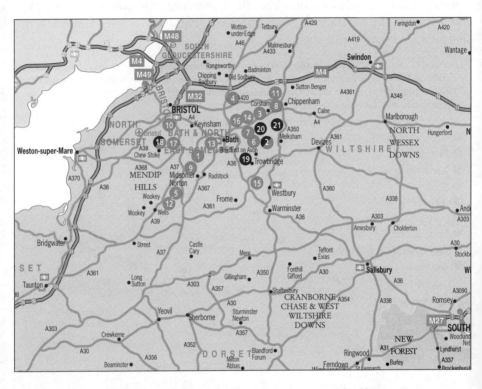

Key

1 Bed & Breakfast

1 Self-Catering

1 B&B and SC

1 Camping Barns

1 Camping & Caravanning

Though modern in name, this county has a wealth of history. Its namesake, the beautiful city of Bath, is a World Heritage site famed for its Roman remains, in the shape of the fascinating Roman Baths, and elegant Georgian architecture. The whole city is alive with unusual shops, street entertainment and pavement cafes, while nearby Bristol will keep you busy for days. Around Bath, the lovely countryside rolling away to the Mendip Hills is just as noteworthy as the city attractions. Picturesque villages with charming country pubs are too numerous to mention. You can walk or cycle the newly-restored Kennet and Avon Canal, sail the lakes at Blagdon and Chew Valley or, if that sounds too energetic, try the local cider on one of our farms.

If you would like help in finding suitable farm accommodation, turn to the full listing of FHB Groups on pages 392 to 395 to find appropriate contact details for this area.

Bed and Breakfast
(and evening meal)

Barrow Vale Farm, Farmborough, Bath BA3 1BL ①

Cherilyn Langley
☎ 01761 470300
[BB] From £19–£20
Sleeps 6
☺(5) ⚡ ⛺ ⚓
♦♦♦♦

Situated between the historic cities of Bath and Wells, we offer a high standard of accommodation – tastefully furnished en suite bedrooms, TV lounge and conservatory for guests' use overlooking the garden. Cheddar, Longleat and Weston-super-Mare are all within easy reach. Local eating houses close by. Open all year except Christmas and New Year.

Beeches Farmhouse, Holt Road, Bradford-on-Avon, Wiltshire BA15 1TS ②

Mrs Sharon Gover
☎/Fax 01225 863475
Mobile 0374 607417
[BB] From £25–£30
Sleeps 12
⊕ ☺ ⚡ ⊡ ⚓ ⛺ ⊛
♦♦♦♦♦

Idyllic 18th century farmhouse and recently converted old dairy and old cart house in rural setting east of Bath. Family, double and twin rooms, all en suite and decorated with original country pine furnishings to a very high standard. Exposed beams, breakfast in Victorian-style conservatory overlooking a running stream. Free range ducks and hens – collect your own eggs for breakfast. Riding and golf nearby. Brochure. Closed Christmas. E-mail: beeches-farmhouse@1way.co.uk

---

Church Farm, Hartham Park, Corsham, Nr Chippenham, Wiltshire SN13 0PU ③

Mrs Kate Jones
☎/Fax 01249 715180
Mobile 07977 910775
[BB] From £20–£22.50
Sleeps 6
☺ 🐴 ⚡ 🧍 🚗 ⚓ 🐕 ⛺
♦♦♦♦

Our Cotswold stone farmhouse enjoys a secluded position with wonderful views across the adjoining valley and fields of our dairy/beef farm. Lovely walks and riding close by, as are pretty villages like Lacock and Castle Combe. Easy access to Bath (8 miles), M4 (4 miles), award-winning local pubs/restaurants. Family and double room, both en suite, single room with private shower, all with TV, CH and tea/coffee. Hearty breakfasts. Closed Christmas and New Year. E-mail: kmjbandb@aol.com

---

Fairfield Farm, Upper Wraxall, Chippenham, Wiltshire SN14 7AG ④

Julie McDonough
☎ 01225 891750
Fax 01225 891050
[BB] From £20–£25
Sleeps 4
☺ ⚡ ⛺ ⚓ ⊛
♦♦♦♦

Fairfield is a friendly family farmhouse in Beaufort country, 8 miles from Georgian Bath, 3 miles from beautiful Castle Combe on route for Bristol (12 miles). Large garden, wonderful views. 1 double/family room, 1 twin, both with private bathrooms, TV and tea/coffee-making facilities. Excellent pubs nearby. A warm welcome awaits you. Closed Christmas. E-mail: mcdonoug@globalnet.co.uk

---

Franklyns Farm, Chewton, Mendip, Bath BA3 4NB ⑤

Mrs Betty Clothier
☎/Fax 01761 241372
[BB] From £19–£20
Sleeps 6
☺ 🐴 ⚓
♦♦♦

Come and unwind in the heart of the Mendip Hills. Wells, Cheddar, Bath, Bristol and Longleat are all within ½ hour's drive. Comfortable en suite bedrooms, all with TV. Delicious breakfasts. One-acre garden plus tennis court. Situated just off A39 at Chewton on B3114 to Emborough. Open all year. *Associate.*

6   **Great Ashley Farm,** Ashley Lane, Bradford-on-Avon, Wiltshire BA15 2PP

Helen Rawlings
☎/Fax 01225 864563
BB From £20
Sleeps 5
🐕 ½ 🎪 ♨
◆◆◆◆

Come and enjoy our lovely secluded farmhouse overlooking a large natural pond in AONB minutes from Bath and Bradford-on-Avon. The house is decorated with taste, imagination and care, offering delightful en suite bedrooms with every home from home comfort. An ideal place to relax and unwind. Great hospitality, delicious breakfast. Convenient for M4, Stonehenge, Lacock, Salisbury, Avebury, Corsham. Open all year except Christmas.

7   **Hatt Farm,** Old Jockey, Box, Nr Bath, Wiltshire SN13 8DJ

Mrs Carol Pope
☎ 01225 742989
Fax 01225 742779
BB From £20–£25
Sleeps 4
🐕 ½ ♨ 🎪 ⊛
◆◆◆◆

Extremely comfortable Georgian farmhouse in peaceful surroundings. Scrumptious breakfasts served overlooking beautiful countryside views. What could be nicer than sitting by a log fire in winter or enjoying the garden in summer? Lovely walks and good golfing nearby. Ideal for touring Wiltshire and the Cotswolds yet only 15 mins' drive to Bath. One twin with en suite shower, one double/family with private bathroom, both with tea/coffee. CH. Guests' lounge. Closed Christmas and New Year.

8   **Home Farm,** Harts Lane, Biddestone, Chippenham, Wilts SN14 7DQ

Ian & Audrey Smith
☎ 01249 714475
Fax 01249 701488
BB From £20–£25
Sleeps 9
🐕 ½ ♨ 🎪 ⊛
◆◆◆◆

A warm welcome awaits you in this 17th century farmhouse on a family-run working mixed farm. Set in beautiful Biddestone just a stroll across village green from the pub. Ideally situated for Bath, Castle Combe and Lacock, Stonehenge, Avebury, Longleat, etc. All rooms have colour TV, tea and coffee; two en suite, the other has private bathroom. Open all year.
E-mail: smith@homefarmb-b.freeserve.co.uk

9   **Home Farm,** Farrington Gurney, Bristol BS39 6UB

Tish and Andy Jeffery
☎/Fax 01761 452287
BB From £15–£30
Sleeps 6
🐕 ½ ♨ 🎪 ⅌
◆◆◆◆

Our beautifully refurbished 17th century farmhouse and 230-acre mixed farm is set on the northern edge of the Mendips. We offer a friendly welcome and delicious homemade breakfast. One double with four-poster, one four-bedded family room, both en-suite with full facilities. Lounge with woodburner, lovely garden. We are well placed for Bath, Wells, Cheddar, Longleat. Golf course next door. Open Feb–Nov. E-mail: tish_andy@tish-andy.freeserve.co.uk

10   **The Model Farm,** Norton Malreward, Pensford, Bristol BS39 4HA

Margaret Hasell
☎ 01275 832144
BB From £18–£22
Sleeps 6
🐕 ♨ ⊛
◆◆◆

The farmhouse is situated 2 miles off the A37 in a peaceful hamlet, nestling under the Dundry Hills. A working arable and beef farm in easy reach of Bristol, Bath, and many other interesting places. The accommodation consists of 1 family room and 1 double room, both en suite. Guests' lounge and dining room. Open all year except Christmas and New Year.

11   **Oakfield Farm,** Easton Piercy Lane, Yatton Keynell, Chippenham, Wiltshire SN14 6JU

Mrs Margaret Read
☎ 01249 782355
Fax 01249 783458
BB From £20–£25
Sleeps 6
🐕 🎪 ½ ♨ ⊛
◆◆◆◆

Friendly welcome in Cotswold stone farmhouse with fine views over open countryside. On working livestock farm in a quiet location, excellent for wildlife. One en suite double/family room, 1 double and 1 twin room, all with tea/coffee-making facilities and colour TV. Full central heating. Ideal base for visiting Bath, Castle Combe, Stonehenge and the Cotswolds. Open Mar–Nov.

Pantiles, Bathway, Chewton Mendip, Nr Bath BA3 4NS   ⑫

Pat Hellard
☎ **01761 241519**
BB **From £19–£22**
Sleeps 6
⟍ ⊕ 🛏 ⅓ 🎒
◆◆◆◆

Delightful house with views over Mendip countryside. Sample the locally baked bread and free range eggs. Ideal base for visits to Bath, Wells, Cheddar, Glastonbury. We offer 3 rooms all with private facilities, colour TV and hospitality trays. Early booking advised. Open all year.

Pennsylvania Farm, Newton St Loe, Bath BA2 9JD   ⑬

Peggy Foster
☎/Fax **01225 314912**
BB **From £20–£25**
Sleeps 6
⟍ ⅓ 🎒 ⚒
◆◆◆◆

Pennsylvania Farm is set in 280 acres of beautiful countryside close to Bath, Bristol, Cheddar and Wells. The farmhouse is a listed 17th century building which is well appointed, warm and comfortable. It has one double en suite, one twin/double en suite and one double with private facilities. Open all year. *Associate.*
E-mail: pennsfarm1@aol.com

Pickwick Lodge Farm, Guyers Lane, Corsham, Wiltshire SN13 0PS   ⑭

Gill Stafford
☎ **01249 712207**
Fax **01249 701904**
BB **From £20–£25**
Sleeps 6
⟍ ⅓ 🎒 ⚒ ⊛
◆◆◆◆

Enjoy a stay at our beautiful home set in wonderful countryside where you can see rabbits, pheasant and occasionally deer. Relax in our garden having started the day with a hearty delicious breakfast. Bath, NT properties, Corsham Court, Stonehenge and many interesting villages nearby. Three well appointed and tastefully furnished rooms with en suite/private facilities, hospitality tray, home made biscuits. Closed Christmas and New Year.
E-mail: b&b@pickwicklodge.freeserve.co.uk

Rode Farm, Rode, Bath BA3 6QQ   ⑮

Mrs Sarah Hawker
☎ **01373 831479**
BB **From £19–£25**
Sleeps 6
⟍ 🛏 ⅓ 🎒
◆◆◆

17th century traditional farmhouse on working dairy farm. Peaceful location yet conveniently situated for Bath, Longleat, Stourhead and Stonehenge. Heated outdoor pool with toilet, shower and changing facilities and barbecue available for guests, as is a hard tennis court. Perfect for a relaxing country holiday. Open all year except Christmas.

Saltbox Farm, Drewetts Mill Lane, Box, Corsham, Wiltshire SN13 8PT   ⑯

Mary Gregory
☎ **01225 742608**
BB **From £20–£23**
Sleeps 4
⟍ ⅓ ⟲ ⚒ 🎒 ⊛
◆◆◆

Mary and Tony invite you to relax in their 18th century farmhouse surrounded by the unspoilt Box Valley, offering scenic walks in a wildlife and conservation area. Centrally situated for touring the West Country and Bath. One double en suite, one twin/family room with guests' bathroom, both with tea/coffee. Visitors' lounge/diner with colour TV, CH. Special rates for 3/4 day breaks. Open Feb–Dec.

Valley Farm, Sandy Lane, Stanton Drew, Nr. Bristol BS39 4EL   ⑰

Mrs Doreen Keel
☎ **01275 332723**
BB **From £20–£26**
Sleeps 6
⊕ ⟍ ⅓ 🎒 ⚒
◆◆◆◆

Modern farmhouse situated on the edge of an ancient village near the river Chew, with Druid Stones and many footpaths to walk. Near the Chew Valley Lakes renowned for trout fishing and in easy reach of Bath, Bristol, Wells and Cheddar. Stanton Drew is off A368 Bath to Weston-super-Mare road or the B3130 road. There are 3 bedrooms, 2 en suite and 1 private bathroom, all with TV and coffee/tea making facilities, also guests' lounge.

18 **Woodbarn Farm,** Denny Lane, Chew Magna, Bristol BS40 8SZ

Mrs Judi Hasell
☎/Fax 01275 332599
🅱️ From £19–£23
Sleeps 6
🐕(3) ✄ 🔥
♦♦♦

Woodbarn is 5 minutes from Chew Valley Lake in an Area of Outstanding Natural Beauty. Chew Magna is a large village with pretty cottages, Georgian houses and is central for touring. There are two en suite bedrooms, one double and one family, both with tea trays. Guests' lounge and dining room. Open all year except Christmas and New Year.

Self-Catering

19 **Church Farm Cottages,** Winsley, Bradford-on-Avon, Wiltshire BA15 2JH

Trish Bowles
☎/Fax 01225 722246
Mobile 0468 543027
🆂 From £170–£330
Sleeps 2–4 + cot
🐎 🏇 ✄ ⌂ 🛉 🐎 🔥 ☂ 🌀
🏅🏅🏅🏅 *Commended*

Five newly converted single-storey cottages with original features. Luxuriously appointed. Four poster bed. On outskirts of village within 500 metres of pub and shop. Bath 5 miles. Kennet and Avon canal ¾ mile for cycling, walking, boating and fishing. Picturesque touring caravan/campsite with electricity and facilities. Brochure available. Open all year.
E-mail: churchfarmcottages@compuserve.com

2 **Pig-Wig Cottage,** Beeches Farmhouse, Holt Road, Bradford-on-Avon, Wiltshire BA15 1TS

Mrs Sharon Gover
☎/Fax 01225 863475
Mobile 0374 607417
🆂 From £250–£450
Sleeps 4 + cot
🐄 🐕 ✄ ⌂ 🔥 🌀
🏅🏅🏅🏅 *Highly Commended*

South-facing cottage overlooking open countryside. Luxurious, spacious accommodation with olde worlde charm, exposed beams, woodburner. Barbecue and patio furniture. Play area and tree house. Free range ducks and chickens. Collect your own eggs for breakfast. Golf and pony trekking nearby. Ideal for Bath, Lacock, Castle Combe, Wells, Stonehenge and Longleat. Electricity and linen included. Brochure. Open all year.
E-mail: beeches-farmhouse@1way.co.uk

18 **Stable & Denny Cottages,** Woodbarn Farm, Denny Lane, Chew Magna, Bristol BS40 8SZ

Mrs Judi Hasell
☎/Fax 01275 332599
🆂 From £200–£400
Sleep 2/6
♿ 🐎 ✄ 🔥
🏅🏅🏅 – 🏅🏅🏅🏅
Highly Commended

Stone-built barn conversion on farm, close to Chew Valley Lake, 30 minutes from Bath, Wells, Bristol, Cheddar. Stable Cottage, just for two, has its own patio. Denny Cottage, for 6, has 2 bedrooms, 2 bathrooms, lounge, kitchen/diner and is suitable for disabled guests. Beautiful countryside, peaceful location. Short breaks available. Open all year.

20 **Wadswick Barns,** Manor Farm, Wadswick, Corsham, Wiltshire SN13 8JB

Carolyn Barton
☎ 01225 810733
Fax 01225 810307
🆂 From £312–£531
Sleeps 4–7
🐕 🏇 ✄ 🔥 🔥 ☂
🏅🏅🏅🏅 *Highly Commended*

Three beautifully converted 16th century farm buildings, situated in the peaceful hamlet of Wadswick. Furnished to a very high standard with a wealth of original features, natural beams, gas stoves. Private gardens and patios. Close to Bath, Lacock, Castle Combe and Corsham. Open all year. E-mail: wadswick@compuserve.com

Wick Farm, Lacock, Chippenham, Wiltshire SN15 2LU

Philip and Sue King
☎ **01249 730244**
Fax 01249 730072
[SC] **From £170–£395**
Sleeps 4/5 + cot
🐕 ✂ 🍳 🍴 ☕ 🍵 ◎
🎣 🎣 🎣 *Highly Commended*

Philip and Sue invite you to their working farm in The Cheese House or Cyder House, where original cyder press remains, also stepped fireplace with woodburning stove. Some windows in Cheese have original shutters with gallery as extra seating area with portable TV. Both properties have exposed timbers, traditional furnishings. Linen and towels included. Coarse fishing on own lake. Brochure available. Open all year.

㉑

CONFIRM BOOKINGS

Disappointments can arise from misunderstandings over the telephone. Please write to confirm your booking.

USE THE INDEX

The comprehensive Index shows which farms offer access to disabled visitors; caravanning/camping facilities; the chance to participate on a working farm; stabling/grazing for visiting horses; en suite rooms; a welcome to business people; acceptance of *Stay on a Farm* gift tokens.

Our Internet address is
http://www.webscape.co.uk/farmaccom/

STAY ON A FARM GIFT TOKENS

If you have enjoyed your Stay on a Farm, why not treat your friends and relatives to *Stay on a Farm* gift tokens? Available from the Bureau office (tel: 024 7669 6909), they can be redeemed against accommodation and are accepted by the majority of farms (see Index). Please check when booking to avoid disappointment.

Somerset

Exmoor National Park, Quantock Hills & Mendip Hills

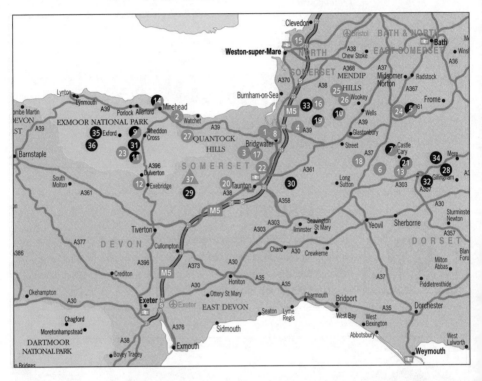

Key

Key

- **1** Bed & Breakfast
- **1** Self-Catering
- **1** B&B and SC
- **1** Camping Barns
- **1** Camping & Caravanning

Originally named by the Saxons as the 'Summer Land', this is a county full of contrasts from ancient gorges to the waterways of the Somerset Levels. We have a wealth of National Trust properties with beautiful buildings and fragrant gardens. The energetic can go caving, cycle or ramble through our wonderful countryside and Exmoor National Park. In our rural museums you can learn about traditional local crafts such as willow basket weaving and paper, cheese and cider making. Children will thrill to the adventure of the legendary Witch of Wookey Hole and the whole family will enjoy a 'bucket and spade' day at one of our coastal resorts, rounded off with a delicious cream tea!

If you would like help in finding suitable farm accommodation, turn to the full listing of FHB Groups on pages 392 to 395 to find appropriate contact details for this area.

Bed and Breakfast
(and evening meal)

Ash-Wembdon Farm, Hollow Lane, Wembdon, Bridgwater, Somerset TA5 2BD   ①

Mrs Mary Rowe
☎ 01278 453097
Mobile 0402 272755
Fax 01278 445856
BB From £20
Sleeps 6
⌂(10) ⚹ 🖭 🛉 🛏 ⊛
♦♦♦♦ Silver Award

Enjoy a refreshing and memorable stay at our 17th century farmhouse near the Quantocks Hills. Ideal for touring Somerset, Bath, Wells, North Devon, NT properties. Excellent golfing and walking – Parret Trail at our back gate. Warm romantic en suite rooms, with tea/coffee, colour TV. Superb breakfasts using local produce. Landscaped gardens, off road parking. Tucked away yet easy to find. "A gem of a place for all seasons." E-mail: mary.rowe@btinternet.com

---

Binham Farm, Old Cleeve, Minehead, Somerset TA24 6HX   ②

Mrs S Bigwood
☎/Fax 01984 640222
BB From £17–£20
Sleeps 6
⌂ 🛉 ⚹ 🏃 🔥 🛏 🛏
Awaiting new rating

Predominantly 17th-century Jacobean farmhouse on a working family farm in an idyllic setting close to the Exmoor National Park and Quantock Hills. A few minutes walk across our fields to Blue Anchor sea front and the West Somerset Steam Railway. Comfortably furnished bedrooms with en suite facilities available, private lounge with colour TV, mediaeval dining hall. Full CH. Open all year. E-mail: sheralynn@sheralynn.freeserve.co.uk

---

Blackmore Farm, Blackmore Lane, Cannington, Bridgwater, Somerset TA5 2NE   ③

Mrs Ann Dyer
☎ 01278 653442
Fax 01278 653427
BB From £21–£25
Sleeps 8
🛏 ⌂ ⚹ 🖭 ☂ 🛏 ⊛
♦♦♦♦♦

A tastefully restored and furnished 14th century manor house, set in rolling countryside with views to the Quantock Hills. Rooms with oak bedsteads and four poster beds, all en suite with full central heating. Facilities for disabled guests. As featured in *Country Living* magazine. Within easy reach of Exmoor, West Somerset coast, Taunton, Wells and Glastonbury. Open all year. E-mail:dyerfarm@aol.com.uk

---

Brookhayes Farm, Bell Lane, Cossington, Bridgwater, Somerset TA7 8LR   ④

Mrs Susan Bell
☎/Fax 01278 722559
BB From £20–£22
Sleeps 6
⌂ 🛉 ⚹ 🛏
♦♦♦

Working dairy farm with outstanding views over moors and hills. Situated between Bridgwater and Glastonbury on the edge of lovely village of Cossington. All rooms en suite plus family room. Large garden. Also good fishing nearby. Good pub within walking distance for evening meal – always a warm welcome. Open all year.

Burnt House Farm, Waterlip, West Cranmore, Nr Shepton Mallet, Somerset BA4 4RN   ⑤

Pam Hoddinott
☎ 01749 880280
Fax 01749 880004
BB From £24–£30
Sleeps 6
⌂(4) ⚹ 🛏 🔥
♦♦♦♦ Silver Award

Totally refurbished period farmhouse retaining inglenook, beams and pine floors. Bedrooms have hospitality tuck tray, TV, trouser press, hairdryer. Garden has summerhouse, hot spa for 6, patio. Games room with full-sized snooker table, table tennis, darts. Garage. Profuse, choice, delectable breakfasts to sustain all day! Attentive service and a warm welcome are assured. Open all year. See colour ad on page 41.

6   **Cary Fitzpaine,** Yeovil, Somerset BA22 8JB

Mrs Susie Crang
☎ 01458 223250
Fax 01458 223372
BB From £19–£22
EM From £9
Sleeps 6

Gracious Georgian manor farmhouse set in two acres of gardens on 600-acre working farm comprising of sheep, cattle, horses and arable. There is a river running through the farm with an abundance of wildlife. The bedrooms are large and attractively decorated, all en suite. Peaceful, relaxed setting. Open all year. E-mail:acrang@aol.com

7   **Clanville Manor,** Castle Cary, Somerset BA7 7PJ

Mrs Sally Snook
☎ 01963 350124/350313
Fax 01963 350313
Mobile 07966 512732
BB From £17.50–£25
Sleeps 6

Explore Somerset, Bath, Wells and Glastonbury from an elegant Georgian farmhouse on a working dairy farm. Only 2 miles from Castle Cary, with riverbank walks. Outdoor heated pool in summer. En suite and family room available and all rooms have colour TV and tea/coffee-making facilities. Safe parking. Full CH. Open all year. AA QQQQ Selected. E-mail: clanville@aol.com

8   **Cokerhurst Farm,** 87 Wembdon Hill, Bridgwater, Somerset TA6 7QA

Derrick and Diana Chappell
☎/Fax 01278 422330
Mobile 07850 692065
BB From £25
Sleeps 6

We would like to welcome you into our home, a 16th century Somerset longhouse. We have 3 pretty en suite bedrooms, all with comfortable beds, TV, CH, tea/coffee facilities. A good hearty breakfast is served to you in the dining room overlooking the garden and lake beyond. Good central location for exploring the 'Cider' county of Somerset. Open all year except Christmas. E-mail: cokerhurst@clara.net

9   **Cutthorne Farm,** Luckwell Bridge, Wheddon Cross, Somerset TA24 7EW

Ann Durbin
☎/Fax 01643 831255
BB From £25
EM From £15
Sleeps 6
◌(12) ♈ ⚤ ☞ ⚔ ▪ ⁑ ⊛
♦♦♦♦ Gold Award

Tucked away in the heart of Exmoor, Cutthorne is truly 'off the beaten track'. Share our peaceful home overlooking private trout lakes and valley. The pretty bedrooms all have bathrooms, and one even a four-poster bed. A choice of traditional farmhouse fayre is served in the sunny dining room, using local meat and organic vegetables. Open all year except Christmas.

10   **Double-Gate Farm,** Godney, Nr Wells, Somerset BA5 1RX

Mrs H Millard
☎ 01458 832217
Fax 01458 835612
BB From £22.50
Sleeps 8
♦♦♦♦ Gold Award

Situated on the banks of the River Sheppey, this lovely old Georgian farmhouse offers comfortable guests' lounge, games room and en suite bedrooms with tea/coffee facilities, colour TVs and CH. Guests' launderette. Lovely flower garden, outdoor breakfast in summer. Ideal base for touring, cycling, birdwatching, etc. Evening meals available in nearby village inn. AA QQQQQ and RAC acclaimed. Closed Christmas and New Year. E-mail: doublegate.demon.co.uk

11   **Highercombe Farm,** Dulverton, Somerset TA22 9PT

Abigail Humphrey
☎/Fax 01398 323616
BB From £20–£24
EM £15
Sleeps 6
◌(6) ♈ ⁑ ⚔
♦♦♦ Silver Award

A 450-acre working farm on the edge of the moor. We have spectacular 60-mile views and red deer can often be seen from the farmhouse. Pretty en suite rooms with tea/coffee facilities and colour TV. Large guest lounge with inglenook and bay window where breakfast is served. A relaxed atmosphere, a friendly welcome, personal service and quality food. Complimentary farm tours. Open Mar–Nov. E-mail: abigail@highercombe.demon.co.uk

Higher Langridge Farm, Exebridge, Dulverton, Somerset TA22 9RR

Gill Summers
☎/Fax 01398 323999
[BB] From £20–£25
EM From £12.50
Sleeps 6
♿ ⅍ ♨ ⁑ ◎
♦♦♦♦

Come and enjoy comfort, good food and warm hospitality in our 17th century farmhouse, our family's home since the late 1800s. Our working farm is set amidst superbly peaceful countryside on the edge of Exmoor National Park where red deer and other wildlife are plentiful. En suite/private bathrooms and tea/coffee-making facilities. Central heating throughout and log fires in winter. Open all year. E-mail: gill.langridge@ukf.net

---

Hill Ash Farm, Woolston, North Cadbury, Yeovil, Somerset BA22 7BL

Mrs Jane Pearse
☎/Fax 01963 440332
Mobile 0498 835173
[BB] From £22–£25
Sleeps 6
⅍ ♨ ◎
♦♦♦♦ Silver Award

This lovely thatched house, a listed building constructed in 1766, is set in a beautiful hamlet of south Somerset 1½ miles from A303. It is an ideal centre for visiting the many tourist attractions and NT gardens in Somerset and Dorset. 2 double en suite rooms and 2 singles, all with tea/coffee-making facilities, full central heating. Open Mar–Oct.

Hindon Farm, Near Minehead, Somerset TA24 8SH

Penny & Roger Webber
☎/Fax 01643 705244
[BB] From £20–£22
EM From £15
Sleeps 6
♿ ⅀ ⅍ ⅍ ⁂ ♨ ⁑
♦♦♦

Escape to our organic farm in peaceful Exmoor valley (Minehead 3 miles, Selworthy 1 mile for cream teas!) Wander our 500-acres and adjoining heather moors to coast path or stroll our nature trail. Relax by the stream while ducks dabble and donkeys dawdle. DIY stables and outdoor arena. 18th century farmhouse with 20th century hospitality. Pretty bedrooms, delicious breakfasts (own produce). Featured on TV and in *Which? Best B&B*. Brochure.
E-mail: rogpenweb@virgin.com

Icelton Farm, Wick-St-Lawrence, Weston-super-Mare, North Somerset BS22 7YJ

Mrs Elizabeth Parsons
☎ 01934 515704
[BB] From £16–£18
Sleeps 5
♿(2) ♨
♦♦♦

Icelton is a working dairy/sheep farm, just off the M5 (jct21). Ideal for touring Wells, Cheddar, and Mendip Hills. This listed farmhouse offers double room with H/C, family room with H/C and shower. Tea/coffee-making facilities. Oak-beamed dining room and lounge, both with inglenook fireplaces. English breakfast. Good pubs and restaurants close at hand. No dogs. Open Mar–Nov.

Laurel Farm, The Causeway, Mark, Nr Highbridge, Somerset TA9 4PZ

Mrs Bernice Puddy
☎ 01278 641216
Fax 01278 641447
[BB] From £16.50–£19
Sleeps 6
♿ ⅍
♦♦

Grade II listed farmhouse on 170-acre working farm of Holstien cows. Ideal overnight stop or touring centre for Cheddar, Wells, Mendips, Quantocks and Dunster. Burnham-on-Sea 5 miles, M5 J22 2 miles. All rooms en suite with CH, electric blankets and tea/coffee-making facilities. Lounge with colour TV, log fires Sept–May. Open all year. *Associate.*

Lower Clavelshay Farm, Clavelshay, North Petherton, Bridgwater, Somerset TA6 6PJ 

Sue Milverton
☎/Fax 01278 662347
[BB] From £17–£22
EM From £10
Sleeps 6
♿ ⅍ ⅍ Å ♨ ⌣
Awaiting new rating

Simple pleasures – beautiful countryside, long walks, wildlife, wild flowers, log fires, starry nights, comfy beds, peace and tranquillity, good food, good books and good humour. Great hospitality in a wonderful setting – like staying with friends. Come soon! (Featured on BBC *Countryfile*, winner of 'Working Country' category in Photo '98.)

18 Lower Farm, Kingweston, Somerton, Somerset TA11 6BA

David & Jane Sedgman
☎ **01458 223237**
Fax **01458 223276**
🅱 **From £22**
Sleeps 5
♨(6) ⚒ ⊞ 🐾 🛢 🛉
◆◆◆◆

This Grade II listed farmhouse, sited in a conservation area and overlooking a wide stretch of open country, was formerly a coaching inn and retains many of its original features. The attractive rooms are excellently equipped to ensure your every comfort. Well placed to visit Wells, Glastonbury and Bath. Good country pubs nearby. AA QQQ and RAC Acclaimed. Open all year except Christmas and New Year.
E-mail: lowerfarm@kingweston.demon.co.uk

19 New House Farm, Burtle Road, Westhay, Nr Glastonbury, Somerset BA6 9TT

Mrs M Bell
☎ **01458 860238**
Fax **01458 860568**
🅱 **From £22–£24**
EM From £13
Sleeps 5
♨ 🐓 ⚒ 🛢
◆◆◆◆

Large Victorian farmhouse on dairy farm. Central for touring Wells, Cheddar, etc. Accommodation comprises of double room and 1 family room both en suite with colour TV, tea/coffee facilities, hair drier, etc. Lounge with colour TV, separate dining room, also sun lounge, CH throughout, plenty of local fishing. Open all year except Christmas and New Year. See colour ad on page 41.
E-mail: info@bellfarm2freeserve.co.uk

20 North Down Farm, Pyncombe Lane, Wiveliscombe, Taunton, Somerset TA4 2BL

Jenny Blackshaw
☎ **01984 623730**
🅱 **From £19**
EM From £10
Sleeps 6
♨ 🐓 🐕 🛢 🛉
◆◆◆

Family-run stock farm set on edge of Exmoor in Lorna Doone country. 10 miles Taunton, 1 mile Wiveliscombe, 7 miles M5 J26. Peaceful surroundings and magnificent views over rolling countryside. Home grown produce. Attractively furnished, comfortable rooms, all en suite with full central heating and double glazing. Golf, riding, fishing and country sports nearby. Open all year except Christmas. *Associate.*

21 Orchard Farm, Cockhill, Castle Cary, Somerset BA7 7NY

Olive Boyer
☎/Fax **01963 350418**
🅱 **From £18–£20**
Sleeps 5
♨ 🐓 ⊞ 🛉 🛢 Ⓢ
◆◆◆

Our pleasure is your comfort. We welcome you with tea and homemade cakes in the conservatory or garden. Quiet, beautiful surroundings. Two en suite bedrooms with colour TV, radio, alarm clock, tea/coffee. Newspapers at breakfast. Bath, Longleat, Stourhead, Yeovilton Air and Haynes Motor Museums close, also many NT properties. Castle Cary with many shops and eating places 1½ miles. Open all year.

22 Prockters Farm, West Monkton, Taunton, Somerset TA2 8QN

Dianne Besley
☎/Fax **01823 412269**
🅱 **From £20–£23**
Sleeps 10
♨ 🐓 ⚒ 🐕 ⊞ 🛢
◆◆◆

Lovely 17th century farmhouse, full of character with beams and log fires, surrounded by a large garden and family-run farm. Ground floor en suite rooms suitable for disabled guests. Ideally placed to explore Exmoor and Quantock Hills, coast nearby. Taunton and motorway only 2 miles away. Two good pubs nearby offering excellent food and hospitality. Open all year. *Associate.*

23 Springfield Farm, Ashwick Lane, Dulverton, Somerset TA22 9QD

Mrs Patricia Vellacott
☎/Fax **01398 323722**
🅱 **From £20–£25**
EM From £13
Sleeps 6
♨ 🐓 ⚒ 🛢 Ⓢ
◆◆◆◆

A warm welcome awaits you at our 270-acre Exmoor farm. Peacefully situated between Tarr Steps and Dulverton, overlooking the River Barle valley with magnificent moorland and woodland views. Comfortable accommodation and delicious farmhouse meals. All bedrooms have en suite or private facilities and beverage trays. Guests' sitting room with colour TV. Large dining room leading onto patio and garden. Garage on request. Open Easter–Nov.

Temple House Farm, Doulting, Shepton Mallet BA4 4RQ   (24)

Mrs Veronica Reakes
☎ **01749 880294**
Fax **01749 880688**
⊞ From **£25**
EM From **£10**
Sleeps 5
🐕(2) ✗ ♨ ᛉ
♦♦♦

Temple House Farm is a family-run dairy farm situated on the eastern end of the Mendip Hills. A 400-year old listed farmhouse with all facilities, set in a rural area within easy reach of the Royal Bath and West Showground, Wells, Bath and many local attractions. All fresh produce used, hearty evening meals also available. Open all year.

Tor Farm Guesthouse, Nyland, Cheddar, Somerset BS27 3UD   (25)

Mr & Mrs Ladd
☎/Fax **01934 743710**
⊞ From **£21–£23**
EM From **£10**
Sleeps 16
🐎 🐕 ⊞ ♨
♦♦♦♦

Our working farm is situated three miles from Cheddar in open countryside. The house has full central heating (log fires on colder evenings) and for those long hot days a heated swimming pool in the garden. Bath, Cheddar, Wells, Glastonbury and the coast close by. Open all year except Christmas. E-mail: bcjbkj@aol.com

---

Townsend Farm, Sand, Wedmore, Somerset BS28 4XH   (26)

Sarah Willcox
☎ **01934 712342**
Fax **01934 712405**
⊞ From **£20–£22**
Sleeps 6
🐕(5) 🐎 ✗ ♨
♦♦♦

Townsend Farm is a working dairy farm, set in peaceful countryside with views of the Mendip hills, close to Wells, Cheddar and Glastonbury, 6 miles from M5 (jct22). The spacious Victorian farmhouse offers comfortable accommodation and a friendly atmosphere, traditional English breakfast served in dining room, relaxing separate TV lounge. All bedrooms have TV, en suite available. Open Mar–Nov.

Wood Advent Farm, Roadwater, Exmoor National Park, Somerset TA23 0RR   (27)

Diana Brewer
☎/Fax **01984 640920**
⊞ From **£20–£25**
EM **£15**
Sleeps 8
🐕(10) 🐎 ⊞ ⚓ ᛉ ♨ ⊚
Awaiting new rating

Peace and tranquillity at our listed farmhouse in the Exmoor countryside. Well-marked footpaths go for miles! Four en suite bedrooms with TV and hospitality trays, glorious views. Two large reception rooms and dining room where delicious Exmoor dishes are served with good wines. Heated pool, enjoy afternoon tea in the large gardens. Wonderful base for the West Country. We look forward to welcoming you. Open all year. See colour ad on page 42. E-mail: jddibrewer@aol.com

Self-Catering

Cockhill Farm & Orchard Farm, Cockhill, Castle Cary, Somerset BA7 7NY   (21)

Olive Boyer
☎/Fax **01963 350418**
⊞ From **£150–£400**
Sleep 4/6
🐎 🐕 ⊞ ♨ ᛉ ⊚
🐾🐾🐾 – 🐾🐾🐾🐾
Up to Commended

An attractive listed farmhouse overlooking beautiful countryside, with 3 bedrooms and fully equipped with TV, dishwasher, washing machine and spin dryer. Also 2 attractive cottages converted from a Somerset barn, both fully equipped, electricity and linen inclusive. Bath, Longleat, Stourhead, Yeovilton Air and Haynes Motor Museums and many NT properties nearby. Castle Cary with many shops and eating places 1½ miles. Open all year.

19 **The Courtyard,** c/o New House Farm, Burtle Road, Westhay, Nr Glastonbury, Somerset BA6 9TT

Mr & Mrs P Bell
☎ 01458 860238
Fax 01458 860568
🆂 From £150–£420
Sleeps 6
⏰ 🐴 ♿
🐾🐾🐾🐾 *Highly Commended*

The Courtyard is a converted barn which sleeps up to 4 adults and 2 children. Its situation on a dairy farm on the Somerset Levels makes it central for touring Wells, Cheddar, Bath, etc. Superbly equipped, including colour TV, washing machine, microwave, tumble dryer. Bed-linen, electricity and heating included. Good local fishing. Open all year. E-mail: info@bellfarm2freeserve.co.uk

9 **Cutthorne Farm,** Luckwell Bridge, Wheddon Cross, Somerset TA24 7EW

Ann Durbin
☎/Fax 01643 831255
🆂 From £200–£495
Sleeps 4
⏰ 🐴 🍴 🎯 🐾 ♿ ⊚
🐾🐾🐾🐾
Highly Commended

'What a wonderful position' – the most frequent comment we hear. Nestling in the heart of Exmoor, we offer two attractive barn conversions on side of farmhouse. These peaceful havens overlook our own trout lakes and valley. Close to Lynton and Lynmouth, Tarr Steps and Dunster, also small unspoilt beaches. Home-cooked meals may be taken in the farmhouse. Open all year.

10 **Double-Gate Farm,** Godney, Nr Wells, Somerset BA5 1RX

Hilary Millard
☎ 01458 832217
Fax 01458 835612
🆂 From £175–£750
Sleeps 11
♿⏰🍴🏠♿
🐾🐾🐾 *Highly Commended*

The Old Cart House and Swallow Barn are delightful barn conversions, both furnished to an excellent standard. Heating, electricity, linen and towels included. All bedrooms are en suite (one ground floor) with colour TV. Games room with full-size snooker table, table tennis, darts, etc. Guests' laundrette. Ideal for touring, cycling, bird watching, fishing. Village inn nearby for meals. (minimum 5 nights' occupation.) Open all year. E-mail: hilary@doublegate.demon.co.uk

28 **Hale Farm,** Cucklington, Wincanton, Somerset BA9 9PN

Mrs Pat David
☎ 01963 33342
🆂 From £75–£210
Sleeps 2/4
⏰ 🐴 ♿
🐾🐾 *Approved*

Set in a peaceful, but not isolated, position on edge of village, only 2 miles from A303. Ideal touring. Period converted former cowshed, comfortable and well equipped. One twin and one double bedroom, bathroom, kitchen, sitting room. All electric (coin meter). Linen supplied. Smaller unit also available, sleeping two. Open all year.

29 **Halsdown Farm,** Waterrow, Taunton, Somerset TA4 2QU

Mrs Ann James
☎ 01984 623493
🆂 From £190–£400
Sleeps 4/5
⏰ 🐴 ♿
🐾🐾🐾 *Commended*

Set in a spectacular position on the edge of the Brendon Hills, this is an ideal base from which to explore the wonderfully unspoilt countryside of West Somerset and Exmoor. We offer two attractive and well-equipped cottages with spacious gardens and children's play area. Visitors are welcome to walk our family farm and enjoy the animals. Open all year. *Associate.*

11 **Highercombe Farm,** Dulverton, Somerset TA22 9PT

Abigail Humphrey
☎/Fax 01398 323616
🆂 From £190–£360
Sleeps 5
⏰ 🐴 🐾 🎯
🐾🐾🐾🐾 *Commended*

Self-contained wing of large farmhouse on 450-acre working farm next to the moor. Well furnished in cottage style. Private entrance, large gardens, spectacular views. 2 bedrooms, bathroom, large lounge/dining room with colour TV, CD player/radio, woodburner. Modern pine kitchen. Linen, CH, hot water, logs included. Use of washing machine/dryer. Evening meals arranged, babysitting service. Electricity pound coin meter. Open all year. E-mail: abigail@highercombe.demon.co.uk

Hindon Farmhouse Cottage, Hindon Farm, Nr Minehead, Somerset TA24 8SH 14

Penny & Roger Webber
☎/Fax 01643 705244
SC From £250–£550
Sleeps 6
Commended

18th century cottage/wing of Exmoor farmhouse on 500-acres between Minehead and Selworthy (short walk for cream teas!). Spot wildlife on our farm trail, sea views from the heather moors adjoining fields. Tastefully furnished with original fireplace, log burner. Living/dining/kitchen, CH, colour TV, video and all mod cons. 1 double en suite, 2 twins with bathroom. Linen and towels provided. Breakfast and evening meal by arrangement. Featured on TV. Brochure. E-mail: rogpenweb@virgin.com

Holly Farm, Holly Cottage, Stoke St. Gregory, Taunton TA3 6HS 30

Liz Smith
☎ 01823 490828
Fax 01823 490590
SC From £170–£380
Sleep 4/6
Highly Commended

Come and stay in one of our 5 spacious cottages converted from old stone long barns. Each has its own private, enclosed garden and there is a games barn for the energetic. Plenty of fishing, horse riding or walking and an excellent selection of pub grub and restaurants nearby so give the cook a holiday too. Mobile 0777 599 3716. Open all year. E-mail: RobHembrow@btinternet.com

Leigh Holt, Burnt House Farm, Waterlip, West Cranmore, Nr Shepton Mallet, Somerset BA4 4RN 5

Pam Hoddinott
☎ 01749 880280
Fax 01749 880004
SC From £180–£490
Sleeps 5
(4)
Highly Commended

Luxuriously converted and well-appointed carthouse (ground floor) in central Somerset with lovely Mendip views. Every facility included, no hidden extra cost. Garden with summerhouse, hot spa for 6, patio. Games room with full-sized snooker table, table tennis and darts. Garage. Attentive service assured. £50 prize for cleanest-left let! Apply for brochure. Open all year. See colour ad on page 41.

Liscombe Farm, Winsford, Dulverton, Somerset TA22 9QA 31

Sally Wade
☎/Fax 01643 851551
SC From £100–£650
Sleeps 2/9 + cot
Commended

Liscombe is a 385-acre beef and sheep farm in Exmoor National Park. Peaceful, spacious farmhouse and two converted barns, each furnished to a high standard with CH, dishwasher, washing machine, drier, hi-fi, video – everything to make a relaxing holiday. Perfect for walking, riding or fishing. Cosy log fires, garden, play area and barbecue. Stabling available. Open all year.

Lois Barns, Lois Farm, Horsington, Templecombe, Somerset BA8 0EW 32

Paul & Penny Constant
☎/Fax 01963 370496
SC From £189–£411
Sleeps 4/6
Commended

In the heart of the Blackmore Vale, Lois Barns are situated on a small sheep farm surrounded by meadow fields. Light and spacious, both barns have south-facing patios and are fully equipped. CH, electricity and linen are all inclusive. Walk, bike, drive or simply enjoy the quiet of our rural landscape. Phone/fax for a brochure. Open all year. E-mail: p.constant@talk21.com

Pear Tree Cottage, Northwick Farm, Northwick Road, Mark, Highbridge, Somerset TA9 4PG 33

Mrs Susan Slocombe
☎ 01278 641228
SC From £175–£350
Sleeps 6
(5)
Highly Commended

Situated on the Somerset Levels in an area of outstanding natural beauty. Recent barn conversion. Luxurious and comfortable with beautifully co-ordinated fabrics and furnishings. Perfect for a peaceful relaxing holiday and an ideal base for touring this part of the West Country. Excellent facilities nearby for golf, fishing and riding and only 4 miles from coast. Open all year.

34 **Pigsty, Cowstall & Bullpen Cottages,** Barrow Lane Farm, Charlton Musgrove, Wincanton, Somerset BA9 8HJ

Mrs Chris Chilcott
/Fax 01963 33217
SC From £160–£320
Sleeps 5–8 + cot
Commended

Pigsty, Cowstall and Bullpen Cottages are conversions from the appropriate farm buildings in rural Somerset. Pleasant garden, barbecue and games room. Pets welcome. Please send for brochure. Open all year.

7 **The Tallet,** Clanville Manor, Castle Cary, Somerset BA7 7PJ

Mrs Sally Snook
01963 350124/350313
Fax 01963 350313
Mobile 07966 512732
SC From £200–£400
Sleeps 4/5 + cot
Highly Commended

In summer, walk or picnic beside the river, swim in the heated pool or play games in the walled garden. Watch the milking, help collect the eggs. Take a cosy short break in winter and curl up in front of the fire. Newly fitted kitchen with dishwasher and freezer. Double room, bunk room and cot. All-inclusive rent and starter pack. Brochure. Open all year. E-mail: clanville@aol.com

35 **Westermill Farm,** Exford, Nr Minehead, Somerset TA24 7NJ

The Edwards family
01643 831238
Fax 01643 831660
SC From £139–£399
Sleep 4/8
–
Commended

Six delightful log cottages (David Bellamy Conservation Gold Award) in grass paddocks on side of valley by a river. Log fires and double glazing in two cottages. Also bright, comfortable cottage adjoining the farmhouse overlooks the river. Patio, garage. Four waymarked walks over 500-acre farm in centre of Exmoor. 2½ miles shallow river, fishing, bathing. Laundry, payphone, information centre, seasonal small shop. Open all year.

36 **Wintershead Farm,** Simonsbath, Exmoor, Somerset TA24 7LF

Jane Styles
01643 831222
Fax 01643 831628
SC From £125–£495
Sleeps 1–6 + cot
–
Highly Commended

Forget the pressures of everyday life and unwind in one of our warm and cosy cottages. Hidden away in the hills of Exmoor where the views are breathtaking, most of the traffic has four legs and the only street lighting is the stars above. You can relax after a wonderful day's exploring, with comfy sofas, log fires, central heating and lots of hot water. Short breaks available Nov–Mar. Colour brochure. Open all year.

Camping and Caravanning

37 **Oxenleaze Farm Caravans,** Chipstable, Wiveliscombe, Somerset TA4 2QH

Marian/Elaine Rottenbury
/Fax 01984 623427
SC From £85–£350
Sleeps 6
★★★★

A small, family-owned site on a real working farm bordering Exmoor. Amidst magnificent countryside, enjoy the 'peace and quiet' of this picturesque site and idyllic location, staying in luxury and super-luxury caravans. Facilities include excellent free coarse fishing, indoor heated pool, games room, children's play area, laundry room, pay phone. Colour brochure available. Open Easter–Oct. See colour ad on page 42.

North Devon

Exmoor National Park, North Devon Coast
& Taw & Torridge Valleys

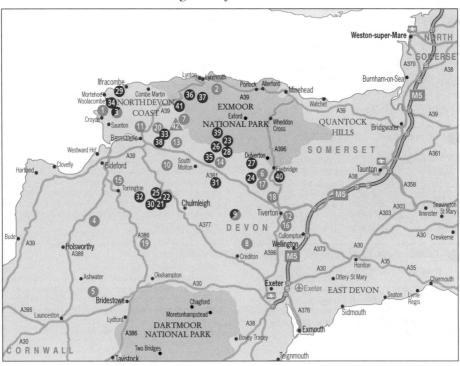

Key

- **1** Bed & Breakfast
- **1** Self-Catering
- **1** B&B and SC
- **1** Camping Barns
- **1** Camping & Caravanning

The land of wild secrets and dramatic contrast, from golden sands to the deepest heartland of Domesday hamlets. Plan a voyage of discovery from quaint fishing villages like cobbled Clovelly to the famous Tarka Trail. Journey through the Devonshire Dales of rolling hills, the gentler Taw and Torridge Valleys to the historic Tamar river. Ramble the wild moorlands of Exmoor and the Quantock Hills where dramatic scenery sweeps down to the Bristol Channel. Soak up romantic legends of yesteryear and explore the country lanes in search of hidden curiosities. Explore gardens and traditional industries – pottery, crystal and sheepskin. Indulge in West Country fayre, cream teas and the magic of this unspoilt county.

If you would like help in finding suitable farm accommodation, turn to the full listing of FHB Groups on pages 392 to 395 to find appropriate contact details for this area.

Bed and Breakfast
(and evening meal)

---

1 Combas Farm, Putsborough, Croyde, North Devon EX33 1PH

Mrs Gwen Adams
☎ 01271 890398
BB From £19–£25
EM From £11
Sleeps 11
☡ ☗ Å ⬛ ⊛
♦♦♦

140-acre stock farm nestling in its own secluded valley ('idyllic' – guest's description) just 15 mins' walk from miles of golden sands (5 mins from the village pub!). Many repeat bookings confirm claims to a warm welcome and high standard of home cooking using home produce. Wisteria rambles over this 17th century longhouse overlooking a lovely garden and unspoiled view. In *'Which' Good B&B Guide*. Colour brochure. Closed Christmas & lambing time. See colour ad on page 43.

---

2 Coombe Farm, Countisbury, Lynton, Exmoor, Devon EX35 6NF

Rosemary & Susan Pile
☎/Fax 01598 741236
BB From £19–£23
Sleeps 14
☡ ☗ ✂ ⊞ ⬛ ⊛
♦♦♦

Comfortable 17th century farmhouse set on a hillside between picturesque Lynmouth and the legendary Doone Valley. Delicious breakfast with homemade bread and marmalade, served in large beamed dining room, will set you up for the day exploring Exmoor, then relax in the lounge with colour TV and plan for tomorrow. 2 bedrooms with shower en suite, 3 with H/C, all with hot drinks facilities. Open Mar–end Nov.

---

3 Denham Farm, North Buckland, Braunton, North Devon EX33 1HY

Mrs Jean Barnes
☎/Fax 01271 890297
BB From £25–£28
Sleeps 24
☡ ✂ ⊞ ☼ ⬛ ⊛
♦♦♦♦ Silver Award

A Happy Holiday Recipe
Take a lovely warm farmhouse, pretty en suite bedrooms, a pinch of fun and laughter, mix with nearby attractions and miles of golden sand. Surround with green fields, country walks, keep amused with small pets and games room. Serve up with a warm smile and return for a repeat helping. Open Jan–Nov. See colour ad on page 43.

---

4 Forda Farm, Thornbury, Holsworthy, North Devon EX22 7BS

Mrs Valerie Wood
☎ 01409 261369
BB From £16–£20
EM From £10
Sleeps 5
☡ ✂ ⬛ ⊛
♦♦♦

Roddy and Val invite you to stay on their livestock farm set in a peaceful location four miles from the market town of Holsworthy. Comfortable lounge with exposed beams and inglenook fireplace. Day trips to the North Cornish coast, Rosemoor Gardens, Dartmoor and National Trust properties are highly recommended. Open all year.

---

5 Frankaborough Farm, Broadwoodwidger, Lifton, Devon PL16 0JS

Linda Banbury
☎ 01409 211308
BB From £15
Sleeps 4
☡ ☗ ⬛ ☇ ☈
♦♦

A warm welcome awaits you in our traditional 17th century farmhouse set in beautiful countryside near to Roadford Lake and Dartmoor. Easily accessible to both coasts. Tea on arrival. Children most welcome. Comfortable rooms with H & C, colour TV and tea/coffee-making facilities. Beautiful gardens and summerhouse. Open all year.

Harton Farm, Oakford, Tiverton, Devon EX16 9HH   ⑥

Mrs Lindy Head
☎/Fax 01398 351209
[BB] From £16–£17
EM From £8
Sleeps 6
🦢(4) �)= ♣ 🌲 🍴 ⊚
♦♦♦

Country fare at its best, in peaceful surroundings, with additive-free home-grown meat and vegetables. Meet the sheep, relax in the comfortable old stone farmhouse, explore wonderful countryside and return home revitalised – the perfect get-away-from-it-all break. Vegetarian menu on request. Tea-making facilities, home-spun wool available. Farm walk with nature notes, friendly animals. Reduction for children. Open all year (closed Christmas & New Year). E-mail: harton@eclipse.co.uk

Haxton Down Farm, Bratton Fleming, Barnstaple, Devon EX32 7JL   ⑦

Mrs Pat Burge
☎/Fax 01598 710275
[BB] From £17–£20
EM From £9
Sleeps 5
🦢 🐴 🌲 ♣ ⊚
♦♦♦

Relax among leafy lanes and wonderful scenery on our working stock farm nestling in a peaceful valley. 17th century farmhouse offers warmth and comfort with private or en suite facilities, CTV, tea trays and a warm welcome to all ages. Delicious food with hearty breakfasts and tempting 4-course dinners. Close to beach and moor and attractions galore. Give North Devon a try – you'll be pleased you did. Ring for brochure please. Open Easter–Nov.

Hayne Farm, Cheriton Fitzpaine, Crediton, Devon EX17 4HR   ⑧

Mrs Margaret Reed
☎/Fax 01363 866392
[BB] From £16
EM From £7
Sleeps 6
🦢 🥾 💬 ♣
♦

Guests are welcome to our 17th century working farm situated between Cadeleigh and Cheriton Fitzpaine. Exeter 9 miles, Tiverton 8 miles. South and north coasts, Exmoor and Dartmouth are within easy reach. Many great tourist attractions around, three local pubs to visit. Summerhouse overlooking pond with ducks. Open all year except Christmas.

Hele Barton, Black Dog, Thelbridge, Crediton, Devon EX17 4QJ   ⑨

Mrs Gillian Gillbard
☎/Fax 01884 860278
[BB] From £16
Sleeps 4
🦢 ♣ ⊚
♦♦♦

Relax amid peaceful surroundings with lovely views from our 17th century thatched farmhouse on family-run 273-acre beef and sheep farm. Ideal position just off B3042, 2 miles B3137 pub/restaurant just ½ mile. Double or twin rooms (en suite.available). Guests return year after year. Send for a brochure and the cream tea is waiting to welcome you. Open all year except Christmas and New Year. E-mail: gillbard@eclipse.co.uk

Higher Biddacott Farm, Chittlehampton, Umberleigh, Devon EX37 9PY   ⑩

Mrs Fiona Waterer
☎/Fax 01769 540222
[BB] From £15–£20
Sleeps 6
🦢 🐴 🥾 🏹 🐎 ♣ 🍴 🌲
♦♦♦

Wake up to a view of rolling Devon countryside, a scrumptious breakfast and the sound of shire horses going out to work on a traditional working farm. Biddacott's mediaeval farmhouse provides log fires and a plasterwork ceiling. Exmoor and beautiful coastline are close at hand. Open all year except Christmas.

Home Park Farm, Lower Blakewell, Muddiford, Barnstaple, North Devon EX31 4ET   ⑪

Mrs Mari Lethaby
☎/Fax 01271 342955
[BB] From £15–£20
EM From £8.50
Sleeps 6
🦢 🥾 ♣ ⊚
♦♦♦♦

Paradise for a country and garden lover. Panoramic scenic views combined with warm hospitality, genuine farmhouse cuisine and a relaxing, tranquil atmosphere await you at Home Park. All rooms en suite, TV, hair dryer, hospitality tray. Four-poster beds. CH. Many extras including laundry. Conveniently positioned for Exmoor, N. Devon coast. Many repeat bookings confirm excellent accommodation. 2 miles north of Barnstaple. RAC acclaimed. AA QQQQ. Closed Christmas.

---

12 Hornhill Farmhouse, Exeter Hill, Tiverton, Devon EX16 4PL

Barbara Pugsley
☎/Fax 01884 253352
🅱🅱 From £20–£25
EM £12.50
Sleeps 6
🌣(10) 🐾 ⊞ ⅄ 🛋 ⊛
♦♦♦♦♦ *(AA Inspected)*

If you appreciate relaxation with comfortable beds (one Victorian four-poster and one ground floor), private bathrooms, good breakfasts, on-site parking and no smoking, come and stay with us. Our 17th century farmhouse has superb views and is surrounded by fields. You will be most welcome. Recommended by *Which? Good B&B Guide.* Evening meal by arrangement only. Open all year.

---

13 Huxtable Farm, West Buckland, Barnstaple, North Devon EX32 0SR

Jackie & Antony Payne
☎/Fax 01598 760254
🅱🅱 From £24–£25
EM £15
Sleeps 17
🌣 ⅄ ⊞ 🧍 🛋 ☆ ⊛
♦♦♦♦

Enjoy a 4-course candlelit dinner of farm/local produce with a glass of complimentary homemade wine in the medieval dining room of this 16th century Devon longhouse. Secluded sheep farm with abundant wildlife. En suite bedrooms with TV. Log fires, fitness room, sauna, games room and tennis court. Reductions for short/long breaks out of season and for children (£10). Free informative brochure. Open Feb–Nov and New Year.
E-mail: jackie@huxhilton.enterprise-plc.com

---

14 Kerscott Farm, Ash Mill, South Molton, North Devon EX36 4QG

Mrs Theresa Sampson
☎ 01769 550262
🅱🅱 From £19–£20
EM £8.50
Sleeps 6
⅄ 🛋
♦♦♦♦♦ Gold Award

Peaceful, olde worlde16th century Exmoor working farm mentioned in Domesday Book (1086). Fascinating interior/ antiques – a rare find. Superb elevated position overlooking Exmoor National Park and surrounding countryside. Pretty en suite bedrooms with colour TV. Varied, excellent and hearty homemade food including bread and preserves. Spring water. Non-smokers only. Finalist 1999 AA Landlady of the Year. Open Feb–Nov.

---

15 Locksbeam Farm, Torrington, North Devon EX38 7EZ

Mrs Tracey Martin
☎/Fax 01805 623213
🅱🅱 From £20–£24.50
EM From £10
Sleeps 12 + cot
🌣 🧍 ⊶ 🛋 ⊛
♦♦♦♦

A warm welcome awaits you on our family-run dairy farm, offering peace and tranquillity to all who visit. Refurbished farmhouse offers delicious home cooking and comfortable accommodation. All bedrooms en suite with tea tray, colour TV and hairdryer. Large, inviting lounges, open fires and full CH. Traditional English breakfast, optional evening meal. Adjoining local golf course/fishing. Come, relax and enjoy. Open all year except Christmas.

---

16 Lower Collipriest Farm, Tiverton, Devon EX16 4PT

Mrs Linda Olive
☎/Fax 01884 252321
🅱🅱 From £21–£23
EM From £12
Sleeps 6
⅄ ⊞ 🛋 ☆ ⊷ ⊛
♦♦♦♦

Come and relax and enjoy the beauty of the Exe Valley in our 17th century thatched farmhouse. Comfortable lounge with inglenook fireplace and oak beams. Colour TV. Central heating throughout. Twin/single rooms with bathroom en suite, tea/coffee-making facilities. Delicious, traditional fresh cooking with our/local produce. Lovely walks over 220-acre dairy farm, conservation pond/woodland area. An AA award-winning farm. Open Feb–Oct. Brochure available.

---

17 Newhouse Farm, Oakford, Tiverton, Devon EX16 9JE

Mrs Anne Boldry
☎/Fax 01398 351347
🅱🅱 From £20–£22
EM From £12
Sleeps 4
⅄ ⅌ 🛋 ☆ ⊛
♦♦♦♦ *(AA Inspected)*

A perfect base for discovering Devon, our 17th century farmhouse is close to Exmoor. Tastefully and comfortably furnished featuring oak beams and inglenook. Bedrooms have CH, CTV, tea trays, en suite bathrooms. We aim to provide the best of farmhouse cooking and hospitality. West Country Cooking Best Farmhouse award. Recommended by *Which? Good B&B Guide.* Weekly reductions. Open all year (closed Christmas).

Quoit-at-Cross Farm, Stoodleigh, Tiverton, Devon EX16 9PJ

Mrs Linda Hill
☎ 01398 351280
Fax 01398 351351
BB From £19
EM From £11
Sleeps 6
🖙 ⅍ ⅋ ◎
♦♦♦

Beautiful 17th century farmhouse in conservation village. Unwind in the comfort of our home. Make *yourself* at home. Enjoy panoramic views, take a stroll around the lanes and return to a delicious evening meal. Attractive, co-ordinated bedrooms, all en-suite. Full English breakfast. Ideal location for National Trust properties, beaches and Exmoor. Open Apr–Dec.

Seldon Farm, Monkokehampton, Winkleigh, Devon EX19 8RY

Mary Case
☎ 01837 810312
BB From £16–£17
Sleeps 6
🖙 ⼂ 🐎 ⅌
♦♦

Relax in our delightful 17th century farmhouse situated in beautiful unspoilt part of the Devonshire countryside. Ideal for touring Dartmoor and Exmoor. Tarka Trail nearby, Rosemoor Gardens a short drive. Two double, one family room, all with H&C and tea/coffee-making facilities. Reductions for weekly bookings and children. Open Easter–Nov.

Waytown Farm, Shirwell, Barnstaple, North Devon EX31 4JN

Hazel Kingdon
☎/Fax 01271 850396
BB From £18.50–£21
EM From £10.50
Sleeps 10
🖙 ⼂ ⅌ ◎
♦♦♦♦

Enjoy a relaxing, peaceful holiday set in the beautiful rolling countryside of North Devon. We have a family-run beef and sheep farm, easily found just three miles north of Barnstaple. Our 17th century farmhouse offers comfortable, well-appointed bedrooms with superb views. Traditional farmhouse cooking. Send for colour brochure. Reductions for weekly bookings. Open all year except Christmas. E-mail: hazel@waytown.enterprise-plc.com

---

Self-Catering

Barley Cottage & Old Granary, c/o Denham Farm, North Buckland, Braunton, North Devon EX33 1HY

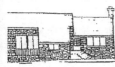

Jean Barnes
☎/Fax 01271 890297
SC £160–£635
Sleeps 4/8
🖙 ⼂ 🗃 ♨ ⅌ ◎
🐾🐾🐾🐾 *Commended*

Nowhere is far away. Ideally based for beaches, Exmoor, towns and attractions. Walk our country lanes or simply relax in comfort. Play area and games room for the young at heart. Enjoy lazy days and barbecues, a slower pace of lifestyle and pure Devonian hospitality. Open all year. See colour ad on page 43.

Beech Grove, East Westacott, Riddlecombe, Chulmleigh, Devon EX18 7PF

Thomas & Joyce Middleton
☎/Fax 01769 520210
SC From £150–£395
Sleeps 4/6
🖙 ♨ ⅌ ◎
🐾🐾🐾🐾 *Commended*

Come, relax in peaceful, idyllic surroundings amidst the beauty of unspoilt countryside – flower filled hedgerows, singing birds, skipping lambs, nature in abundance! Superbly equipped, warm and comfortable bungalow, lovingly cared for. Cot available. Lovely views over green fields and pretty gardens with sunny patio. Large games room for all ages. Friendly farmers nearby. Within easy reach of moors and sandy beaches. Brochure tells all. Open all year.

22 Bridleway Cottages, Golland Farm, Golland Lane, Burrington, Umberleigh, Devon EX18 9JP

Fiona Lincoln-Gordon
☎/Fax 01769 520263
⚏ From £160
Sleeps 2–6
⚏⚏⚏⚏⚏⚏⚏⚏
⚏⚏⚏⚏ *Commended*

Beautiful barns traditionally restored with much character on small organic farm. Very well equipped. Take in the peace and tranquillity with fantastic views of the unpolluted Taw Valley. Private walks/fishing, rare breed animals, organic produce available. Relax and unwind in the heart of Devon. Painting courses available – colour brochure. Open all year. E-mail: golland@btinternet.com

23 Churchtown Farm, West Anstey, South Molton, Devon EX36 3PE

Mrs Nicky Tarr
☎/Fax 01398 341391
⚏ From £100–£475
Sleeps 8
⚏⚏⚏⚏⚏⚏⚏⚏
⚏⚏⚏⚏ *Commended*

Enjoy a characteristic, spacious and attractively furnished half of Devon longhouse set in 200 acres of working farm adjoining moorland. Farmyard animals and pony rides. Beautiful secluded garden, barbecue, stocked fish ponds. 3 bedrooms, lounge with TV, video and woodburner, dining hall, well equipped kitchen, bathroom, CH. Linen included. Washing/drying facilities. Babysitting. Ideal family/walking holiday destination. Open all year.

24 Coombe Cottage, Oakford, Tiverton, Devon EX16 9HF

Mrs Mary Reed
☎ 01398 351281
Fax 01398 351211
⚏ From £115–£330
Sleeps 3/4
⚏⚏⚏⚏
⚏⚏⚏⚏ *Commended*

Set deep in the heart of Devon's beautiful countryside, this charming, well-maintained annexe is ideally situated for exploring Exmoor. If you prefer, you can relax and enjoy the peaceful surroundings in our picturesque garden with its pond and summerhouse. An adjoining paddock is available for your pets to play in. Open all year. *Associate.*

25 Country Ways, Little Knowle Farm, High Bickington, Umberleigh, Devon EX37 9BJ

Kate Price
☎/Fax 01769 560503
⚏ From £170–£525
Sleeps 2–6 + cot
⚏⚏⚏⚏⚏ – ⚏⚏⚏⚏
Highly Commended

Beautifully converted stone barns hidden away on a small farm with magnificent views across the Devonshire Dales. Warm and well-equipped, incredibly peaceful with lovely gardens. Walks through ancient woodland. Rare breeds with lots of friendly animals. Children's play area. Within easy reach of Exmoor, Barnstaple and the coast. One unit ideal for wheelchairs. Three day breaks from £85. Open all year. E-mail: kate.price@virgin.net

26 Drewstone Farm, South Molton, North Devon EX36 3EF

Ruth Ley
☎ 01769 572337
⚏ From £160–£395
Sleeps 6
⚏⚏⚏⚏⚏
⚏⚏⚏⚏⚏ – ⚏⚏⚏⚏⚏
Commended

Escape to farm tranquillity on edge of Exmoor. 16th century luxury cottage and converted barn with beams, woodburner, colour TV, fitted carpets, phone, dishwasher, washing machine. 3/4 bedrooms, bath-shower room. Fully equipped oak kitchen/diner and lounge with panoramic views. Enclosed lawn, children's games room, animals, freedom to explore the farm. Country walks, clay-pigeon shooting, trout lake. Open all year.

27 Dunsley Farm, West Anstey, South Molton, Devon EX36 3PF

Mrs Mary Robins
☎ 01398 341246
⚏ From £90–£375
Sleeps 5
⚏⚏⚏⚏
⚏⚏⚏⚏ *Commended*

Self-contained cottage forming part of 16th century farmhouse, overlooks meadows and woodland valley. Access off a quiet country road. 2 bedrooms (accommodate 5 people), bathroom, large lounge/diner with colour TV. Large modern equipped kitchen, electric heating (£1 meter). Linen provided, pets welcome. Coarse fishing available on farm. Dulverton 6 miles. Open all year.

Dunsley Mill, West Anstey, South Molton, Devon EX36 3PF

Helen Sparrow
☎/Fax 01398 341374
🅂🄲 From £150–£450
Sleeps 6
🌙 ♒ 🛢 🐎 ✕ 🐾 ♘
🐾 🐾 🐾 🐾 *Highly Commended*

Beautifully converted detached stone barn set in 30 acres in an idyllic riverside situation. Three bedrooms, 2 doubles, 1 twin. Dishwasher, microwave, electric oven, washing machine. Linen and towels provided. Children, dogs and horses welcome. Bridleways adjoin the property. Fishing, hunting and shooting all in the vicinity. Open all year.

Lower Campscott Farm, Lee, Ilfracombe, Devon EX34 8LS

Mrs Margaret Cowell
☎ 01271 863479
🅂🄲 From £186–£490
Sleeps 4/8
🌙 ✂ 🎣 🏹 🐎 🛢 ♘
🐾 🐾 *Up to Commended*

Our four cottages have been converted from the farm's original buildings. All have fitted carpets, colour TV, fridge and microwave, the largest ones have freezers. Communal laundry room. Variety of farm animal pets for children to make friends with. Situated at the head of the Fuchsia Valley with a footpath to the village and beach 1½ miles away. Open all year.
E-mail: setaside@email.msn.com

Manor Farm, Riddlecombe, Chulmleigh, North Devon EX18 7NX

Eveline Gay
☎/Fax 01769 520335
🅂🄲 From £190
Sleeps 7/8 + cot
🌙 🐎 🛢 ♘ ◉
🐾 🐾 🐾 🐾 *Commended*

'An Alladin's cave.' This is how children and parents have described our superb games room, which includes a play cottage, ride-on toys (including tractors!), pool, table tennis and much more. Picturesque farmhouse with 3 bedrooms in idyllic setting on real working farm. Meet Doris our adorable cow, collect eggs, watch milking, feed lambs. Children will love the farm experience. Excellent heating for all seasons. Cleanliness assured.

Nethercott Manor Farm, Rose Ash, South Molton, North Devon EX36 4RE

Carol Woollacott
☎/Fax 01769 550483
🅂🄲 From £100–£425
Sleeps 4 and 7
🌙 🐎 🏹 🐎 ✕ ♘ 🛢 ◉
🐾 🐾 🐾 *Up to Commended*

Welcome to Nethercott! Situated in the heart of the Devonshire dales – explore the farm, Exmoor and beautiful coast. Three cottages within traditional thatched farmhouse. Comfortably furnished, cosy and warm atmosphere, woodburners, oak beams, nooks and crannies. Trout pond, games room with skittles, pool table, tennis, darts. Barbecue or relax. Open all year. See colour ad on page 44.

Northcott Barton Farm, Ashreigney, Chulmleigh, Devon EX18 7PR

Mrs Sandra Gay
☎/Fax 01769 520259
🅂🄲 From £170
Sleeps 7/8 + cot
🌙 🐎 🛢 ♘
🐾 🐾 🐾 *Commended*

Unwind and relax country-style. Glorious countryside and farm to explore. Beautifully equipped, warm and comfy three bedroomed cottage offers character beams and log fire, plus video, microwave, washer, freezer, etc. Children love helping feed lambs and calves. Collect eggs for breakfast and see the cows come home for milking.

The Old Granary, Bampfield Farm, Goodleigh, Barnstaple, North Devon EX32 7NR

Lynda Thorne
☎/Fax 01271 346566
🅂🄲 From £200–£620
Sleeps 6/8 + cots
🌙 🏹 🛢
🐾 🐾 🐾 🐾 *Commended*

Recently converted from a granary, this delightful detached cottage is situated near the picturesque village of Goodleigh on a 200-acre dairy farm. Spacious accommodation, beamed ceilings, woodburner and 'olde worlde' cottage ambience. Dishwasher, washer/dryer, microwave, CH. En suite master bedroom, family bathroom, separate WC. Play area, barbecue. Ideal for north coast/Exmoor and Barnstaple. Open all year.
E-mail: lynda@bampfieldfm.freeserve.co.uk

34 Pickwell Barton Holiday Cottages, Pickwell Barton, Georgeham, Braunton, North Devon EX33 1LA

Mrs Sheila Cook
☎/Fax 01271 890987
[SC] From £170–£430
Sleeps 7/8
🐕 ♨ 🕭
🐾🐾 Commended

Visit Pickwell Barton and you have the best of both worlds – gorgeous country walks with a fantastic view of Putsborough, Woolacombe beach. Stroll across our fields in the evening to view the sun setting into the ocean. Each cottage has 3 bedrooms on our sheep and arable farm just 20 minutes' walk to the golden, sandy beach. Warm, cosy open fires in winter. Open all year.

35 Stable Cottage, Pitt Farm, North Molton, North Devon EX36 3JR

Mrs Gladys Ayre
☎ 01598 740285
[SC] From £160–£395
Sleeps 5/6
🐕 ✂
🐾🐾🐾 Commended

Enjoy peaceful surroundings at our charming cottage, set in unspoilt Exmoor countryside, 1 mile from village shops, pubs, garage, equipped to high standard with night storage heating throughout. 3 bedrooms. Bath/shower/ beamed lounge with woodburner. Colour TV, oak fitted kitchen/diner. Autowasher, fridge, microwave, etc. Own patio. Barbecue. Pond with ducks and geese. Freedom to explore the farm. Open all year.

36 West Ilkerton Farm, Barbrook, Lynton, North Devon EX35 6QA

Chris & Victoria Eveleigh
☎/Fax 01598 752310
[SC] From £190–£480
Sleeps 6 + cot
🐕 ✂ 🕭 🐎 🐈 ♨ ⊕
🐾🐾🐾🐾 Commended

Luxurious semi-detached cottage on secluded hill farm bordering open moor. Sheep, cattle, carthorses and Exmoor ponies. Coast 3 miles, riding ½ mile. 3 bedrooms (2 king size, 1 twin) 2 bathrooms, living/dining room, kitchen (Rayburn and full range of appliances). CH. TV, video. Baby equipment and evening babysitting. Children, dogs and horses welcome. Special winter breaks from £95. Ideal for walking, riding, family farm holidays. Open all year.

37 Whitefield Barton, Challacombe, Barnstaple, Devon EX31 4TU

Rosemarie Kingdon
☎ 01598 763271
[SC] From £100–£375
Sleeps 6 + cot
🐕 ♨ 🕭
🐾🐾🐾 Commended

Spacious characteristic accommodation in half of 16th century farmhouse with modern luxuries. Tastefully furnished to high standard. Warm cosy lounge, well equipped kitchen, family & twin rooms, bathroom/shower, babysitting. Ample parking. Private patio, BBQ, streamed garden. Linen & electricity incl. Peaceful surroundings with scenic walks and farm animals on 200-acre farm. Central for beaches, moors. Open May–Dec.

9 White Witches and Stable Lodge, Hele Barton, Black Dog, Thelbridge, Crediton, Devon EX17 4QJ

Mrs Gillian Gillbard
☎/Fax 01884 860278
[SC] From £150–£450
Sleeps 2–6/8 + cot
🏠 🐕 ✂ 🕭 ⊕
🐾🐾🐾 Up to Highly Commended

Dream of a pretty, well-equipped thatched cottage in the country with a garden leading to fields with a river meandering by. Listen to the birds singing on a summer evening or enjoy cosy nights by an open fire, or the luxury of en suite bedrooms and a four-poster bed in our listed barn. Sounds like heaven? Well this is reality. Send for a brochure and we shall be here to welcome you. Open all year. E-mail: gillbard@eclipse.co.uk

38 Willesleigh Farm, Goodleigh, Barnstaple, North Devon EX32 7NA

Charles & Anne Esmond-Cole
☎/Fax 01271 343763
[SC] From £160–£660
Sleeps 6 + cot
🐕 ✂ ⊕
🐾🐾🐾 Highly Commended

86-acre family-run dairy farm in glorious countryside, ½ mile from village, within ½ hour's drive of dramatic coastlines, Exmoor, glorious gardens, superb walks. Lovingly cared for, The Cottage and The Gatehouse welcome all ages and abilities to year-round comfort and peace. Enclosed heated swimming pool May–Oct. Open all year.

Wintershead Farm, Simonsbath, Exmoor, Somerset TA24 7LF   39

Jane Styles
☎ 01643 831222
Fax 01643 831628
SC From £125–£495
Sleeps 1–6 + cot
🛇 🏊 🛖
♟♟ – ♟♟♟♟
Highly Commended

Forget the pressures of everyday life and unwind in one of our warm and cosy cottages. Hidden away in the hills of Exmoor where the views are breathtaking, most of the traffic has four legs and the only street lighting is the stars above. You can relax after a wonderful day's exploring, with comfy sofas, log fires, central heating and lots of hot water. Short breaks available Nov–Mar. Colour brochure. Open all year.

Wonham Barton, Bampton, Tiverton, Devon EX16 9JZ   40

Anne McLean Williams
☎/Fax 01398 331312
SC From £125–£298
Sleeps 4/6
🛇 🏊 ⊞ ⅄ 🎋 🍴 🎺
♟♟♟ *Commended*

Conveniently explore sleepy Devon from our friendly, comfortable farmhouse wing overlooking the Exe Valley. Discover Domesday hamlets, majestic moorland, dramatic coastlines – or enjoy country pursuits and leisurely cream teas. Children are fascinated by soaring buzzards, Exmoor red deer and traditional shepherding on horseback with skilled Border Collies. TV drama and films have been made here; you too can share our secrets. Tell us when you are coming! Open all year.

Yelland Cottage, c/o West Whitefield Farm, Challacombe, Barnstaple, Devon EX31 4TU   41

Jean Kingdon
☎ 01598 763433
SC From £130–£290
Sleeps 6
🛇 🏊 🎋
♟♟♟ *Approved*

Semi-detached cosy farm cottage on working hill farm amidst beautiful countryside within easy reach of village pub and shop. Log fire, Rayburn plus electric conveniences. Relaxing lounge, colour TV. Linen provided. Friendly, relaxed atmosphere with farm animals. Spacious garden with ample parking. Ideal for beaches, walking, fishing, riding and touring North Devon. Open all year.

Camping and Caravanning

Welcombe Farm, Charles, Nr Barnstaple, North Devon EX32 7PU   42

Mrs Margaret Faulkner
☎/Fax 01598 710440
SC From £100–£270
Sleeps 4/5
🛇 🏊 ⅄ 🚐 🍴
Tourist Board Inspected

Imaginative private setting for a luxury caravan holiday. Comfortable and peaceful, with full facilities, two bedrooms and heating throughout. Small, family run farm with dairy cows and sheep, on the foothills of Exmoor. Panoramic views of hills and valleys from enclosed garden. Close to Tarka Trail and easy reach of sandy beaches, moors and gardens. Wildlife in abundance. Open Easter–Oct.

FARM HOLIDAY BUREAU

Please mention **Stay on a Farm** when booking

Wiltshire

Stonehenge, Avebury, Wiltshire White Horses
& the Ridge Way

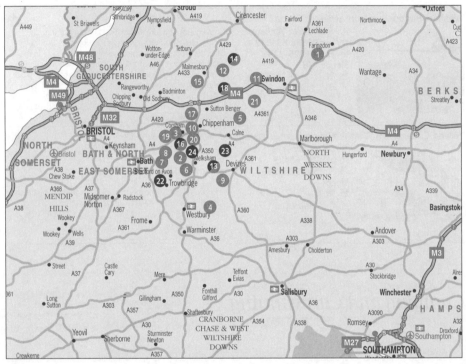

Key

1 Bed & Breakfast

1 Self-Catering

1 B&B and SC

1 Camping Barns

1 Camping &
Caravanning

Although easily accessible from London, Wiltshire offers some of the best of rural England. Its wide, peaceful downland is rich in historic interest, with Stonehenge, Avebury and Silbury Hill standing out on the rolling green plain. Picturesque villages such as Castle Combe and Lacock lie tucked away in the valleys and just over the county border lies the Georgian city of Bath. Six hundred years of building are displayed in the magnificent collection of historic homes – Longleat, Bowood House, Corsham Court, Sheldon Manor... Walk the ancient Ridge way Path or along the Kennet and Avon Canal, now restored along much of its route. Once here, you'll see why almost half the county is designated an Area of Outstanding Natural Beauty.

If you would like help in finding suitable farm accommodation, turn to the full listing of FHB Groups on pages 392 to 395 to find appropriate contact details for this area.

Bed and Breakfast
(and evening meal)

Ashen Copse Farm, Coleshill, Highworth, Nr Swindon, Wiltshire SN6 7PU   ①

Pat Hoddinott
☎ 01367 240175
Fax 01367 241418
BB From £21–£25
Sleeps 6
🐴 ✂ 🎋 📠 ⊛
♦♦♦

Our National Trust beef/arable farm is an ideal setting for peace and quiet. Watch the wildlife during wonderful walks in beautiful countryside. Explore pretty Cotswold villages and attractions. Good food, golf and riding nearby. M4 11 miles. 1 family en suite, 1 twin and 1 single bedroom in comfortable 17th century farmhouse. Open all year except Christmas Day. E-mail: pat@hodd.demon.co.uk

---

Boyds Farm, Gastard, Nr Corsham, Wiltshire SN13 9PT   ②

Dorothy Robinson
☎/Fax 01249 713146
BB From £20–£25
Sleeps 6
🐴 ✂ 📠 🎋 ⊛
♦♦♦♦ Silver Award

Enjoy a relaxing stay on our arable farm situated in the peace and tranquillity of the unspoilt Wiltshire countryside. Our delightful 16th century farmhouse, featured by the *Daily Express, Observer* and *Daily Mail* accommodates families, couples and individuals. All rooms have en suite/private facilities and TV. Guests' own lounge with woodburning stove. Easy access to M4, Bath, Lacock, Castle Combe, Stonehenge, Bradford-on-Avon. Excellent pub food close by. Closed Christmas & New Year.

Church Farm, Hartham Park, Corsham, Nr Chippenham, Wiltshire SN13 0PU   ③

Mrs Kate Jones
☎/Fax 01249 715180
Mobile 07977 910775
BB From £20–£22.50
Sleeps 6
🐴 🐓 ✂ 👤 🚜 📠 🐕 🎋
♦♦♦♦

Our Cotswold stone farmhouse enjoys a secluded position with wonderful views across the adjoining valley and fields of our dairy/beef farm. Lovely walks and riding close by, as are pretty villages like Lacock and Castle Combe. Easy access to Bath (8 miles), M4 (4 miles), award-winning local pubs/restaurants. Family and double room, both en suite, single room with private shower, all with TV, CH and tea/coffee. Hearty breakfasts. Closed Christmas and New Year. E-mail: kmjbandb@aol.com

---

Church Farm, Steeple Ashton, Trowbridge, Wiltshire BA14 6EL   ④

Susan Cottle
☎ 01380 870518
BB From £18.50–£20
Sleeps 4
🐴 🐓 ☕ 🎋 📠 ⊛
♦♦♦♦

Lovely old farmhouse dating back to 16th century in centre of beautiful village. Ideally situated for Bath, Salisbury, Longleat, Stourhead, Castle Combe. Lacock, Avebury. Spacious rooms, one double with H&C, one family, tea/coffee facilities. Guests' bathroom. Homely atmosphere, use of lounge, TV. Log fire in winter. Tea and homemade cake on arrival. No smoking in bedrooms. Open all year except Christmas and New Year. E-mail: church.farm@farmline.com

---

Friday Street Farm, Christian Malford, Chippenham, Wiltshire SN15 4BU   ⑤

Mrs Linda Di Claudio
☎/Fax 01249 720146
BB From £22.50–£25
EM From £12.50
Sleeps 2
✂ 📠 🐎 🎋
♦♦♦♦

An absolutely delightful 17th century farmhouse with a wealth of character, peace and relaxation. Low ceilings, beams, log fires and excellent candlelit dinners add to the ambience. Accommodation is in one double room en suite with private sitting/dinning room. A truly lovely home, an ideal base for exploring this attractive area. Open all year. *Associate.*

---

6   **Frying Pan Farm,** Broughton Gifford, Melksham, Wiltshire SN12 8LL

Barbara Pullen
☎ 01225 702343
Fax 01225 793652
🅱 From £20–£25
Sleeps 4
🐎(2) ⚬ 🎇 🛅
♦♦♦

A warm welcome awaits you at our 17th century farmhouse situated 1 mile from Melksham making it ideally positioned for visiting Bath, Bradford-on-Avon, Lacock and numerous National Trust properties. The cosy accommodation consists of one double and one twin, both en suite, with tea/coffee facilities and TV. Good pub food in village 1 mile. Closed Christmas and New Year.

7   **Great Ashley Farm,** Ashley Lane, Bradford-on-Avon, Wiltshire BA15 2PP

Helen Rawlings
☎/Fax 01225 864563
🅱 From £20
Sleeps 5
🐎 ⚬ 🎇 🛅
♦♦♦♦

Come and enjoy our lovely secluded farmhouse overlooking a large natural pond in AONB minutes from Bath and Bradford-on-Avon. The house is decorated with taste, imagination and care, offering delightful en suite bedrooms with every home from home comfort. An ideal place to relax and unwind. Great hospitality, delicious breakfast. Convenient for M4, Stonehenge, Lacock, Salisbury, Avebury, Corsham. Open all year except Christmas.

8   **Hatt Farm,** Old Jockey, Box, Nr Bath, Wiltshire SN13 8DJ

Mrs Carol Pope
☎ 01225 742989
Fax 01225 742779
🅱 From £20–£25
Sleeps 4
🐎 ⚬ 🛅 🎇 ⓖ
♦♦♦♦

Extremely comfortable Georgian farmhouse in peaceful surroundings. Scrumptious breakfasts served overlooking beautiful countryside views. What could be nicer than sitting by a log fire in winter or enjoying the garden in summer? Lovely walks and good golfing nearby. Ideal for touring Wiltshire and the Cotswolds yet only 15 mins' drive to Bath. One twin with en suite shower, one double/family with private bathroom, both with tea/coffee. CH. Guests' lounge. Closed Christmas and New Year.

9   **Higher Green Farm,** Poulshot, Devizes, Wiltshire SN10 1RW

Marlene & Malcolm Nixon
☎/Fax 01380 828355
🅱 From £18
Sleeps 6
🐎 🎇 ⚬ 🛅
♦♦♦

Welcome to our peaceful 17th century timbered farmhouse facing village green and cricket pitch. Excellent traditional inn nearby. Our dairy farm is situated between Bath and Salisbury, close to many National Trust properties. Ideal for Stonehenge, Longleat, Avebury and Lacock. 1 double, 1 twin, 2 single rooms. Tea-making facilities. Guests' lounge, colour TV. Take A361 from Devizes, after 2 miles left to Poulshot, farm opposite Raven Inn. Open Mar–Nov.

10   **Home Farm,** Harts Lane, Biddestone, Chippenham, Wilts SN14 7DQ

Ian & Audrey Smith
☎ 01249 714475
Fax 01249 701488
🅱 From £20–£25
Sleeps 9
🐎 ⚬ 🛅 🎇 ⓖ
♦♦♦♦

A warm welcome awaits you in this 17th century farmhouse on a family-run working mixed farm. Set in beautiful Biddestone just a stroll across village green from the pub. Ideally situated for Bath, Castle Combe and Lacock, Stonehenge, Avebury, Longleat, etc. All rooms have colour TV, tea and coffee; two en suite, the other has private bathroom. Open all year.
E-mail: smith@homefarmb-b.freeserve.co.uk

11   **Leighfield Lodge Farm,** Malmesbury Road, Leigh, Swindon, Wiltshire SN6 6RH

Mrs Claire Read
☎/Fax 01666 860241
🅱 From £22.50
Sleeps 6
🐎 ⚬ 🔲 🛅 ⓖ
♦♦♦♦

Imagine a lovely old farmhouse in a truly rural setting. Step inside and discover comfortable en suite rooms with crisp cotton bedlinen. Relax in the sitting room in front of a warm fire, after explororing the Cotswolds or Wiltshire Downs. Children will enjoy meeting the Jersey cows and may even see the wild deer! Open all year.

Lovett Farm, Little Somerford, Nr Malmesbury, Wiltshire SN15 5BP   ⑫

Susan Barnes
☎/Fax 01666 823268
Mobile 07808 858612
⬛ From £22–£25
Sleeps 4
⌂(5) ♨ ⅍ ♨ ⍟
♦♦♦♦

Enjoy traditional hospitality at our delightful farmhouse on a working farm with beautiful views. Two attractive double and twin en suite bedrooms, each with tea/coffee-making facilities and colour TV. Full central heating. Guests' dining room/ lounge. Log fires in winter. Convenient M4, Bath, Cotswolds, Lacock and Stonehenge. Excellent food pubs nearby. Open all year except Christmas.

Lower Foxhangers Farm, Rowde, Devizes, Wiltshire SN10 1SS   ⑬

Cynthia & Colin Fletcher
☎/Fax 01380 828254
⬛ From £20–£22.50
Sleeps 6
⌂(5) ♯ ⅍ ♨ ⎐(touring & static)
♨ ♨ ♨ ⍟
♦♦♦

We expectantly await your visit to our 18th century farmhouse alongside the canal with its gaily painted narrow boats. Assist boats through the locks whilst strolling to the pubs. Ideal for walking, cycling, fishing, boating. Easy reach Stonehenge/Bath. Also available for hire our new 40'–60' narrowboats. Twin, double and family rooms, all en suite with TV and hospitality tray. Self-catering units and small campsite with electricity, toilets/shower. Open May–Oct. E-mail: fletcher@foxcanhol.freeserve.co.uk

---

Lower Stonehill Farm, Charlton, Malmesbury, Wiltshire SN16 9DY   ⑭

Mrs Edna Edwards
☎/Fax 01666 823310
⬛ From £19
Sleeps 6
⌂ ♯ ♨
♦♦♦♦

Large Cotswold stone 15th century farmhouse on working dairy farm in the lush, rolling countryside on the Wilts/Glos border. Three comfortable rooms, 1 en suite, all with tea/coffee facilities. Children and dogs welcome. Delicious full English breakfast served in guests' sitting/dining room or garden if fine. Central for Oxford, Bath, Stratford, Stonehenge and the Cotswolds. On the B4040 3½ miles from historic Malmesbury. Open all year.

Manor Farm, Corston, Malmesbury, Wiltshire SN16 0HF   ⑮

Mrs Ross Eavis
☎ 01666 822148
Fax 01666 826565
⬛ From £20–£28
Sleeps 12
⌂(12) ⅍ ⊞ ♨ ⍟
♦♦♦♦

Manor Farm is very easy to find just 3 miles north of M4 J17. Cotswold stone farmhouse full of character and very homely. Six rooms, four en suite all with colour TV and hospitality tray. Large gardens to while away the time or visit local pub just down the road. As featured in the *Daily Express*. Closed Christmas.

Manor Farm, Wadswick, Box, Corsham, Wiltshire SN13 8JB   ⑯

Carolyn Barton
☎ 01225 810733
Fax 01225 810307
⬛ From £22.50–£25
Sleeps 6
⌂(5) ⅍ ♞ ⊞ ♨
♦♦♦♦

Visit our arable and horse farm nestling in the quiet hamlet of Wadswick. We are only 7 miles from Bath yet close to Lacock and other beautiful villages. Our 16th century farmhouse has large, spacious rooms, all en suite with tea/coffee making facilities and colour TV. Stabling and riding by arrangement. Open Mar–Nov. E-mail: wadswick@compuserve.com

---

Oakfield Farm, Easton Piercy Lane, Yatton Keynell, Chippenham, Wiltshire SN14 6JU   ⑰

Mrs Margaret Read
☎ 01249 782355
Fax 01249 783458
⬛ From £20
Sleeps 6
⌂ ♯ ⅍ ♨ ⍟
♦♦♦♦

Friendly welcome in Cotswold stone farmhouse with fine views over open countryside. On working livestock farm in a quiet location, excellent for wildlife. One en suite double/family room, 1 double and 1 twin room, all with tea/coffee-making facilities and colour TV. Full central heating. Ideal base for visiting Bath, Castle Combe, Stonehenge and the Cotswolds. Open Mar–Nov.

18 **Olivemead Farm,** Olivemead Lane, Dauntsey, nr Chippenham, Wiltshire SN15 4JQ

Suzanne Candy
☎/Fax 01666 510205
Mobile 07974 815305
[BB] From £18–£24
Sleeps 6
ᘉ 🐕 ⅄ 🛉 🛄 🎠 ⊛
◆◆

Relax and enjoy the warm, informal hospitality at our delightful 18th century farmhouse on a working dairy farm. Thoughtfully decorated twin, double, family rooms with washbasin, colour TV. Tea/coffee facilities. Generous breakfasts. Oak beamed dining room/lounge for guests' exclusive use. Large garden, play area, cot, highchair. Convenient M4, Bath, Cotswolds, Salisbury. Open all year except Christmas and New Year.
E-mail: olivemead@farming.co.uk

19 **Pickwick Lodge Farm,** Guyers Lane, Corsham, Wiltshire SN13 0PS

Gill Stafford
☎ 01249 712207
Fax 01249 701904
[BB] From £20–£25
Sleeps 6
ᘉ ⅄ 🛉 🎠 ⊛
◆◆◆◆

Enjoy a stay at our beautiful home set in wonderful countryside where you can see rabbits, pheasant and occasionally deer. Relax in our garden having started the day with a hearty delicious breakfast. Bath, NT properties, Corsham Court, Stonehenge and many interesting villages nearby. Three well appointed and tastefully furnished rooms with en suite/private facilities, hospitality tray, home made biscuits. Closed Christmas and New Year.
E-mail: b&b@pickwicklodge.freeserve.co.uk

20 **Thingley Court Farm,** Thingley, Corsham, Wiltshire SN13 9QQ

Zoe Sully
☎ 01249 713617
Mobile 07050 128466
[BB] From £20–£25
Sleeps 4
ᘉ 🐔 🛄 🎠
◆◆◆

Relax and unwind in comfort in our 15th century farmhouse situated between Lacock and Corsham, not far from Bath and easily accessible from the M4. Large lounge with log fire. One en suite and one twin room with private facilities. Central heating throughout. Open all year.

21 **Tockenham Court Farm,** Tockenham, Nr Swindon, Wiltshire SN4 7PH

Mrs Elizabeth Bennett
☎/Fax 01793 852315
Mobile 0831 341310
[BB] From £22–£25
Sleeps 6
ᘉ(5) 🐔 🛄
◆◆◆◆

Welcome to our Grade II listed 16th century court house. We have 1 double room with private shower room and toilet, 1 double room with private bathroom and toilet, 1 en suite room. CH, tea/coffee facilities and colour TV. Guests' own sitting room.

Self-Catering

22 **Church Farm Cottages,** Winsley, Bradford-on-Avon, Wiltshire BA15 2JH

Trish Bowles
☎/Fax 01225 722246
Mobile 0468 543027
[SC] From £170–£330
Sleeps 2–4 + cot
ᘉ 🐕 ⅄ 🖽 👤 🛁 🛄 🎏 ⊛
🐾 🐾 🐾 🐾 Commended

Five newly converted single-storey cottages with original features. Luxuriously appointed. Four poster bed. On outskirts of village within 500 metres of pub and shop. Bath 5 miles. Kennet and Avon canal ¾ mile for cycling, walking, boating and fishing. Picturesque touring caravan/campsite with electricity and facilities. Brochure available. Open all year.
E-mail: churchfarmcottages@compuserve.com

Home Farm Barn and The Derby, Home Farm, Heddington, Nr Calne, Wiltshire SN11 0PL

Mrs Janet Tyler
☎/Fax 01380 850523
SC From £150–£395
Sleep 2/5
🐕 🐎 💼 ®
⚘⚘⚘⚘ *Commended*

Home Farm is a large dairy and arable farm in village centre with its own private lake and offering unbeatable downland walks with panoramic views (SSSI). Riding school and golf course adjoin the farm. Also bungalow-style stable conversion set in idyllic courtyard. Sleeps 2. Colour brochure. E mail: W.S.Tyler@farmline.com

---

Lower Foxhangers Farm, Rowde, Devizes, Wiltshire SN10 1SS

Cynthia & Colin Fletcher
☎ 01380 828254/828795
Fax 01380 828254
SC From £170–£230
Sleeps 4/6
🐕 🐎 ⚥ 🐎 🚐(touring and static)
🐿 🐎 💼 ®
Tourist Board Inspected

Enjoy your holiday with us on our small farm/marina with its diverse attractions. Relax on the patio of your rural retreat. We have four holiday mobile homes. Hear the near musical clatter of the windlass heralding the lock gate opening and the arrival of yet another narrow boat. Hire one of our new narrowboats and cruise to Bath and back. Also B&B and small campsite with electricity and facilities. Open Apr–Nov. E-mail: fletcher@foxcanhol.freeserve.co.uk

---

Stonehill Farm, Charlton, Malmesbury, Wiltshire SN16 9DY

Mrs Edna Edwards
☎/Fax 01666 823310
SC From £180–£230
Sleeps 2/3
🐿 🐎 💼
⚘⚘⚘ *Commended*

Stonehill is a family-run dairy farm on the Wilts/Glos border, 3 miles from Malmesbury and 8 miles M4. The Cow Byre and Bull Pen are converted cowsheds, comfortably furnished with double bed, bathroom, fitted kitchen/diner and lounge. Full CH, colour TV, microwave, all power and linen included. Facing south-west with gravel patio and garden chairs. Open all year.

Swallow Cottage, Olivemead Farm, Olivemead Lane, Dauntsey, nr Chippenham, Wilts SN15 4JQ

Suzanne Candy
☎/Fax 01666 510205
Mobile 07974 815305
SC From £200–£350
Sleeps 6 + 2
🐿 🐎 ⚥ 💼 🐎 ®
⚘⚘⚘⚘ *Commended*

Imagine a delightful, comfortable, well-equipped cottage on a working dairy farm. Newly converted to offer the luxuries of modern living but retaining its traditional features. Bed settee available for extra guests. Perfectly positioned for days out in Wiltshire, Bath and the Cotswolds. Plenty to do for all the family even on the wettest of days. Brochure available. Open all year. E-mail: olivemead@farming.co.uk

---

Wadswick Barns, Manor Farm, Wadswick, Corsham, Wiltshire SN13 8JB

Carolyn Barton
☎ 01225 810733
Fax 01225 810307
SC From £312–£531
Sleeps 4–7
🐿 🐎 ⚥ 💼 ▣ 🐎
⚘⚘⚘⚘⚘ *Highly Commended*

Three beautifully converted 16th century farm buildings, situated in the peaceful hamlet of Wadswick. Furnished to a very high standard with a wealth of original features, natural beams, gas stoves. Private gardens and patios. Close to Bath, Lacock, Castle Combe and Corsham. Open all year. E-mail: wadswick@compuserve.com

---

Wick Farm, Lacock, Chippenham, Wiltshire SN15 2LU

Philip and Sue King
☎ 01249 730244
Fax 01249 730072
SC From £170–£395
Sleeps 4/5 + cot
🐿 ⚥ 🚐 💼 🐎 🐎 ®
⚘⚘⚘ *Highly Commended*

Philip and Sue invite you to their working farm in The Cheese House or Cyder House, where original cyder press remains, also stepped fireplace with woodburning stove. Some windows in Cheese have original shutters with gallery as extra seating area with portable TV. Both properties have exposed timbers, traditional furnishings. Linen and towels included. Coarse fishing on own lake. Brochure available. Open all year.

Dorset

Hardy Country, Lyme Regis & Dorset Coast

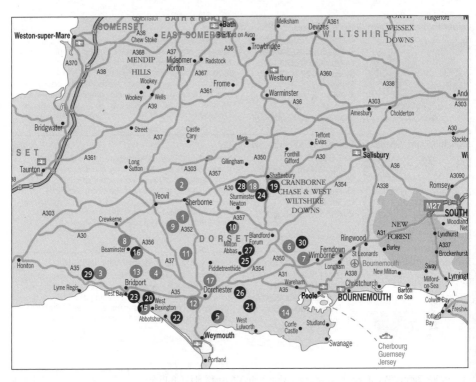

Key

1 Bed & Breakfast

1 Self-Catering

1 B&B and SC

1 Camping Barns

1 Camping & Caravanning

With its mild south coast climate, Dorset is a county for all seasons. In West Dorset, with its pretty villages, interesting coastline and unspoilt countryside, you can fish, enjoy watersports, hunt for fossils or wander the footpaths. North Dorset, with its unchanged pastureland and valleys, may remind you of Thomas Hardy's Wessex. There are so many attractive places, for instance Gold Hill at Shaftesbury and Milton Abbey. The rolling downland of East Dorset is within easy distance of Blandford, Wimborne, Poole and Bournemouth with their attractions and theatres. South Dorset and the Isle of Purbeck have wonderful beaches, heathland and areas of historical interest. The county footpath network is unsurpassed, taking in hidden valleys, dramatic hills, unspoilt villages and the glorious scenery of the Coastal Way. 'There never was a finer county' declared Charles II.

If you would like help in finding suitable farm accommodation, turn to the full listing of FHB Groups on pages 392 to 395 to find appropriate contact details for this area.

Bed and Breakfast
(and evening meal)

Almshouse Farm, Hermitage, Holnest, Sherborne, Dorset DT9 6HA   ①

Mrs Jenny Mayo
☎/Fax 01963 210296
BB From £20–£25
Sleeps 6
☼(10) 🏠 ®
♦♦♦♦

Spoil yourself and stay on our traditional working dairy farm situated in a totally unspoiled part of Dorset. Listed farmhouse retains its age and beauty whilst boasting every modern convenience. Wander the charming garden, surrounding fields or lanes and build an appetite for a real farmhouse breakfast. Golf, fishing and riding nearby. AA QQQQ selected. Open Feb–Dec.

Ashclose Farm, Blackford Road, Charlton Horethorne, Sherborne, Dorset DT9 4PG   ②

Babs & Henry Gooding
☎ 01963 220360
BB From £15.50–£18
Sleeps 5/6
☼ 🐴 🏠
♦♦♦

Comfortable farmhouse in peaceful countryside with super views. Friendly welcome and quiet, relaxed atmosphere. There is an attractive one-acre garden and large conservatory where our guests may enjoy the view. Large private lounge with colour TV/Sky. Children welcome. Comfortably furnished bedrooms (double, twin and single). Good central location for exploring this area. Open all year. *Associate.*
E-mail: gooding@ashclosefarm.freeserve.co.uk

Cardsmill Farm, Whitchurch Canonicorum, Bridport, Dorset DT6 6RP   ③

Mrs Sue M Johnson
☎/Fax 01297 489375
BB From £17–£22
Sleeps 6
☼ 🐕 🐴 🏠 🍴 ®
♦♦♦

Freedom to wander around and watch on this working family farm. Nature walks to the village and pub via the woods and fields. Ideal for family and friends to visit the beach, go fossil hunting, touring and walking. One double and one family room both en suite with colour TV and tea/coffee tray. Lounge with CTV and inglenook fireplace. English and varied breakfasts. A warm welcome guaranteed. Open Feb–Nov.

Colesmoor Farm, Toller Porcorum, Dorchester, Dorset DT2 0DU   ④

Mrs Rachael Geddes
☎ 01300 320812
Fax 01300 321402
BB From £20
EM From £9.50
Sleeps 4
☼ ⅙ 🍴 🏠 ®
♦♦♦♦

Colesmoor Farm, reached by its own private track, is surrounded by peaceful countryside with extensive views. We offer a choice of breakfasts with homebaked bread. Our ground floor accommodation consists of a double and a twin/double room. Both rooms have well-equipped en suite bathrooms, CTV and hot drink facilities. Excellent choice of pubs and restaurants nearby. Brochure. Closed Mar, Apr & Dec. E-mail: geddes.colesmoor@eclipse.co.uk

---

Halls Farm, Church Lane, Osmington, Nr Weymouth, Dorset DT3 6EW   ⑤

Karen-Lee Knott
☎ 01305 837068
BB From £20–£24
EM From £10
Sleeps 4
☼ 🐴 ⅙ 🏠 🍴
Applied

Set in a secluded rural location, enjoying stunning views of the White Horse valley, this traditional farmhouse offers two attractive double en suite rooms with large guests' lounge and dining room area. Good pubs within walking distance and brilliant access to footpaths, bridleways and the coast. A superb base to explore all that Dorset has to offer. Stabling available. Open all year.

6   **Hemsworth Farm,** Hemsworth, Witchampton, Nr Wimborne, Dorset BH21 5BN

Mrs A C Tory
☎ 01258 840216
Fax 01258 841278
BB From £25
Sleeps 6
☗ ☖ ⅄ ▲ ☂ ☼ ♞
♦♦♦♦

Working family farm of approx 800 acres, mainly arable, but with horses, ponies, cattle, sheep and pigs, and situated in unspoilt countryside with only one other farmhouse in sight! Easy access to Bournemouth, Salisbury, Dorchester and the New Forest. Spacious en suite rooms, 3 double, 1 twin, all with colour TV, tea/coffee-making facilities. Excellent local pubs in the area. Open all year except Christmas.

7   **Henbury Farm,** Dorchester Road, Sturminster Marshall, Wimborne, Dorset BH21 3RN

Sue & Jonathan Tory
☎ 01258 857306
Fax 01258 857928
BB From £21–£25
Sleeps 6
☒(10) ▲ ☂
♦♦♦♦

300-year-old farmhouse facing large front lawn and pond, situated on 200-acre farm. Guests' lounge with colour TV. Near to New Forest and 15 minutes' drive from sandy beaches. Numerous local restaurants to meet your evening requirements. Many local attractions and country walks. Ideally situated for a great holiday. En suite facilities available. Open all year except Christmas.

8   **Higher Langdon,** Beaminster, Dorset DT8 3NN

Judy Thompson
☎ 01308 862537
Fax 01308 863532
BB From £20–£25
EM From £15
Sleeps 4
☒ ☂ ▲ ♞
♦♦♦

Tucked away in the green folds of West Dorset, at the end of long quiet lane is our stone built, unstuffy farmhouse with rambling character, big log-fired drawing room and loads of space. 9 miles to coast. Farmyard animals and tennis court make sure everyone can relax! En suite rooms. E-mail: a.j.thompson@farming.co.uk

9   **Huntsbridge Farm,** Batcombe Road, Leigh, Nr Sherborne, Dorset DT9 6JA

Mrs Su Read
☎/Fax 01935 872150
BB From £22
Sleeps 6
☒ ⅄ ⊞ ☂ ▲ ◉
♦♦♦♦♦ Silver Award

Family-run dairy farm situated in open countryside in the beautiful part of Dorset Thomas Hardy chose for his novel 'The Woodlanders'. Tastefully furnished bedrooms, 2 double (one with four-poster) and 1 twin, all en suite with tea/ coffee facilities, colour TV, radio/alarm and full CH. Weekly price from £20 per night. Farmhouse breakfast served in conservatory overlooking garden and fields. So why not come and relax 'far from the madding crowd'? Open Feb–mid Dec.

10   **Lower Fifehead Farm,** Fifehead St Quinton, Sturminster Newton, Dorset DT10 2AP

Mrs Jill Miller
☎/Fax 01258 817335
BB From £17.50–£25
Sleeps 4
☗ ☖ ▲ ⅄ ☂ ☼ ◉
♦♦♦

Come and stay with us on a working farm in our 17th century listed farmhouse mentioned in Nicolas Pense's and Jo Draper's Dorset books for its architectural interest. En suite or private bathroom, tea/coffee, guests' sitting room. Large peaceful garden, green fields, ideal for relaxing, walking or touring Dorset beauty spots. Riding easily arranged. Open all year.

11   **Magiston Farm,** Sydling St Nicholas, Dorchester, Dorset DT2 9NR

Mrs T Barraclough
☎ 01300 320295
BB From £18.50
EM From £9.50
Sleeps 6
☒(10) ☖ ▲ ☂
♦♦

Magiston is a 16th century farmhouse with inglenook fireplace and antique furniture. A river runs through the well-kept garden. The 400-acre working farm is in a peaceful valley in Thomas Hardy Country. Tea/coffee-making facilities. Evening meal on request. Open all year except Christmas. Associate.

Maiden Castle Farm, Dorchester, Dorset DT2 9PR

Hilary Hoskin
☎ 01305 262356
Fax 01305 251085
BB From £23–£26
Sleeps 6
🐕 🐈 🏠 ⊚
♦♦♦♦ Silver Award

Our large working farm, 1 mile from Dorchester and 7 miles from Weymouth in the heart of Hardy country, enjoys magnificent views of Maiden Castle and the surrounding countryside. En-suite bedrooms with CH, TV, tea-making facilities and a telephone for guests' use combine to offer comfort, peace and quiet – ideal for the perfect holiday. Babysitting by arrangement. Open all year.

New House Farm, Mangerton Lane, Bradpole, Bridport, Dorset DT6 3SF

Jane Greening
☎/Fax 01308 422884
BB From £20
EM From £10
Sleeps 6
🐕 🐈 🏠 ⊚
♦♦♦

Modern, comfortable farmhouse set in the rural Dorset hills. Near coast (2½ miles). A warm welcome to guests. Two family rooms, both en suite. Lots to do and see in this historically beautiful area. Course fishing lake. Evening meals available subject to prior reservation. Open all year except Christmas.

Priory Farm, East Holme, Wareham, Dorset BH20 6AG

Mrs Jenny Goldsack
☎/Fax 01929 553832
BB From £19–£25
EM From £14.95
Sleeps 6
🐕 🐈 🏠 ⊚
♦♦♦♦

A 16th century thatched family farmhouse in a quiet backwater of the Isle of Purbeck. It is here that our cows graze the water meadows of the Frome Valley and where we aim to provide you with a warm, friendly, relaxed atmosphere after your days out exploring coast and countryside. Open all year except Christmas and New Year. E-mail: goldpriory@aol.com

Rudge Farm, Chilcombe, Bridport, Dorset DT6 4NF

Sue Diment
☎ 01308 482630
Fax 01308 482635
BB From £24–£26
Sleeps 8
🐕 🏠 ⊚
♦♦♦♦ Silver Award

Peacefully situated in the beautiful Bride Valley, just over 2 miles from the sea. After a day spent exploring the lovely West Dorset countryside, relax in our comfortably furnished farmhouse or the adjacent converted barn. Then try one of the many good local pubs and restaurants. All rooms are en suite with TV and tea tray and have far reaching views. Open all year except Christmas. E-mail: sue@rudge-farm.co.uk

Watermeadow House, Bridge Farm, Hooke, Beaminster, Dorset DT8 3PD

Mrs Pauline Wallbridge
☎/Fax 01308 862619
BB From £20–£25
Sleeps 6
🐕 🏠 ⊚
♦♦♦♦

Watermeadow House stands amidst beautiful countryside on the edge of the small village of Hooke. All bedrooms enjoy splendid rural views and overlook the river Hooke which meanders close by the garden where guests are welcome to sit. One double room with private bathroom, one family with en suite shower room. Breakfast is served in the sunlounge which attracts the morning sun. Perfect for those seeking peace and quiet in a friendly atmosphere. Open Mar–Nov.

Yalbury Park, Frome Whitfield Farm, Dorchester, Dorset DT2 7SE

Tom and Ann Bamlet
☎ 01305 250336
Fax 01305 260070
BB From £22–£25
Sleeps 6
🐕 🏠 ⊚
♦♦♦♦

Stone farmhouse with large garden in parkland to River Frome. Warm and welcoming for all country lovers. All rooms en-suite have TV, tea/coffee-making facilities, fridge, hairdrier. 1 double with french windows to garden, 2 family rooms. Traditional farmhouse breakfasts. Ideal for walking, beaches, fishing, riding and all country pursuits. Open all year.

18 Yew House Farm, Husseys, New Street, Marnhull, Sturminster Newton, Dorset DT10 1PD

Gil Espley
☎ 01258 820412
Fax 01258 821044
[BB] From £22.50–£25
Sleeps 6
☺ ⚲ 🍴 ⚓ ⊕
♦♦♦♦ Silver Award

Spacious family house of character in quiet location with superb views over open countryside. No longer a working farm, we welcome guests to enjoy our hospitality. Excellent area for walking, coarse fishing and sightseeing. Two double rooms, 1 twin, all en suite with tea/coffee-making facilities and colour TV. Open all year.

Self-Catering

19 Buddens Farm, Twyford, Shaftesbury, Dorset SP7 0JE

Sarah Gulliford
☎/Fax 01747 811433
[SC] From £120–£600
Sleeps 2/6 + cot
⛲ ⚲ 🍴 🏇 ⚓ 🎿 ⚓ ⊕
⚹⚹⚹⚹ Commended

HARRASSED? Have a real farm holiday, guests welcome to help feed pigs, sheep, chickens and goats and watch cows being milked. Pony rides over farm. Set in rolling hills and patchwork fields. Relax in superb farmhouse and cottage accommodation. Comfortably furnished, woodburners, dishwasher, colour TV, laundry room, outdoor swimming pool. Fully equipped for babies and children. Open all year. See colour ad on page 44.

20 Daisy Down, Puncknowle Manor Farm, Puncknowle, Dorchester, Dorset DT2 9BJ

Susan Ikin
☎ 01308 897692
Fax 01308 898022
[SC] From £250–£600
Sleeps 6
⛲ 🍴 ⚓ ⚓ 🏇
⚹⚹⚹⚹ Highly
Commended

Pretty farm cottage in Bride Valley, 5 minutes' drive from spectacular coastline and beach. Recently refurbished and equipped to a very high standard. Three bedrooms, downstairs cloakroom with shower, upstairs bathroom. Sitting room with open fireplace and dinning area. TV video, CH. Price is fully inclusive. Open all year.

21 Glebe Cottage, c/o Glebe House, Moreton, Dorchester, Dorset DT2 8RQ

Carol Gibbens
☎ 01929 462468
[SC] From £140–£280
Sleeps 4
⛲
⚹⚹ Approved

Glebe Cottage is set in an old rectory garden in the peaceful farming village of Moreton, famous for its church windows engraved by Laurence Whistler and burial place of Lawrence of Arabia. It is a wildlife haven. The cottage is detached, is on one floor with 2 double bedrooms, kitchen, living room, bathroom, night storage heating and has its own garden. Open all year.

22 Gorwell Farm, Abbotsbury, Weymouth, Dorset DT3 4JX

Mrs Mary Pengelly
☎ 01305 871401
Fax 01305 871441
[SC] From £160–£600
Sleeps 1–8 + cot
⛲ 🐄 ⚲ ⊞ 🎿 🏇 🍴 ⚓ ⊕
⚹⚹⚹⚹ Commended

Relax, unwind and enjoy peaceful and natural surroundings at Gorwell Farm. A family farm in its own scenic valley with lambs in the spring and calves in the summer. Comfortable, well equipped, warm accommo-dation with log fires. 2 miles from Abbotsbury and the Chesil Beach. Explore the coastal path crossing our farm or enjoy watersports, fishing, birdwatching and riding locally. Wildlife in abundance. Winter short breaks. Open all year. E-mail: gorwell.farm@wdi.co.uk

---

Graston Farm Cottage, Graston Farm, Burton Bradstock, Bridport, Dorset DT6 4NG

Mrs Sylvia Bailey
☎ 01308 897603
Fax 01308 897016
🆂 From £160–£480
Sleeps 7–9
🐕 🛇 ☕ 🎄 ⚓ 🌀
ℯℯ ℯ Commended

This spacious detached cottage is situated on a dairy farm in the beautiful Bride Valley one mile from Burton Bradstock and the sea. Three bedrooms (1 double, 1 double and single, 1 twin), two bathrooms, sitting room with woodburning stove, large well equipped kitchen/dining room and a further room with bed-settee. Open all year.

Halls Farm Cottage, Church Lane, Osmington, Nr Weymouth, Dorset DT3 6EW

Karen-Lee Knott
☎ 01305 837068
🆂 From £190–£360
Sleeps 6
🐕 🐎 🔪 ⚓ 🎄
Applied

Set in a secluded rural location enjoying stunning views of the White Horse valley, this traditional 200-acre farm offers an extremely comfortable, well-equipped three bedroomed cottage. Recently converted from 19th century farm buildings, the cottage retains a wealth of character and overlooks a gravelled stable courtyard. Good pubs within walking distance and brilliant access to footpaths, bridleways and the coast. Open all year.

Hartgrove Farm Cottages, Hartgrove, Shaftesbury, Dorset SP7 0JY

Mrs Susan Smart
☎ 01747 811830
Fax 01747 811066
🆂 From £180–£530
Sleeps 2/5 + cot
♿🐕🐎🔪🎄⚓☕🌀🐎🌀
ℯℯℯℯ Up to Highly
Commended

Come and meet Daisy and Tempo, our two friendly goats, and Whisper the pony. Watch the cows being milked. Feed a lamb or collect eggs. All in glorious country with breathtaking views. Four award-winning cottages and farmhouse flat. Log fires and beams. Tennis court, games barn. Free local swimming. Lovely village pubs. Brochure. Open all year. See colour ad on page 45.
E-mail: smart@hartgrove.demon.co.uk

Lower Fifehead Farm, Fifehead St Quinton, Sturminster Newton, Dorset DT10 2AP

Mrs Jill Miller
☎/Fax 01258 817335
🆂 From £100–£300
Sleeps 2/5
🐕 🐎 ⚓ 🌾 ☕ 🎄 🌀
ℯℯℯℯ Commended

Come and join us on our 400-acre dairy farm in beautiful, peaceful North Dorset staying in the cottage (sleeps 4/5) or flat (2/3). Situated in the heart of Hardy's Blackmore Vale within easy reach of many beauty spots. Large garden, friendly atmosphere.

Luccombe Farm, Milton Abbas, Blandford, Dorset DT11 0BE

Murray & Amanda Kayll
☎ 01258 880558
Fax 01258 881384
🆂 From £160–£650
Sleeps 2–7
🚶🐕🐎🛇♿⚓🌾☕🎄🌀
ℯℯℯ – ℯℯℯℯ Up to
Highly Commended

Our traditional barn conversions lie in a secluded hidden valley, deep in rolling downland. Beauty, peace and history surround you. Comfortable, well equipped and sleeping 2–7, they stand around a pond in landscaped grounds. Riding, fishing, sailing, clay shooting, good walking, cycling, etc. on farm or locally. Telephone, games room, tennis court and laundry room all available. Open all year.

Old Dairy Cottage, c/o Clyffe Farm, Tincleton, Dorchester, Dorset DT2 8QR (26)

Rosemary Coleman
☎ 01305 848252
Fax 01305 848702
🆂 From £195–£475
Sleeps 2/6 + cot
🐕 ☕ ⚓ 🎄 🌀
ℯℯℯ ℯ Commended

Attractive, comfortably furnished character cottage, cosy with beams, inglenook, garden and CH. Interesting working dairy farm – magnificent wildlife on our ponds and rivers. Fishing, birdwatching, walking, cycling, golf, riding and swimming locally. All year round interest, beautiful spring flowers. Historical houses and gardens and heritage coastline within easy reach. Good value winter breaks. Open all year.

16 **Orchard End,** Hooke, Beaminster, Dorset DT8 3PD

Mrs Pauline Wallbridge
☎/Fax 01308 862619
[SC] From £200–£400
Sleeps 6
ॐ ★ ← ▲ ※
♪♫♪♫ *Approved*

Stone-built bungalow on edge of small village of Hooke. Peaceful situation on our dairy farm, large garden, driveway and garage. Three comfortable bedrooms, 2 double, 1 twin. Large sitting room with dining area, well equipped kitchen. Lovely walking area. Price includes bedlinen, towels, electricity, VAT. Open all year.

27 **Park Farm,** Milton Abbas, Blandford Forum, Dorset DT11 0AX

Mrs A Burch
☎ 01258 880828
Fax 01258 881788
[SC] From £150–£600
Sleeps 5–10 + cot
ॐ ★ ⅍ ⅄ ⏆ ☀ ※ ▲ ⅍ ◉
♪♫♪ – ♪♫♪♫ *Up to*
Highly Commended

Two thatched cottages in Grade II listed Dorset barn. Very interesting and sympathetic conversions. Stunning views over the farm to Poole harbour and Purbecks. Peaceful and tranquil, ideal to unwind. Bring your old clothes and even your horse and explore the heart of Dorset. Superb woodland walks and rides in conservation area. Coastal path and beaches 30 minutes' drive. Open all year. E-mail: burch@miltonpark.freeserve.co.uk

15 **Rudge Farm Cottages,** Chilcombe, Bridport, Dorset DT6 4NF

Sue Diment
☎ 01308 482630
Fax 01308 482635
[SC] From £200–£545
Sleep 2–6
⅍ ॐ ☀ ※ ▲ ◉
♪♫♪♫
Highly Commended

Rudge is a peacefully situated livestock farm in the beautiful Bride Valley, just over 2 miles from the sea. The old farm buildings have been converted into superbly comfortable cottages, around a flower-decked cobbled yard, enjoying open views towards our lake and the countryside beyond. Ideal for a family holiday or relaxing short break. Open all year. E-mail: sue@rudge-farm.co.uk

28 **Top Stall,** Factory Farm, Fifehead Magdalen, Gillingham, Dorset SP8 5RS

Kathy Jeanes
☎/Fax 01258 820022
[SC] From £200–£400
Sleeps 5 + cot
⅍ ॐ ★ ⅄ ←
♪♫♪ *Highly Commended*

Tastefully converted cow stall adjoining listed farmhouse on a dairy farm, formerly a woollen mill. 'Top Stall' has a walled garden with barbecue. It is well equipped throughout. Babysitting can be arranged. Ideal for fishing and walking or just relaxing. Longleat, Stourhead, Bath or the coast all within 30 miles. Open all year.

29 **Westover Farm Cottages,** Wootton Fitzpaine, Bridport, Dorset DT6 6NE

Debby Snook
☎ 01297 560451
[SC] From £175–£495
Sleeps 6/7
ॐ ★ ▲ ⅍ ※ ◉
♪♫♪♫ *Commended*

Enjoy the rural tranquillity of Westover Dairy Farm. Two spacious, comfortable three-bedroomed cottages, well furnished and equipped and situated 1½ miles from the sea of Charmouth. With open fires, woodburning stoves, inglenooks and large secluded gardens, they make an ideal base for discovering delightful West Dorset and its world-famous coastline and countryside. Open all year. E-mail: wfcottages@aol.com

30 **White Cottage,** Tarrant Crawford Farm, Blandford, Dorset DT11 9HY

Mrs Jan Tory
☎ 01258 857417
Fax 01258 857218
[SC] From £250–£400
Sleeps 6
ॐ ⅄ ▲ ←
♪♫♪ *Commended*

Enjoy a welcome in a modernised, extremely comfortable cob cottage with enclosed garden. On 550-acre family-run dairy/arable farm. Three bedrooms, CTV, CH, 2 WCs, washing machine, microwave. Ideal for exploring coast, National Trust properties – beach 20 mins. Children welcome, no pets please. Open Mar–Oct.

South, East & West Devon

Dartmoor National Park, Devonshire Heartland,
South & East Devon Coasts

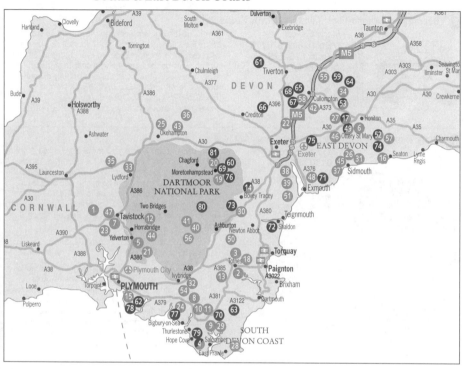

Key

- (1) Bed & Breakfast
- (1) Self-Catering
- (1) B&B and SC
- [1] Camping Barns
- (1) Camping & Caravanning

With its thatched cottages, lush meadows, steeply wooded valleys, rivers and streams, this is a special place. The 365 spectacular square miles of Dartmoor are wild, open and free. They stretch down to the sandy beaches and coves through the hamlets of the South coast. Ancient small country towns and villages are unspoilt and tempt you to stop and browse.

Taste delicious clotted cream teas, fresh fish from our local fishermen, ciders from traditional orchards or the huge selection of cheeses for which the county is famous. History comes alive in the cities; visit the treasures of the National Trust properties, castles and abbeys. Walk the coastal paths, catch a glimpse of the wildlife. There is something for everyone in this part of 'heaven in Devon'.

If you would like help in finding suitable farm accommodation, turn to the full listing of FHB Groups on pages 392 to 395 to find appropriate contact details for this area.

Bed and Breakfast
(and evening meal)

1 Beera Farm, Milton Abbot, Tavistock, Devon PL19 8PL

Hilary Tucker
☎/Fax 01822 870216
BB From £20–£25
EM From £9.50
Sleeps 6
⎵ ♞ ✂ ♨ ⊚
♦♦♦♦

Come and relax on our beef and sheep farm on the banks of the River Tamar. On arrival treat yourself to a cream tea and enjoy excellent home cooked evening meals. Sit in the garden, walk on the farm, visit National Trust properties or many other local attractions. Stay in tastefully decorated rooms, one with four-poster bed, all with tea/coffee-making facilities and TV. Open all year.
E-mail: robert.tucker@farming.co.uk

2 Berry Farm, Berry Pomeroy, Totnes, Devon TQ9 6LG

Mrs Geraldine Nicholls
☎ 01803 863231
BB From £16
EM From £10
Sleeps 6
⎵ ♞ ✂ ♨ ♠ ⊚
♦

A friendly welcome awaits you at our large mixed, traditional working farm situated 1½ miles from Totnes town. Pretty, spacious rooms, with tea/coffee facilities, washbasins – one family, one twin, also one double en suite. Bathroom, shower, separate toilet. Guests' lounge and dining room, colour TV. Enjoy delicious home cooking. Superb base for touring coast/moors. Parking. Open all year.

3 Buckyette Farm, Buckyette, Littlehempston, Totnes, Devon TQ9 6ND

Mrs EP Miller
☎/Fax 01803 762638
BB From £19–£25
Sleeps 16
⎵ ✂
♦♦♦

The farmhouse was built in the era of Victorian elegance with lovely views over the valley. Nearby are Totnes, Dartington cultural centre, steam railways, River Dart for fishing and several golf courses welcoming visitors, so don't forget your handicap card. Many other leisure activities. Beds have cotton sheets. Large garden, croquet lawn. Breakfast with locally produced bacon and sausages and homemade rolls. Open Mar–Nov.

4 Burton Farm, Galmpton, Kingsbridge, South Devon TQ7 3EY

Anne Rossiter
☎/Fax 01548 561210
BB From £24–£28
EM From £13
Sleeps 24
⎵ ⊞ ♠ ♨ ⊚
♦♦♦♦

Working dairy and sheep farm situated in the valley running towards Hope Cove. 3 miles from famous sailing haunt of Salcombe. Walking, beaches, sailing, windsurfing, bathing, diving, fishing. Guests welcome to enjoy the farm's activities when possible. Traditional farmhouse cooking, home produce (clotted cream, etc). 4 course dinner. Access to rooms at all times. En suite available and washbasins. Tea-making facilities, TV. Closed Christmas Day.

5 Callisham Farm, Meavy, Yelverton, Devon PL20 6PS

Esmé Wills
☎/Fax 01822 853901
BB From £18–£25
Sleeps 6
⎵ ✂ ♞ ♥ ♠ ♨ ⊚
♦♦♦

Traditional Dartmoor farmhouse nestling in the pretty Meavy valley. Perfect for walking and fishing – riding and golf nearby. A warm welcome, comfortable beds and huge breakfasts await you. ¼ mile from 12th century inn and picturesque village. Homely atmosphere with all comforts, log fires in winter. Full central heating. Open all year.

Catshayes Farm, Gittisham, Honiton, Devon EX14 0AE ⑥

Mrs Christine Broom
☎/Fax 01404 850302
🅱 From £16.50–£18.50
EM From £8.50
Sleeps 6
🐂 ♔ ✄ ⬛ ⊚
♦♦

Countryside lovers will enjoy the peace and tranquillity of our 15th century thatched Devon longhouse on our working dairy farm. Near charming thatched village, market town, woodland walks. Abundance of wildlife and panoramic views. Shooting and riding by arrangement. Log fires, oak beams, farmhouse cooking. Studio nearby offering creative and personal development workshops. Open all year.

Colcharton Farm, Gulworthy, Tavistock, Devon PL19 8HU ⑦

Mrs Lowenna Edwards
☎/Fax 01822 616435
🅱 From £19–£22
EM From £10
Sleeps 6
🐂 ♔ ✄ ♠ ⬛ ♎
♦♦♦♦

Enjoy every home comfort in tasteful surroundings – good food and hearty breakfasts a speciality. We are situated in quiet and peaceful surroundings, central for touring, with splendid Dartmoor views. Relax in a charming garden or beside a cosy log fire. Good eating houses and National Trust properties nearby. Only 2 miles from beautiful historic town of Tavistock. Open all year.

Combe Farm, Loddiswell, Kingsbridge, Devon TQ7 4DT ⑧

Nicola Herbert
☎/Fax 01548 550560
🅱 From £19.50–£24
EM From £15
Sleeps 6
🐂 ✄ ⬛
♦♦♦♦

Beautiful Grade II listed Georgian farmhouse, completely renovated in 1994, nestling in small valley down private drive. Twelve acres with sheep, poultry, cats and dogs. One double en suite, two twins with shared bathroom, all with CH and tea/coffee-making facilities. Sitting room with colour TV/video and woodburner. Outdoor swimming pool. Open all year except Christmas.

Coombe Farm, Kingsbridge, South Devon TQ7 4AB ⑨

Beni & Jonathan Robinson
☎/Fax 01548 852038
🅱 From £20–£22.50
Sleeps 6
🐂(12) ✄ ☛
♦♦♦

Come and enjoy the peace and beauty of Devon in our lovely 16th century farmhouse. Wonderful breakfast, large elegant rooms, all en suite with colour TV, hot drink facilities. Artists have use of an art studio, and fishermen the well known Coombe Water fishery. Open Mar–Nov.

Court Barton Farmhouse, Aveton Gifford, Kingsbridge, Devon TQ7 4LE ⑩

John & Jill Balkwill
☎ 01548 550312
Fax 01548 550128
🅱 From £20–£30
Sleeps 16
🐂 ⊞ ♣ ♠ ⊚
♦♦♦♦

Delightful 16th century listed manor farmhouse set in extensive gardens and situated on 40-acre farm. Seven bedrooms, mostly en suite, all with colour TV. Sunny breakfast room to enjoy delicious country farmhouse breakfasts and log fires in the comfortable lounge in colder weather. Close to moorland, beaches, ideal centre for walking, sailing, fishing, birdwatching. Open all year except Christmas. E-mail: jill@courtbarton.co.uk

Crannacombe Farm, Hazelwood, Loddiswell, Nr Kingsbridge, South Devon TQ7 4DX ⑪

Shirley & Stephen Bradley
☎ 01548 550256
🅱 From £20
Sleeps 4
🐂 ✄ ♠ ⬛
♦♦♦

In an Area of Outstanding Natural Beauty near Kingsbridge, a working farm also producing organic cider and apple juice. The Georgian farmhouse, is comfortable, informal, absolutely peaceful. Two double bedrooms with private bathrooms and TV. Lovely walks, stunning views and a clean river to paddle, play and picnic by. 15 minutes beach, 20 minutes Dartmouth and Salcombe.

---

12 Eggworthy Farm, Sampford Spiney, Yelverton, Devon PL20 6LJ

Linda Landick
☎ 01822 852142
BB From £18–£20
Sleeps 6
♿ ⊀ ⅍ ▦
♦♦♦

Away-from-it-all Dartmoor working farm with secluded gardens and beautiful moorland walks. Relax and enjoy our comfortable rooms with colour TV, tea/coffee-making facilities, H&C. One room en suite, one with private bathroom. Small room available with bunk beds for children. Full English breakfast. Pets welcome. We look forward to seeing you. Open all year except Christmas.

---

13 Foales Leigh, Harberton, Totnes, Devon TQ9 7SS

Carol Chudley
☎/Fax 01803 862365
BB From £20–£25
Sleeps 6
♿(5) ⅍ ⊼ ▦ ⊛
♦♦♦♦

A charming 16th century farmhouse in traditional courtyard setting. This family farm is situated in peaceful, unspoilt countryside within easy reach of beaches, moors and towns. Comfortable accommodation includes large oak-beamed lounge and 3 spacious bedrooms: 1 double, 1 family, 1 twin, all en suite with TV, CH and beverage trays. Delicious Aga-cooked breakfast. Closed Christmas & New Year.

---

14 Frost Farm, Hennock, Bovey Tracey, South Devon TQ13 9PP

Linda Harvey
☎/Fax 01626 833266
BB From £20–£22
EM From £10
Sleeps 6
♿ ⅍ ▦
♦♦♦

Working organic farm, cosy and comfortable with relaxing homely atmosphere. Spacious bedrooms (one ground floor) with colour TV, CH, tea/coffee-making facilities and comfy sofas. Excellent en suites. Breakfast is great too! Bovey Tracey 2 miles, on edge of Dartmoor with its craft, pottery, heritage and glass centres. Walks, pubs, shops galore. Brochure. Open Mar–Nov.

---

15 Gabber Farm, Down Thomas, Plymouth, Devon PL9 0AW

Margaret MacBean
☎/Fax 01752 862269
BB From £17–£19
EM From £10
Sleeps 12
♿ ⊀ ⊼ ▦ ⊛
♦♦♦

A warm welcome is assured on this working dairy farm in an area of outstanding natural beauty. Situated on the coast near Plymouth with lovely walks and within easy reach of the beaches. Good home cooking, hot drinks facilities in all rooms, double and family with en suite showers. Open all year. E-mail: margaret@lineone.net

---

16 Gatcombe Farm, Seaton, Devon EX12 3AA

Julie Reed
☎ 01297 21235
Fax 01297 23010
BB From £16.50–£20
Sleeps 6
⅍ ⊼ ▦ ⅌
♦♦♦

Only 5 minutes from the coast, Gatcombe is a family-run dairy farm in the beautiful Axe valley. Spacious farmhouse with double, twin and family rooms with washbasins. Guests' dining room and lounge with traditional beams, stonework and woodburner. Tea/coffee-making facilities, TV, video, large enclosed gardens. Hearty breakfasts, many local inns. Open Feb–Nov.

---

17 Godford Farm, Awliscombe, Honiton, Devon EX14 0PW

Sally Lawrence
☎/Fax 01404 42825
BB From £17–£21
Sleeps 6
♿ ▦ ⊼ ⊛
♦♦♦♦

We invite you to stay on this family-run dairy farm, set in a beautiful river valley. Listed farmhouse with large sitting and dining rooms. Colour TV. Central heating. Drinks facilities in bedrooms. Scrumptious Devonshire breakfasts, local meat, homemade preserves. Delightful area for walking and wildlife. Cot and highchair provided. Family and twin room, en suite/ private bathrooms. Child reductions. Brochure. Open Easter–Oct.

Great Court Farm, Weston Lane, Totnes, Devon TQ9 6LB   (18)

Janet Hooper
☎/Fax 01803 862326
BB From £16.50–£18.50
EM From £10
Sleeps 6
🐾 🍴 🐎 ®
♦♦♦♦

Relax and enjoy the warm hospitality and country cuisine in our Victorian farmhouse overlooking the historic town of Totnes and surrounding countryside. Dairy farm with lanes and fields running down to River Dart. Ideal for coast and Dartmoor. Spacious double/family rooms have tea/coffee facilities, washbasins, TV, CH. Twin room en suite, WC and basin. Guests' bathroom, shower. Lounge, garden. South Hams Accommodation Award winner 1998. Open all year.

Great Sloncombe Farm, Moretonhampstead, Newton Abbot, Devon TQ13 8QF   (19)

Mrs Trudie Merchant
☎/Fax 01647 440595
BB From £22–£23
EM From £12
Sleeps 6
🐾(8) 🐎 🍴 🐎 🐎 🐖 ®
♦♦♦♦ Silver Award

Share the magic of Dartmoor all year round whilst staying in our lovely 13th century farmhouse. A working dairy farm set amongst meadows and woodland, abundant in wild flowers and animals. A welcoming place to relax and explore Devon. Comfortable double and twin rooms all en suite with central heating, TV. Plenty of delicious home-cooked Devonshire food. Open all year.

Great Wooston Farm, Moretonhampstead, Newton Abbot, Devon TQ13 8QA   (20)

Mary Cuming
☎/Fax 01647 440367
BB From £20–£22
Sleeps 6
🐾(8) 🍴 🐖 🐖 ®
♦♦♦♦

Great Wooston, once owned by Lord Hambledon, is situated above the Teign Valley in the Dartmoor National Park, with views over open moorland. Plenty of walks, golf, fishing and riding nearby. The farmhouse is surrounded by a delightful ½-acre garden. 3 pleasant bedrooms, 2 en suite, 1 with 4-poster, 1 with private bathroom. Excellent breakfasts. Guests' lounge to relax in after a day exploring the Devon countryside. Open all year.

Greenwell Farm, Nr Meavy, Yelverton, Plymouth, Devon PL20 6PY   (21)

Bridget Cole
☎/Fax 01822 853563
BB From £22–£25
EM From £14.50
Sleeps 6
🐎 🐖 ®
♦♦♦♦

Fresh country air, breathtaking views and scrumptious farmhouse cuisine. This busy farming family welcomes you to share the countryside and wildlife. Greenwell nestles on the slopes of Dartmoor and is ideal for walking. Touring Devon and Cornwall is easy with many gardens and National Trust properties locally or you may just prefer to relax and enjoy the peace and tranquillity. Licensed, brochure available. Open all year (closed Christmas). E-mail: greenwellfarm@btconnect.com

Hayne House, Silverton, Exeter, Devon EX5 4HE   (22)

Mrs L Kelly
☎/Fax 01392 860725
BB From £16–£20
Sleeps 6
🐾 🍴 🐖 ®
♦♦♦

Explore Devon from our spacious and elegant Georgian farmhouse in delightful rural location. Centrally situated for touring coast, moors and NT properties. Killerton House is close by. 1 family, 1 twin room, both with private bath, 1 single with H&C, all with tea/coffee. Separate drawing room with colour TV and dining room. Tea and homemade cake on arrival. Nearby Inns for good food. Open Apr–Oct.

Hele Farm, Gulworthy, Tavistock, Devon PL19 8PA   (23)

Mrs Rosemary Steer
☎ 01822 833084
BB From £18–£20
Sleeps 5
🐾 🐎 🍴 🐖
♦♦♦

A welcoming tea awaits you at the architecturally listed farmhouse (1780) on our working dairy farm which is farmed organically. Two fully en suite bedrooms with CH and tea/coffee. Central location for Dartmoor, both coasts and National Trust properties. Abundant good pubs and restaurants nearby. Dogs accepted. Open Apr–Oct.

24 Helliers Farm, Ashford, Aveton Gifford, Kingsbridge, Devon TQ7 4ND

Christine Lancaster
☎/Fax 01548 550689
BB From £20–£25
Sleeps 9
🐴 ⚡ 🐕 📱
♦♦♦♦

Small working sheep farm on a hillside set in the heart of Devon's unspoilt countryside. An ideal spot for touring the coast, Dartmoor, Plymouth, NT houses and walks. Family room with own private bathroom, double and twin both en suite and a single room, all tastefully appointed with washbasins and tea/coffee facilities. Comfortable lounge with TV. Dining room where excellent breakfasts, using local produce, are served.

25 Higher Cadham Farm, Jacobstowe, Okehampton, Devon EX20 3RB

John & Jenny King
☎ 01837 851647
Fax 01837 851410
BB From £18.50–£25
EM From £10
Sleeps 17
🐴 🐓 ♿ 📱 🎯 ◎
♦♦♦♦

Superb farmhouse accommodation, tasty home cooking, and breathtaking Devon scenery, that's the appetising recipe on offer at Higher Cadham in the heart of Tarka Country. Facilities for the less agile, en suite, flexible meal times, riverside walks and lots more! Ring for a brochure and details of our special offers. Open all year except Christmas and New Year.

26 Higher Coombe Farm, Tipton St John, Sidmouth, Devon EX10 0AX

Kerstin Farmer
☎/Fax 01404 813385
BB From £18–£22
Sleeps 10
🐴 🐓 📱 ◎
♦♦♦

Find a warm, friendly welcome and comfortable, fully equipped rooms in our Victorian farmhouse, family owned since 1913. We offer total relaxation and a superb breakfast. After exploring East Devon's towns and villages, rolling countryside and beaches, take tea on the patio overlooking mature garden. Ideal for families. Easily reached, 4 miles inland from Sidmouth. Open Mar–Dec.

27 Higher Curscombe Farm, Feniton, Honiton, Devon EX14 0EU

Mrs Marguerite Coker
☎ 01404 850265
BB From £18–£20
Em From £10
Sleeps 6
🐴 🐓 📱 🎯
♦♦

A warm welcome awaits you at this family-run dairy farm set in picturesque countryside. Homely, comfortable accommodation. Guests' lounge with inglenook, colour TV, video and board games. Separate dining room where traditional farmhouse food is served. Bedrooms have tea/coffee-making facilities and convector heating. Open Apr–Oct.

28 Higher Kellaton Farm, Kellaton, Kingsbridge, Devon TQ7 2ES

Mrs Angela Foale
☎/Fax 01548 511514
BB From £17.50–£20
EM From £9
Sleeps 6
🐴 🐓 ⚡ 📱 🎯
♦♦♦

Our traditional, family-worked farm welcomes you to an area of peaceful and natural unspoilt beauty. Friendly farm animals. Children welcome. Nearby safe, sandy beaches, coastal walks and family attractions. Georgian farmhouse with attractive gardens. Comfortable, well furnished, spacious rooms. Guests' own lounge. Delicious Aga cooking, flexible meal times. Tea/coffee-making facilities. Open Easter–Oct.

29 Higher Stancombe Farm, Sherford, Kingsbridge, Devon TQ7 2BG

Jenny Tucker
☎/Fax 01548 531013
BB From £19–£25
EM From £10
Sleeps 6
🐴 🐓 ⚡ 🚶 📱 🎯 🎯 🎯
♦♦♦♦

Find a warm welcome, space, peace and quiet with unsurpassed rural views to the coast. Situated in the heart of the South Hams, close to the historic towns of Totnes and Dartmouth and the Slapton nature reserve. Working family farm with lovely walks and riding. Stabling available. Rooms are en suite or have private bathroom, all with colour TV and beverage tray. Open all year except Christmas. E-mail: jentuc@globalnet.co.uk

---

Higher Venton Farm, Widecombe-in-the-Moor, Newton Abbot, South Devon TQ13 7TF   **30**

Helen Hicks
☎ **01364 621235**
Fax **01364 621382**
BB From **£20–£23**
EM From **£10**
Sleeps **6**
☺(5) ᛏ ♨
◆ ◆

A friendly welcome awaits you at Higher Venton Farm, a 16th century thatched farmhouse and working farm. Peaceful and relaxing, ideal for touring Dartmoor. Riding stables nearby. Coast 16 miles, ½ mile from Widecombe village. Good local eating places recommended. 2 double en suite with colour TV and 1 twin with washbasin. CH, tea/ coffee-making facilities, lounge with colour TV. Open all year except Christmas.

Higher Weston Farm, Weston, Nr Sidmouth, Devon EX10 0PH   **31**

Sandy MacFadyen
☎ **01395 513741**
BB From **£19–£23**
Sleeps **6**
☺ ᛏ ♞ ♨ ✂ ◉
◆ ◆ ◆ ◆

Enjoy a relaxed, comfortable holiday in superb Heritage coast location, 3 miles from Sidmouth. Fully equipped en suite rooms, comfortable lounge. Breakfast menu includes vegetarian. Lovely garden, croquet, badminton, stabling available. Conservation award winning, working farm. Fields extend to coastal footpath, superb views of Lyme Bay, and to unspoilt Combe and beach. Closed Jan.

Hillhead Farm, Ugborough, Ivybridge, Devon PL21 0HQ   **32**

Mrs J Johns
☎ **01752 892674**
Fax **01752 690111**
BB From **£18–£22**
EM From **£12.50**
Sleeps **6**
☺ ᛏ ⅄ ⚔ ♨ ✂ ↩ ◉
◆ ◆ ◆ ◆

Views over rolling South Devon countryside make this friendly farmhouse an ideal place to stay. Breakfast in our sunny conservatory and enjoy candlelit dinners in the comfortably elegant dining room. Feast on home-reared meat from the farm and vegetables from our organic garden. Pretty bedrooms with generous bathrooms (bath and shower) two en suites, one with private bathroom. Closed Christmas.

The Knole Farm, Bridestowe, Okehampton, Devon EX20 4HA   **33**

Mrs Mavis Bickle
☎/Fax **01837 861241**
BB From **£20–£22**
EM From **£10**
Sleeps **8**
☺ ᛏ ♨
◆ ◆ ◆ ◆ Silver Award

Family working farm in area of outstanding beauty overlooking Dartmoor. Farmhouse with spacious rooms, large garden, sunlounge. Enjoy good home cooking. Ideally based to visit numerous places of interest with birdwatching, horseriding, fishing and walking for the energetic. En suite rooms available. Breakfast to your choice, four-course evening meal optional.

Lane End Farm, Broadhembury, Honiton, Devon EX14 0LU   **34**

Mrs Molly Bennett
☎/Fax **01404 841563**
BB From **£16–£20**
EM From **£8.50**
Sleeps **6**
☺ ᛏ ♨ ♨ ◉
◆ ◆ ◆

At Lane End Farm you will enjoy delicious home cooking in glorious surroundings. Panoramic views of the Blackdown Hills, an Area of Outstanding Natural Beauty. With cattle and sheep grazing, floral gardens all within walking distance of the unspoilt thatched village of Broadhembury. Tea/ coffee facilities in bedrooms (2 en suite). CH, colour TV. Colour brochure. Children reduced rates. Evening meals optional. Open all year.

Little Bidlake Farm, Bridestowe, Okehampton, Devon EX20 4NS   **35**

Jo Down
☎/Fax **01837 861233**
BB From **£17–£18**
EM From **£9**
Sleeps **6**
☺ ᛏ ♞ ↩ ♨ ♨
◆ ◆ ◆

We are a working dairy/beef farm which is family run. Come and unwind in a relaxed atmosphere and enjoy traditional farmhouse fare. Walking, riding, golf and fishing can easily be arranged and Dartmoor is on our doorstep. Kennels and stabling available, as are packed lunches. Phone/fax for details. Open Mar–Nov.
E-mail: bidlakefm@aol.com

---

36   **Lower Nichols Nymet Farm,** North Tawton, Devon EX20 2BW

Mrs Jane Pyle
☎/Fax 01363 82510
⌷ᴮᴮ From £20–£22.50
EM From £10
Sleeps 6
⛺ ⅍ 🅰 ☜ 🐾 ◎
♦♦♦♦ Silver Award

We offer a haven of comfort and rest on a modern working dairy farm and provide the perfect base for exploring the beauties of the West Country. Residents' lounge, colour TV. All rooms en suite, plus tea/coffee-making facilities. An ideal holiday centre – beaches, golf, good walks, riding, fishing, fine houses and gardens nearby to visit. Open Easter–Oct (incl).

---

37   **Lower Pinn Farm,** Peak Hill, Sidmouth, Devon EX10 0NN

Elizabeth Tancock
☎/Fax 01395 513733
⌷ᴮᴮ From £19–£22
Sleeps 6
⛺ 🐓 🛁 🐾 ◎
♦♦♦♦

A friendly welcome and comfortable, spacious rooms await you at Lower Pinn. 2 miles west of the coastal resort of Sidmouth. Many coastal and country walks. Bedrooms are en suite, fully centrally heated and have colour TV, hot drink making facilities. Own keys for access at all times. Guests' lounge, dining room with separate tables. Good hearty breakfasts. Ample parking. Several local pubs and restaurants. Open most of the year.

---

38   **Lower Thornton Farm,** Kenn, Exeter, Devon EX6 7XH

Mrs Alison Clack
☎/Fax 01392 833434
Mobile 07970 972012
⌷ᴮᴮ From £18
Sleeps 6
⛺ ⅍ 🛁
♦♦♦♦

Come and relax at our secluded family farm with panoramic views. Just 2 miles from A38. Ideal base to visit Exeter, Torquay, Dartmoor, coast and racecourse. Our ground floor bedrooms are spacious and comfortable. One room en suite opening onto patio and garden, other has private bathroom. Both with tea/coffee facilities. Guests' lounge, colour TV, CH throughout. Child reductions. Open all year.

---

39   **Mill Farm,** Kenton, Exeter, Devon EX6 8JR

Delia Lambert
☎ 01392 832471
⌷ᴮᴮ From £19
Sleeps 10
⛺ 🛁
♦♦♦♦

Mill Farm – a charming farmhouse. All five delightful, sunny en suite bedrooms have colour TV. Lovely rural setting. Ideal base to explore Devon. Good parking. Very easy to find. Don't miss out. Send for a brochure now!

---

40   **Mill Leat Farm,** Holne, Ashburton, Newton Abbot, Devon TQ13 7RZ

Dawn Cleave
☎/Fax 01364 631283
⌷ᴮᴮ From £17–£20
EM From £10
Sleeps 6
⛺ 🐓 🐾 🛁 ◎
♦♦♦

200-acre hill farm situated on the edge of Dartmoor, an ideal place for touring Devon's beautiful countryside, moorland or beaches. Comfortable accommodation in 18th century farmhouse with large spacious bedrooms, en suite available, with tea/coffee facilities. Very peaceful surroundings, just right for relaxing. Closed Christmas.

---

41   **New Cott Farm,** Poundsgate, nr Ashburton, Newton Abbot, Devon TQ13 7PD

Margaret Phipps
☎/Fax 01364 631421
⌷ᴮᴮ From £20–£21
EM From £11.50
Sleeps 8
🧍 ⛺(5) ⅍ 🛁 ◎
♦♦♦♦

A friendly welcome, beautiful views, pleasing accommodation at New Cott, a working farm in the Dartmoor National Park. Relax in our conservatory after enjoying the freedom and tranquillity of open moorland, the Dart Valley or one of the many attractions in Devon. Lots of lovely homemade food. Tea/coffee/chocolate in your en suite bedroom. Weekly reductions. Ideal for less able guests. OS: SY 703727. Closed Christmas Day.

Newcourt Barton, Langford, Cullompton, Devon EX15 1SE ㊷

Mrs Helen Hitt
☎/Fax 01884 277326
🆎 From £16–£20
Sleeps 6
🐕 🛏 🛋 🚗 🍴 ☕
♦♦♦

A friendly welcome awaits you at Newcourt Barton. Quietly situated just 3 miles from M5/J28, an ideal base for touring Devon's coast and countryside with many attractions nearby. Enjoy our large garden with grass tennis court or coarse fishing on farm. One twin/double en suite, one family room with private bathroom. Tea/coffee facilities, cot, highchair. Guests' own TV lounge, dining room. Child reductions. Local inn and restaurants for evening meal. Closed Christmas.

Oaklands Farm, North Tawton, Okehampton, Devon EX20 2BQ ㊸

Winifred Headon
☎ 01837 82340
🆎 From £18–£19
Sleeps 5
🐕 🐎 🛋
♦♦♦

A warm welcome awaits you at Oaklands, a 130-acre farm in the centre of Devon. Easy to find on a level drive from a good road. Traditional farmhouse cooking with ample of everything. Heating, TV and electric blankets in bedrooms. Lounge with colour TV. Pleasant gardens. Open Mar–Nov.

Peek Hill Farm, Dousland, Yelverton, Devon PL20 6PD ㊹

Justine Colton
☎/Fax 01822 854808
🆎 From £17–£20
EM From £10
Sleeps 6
🐕 🛏 ✄ 🛋 ⊚
♦♦♦

Sizzling sausages, new laid eggs. Comfy beds to rest your legs. Dartmoor to Bodmin quite a view, TV, kettle too. Take a hike, hire a bike, the choice is yours to view the moors. Yummy cream teas – have one on us! Need a picnic, it's no fuss. Pack a bag, come away, promise of a pleasant stay. Open all year except Christmas.
E-mail: peekhillfarm@farming.com

Pinn Barton Farm, Pinn Lane, Peak Hill, Sidmouth, Devon EX10 0NN ㊺

Betty Sage
☎/Fax 01395 514004
🆎 From £20–£22
Sleeps 6
🐕(3) 🛏 🛋 ⊚
♦♦♦♦

Enjoy a warm welcome on our 330-acre farm by the coast, 2 miles from Sidmouth seafront. Lovely walks in Area of Outstanding Natural Beauty. Comfortable bedrooms (all en suite) with CH, colour TV, hot drink facilities, electric blankets, access at all times. TV lounge and dining room with separate tables. Substantial breakfast, bedtime drinks. Many restaurants, inns and places to visit nearby. Open most of the year. See colour ad on page 45.

Pitt Farm, Fairmile, Ottery St Mary, Devon EX11 1NL ㊻

Susan Hansford
☎/Fax 01404 812439
🆎 From £18–£20
Sleeps 14
🐕 🔳 🛋 ⊚
♦♦♦♦

A warm family atmosphere awaits you at this 16th century thatched farmhouse which nestles in the picturesque Otter Valley ½ mile from A30 on B3176. Within easy reach of all East Devon resorts and pleasure facilities. A working cattle/arable farm surrounded by lovely countryside and rural walks. Family, double and twin rooms. Lounge with colour TV. Fire certificate. Open Mar–Nov.

Rubbytown Farm, Gulworthy, Tavistock, Devon PL19 8PA ㊼

Mary Steer
☎/Fax 01822 832493
🆎 From £20–£25
EM From £12
Sleeps 6
🐕(12) ✄ 🌿 🛋
♦♦♦♦

Stay in our lovely old farmhouse and sleep in four-poster beds. Enjoy woodland walks. There is abundant wildlife, you may see deer if you are lucky and at dusk the foxes and badgers at play. Help with feeding the calves. Good farmhouse cooking with evening meals served by candlelight. St Mellion Golf and Country Club nearby. 2 double, 4 posters, en suite, 1 twin with private bathroom. Evening meal served by candlelight by prior arrangement. Closed Christmas.

48 **Rydon Farm,** Woodbury, Exeter, Devon EX5 1LB

Sally Glanvill
☎/Fax 01395 232341
BB From £23–£27
Sleeps 6
☒ ♙ ▦
◆◆◆◆

Come and enjoy the peaceful tranquillity of our 16th century Devon longhouse on a working dairy farm. Exposed beams and inglenook fireplace. Bedrooms with tea/coffee facilities, hairdryers, full CH, private or en suite bathrooms. Romantic four-poster. Full English breakfast with free range eggs. Several local pubs and restaurants. AA QQQQ Selected. Open all year.

49 **Skinners Ash Farm,** Fenny Bridges, Honiton, Devon EX14 0BH

Mrs Jill Godfrey
☎/Fax 01404 850231
BB From £18–£20
EM From £10
Sleeps 6
☒ ♙ ⚘ ▦ ◉
◆◆◆

Have fun on our family-run rare breeds farm situated in the Otter Valley. Relax in our 16th century farmhouse. Guests' lounge with TV and video. The comfortable bedrooms have TV and tea tray. Access at all times. Cot and highchair available. Scrumptious breakfast and meals. Enjoy pony rides, collect your own eggs. Near local beaches and tourist attractions. Colour brochure. Open all year.

50 **Sladesdown Farm,** Landscove, Ashburton, Devon TQ13 7ND

Mr & Mrs J Haddy
☎ 01364 653973
BB From £19.50–£22.50
Sleeps 6
☒ ⚘ ▦ ⚘
◆◆◆◆

A warm welcome awaits you at Sladesdown Farm, set in the heart of the country with peaceful, scenic walks. Close to the moors and coast yet only two miles off the A38. Two spacious attractive bedrooms, en suite with sitting area, TV and hot drinks facilities. Open Mar–Nov.

51 **Smallacombe Farm,** Aller Valley, Dawlish, Devon EX7 0PS

Mrs Alison Thomson
☎ 01626 862536
BB From £16.50–£18
EM From £10
Sleeps 6
☒ ♙ ⚘ ▦
◆◆◆

Off the beaten track, yet only two miles from Dawlish and the beach. Enjoy the best of both worlds, 'country and coast'. Children play freely with no fear of busy roads. Meet our 3 friendly dogs. Relax in the peaceful surroundings and homely atmosphere. 2 double rooms, 1 twin room, family unit available, en suite. Fridges in bedrooms. Reductions for children, weekly discounts. Ring or write for brochure. Open all year.

52 **Smallicombe Farm,** Northleigh, Colyton, Devon EX24 6BU

Maggie Todd
☎ 01404 831310
Fax 01404 831431
BB From £18.50–£22.50
EM From £9.50
Sleeps 6
♙ ☒ ⚘ ▦ ⚘ ⚘ ◉
◆◆◆◆

Taste real pork, bacon and sausages from our prize-winning rare breed pigs in idyllic setting little changed over the centuries. Meet traditional farm animals and watch the surrounding wildlife. Explore coast and country in this unspoilt corner of Devon. Featured in *Guide to Good Food in the West Country*. Family or ground floor twin/double room, all en suite. Laundry, games room with Devon skittles, snooker and table tennis. Open all year.
E-mail: maggie_todd@yahoo.com

53 **Stafford Barton,** Broadhembury, Honiton, Devon EX14 0LU

Anne Barons
☎/Fax 01404 841403
BB From £20–£25
EM From £10
Sleeps 6
☒ ♙ ⚘ ▦ ◉
◆◆◆◆◆
Gold Award

Come and share our lovely home for a holiday treat. We are situated beneath the Blackdown Hills, ¼ mile from picturesque thatched village. Glorious walks through woodland and country lanes. Roam our farm and meet cows, pigs, ducks and hens. Double and twin rooms, all en suite with colour TV, etc. Large lounge/dining room overlooking beautiful garden. Delicious home cooking using own produce. Table licence. Weekly terms. Brochure. Open all year. E-mail: anne@devonfarms.co.uk

Venn Farm, Ugborough, Ivybridge, Devon PL21 0PE

Pat Stephens
☎/Fax 01364 73240
BB From £21–£24
EM £11
Sleeps 11
🐴(8) 🐕 🏠 ✦
♦♦♦

We are well placed to offer you a peaceful and relaxing holiday 'off the beaten track'. Secluded gardens, streams, Gypsy caravan, an abundance of fresh local produce. Our guests become friends and keep returning. Carve your own roasts, still popular after 20 years. Also two bedroomed ground floor garden cottage for B&B guests. Open Feb–Nov.

Weir Mill Farm, Jaycroft, Willand, Cullompton, Devon EX15 2RE

Rita Parish
☎ 01884 820803
Fax 01884 820973
BB From £19–£21
EM From £11
Sleeps 6
🐴 🏠 ⊚
♦♦♦♦ Silver Award

Luxurious rooms, beautiful views and peaceful surroundings make Weir Mill, in the beautiful Culm Valley, something very special. Only 3 miles from M5 J27, giving easy access to coasts, moors and NT properties. There is one double en suite, one family en suite and one double room with private bathroom. All have CH, TV and tea/coffee-making facilities. Large garden, ample parking. Open all year.

Wellpritton Farm, Holne, Ashburton, Newton Abbot, South Devon TQ13 7RX

Sue Gifford
☎ 01364 631273
BB From £19
EM From £9
Sleeps 11
🐴 🐕 🏠 ⊚
♦♦♦

Delightful character farmhouse set in Dartmoor National Park with beautiful views. Exposed beams, woodburner, scrumptious farmhouse cuisine. An ideal base, 3 miles from A38, within easy reach of all main attractions and NT properties. Perfect for staying off the beaten track. Elizabeth Gundrey recommended. Riviera Care Award winner. Brochure available. Open all year.

Wiscombe Linhaye Farm, Southleigh, Colyton, Devon EX24 6JF ⑤⑦

Sheila Rabjohns
☎/Fax 01404 871342
BB From £20–£25
EM From £10
Sleeps 6
🧍 🐴(10) 🐕 ⚹ 🏠 ⊚
♦♦♦

A spacious farm bungalow on a small working farm in quiet countryside but in easy reach of Sidmouth, the Donkey Sanctuary and Lyme Regis. Ideal for senior citizens and those who cannot use stairs. Private en suite bathrooms. Drink facilities, TV and hair dryers in all bedrooms. Separate dining tables. Home/local produce. Open Mar–Oct.

Wishay Farm, Trinity, Cullompton, Devon EX15 1PE ⑤⑧

Mrs Sylvia Baker
☎/Fax 01884 33223
BB From £16–£18
Sleeps 6
🐴 ⚹ 🏠 ⊚
♦♦♦

Comfortable and spacious 17th century farmhouse, set amid the peace and seclusion of the countryside. Ideal base for touring. Comfortable lounge with colour TV. Central heating. 1 family room with en suite bathroom, double with separate guests' bathroom, both with colour TV, fridge and tea/coffee-making facilities. Children welcome. Open Feb–Nov.

FARM HOLIDAY BUREAU

Please mention *Stay on a Farm* when booking

Self-Catering

---

49 Bertie's and Porky's Barns, Skinners Ash Farm, Fenny Bridges, Honiton, Devon EX14 0BH

Mrs J S Godfrey
☎/Fax 01404 850231
SC From £180–£450
EM £10
Sleep 5/7
🐕 🐎 ✂ 🛏 ⚓ ⊚
♟♟♟♟ Up to Highly
Commended

Have fun on our family-run rare breeds farm situated in the Otter Valley. The luxury barns have colour TV, cot, highchair and well-fitted kitchens. Enjoy pony rides, collect your own eggs. Meals available. Near local beaches and tourist attractions. Send for colour brochure. Open all year.

---

59 Bodmiscombe Farm, Blackborough, Cullompton, Devon EX15 2HR

Mrs Brenda Northam
☎/Fax 01884 266315
SC From £115–£310
Sleeps 4 + cot
🐕 🐎 ✂ 🍴 ⚓ ⊚
♟♟♟ Commended

For three generations our family has been farming in this tiny peaceful hamlet set in the Blackdown Hills now designated an Area of Outstanding Natural Beauty. The self-contained part of our 17th century farmhouse with beamed ceilings is furnished to a high standard. Cleanliness and comfort guaranteed. Come and share 200 acres of rolling Devonshire countryside with us. Nature trails, private fishing. Looking forward to meeting you! Open all year.

---

60 Budleigh Farm, Moretonhampstead, Devon TQ13 8SB

Mrs Judith Harvey
☎ 01647 440835
Fax 01647 440436
SC From £110–£388
Sleeps 2–6
👤 🐎 🐕 ⊞ 🧍 🚗 🍴 ⚓ ⊚
♟♟ – ♟♟♟
Commended

Seven properties, created with flair from traditional granite barns, on a farm at the end of a stunning valley in the Dartmoor National Park – rural but not remote. Superb gardens, delightful pubs, beaches and castles are not too far away. Come especially in May when the bluebells turn the woods to a smoky haze. Open all year.
E-mail: farmleigh@aol.com

---

4 Burton Farm Cottages, Burton Farm, Galmpton, Kingsbridge, South Devon TQ7 3EY

Anne Rossiter
☎/Fax 01548 561210
SC From £75–£525
Sleeps 4/5 + cot
🐕 🐎 ✂ ⚓ ⚓ ⊚
♟♟♟♟ Commended

Situated in a pretty hamlet adjoining open farmland, 5 mins walk from farm, these cob and slate cottages are 5 miles from Kingsbridge, 3 miles from sailing haunt of Salcombe and 1 mile from lovely beaches of Hope Cove and Thurlestone. Traditionally decorated and furnished, many original features with stone-built fireplaces and electric heating. Guests welcome to enjoy farm activities. Meals (from £13) available on request.

---

61 Cider Cottage, c/o Great Bradley Farm, Withleigh Cross, Tiverton, Devon EX16 8JL

Mrs Sylvia Hann
☎/Fax 01884 256946
SC From £180–£380
Sleeps 2–5 + cot
🐎 ✂ ⚓ ⊚
♟♟♟♟ Highly
Commended

This charming cottage, its oak beams hung with cider jars, is cosy, warm, bright and comfortable. It has, we think, the best view in Devon, always changing with the light and seasons. Lean on the gate and watch the cows come home, or laze in the garden with a book. Then at the end of a happy day out, tuck freshly bathed children into bed, enjoy a glass of wine and relax. Lovely! Open all year.

Coombe Farm Cottage, Wembury Road, Plymstock, Plymouth, Devon PL9 0DE

Suzanne MacBean
☎/Fax 01752 401730
⑤ᶜ From £150–£400
Sleeps 5/6
ᗒ ᛘ ⅍ ▥
ℐℐℐℐ *Commended*

A warm welcome with tea and cake awaits you to our comfortable and homely cottage, set in a peaceful valley on a working dairy farm. Close to beaches, moor and city centre. Off road parking, linen and towels included, small garden with barbecue. Pets welcome by arrangement. Open all year.

Dittiscombe Farm Cottages, Slapton, Kingsbridge, Devon TQ7 2QF

Ruth Saunders
☎ 01548 521272
Fax 01548 521425
⑤ᶜ From £185–£600
Sleeps 2–8 + cot
ᗒ ᛘ ⅍ ▥
ℐℐℐℐ *Up to Highly Commended*

Relax in one of our individual stone cottages which nestle in our private conservation valley. Just two miles from historic Slapton Village, beaches and the spectacular Coast Path, this is ideal country for dog walking, bird watching, fishing and just pure relaxation. Horse riding and livery. Woodburners. Airbaths/sauna. Children's playground. Pets welcome. Brochure. Open all year. *Associate.*

Droughtwell Farm, Sheldon, Honiton, Devon EX14 0QW

Mrs Sue Cochrane
☎ 01404 841349
⑤ᶜ From £140–£240
Sleeps 2 + cot
ᗒ ᛘ ▥
ℐℐℐ *Commended*

Come to a cosy, comfortable self-contained wing of our farmhouse, with log fire. We are a small working sheep farm in peaceful countryside. Lovely walks in fields and forest where foxes, badgers, roe deer and a great variety of birds can be seen. Open all year.

Five Elms, Bradninch, Exeter, Devon EX5 4RD

Mrs Eileen Persey
☎ 01392 881526
Fax 01392 881249
⑤ᶜ From £160–£550
Sleeps 8 + cot
ᗒ ᗦ ▥ ᛘ
ℐℐℐℐ – ℐℐℐℐ
Commended

Secluded luxury four-bedroomed bungalow overlooking the peaceful Colebrook Valley with easy access to Exmoor, Dartmoor and beaches. Ideal for summer holidays or short breaks. Golf, sports centre, NT properties, country pubs nearby. Explore the footpaths, visit the award-winning dairy unit, fish the 5km of river, enjoy the superb scenery and wildlife on this 400-acre farm. Sorry no pets. Open all year. E-mail: persey.park@btinternet.com

Fursdon, Cadbury, Exeter, Devon EX5 5JS

Mrs Catriona Fursdon
☎/Fax 01392 860860
⑤ᶜ From £168–£595
Sleeps 4–8
ᗒ ᛘ ⊞ ᗦ ▥ ᛘ ◉
ℐℐℐℐ *Commended*

Half an hour from the cathedral city of Exeter in hills above Exe Valley. Comfort and care assured in two manor house apartments and two cottages, surrounded by garden, woods, pasture and corn! Friendly flock of black sheep. Grass tennis court, barbecues, football, table tennis, woodland walks – acres of freedom. Open all year. E-mail: fursdon@eclipse.co.uk

The Garden Lodge, Stafford Barton, Broadhembury, Honiton, Devon EX14 0LU

Mrs Anne Barons
☎/Fax 01404 841403
⑤ᶜ From £285–£340
Sleeps 4
ᗒ ᛘ ◉
ℐℐℐℐ *Commended*

In need of a break? Then come and relax in our spacious Garden Lodge. Enjoy the beautiful scenery and garden. Watch the sun set over the Blackdown Hills. Stroll into nearby idyllic thatched village with pub and shop. Plenty to see and do. Lovely farm walks with lots of animals. Meals also available in farmhouse. Brochure available. Open all year. E-mail: anne@devonfarms.co.uk

67 Hele Payne Farm, Hele, Exeter, Devon EX5 4PH

Irene and Sally Maynard
☎ 01392 881530/881356
Fax 01392 881530
SC From £180–£430
Sleeps 3/5/6
🐎🐈🛁🎭🎣
🐾🐾🐾🐾 *Up to Highly Commended*

Relax in our outdoor heated swimming pool and slip into the tranquillity of rural life as recently featured on BBC 1's *Holiday* programme. Explore our dairy farm – children may help to feed the baby calves. All three cottages are surrounded by beautiful gardens, ideal for barbecues, and have colour TV, bed linen, laundry room, cot, highchair and CH. Games barn with pool, table tennis etc provides fun for any age. Open all year.

---

68 Highdown Farm, Bradninch, Exeter, Devon EX5 4LT

Mrs Sandra Vallis
☎ 01392 881028
Fax 01392 881272
SC From £120–£530
Sleeps 2/4/7 + cot
🐎🐈🛁
🐾🐾🐾🐾 *Highly Commended*

Situated high above the Culm Valley, Highdown, an organic Duchy of Cornwall mixed/dairy farm, boasts spectacular views, an abundance of wildlife and lovely walks. We have three warm and welcoming cottages to choose from, all tastefully decorated and furnished, each with its own garden. An ideal holiday base whatever the season. Open all year.

---

69 Howton Linhay, Great Howton Farm, Moretonhampstead, Newton Abbot, Devon TQ13 8PP

Jane & Alastair Wimberley
☎/Fax 01647 440100
SC From £225–£475
Sleeps 6
🐎🐕🧍🛁🎭🎣
🐾🐾🐾🐾 *Commended*

Comfortable, well-designed barn conversion standing in its own garden. Spacious accommodation with well-equipped kitchen. Working livestock family farm with ponds, streams and woodland walks. Easy access to open moorland with its wonderful scenery, walking, cycling, horseriding, other outdoor pursuits and many tourist attractions. Open all year.

---

70 Ledstone Farm, Ledstone, Kingsbridge, South Devon TQ7 2HQ

Ann Lidstone
☎/Fax 01548 852662
SC From £210–£273
Sleeps 2/3
🐎✂🐈
🐾🐾🐾🐾
Highly Commended

In a tiny village near Kingsbridge we offer a choice of two converted haylofts. The Loft has two bedrooms and Swallow Barn one bedroom. Both have living rooms with corner kitchens, lots of extras. Lovely locations and a happy, comfortable atmosphere. Phone, towels, VCR, etc. Convenience and contentment guaranteed. Open all year.

---

71 Lemprice Farm, Yettington, Budleigh Salterton, Devon EX9 7BW

Mrs Hanneke Coates
☎ 01395 567037
Fax 01395 567585
SC From £240–£550
Sleeps 4–6
👵🐎🐕🎭🛁
🐾🐾🐾 – 🐾🐾🐾🐾
Highly Commended

National award winning stone barn cottages suitable for disabled. Exceptional walking area of outstanding natural beauty and scientific interest. Home of the rare barn owl. All cottage gardens overlook small lake and marshes abundant with wildlife, hills and open countryside beyond. All linen and electricity included. Dogs by arrangement only. Three miles to beach. Brochure. Open Easter–Nov. E-mail: dickcoates@compuserve.com.uk

---

72 Longmeadow Farm, Coombe Road, Ringmore, Shaldon, Teignmouth, Devon TQ14 0EX

Mrs Anne Mann
☎ 01626 872732
Fax 01626 872323
SC From £175–£315
Sleeps 4
🐎🧍📺🛁
🐾🐾🐾 *Approved*

Enjoy the best of both worlds on our South Devon farm set in lovely countryside but less than a mile from the beach and Shaldon village. Comfortable accommodation (in two units each sleeping 4) adjoining traditional style farmhouse overlooking estuary. Garden, patio, barbecue. Ideal location for touring coast, moors. Walks, fishing, riding nearby. Ample parking. Brochure available. Open all year.

Lookweep Farm, Liverton, Newton Abbot, Devon TQ12 6HT

Jon & Sue Peters
☎ 01626 833277
SC From £210–£435
Sleeps 5
🐕 🐈 🛏 ♿
♪♪♪♪ *Commended*

Perfectly placed to explore Dartmoor, the stunning coastline, charming villages and towns of South Devon. Just two attractive, well-equipped stone cottages surrounded by open farmland and woods in tranquil setting within two miles of Bovey Tracey and of Haytor. Own gardens, ample parking, heated pool and splendid walks right on your doorstep.
E-mail: holiday@lookweep.co.uk

Lovehayne Farm Cottages, Lovehayne Farm, Southleigh, Colyton, Devon EX24 6JE

Mrs Philippa Bignell
☎/Fax 01404 871216
SC From £175–£595
Sleep 4/8 + cot
🐕 🐈 🎾 ♿
♪♪♪♪ *Commended*

Delightful cottages in secluded private valley. Explore our 200-acre mixed farm with woods and streams, abundant wildlife, horses and sheep. In an Area of Outstanding Natural Beauty, 3 miles from the sea at Branscombe. Hard tennis court. Bedlinen provided, Central heating. Brochure available. Open Apr–Nov.
E-mail: cottages@fairway.globalnet.co.uk

Middle Cobden Farm, Whimple, Exeter, Devon EX5 2PZ

Mrs Cathie Cottey
☎ 01404 822276
SC From £170–£385
Sleeps 6
🐕 ✄
♪♪♪ *Approved*

A warm and friendly welcome awaits you on our real working dairy farm. Peace and quiet with comfortable surroundings offered in half of our farmhouse. Self-contained, the accommodation offers large lounge, kitchen/diner, family room, twin room and bathroom. Easy access to M5, Exeter and East Devon resorts. Brochure available. Open all year.

Narramore Farm Cottages, Narramore Farm, Moretonhampstead, Devon TQ13 8QT

Sue Horn
☎ 01647 440455
Fax 01647 440031
SC From £85–£500
Sleeps 2–6
🐕 🐈 🛏 ♿
♪♪♪ – ♪♪♪♪ *Up to*
Highly Commended

Stressed out? Let Narramore work its magic on you! Six comfortable cottages situated on 107-acre horse stud/deer farm. A really warm pool, bubbling hot spa, satellite TV, games/laundry room, payphone, play area, fishing lake, boat, barbecue, small animals plus the opportunity to badgerwatch amidst glorious countryside – all these make us special. Colour brochure. Open all year.
E-mail: narramore@btinternet.com

Oldaport Farm Cottages, Modbury, Ivybridge, Devon PL21 0TG

Miss C Evans
☎ 01548 830842
Fax 01548 830998
SC From £149–£441
Sleep 2/6
🐕 🛏 ♿
♪♪♪ – ♪♪♪♪
Highly Commended

Oldaport is a small sheep farm of 70 acres, lying in the Erme Valley, and offering lovely views of the countryside. The four cottages, which sleep 2/6, were redundant stone barns which have been carefully converted into comfortable holiday homes. All fully equipped, heating in all rooms. Sandy beaches nearby, Dartmoor 8 miles. Excellent birdwatching. No dogs in high season. Brochure available. Open all year.
E-mail: cathy.evans@dial.pipex.com.uk

Otter Holt and Owl Hayes, c/o Godford Farm, Awliscombe, Honiton, Devon EX14 0PW

Sally Lawrence
☎/Fax 01404 42825
SC From £120–£350
Sleeps 4 + cot
🐕 🎾 ♿ ◉
♪♪♪ *Commended*

Come and see where the hayracks are in our beautiful barn cottages, one of the many features that make them unique. Each cottage has beamed lounge with colour TV/video, pine kitchen/diner with washer/dryer, microwave, fridge/freezer. CH. 2 bedrooms (linen incl). Walkers' paradise, wildlife abundant. Floral gardens, games barn, pets and calves to feed. Farm map. Children welcome, large play area. Cot available. Brochure. Open all year.

52 **Smallicombe Farm,** Northleigh, Colyton, Devon EX24 6BU

Maggie Todd
☎ 01404 831310
Fax 01404 831431
sc From £95–£695
Sleeps 2–8
♠ ☎ ♨ ♞ ☂ ◎
♟♟♟ – ♟♟♟♟ *Up to*
Highly Commended

Escape the stresses of modern living to converted barns in idyllic rural setting little changed over the centuries. Meet our traditional farm animals and watch for the surrounding wildlife. Try Devon skittles in our games room. Explore coast and country in this unspoilt corner of Devon. ETB 'England for Excellence' Award 1995. Holiday Care Service 'Best Self-Catering Accommodation' 1996. Open all year.
E-mail: maggie_todd@yahoo.com

14 **Stickwick Holiday Homes,** c/o Frost Farm, Hennock, Bovey Tracey, South Devon TQ13 9PP

Linda Harvey
☎/Fax 01626 833266
sc From £125–£1,300
Sleeps 2–12
☎ ♞
♟♟♟♟ – ♟♟♟♟♟
Commended

These holiday homes are a joy to stay in. Georgian house dating from 1780. Grand atmosphere, period furnishings (sleeps 12/14). Character farmhouse with beams, original features and woodburner (sleeps 6/7). Pretty cottage ideal for two for a get-away break (sleeps 2/5). Gardens, games barn, friendly farm animals. Near Bovey Tracey, glass/pottery/craft/heritage centres, walks, pubs and shops. Brochure. Open all year.
E-mail: postmaster@hennock.org.uk

78 **Traine Farm,** Wembury, Plymouth, Devon PL9 0EW

Sheila Rowland
☎/Fax 01752 862264
sc From £110–£385
Sleeps 5 (+ 2) + cot
☎ ♞ ♨ ☂ ♨ ◎
♟♟♟ *Commended*

Come and enjoy a relaxed holiday in lovely surroundings, on farm overlooking village of Wembury and beautiful heritage coastline. Ideal for families, children can enjoy rockpool rambling, pony rides. Good centre for walking with waymarked trails through the farm. Sailing, diving, golf nearby. Short breaks. Open all year.
E-mail: rowland.trainefarm@eclipse.co.uk

79 **Withymore Cottage,** Withymore Farm, Malborough, Kingsbridge, South Devon TQ7 3ED

Mrs Jo Hocking
☎/Fax 01548 561275
sc From £150–£450
Sleeps 6 + cot
☎ ♞ ♥ ♨ ☂
♟♟♟♟ *Commended*

Recently modernised cottage nestling in a peaceful valley on a family-run dairy farm within a short distance of Salcombe. Very comfortable and furnished to a high standard throughout. Colour TV, bed linen, CH. Well equipped kitchen. Large enclosed garden. Ideal centre for family holiday with many beaches, sailing, fishing, golf, horse riding and spectacular coastal walks. Open all year.

80 **Wooder Manor,** Widecombe-in-the-Moor, Newton Abbot, Devon TQ13 7TR

Mrs Angela Bell
☎/Fax 01364 621391
sc From £120–£870
Sleeps 2/16
♠ ☎ ♞ ♨ ♨
♟♟♟ – ♟♟♟♟
Commended

Cottages and converted coachhouse on 150-acre family farm, nestled in picturesque valley surrounded by unspoilt woodland, moors and granite tors. Peaceful location, central for touring Devon and exploring Dartmoor by foot or on horseback. Clean and fully equipped. Colour TVs, laundry facilities, microwaves, CH. Gardens, courtyard for easy parking. Good food at local inn (½ mile). Choose a property to suit from our colour brochure. Two ground floor units suitable for disabled guests. Open all year.

81 **Yarningale,** Exeter Road, Moretonhampstead, Newton Abbot, Devon TQ13 8SW

Sarah Radcliffe
☎/Fax 01647 440560
sc From £150–£350
Sleeps 6
☎ ♞ ✂ ☂ ◎
♟♟♟ *Commended*

A secluded, tranquil property offering exceptional panoramic views of Dartmoor. An individual, totally private self-contained flat offering two large double (or triple) bedrooms, each with their own bathroom, lounge, kitchen/diner. Ample level parking. Stables/kennels available. Superb walking country – 500 acres of open moorland within 5 minutes of house.

Cornwall

Bodmin Moor, North & South Cornwall Coasts, Land's End
& St Michael's Mount

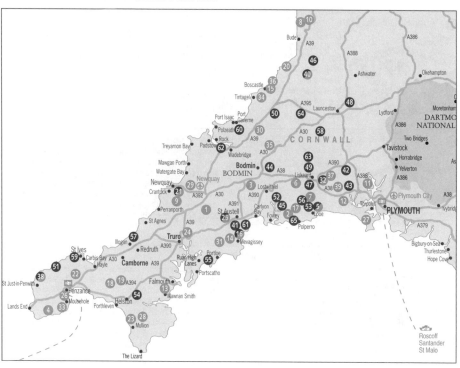

Key

1 Bed & Breakfast

1 Self-Catering

1 B&B and SC

1 Camping Barns

1 Camping & Caravanning

Cornwall has a coastline of 326 miles, varying from wonderful stretches of firm, golden sands and soaring cliffs on the north coast, to tiny coves, picturesque fishing villages and sheltered, wooded estuaries in the south. Beaches from Bude to St Ives are famous for the exhilarating Atlantic surf, while Looe, Fowey, Mevagissey and Falmouth are ideal for sailing, fishing and windsurfing. Inland lies the atmospheric Bodmin Moor with its mysterious standing stones. Visitors have a wide choice of art galleries, potteries, famous gardens and National Trust properties such as St Michael's Mount, Lanhydrock and Trelissick, while Arthurian Tintagel sums up the mystical quality of Cornwall.

If you would like help in finding suitable farm accommodation, turn to the full listing of FHB Groups on pages 392 to 395 to find appropriate contact details for this area.

Bed and Breakfast
(and evening meal)

---

1 Arrallas, Ladock, Truro, Cornwall TR2 4NP

Mrs Barbara Holt
☎ 01872 510379
Fax 01872 510200
[BB] From £22
Sleeps 6
⌂(12) ⌖ ♨ ⚘ ⊚
♦♦♦♦♦ Silver Award

Luxurious rooms, beautiful views, peaceful surroundings and the magic of birdsong make Arrallas something very special. The warm welcome and personal attention to our guests make your holiday with us one to remember. Come and be pampered, walk through our woods, watch for the barn owls. Listen for the woodpeckers, laze in the garden. (Phone for directions.) Open all year except Christmas and New Year.

---

2 Bake Farm, Pelynt, Looe, Cornwall PL13 2QQ

Doreen Eastley
☎/Fax 01503 220244
[BB] From £17–£19
Sleeps 6
⌂(3) ⌖
♦♦♦

A warm welcome and good farmhouse breakfasts await you at this listed farmhouse bearing the Trelawney coat of arms (1610). The family-run working farm, set in quiet and peaceful surroundings, is situated midway between Looe and Fowey, the home of author Daphne du Maurier. An ideal base from which to explore Cornwall, with coastal paths, riding and fishing all nearby. Open Apr–Oct.

---

3 Bokiddick Farm, Lanivet, Bodmin, Cornwall PL30 5HP

Gill Hugo
☎/Fax 01208 831481
[BB] From £20–£22
Sleeps 5
⌂(3) ⌖ ♨ ⊚
♦♦♦♦ Gold Award

Lovely Georgian farmhouse with oak beams and wood panelling, in peaceful location nestling in beautiful countryside with magnificent views. Our 180-acre dairy farm is central for touring all of Cornwall. Close to NT Lanhydrock House. Lovely en suite bedrooms, delicious breakfasts cooked on the Aga. The warmest of welcomes awaits you. Open all year except Christmas and New Year.

---

4 Boskenna Home Farm, St Buryan, Penzance, Cornwall TR19 6DQ

Julia Hosking
☎/Fax 01736 810705
[BB] From £20–£22
Sleeps 6
⌂ ⌖ ♨ ⊚
♦♦♦♦

Our 17th century listed farmhouse which has been in our family for generations lies in the far west of Cornwall close to Land's End, nestling south of the rugged moorland, near the coastal path. Stay on our working dairy farm, with Guernsey cows, farm pets and Redde-Wood the pony. Open Mar–Nov.

---

5 Bucklawren Farm, St Martin-by-Looe, Cornwall PL13 1NZ

Mrs Jean Henly
☎ 01503 240738
Fax 01503 240481
[BB] From £20–£23
EM From £11
Sleeps 14
⌂(5) ⊞ ♨ ⚭ ⊚
♦♦♦♦

Tucked away in the Cornish countryside is Bucklawren, a beautiful Domesday hamlet. The delightful 19th century farmhouse enjoys spectacular sea views over Looe Bay. Come and enjoy good food, comfort and relaxation. An award-winning farm where every effort is made to ensure you have a memorable stay. Open mid Mar–Oct.
E-mail: bucklawren@compuserve.com

Caduscott, Dobwalls, Liskeard, Cornwall PL14 4NG ⑥

Lindsay Pendray
☎/Fax 01579 320262
BB From £17–£21
Sleeps 4
☙ ⅍ ▥ ◉
♦♦♦

Sweet dreams and restful nights broken only by the owl's hooting in the clear night sky; from stargazers to shellseekers, all the ingredients are here to match your mood! A positive approach to all your needs. Log fires to brighten your return after days spent on the rugged cliffs or exploring the sheltered valleys. Open Apr–Sept incl. Easter. E-mail: caduscott@farmline.com

Carglonnon Farm, Duloe, Liskeard, Cornwall PL14 4QA ⑦

Mrs Ann Bray
☎/Fax 01579 320210
BB From £18–£19
Sleeps 6
☙(5) ⅍ ⚲ ▥
♦♦♦

A lovely 18th century Georgian farmhouse which is part of the Duchy of Cornwall Estate. A working mixed farm of 230 acres, situated 4½ miles from fishing port of Looe. Forestry walks from farm. Golf, horse-riding, Theme Park, coastal walking, moors all nearby. Two doubles en suite. One twin with private bathroom. Tea/coffee-making facilities, central heating. Open all year except Christmas.

Cornakey Farm, Morwenstow, Bude, Cornwall EX23 9SS ⑧

Mrs Monica Heywood
☎ 01288 331260
BB From £17–£20
EM From £9
Sleeps 6
☙ ⅍ ⚲ ▥
♦♦

This is a 220–acre mixed coastal farm with extensive views of sea and Lundy island from bedrooms and bathroom. Good touring centre with easy reach of quiet beaches. The farmhouse offers one family room en suite and two double rooms. Bathroom, toilet, lounge (colour TV), dining room. Children welcome at reduced rates. Cot, highchair, baby-sitting. Good home cooking with fresh vegetables. Open Jan–Nov.

Degembris Farmhouse, St Newlyn East, Newquay, Cornwall TR8 5HY ⑨

Kathy Woodley
☎ 01872 510555
Fax 01872 510230
BB From £20–£22
EM From £12.50
Sleeps 12
☙ ⅍ ▤ ▥ ◉
♦♦♦♦

Degembris nestles in a south facing hillside overlooking a beautiful wooded valley. Its low beams and log fires make this listed 18th century farmhouse a delight. Come inside (mind your head!) and enjoy the charming Georgian surroundings, complete with creaky floorboards! Take a stroll along our farm trail that wanders through woodland and fields of corn. Open all year except Christmas. E-mail: kath@tally-connect.co.uk

East Woolley Farm, Morewenstow, Bude, Cornwall EX23 9PP ⑩

Julia Dauncey
☎/Fax 01288 331525
BB From £19–£22
Sleeps 6
☙ ⅍ ▥ ⚲
♦♦♦

East Woolley is a small dairy farm situated in a peaceful hamlet just ½ mile off the A39, with magnificent cliff walks and beaches nearby. The accommodation consists of self-contained rooms in a converted barn around the courtyard. Breakfast is served in the farmhouse. Guests are welcome to sit and relax in the conservatory. Open all year.

Haye Farm, Landulph, Saltash, Cornwall PL12 6QQ ⑪

Valerie Willcocks
☎/Fax 01752 842786
BB From £18.50–£20
EM From £11
Sleeps 4
☙ ⅍ ▥ ⚲
♦♦♦

Relax in a tranquil setting, a family farm on the banks of the River Tamar. We have pedigree cows and calves, old English game fowl, for the keen birdwatchers marsh and estuary birds and footpaths for walkers. Ideal for touring Cornwall and Devon. Comfortable en suite accommodation. Guests' lounge with log fire. A warm welcome awaits you with delicious farmhouse cooking. Open Mar–Nov.

12 Hendra Farm, Polbathic, Torpoint, Cornwall PL11 3DT

Mrs A Hoskin
☎/Fax 01503 250225
BB From £18–£20
Sleeps 5
♨ ⅃ ▩ ◉
♦♦♦

Hendra is a working farm situated in an area of outstanding natural beauty. The fishing port of Looe is 6 miles, and safe bathing beaches of Downderry and Seaton only 2 miles. The main shopping centre of Plymouth is within ½ hours travelling. TV lounge. Family room with en suite shower and WC. Babysitting. Open Easter–Nov.

---

13 Higher Kergilliack Farm, Budock, Falmouth, Cornwall TR11 5PB

Jean Pengelly
☎ 01326 372271
BB From £19.50–£20
Sleeps 6
♨ ⅃ Å ♠ ⚛ ▩
♦♦♦

18th century Georgian listed farmhouse on 130-acre dairy farm, former residence of Bishop of Exeter. Overlooks Falmouth Bay and near the seal sanctuary. See the flowers in the hedgerows and daffodil fields. Trebah, Trelissick and Glendurgan Gardens 15 mins. 1 double with en suite WC and shower, 1 twin/family with en suite WC and bath. Take 2nd right on A39 at Hillhead roundabout. Open all year.

---

14 Higher Kestle Farm, St Ewe, Near Mevagissey, St Austell, Cornwall PL26 6EP

Vicky Lobb
☎/Fax 01726 842001
BB From £18–£25
Sleeps 6
♨(12) ⅃ ☞ ⚛
♦♦♦♦ Silver Award

Unwind in our tastefully restored Grade II listed farmhouse, boasting beautiful views from our three pretty bedrooms (two en suite). Picturesque Mevagissey, beaches and footpaths nearby. After a hearty breakfast take a stroll through our woodlands to the 'Lost Gardens of Heligan' or explore our trout lakes. A warm welcome awaits you. Open Mar–Oct.
E-mail: vicky@higherkestle.freeserve.co.uk

---

15 Home Farm, Minster, Boscastle, Cornwall PL35 0BN

Jackie Haddy
☎/Fax 01840 250195
BB From £17–£19.50
Sleeps 6
♨ ⅃ ♠ ▩ ⚛
♦♦♦

A warm welcome awaits you at Home Farm, our family working farm situated overlooking picturesque Boscastle and the Atlantic coastline. The farm is surrounded by National Trust countryside and walks. The traditional farmhouse has three tastefully decorated bedrooms. Delicious farmhouse breakfasts, homemade bread and plenty of Cornish hospitality. Open all year except Christmas.

---

16 Kerryanna Country House, Treleaven Farm, Mevagissey, Cornwall PL26 6RZ

Linda Hennah
☎/Fax 01726 843558
BB From £23–£27
EM £12
Sleeps 14
♨(5) ⊞ ▩ ◉
♦♦♦♦

Surrounded by farmland, wildlife and flowers, the farm is only 8 minutes' walk from the centre of Mevagissey. Romantic en suite bedrooms with TV and beverage tray. Beautiful gardens with heated outdoor pool and stunning views. Games barn, putting green. Hearty breakfasts and delicious evening meals. A warm welcome assured. Mentioned in the *Daily Telegraph* and Gill Charlton's *A Week in Cornwall*. Open Mar–Oct.

---

17 Little Larnick Farm, Pelynt, Looe, Cornwall PL13 2NB

Angela Eastley
☎/Fax 01503 262837
BB From £19–£22
Sleeps 12
♨(3) ⅃ ▩ ◉
♦♦♦♦

Little Larnick is situated in a sheltered part of the West Looe river valley. Walk to the bustling fishing town of Looe from our working dairy farm and along the coastal path to picturesque Polperro. The farmhouse offers twin, double and family en suite rooms or stay in our barn suite for a unique experience. Open all year except Christmas

Little Pengwedna Farm, Helston, Cornwall TR13 0AY

Iris White
☎ 01736 850649
Fax 01736 850489
BB From £20–£25
Sleeps 10
ঠ ㅏ ㉫ 🎴 🛠 ⑧
◆◆◆◆

A friendly Cornish welcome and hearty home-cooked breakfast make a stay at this charming farmhouse a real treat. Ideally positioned for touring either coast, you'll find this 19th century granite house prettily and comfortably decorated with original paintings and fresh flowers. It's easily reached, on the B3302 between Helston and Hayle. Open all year (Christmas by arrangement).

Longstone Farm, Trenear, Helston, Cornwall TR13 0HG

Gillian Lawrance
☎/Fax 01326 572483
BB From £18–£20
EM From £9
Sleeps 12
ঠ ㅏ ㅊ 🛠 ⑧
◆◆◆

Enjoy the warm and friendly atmosphere of our home which is off the beaten track overlooking rolling fields and peaceful countryside. Central for sandy beaches and many attractions, particularly Flambards. All bedrooms en suite or private facilities. Delicious meals using local produce, attractively presented in our dining room overlooking spacious garden. Relax and unwind in our TV lounge and sunlounge. Open Mar–Oct.

Lower Tresmorn Farm, Crackington Haven, Bude, Cornwall EX23 0NU

Rachel Crocker
☎/Fax 01840 230667
BB From £20–£25
EM From £14
Sleeps 11
ঠ(8) ㅊ 🛠 ⚡ ⚑ ⑧
◆◆◆◆

Beautiful medieval farmhouse situated on a secluded National Trust clifftop farm, just north of a sandy cove at Crackington Haven. Massive oak beams, granite fireplace, real fires, fine furnishings and superb home cooking. Stunning coastal walks from the front door. A lovely welcoming place to stay, whatever the season. Open all year except Christmas.

Manuels Farm, Quintrell Downs, Newquay, Cornwall TR8 4NY

Mrs Jean Wilson
☎/Fax 01637 873577
BB From £18.50–£22
Sleeps 6
ঠ ㅏ ㅊ 🛠 ⚡ ⚑ 🛠 ⑧
◆◆◆◆

A delightful 17th century farmhouse situated in a sheltered valley, 2 miles from Newquay's magnificent beaches. Bedrooms have brass beds and window seats overlooking the charming gardens, and are enhanced by antique and pine furniture. There is a lounge and fascinating dining room with huge inglenook fireplace and antique dining table around which guests gather for substantial farmhouse breakfasts. Closed Christmas.

Menwidden Farm, Ludgvan, Penzance, Cornwall TR20 8BN

Mrs C E Quick
☎ 01736 740415
BB From £16.50–£20
EM From £7
Sleeps 9
ঠ ㅏ ㅊ 🛠 ⚡
◆◆◆

Centrally situated in West Cornwall, we offer good home cooking and comfortable beds. A warm welcome awaits you and we try to make your stay a happy one. Turn towards Ludgvan at Crowlas crossroads on A30, third right signposted Vellandweth, one mile up road, last farm on left. *Associate.*

Polhormon Farm, Polhormon Lane, Mullion, Helston, Cornwall TR12 7JE

Alice Harry
☎/Fax 01326 240304
BB From £17–£20
Sleeps 8
ঠ ㅏ ㅊ ⑧
◆◆◆

Treat yourselves to a relaxing Cornish break in our comfortable Georgian farmhouse. Spectacular views over the sea and sandy Poldhu beach on the unspoilt Lizard Peninsula. Watch the milking or help feed our newborn calves. Ideal base for beaches, cliffwalking or boat trips around Mullion Island with local fisherman, Barry. Scrumptious breakfasts. Open Easter–Oct.

24 **Polsue Manor Farm,** Tresillian, Truro, Cornwall TR2 4BP

Geraldine Holliday
☎ 01872 520234
Fax 01872 520616
BB From £18–£24
EM From £11
Sleeps 14
⮜ 🐓 🐖 🐄 ❦ ⊚
♦♦♦

The farmhouse on this 190-acre working farm, set in glorious countryside, overlooks the tidal Tresillian River and one of the prettiest parts of Cornwall, 'gateway' to the Roseland Peninsula. Beautiful cathedral city of Truro 2 miles. Centrally situated between north and south coasts, ideal centre for touring Cornwall. Delightful woodland and estuary walks. Traditional home cooking, comfortable, relaxed atmosphere. Open most of year but not Christmas.

25 **Poltarrow Farm,** St Mewan, St Austell, Cornwall PL26 7DR

Judith Nancarrow
☎/Fax 01726 67111
BB From £22–£25
Sleeps 12
⮜ ⊞ ☕ 🐄 🛄 ⊚
♦♦♦♦

Our period farmhouse is situated on the south coast between St Austell and the cathedral city of Truro. Poltarrow offers pretty en suite bedrooms, a hearty Cornish breakfast and the luxury of an indoor swimming pool. A few minutes' drive takes you to the coast, gardens (particularly Heligan) local inns and restaurants. Open all year except Christmas.

26 **Rose Farm,** Chyanhal, Buryas Bridge, Penzance, Cornwall TR19 6AN

Mrs Penny Lally
☎/Fax 01736 731808
BB From £20–£27
Sleeps 8
⮜ ⊞ 🐄 🛄
♦♦♦

Rose Farm is a small working farm in a little hamlet close to the picturesque fishing villages of Mousehole and Newlyn and 7 miles from Lands End. The 200-year-old granite farmhouse is cosy with pretty, en suite rooms. 1 double, 1 family suite and a romantic 15th century four poster room in barn annexe. We have all manner of animals, from pedigree cattle to pot-bellied pigs! Open all year (closed Christmas).

27 **Stone Farm,** Whitsand Bay, Millbrook, Torpoint, Cornwall PL10 1JJ

Mrs Sarah Blake
☎/Fax 01752 822267
BB From £17–£22
Sleeps 6
⮜ 🐄 🛄
♦♦♦

Dairy farm 400 yards from the cliff path leading to miles of sandy beaches in an Area of Outstanding Natural Beauty, with panoramic views from Rame to Looe. Large garden with croquet lawn. Everyone can help feed the animals or watch the milking. Children's pony rides and games room. Open all year except Christmas.

28 **Tregaddra Farm,** Cury, Cross Lanes, Helston, Cornwall TR12 7BB

June Lugg
☎/Fax 01326 240235
BB From £19.50–£25
EM From £10
Sleeps 17
⮜ ✄ ⊞ 🛄 ⊚
♦♦♦♦

If you want stress-free relaxation, fresh air and freedom, Tregaddra, a working farm, is a fantastic place to stay. Situated in an Area of Outstanding Natural Beauty, our views of rolling countryside are unrivalled. Pretty en suite bedrooms, two with balconies. All-weather tennis court, heated outdoor pool and large peaceful garden. A warm 'farming family' welcome awaits you. Open all year except Christmas. See colour ad on page 46.

29 **Tregaswith Farmhouse,** Tregaswith, near Newquay, Cornwall TR8 4HY

John & Jacqui Elsom
☎/Fax 01637 881181
BB From £22–£25
EM From £14
Sleeps 6
⮜ 🐓 ✄ 🐄 🛄 ⊚
♦♦♦♦

Tregaswith is a small hamlet between Newquay and Padstow. Five minutes' drive to beaches and several National Trust properties near. The elegant farmhouse built over 250 years ago, now a smallholding with many friendly animals. Pony rides and an introduction to carriage driving can be arranged. We have a reputation for delicious food. 3 beautiful bedrooms, all en suite. Antiques and oak beams throughout. Open all year.

Tregellist Farm, Tregellist, St Kew, Bodmin, Cornwall PL30 3HG   30

Mrs Jill Cleave
☎ **01208 880537**
BB **From £20–£22**
Sleeps 6
🐎 ▪
♦♦♦

A warm welcome awaits you at this 130-acre working farm set in beautiful countryside. Situated close to the North Cornwall beaches and the Camel Trail. All bedrooms are en suite with tea/coffee-making facilities. Traditional farmhouse fare is served. Open Feb–Nov. *Associate.*

Tregonan, Tregony, Truro, Cornwall TR2 5SN   31

Sandra Collins
☎/Fax **01872 530249**
BB **From £17–£24**
Sleeps 6
🐎 ▪ ⊚
♦♦♦♦

Discover Tregonan, a spacious, comfortable farmhouse tucked away down a ½-mile private lane and set in a secluded garden amidst our 300-acre farm. A choice of one double room, one twin or one double en suite. 6 miles west of Mevagissey, we are on the threshold of the Roseland Peninsula, with a good selection of gardens, walks, beaches and eating places locally. Open Mar–Nov.

Tregondale Farm, Menheniot, Liskeard, Cornwall PL14 3RG   32

Stephanie Rowe
☎/Fax **01579 342407**
BB **From £20–£22.50**
EM From £10
Sleeps 6
🐎(3) ⅍ ☂ ▪ ⚜ ⊚
♦♦♦♦

Feeling like a break? Relax in style in the peace of the countryside near the coast. Three charming en suite bedrooms with TV/radio. Home produce a speciality. Play tennis, explore the woodland farm trail. See pedigree cattle, lambs in spring amidst wildlife and flowers. Activities arranged, golf, cycling, walking and fishing. A warm welcome awaits you. Open all year. See colour ad on page 46.

Tregurnow Farm, St Buryan, Penzance, Cornwall TR19 6BL   33

Edwina Jeffery
☎/Fax **01736 810255**
BB **From £20–£25**
Sleeps 6
🐎 🐓 ⅍ ⊡ ☂ ▪
♦♦♦

Our tastefully furnished farmhouse is situated in a magnificent coastal position above Lamorna Cove. Ideal base for the South West Way, Minack Theatre, Land's End, The Tate and beaches. Romantic four-poster. Spectacular views across Mount's Bay. Superb Aga-cooked breakfasts. We combine comfort and luxury with peace and tranquillity. Open Mar–Oct.
E-mail: tregurno@eurobell.co.uk

Trehane Farm, Trevalga, Boscastle, Cornwall PL35 0EB   34

Sarah James
☎/Fax **01840 250510**
BB **From £20–£22**
EM From £10
Sleeps 4
🐎 🐓 ⅍ 🦌 ☂ ☂ ▪ ⊚
♦♦♦

Our traditional farmhouse is in a magnificent position overlooking the sea and wild rugged coastline of North Cornwall. Peaceful and secluded situation, close to the Coastal Path and hidden coves. Plenty of wholesome local food, homemade bread and exciting vegetarian concoctions. Two pretty en suite rooms, warm and cosy with spectacular views. Brochure available. Open Feb–Nov.

Trehudreth Farm, Blisland, Bodmin, Cornwall PL30 4JW   35

Robin Grace
☎/Fax **01208 851460**
BB **From £20–£26**
EM From £15
Sleeps 8
🐎(8) ⅍ ▪
♦♦♦♦

If you want to relax in the peace and tranquillity of the beautiful countryside and enjoy the niceties of life, come and stay with Rob and Sue at Trehudreth, our traditional family farm, mentioned in the Doomsday Book. Our rooms have exposed beams, antique furniture and quality furnishings. We are ideally situated for touring, being only 14 miles from each coast. Heligan, other gardens and NT properties close by. Open Easter–Oct.
E-mail: grace@trehudreth.co.uk

36 Trerosewill Farm, Paradise, Boscastle, Cornwall PL35 0DL

Mrs Cheryl Nicholls
☎/Fax 01840 250545
BB From £19–£29.50
Sleeps 13
☆ ⚡ 🖽 🛁 ⊚
♦♦♦♦ Silver Award

Luxurious farmhouse offering bed & breakfast on a working farm. Situated a short walk from the picturesque village of Boscastle. All rooms equipped to the highest standards and there are unsurpassed panoramic sea views of Lundy Island and the North Devon coast from most rooms. Traditional farmhouse fare. Special spring/autumn breaks. FHG award winner. Open all year except Christmas and New Year.
E-mail: nicholls@trerosewill.telme.com

37 Tresulgan Farm, Nr Menheniot, Liskeard, Cornwall PL14 3PU

Mrs E Elford
☎/Fax 01503 240268
BB From £20–£25
EM From £10
Sleeps 6
☆(2) ⚡ ⚡ 🛁 ⊚
♦♦♦

This attractive 17th century farmhouse, with its original oak-beamed dining room serving delicious meals and homemade cream, is set on a working dairy farm which has superb views of the Seaton Valley. Pretty en suite rooms offering every comfort. Watch the milking, help with the calves or just simply relax. Open all year. See colour ad on page 47. E-mail: tresulgan@elfordnet.co.uk

38 Trewellard Manor Farm, Pendeen, Penzance, Cornwall TR19 7SU

Mrs Marion Bailey
☎/Fax 01736 788526
BB £20
Sleeps 6
☆ ⚡ 🛁 ⊚
♦♦♦♦

The farm is situated in a superb coastal position between Lands End and St Ives. We offer a friendly, relaxed atmosphere with seasonal fires and CH. 3 bedrooms (2 en suite, 1 with private bathroom) all with tea/coffee facilities. Use of swimming pool (June–Sept) with good beaches within easy reach. Golf available nearby. This is an outstanding area for walking, either inland or on the coast path. Open all year (closed Christmas).

39 Trewint Farm, Menheniot, Liskeard, Cornwall PL14 3RE

Elizabeth Rowe
☎/Fax 01579 347155
BB From £18–£22
EM From £10
Sleeps 6
☆ ⚡ 🛁 ⊚
♦♦♦

Ideally situated only minutes from the A38, yet in peaceful, tranquil surroundings. After a Cornish cream tea, wander around our 200-acre working farm known for its prize-winning pedigree cattle. Meet Rusty the pony and Lucy the lamb in pets' corner. En suite rooms with matching decor. Breakfast overlooking the garden watching the birds while you enjoy the farmhouse fare using home/local meats and produce. Open all year except Christmas and New Year.

40 Wheatley Farm, Maxworthy, Launceston, Cornwall PL15 8LY

Valerie Griffin
☎/Fax 01566 781232
BB From £18–£23
EM From £13.50
Sleeps 12
☆ ⚡ 🖽 🛁 🎆 ⊚
♦♦♦♦ Silver Award

Come and join us at Wheatley Farm – we'd like you to think of the farmhouse as your home. Linger over breakfast, dinner in serene dining room with granite fireplace. From soup course to desert, we serve only fresh homemade food using only local produce. West Country winner of England for Excellence award. Explore this special corner of Cornwall. Superb walks, stunning coastline nearby.

Please mention *Stay on a Farm* when booking

Self-Catering

Beechleigh Cottage, Tregondale Farm, Menheniot, Liskeard, Cornwall PL14 3RG

Stephanie Rowe
☎/Fax 01579 342407
SC From £95–£425
Sleeps 2/4 + cot
🐎 🐕 💝 🏖 🎾 ◎
♟♟♟♟ *Highly Commended*

In the leigh of our farmhouse beech tree, this peaceful, attractive character cottage nestles. Warm and cosy in winter, barbecue on the patio in summer, play tennis. Explore the woodland farm trail. Hear birds singing, enjoy wild flowers and lambs in Spring. See pedigree South Devon cattle, naturally reared. Special activities arranged – golf, cycling, fishing. A warm welcome awaits you – come and discover the beauty of Cornwall. Open all year.

Bosinver Farm, Trelowth, St Austell, Cornwall PL26 7DT

Pat Smith
☎/Fax 01726 72128
SC From £120–£985
Sleeps 2–10
🐎 🐕 🏖 🎾 💝 🎾 ◎
♟♟♟ – ♟♟♟♟
Up to Commended

Nestling in a hidden valley near the sea and Lost Gardens of Heligan, our small farm has friendly animals and ponies. 16th century thatched farmhouse or cottages, privately set in their own mature gardens surrounded by wildflower meadows and 8 other lodges. Fishing, tennis, swimming pool and a short walk to the village pub.
E-mail: bosinver@holidays2000.freeserve.co.uk

Bucklawren Farm, St Martin-by-Looe, Cornwall PL13 1NZ

Mrs Jean Henly
☎ 01503 240738
Fax 01503 240481
SC From £120–£750
Sleeps 2–8
🐎 🐕 🏖 💝 🎾 ◎
♟♟♟♟ *Highly Commended*

Step back in time and enjoy our character cottages, tastefully converted and furnished to a high standard. Come and enjoy our spectacular scenery with exceptional sea views. Plenty to do with walks, golf, fishing, all close by. An award-winning farm where you can come and discover a true Cornish farm holiday. Open all year.
E-mail: bucklawren@compuserve.com

Cadson Manor Farm, Callington, Cornwall PL17 7HW

Brenda Crago
☎/Fax 01579 383969
SC From £210–£550
Sleeps 6 + cot
🐎 🍴 🏕 💤 🎾 💝 ◎
♟♟♟♟ *Highly Commended*

Wing of manor house with large garden on 200-acre working farm set in the beautiful Lynher Valley with lovely views of two-acre fishing lake and historic Cadson Bury. Three pretty bedrooms, bathroom, lounge/diner and separate kitchen, all tastefully decorated and equipped to a very high standard. Cosy and comfortable. Farm and river walks. Open all year.
E-mail: greenstock@callington.swinternet.co.uk

The Coach House, c/o Lantallack Farm, Landrake, Nr Saltash, Cornwall PL12 5AE

Nicky Walker
☎/Fax 01752 851281
SC From £245–£595
Sleeps 6/7 + cot
🐎 🍴 🎾 🏖
♟♟♟♟ *Highly Commended*

Georgian farm coach house, extremely comfortable with outstanding views across undulating countryside and wooded valleys. The perfect retreat for a relaxing holiday. We keep ponies, sheep, ducks, hens and a pig called Polly. Golf at St Mellion, 10 mins. away. Close to sea and moors. 2 bathrooms, log fire, CH, phone, microwave, dishwasher and games room. Linen/electricity inclusive. Art classes available. Open May–Oct.

---

44 **Glynn Barton Farm Cottages,** Glynn Barton, Cardinham, Bodmin, Cornwall PL30 4AX

Diana Mindel
☎/Fax 01208 821375
SC From £150–£590
Sleeps 2/6
🐕 ♿ 🎾 ◎
♟♟♟♟ *Commended*

Whatever the season, make the most of our comfortable cottages – four poster, wood beams and traditional cast iron stove. From your cottage enjoy beautiful views and take woodland or farmland walks. Play tennis or relax by heated pool in walled 'Mediterranean' atmosphere. Central for golf, beaches, cycling, fishing, horseriding and gardens. Open all year.
E-mail: tony@tmindel.freeserve.co.uk

---

45 **Katie's Cottage,** Bocaddon, Lanreath, Looe, Cornwall PL13 2PG

Mrs Alison Maiklem
☎/Fax 01503 220192
SC From £150–£430
Sleeps 4
↟ 🐕 ⅄
♟♟♟♟ *Highly Commended*

A warm welcome awaits you all the year round at this tastefully converted barn situated in peaceful countryside, on our 350-acre dairy farm. Central heating, fully equipped kitchen, wheelchair access, close parking. Six miles from fishing villages and beaches. Central for wonderful gardens, walks and children's entertainments. Open all year. See colour ad on page 47.
E-mail: bocaddon@aol.com

---

46 **Leigh Manor Farm Cottages,** Week St Mary, Holsworthy, Devon EX22 6XB

Michael & Annie Bucknell
☎ 01288 341421
Fax 01288 341100
SC From £190–£950
Sleeps 2–8
🐕 🎠 ⛶ ♿ ♟ 🎾 ◎
♟♟♟♟ – ♟♟♟♟♟
Highly Commended

For your perfect relaxing holiday… a beautiful 16th century manor house and courtyard barns peacefully set down a private lane, yet close to the spectacular Cornish coast. Rambling gardens, farm walks, wildlife, coarse fishing, safe play areas, animals to pet, pony-trap rides, games room, barbecue. Properties luxuriously equipped including four-poster bed, Aga, woodburner, CH. All linen, towels and fuel included. Brochure. Open all year.
E-mail: michael.bucknell@virgin.net

---

47 **Lodge Barton Farm,** Liskeard, Cornwall PL14 4JX

Rosanne Hodin
☎/Fax 01579 344432
SC From £120–£400
Sleeps 2/5 + cot
🐕 🎠 ⛶ ♿ 🎾
♟♟♟♟ *Commended*

Lodge Barton is set in a beautiful river valley flanked by woodland. We keep goats and also have ducks, hens and geese. Everyone can help collecting eggs and feeding. Our character cottages are luxuriously equipped including heating, woodburners, video, linen, laundry room, private gardens and playground. We are close to sea, moors, sailing, windsurfing, riding, fishing, golf. Open all year.
E-mail: lodgebart@aol.com

---

48 **Lower Dutson Farm,** Launceston, Cornwall PL15 9SP

Mrs Kathryn Broad
☎/Fax 01566 776456
SC From £120–£400
Sleeps 6
🐕 🎠 ⛶ 🎾
♟♟♟♟ *Commended*

A warm welcome awaits you at our 17th century farmhouse, centrally situated for Devon, Cornwall, Dartmoor and Bodmin Moors. Wander across to the River Tamar or coarse lake (good fishing available). Fully equipped kitchen, microwave, washing machine, tumble dryer, electric cooker, colour TV, storage heaters, two bathrooms. Open all year.

---

49 **Lower Trengale Farm,** Liskeard, Cornwall PL14 6HF

Louise Kidd
☎ 01579 321019
Fax 01579 321432
SC From £140–£495
Sleep 4–6
🐕 🎠 ♿ ◎
♟♟♟♟ *Highly Commended*

A small farm, set in beautiful countryside, offering three comfortable and well equipped cottages with woodburners, videos and dishwashers. Super for children with playground and games room. Lovely views from the garden. Ideally located for beaches, moors, golfing, fishing and walking. All linen, cots, highchairs supplied. Open all year. E-mail: lkidd@eurobell.co.uk

---

Manuels Farm, Quintrell Downs, Newquay, Cornwall TR8 4NY　㉑

Alan & Jean Wilson
☎/Fax 01637 873577
[SC] From £100–£575
Sleeps 2/5 + cot
🐕🐎🐴♨🛁⚓
🏇🏇🏇 *Commended*

Imagine a family holiday close to Newquay's magnificent beaches but tucked away in your own quiet valley. Secluded from the crowd but perfectly placed for touring, walking and riding. Your own character cottage in the country, on the farm, with gardens, flowers, pets and farm animals around you. The children will enjoy the calves, tractor and ponies while you relax. Electricity and linen included. Short breaks available. Open all year.

Old Newham Farm, Otterham, Camelford, Cornwall PL32 9SR　㊿

Mrs Mary Purdue
☎ 01840 230470
Fax 01840 230303
[SC] From £120–£495
Sleeps 2–4
🐕🐎🐈♨🛁♨
🏇🏇🏇🏇 *Commended*

Three individual stone and slate cottages around an old farmyard dating back to medieval times, at the end of a quiet country lane. Our 30-acre farm is managed in a traditional way with cattle, sheep and other small animals for the children. Here you can find the peace of the Cornish countryside yet be only 3 miles from the most spectacular coastline in the area. Cottages with character, open fire, CH. Open all year.

Polmina, Bosigran Farm, Pendeen, Penzance TR20 8YX　㊿

Liz Scambler
☎/Fax 01736 796940
[SC] From £190–£380
Sleeps 2
✂🛁♨
🏇🏇🏇 *Highly Commended*

Explore the rugged, beautiful coastline of West Penwith where wild Atlantic meets heather-covered moor. Stay in our former hayloft, stylishly converted into studio-type living for two. Explore our organic farm, wander down to the cove, maybe watch the seals, listen to the nightjar hiding in the hills. Open all year.
E-mail: bosigran@bigfoot.com

Poltarrow Farm, St Mewan, St Austell, Cornwall PL26 7DR　㉕

Judith Nancarrow
☎/Fax 01726 67111
[SC] From £100–£675
Sleeps 2/6
🧍🐎🐕🚲🍴♨🛁⚓
🏇🏇🏇🏇 *Up to Highly Commended*

There can be no more perfect way to discover Cornwall than to stay in a cottage with rustic charm and the comforts of a modern home. Add to that: an indoor pool for that touch of luxury; wheelchair access; a few minutes' drive to beaches and gardens (particularly Heligan); farm trail, fishing and pets; short breaks. Open all year.

Tredethick Farm Cottages, Little Bakes, Tredethick, Lostwithiel, Cornwall PL22 0LE　㊼

Tim & Nicky Reed
☎/Fax 01208 873618
[SC] From £145–£680
Sleeps 2–6
🐕🐎✂🚲🍴♨🛁⚓🎾🏇
🏇🏇🏇🏇 *Highly Commended*

Winner of the 1999 West Country Best Self Catering Holiday of the Year. Need we say more!
E-mail: tredethick@zetnet.co.uk

Tredinnick Farm, Duloe, Liskeard, Cornwall PL14 4PJ　㊾

Mrs Angela Barrett
☎ 01503 262997
Fax 01503 265554
[SC] From £125–£735
Sleeps 2/10 (+ cot)
🐕🛁⚓
🏇🏇🏇🏇 *Highly Commended*

Enjoy a warm welcome at our spacious farmhouse set in the beautiful rolling countryside. The two wings are decorated to a high standard and are fully equipped. In your own secluded garden you can easily unwind and get away from it all, or within a few miles discover the delights of Looe and the historic fishing village of Polperro. Open all year.

---

54   **Tregevis Farm,** St Martin, Helston, Cornwall TR12 6DN

Julie Bray
☎/Fax 01326 231265
🆂🅲 From £220–£490
Sleeps 6
🌣 ⚥ 🎠
🐾🐾🐾 *Highly Commended*

Come and relax at Tregevis, a working dairy farm in the picturesque Helford River area, just ½ mile from the little village of St. Martin and 5 miles from sandy beaches. The accommodation is a self-contained, spacious part of the farmhouse, very comfortable, well equipped and with a games room. The large lawn area with swings will prove popular with children, as will our farm animals. Open Mar–Oct.

---

55   **Trelagossick Farm,** Ruan High Lanes, Truro, Cornwall TR2 5JU

Mrs Rachel Carbis
☎ 01872 501338
🆂🅲 From £130–£350
Sleeps 3/6 + cot
🌣 ⚥ 🐎 🐾 ♥ 🎠
Applied

Welcome to Trelagossick, a 190-acre dairy farm on the Roseland Peninsula. Two individual self-contained wings of the 17th century farmhouse with one and three bedrooms. Linen and electricity included. Explore the South Coast Footpath and sandy beaches just 3 miles away. Peaceful countryside views. Flexible breaks. Brochure available. Open all year. *Associate.*

---

16   **Treleaven Farm Cottages,** Treleaven Farm, Mevagissey, Cornwall PL26 6RZ

Mrs Linda Hennah
☎/Fax 01726 843558
🆂🅲 From £190–£600
Sleep 4–6
🐎 🎠 ◉
🐾🐾🐾 *Highly Commended*

Surrounded by rambling countryside, wildlife and flowers, the farm is only 8 minutes' walk from the centre of Mevagissey. Each cottage has luxury pine fitted kitchen with dishwasher, microwave, fridge/freezer and cooker. Lovely bathroom with shower, cosy lounge with TV, video and hi-fi. Some en suite bedrooms. CH included. Linen and electricity inclusive. Laundry room. Ample parking. Games barn. Next to Heligan Gardens and central for touring. Open all year.

---

56   **Tremadart Farm,** Duloe, Liskeard, Cornwall PL14 4PE

Evelyn Julian
☎/Fax 01503 262855
🆂🅲 From £200–£725
Sleeps 2–12
🐎 🍴 ◉
🐾🐾🐾 *Commended*

We welcome you to our Victorian farmhouse set in a large, secluded garden and within walking distance of local shop and pub which serves excellent food. Enjoy a working farm set in beautiful countryside with woodland paths, riverside walks and close to Looe for beaches, walking, cycling, horse riding and fishing. Open all year.

---

57   **Trengove Farm,** Cot Road, Illogan, Redruth, Cornwall TR16 4PU

Mrs Lindsey Richards
☎ 01209 843008
Fax 01209 843682
🆂🅲 From £130–£470
Sleeps 2–6/7
🌣 🏃 🍴 🎠 ◉
🐾🐾🐾 *Up to Highly Commended*

A courtyard of charming, traditional cottages, all individually furnished. Stroll gently down through the woods to Portreath, a sandy beach, popular with families and surfers. Drive along the spectacular coast to the golden beaches of St Ives Bay. An ideal location for walking, swimming, touring or just switching off! Open all year. E-mail: richards@trengovefarm.freeserve.co.uk

---

58   **Trevadlock Farm Cottages,** Trevadlock Farm, Trevadlock, Congdon's Shop, Launceston, Cornwall PL15 7PW

Mrs Barbara Sleep
☎/Fax 01566 782239
🆂🅲 From £120–£560
Sleeps 3/6
🌣 ⚥ 🍴 🎠 ◉
🐾🐾🐾🐾 *Highly Commended*

A truly Cornish welcome awaits you at Trevadlock Farm, offering a wonderful retreat, in one of our beautifully restored cottages. Log fires, dishwasher, TV/video and much more. Ideally situated for both coasts, walk the moors, visit Jamaica Inn, explore the many gardens, or golf at St Mellion – Trevadlock is perfectly placed. Open all year. E-mail: trevadlockfarm@compuserve.com

Trevalgan Farm, St Ives, Cornwall TR26 3BJ　　59

Jean Osborne
☎/Fax 01736 796433
⑤ From £180–£460
Sleeps 2/6
ঽ⊼⊞⋆∿♨⊛
ℓℓℓℓ *Commended*

Trevalgan is a coastal stock-rearing farm surrounded by magnificent scenery, just 2 miles from St Ives. Enjoy walking our farm trail to the cliffs overlooking the sea, a paradise for nature lovers. Traditional granite barns have been carefully converted into 7 lovely holiday homes around an attractive courtyard. Land's End, St Michael's Mount, Mousehole and Lamorna within easy reach by car. Open all year.

Trevathan Farm, St Endellion, Port Isaac, Cornwall PL29 3TT　　60

Jo Symons
☎/Fax 01208 880248
⑤ From £150–£960
Sleeps 2–12
ঽ⊼♨⊛
ℓℓℓℓℓ – ℓℓℓℓℓ
Highly Commended

Enjoy a taste of country life on our family-run working farm. Beautiful cottages with panoramic views, own gardens and barbecues. Friendly animals, tennis and volleyball courts, games room, children's play area. Sandy beaches, sailing, surfing, golf and riding within 3 miles. Also large period house sleeping 12, golf and moors 2 miles, sea 5 miles. Open all year.

Trevissick Manor, Trevissick Farm, Trenarren, St Austell, Cornwall PL26 6BQ　　61

Anita Treleaven
☎/Fax 01726 72954
⑤ From £140–£400
Sleeps 2–4 + cot
ঽ⊼♨⋆
ℓℓℓℓ *Commended*

The east wing of the manor farmhouse on our coastal mixed farm is situated between St Austell and Mevagissey Bays. Spectacular views across the gardens down the valley to the sea. Ideal for a couple or family. Meet the animals, view the milking, play tennis or take the farm trial to Hallane Cove. Near sandy beaches, sailing, watersports, cycling, 18-hole golf. Heligan Gardens 5–10 mins. Open all year.

Trevorrick Farm, St Issey, Wadebridge, Cornwall PL27 7QH　　62

Alice & Bryan Mealing
☎ 01841 540574
⑤ From £169–£599
Sleeps 2–6
⋏ঽ⊼⊞♨⋆⊛
ℓ – ℓℓℓℓ *Up to*
Highly Commended

Come and stay in our luxury stone cottages. Heated indoor swimming pool, children's play area, full-sized snooker, pool table and table tennis. Laundry and pay phone. Safe sandy beaches and numerous attractions nearby, also surfing beaches. Footpath from front door to Padstow, Camel Trail, Saints Way and Coastal Path. Open all year. *Associate.*

Trewalla Farm Cottages, Trewalla Farm, Minions, Liskeard, Cornwall PL14 6ED　　63

Fiona Cotter
☎/Fax 01579 342385
⑤ From £220–£435
Sleeps 3/4 (+ cot)
ঽ⊼∿
ℓℓℓ *Commended*

Our small, traditionally-run farm on Bodmin Moor has rare breed pigs, sheep, hens and geese. All free-range and very friendly. Our three cottages are beautifully furnished and very well equipped. Their moorland setting offers perfect peace, wonderful views, ideal walking country and a good base for exploring – if you can tear yourself away! Linen and electricity included. Open Mar–Dec and New Year.

Trewellard Manor Farm Cottages, Pendeen, Penzance, Cornwall TR19 7SU　　38

Mrs Marion Bailey
☎/Fax 01736 788526
⑤ From £165–£435
Sleeps 4/5
ঽ⊼♨⊛
ℓℓℓℓ *Commended*

In the heart of Poldark Country, between Land's End and St Ives, attractive stone cottages converted from old stables. Situated across courtyard from owner's farmhouse and swimming pool (June–Sept). On edge of village within easy reach of beaches and coast path. Special winter short breaks. Open all year.

64 **Trewithen Country Lodges,** Trewithen Farm, Laneast, Launceston, Cornwall PL15 8PW

Mrs Margaret Colwill
☎/Fax 01566 86343
SC From £200–£415
Sleeps 4 + cot
🛏 ⛓ ◉
♟ ♟ ♟ ♟ Commended

Come down to our Cornish farm and stay,
Where the hedgerows are wonderful, changing each day,
Two Scandinavian lodges, beautifully designed,
Away from the noise, relax and unwind,
Tastefully furnished and cosy as pie,
Fun for the family and jacuzzi to try,
Panoramic views of the surrounding moors,
Enjoy animals and walks in the great outdoors.

65 **West Kellow Farm,** Lansallos, Looe, Cornwall PL13 2QL

Mrs E Julian
☎/Fax 01503 262855
SC From £200–£650
Sleeps 2–10
🛏 🍴 ◉
♟ ♟ ♟ ♟ Up to Highly
Commended

Come and relax with your family and friends in this
spacious Victorian farmhouse. Enjoy the peace and quiet
amidst beautiful countryside, only one mile from
picturesque Polperro. Also two individually designed
character cottages with private gardens. Games room.
Country and coastal walks, horse riding, cycling, golf and
fishing close by. Open all year.

40 **Wheatley Farm Cottages,** Maxworthy, Launceston, Cornwall PL15 8LY

Valerie Griffin
☎/Fax 01566 781232
SC From £100–£575
Sleep 4/7
🛏 ⛓ 🐴 🍴 🐎 ◉
♟ ♟ ♟ ♟ Highly
Commended

Two idyllic stone-built cottages, bursting with charm and
special atmosphere, each set in its own grounds. Slate
floors, rugs, beams, granite lintels, woodburners and much
more await you at Wheatley, a working farm. Every
comfort for the perfect holiday. Nearby are the sandy
beaches of the spectacular Cornish coast. Children's play
area, pony rides, farm animals to visit. Open all year.
E-mail: wheatleyfrm@compuserve.com

CONFIRM BOOKINGS

Disappointments can arise from misunderstandings over the telephone.
Please write to confirm your booking.

USE THE INDEX

FARM HOLIDAY
BUREAU

The comprehensive Index shows which farms offer access to disabled visitors;
caravanning/camping facilities; the chance to participate on a working farm;
stabling/grazing for visiting horses; en suite rooms; a welcome to business people;
acceptance of *Stay on a Farm* gift tokens.

Wales

Farm entries in this section are listed under those tourism areas shown in green on the key map. The index below the map gives the appropriate page numbers. You will see that we have listed the tourism areas geographically so that you can turn more easily to find farms in neighbouring tourism areas.

At the start of each tourism area section is a detailed map with numbered symbols indicating the location of each farm. Different symbols denote different types of accommodation; see the key below each tourism area map. Farm entries are listed alphabetically under type of accommodation. Some farms offer more than one type of accommodation and therefore have more than one entry.

❶ *The Isle of Anglesey*
❷ *Snowdonia – Mountains & Coast*
❸ *The North Wales Coast & Borderlands*
❹ *Ceredigion, Cardigan Bay*
❺ *Mid Wales, Lakes & Mountains*
❻ *Pembrokeshire*
❼ *Carmarthenshire*
❽ *Wye Valley & Vale of Usk*
❾ *Valleys of South Wales*
❿ *Swansea Bay*
⓫ *Cardiff & Glamorgan Heritage Coast*

KEY MAP TO WALES

The Isle of Anglesey

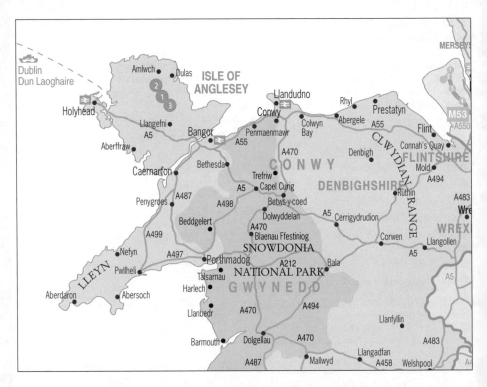

Anglesey, known as the 'Mother of Wales', is a largely agricultural island. The signs are everywhere, from the inland cornfields to the coastal pastures, and from the whitewashed cottages of the smallholdings to the 'home farms' of the great country estates. Anglesey's history is written in the stone of its prehistoric burial chambers and tall standing stones, Roman walls, the little churches and chapels, and the ramparts of Beaumaris Castle which serve as a reminder of the invaders from across the border. Holiday makers will find that the island's lovely coast – much of it an Area of Outstanding Natural Beauty – includes some of Europe's most thrilling beaches.

If you would like help in finding suitable farm accommodation, turn to the full listing of FHB Groups on pages 392 to 395 to find appropriate contact details for this area.

Bed and Breakfast
(and evening meal)

Drws-y-Coed, Llannerch-y-medd, Isle of Anglesey LL71 8AD   ①

Mrs Jane Bown
☎/Fax **01248 470473**
BB **From £21.50–£23.50**
Sleeps 6

★★★★
FARM

Enjoy excellent hospitality, food and tranquil surroundings with panoramic views of Snowdonia. Centrally situated to explore Anglesey's coastline and attractions. 25 minutes to Holyhead Port. Comfortable en suite bedrooms with all facilities. Inviting spacious lounge with log-fire. Interesting historical farmstead and private walks on a 550-acre mixed farm. Games room. WTB Farmhouse Award, Farm Holiday Guide Diploma Award. Open all year except Christmas.

Llwydiarth Fawr, Llanerchymedd, Isle of Anglesey LL71 8DF   ②

Mrs Margaret Hughes
☎ **01248 470321/470540**
BB **£25**
Sleeps 6
Applied

Secluded Georgian mansion set in 850 acres of woodland and farmland. Ideal touring base for island's coastline, Snowdonia and North Wales coast. Nearby is Llyn Alaw for trout fishing. Reputation for excellent food using farm and local produce. En suite bedrooms. TV, CH, log fires. Walks and private fishing. Winner of the BBC 'Welsh Farm housewife of the Year' competition. Member of Taste of Wales. Warmest Welcome Award 1993. Closed Christmas.

Mynydd Mwyn Mawr, Llannerch-y-Medd, Ynys Môn, Isle of Anglesey LL71 7AG   ③

Sarah Astley
☎ **01248 470276**
BB **From £20**
Sleeps 6

★★★
FARM

Peacefully situated in central Anglesey, Mynydd Mwyn Mawr is 'off the beaten track', an ideal place to get away from it all. Our farmhouse is set in 220 acres where we grow fodder crops and breed Farm Assured Welsh beef and lamb. Comfortable accommodation with en suite facilities and family suite, spacious centrally heated rooms with colour TV and usual facilities. A warm welcome is assured at our busy working farm. Open all year.
E-mail: sarahastley@zetnet.co.uk

NO ANSWER?
Farmers are mostly out and about during the day.
Try to telephone before 9.30am or after 4pm.

USE THE INDEX

FARM HOLIDAY
BUREAU

The comprehensive Index shows which farms offer access to disabled visitors; caravanning/camping facilities; the chance to participate on a working farm; stabling/grazing for visiting horses; en suite rooms; a welcome to business people; acceptance of *Stay on a Farm* gift tokens.

Snowdonia – Mountains & Coast

In & around Snowdonia National Park

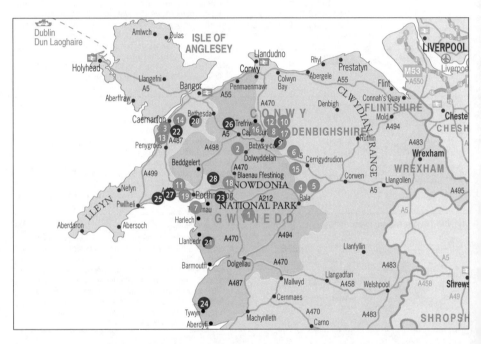

Key

1 Bed & Breakfast

1 Self-Catering

1 B&B and SC

1 Camping Barns

⚠ Camping & Caravanning

Snowdonia, with its breathtaking scenery, is renowned as one of Britain's most beautiful National Parks. There is so much to see and do, and in such a dramatic setting. Now so accessible, Snowdonia is a perfect location for holidays and short breaks in any season. Relax on our many beaches; walk or ride up Mount Snowdon; climb Cader Idris or the Cnicht (known as the Welsh Matterhorn); ride the seven Great Little Trains of Wales; visit a Victorian mine; tour historic castles and numerous National Trust properties with their magnificent gardens; enjoy exciting water sports, riding, golf, bird watching, forests and coastal walks. Above all, enjoy the peace, tranquillity and friendliness of our unique culture in this the heartland of the Welsh language.

If you would like help in finding suitable farm accommodation, turn to the full listing of FHB Groups on pages 392 to 395 to find appropriate contact details for this area.

Bed and Breakfast
(and evening meal)

Bryn Celynog Farm, Cwm Prysor, Trawsfynydd, Gwynedd LL41 4TR   (1)

Mrs G E Hughes
☎/**Fax 01766 540378**
[BB] **From £19–£21**
Sleeps 6
⛅ 🐏 ⅍ ☂ 🎠 🛍 ◉
★★★
FARM

Relax in peaceful setting with splendid views of Cwmprysor Valley, on 700-acre working beef and sheep farm 3 miles from Trawsfynydd village. Spacious twin, double and family bedrooms, one en suite, all with washbasins, beverage trays. Guests' lounge with colour TV, log fire. Reputation for excellent food and friendliness. Welsh speaking. WTB Farmhouse Award. Open all year except Christmas.

Bryn Tirion Farm, Dolwyddelan, Betws-y-Coed, Conwy LL25 0JD   (2)

Mrs Caroline Price
☎ **01690 750366**
[BB] **From £17–£23**
Sleeps 6
⛅ ⅍ ⋏ 🚐 🛍 🎠
★
FARM

A conveniently located working farm adjacent to the A470 road at the foot of the ancient Dolwyddelan Castle. The farm is within ¾ mile of the tranquil village with its usual rural amenities in the renowned picturesque Lledr Valley. Open all year.

Cae'r Efail Farm, Llanfaglan, Caernarfon, Gwynedd LL54 5RE   (3)

Mrs Mari Williams
☎ **01286 676226/672824**
Fax 01286 676226
[BB] **From £20–£25**
EM From £12
Sleeps 4
⛅ 🐏 🛍 🎠 ◉
★★★★
FARM

Modernised farmhouse enjoying perfect tranquillity and seclusion with splendid views of Snowdonia and the Menai Straits. Central for Snowdonia, Isle of Anglesey, Llŷn Peninsula and all attractions of North Wales. Caernarfon only 2 miles. Homely atmosphere and warm welcome. Good home cooking. En suite bedrooms with colour TV, hairdryer and tea/coffee facilities. TV/video lounge and separate dining room. WTB Farmhouse Award. Open Easter–Oct.

Cwm Hwylfod, Cefn-Ddwysarn, Bala, Gwynedd LL23 7LN   (4)

Joan Best
☎/**Fax 01678 530310**
[BB] **From £16–£18**
Sleeps 6
⛅ 🎠 🛍 🎠 ◉
★★★
FARM

Set in hills near Bala, our 400-year-old farmhouse is warm and welcoming. The views are spectacular. Animals abound and everyone, especially children, can take part in farm activities. Bedrooms have washbasins and tea making facilities. The guest lounge has TV, books and games. Full central heating. All diets catered for. Open all year except Christmas Day.

Erw Feurig Farm, Cefn-Ddwysarn, Bala, Gwynedd LL23 7LL   (5)

Glenys Jones
☎/**Fax 01678 530262**
[BB] **From £17–£20**
Sleeps 9
⛅ ⅍ ☂ ◉
★★★
FARM

Facing the Berwyn Mountains, Erw Feurig is a guesthouse set on the 200-acre family farm, 3½ miles from Bala. The old farm cottage has been extended to provide modern, comfortable accommodation in family, double and twin rooms, some en suite. All bedrooms have heating, colour TV and tea/coffee. Separate guests' dining room and lounge. Good home cooking using local produce. Coarse fishing on the farm. WTB Farmhouse Award. Open all year except Christmas.

6 **Frongoch Farm,** Frongoch, Bala, Gwynedd LL23 7NT

Carys Davies
☎/Fax 01678 520483
🅱 From £18–£20
Sleeps 6
🐾 ⅟ ⚘ 🎋 ⓦ
Applied

Enjoy a relaxed, friendly stay in our old historic farmhouse. Traditionally furnished, log fires, oak beams. All bedrooms have en suite/private facilities, TV, radio, tea/coffee. Perfect for unwinding or exploring Snowdonia and its magnificent countryside. Walks, fishing, water sports, leisure centre, all close by. Good home cooking. WTB Farmhouse Award. Brochure. Open all year except Christmas.

7 **Gwrach Ynys,** Talsarnau, Nr Harlech, Gwynedd LL47 6TS

Mrs Deborah Williams
☎ 01766 780742
Fax 01766 781199
🅱 From £22–£25
Sleeps 15
🐾(3) ⓔ ⅟ 🏠 ⓦ
★★★★
COUNTRY HOUSE

Relax in the peace and comfort of our secluded Edwardian House. Conveniently located, close to sea and mountains with many tourist attractions nearby. Ideal golfing, rambling, birdwatching area. En suite bedrooms, individually decorated and furnished to a high standard. Two comfortable guest lounges and a separate dining room. WTB Farmhouse Award. AA Selected. Open Mar–Oct.

8 **Hendre Wen Farm,** Betws Road, Llanrwst, Conwy LL26 0PY

Grace Ann Roberts
☎ 01690 710339
🅱 From £16–£18
Sleeps 6
🐾(5) 🐕 ⅟ 🅔 🏠 🎋
★★★
FARM

Hendre Wen farmhouse dates back to 1600 and has retained its character with oak beams, floor and doors. Even the oak partitions between bedrooms are original. You will find a traditional Welsh welcome, where the proprietors really take pride in looking after their guests. Nothing is too much trouble, which is why so many people return every year. Open Mar–Nov.

9 **Llannerch Goch,** Capel Garmon, Betws-y-Coed, Conwy LL26 0RL

Eirian Ifan
☎ 01690 710261
🅱 From £18–£22
Sleeps 6
🐾 🏠
★★★★
COUNTRY HOUSE

This charming 17th century former rectory, now a smallholding, is 2 miles from the picturesque village of Betws-y-Coed, offering superb views of the Snowdonia mountain range. Perfectly located for Bodnant Gardens, Portmeirion, Slate Caverns and numerous NT properties. All bedrooms are en suite with beverage facilities and TV. Relax in our garden with water pump and ponds. Pub/restaurant 400 yards. Pool room. Brochure. Open all year.

10 **Llwyn Goronwy,** Carmel, Llanrwst, Conwy LL26 0PD

Mrs Margaret Evans
☎ 01492 640335
🅱 From £18
Sleeps 4
🐾 🐎 ⅟ 🏠 🎋
★★★
FARM

Award-winning dairy and sheep family farm commanding spectacular views of the Snowdonia range. Llwyn Goronwy is situated high above the Conwy Valley within easy reach of the North Wales coast and Snowdonia. The renovated farmhouse combines modern comforts with a taste of the past. Home cooking and Welsh welcome. Open Apr–Oct.

11 **Llwyn Mafon Isaf,** Criccieth, Gwynedd LL52 0RE

Mrs Buddug Anwyl Jones
☎ 01766 530618
🅱 From £18–£20
Sleeps 6
🐾 🐓 🅐 ⚑ 🏠 🎋
★★★
FARM

Traditional 17th century farmhouse, sympathetically modernised and offering superb views of Cardigan Bay and the Snowdonia mountain range. Two double en suite bedrooms, a spacious single bedroom and 1 twin bedroom, both with private bathroom. Relax in the comfortable beamed lounge with colour TV and enjoy a hearty breakfast on separate tables in the dining room. Please ring for directions. Open Apr–Oct.

Nant-y-Glyn Isaf, Tafarn-y-Fedw, Llanrwst, Conwy LL26 0NN   (12)

Mai Evans
☎/Fax 01492 640327
[BB] From £19.50–£20
Sleeps 6
ɔ(8) ✄ ■ ✿
★★★
FARM

Beautiful old stone farmhouse on a working beef and sheep farm, set in a lovely garden with spectacular views of Snowdonia. Spacious, comfortable rooms. The dining room is in the conservatory, with opportunity to watch the sheep and cattle in the fields nearby. There is a badger sett on the farm and plenty of walks. Open all year.

Pengwern, Saron, Llanwnda, Caernarfon, Gwynedd LL54 5UH   (13)

G & J Lloyd Rowlands
☎/Fax 01286 831500
Mobile 0378 411780
[BB] From £20–£25
EM From £12.50
Sleeps 6
ɔ ✄ [£] ■ ✿ ✽ ●
★★★★
FARM

Charming, spacious farmhouse of character, situated between mountains and sea. Unobstructed views of Snowdonia. Well appointed bedrooms, all with en suite bathrooms. Set in 130 acres of land which runs down to Foryd Bay. Jane has a cookery diploma and provides the excellent meals with farmhouse fresh food, including home-produced beef and lamb. Excellent access. Open Feb–Nov. E-mail: jhjgr@enterprise.net

---

Plas Tirion Farm, Llanrug, Caernarfon, Gwynedd LL55 4PY   (14)

C H Mackinnon
☎/Fax 01286 673190
[BB] From £20–£25
EM From £13
Sleeps 6
ɔ ●

★★★
FARM

Peacefully located in 300 acres of lowland pastures, commanding panoramic views of Snowdonia and historic Caernarfon. Ideally situated for touring North Wales. Traditional stone farmhouse, offering guests warm and comfortable accommodation. All en suite bedrooms with beverage facilities and TV. Mid-week breaks Apr–May and Sept–Oct. Open Apr–Oct.

Rhydydefaid Farm, Frongoch, Bala, Gwynedd LL23 7NT   (15)

Olwen Davies
☎/Fax 01678 520456
[BB] From £17.50–£18.50
Sleeps 6
ɔ ✝ ✄ ■ ☙ ✿ ●
★★★
FARM

A true Welsh welcome awaits you at our traditional Welsh stone farmhouse. 3 miles from Bala in secluded position. 100-acre working farm. Oak beamed lounge with inglenook fireplace. Three comfortable bedrooms with CH, 1 with exposed beams and trusses, 2 en suite. All with tea/coffee-making facilities. Ideal for touring Snowdonia. Open all year except Christmas.

Tan-yr-Eglwys Farm, Llanrhychwyn, Trefriw, Llanrwst, North Wales LL27 0YJ   (16)

Mrs M Metcalfe
☎/Fax 01492 640547
[BB] From £16–£20
EM From £10
Sleeps 6
ɔ(8) ✝ ✄ ✿
★★★
FARM

Tan-yr-Eglwys is a modernised farmhouse. All rooms have H&C and tea/coffee-making facilities. Llanrhychwyn is a small hamlet above the Conwy Valley between Trefriw and Llanrwst, an ideal haven for country lovers, hill walkers and bird watchers. A homely welcome and wholesome home cooking are assured. Packed lunches available with pleasure. Open Mar–Oct.

Tyddyn Du, Nant-y-Rhiw, Llanrwst, Conwy LL26 0TG   (17)

Mrs Menna Williams
☎ 01492 640189
[BB] From £17–£20
Sleeps 4
ɔ ✄ ■
★★
FARM

Tyddyn Du is a traditional farmhouse offering a homely Welsh welcome. It has oak doors and deep windowsills, evoking a sense of the past. The rooms have recently been decorated. Substantial garden where you can sit and enjoy spectacular views of the Snowdonia Range. The farm itself is a busy one, keeping Welsh Black Cattle and Welsh Mountain Sheep. Within 5 miles of Betws-y-Coed and attractions and 20 minutes from coast. Open Apr–Nov.

18 Tyddyn Du Farm, Gellilydan, Ffestiniog, nr Porthmadog, Gwynedd LL41 4RB

Paula Williams
☎/Fax 01766 590281
BB From £20–£28
EM From £13
Sleeps 8
🐕🐎🕺🎺🛄🎿☕
★★★★
FARM

Enchanting 400 year-old farmhouse on our working sheep farm, set amidst spectacular scenery in superb central Snowdonia location. A specially relaxing farm holiday – private luxury barn and stable suites in unique position with patio window garden, jacuzzi bath and shower, fridge and microwave. Delicious farmhouse cuisine. Weekly dinner B&B from £190-£260. Open all year (no meals Christmas Day). E-mail: tyddyndufarm@btinternet.com

19 Tyddyn Iolyn, Pentrefelin, Nr Criccieth, Gwynedd LL52 0RB

Charlotte Lowe
☎/Fax 01766 522509
BB From £20–£30
EM From £14
Sleeps 12
🐕🐎🕺🐎🛄🎿☕
★★★
FARM

Lovingly restored, secluded 16th century oak-beamed farmhouse, set in idyllic farmland. Breathtaking views of Snowdonia and coastline. Perfect base for exploring Portmeirion, Snowdonia, Llŷn Peninsula. Five en suites (including 4-poster) and luxury stables, all with beverage trays. Traditional cooking/vegetarian, candlelit dinners, homemade jams. Abundance of books/local information. Cats, chickens, ponies. Farm Tourism Award. AA 3 diamonds. Closed Christmas Day. E-mail: tiol@nildram.co.uk

20 Ty-Mawr Farm, Llanddeiniolen, Caernarfon, Gwynedd LL55 3AD

Mrs Jane Llewelyn Pierce
☎/Fax 01248 670147
BB From £16–£25
EM From £12.50
Sleeps 6
🐕🛄☕
★★★
FARM

Charming, warm country farmhouse on 100-acre farm with superb views of Snowdonia mountain range. Ideal for touring North Wales and Anglesey. Caernarfon only 5 miles. All rooms have en suite bathrooms, TV and tea and coffee facilities. Two lounges with wood fires and a separate dining room. Good home cooking. Ample parking area. Open all year. E-mail: jane@tymawrfarm.freeserve.co.uk

21 Ystumgwern Hall Farm, Dyffryn Ardudwy, Gwynedd LL44 2DD

Jane E Williams
☎ 01341 247249
Fax 01341 247171
BB From £23–£25
Sleeps 16
🐕🐎🕺🎺🛄🎿☕
★★★★
FARM

A warm Welsh welcome awaits you at Ystumgwern where the mountains of Snowdonia slope down to the sea. The traditional 16th century farmhouse has a wealth of antiques and heavy oak timbers creating a luxurious homely atmosphere. Each bedroom is charmingly decorated with many extras including the luxury of a well-equipped kitchen and its own lounge with colour TV and video. Farmhouse Award. Colour brochure sent with pleasure. Open all year.

Self-Catering

22 Bryn Beddau, Bontnewydd, Caernarfon, Gwynedd LL54 7YE

Eleri Carrog
☎ 01286 830117/673795
Fax 01286 675664
SC From £120–£375
Sleeps 5
🐕🐎🕺🛄🎺🎿

Cosy stone–built stable cottage with views of mountains and sea. Excellent centre for walks, touring, lovely beaches and Snowdonia. Secluded setting yet only 3 miles from Caernarfon. Lovely gallery bedroom with graceful arch windows, twin room, cot. Ideal for families or that romantic break. Spacious beamed lounge of great character and many books. Patio, barbecue. "Croeso Cymreig". Open all year. E-mail: eleri.carrog@virgin.net

Caerwych Farmhouse, Llandecwyn, Talsarnau, Near Harlech, Gwynedd LL47 6YT (23)

Richard Williams-Ellis
☎ 01766 770913/771270
[sc] From £200–£450
Sleeps 9/10
🐕 🐎 🚶 ⚘
〰️〰️〰️

Secluded and set in marvellous scenic countryside with stupendous views to the sea. We are a typically traditional sheep farm but also breed horses and are replanting ancient woodlands. The stone farmhouse is old, large and handsome. Central heating throughout. Five bedrooms. Perfection for walkers. Accompanied trail riding in the mountains. Open all year.

Cartref, Ty Newydd, Llanegryn, Tywyn, Gwynedd LL36 9SR (24)

Ian & Catrin Rutherford
☎/Fax 01654 711726
[sc] From £120–£450
Sleeps 4
🐕 🚶 ⬛ ●
〰️〰️〰️〰️

An attractive cottage in the charming hamlet of Llanegryn nestling in the Dysynni Valley at the foot of Cader Idris in the Snowdonia National Park. Convenient for walking, swimming, golfing etc. and 2½ miles from the beach. Tastefully decorated, storage heaters, washing machine, private garden. Ideal for summer or winter breaks. Open all year. E-mail: cartref@corris-wales.co.uk

---

Chwilog Fawr, Chwilog, Pwllheli, Gwynedd LL53 6SW (25)

Catherine Jones
☎/Fax 01766 810506
[sc] From £125–£550
Sleeps 2/6
🐕 🚶 👤 🦽 ⬤ ⬛ 🎾 ●
〰️〰️〰️〰️ – 〰️〰️〰️〰️〰️

Enjoy the comforts of a home from home holiday with panoramic views of the Welsh coastline while sheep and cattle graze peacefully nearby. Walk along the footpath pass the fishing lake to the village or down to the beach (3 miles). Choice of accommodation to suit you – traditional Welsh farmhouse, chalets or caravans. Request our colour brochure today.

Dol-Llech, Capel Curig, Betws-y-Coed LL28 5SB (26)

Gwen Williams
☎ 01492 580391
[sc] From £150–£280
Sleeps 7
🐕 🚶 🦽 ⬛ 🎾
〰️〰️

Perfectly situated in the heart of Snowdonia National Park, ideal for outdoor activities and Plas-y-Brenin. Beams, slate fireplace, mountain views from all main rooms. Barbecue and picnic table. Shop 1 mile, pub and restaurant 1½ miles. Guests welcome to walk owners' 400-acre hill farm, fish and enjoy wildlife. Open all year.

Dwyfach Cottages, Pen-y-Bryn, Chwilog, Pwllheli, Gwynedd LL53 6SX (27)

Mrs Sulwen Edwards
☎ 01766 810208
Fax 01766 810064
[sc] From £100–£550
Sleeps 2–8
🐕 🚶 🦽 ⬛ 🎾 ●
〰️〰️〰️〰️〰️

We offer a choice of luxury accommodation for the discerning. Enjoy a memorable holiday in our tastefully restored farmhouse or bungalow. Both are set in their own garden with permanent barbecue and enjoy panoramic views of Cardigan Bay and Snowdonia. Here you will find peace and tranquillity yet be within easy reach of towns, beaches, tourist attractions, fishing and shooting, children's play area. Open all year.

Garth-y-Foel, Croesor, Penrhyndeudraeth, Gwynedd LL48 6SR (28)

Richard Williams-Ellis
☎ 01766 770913
[sc] From £200–£400
Sleeps 6
🐕 🚶 👤 🐎 🦽 ⚘
〰️

Absolute seclusion! And set in its own gentle, park-like, miniature valley with views to the sea in this otherwise wild mountain landscape – an unexpected, special, compelling place. Own wooded 90 acres include river with falls, pools and firewood for free. Oil, Aga and CH. 3/4 bedrooms (plus there's a large bell tent!). Be forewarned about the rough, narrow, gated and bridged access track. Open all year.

20 **Hafod & Hendre,** c/o Ty-Mawr Farm, Llanddeiniolen, Caernarfon, Gwynedd LL55 3AD

Mrs Jane Llewelyn Pierce
☎/Fax 01248 670147
⑤ From £100–£450
Sleeps 2/5
🐕 🐎 🛏 ⓐ
🐞 🐞 🐞 🐞 🐞

Two luxurious, self-catering converted granaries situated in a private courtyard on our working farm. Hafod sleeps three and Hendre five. Both are centrally heated and have wood burning stoves. CH, electricity, towels and full bedding included in price. Caernarfon 5 miles, Snowdon 4 miles. Brochures available. Open all year.
E-mail: jane@tymawrfarm.freeserve.co.uk

9 **The Old Coach House,** Capel Garmon, Betws-y-Coed, Conwy LL26 0RL

Eirian Ifan
☎ 01690 710261
⑤ From £185–£424
Sleeps 6
🐕 🐎 🛏
🐞 🐞 🐞 🐞 🐞

A luxurious 17th century oak-beamed coach house with many original features, full of character and atmosphere, lovingly restored by the owner. Perfect location, 2 miles from Betws-y-Coed, for touring and walking Snowdonia. French doors to kitchen/dining room, bathroom with shower, one double with canopy bed, one twin, sofa bed in upstairs lounge. Fully equipped with modern amenities, linen included. Barbecue, pool room. Brochure. Open all year.

21 **Ynys,** Ystumgwern, Dyffryn Ardudwy, Gwynedd LL44 2DD

Jane & John Williams
☎ 01341 247249
Fax 01341 247171
⑤ From £140–£690
Sleeps 2–8
🧍 🐎 🐕 🛏 🎾 ⓧ ⓐ
🐞 🐞 🐞 🐞 🐞

A taste of luxury with cosy, relaxed atmosphere. Situated between sea and mountains. 16th century farmhouse and barn conversions furnished and equipped to the highest standards. Oak beams, inglenook fireplace, gas CH. From one to four bedrooms, many en suite. Laundry room, play area. Barbecue, picnic table. Ample parking via private drive. Farmhouse Award. Warm welcome to all. Colour brochure available. Open all year.

FARM HOLIDAY
BUREAU

Please mention *Stay on a Farm* when booking

NO ANSWER?

Farmers are mostly out and about during the day.
Try to telephone before 9.30am or after 4pm.

FARM HOLIDAY
BUREAU

Our Internet address is
http://www.webscape.co.uk/farmaccom/

Snowdonia – Mountains & Coast

The Lleyn Peninsula

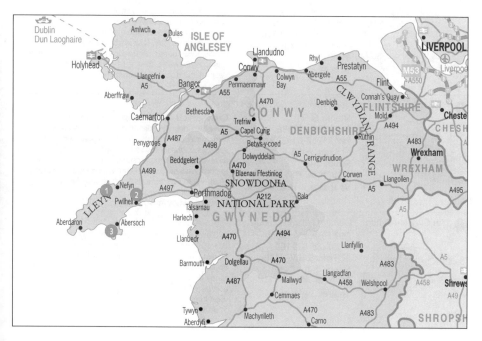

Key

 Bed & Breakfast

 Self-Catering

 B&B and SC

 Camping Barns

 Camping & Caravanning

The Lleyn promontory, 13 miles west of Snowdonia, is an environmentally sensitive area with a 50-mile heritage coast of rocky headlands and numerous sandy or shell-strewn bays. This is the habitat of seals, rare plants and birds, a haven for nature lovers where the Gulf Stream affords a temperate climate all year and Mediterranean plants flourish. It offers three Blue Flag beaches, many coastal and rural forest walks, sea, river and coarse fishing, water sports and sailing. You can relax on the beach viewing the mountainous hinterland or scale Snowdon, an hour's drive away. Castles, miniature railways, attractions and seven golf courses within 20 miles – all tastes are catered for here, a two-hour drive from Chester.

If you would like help in finding suitable farm accommodation, turn to the full listing of FHB Groups on pages 392 to 395 to find appropriate contact details for this area.

Self-Catering

---

1 **Cefnamwlch,** Tudweiliog, Pwllheli, Gwynedd LL53 8AX

Mrs R Wynne-Finch
☎ 01758 770209
Fax 01758 770548
SC From £120–£310
Sleeps 4/6 + cot

Houses 1 & 2 sleep 6 in 3 double bedrooms. Cot available. Converted from wing of owner's 17th century manor farmhouse on ancient Welsh estate. Situated in beautiful woodland setting 1 mile from village of Tudweiliog, along rhododendron drive. Easy reach sandy beaches, golf course. Ideal touring centre. Colour TV, tumble dryer and spindryer. Play area. Electric £1 meter. Ty Thimble Cottage sleeps 4 in 2 double bedrooms.

---

2 **Gwynfryn Farm,** Gwynfryn, Pwllheli, Gwynedd LL53 5UF

Sharon B Ellis
☎ 01758 612536
Fax 01758 614324
SC From £155
Sleeps 2–8

Our **organic** dairy farm is a peaceful haven for nature lovers, yet only 1½ miles from Pwllheli. Cottages for romantic couples/houses 4–8 persons, all personally supervised, quality assured. Snowdon 25 miles, sea 2 miles. Beds made up, storage/central heating. Electricity included in price. Mini breaks Oct–Mar. Cooked dishes to order. Gold Award Welcome Host. Farmhouse Award. Colour brochure. Open all year.
E-mail: sian@gwynfryn.freeserve.co.uk

---

3 **Tai Gwyliau Tyndon Holiday Cottages,** c/o Penlan, Rhos Isaf, Caernarfon, Gwynedd LL54 7NG

Mrs Elisabeth Evans
☎ 01286 831184
SC From £109–£420
Sleeps 2–8

120 acre sheep farm on the beautiful Llŷn heritage coast. Peaceful and relaxing self-catering units. 1 mile from Llanengan with its country pub and 6th century church. Boating resort of Abersoch only 2 miles away. Beautiful sandy beach of Porthneigwl within 200 yards (with private access). Most cottages have glorious views of the bay. Ideal family holiday. Personal supervision. Free brochure. Short breaks. Open Feb–Nov.

Our farms offer a range of facilities that are illustrated by symbols in each entry. Turn to page 14 for an explanation of the symbols.

FOLLOW THE COUNTRY CODE

Leave nothing but footprints,
Take nothing but photographs,
Kill nothing but time!

Snowdonia – Mountains & Coast

Southern National Park & Cader Idris

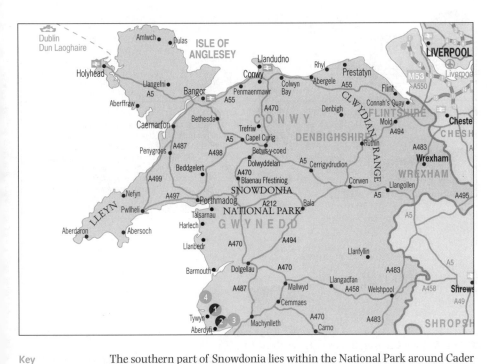

Key

- **1** Bed & Breakfast
- **1** Self-Catering
- **1** B&B and SC
- **1** Camping Barns
- **1** Camping & Caravanning

The southern part of Snowdonia lies within the National Park around Cader Idris, one of the highest peaks in Wales. On our traditional Welsh working farms we offer a warm, friendly welcome, 'croeso' to our guests. See the animals or just relax in an exciting area of contrasts, from the golden beaches of the coast to hills and mountains. There is something for everyone, from fishing lakes, forest visitor centres and castles to the unspoilt market town of Dolgellau, the picturesque valley of Talyllyn and the historic town of Machynlleth with Celtica and the Alternative Technology Centre nearby. The green countryside entices walkers, explorers and cyclists to this area of unspoilt beauty and tranquillity.

If you would like help in finding suitable farm accommodation, turn to the full listing of FHB Groups on pages 392 to 395 to find appropriate contact details for this area.

Bed and Breakfast
(and evening meal)

---

❶ Cynfal Farm, Bryncrug, Tywyn, Gwynedd LL36 9RB

Mrs Carys Evans
☎/Fax 01654 711703
[BB] From £19–£22
Sleeps 6
🐕 ⚡ 🎿 🚬

★★★
FARM

Mixed working farm, magnificently situated with panoramic views of mountains and sea. Talyllyn narrow gauge steam railway runs within 150 yards of the house and the farm has its own halt. Three spacious bedrooms, two double en suite and one twin with private facilities, all with beverage trays, TV and hairdrier. Ideal area for touring and only two miles from beach. Brochure. Open Mar–Nov.

---

❷ Gogarth Hall Farm, Gogarth, Pennal, Machynlleth, Powys SY20 9LB

Deilwen Breese
☎/Fax 01654 791235
[BB] From £18–£22
EM From £8–£12
Sleeps 6
🐕 ⚡ 💺 🎿 💼 🚬

★★★★
FARM

It's a pleasure to welcome guests for a quiet, relaxing stay. Feel the warmth and quality of a Welsh welcome in traditional style on our farm in magnificent setting overlooking the Dovey estuary opening to Cardigan Bay. Aberdovey beach 4 miles. En suite facilities, guests' sitting and dining rooms. See the farm animals and wildlife (kites, barn owls, etc). Farmhouse Award. Brochure. Open all year except Christmas Day.
E-mail: gogarthhallfarmholidays@aol.com

Self-Catering

---

❶ Cynfal Farm Cottages, Bryncrug, Tywyn, Gwynedd, LL36 9RB

Mrs Carys Evans
☎/Fax 01654 711703
[SC] From £160–£425
Sleeps 5
🐕 ⚡ 🎿 🚬

🏠🏠🏠🏠🏠

A perfect holiday location for couples or families seeking something rather special. Luxury barn conversion with en suite bedrooms. Fully equipped pine kitchen with dishwasher, washing machine, tumble drier, fridge and freezer. Oil central heating, logs, bedding and towels inclusive. Only two miles from beach and within easy reach of numerous attractions. Brochure. Open all year.

---

❷ Gogarth Hall Farm, Gogarth, Pennal, Machynlleth, Powys SY20 9LB

Deilwen Breese
☎/Fax 01654 791235
[SC] From £100–£500
Sleeps 6
🐕 ⚡ 💺 🎿 💼 🚬

🏠🏠🏠🏠🏠

Welcome to four various properties in unique settings at Gogarth with magnificent views of the Dovey estuary opening to Cardigan Bay. The coach house, farmhouse and caravan are luxury properties where you can see rare birds, take beautiful walks or just relax. Cwmffernol is uniquely set in a tranquil valley by the river, surrounded by hills and mountains. Aberdovey golden sands, Alternative Technology Centre and Celtica nearby. Open all year.
E-mail: gogarthhallfarmholidays@aol.com

Penmaenbach Farm Cottages, Cwrt, Pennal, Machynlleth, Powys SY20 9LD ❸

Mrs Shana Rees
☎/Fax 01654 791616
⟦SC⟧ From £160–£450
Sleep 4–6
🛏 🐕 ⚓ ▪

We offer a choice of luxury accommodation at our three farm cottages. Laundry/games room, tennis court, free use of owners' heated open air swimming pool. Ideally located with Aberdovey beach, Talyllyn Railway, Celtica, Centre for Alternative Technology and lots more all within 8 miles. Children are welcome to see the farm animals and feed the hens. Colour brochure. Open all year.
E-mail: farm cott@aol.com!

Plas y Nant Cottages, c/o Henblas, Llwyngwril, Gwynedd LL37 2QA ❹

Mrs Swancott Pugh
☎/Fax 01341 250350
⟦SC⟧ From £180–£400
Sleep 4–6
🐎 ▪ 🅿

Situated on a working farm overlooking Cardigan Bay, these four stone cottages have been tastefully converted from farm buildings. All have two bedrooms, linen supplied. Utility room, paved courtyard. All-inclusive price. Ideal for walking, climbing and swimming. Golf, riding and fishing available within 8 miles. Welsh-speaking family. Open all year. See colour ad on page 48.

STAY ON A FARM GIFT TOKENS

FARM HOLIDAY BUREAU

If you have enjoyed your Stay on a Farm, why not treat your friends and relatives to *Stay on a Farm* gift tokens? Available from the Bureau office (tel: 024 7669 6909), they can be redeemed against accommodation and are accepted by the majority of farms (see Index). Please check when booking to avoid disappointment.

THE 1000+ BUREAU MEMBERS OFFER A UNIQUE LINK TO CUSTOMERS ACROSS THE UK

FARM HOLIDAY BUREAU

All Bureau members belong to a local Group. Each member can refer you to an equally high quality member within the Group... or across the UK: England, Northern Ireland, Scotland, Wales.

FOLLOW THE COUNTRY CODE

Leave nothing but footprints,
Take nothing but photographs,
Kill nothing but time!

The North Wales Coast & Borderlands

Vale of Clwyd, Llandudno, Bodnant Gardens, Colwyn Bay, Rhyl, Prestatyn, Chester & Clwydian Range

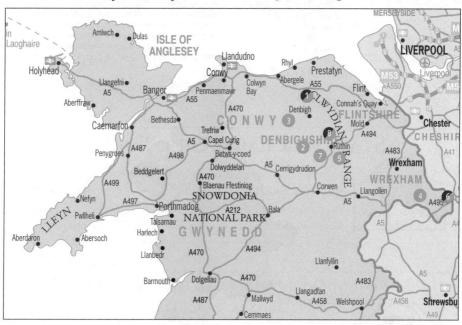

Key

1 Bed & Breakfast

1 Self-Catering

1 B&B and SC

1 Camping Barns

1 Camping & Caravanning

Pride of this area is the Clwydian Range of rolling hills overlooking the Vale of Clwyd and the Denbigh Moors beyond. St Asaph, at the head of the Vale, might appear to be a large village, but it is also a 'city' with one of the oldest cathedrals in Wales. Further into Clwyd lies Ruthin with its castle and 'Maen Huail' stone where King Arthur is said to have beheaded his rival in love. Visit Ruthin's craft centre and those at Afon-wen and Llanasa. Craft of a different nature are to be found in Llangollen where horse-drawn barges glide along the Shropshire Union Canal. Catch the International Eisteddfod here, try a world-class theatre production in Mold or visit the National Trust's Erddig near Wrexham.

If you would like help in finding suitable farm accommodation, turn to the full listing of FHB Groups on pages 392 to 395 to find appropriate contact details for this area.

Bed and Breakfast
(and evening meal)

Bach-y-Graig, Tremeirchion, St Asaph LL17 0UH   ❶

Anwen Roberts
☎/Fax 01745 730627
[BB] From £20–£25
EM From £9
Sleeps 6
⌖ ⛸ 🖴 🐾 ☂ ◉
★★★★
FARM

A 16th century listed farmhouse nestling at the foot of the Clwydian Range with beautiful views of the surrounding countryside. Highest standard of traditional furnishings and decor, en suite, TVs, tea/coffee-making facilities in bedrooms, full CH, beamed inglenook fireplace with log fires. Central for North Wales, Chester, coast 9 miles. Games room. 40 acre woodland trail. WTB Farmhouse Award. AA selected award. Closed Christmas/New Year.

Bryncoch, Clawddnewydd, Ruthin, Denbighshire LL15 2NA   ❷

Gaenor Lloyd Jones
☎/Fax 01824 750603
[BB] From £15–£18
EM From £8
Sleeps 6
🐾 🖴 ☂ ◉
★★
FARM

Bryncoch is a working farm situated on the B5105 Ruthin-Cerrig y Drudion road on the edge of Clocaenog Forest overlooking the Vale of Clwyd. 4 miles from Ruthin with its medieval castle and historic buildings. Convenient base for Chester, Snowdonia and North Wales coast. Enjoy delicious home cooking using local produce. Families welcome. Croeso Cynnes. Welcome Host Gold Award. Open Mar-Oct

Fron-Haul, Bodfari, Denbigh, Denbighshire LL16 4DY   ❸

Gwladys M Edwards
☎/Fax 01745 710301
[BB] From £19–£20.50
EM From £10.50
Sleeps 6
🐾 🐓 ⌖ Å 🖴 ◉
★★★
FARM

Discover an oasis of calm and taste. Fron-Haul dominates the high ground above the Wheeler Valley with superb views of the Vale of Clwyd and Snowdonia. Easily accessible from the A55 expressway, just a short distance from Chester and the North Wales coast. The farm supplies the freshest, best quality vegetables, Welsh lamb, etc for the varied farmhouse menu. Truly a Taste of Wales. Open all year. E-mail: fronhaul@pantglasbodfari.freeserve.co.uk

Horseman's Green Farm, Horseman's Green, Nr Wrexham SY13 3EA   ❹

Mrs Gillian Huxley
☎ 01948 830480
Fax 01948 780552
[BB] From £22–£28
Sleeps 4
🐾 ⌖ 🖴 🐓 ☂ ◉
★★
FARM

A very special Grade I listed 14th century hall house, of the North Welsh Marches, with many original timbers including a rare aisle truss. Very comfortable accommodation with all private facilities and galleried sitting room. Convenient for Chester, Shrewsbury and Llangollen, the hills and coasts of North Wales within easy reach. Excellent unspoilt walking. Local and home made produce. Open all year except Christmas.

Llainwen Ucha, Pentrecelyn, Ruthin, Denbighshire LL15 2HL   ❺

Elizabeth Parry
☎ 01978 790253
[BB] From £16–£17
EM From £8
Sleeps 5
🐾 ⌖ ◉
★★
FARM

Our 130 acre farm overlooks the beautiful Vale of Clwyd. Centrally situated to coast, Snowdonia, Chester and Llangollen. Modern house with 2 pleasant bedrooms to accommodate 5 persons. CH and good home cooking, a warm welcome to visitors throughout the year. Take A525 from Ruthin towards Wrexham; after 4 miles turn left after college, we are a mile up this road. Open all year except Christmas and New Year.

6 **Mill House,** Higher Wych, Malpas, Cheshire SY14 7JR

Chris & Angela Smith
☎ 01948 780362
Fax 01948 780566
BB From £20
EM From £10
Sleeps 4
ら ⓖ ▄ ⓦ
★★★
GUEST HOUSE

Modernised Mill House on the Cheshire/Clwyd border in a quiet valley, convenient for visiting Chester, Shrewsbury and North Wales. The house is centrally heated and has an open log fire in the lounge. Bedrooms have washbasins, radios and tea-making facilities. 1 bedroom has an en suite shower and WC. Reductions for children and senior citizens. Open Jan–Nov.
E-mail: toni@videoactive.freeserve.co.uk

7 **Tyddyn Chambers,** Pwllglas, Ruthin, Denbighshire LL15 2LS

Mrs Ella Williams
☎ 01824 750683
BB From £16–£20
EM From £9
Sleeps 6
ら ▄ ⓦ
★★
FARM

A traditional sheep and dairy farm set in scenic countryside with close proximity to Snowdonia and many other North Wales attractions. Your hosts are a typical Welsh-speaking musical family. Your stay will be enhanced by tasting our home-fare cooking and enjoyment of the peaceful surroundings. Croeso/welcome. Open all year except Christmas and New Year.

Self-Catering

1 **Bach-y-Graig,** Tremeirchion, St Asaph LL17 0UH

Anwen Roberts
☎/Fax 01745 730627
SC From £90–£375
Sleeps 6 + cot
ら ⅄ ▄ ⌖ ⓦ
⚜ ⚜ ⚜ ⚜ ⚜

Stay on a working dairy farm in this 16th century farmhouse, retaining the charm but offering comforts and convenience of modern living in high standard accommodation. Dark oak, fully equipped kitchen. 3 bedrooms, 1 four-poster bed. Bathroom with shower/bath. Downstairs toilet, CTV heating. Log fires. Linen provided. Games room, large garden with swings. Central for Chester, Snowdonia and coastal resorts. No pets. Open all year.

6 **The Granary,** c/o Mill House, Higher Wych, Malpas, Cheshire SY14 7JR

Chris & Angela Smith
☎ 01948 780362
Fax 01948 780566
SC From £90–£180
Sleeps 4/5 + cot
ら ▄ ⓦ
⚜ ⚜ ⚜ ⚜

The Granary is a self-contained bungalow adjacent to Mill House. Sleeps 4/5 in 2 double bedrooms, kitchen/living area, shower and WC. CH. Cot and babysitting available. Situated in a quiet valley with a small stream in the garden. Convenient for visiting Chester, Shrewsbury and North Wales. Open May–Nov.
E-mail: toni@videoactive.freeserve.co.uk

8 **Tyddyn Isaf,** Rhewl, Ruthin, Denbighshire LL15 1UH

Elsie Jones
☎ 01824 703142/703367
SC From £90–£260
Sleeps 2–6 + cot
ら ⅄ ▄ ⓦ
⚜ ⚜ ⚜ ⚜

Stay in self-contained part of farmhouse or recently converted granary in picturesque Vale of Clwyd. Both fully equipped to high standard. Farmhouse has kitchen lounge/diner, 2 bedrooms sleeping 4/6, bathroom, separate toilet. Granary has 1 bedroom with vanity unit, sofa bed in lounge, sleeps 2/4, shower room. 3 miles from Ruthin and within easy reach of Chester, the coast, Snowdonia. Bedlinen provided. No pets. Open all year.

Ceredigion, Cardigan Bay

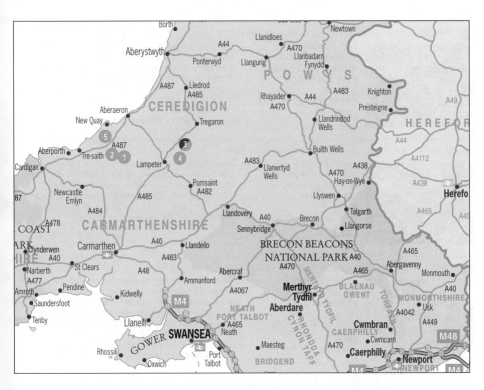

Key

1 Bed & Breakfast

1 Self-Catering

1 B&B and SC

1 Camping Barns

1 Camping & Caravanning

The magic of Cardiganshire will enchant you with its gentle mountains and 52 miles of unspoilt coastline encircling pastureland threaded with salmon rivers and providing a haven for wildlife. The coastline, with its safe, sandy beaches and spectacular walks, stretches from Cardigan to the university town of Aberystwyth. The county's main river, the Teifi, is shared by fishermen, canoeists and the famous coracle men of Cenarth. Woollen mills, potteries and Celtic crafts abound. Here, in the ancient kingdom of Ceredigion, a rural way of life persists in the small farms and villages where Welsh is still the first language. Come and join us.

If you would like help in finding suitable farm accommodation, turn to the full listing of FHB Groups on pages 392 to 395 to find appropriate contact details for this area.

Bed and Breakfast
(and evening meal)

---

1 **Broniwan,** Rhydlewis, Llandyssul, Ceredigion SA44 5PF

Carole Jacobs
☎/Fax 01239 851261
BB From £21.50–£23
EM From £12.50
Sleeps 4
☺(10) 🐾 ⅍ 🛁 ☂ ♨ ◉
★★★
FARM

Unwind in the peace of our traditional Cardiganshire home. Our small farm, 10 minutes' drive from National Trust sandy beaches at Penbryn, has quiet gardens with views of the Preseli Hills. Great walks. We use our own organic produce for generous meals (including vegetarian). En suite/private facilities. Reduced weekly terms. WTB Farmhouse Award.
E-mail: 101535.2310@compuserve.com.uk

---

2 **Llwyn yr Eos,** Rhydlewis, Llandyssul, Ceredigion SA44 5QU

Judith Rodwell
☎/Fax 01239 851268
BB From £19–£21
EM From £11
Sleeps 5
☺ ⅍ 🛁 ☜ ☂ ☂
★★★
FARM

Escape to our sheep farm in the beautiful Teifi valley. Comfortable, south-facing en suite bedrooms with superb views. Watch buzzards and red kites on the farm or dolphins and seals off the coast 10 minutes' drive away. Good food using fresh local produce with fruit and vegetables from the garden. Open all year.
E-mail: jmr@rhydl.freeserve.co.uk

---

3 **Pant-Teg,** Llanfair Clydogau, Lampeter, Ceredigion SA48 8LL

Mrs Pat Brown
☎ 01570 493416
BB From £20–£22
Sleeps 5
☺(6) 🐾 ⅍ 🛁 ☂ ◉
★★★
GUEST HOUSE

Welcome to Pant-Teg! Once an old stone hill farm, now a peaceful country home, it rests on the gentle mountainside with magnificent views. Red kites wheel overhead and wildlife surrounds us. Beautiful lawned gardens, pond, meandering brook. Enticing meals, vegetarian if preferred, served in our charming conservatory. Cosy woodburner and en suite facilities. Come and join us! Open all year except Christmas.

---

4 **Pentre Farm,** Llanfair Clydogau, Lampeter, Ceredigion SA48 8LE

Eleri Davies
☎/Fax 01570 493313
BB £20
EM From £10
Sleeps 6
🧍 ☺ ⅍ 🛁 ☜ ☂ ◉
★★★
FARM

Pentre, a family farm overlooks the Teifi Valley. Comfortable en suite accommodation in large 1870 stonebuilt farmhouse and recently converted carthouse with attractive four-poster beds. Excellent farmhouse fare using fresh local produce reflecting a taste of Wales. Peaceful countryside walks, free fishing for salmon and trout. Brochure supplied. Open Apr–Oct.

---

5 **Wervil Grange Farm,** Pentregat, Nr Llangranog, Llandyssul, Ceredigion SA44 6HW

Ionwen Lewis
☎/Fax 01239 654252
BB From £20–£25
Sleeps 6
☺ 🐾 ⅍ 👤 🐎 ☂ 🛁 ☜ ☂ ◉
Applied

A very warm welcome awaits you in this superb de luxe Welsh Georgian farmhouse, offering a very high standard of accommodation. All bedrooms en suite with colour TV. The house has been beautifully decorated and furnished and has a very relaxed atmosphere. Enjoy the true 'Taste of Wales' with mouth-watering food and wine, mostly grown on the farm or locally supplied. Free coarse and trout fishing for guests. Just off the A487, halfway between the Georgian towns of Aberaeron and Cardigan.

Self-Catering

Pant-Teg Studio Cottage, Llanfair Clydogau, Lampeter, Ceredigion SA48 8LL   ③

Mrs Pat Brown
☎ 01570 493416
SC **From £150–£325**
Sleeps 4–6
⛺(3) 🐕 ✂ 🛁 🌯 ⓐ
🌺 🌺 🌺 🌺

Set on the bank, its patio area next to our tumbling brook, and surrounded by meadows of grazing sheep, Pant-Teg Studio, tastefully converted, fully equipped and with en suite facilities, shares the beautiful views and tranquil gardens of the main farmhouse, whilst offering privacy and independence. Coast and countryside abound with wildlife and our peaceful haven is a perfect base from which to explore – or just relax! Brochure available. Open all year.

FINDING YOUR ACCOMMODATION

The local FHB Group contacts listed on page 392 can always help you find a vacancy in your chosen area.

STAY ON A FARM GIFT TOKENS

If you have enjoyed your Stay on a Farm, why not treat your friends and relatives to *Stay on a Farm* gift tokens? Available from the Bureau office (tel: 024 7669 6909), they can be redeemed against accommodation and are accepted by the majority of farms (see Index). Please check when booking to avoid disappointment.

Our Internet address is
http://www.webscape.co.uk/farmaccom/

Mid Wales, Lakes & Mountains

Montgomeryshire, Heart of Wales

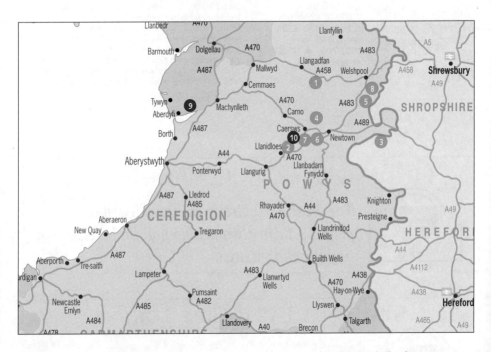

Key

1 Bed & Breakfast

1 Self-Catering

1 B&B and SC

1 Camping Barns

1 Camping & Caravanning

Welcome to Montgomeryshire and to a holiday that harks back to a time and a place you thought had long since disappeared, with log fires, honest-to-goodness farmhouse food, clear country air and magnificent scenery. Every 'Heart of Wales' farmhouse is set in glorious unspoilt countryside, with walks starting from the front door. Even in summer you'll miss the crowds, and you probably won't see anything but scenery and wildlife, as Montgomeryshire is still 'Wales' best-kept secret'! We'll give you memories you can take home and treasure for a long time to come – and that's what makes a Heart of Wales holiday that extra bit special.

If you would like help in finding suitable farm accommodation, turn to the full listing of FHB Groups on pages 392 to 395 to find appropriate contact details for this area.

Bed and Breakfast
(and evening meal)

Cwmllwynog, Llanfair Caereinion,Welshpool, Powys SY21 0HF ①

Joyce Cornes
☎/Fax 01938 810791
BB From £20
EM From £10
Sleeps 4
🐎 🐕 🏠 🛎 🐾 ☺
★★★
FARM

Built in the early 17th century Cwmllwynog is a traditional long farmhouse of character on a working dairy farm. We have a spacious garden with a stream at the bottom and a lot of unusual plants. All bedrooms have colour TV and drink making facilities. Double room en suite, twin with hot and cold and private bathroom. Delicious home-cooked meals cooked. Just for you! We can help you with routes. WTB Farmhouse Award. Open Jan–Nov.

Dol-Llys Farm, Llanidloes, Powys SY18 6JA ②

Olwen S Evans
☎ 01686 412694
BB From £18–£20
Sleeps 6
🐎(5) 🅰 🐎 🐾 🛎 🐾 ☺
★★★
FARM

Dol-Llys is a working farm situated on the banks of the River Severn. This intriguing farmhouse has many levels and small staircases with character throughout. Three en suite bedrooms with all facilities. Ideal for walking, fishing and birdwatching yet within walking distance of the historic town of Llanidloes. Open Apr–Oct.

The Drewin Farm, Churchstoke, Montgomery, Powys SY15 6TW ③

Mrs Ceinwen Richards
☎/Fax 01588 620325
BB From £20
EM From £10
Sleeps 5
🐎 🍴 🅰 🐾 🛎 ☺
★★★
FARM

Relax in our 17th century farmhouse which has a wealth of charm and character, with original features such as exposed beams and inglenook fireplace. En suite bedrooms with TV and drinks facilities. Offa's Dyke footpath runs through the farm, from which its elevated position, commands outstanding views of the surrounding countryside. Warm Welsh welcome, kettle always on the boil. AA Selected, WTB Farmhouse Award. Open Mar–Oct. E-mail: ceinwen@drewin.freeserve.co.uk

---

Dyffryn Farm, Aberhafesp, Newtown, Powys SY16 3JD ④

Dave & Sue Jones
☎ 01686 688817
Fax 01686 688324
BB From £23–£26
EM From £14
Sleeps 6
🐎 🍴 🐾 🛎 ☺
★★★★
FARM

Set on the banks of a stream, Dyffryn has luxurious, en suite accommodation, full central heating and pretty decor. Lovely walks along stream and in woods, lakes and nature reserve nearby. Traditional farmhouse fare including vegetarian specialities. Walkers and cyclists welcome. 'Come and enjoy life on a Welsh hill farm – you might want to stay!' Open all year.
Mobile 0585 206412 E-mail: daveandsue@clara.net

Little Brompton Farm, Montgomery, Powys SY15 6HY ⑤

Gaynor Bright
☎/Fax 01686 668371
BB From £20–£21
EM From £10
Sleeps 6
🐎 🐕 🍴 🅰 🐎 🐾 🛎 🐾 ☺
★★★
FARM

A true oasis of tranquillity in beautiful scenery, this 17th century oak framed farmhouse on working farm offers friendly hospitality. Pretty rooms enhanced by quality furnishings and antiques, all amenities, en suites available. Traditional farmhouse cooking (evening meals by arrangement). Offa's Dyke footpath runs through farm. WTB Farmhouse Award. AA selected. Welcome Host. Situated 2 miles east of Montgomery on B4385. Open all year.

6   **Llettyderyn,** Mochdre, Newtown, Powys SY16 4JY

Mrs Margaret Jandrell
☎ 01686 626131
[BB] From £20–£27
EM From £12
Sleeps 6
🧍 🐂 🐕 ♨ 🎱
★★★
FARM

Llettyderyn – a restored 18th century farmhouse with exposed beams, inglenook fireplace and traditional parlour. A working farm rearing sheep and beef. 2 miles from Newtown; an ideal base for touring Mid-Wales. Excellent farmhouse cooking, with home-made bread. Vegetarians catered for. Double and twin-bedded rooms en suite, tea-making facilities and TV. Full CH. Ample parking. Welcome Host Gold Award. Open all year.

7   **Lower Gwerneirin Farm,** Llandinam, Powys SY17 5DD

Mrs Anne Brown
☎ 01686 688286
[BB] From £20–£25
EM From £12
Sleeps 4
🐂 ⚲ ♨ 🎠 ⟨ 🎱
★★★
FARM

Beautifully situated in the Severn Valley, the farmhouse is a spacious Victorian dwelling offering comfortable accommodation. All rooms have CH, drinks facilities and colour TV. One double and 1 twin en suite. Guests lounge with log fire. Fishing in own trout pool. We have a wealth of wildlife. Ideally located for exploring Mid Wales. Large garden with beautiful views. Superb home cooking. Open all year.

8   **Moat Farm,** Welshpool, Powys SY21 8SE

Gwyneth Jones
☎/Fax 01938 553179
[BB] From £20–£25
EM From £11
Sleeps 6
🐂 🎠 ⚲ ♨ 🎱
★★★
FARM

Moat Farm is a 260-acre dairy farm set in the beautiful Severn Valley. The 17th century farmhouse offers warm and comfortable accommodation with good home cooking served in a fine timbered dining room, traditionally furnished with Welsh dresser. All rooms en suite with tea/ coffee facilities and colour TV. Quiet lounge, pool table and spacious garden. Good touring centre. Near Powis Castle. Golf, riding and fishing nearby. Open Mar–Nov.

Self-Catering

9   **Penmaenbach Farm Cottages,** Cwrt, Pennal, Machynlleth, Powys SY20 9LD

Mrs Shana Rees
☎/Fax 01654 791616
[SC] From £160–£450
Sleep 4–6
🐓 ⟋ 🎠 ♨
🐾 🐾 🐾 🐾 🐾

We offer a choice of luxury accommodation at our three farm cottages. Laundry/games room, tennis court, free use of owners' heated open air swimming pool. Ideally located with Aberdovey beach, Talyllyn Railway, Celtica, Centre for Alternative Technology and lots more all within 8 miles. Children are welcome to see the farm animals and feed the hens. Colour brochure. Open all year.
E-mail: farm cott@aol.com!

10   **Red House,** Trefeglwys, Nr Caersws, Powys SY17 5PN

Gwyneth Williams
☎ 01686 688194
[SC] From £150
Sleeps 5 + cot
🐂 ⚲ 🎱
🐾 🐾 🐾 🐾

A highly furnished, self-contained part of the farmhouse, situated on a mixed working family farm. Panoramic views, unspoilt scenery and the tranquillity of the Trannon Valley. Ideal base for touring Mid Wales. Golf, riding and fishing available within 6 miles. Llanidloes 6 miles. Guests' comfort is the priority. Log fire, oak beams, garden with furniture, ample parking and wildlife. Open all year.

Mid Wales, Lakes & Mountains

Radnor

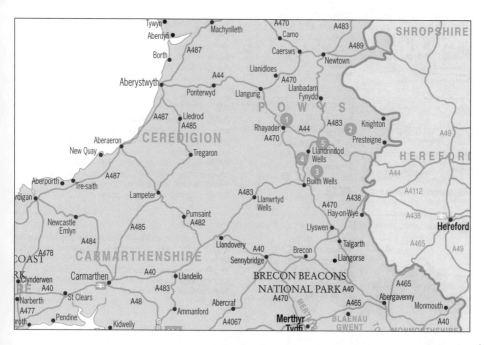

Radnorshire is an undiscovered jewel set on the borders of England and Wales. How is it that a land so fought over in the past could be so friendly now? Our castles are romantic ruins but it takes little imagination to picture ancient hard-fought battles. Now, though, you can wander or ride over wide open hills, through dark forests or beside serene lakes in a countryside vibrant with wildlife such as dragonflies, butterflies, badgers and red kite. There are sports and attractions for young and old from Victorian Week in summer to rally driving, from fishing to trotting races and sheepdog trials. We have wonderful museums and churches, craft centres, the Powys Observatory, spa towns and even the winner of the 1998 Village of the Year award. If you come to our land of fresh clean air and skies, where the stars seem to reach down and touch you, you will want to return.

If you would like help in finding suitable farm accommodation, turn to the full listing of FHB Groups on pages 392 to 395 to find appropriate contact details for this area.

Bed and Breakfast
(and evening meal)

---

① Beili Neuadd, Rhayader, Powys LD6 5NS

Mrs Ann Edwards
☎/Fax 01597 810211
BB From £19.50–£21
Sleeps 6
⌂(8) ⚲ ⚱ ♨ ⚰ ☂ ✿ ◉
★★★
FARM

An attractive 16th century stone-built farmhouse set amidst beautiful countryside in a quiet, secluded position approx. 2 miles from small market town of Rhayader. Guests are assured of every comfort with CH, log fires and well appointed accommodation in single, double and twin bedded rooms, all with private facilities. WTB Farmhouse Award winner. We look forward to welcoming you to this lovely part of Wales. Open all year except Christmas.

---

② Cefnsuran Farm, Llangunllo, Knighton, Powys LD7 1SL

Gill Morgan
☎/Fax 01547 550219
BB From £21–£25
EM From £10.50
Sleeps 6
⌂ ⚱ ♨ ⚰ ☂ ◉
★★★
FARM

Cefnsuran is a 16th century farmhouse set in isolated valley with large gardens and extremely picturesque countryside. 5 mins from A483. Recently refurbished, it retains its farmhouse feel with woodburning inglenook fireplaces and exposed beams. High standard of traditional cooking using fresh local produce whenever possible. Vegetarian and special diets. Open all year.
E-mail: cefn@suran.freeserve.co.uk

---

③ Gaer Farm, Hundred House, Llandrindod Wells, Powys LD1 5RU

Patricia Harley
☎/Fax 01982 570208
BB From £17.50–£20
EM From £12
Sleeps 8
⌂ ♨ ☂ ◉
★
FARM

A warm welcome awaits you in our converted barn set in a quiet, scenic valley with interesting walks and ideal for birdwatching. Good access to Mid Wales and the Royal Welsh Showground. Ground floor accommodation. Evening meals by prior arrangement using own produce when available. Open all year.

---

④ Holly Farm, Howey, Llandrindod Wells, Powys LD1 5PP

Mrs Ruth Jones
☎ 01597 822402
BB From £19–£24
EM From £10
Sleeps 10
⌂ ♨ ◉
★★★
FARM

Working farm with tastefully restored farmhouse dating back to Tudor times. Ideal base from which to explore this scenic and wonderful part of Mid Wales, excellent for walking, birdwatching, cycling or relaxing. En suite rooms with colour TV and beverage tray. Two lounges, delicious cuisine using farm produce. Tourism award. Safe parking. AA 4 Diamonds. Brochure. Open all year.

---

⑤ Neuadd Farm, Penybont, Llandrindod Wells, Powys LD1 5SW

Peter & Jackie Longley
☎/Fax 01597 822571
BB From £20–£23
EM From £11
Sleeps 6
⌂(10) ⚰ ♨ ⚰ ☂ ◉
★★★★
FARM

Enjoy a relaxing break in our comfortably furnished 16th century farmhouse looking over the lovely Ithon Valley. Historic location with no traffic. Separate guests' sitting and dining rooms, both with inglenook fireplaces. Good traditional home cooking. Ideal for exploring Mid Wales or walk direct from our door. Brochure available. Open all year except Christmas.

Mid Wales, Lakes & Mountains

Brecon Beacons National Park & Black Mountains

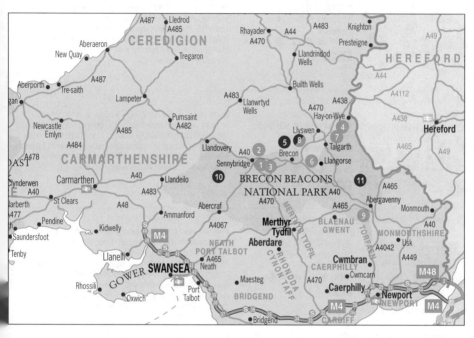

Key

- 1 Bed & Breakfast
- 1 Self-Catering
- 1 B&B and SC
- 1 Camping Barns
- 1 Camping & Caravanning

The Brecon Beacons National Park is a captivatingly varied landscape dominated by wilderness and natural beauty, a haven for wildlife. Here you can take a guided walk or enjoy pony trekking, climbing, caving, cycling, sailing, fishing or walking at any level of ability. The numerous attractions include Dan-yr-Ogof Showcaves and Shire Horse Centre, Big Pit Colliery, Llangorse Rope Centre and the National Park Visitors Centre. There are craft shops, castles, historic sites, antique shops and so much more. Fascinating towns such as Brecon, Hay-on-Wye and Talgarth let you experience Welsh culture from agricultural markets to local choirs. Sample home cooking at its best when you stay at one of our farmhouses. You can be sure there will be a warm welcome in the hillside – why not discover the area for yourself?

If you would like help in finding suitable farm accommodation, turn to the full listing of FHB Groups on pages 392 to 395 to find appropriate contact details for this area.

Bed and Breakfast
(and evening meal)

---

1 Blaencar Farm, Sennybridge, Brecon, Powys LD3 8HA

Mrs Carol Morgan
☎ 01874 636610
🆔 From £20–£24
Sleeps 6
🐴 ⅍ 🏠 ☜ 🐎 ⚫
★★★★★
FARM

Tastefully restored farmhouse with oak beams and inglenooks on working upland family farm. Quality en suite bedrooms with hospitality tray and colour TV. Peaceful, accessible location in the heart of the Brecon Beacons National Park. Pleasant 15-minute walk to traditional country pub for meals. Private fishing. Welcome Host Gold. Open all year.

---

2 Bryn y Fedwen Farm, Trallong Common, Sennybridge, Brecon, Powys LD3 8HW

Mrs Mary Adams
☎ /Fax 01874 636505
🆔 From £22–£25
EM From £12
Sleeps 6
🐴 ⅍ 🏠 🐎 ⚫
★★★★
FARM

Enjoy peace and quiet at Bryn y Fedwen, a family-run sheep farm situated between Brecon and Sennybridge overlooking the National Park and Usk Valley. Lovely farm walks with wildlife. Comfortable, spacious en suite bedrooms. Tastefully furnished TV lounge with log fire. Personal attention and good home cooking. WTB Farmhouse Award.

---

3 Cwmcamlais Uchaf Farm, Cwmcamlais, Sennybridge, Brecon, Powys LD3 8TD

Mrs Jean Phillips
☎/Fax 01874 636376
🆔 From £20–£21
Sleeps 6
🐴(8) 🐦 ⅍ 🏠 🐎 ⚫
★★★
FARM

Cwmcamlais Uchaf is a working farm situated on the route of a popular walk in the Brecon Beacons National Park. 1 mile off the A40 between Brecon and Sennybridge. Our 16th century farmhouse has exposed beams and stonework, inglenook fireplace and tastefully decorated bedrooms (2 double en suite, one twin with own shower room, all with tea/coffee). The River Camlais with its waterfalls, flows through the farmland. A warm Welsh welcome awaits you. Closed Christmas.

---

4 Ffordd-Fawr Farmhouse, Fforddfawr, Glasbury, Hay-on-Wye, Hereford HR3 5PT

Mrs Barbara Eckley
☎/Fax 01497 847332
🆔 From £18–£21
Sleeps 6
🏃 🐴(8) ⅍ 🏃 🏠 🐎 ⚫
★★★
FARM

Charming 17th century farmhouse set in idyllic open countryside, nestling between the Black Mountains and Radnor hills, 3 miles from the famous bookshops of Hay-on-Wye. The three en suite bedrooms each have their own individual charm and enjoy views over the countryside. The farm is bordered by the River Wye and is noted for its birdlife and natural beauty. A perfect place to rest and relax. Open all year.

---

5 The Hayloft, Cae Crwn, Battle, Brecon, Powys LD3 9RW

Mrs Jill Derbyshire
☎/Fax 01874 625397
🆔 From £22.50–£25
EM From £10
Sleeps 4
🐴 ⅍ 🏠
★★★
FARM

Delightfully situated small holding with breathtaking views of the Brecon Beacons. Excellent hill walking and cycling. Ideal location for exploring the National Park and surrounding countryside. Luxury self-contained, two-bedroomed accommodation in converted hayloft with drying room. Seasonal farm produce, good home cooking and a warm welcome. *Associate*.
E-mail: jill@caecrwn.demon.co.uk

Highgrove Farm, Llanhamlach, Brecon, Powys LD3 7SU

Mrs Ruth Williams
☎ 01874 665489
BB From £20–£25
Sleeps 6

★★★★
FARM

Highgrove, situated between Brecon and Llangorse Lake in the National Park, is a 16th century farmhouse in a superb position overlooking the Brecon Beacons. Conservation award for renovation. A comfortable base for relaxing, touring and exploring. Good choice of restaurants and pubs for evening meals nearby. Open all year.

Lodge Farm, Talgarth, Brecon, Powys LD3 0DP

Mrs Marion Meredith
☎/Fax 01874 711244
BB From £20–£22
EM From £13
Sleeps 6

★★★
FARM

Enjoy the tranquillity on this working farm nestling in the Brecon Beacons National Park. Relax in cottage-style garden with spectacular mountain views, wander along country lanes with direct access to common and mountains. Return to 18th century house for interesting homemade meals including vegetarian. Dining room has inglenook and flagstone floor. Retire to cosy en suite period furnished bedrooms. Talgarth 1½ miles, Hay-on-Wye 8 miles. Open all year.

Trehenry Farm, Felinfach, Llandefalle, Brecon, Powys LD3 0UN

Mrs Theresa Jones
☎/Fax 01874 754312
BB From £18–£21
Sleeps 8

★★★
FARM

Trehenry is a 200 acre mixed farm situated east of Brecon, 1 mile off A470. The impressive 18th century farmhouse with breathtaking views, inglenook fireplaces and exposed beams offers comfortable accommodation, good food and cosy rooms. TV lounge, separate dining tables, central heating, tea-making facilities, all rooms en suite. Brochure on request. Farmhouse Award winner. Open all year except Christmas.

The Wenallt Farm, Gilwern, near Abergavenny, Monmouthshire NP7 0HP

The Harris Family
☎/Fax 01873 830694
BB From £19.50–£24
EM From £12
Sleeps 8

★★
FARM

A 16th century Welsh longhouse set in 50 acres of farmland in the Brecon Beacons National Park commanding magnificent views over the Usk Valley. Retaining all its old charm with oak beams, inglenook fireplace, yet offering a high standard with en suite bedrooms, good food and a warm welcome. An ideal base from which to see Wales and the surrounding areas. Licensed. AA listed. Brochure available. Open all year.

Self-Catering

Gwydre Cottage, Gwydre, Llanddeusant, Llangadog, Carmarthenshire SA19 9YS

Mrs D J Price
☎ 01550 740242
SC From £200–£360
Sleeps 6 + cot

Gwydre Cottage is situated at the foot of the Brecon Beacons on a working farm where you are welcome to lend a hand. With rolling acres to explore, feel the fresh hill breezes and see the breathtaking scenery. Ideal for birdwatching (red kites, etc). Inglenook fireplace. Linen and towels provided. Safe, large lawn. Open Mar–Nov.

8 **Trehenry Farm,** Felinfach, Llandefalle, Brecon, Powys LD3 0UN

Mrs Theresa Jones
☎/Fax 01874 754312
SC From £200–£500
Sleeps 8

For a holiday to remember then come to Trehenry 200 acre working farm. Tranquillity surrounded by breathtaking views. 17th century farmhouse modernised to a high standard with oak beams, inglenook fireplace. 3 bedrooms, 2 en suite, 1 private. Bed settee in second lounge. Very well equipped kitchen, lounge with TV, video, CH, wood stove. Price includes linen, electric, heating. Brochure. Open all year.

11 **Upper Bettws Farm,** Fforest Coalpit, Abergavenny, Monmouthshire NP7 7LH

Bronwen Lloyd
☎/Fax 01873 890141
SC From £135–£260
Sleep 2/3

Two delightfully restored stone cottages on 17th century farm. Hidden away high in the Black Mountains with exceptional, panoramic views of the Sugar Loaf Mountain and Bettws Valley, yet only 10 minutes from Abergavenny. This is the perfect location for a peaceful and relaxing holiday with miles of uninterrupted walking on the doorstep. Open all year. E-mail: bettwsbron@talk21.com

CONFIRM BOOKINGS

Disappointments can arise from misunderstandings over the telephone. Please write to confirm your booking.

THE 1000+ BUREAU MEMBERS OFFER A UNIQUE LINK TO CUSTOMERS ACROSS THE UK

FARM HOLIDAY BUREAU

All Bureau members belong to a local Group. Each member can refer you to an equally high quality member within the Group... or across the UK: England, Northern Ireland, Scotland, Wales.

FOLLOW THE COUNTRY CODE

Leave nothing but footprints,
Take nothing but photographs,
Kill nothing but time!

Pembrokeshire

Britain's coastal National Park

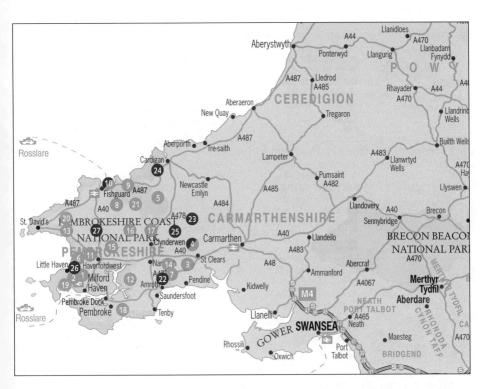

Key

1 Bed & Breakfast

1 Self-Catering

1 B&B and SC

1 Camping Barns

1 Camping & Caravanning

Pembrokeshire, Britain's only coastal National Park, has lovely sandy beaches, bird sanctuary islands and a coastal path offering 200 miles of varied walking and breathtaking views across the Irish Sea. In contrast, the heart of the countryside, with the tranquil, wooded creeks of the Cleddau estuary and the peaceful, rolling uplands of the Preseli Hills, provides an idyllic rural setting for a relaxing holiday. Pembrokeshire is rich in history with dramatic castles, stone circles and the beautiful cathedral at St David's. As for activities, there's something for everyone – water sports, riding, fishing, attractions and theme parks for all the family. Pembrokeshire has a special appeal in all seasons – come and see us soon.

If you would like help in finding suitable farm accommodation, turn to the full listing of FHB Groups on pages 392 to 395 to find appropriate contact details for this area.

Bed and Breakfast
(and evening meal)

---

① Barley Villa, Walwyns Castle, Nr Broad Haven, Haverfordwest, Pembrokeshire SA62 3EB

Sandra Davies
☎ **01437 781254**
▣ **From £17–£20**
EM From £12.50
Sleeps 4
🐶(10) ⚥ ⚓ ◉
★★★
FARM

Our spacious family homestead and smallholding overlooks a nature reserve and woodland abundant with wildlife. Ideally situated for bird islands, sandy bays, coastal path and walks. Double and twin rooms with tea-making facilities, en suite available. TV lounge, parking, packed lunches, special diets. A non-smoking establishment. Warm welcome. Open Mar–Nov.
E-mail: barley-villa@pfh.co.uk

---

② The Bower Farm, Little Haven, Haverfordwest, Pembrokeshire SA62 3TY

John Birt-Llewellin
☎ **01437 781554**
Fax **01437 781940**
▣ **From £20–£30**
EM £18
Sleeps 12
🐶 🐴 🏕 ⚔ 🚴 ⚓ 🎾 ⚓ ◉
★★★
FARM

An extensively modernised traditional farmhouse on working sheep farm offering peace, warmth, comfort and friendliness to the casual or longer stay visitor. Run by local historic family. Dogs, horses (livery available) and children welcome. Walking distance of Broad Haven beach and coast path. Impressive sea views over St Brides Bay and islands. All rooms en suite. Licensed. Farmhouse Dragon Award. WTB Farmhouse Award. Open all year.
E-mail: bowerfarm@lineone.net

---

③ Brunant Farm, Whitland, Carmarthenshire SA34 0LX

Mrs O Ebsworth
☎/Fax **01994 240421**
▣ **From £22–£24**
EM £12
Sleeps 6
🐶 🎾 ⚥ ⚓ ◉
★★★
FARM

'Never enough time to enjoy this to the full, never enough words to say how splendid it was': John Carter, Thames TV (Wish You Were Here). Welcome to our 200 year old farmhouse centrally situated for touring, beaches, walking, golf or just relaxing. Comfortable, spacious bedrooms, all en suite, tea/coffee, TV, hairdriers. Good home cooking. Comfortable lounge, separate tables in dining room. Open Easter–Oct.

---

④ Cilpost Farm, Whitland, Carmarthenshire SA34 0RP

Ann Lewis
☎ **01994 240280**
▣ **From £17–£23**
EM From £8.50
Sleeps 4
🐶 🐴 ⚓ 🎾 ⚔
Applied

Our 300-year old farmhouse has been tastefully modernised to provide every modern amenity, including en suite facilities, central heating, colour TV in every bedroom, and is just 7 miles from the coast. The heated indoor swimming pool and snooker room are set amidst extensive lawns providing absolute safety for our younger visitors. You are warmly welcomed. Open Apr–Sept.

---

⑤ Dolau Isaf Farm, Mynachlog-ddu, Clunderwen, Pembrokeshire SA66 7SB

Mrs V C Lockton
☎/Fax **01994 419327**
▣ **From £20–£22**
EM From £12.50
Sleeps 4
🐶 🎾 ⚥ ⚓ 🏕 ⚔ ⚓ ◉
★★★
FARM

Nestling in the Preseli Hills, our traditional stone farmhouse is the perfect starting point to discover Pembrokeshire. From our welcoming bedrooms you can enjoy the superb views and watch the sheep and mohair goats. Enjoy a real farmhouse breakfast with our own free-range eggs, honey and homemade marmalade. Walkers catered for. Riding and fishing nearby. WTB Farmhouse Award. Closed Christmas. E-mail: dolau-isaf@pfh.co.uk

---

East Hook Farm, Portfield Gate, Haverfordwest, Pembrokeshire SA62 3LN

Mrs Jen Patrick
☎/Fax 01437 762211
BB From £20–£25
EM From £14
Sleeps 6
🐾 ⌘ ⅙ ♿

★★★
FARM

East Hook is a beef and sheep farm situated 3 miles west of Haverfordwest and surrounded by unspoilt countryside. Relax in the peaceful atmosphere of our Georgian farmhouse. Spacious double/twin rooms, en suite with TV, CH and tea/coffee-making facilities. Family suite available. Ideal for walking, touring or unwinding. Enjoy our selection of farmhouse cooking. Open Mar–Christmas.

East Llanteg Farm, Llanteg, Narberth, Pembrokeshire SA67 8QA

Susan Lloyd
☎ 01834 831336
BB From £15–£20
EM From £10
Sleeps 5
🐾(8) 🐕 ⅙ ⌘ 🐈 ♨ ⊚

★★
FARM

Guests are assured of a warm welcome, traditional home cooking and a relaxed, friendly atmosphere at our comfortable farmhouse. Conveniently located just minutes from the beaches of Amroth and Tenby and renowned Pembrokeshire Coastal Path. Comfortable bedrooms with private bathrooms and all facilities including colour TV. Guests' lounge. Open all year.

Erw-Lon Farm, Pontfaen, Fishguard, Pembrokeshire SA65 9TS

Mrs Lilwen McAllister
☎ 01348 881297
BB From £19–£25
EM From £12
Sleeps 6
🐾(5) ⊚

★★★
FARM

A peaceful working farm where a warm welcome awaits you and the atmosphere is relaxed and comfortable. The farm is in the Pembrokeshire Coast National Park overlooking the beautiful Gwaun Valley. Central for walking the Preseli Hills or sandy beaches and 10 mins' drive from Fishguard harbour and travel to Ireland. Open Mar–Nov. *Associate.*

Fron Isaf, Y Cross, Dinas Cross, Newport, Pembrokeshire SA42 0SW

Mrs Claire Urwin
☎ 01348 811339
BB From £20
EM From £14
Sleeps 5
🐾 🐕 ⌘ ♨ 🐈 ⊚

★★
FARM

Quiet farm in the National Park enjoying panoramic views of coast and Preseli Hills. Two beaches within 1½ miles. Map ref SN 018 384. Bedrooms overlook the sea and have tea/coffee-making facilities. Lounge has books, maps, TV and woodburner. Friendly, relaxed atmosphere. Packed lunches and vegetarian meals available. Pub nearby. Open Apr–Oct.

Gilfach Goch Farmhouse, Fishguard, Pembrokeshire SA65 9SR

June Devonald
☎/Fax 01348 873871
BB From £23–£25
EM £13
Sleeps 16
🐾 ⅙ ⌘ ⊚

★★★
FARM

Charming farmhouse with attractive grounds in National Park for people who want somewhere relaxing, peaceful and very comfortable. Oak beams, stone walls, ingle-nook, pretty bedrooms (en suite), magnificent views to the sea. Small holding with friendly animals and friendly Welsh people too! Superb meals – own produce giving variety, quality and quantity. Residential licence, fire certificate, pay phone. Farmhouse Award. Open Easter–Nov.
E-mail: devgg@netwales.co.uk

Knock Farm, Camrose, Haverfordwest, Pembrokeshire SA62 6HW

Judith Williams
☎/Fax 01437 762208
BB From £17–£25
EM From £10
Sleeps 6
🐾 🐕 ⟲ ⌘

★★★
FARM

For a 'home from home' informal atmosphere, stay on our family-run dairy farm. Situated in central Pembrokeshire, peacefully tucked away in a picturesque valley amidst trees and wildlife pond (a haven for nature lovers). Only ten minutes from Pembrokeshire's sandy beaches and walks. All bedrooms have beverage facilities, one en suite. Open Mar–Nov.

12 Knowles Farm, Lawrenny, Kilgetty, Pembrokeshire SA68 0PX

Mrs Virginia Lort-Phillips
☎ 01834 891221
Fax 01834 891344
[BB] From £20
EM From £10
Sleeps 6
🛇 🐕 ⅍ ⅄ ♨ 🍴 ☎
★★★
FARM

Home from home only better, as we do the work while you relax in total tranquillity. Look out over land sloping down to the shores of the upper Cleddau; wander through the garden and fields to waymarked walks or venture a little further to our lovely coastline. Bring a boat and explore the estuary or just stay put and unwind. Fishing, riding, birdwatching and much more. People and their pets very welcome. E-mail: owenlp@globalnet.co.uk

13 Lochmeyler Farm, Llandeloy, Pen-y-Cwm, Nr Solva, Haverfordwest, Pembrokeshire SA62 6LL

Mrs Morfydd Jones
☎ 01348 837724
Fax 01348 837622
[BB] From £20–£25
EM £12.50
Sleeps 32
🛇 🐕 Ⓔ ♨ ⅄ ☎
★★★★
FARM

Lochmeyler is a 220-acre dairy farm in the centre of St David's Peninsula, 4 miles from Solva Harbour. Sixteen en suite bedrooms (no smoking in bedrooms), TV. 4-poster beds available. Two lounges, 1 non-smokers. Choice of menus, traditional and vegetarian. RAC 5 diamonds. Member of Taste of Wales, WTB Farmhouse Award. RAC Guesthouse of the Year '93. Licensed, credit cards accepted. Open all year including Christmas. See colour ad on page 48. *Associate.*

14 Lower End Town House, Lampeter Velfrey, Narberth, Pembrokeshire SA67 8UJ

Judy Smith
☎ 01834 831738
[BB] From £20
EM From £12
Sleeps 4 + cot
🛇 🐕 ⅍ ♨ ☎
★★★
FARM

Beef and sheep farm owned and run by a young couple. Recent total refurbishment of the farmhouse has been aimed at recalling the peace and tranquillity of a bygone age whilst incorporating the comforts of a modern one. Easily accessible from the A40. Ideal for touring, walking or just unwinding. Evening meals by arrangement. Babies, dogs, and horses welcome. Open Feb–Nov.

15 Lower Haythog, Spittal, Haverfordwest, Pembrokeshire SA62 5QL

Nesta Thomas
☎/Fax 01437 731279
[BB] From £20
EM From £14
Sleeps 10–12
🛇 🐕 ⅍ 🐎 ⅃ ♨ ☎
★★★★
FARM

Sample the delights of a little country living where the quality of life matters. Join us at our charming old farmhouse on a working farm, 5 miles north of Haverfordwest. Ideal base for touring coast and countryside or just relaxing. Enjoy the peace and tranquillity in a friendly, entertaining atmosphere. Excellent, award-winning food. Well appointed en suite bedrooms, also ground floor rooms. Spacious and interesting gardens. WTB Farmhouse Award. Pay phone. Open all year except Christmas.

16 Penygraig Farm, Puncheston, Haverfordwest, Pembrokeshire SA62 5RJ

Betty Devonald
☎/Fax 01348 881277
[BB] From £18–£20
Sleeps 6
🛇 🐕 ♨ ☎
★★
FARM

A warm welcome awaits you at Penygraig, a working farm, situated near the picturesque Preseli Hills, with plenty of walks, natural trails and places of unspoilt beauty to be enjoyed. The rugged coastline of North Pembrokeshire being not far away. In the spacious dining room good wholesome cooking is served. There is 1 double room en suite, 1 family room. All rooms have tea trays, reductions for children sharing. Open Easter–Oct.
E-mail: bettydevonald@farmersweekly.net

17 Plas-y-Brodyr, Rhydwilym, Llandissilio, Clynderwen SA66 7QH

Mrs Janet Pogson
☎ 01437 563771
Fax 01437 563294
[BB] From £19–£22
EM £15
Sleeps 6
⅍ Ⓔ ⅃ ⅄ ♨ ☎
★★★★
FARM

Our lovingly restored farmhouse in historic Rhydwilym is the place to walk, fish, relax and enjoy silence! Explore Pembrokeshire and West Wales from St Davids to the new National Botanic Gardens. Return to Plas-y-Brodyr, unwind by log fires or walk the farm trail with Bob, our lovable sheepdog. WTB Farmhouse Award. Open all year except Christmas. E-mail: janet@farmhols.freeserve.co.uk

Poyerston Farm, Cosheston, Pembroke, Pembrokeshire SA72 4SJ — (18)

Mrs Sheila Lewis
☎/Fax 01646 651347
Mobile 07973 907665
BB From £20–£25
EM From £15
Sleeps 12
★★★★
FARM

Enjoy a relaxing holiday in our charming Victorian farmhouse on a working farm, nestling between the medieval town of Pembroke and historic village of Carew. Only minutes away are the wonderful beaches and spectacular scenery of the South Pembrokeshire coastline. En suite bedrooms offering comfort and style (some ground floor). Unwind in our guests' lounge or Victorian conservatory overlooking our attractive gardens. Excellent home cooking. No smoking. Open all year except Christmas.

Skerryback, Sandy Haven, St. Ishmaels, Haverfordwest, Pembrokeshire SA62 3DN — (19)

Mrs Margaret Williams
☎ 01646 636598
Fax 01646 636595
BB From £19
EM From £15
Sleeps 4
★★★
FARM

Warm Pembrokeshire welcome in 18th century farmhouse set in an attractive garden surrounded by farmland and the coastal footpath on the doorstep. A haven for walkers and bird lovers. All home comforts, home cooking, en suite available, tea-making facilities and central heating backed up by log fires on chilly evenings. Farmhouse Award.

Torbant Farmhouse, Croesgoch, Haverfordwest, Pembrokeshire SA62 5JN — (20)

Mrs Barbara Charles
☎/Fax 01348 831276
BB From £20–£22
Sleeps 4–6
★
FARM

A warm welcome awaits you at Torbant, peacefully situated near St Davids, 1½ miles from sea. The Pembrokeshire Coast National Park is all around us. Two comfortable bedrooms, both en suite with tea/coffee tray and TV. Useful utility room and cosy lounge with log fire if needed. Open Easter–Nov. E-mail: torbant@pfh.co.uk

Trepant Farm, Morvil, Rosebush, Nr Maenclochog, Pembrokeshire SA66 7RE — (21)

Marilyn Salmon
☎/Fax 01437 532491
BB From £20–£22
EM From £12
Sleeps 4
★★★
FARM

Nestling at the foot of the Preseli hills, our family farm offers a warm Welsh welcome. Ideal base for walking, cycling, pony trekking or just a leisurely drive through the quiet countryside, enjoying the unspoilt views and historical monuments. One double and one twin, both with en suite facilities. Imaginative meals, including vegetarian, using the finest local produce. Food hygiene certificate.

Self-Catering

Blackmoor Farm, Ludchurch, Amroth, Nr Saundersfoot, Pembrokeshire SA67 8PG — (22)

Len & Eve Cornthwaite
☎/Fax 01834 831242
SC From £156–£404
Sleeps 6

Relax in the peaceful and friendly environment of our 36-acre farm. Ideal location for Coastal National Park and beautiful beaches; walking, birdwatching, riding and fishing. Our attractively furnished holiday cottages are light and airy, south facing in a sheltered courtyard setting. Children enjoy rides on Dusty, our friendly donkey. Open Mar–Oct.

23 **Castell Pigyn Cottage,** Llanboidy, Whitland, Carmarthenshire SA34 0LJ

Mrs Marian Davies
☎ 01994 448391
Fax 01994 448755
SC From £150–£350
Sleeps 4
🐕 🛁 💻

🌼 🌼 🌼 🌼

Situated 4 miles north of Whitland in a peaceful area with views of undulating farmland, semi-detached to our farmhouse, the cottage is completely self-contained with 1 double and 1 twin bedded room, each with washbasins and shaver points, bedlinen and towels. Bathroom with bath and shower. Pine kitchen units and dining room furniture. Three piece suite, colour TV, fitted carpets. Own secluded garden with furniture, ample parking. Open all year.

24 **Croft Farm and Celtic Cottages,** Croft, Nr Cardigan, Pembrokeshire SA43 3NT

Andrew & Sylvie Gow
☎ /Fax 01239 615179
SC From £175–£815
Sleeps 2–7
🧍 🐕 🐄 🏐 🛁 💻

🌼 🌼 🌼 🌼 🌼

Luxury indoor heated pool, sauna, spa pool and fitness room complement these lovingly furnished, fully equipped stone cottages. Croft Farm, situated amidst beautiful North Pembrokeshire countryside is near unspoilt, sandy beaches, stunning coastal path and National Park. Help feed Tabitha (pig), Pearl and Hazel (goats) and other friendly farm animals. Open all year. E-mail: croftfarm@bigfoot.com

10 **Gilfach Goch Cottages,** Gilfach Goch, Fishguard, Pembrokeshire SA65 9SR

June Devonald
☎ /Fax 01348 873871
SC From £200–£480
Sleep 5/7
🐕 🐄 🔪 🛁 💻

🌼 🌼 🌼 🌼 🌼

Choose from the 200 year old stone walls, beamed ceiling and inglenook of Garn Madog, or Edwardian elegance, vivid colours and style of Brynawelon, two outstanding renovations in quiet, sheltered location. Panoramic landscape of sea/hills. National Park. Each house has secluded private patio, lawns, parking, woodburner, elec heating, microwave, dishwasher, washing machine. Open all year. E-mail: devgg@netwales.co.uk

25 **Gwarmacwydd,** Llanfallteg, Whitland, Carmarthenshire SA34 0XH

Mrs A Colledge
☎ 01437 563260.
Fax 01437 563839
SC From £100–£398
Sleeps 22
🐕 🐄 🔪 🛶 🛁 💻

🌼 🌼 🌼 🌼

Gwarmacwydd is a country estate of over 450 acres, set in the idyllic Taf river valley, with two miles of trout fishing, woodland and farm walks. Watch the farming and feed new born calves or lambs. Interesting and sandy local beaches at Saundersfoot and Pendine. The spacious character heated stone cottages are nicely furnished and equipped. Electricity and linen included. Open all year. E mail: farm.holidays@btinternet.com

26 **Rogeston Cottages,** Portfield Gate, Haverfordwest, Pembrokeshire SA62 3LH

John & Paula Rees
☎ /Fax 01437 781373
SC From £145–£565
Sleep 2–6
🐕 🛁 🎣 💻

🌼 🌼 🌼 🌼 🌼

Enchanting smallholding tucked away in peaceful countryside yet only 1½ miles to glorious St Brides Bay and National Park coastal footpath. Our scrupulously clean 200-year old natural stone cottages are surrounded by delightful gardens, adjoining croquet and badminton lawns, boules pitch and barbecue area. Farm trail. Pet Jersey cows, hens, ducks. Open all year. E-mail: John@pembrokeshire-cottage-holidays.co.uk

4 **The Stable & Coach House,** Cilpost Farm, Whitland, Carmarthenshire SA34 0RP

Ann Lewis
☎ 01994 240280
SC From £180–£580
Sleep 4/8
🐕 🐄 🛶 🛁 ⛳

🌼 🌼 🌼 🌼

Just 7 miles from the Pembrokeshire coast, The Stable and Coach House are delightful stone-built cottages providing the most luxurious accommodation for eight and four people respectively. Guests are welcomed to use the indoor heated swimming pool and snooker room and, by arrangement, have breakfast or dinner in the main farmhouse. Early booking is recommended. Open Apr–Sept.

Ty Geifr, Pant-y-Crwyn, Letterston, Pembrokeshire SA62 5TU　　　**27**

Jim & Ann Sibley
☎ **01348 840897**
🆂 **From £190–£500**
Sleeps 6
🐕 🐈 💼 🌐

🌻 🌻 🌻 🌻

Cottage in peaceful valley on 80-acre farm with cattle, sheep, ponies, goats, dogs and cats. Ground floor open plan accommodation, fully equipped with kitchen/dining/ lounge, bathroom, shower and bunk bedroom. First floor has twin bedded gallery bedroom and double bedroom. Also cot and high chair. Full CH, electricity and linen (excluding towels) included. Enclosed garden, barbecue. Pets welcome, kennelling available. Open Mar–Dec.

USE THE INDEX

The comprehensive Index shows which farms offer access to disabled visitors; caravanning/camping facilities; the chance to participate on a working farm; stabling/grazing for visiting horses; en suite rooms; a welcome to business people; acceptance of *Stay on a Farm* gift tokens.

STAY ON A FARM GIFT TOKENS

If you have enjoyed your Stay on a Farm, why not treat your friends and relatives to *Stay on a Farm* gift tokens? Available from the Bureau office (tel: 024 7669 6909), they can be redeemed against accommodation and are accepted by the majority of farms (see Index). Please check when booking to avoid disappointment.

FINDING YOUR ACCOMMODATION

The local FHB Group contacts listed on page 392 can always help you find a vacancy in your chosen area.

Our Internet address is
http://www.webscape.co.uk/farmaccom/

Carmarthenshire

West Wales, Swansea Bay & Mumbles

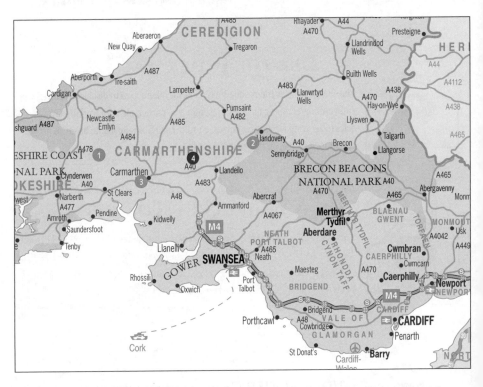

Key

Welcome to Carmarthenshire, at the heart of West Wales, a county of contrasts from the Black Mountain through the tranquil Towy, Teifi and Taf valleys to the picturesque coastal villages and the golden sands of Carmarthen Bay. Welsh is spoken throughout the county adding to the special Celtic atmosphere. All the main towns are steeped in history, many with their own castles such as Kidwelly and Llansteffan near the coast and Carreg Cennen in the hills. Visit Aberglasny Gardens and the new National Botanical Garden of Wales opening Easter 2000. Further south lies the Gower Peninsula, a holiday paradise of glorious beaches, dramatic cliffs, deep valleys and wild moorland. Here you will find charming villages and the popular resort of Mumbles jutting into Swansea Bay.

If you would like help in finding suitable farm accommodation, turn to the full listing of FHB Groups on pages 392 to 395 to find appropriate contact details for this area.

Bed and Breakfast
(and evening meal)

Castell Pigyn Farm, Llanboidy, Whitland, Carmarthenshire SA34 0LJ ①

Marian Davies
☎ **01994 448391**
Fax **01994 448755**
🆎 From **£19–£21**
EM From **£12**
Sleeps **6**
🐎 🔥 ⬤
★★★
FARM

Castell Pigyn is situated 4 miles north of Whitland in a peaceful area with fabulous views of undulating farmland. Accommodation with en suite bedrooms. Lounge with TV, dining room with family tables, good home cooking. CH throughout, ample parking. WTB Farmhouse Award, food hygiene certificate, residential licence. (Also self-catering cottage sleeping 4.) Brochure available. Closed Christmas and New Year.

Cwmgwyn Farm, Llangadog Road, Llandovery, Carmarthenshire SA20 0EQ ②

Marian Lewis
☎ **01550 720410**
Fax **01550 720262**
🆎 **£20–£22**
Sleeps **6**
🐎 ✂ 🐕 ⬤
★★★★
FARM

Welcome to the country on our livestock farm with superb views overlooking the River Towy, 2 miles from Llandovery on A4069. The 17th century farmhouse is full of charm and character with inglenook fireplace, exposed stonework and beams. 3 spacious luxury en suite bedrooms with bath/shower, hairdryer, TV, tea/coffee. Enjoy tranquil riverside setting from garden or picnic area. Ideal for touring mid/South Wales. Open Easter–Nov.

Trebersed Farm, St Peters, Travellers Rest, Carmarthen, Carmarthenshire SA31 3RR ③

Mrs Rosemary Jones
☎ **01267 238182**
Fax **01267 223633**
🆎 From **£19–£25**
Sleeps **6**
🐎 🐕 ✂ 🅱 🔥 ⬤
★★★
FARM

A warm welcome awaits you at our working dairy farm. Wellingtons available! Excellent touring base overlooking thriving market town of Carmarthen, just off main A40. Three comfortable rooms, one family, all en suite, with tea/coffee tray, central heating, radio alarm and colour TV. WTB Farmhouse Award. Open all year except Christmas. E-mail: trebersed.farm@farmline.com

Self-Catering

Pantglas Cottage, Llanfynydd, Carmarthenshire SA32 7BZ ④

Janet Watkins
☎ **01558 668214**
🆂🅲 From **£250–£325**
Sleeps **5**
🐎 🐕 📺 🍴 🔥 🎄
🌺 🌺 🌺 🌺 🌺

Enjoy breathtaking views of the Towy Valley with all its natural wildlife and meandering rivers. A 5-dragon graded cottage with swimming pool and tennis courts, etc within 250 yards. Country parks, the New Botanical Garden of Wales and good-quality restaurants serving excellent local food are just a few of our many attractions. Open all year. Associate.

Wye Valley & Vale of Usk

Brecon Beacons National Park, Monmouth, Monmouthshire
& Brecon Canal

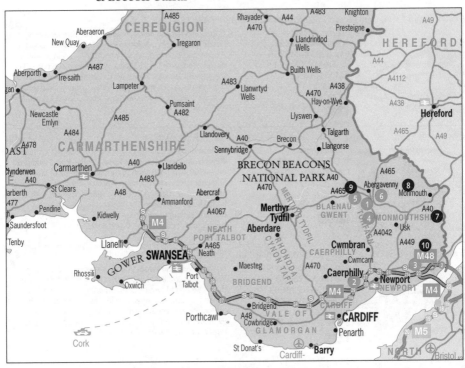

Key

- ⓵ Bed & Breakfast
- ① Self-Catering
- ⓵ B&B and SC
- ☐ Camping Barns
- ▲ Camping & Caravanning

Monmouthshire, where history and legend thrive side by side, is easily accessible from the M4 in an Area of Outstanding Natural Beauty. Discover our treasures: the strategically placed castles of Raglan and Chepstow, beautiful Tintern Abbey immortalised by Wordsworth, Roman ruins and the amphitheatre at Caerleon, and Big Pit Mining Museum. Further north rise the Brecon Beacons National Park and Llanthony Priory, leading you to Hay-on-Wye and its world-famous bookshops. You can unwind on the Monmouthshire and Brecon Canal or play golf on one of our many championship courses. This is the perfect base from which to explore Cardiff, Caerphilly, the Gower Peninsula and the Forest of Dean.

If you would like help in finding suitable farm accommodation, turn to the full listing of FHB Groups on pages 392 to 395 to find appropriate contact details for this area.

Bed and Breakfast
(and evening meal)

Hardwick Farm, Hardwick, Abergavenny, Monmouthshire NP7 9BT   ①

Mrs Carol Jones
☎ 01873 853513
☎/Fax 01873 854238
BB £20
Sleeps 6
ひ ↑ ⅓ ♠
★★★
FARM

A warm welcome awaits you on our family-run dairy farm on the edge of the Brecon Beacons, situated 1 mile from Abergavenny (A4042). Surrounded by mountain views, rolling countryside and bordered by the River Usk. Provides the ideal centre for touring, walking, fishing, pony trekking and exploring castles. Spacious en suite rooms. Brochure available. Open all year except Christmas.

Pentre-Tai Farm, Rhiwderin, Newport, Monmouthshire NP10 8RQ   ②

Susan Proctor
☎/Fax 01633 893284
BB From £19–£25
Sleeps 6
ひ ↑ ⅓ ♠ ♣ ⚙ ♒ ♠ ⚘
★★
FARM

Gateway to Wales. A warm welcome awaits you at our peaceful sheep farm located in the countryside yet only 3 miles from M4. Most rooms en suite, all with TV and beverage facilities. Children welcome at reduced rates. Ideal base for Cardiff and Wye Valley. Perfect stopover en route for Irish ferries. Approved camping and caravan site. Open Feb–Nov.

Penylan Farm, St Brides, Netherwent, Caldicot, Newport, Monmouthshire NP26 3AS   ③

Anne Arthur
☎ 01633 400267
Fax 01633 400997
BB From £20–£25
Sleeps 6
ひ ↑ ⅓ ♠ ⚘ ●
★★★
FARM

Splendid Elizabethan farmhouse with oak beams and inglenook fireplaces. Set on hilltop overlooking beautiful St Brides Valley in rural setting, 2 miles from M4 and Wentwood Forest. Heated indoor swimming pool. Many golf courses (St Pierre, Celtic Manor), castles, excellent eating places. Good overnight stop for Irish ferries. Welsh hospitality assured. Open Mar–Nov.

Ty-Cooke Farm, Mamhilad, Pontypool, Monmouthshire NP4 8QZ   ④

Mrs Marion Price
☎/Fax 01873 880382
BB From £20–£25
Sleeps 6
ひ ⅓ ⚙ ♠ ⚘
★★
FARM

A comfortable 18th century farmhouse set in a cobbled courtyard. The family-run mixed farm is set on the edge of the Brecon Beacons National Park. Goytre Wharf on the Monmouthshire–Brecon Canal is ½ mile away. Ty-Cooke is the ideal centre for exploring the mountains and valleys of South Wales. Open all year.

The Wenallt Farm, Gilwern, near Abergavenny, Monmouthshire NP7 0HP   ⑤

The Harris Family
☎/Fax 01873 830694
BB From £19.50–£24
EM From £12
Sleeps 8
ひ ↑ ♠ ⚘ ⚙ ●
★★
FARM

A 16th century Welsh longhouse set in 50 acres of farmland in the Brecon Beacons National Park commanding magnificent views over the Usk Valley. Retaining all its old charm with oak beams, inglenook fireplace, yet offering a high standard with en suite bedrooms, good food and a warm welcome. An ideal base from which to see Wales and the surrounding areas. Licensed. Brochure available. Open all year.

6 **Werngochlyn Farm,** Llantilio Pertholey, Abergavenny, Monmouthshire NP7 8BN

Mr & Mrs Richard Sage
☎ **01873 857357**
BB **From £18–£22**
Sleeps 6
ﾃﾃﾟﾝﾑﾒﾟ
★
FARM

12th century listed farmhouse under the Skirrid Mountain, 3 miles from Abergavenny market town. Two en suite bedrooms. Indoor heated swimming pool, games room, approved riding centre. Many friendly farm animals. Golf range and golf course ½ mile. Brochure on request.

Self-Catering

7 **Broomy & Purkis Cottages,** Panta Farm, Devauden, Chepstow, Monmouthshire NP16 6PS

Mrs Irene Brooke
☎ **01291 650593**
Fax 01291 650400
SC **From £150–£250**
Sleep 4/5
ﾃﾑﾟ
Applied

Careful conversion of 17th century barn into two self-catering cottages with lovely views over surrounding countryside. 2 miles from Tintern Abbey. Superb unspoilt walks and historic towns nearby. The cottages are tastefully decorated and have electric CH, fitted kitchens and microwaves, colour TV and video. Bedlinen and towels included. Shared laundry room, payphone, enclosed garden. Tennis court, table tennis and delicious homemade ice cream. Open all year.

8 **Granary & Coach House,** Upper Cwm Farm, Brynderi, Llantilio Crossenny, Abergavenny, Mon. NP7 8TG

Ann Ball
☎/**Fax 01873 821236**
SC **From £200–£370**
Sleep 6
ﾃﾟﾑﾟ
⚜ ⚜ ⚜ ⚜

Holidays and short breaks in beautifully converted old barn on working sheep farm. Family accommodation with CH, TV, electricity, bed linen, towels included. Peaceful superb views, ideal for walking, birdwatching, exploring Welsh castles, Brecon Beacons, Wye and Usk Valleys. The Granary (upper) and Coach House (ground) each have 1 double and 2 twin bedrooms, lounge/dining/kitchen, bathroom with shower. Brochure. Open all year.

9 **Hopyard Farm,** Glanbaiden, Govilon, Abergavenny, Monmouthshire NP7 9SE

Diana Blowfield
☎/**Fax 01873 830219**
SC **From £145–£265**
Sleeps 4/5
ﾃﾟﾑﾟ
⚜ ⚜ ⚜

Ideally located on edge of Brecon Beacons between River Usk and Monmouth–Brecon Canal, four cottages converted from old stone barn. Fully furnished, linen, towels and electricity included. Each cottage has small rear garden. Safe children's play area with stunning views of Beacons and Black Mountains. Cycle hire available. Brochure. Open all year.

10 **Parsons Grove,** Earlswood, nr Shirenewton, Chepstow, Monmouthshire NP6 6RD

Frances Marchant
☎/**Fax 01291 641382**
SC **From £135–£360**
Sleep 4/6
ﾃﾟﾝﾑﾟ
⚜ ⚜ ⚜ ⚜

On the edge of beautiful Wye Valley, set in 16 acres of peaceful countryside, with heated swimming pool. Three cottages, furnished to very high standard. Fully carpeted with colour TV, fitted kitchen, refrigerator, cooker, microwave, CH. All linen (duvets) and towels included. Panoramic views of beautiful valley and Wentwood Forest. Riding, golf and fishing nearby. Free use of barbecue, boules, croquet. Brochure. Open Mar–Oct. E-mail: pargrove@aol.com

Northern Ireland

Farm entries in this section are listed under those counties shown in green on the key map. The index below the map gives the appropriate page numbers. You will see that we have listed the counties geographically so that you can turn more easily to find farms in neighbouring Counties.

At the start of each county section is a detailed map with numbered symbols indicating the location of each farm. Different symbols denote different types of accommodation; see the key below each county map. Farm entries are listed alphabetically under type of accommodation. Some farms offer more than one type of accommodation and therefore have more than one entry.

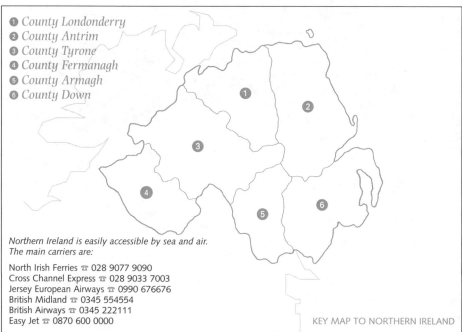

❶ *County Londonderry*
❷ *County Antrim*
❸ *County Tyrone*
❹ *County Fermanagh*
❺ *County Armagh*
❻ *County Down*

Northern Ireland is easily accessible by sea and air. The main carriers are:

North Irish Ferries ☎ 028 9077 9090
Cross Channel Express ☎ 028 9033 7003
Jersey European Airways ☎ 0990 676676
British Midland ☎ 0345 554554
British Airways ☎ 0345 222111
Easy Jet ☎ 0870 600 0000

KEY MAP TO NORTHERN IRELAND

County Londonderry

Sperrin Mountains

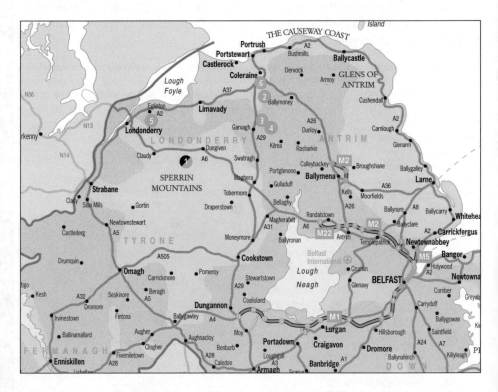

Key

🔵 Bed & Breakfast

⬤ Self-Catering

⬤ B&B and SC

🔲 Camping Barns

🔺 Camping & Caravanning

This is a fertile agricultural county with small farms scattered across the broad, sweeping land and long Atlantic beaches. The city of Londonderry, also known as Derry, is best known for its massive city walls, outstanding museums, two cathedrals and lively cultural scene. In the county's north-east corner is Coleraine which is conveniently close to the seaside resorts of Portstewart and Castlerock for sea angling, golf and children's amusements. For rewarding scenic drives, the Sperrin Mountains are best approached from Limavady and the beautiful Roe Valley Country Park. The Bann river is noted for trout and salmon.

If you would like help in finding suitable farm accommodation, turn to the full listing of FHB Groups on pages 392 to 395 to find appropriate contact details for this area.

Bed and Breakfast
(and evening meal)

Drumcovitt House, 704 Feeny Road, Feeny, Co Londonderry BT47 4SU

Florence Sloan
☎/Fax 028 7778 1224
[BB] From £17–£22
EM From £5–£20
Sleeps 6
🐎 ♿ 🖭 ⚘ 🐾 ⬢
Certified

Listed Georgian farmhouse with established gardens, 2 miles from Banagher Glen. Ideal centre for exploring Sperrins, Derry City, Donegal and the Causeway Coast. Fishing Roe, Faughan. Golf at Derry, Limavady. Archaelogical sites from pre-history onwards. Half mile east of Feeny on B74 off A6 Derry to Belfast. 1 family room, 1 twin, 1 single. Visa/Mastercard/Eurocard/Delta cards accepted. Open all year.
E mail: drumcovitt.feeny@btinternet.com

Greenhill House, 24 Greenhill Road, Aghadowey, Coleraine, Co Londonderry BT51 4EU

Mrs Elizabeth Hegarty
☎ 028 7086 8241
Fax 028 7086 8365
[BB] From £25
EM From £17.50 (booked in advance) Sleeps 14
🖮 🐎 🖭 ♿
3 star

Georgian country guest house (CH). Good views across wooded countryside in the Bann Valley and the Antrim hills. Convenient to Giant's Causeway and north coast for golf, touring, fishing. Six rooms en suite with direct-dial telephones, colour TV, tea/coffee. From Coleraine take A29 south for 7 miles, turn left on B66 and we are on right. Recommended in international guides. Egon Ronay, Taste of Ulster, AA Premier Selected QQQQQ. Open Mar–Oct. E-mail: greenhill.house@btinternet.com

---

Heathfield Farm, 31 Drumcroone Road, Killykergan, Coleraine, Co Londonderry BT51 4EB

Mrs Heather Torrens
☎/Fax 028 2955 8245
[BB] From £20–£22.50
EM From £12.50
Sleeps 6
🐎 🐾 🖭 ⬤ ♿
Certified

Ulster winner of AIB Agr-Tourism Farm Guest House and UDT regional winner. Comfortable 17th century farmhouse on working beef and sheep farm, set in large garden in lovely countryside. Convenient to Giant's Causeway, north coast and superb golf courses. Fishing in River Agivey beside farm. Guests' lounge with log fire. En suite rooms well equipped with many extras. On A29 Garvagh-Coleraine road. Open all year.

Killeague Farm, 157 Drumcroone Road, Blackhill, Coleraine, Co Londonderry BT51 3SG

Margaret Moore
☎/Fax 01265 868229
[BB] From £20
EM From £12
Sleeps 6
🐎 🐾 🍴 ♿ 🐴
Certified

Relax and enjoy the comfort and warm welcome at our 130-acre dairy farm which is on A29, convenient to North Antrim coast, sandy beaches and Giant's Causeway. Stabling on the farm and horse riding can be arranged. Air and sea ports 1 hour's drive. Three en suite luxury bedrooms with tea/coffee. Open fires. TV lounge. Special off-season terms. Open all year.

Killennan House, 40 Killennan Road, Drumahoe, Co Londonderry BT47 3NG

Mrs Averil Campbell
☎/Fax 028 7130 1710
[BB] From £17
Sleeps 6
🐎(4) ♿ ⬤
Certified

A 19th century farmhouse on working farm with spacious gardens close to historic city. Ideal base for touring to Giant's Causeway and Donegal. Airport, fishing, golf, flying and riding nearby. 1 twin, 1 double, 1 family room, all en suite, with CH, colour TV, tea/coffee facilities. A6 Claudy direction from Londonderry, 5m B118 (Eglinton) 1½m left Killenan Road, first right. Open all year.

Tullans Farm, 46 Newmills Road, Coleraine BT52 2JB

Mrs Diana McClelland
☎ 01265 42309
BB From £15–£17
Sleeps 6
ᗘ ⅄ 人 ⊕ ▥
Certified

1 double room en suite, 1 family room with H&C. Farmhouse (central heating) 1 mile from Coleraine. Nearby fishing, swimming pool, bowling, ice-skating, horse riding and birdwatching. Babysitter. Dogs allowed outside. Portstewart/Portrush 5 miles. Golf and sandy beaches 5 miles. Turn off A29 Coleraine bypass (ring road), ½ mile past roundabout (junction A26) into Newmills Road. Open all year.

Self-Catering

Drumcovitt Cottages, 704 Feeny Road, Feeny, Co Londonderry BT47 4SU

Florence Sloan
☎/Fax 028 7778 1224
SC From £265–£360
Sleeps 4/5
ᗘ ᗘ ᚛ ⅏ ▪ ☆ ⋇ ⬡
4 star

Three 4-star cottages, each fully equipped (dishwasher, washer/dryer, microwave, telephone, etc). One wheelchair accessible, all oil centrally heated, two with log fires. Experience Sperrins, Donegal, Giant's Causeway, Derry and much more within an hour's drive from Drumcovitt. Return to quiet 240-acre farm in beautiful Sperrin foothills. Open all year. E-mail: drumcovitt.feeny@btinternet.com

County Antrim

Causeway Coast & Glens of Antrim

Key

🔵1 Bed & Breakfast

🟢1 Self-Catering

🔵1 B&B and SC

⬜1 Camping Barns

🔺1 Camping & Caravanning

To the south east of the county Belfast provides excellent shopping and city entertainment, while in the north west lies the Causeway Coast and famous Giant's Causeway. Between lie the nine Glens of Antrim and their quaint waterfoot villages, the spectacular coast road, Carrickfergus Castle and Antrim with its ancient round tower and splendid park. There's pony trekking near Ballycastle, a spectacular swinging rope bridge at Carrick-a-rede, golf at Royal Portrush, and bathing, boating and fishing along the hundred miles of shore. The Irish Linen Centre at Lisburn recreates Ulster's greatest industry and is a great place for souvenir shopping.

If you would like help in finding suitable farm accommodation, turn to the full listing of FHB Groups on pages 392 to 395 to find appropriate contact details for this area.

Bed and Breakfast
(and evening meal)

---

①   **Beechgrove,** 412 Upper Road, Trooperslane, Carrickfergus, Co Antrim BT38 8TG

Betta Barron
☎/Fax 01960 363304
🅱 From £16–£18
EM From £9.50
Sleeps 13
🛏 🛉 🏃 🐾 🛢 🌸
Certified

A warm welcome awaits you at Beechgrove farmhouse (central heating) on 16 acre mixed farm near sea. Fishing, golf, riding. Knochagh monument, Belfast zoo, leisure centre nearby. 3 single, 1 double, 2 family rooms, 1 twin (all H/C). Babysitter. Dogs allowed (outside). Off A2, 1 mile south of Carrickfergus. Larne 10 miles. Belfast 10 miles. Carrickfergus 3 miles. Open all year.

---

②   **Brown's Country House,** 174 Ballybogey Road, Coleraine, Co Londonderry BT52 2LP

Mrs Jean Brown
☎ 028 2073 2777/1627
Fax 028 2073 1627
🅱 From £20
Sleeps 16
🛉 🛏 🌿 🐾 🛢
Certified

A chalet bungalow with spacious lawns. Central heating. Home baking. On Ballymoney – Portrush road (B62). 2 double bedrooms, 4 twin rooms, 1 family room, 3 ground floor, 1 en suite. Tea/ coffee in all rooms. Babysitter. Dogs allowed (outside). Bushmills 4 miles, Coleraine and Portrush 5 miles. Open all year.

---

③   **Carnside Farm Guest House,** 23 Causeway Road, Giant's Causeway, Bushmills, Co Antrim BT57 8SU

Frances Lynch
☎ 028 2073 1337
🅱 From £14–£20
EM From £10
Sleeps 19
🛏 🛉 🏃
Certified

Farmhouse (central heating) on 200-acre dairy farm. Magnificent coastal view. Fishing, golf, water sports. Old Bushmills Distillery 2 miles has weekday tours. 1 single, 3 double (1 en suite), 1 twin, 3 family rooms (1 en suite), 2 on ground floor, all H&C. Babysitter. Dogs allowed (outside). Bushmills 2 miles, Ballycastle 12 miles, Giant's Causeway ¼ mile. Open Mar–Oct.

---

④   **Cullentra House,** 16 Cloughs Road (off Gaults Road), Cushendall, Co Antrim BT44 0SP

Olive McAuley
☎/Fax 028 2177 1762
🅱 From £14.50–£16.50
Sleeps 6/8
🛉 🛏(2) 🌿 🛢 🌸
Certified

Award-winning country house nestling amidst breathtaking scenery of Antrim Coast and Glens. Golf course, Ballycastle and Giant's Causeway nearby. 1 family room, 1 double and 1 twin, all en suite. TV, tea/coffee-making facilities. Homely atmosphere and warm welcome extended to all guests. Last B&B on Cloughs Road. Open all year.
E-mail: cullentra@ireland-holidays.net

---

⑤   **Neelsgrove Farm,** 51 Carnearney Road, Ahoghill, Ballymena, Co Antrim BT42 2PL

Mrs Margaret Neely
☎ 028 2587 1225
Fax 028 2587 8704
🅱 From £16–£18.50
EM From £10
Sleeps 6
🛏 🌿 🐾 🛢 🌸
Certified

Country house (central heating) in 1 acre of grounds on mixed farm. Home baking. Water skiing 2 miles, golf nearby. 6 miles from Ballymena, 15 miles from International Airport. Convenient to Glens of Antrim and River Bann. Fishermen welcome, tackle space available. 2 double en suite, 1 twin room with H/C. Dogs allowed outside. Car parking. Food hygiene certificate. Open Jan–Nov. E-mail: msneely@btinternet.com

---

Sprucebank, 41 Ballymacombs Road, Portglenone, Co Antrim BT44 8NR   ⑥

Mrs Thomasena Sibbett
☎ **028 2582 2150/1422**
Fax 028 2582 1422
BB **From £16–£18**
Sleeps 8
⟁ ★ ▪
Certified

Relax in the tranquil surroundings of our 18th century farmhouse conveniently situated for touring the province and on route to Ireland's north and west coast. Golf, fishing, forest and river walks nearby. One hour from ports of entry on A54, 1½ miles south west from Portglenone. Open Mar–Oct or by arrangement.
E-mail: portglenone@nacn.org

Valley View, 6a Ballyclough Road, Bushmills, Co Antrim BT57 8TU   ⑦

Valerie McFall
☎ **012657 41608/41319**
Fax 012657 42739
BB **From £16–£18**
Sleeps 19
♿ ⟁ ▥ ⅍ ▪
Certified

Peaceful setting with beautiful views, conveniently located for touring the North Antrim coast and Giant's Causeway. This attractive country house has a homely atmosphere. Relax with tea and home baking on arrival. The six en suite rooms are tastefully decorated and have tea/coffee, TV and hairdrier. Payphone, no smoking. Take B17 to Coleraine for 1 mile, pass Maxol Station, take first left, after 3 miles, on right. Open all year.
E-mail: valerie.mcfall@btinternet.com

CONFIRM BOOKINGS

Disappointments can arise from misunderstandings over the telephone. Please write to confirm your booking.

THE 1000+ BUREAU MEMBERS OFFER A UNIQUE LINK TO CUSTOMERS ACROSS THE UK

All Bureau members belong to a local Group. Each member can refer you to an equally high quality member within the Group... or across the UK: England, Northern Ireland, Scotland, Wales.

STAY ON A FARM GIFT TOKENS

If you have enjoyed your Stay on a Farm, why not treat your friends and relatives to *Stay on a Farm* gift tokens? Available from the Bureau office (tel: 024 7669 6909), they can be redeemed against accommodation and are accepted by the majority of farms (see Index). Please check when booking to avoid disappointment.

County Tyrone

Sperrin Mountains

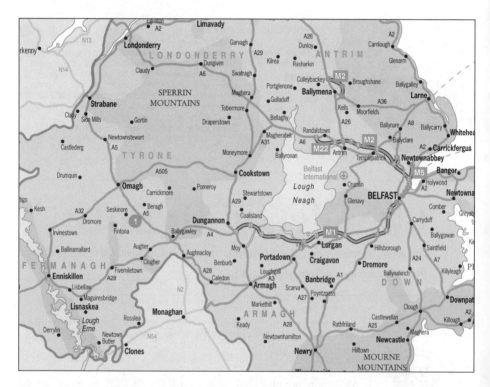

Key

 Bed & Breakfast

 Self-Catering

 B&B and SC

 Camping Barns

 Camping & Caravanning

Between the Sperrins in the north and the green Clogher Valley with its village cathedral in the south lies this county of great historic interest. You can discover its past at the Ulster-American Folk Park and Ulster History Park, both near Omagh, while the story of the Lough Neagh fishing and eel industry is told at Kinturk Cultural Centre, east of Cookstown. A mysterious ceremonial site of stone circles and cairns has recently been discovered at Beaghmore and there are numerous Stone Age and Bronze Age remains in the area. There are forest parks, Gortin Glen and Drum Manor for rambling, excellent fishing near Newtownstewart and market towns such as Dungannon for souvenir Tyrone Crystal.

If you would like help in finding suitable farm accommodation, turn to the full listing of FHB Groups on pages 392 to 395 to find appropriate contact details for this area.

Bed and Breakfast
(and evening meal)

Greenmount Lodge, 58 Greenmount Road, Gortaclare, Omagh, Co Tyrone BT79 0YE

Mrs F Louie Reid
☎ **028 8284 1325**
Fax **028 8284 0019**
[BB] **From £19–£22**
EM From £12.50
Sleeps 22
  ♿ 🐴 🐕 ✂ 📷 🚶 💼
2 star

Farm guest house on 150-acre farm. Superb accommodation, excellent cuisine. Central for sightseeing Fermanagh, Lakeland, the Sperrin Mountains. A5 from Ballygawley to Omagh, left before Carrick Keel pub at Fintona sign 1 mile. Open all year.
E-mail: greenmountlodge@lineone.net

NO ANSWER?
Farmers are mostly out and about during the day.
Try to telephone before 9.30am or after 4pm.

CONFIRM BOOKINGS
Disappointments can arise from misunderstandings over the telephone.
Please write to confirm your booking.

 Please mention *Stay on a Farm* when booking

USE THE INDEX

The comprehensive Index shows which farms offer access to disabled visitors; caravanning/camping facilities; the chance to participate on a working farm; stabling/grazing for visiting horses; en suite rooms; a welcome to business people; acceptance of *Stay on a Farm* gift tokens.

County Fermanagh

Ulster's Lakeland

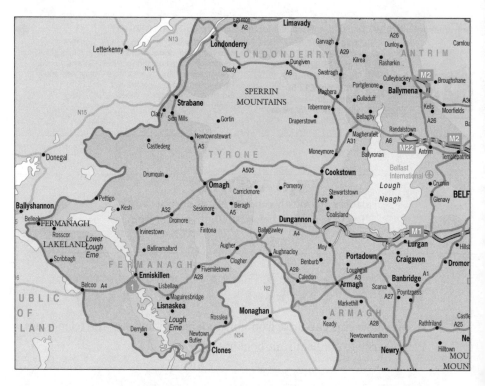

Key

🔴 **1** Bed & Breakfast

🔴 **1** Self-Catering

🟠 **1** B&B and SC

🔲 **1** Camping Barns

🔺 **1** Camping & Caravanning

Ulster's Lakeland spreads its web of waterways, islands, forest and glen, castles and abbey ruins right across the county. Enniskillen, county town and shopping centre, strides the narrows between upper and lower Lough Erne, with the romantic silhouette of the Watergate a famous feature of the waterfront scene. Pleasure boats run daily cruises in summer and boats are available to hire. Golf, water-skiing and even pleasure flying are available nearby. Fishermen need no reminder that these are the waters where record catches are made. Two of Ulster's finest houses in National Trust care, Florence Court and Castle Coole, are in Fermanagh, and there is an underground boat trip at Marble Arch Caves. Visitors to the old pottery at Belleek can watch craftsmen at work on fine porcelain.

If you would like help in finding suitable farm accommodation, turn to the full listing of FHB Groups on pages 392 to 395 to find appropriate contact details for this area.

Bed and Breakfast
(and evening meal)

Riverside Farm Guest House, Gortadrehid, Culkey Post Office, Enniskillen, Co Fermanagh BT92 2FN

Mrs Mary Isobel Fawcett
☎ 028 6632 2725
Fax 028 6632 5822
ⒷⒷ From £16–£18
EM From £6–£8
Sleeps 14
🐕 🏇 🏕 🐟 ⚓ 🎣 ⛺ ⛴
Certified

Farmhouse (central heating) on 65-acre livestock farm. NT properties, fishing, shooting, scenic drives, golfing nearby. 2 family rooms (1 en suite), 3 twin, 1 double, 1 single, all H&C. Babysitter. Dogs allowed outside. Fire certificate. Small parties catered for (max 25). From Enniskillen take A4 for 1½ miles, left (A509) for 1½ miles. Enniskillen 3 miles. Open all year.

County Armagh

The Orchard County

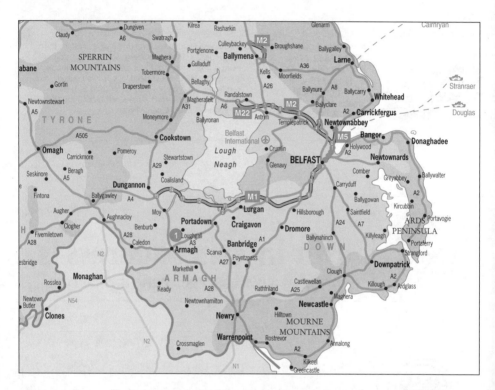

Key

- 🔵 **1** Bed & Breakfast
- 🔴 **1** Self-Catering
- 🟢 **1** B&B and SC
- ⬜ **1** Camping Barns
- 🔺 **1** Camping & Caravanning

Northern Ireland's smallest county rises gently from Lough Neagh's banks, southward through apple orchards, farmland and hill forest to the rocky summit of Slieve Gullion, mountain of Cuchulain. The city of Armagh is a religious capital older than Canterbury, with two cathedrals, the Georgian Mall and a Planetarium and Observatory. Visit the famous hill fort, 'Emain Macha', capital of the kings of Ulster from 600BC and interpreted at the Navan Centre just outside the city. Craigavon has a leisure centre, ski slope and lakes for water sports, and there is sailing on Lough Neagh and angling and canoeing on the Blackwater river.

If you would like help in finding suitable farm accommodation, turn to the full listing of FHB Groups on pages 392 to 395 to find appropriate contact details for this area.

Bed and Breakfast
(and evening meal)

Ballinahinch House, 47 Ballygroobany Road, Richhill, Co Armagh BT61 9NA 

Elizabeth Kee
☎/Fax 01762 870081
🅱 From £15–£20
Sleeps 6/8
⛷ 🐎 🧍 ⊞ 🛏 ⌚ 🛁 ⚱ ⬤
Certified

Early Victorian farmhouse with traditional furnishings, landscaped lawns and rose garden. Tea/coffee-making facilities, home cooking. Shooting over farm. Pony riding, golf, fishing and NT properties nearby. From A3 turn off at junction B131 to Richhill. 2nd road left – Ballyleny Road – go to end, cross roads, straight across – Ballygroobany Road. House 1 mile on left. 1 single, 1 twin, 1 double, 1 family, 1 en suite.

FARM HOLIDAY BUREAU

Please mention *Stay on a Farm* when booking

FARM HOLIDAY BUREAU

STAY ON A FARM GIFT TOKENS

If you have enjoyed your Stay on a Farm, why not treat your friends and relatives to *Stay on a Farm* gift tokens? Available from the Bureau office (tel: 024 7669 6909), they can be redeemed against accommodation and are accepted by the majority of farms (see Index). Please check when booking to avoid disappointment.

LET THE TELEPHONE RING!
Some farmhouses are big places. Let the telephone ring long enough to give the owner time to answer it.

CONFIRM BOOKINGS
Disappointments can arise from misunderstandings over the telephone. Please write to confirm your booking.

County Down

Ards Peninsula & Mourne Mountains

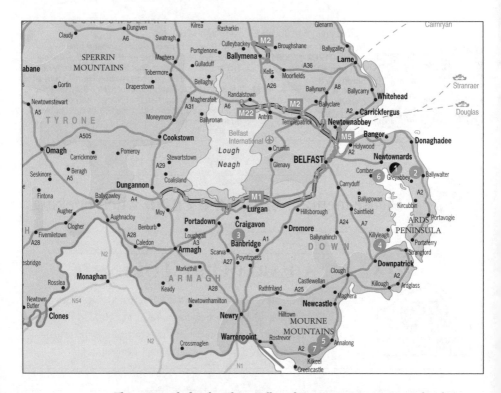

Key

🅐 Bed & Breakfast

🅐 Self-Catering

🅐 B&B and SC

🅐 Camping Barns

🔺 Camping & Caravanning

This area includes the Ulster Folk and Transport Museum at Cultra by Belfast Lough, the ancient shrines of St Patrick's Country round the cathedral hill at Downpatrick, the golden beaches of the Ards Peninsula and the mountainous kingdom of Mourne, an ancient town with some of the richest heritage in Ireland including St Patrick's grave. Lively Newcastle is famous for its seaside festival and there are beautiful historic houses to visit such as Mount Stewart and Castle Ward. Horseriding, sailing, angling and golf are everywhere within reach, there is motor racing at Kirkistown, sea angling in Strangford Lough and an intriguing aquarium at Portaferry.

If you would like help in finding suitable farm accommodation, turn to the full listing of FHB Groups on pages 392 to 395 to find appropriate contact details for this area.

Bed and Breakfast
(and evening meal)

Beechhill Farm, 10 Loughries Road, Newtownards, Co Down BT23 8RN ①

Mrs Joan McKee
☎ **01247 818404**
Fax 01247 812820
ⒷⒷ **From £17.50**
EM From £12
Sleeps 6
🐴 🛏 ⚓ 💼
Certified

Farmhouse on the Ards peninsula on a working farm. 1 double, 1 single, 1 family room (all H/C). Dogs allowed outside. A20 south from Newtownards, 2 miles left at Millisle signpost, right at T junction, left at Loughries School. Newtownards 4 miles, Bangor 8 miles. Open all year except Christmas. E-mail: jr.mckee@virgin.net

---

Greenlea Farm, 48 Dunover Road, Ballywalter, Newtownards, Co Down BT22 2LE ②

Evelyn McIvor
☎/**Fax 012477 58218**
ⒷⒷ **From £15.50–£18**
EM From £6.50–£11
Sleeps 11 (+ cot)
🐴(12) 🛏 ⚓ 💼 ⬡
Certified

Come feel at home in our friendly little home with the big welcome. 5 bedrooms, all with H&C. CH. Large dining room, guests' own sitting room with piano and TV. We provide good food, enjoy people and will make your stay memorable. ½ mile off A2. Yachting, fishing, golf, flying club, racing (Kirkiston), NT properties nearby. Bangor 10 miles, Portaferry 14 miles, Belfast City Airport 20 miles. Open all year.

Mourneview, 32 Drumnascamph Road, Laurencetown, Gilford, Co Down BT63 6DU ③

Esther & Nettie Kerr
☎ **028 4062 6270/4251**
Fax 028 4062 4251
ⒷⒷ **From £17–£20**
Sleeps 8
🧍 🐴(2) 🍴 ☕ ♨ ⚓ ⬡
Certified

Superbly appointed bungalow beautifully designed on 200 acre farm providing a welcoming homely atmosphere. Guests TV lounge, dining room, tea/coffee-making facilities, payphone. Health/hygiene and fire certificates. Good base for touring. Linen. Homelands and participating in the full range of leisure activities nearby. 4 en suite rooms which are also suitable for disabled guests. Open all year except Christmas.
E-mail: mourneview@dialpipex.com

Pheasants' Hill Country House, 37 Killyleagh Road, Downpatrick, Co Down BT30 9BL ④

Janis Bailey
☎/**Fax 028 4461 7246**
Mobile 07710 904135
ⒷⒷ **From £19–£23.50**
EM From £19.50
Sleeps 6
🐴 🛏 🍴 🌳 ♨ ⚓ ⬡
Certified

Luxury Irish country house accommodation, AA 4 Diamonds, in St Patrick's Country beside National Nature Reserve and Strangford Lough (AONB/ASSI). Turf fire, pretty en suite bedrooms, fresh flowers, comfy beds. Delicious Irish cooking, vegetarian available. Market garden, orchard, cottage garden, wildflowers, herbs, rare breeds, pond, stream, woodland. On Ulster Way. Airport 30 minutes. Open all year.
E-mail: pheasants.hill@dnet.co.uk

Sharon Farmhouse, 6 Ballykeel Road, Ballymartin, Kilkeel, Co Down BT34 4PL ⑤

M. Bingham
☎ **028 4176 2521**
ⒷⒷ **From £16–£18**
Sleeps 6
🧍 🐴 🛏 🍴 ⚓ ♨ ⬡
Certified

Farm bungalow – 1 family, 1 twin, 1 single, all with H/C and central heating. Guest bathroom/shower. With excellent sea and mountain views. Situated ideally for mountaineering and 10 minutes from beach. 2 miles from Kilkeel town and fishing port. The area is rich in varied birdlife. Good wholesome home cooked food served in abundance. A warm and welcoming atmosphere. Your comfort is our pleasure. Open all year.

Trench Farm, 35 Ringcreevy Road, Islandhill, Comber, Newtownards, Co Down BT23 5JR

Maureen Hamilton
☎/Fax 028 9187 2558
BB £17.50
Sleeps 6
🐕 🐎 ✂ ▪ ⬡
Certified

Farmhouse on working horticultural farm overlooking Strangford Lough excellent for birdlife. H&C and tea/coffee facilities in all bedrooms. Close to Scrabo Tower and golf course. Public health and hygiene certificate. Take A21 Newtownards Road from Comber, first road on right. Vouchers accepted. Open all year.

 Wyncrest, 30 Main Road, Ballymartin, Kilkeel, Co Down BT34 4NU

Robert & Irene Adair
☎ 028 4176 3012
Fax 028 4176 5988
BB £22
Sleeps 11
🐕 ⓒ ✂ ⓔ ▪
Certified

A warm welcome awaits you at our farm guesthouse where we are renowned for our food and hospitality. Enjoy a holiday in the beautiful 'Mourne' country, a rambler's paradise. Relax in our conservatory and sample our home baking. Most rooms en suite with tea/coffee facilities and colour TV. Visa/Mastercard accepted. Open Apr–Oct.

CONFIRM BOOKINGS

Disappointments can arise from misunderstandings over the telephone. Please write to confirm your booking.

STAY ON A FARM GIFT TOKENS

If you have enjoyed your Stay on a Farm, why not treat your friends and relatives to *Stay on a Farm* gift tokens? Available from the Bureau office (tel: 024 7669 6909), they can be redeemed against accommodation and are accepted by the majority of farms (see Index). Please check when booking to avoid disappointment.

FOLLOW THE COUNTRY CODE

Leave nothing but footprints,
Take nothing but photographs,
Kill nothing but time!

Reference section

FHB Group contacts

Every member of the Farm Holiday Bureau belongs to one of 91 local Groups, each of which has its own nominated contact person. (Occasionally, different contacts are given for bed and breakfast (**B&B**) and self-catering (**SC**) accommodation.) If you need help finding accommodation, try the local Group contacts in your chosen area. They may be able to tell you which members have vacancies.

Listed in the order in which their appropriate counties/tourism areas appear in the guide, FHB Group contacts are as follows:

Scotland

Highlands
Highlands Group
B&B Mrs M Pottie   Tel/Fax 01667 462213
SC Mrs J Masheter   Tel/Fax 01463 782423

Aberdeen & Grampian
Grampian Group
Mrs Patricia Duncan   Tel 01261 851261
Highlands Group (as for *Highlands*)

Argyll, Isles, Loch Lomond, Stirling & Trossachs
Heart of Scotland Group
Mrs Anne Lennox   Tel/Fax 01389 850231

Perthshire
Perthshire Group
Mrs Jo Andrew   Tel/Fax 01350 724254

Angus & City of Dundee
Angus & Dundee Group
B&B Mrs Deanna Lindsay   Tel/Fax 01307 462887
SC Mrs Moira Clarke   Tel/Fax 01575 560213

Kingdom of Fife
Kingdom of Fife Group
Mrs June Weatherup   Tel/Fax 01383 860277

Greater Glasgow & Clyde Valley
Around Glasgow Group
B&B Mrs Elsie Hunter   Tel/Fax 01236 830243
E-mail: hunter@glentore.freeserve.co.uk

SC Mrs Patricia Carmichael   Tel 01899 308336
                                    Fax 01899 308481
E-mail: chiefcarm@aol.com
Heart of Scotland Group
(as for *Argyll, the Isles & Stirling*)

Edinburgh & Lothians
East Lothian – Edinburgh's Coast & Countryside
Mrs M Whiteford   Tel 01620 810327
Heart of Scotland Group
(as for *Argyll, the Isles & Stirling*)

Ayrshire & Arran
Ayrshire & Arran Group
Mrs Agnes Gemmell   Tel/Fax 01292 500225

Dumfries & Galloway
Dumfriesshire (Annandale) Group
B&B Mrs Kate Miller   Tel/Fax 01683 221900

Scottish Borders
Scottish Borders Group
Mrs Ann Prentice   Tel 01361 882811

England

England's North Country

Cumbria
Carlisle's Border Country Group
Mrs Margaret Sisson   Tel/Fax 01228 577219
Central Lakeland Group
Mrs Margaret Harryman   Tel 017687 78544
Eden Valley & North Pennines Group
Mrs Mary Miburn   Tel 017684 86212
Hadrian's Wall, North Cumbria & the Borders Group
Mrs Elizabeth Woodmass   Tel 016977 47285
North Pennines Group
Mrs Susan Huntley   Tel/Fax 01434 381372
South Lakeland Group
Mrs Linda Nicholson   Tel 01229 885277
West Lakeland Group
Mrs Carolyn Heslop   Tel/Fax 01900 824222

Northumberland
Northumberland South Group
Mrs Susan Dart   Tel/Fax 01434 673240

Durham
Durham & its Dales Group
Mrs Helen Lowes   Tel/Fax 01833 621218
North Pennines Group (as for *Cumbria*)

Lancashire
Lancashire Pennines Group
Mrs Carole Mitson   Tel 01282 865301
South Pennines Group
Mrs Charlotte Walsh   Tel 0161 368 4610
                            Fax 0161 367 9106
Vale of Lune, Morecambe Bay
Mrs N Lund   Tel 01524 241458

**Yorkshire – Dales, Brontë Country, South,
West & Harrogate**
Harrogate & Nidderdale Group
Mrs Christine Ryder   Tel 01943 880354
                            Fax 01943 880374
Mrs Sheila Smith   Tel 01423 771040
                            Fax 01423 771515
South & West Yorkshire Group
Mrs Marie Gill   Tel 01924 848339
Yorkshire Dales & Bronte Country Group
Mrs Anne Pearson   Tel 01756 791579

**Yorkshire – Dales (North), Vales, Moors,
Wolds & Coast**
Cleveland & North Yorkshire Borders Group
Mrs Patricia Weighell   Tel/Fax 01642 712312
Herriot's Yorkshire, Moors & Dales Group
B&B Mrs Diana Greenwood   Tel 01748 822152
SC Lady Mary Furness   Tel 01609 748614
Ryedale Group
B&B Mrs Sarah Wood   Tel 01439 798277
SC Mrs Sally Robinson   Tel 01439 798221
Yorkshire Moors, National Park & Coast Group
Mrs Jean & Miss Lorraine Allanson
                            Tel/Fax 01723 859333

Yorkshire – Vale of York & the Wolds
Vale of York & the Wolds Group
Mrs Gill Lamb   Tel 01377 217204

Greater Manchester
South Pennines Group (as for *Lancashire*)

Cheshire
Cheshire Group
Mrs Sue Schofield   Tel 01606 852717

England's Heartland

Derbyshire
Derbyshire Dales & Dovedale Group
B&B Mrs Sylvia Foster   Tel 01335 360346
SC Mrs Janet Hinds   Tel 01335 344504
Peak District Group
Mrs Joy Lomas   Tel/Fax 01629 540250
E-mail: joy.lomas@btinternet.com

Nottinghamshire
Sherwood Forest/Nottinghamshire Group
B&B Mr Esme Stubbs   Tel 0115 963 2310
SC Mrs Anne Lamin   Tel 0115 926 8330

Lincolnshire
Lincolnshire Group
Mrs Gill Grant   Tel 01673 842283

Shropshire
Shrewsbury, Ironbridge & Shropshire Group
Mrs Mary Kennerly   Tel/Fax 01939 270601
South Shropshire Group
Mrs Christine Price   Tel/Fax 01547 530249

Staffordshire
Peak District Group (as for *Derbyshire*)
Staffordshire Group
Mrs Christine Shaw   Tel/Fax 01538 702830

Leicestershire
Leicestershire Group
Mrs Janet Clarke   Tel 0116 260 0472

Herefordshire
Herefordshire Group
B&B Mrs Elizabeth Godsall   Tel 01531 670408
Herefordshire Group (cont)
SC Mrs Judy Wells   Tel 01568 797347
                            Fax 01568 797366

Worcestershire
Worcestershire Group
B&B Mrs Helen Hirons   Tel/Fax 01562 777533
SC Mrs Sarah Goodman   Tel 01299 896500
                            Fax 01299 896065

Gloucestershire
Cotswolds & Royal Forest of Dean Group
Mrs Barbara Scudamore   Tel/Fax 01242 602344

Warwickshire
Warwickshire Group
Miss Deborah Lea — Tel 01295 770652
Fax 01295 770632
Mobile 07775 626458

Northamptonshire
Northamptonshire Group
Mrs Heather Jefferies — Tel 01327 703302

Cambridgeshire
Cambridgeshire Group
Mrs Jean Wiseman — Tel/Fax 01763 838263

Norfolk
Norfolk & Suffolk Group
B&B Mrs Carrie Holl — Tel/Fax 01508 550260
SC Mrs Margaret Langton — Tel/Fax 01473 652210
E-mail: keith.larrington@farmline.com

Suffolk
Norfolk & Suffolk Group (as for *Norfolk*)

South & South East England

Bedfordshire
Bedfordshire Group
B&B Mrs Alison Knowles — Tel/Fax 01442 866541
SC Mrs Ruth Pibworth — Tel 01234 711655
Fax 01234 711855

Oxfordshire
Thames Valley Group
Mrs Jean Kinch — Tel 01367 870279

Buckinghamshire
Thames Valley Group (as for *Oxfordshire*)

Hertfordshire
Hertfordshire Group
Mrs Alison Knowles — Tel/Fax 01442 866541

Essex
Essex Group
Mrs Delia Douse — Tel/Fax 01371 851021

Isle of Wight
Isle of Wight Group
Mrs Judy Noyes — Tel 01983 852582

Surrey
Sussex & Surrey Group
Mrs Gill Hill — Tel 01306 730210

Kent
Kent Group
Mrs Corrine Scutt — Tel 01233 740596

England's West Country

Bath & North East Somerset
Bath & Wells Group
Mrs Elizabeth Parsons — Tel 01934 515704
Bath & Wiltshire Group
Mrs Julie McDonough — Tel 01225 891750

Somerset
Exmoor Coast & Country Group
Mrs Penny Webber — Tel/Fax 01643 705244
Exmoor National Park Group
B&B Mrs Elaine Goodwin — Tel/Fax 01398 331400
SC Mrs Abigail Humphrey — Tel/Fax 01398 323616
Somerset Group
B&B Mrs Jane Sedgman — Tel 01458 223237
Fax 01458 223276
E-mail: lowerfarm@kingweston.demon.co.uk
SC Mrs Liz Smith — Tel/Fax 01823 490828
E-mail: robhembrows@btinternet.com

North Devon
Exmoor National Park Group (as for *Somerset*)
Friendly Farms of West Devon Group
Mrs Jenny King — Tel 01837 851647
Fax 01837 851410
Heart of Devon Group
Mrs Anne McLean Williams — Tel/Fax 01398 331312
North Devon Coast & Country Group
B&B Mrs Pat Burge — Tel 01598 710275
SC Mrs Ruth Ley — Tel 01769 572337

Wiltshire
Bath & Wiltshire Group
(as for *Bath & North East Somerset*)

Dorset
Dorset Group
B&B Mrs Rachel Geddes — Tel 01300 320812
Fax 01300 321402
Mobile 07974 796370
SC Mrs Kathy Jeanes — Tel/Fax 01258 820022
Heart of Dorset Group
Mrs Rosemary Coleman — Tel 01305 848252
Fax 01305 848702

South, East & West Devon
Dartmoor & South Devon Group
Mrs Anne Barons — Tel/Fax 01404 841651

Friendly Farms of West Devon Group
(as for *North Devon*)
Heart of Devon Group
(as for *North Devon*)
Moor to Shore in Devon Group
Mrs Anne Barons   Tel/Fax 01404 841651

Cornwall
Cornish Farm Holidays Group
Mrs Barbara Sleep   Tel/Fax 01566 782239

Wales

Isle of Anglesey
Isle of Anglesey Group
Mrs Sarah Astley   Tel 01248 470276
E-mail: sarahastley@zetnet.co.uk

Snowdonia – Mountains & Coast
Heart of Snowdonia Group
Mrs Paula Williams   Tel/Fax 01766 590281
Llyn Peninsula Group
Mrs Elizabeth Evans   Tel 01286 831184
Snowdonia Group
Mrs Jane Llewelyn Pierce   Tel/Fax 01248 670147
Croeso Nant Conwy
Mrs Eirian Ifan   Tel 01690 710261
Croeso Cader Idris Group
Mrs Deilwen Breese   Tel/Fax 01654 791235

The North Wales Coast & Borderlands
Croeso Dyffryn Clwyd
Mrs Elsie Jones   Tel 01824 703142

Ceredigion, Cardigan Bay
Ceredigion Group
Mrs Eleri Davies   Tel/Fax 01570 493313
Heart of Cardigan Group
Mrs Carole Jacobs   Tel/Fax 01239 851261

Mid Wales, Lakes & Mountains
Brecon Group
Mrs Mary Adams   Tel/Fax 01874 636505

Montgomeryshire – Heart of Wales Group
Mrs Joyce Cornes   Tel 01938 810791
Radnor Group
Mrs Gill Morgan   Tel/Fax 01547 550219

Pembrokeshire
Pembrokeshire Group
Mrs Vivienne Lockton   Tel/Fax 01994 419327

Carmarthenshire
Carmarthenshire Group
Mrs Marian Lewis   Tel 01550 720410
    Fax 01550 720262

Wye Valley & Vale of Usk
Monmouthshire Group
Mrs Sue Proctor   Tel/Fax 01633 893284

Northern Ireland

County Londonderry
County Londonderry Group
Mrs Heather Torrens   Tel/Fax 028 2955 8245

County Tyrone
County Tyrone Group
Mrs Louie Reid   Tel 028 8284 1325
    Fax 028 8284 0019

County Fermanagh
County Fermanagh Group
Mrs Mary Isobel Fawcett   Tel 028 6632 2725
    Fax 028 6632 5822

County Armagh
County Armagh Group
Mrs Elizabeth Kee   Tel/Fax 028 3887 0081

County Down
County Down Group
Miss Esther Kerr   Tel 028 4062 6270/624251
    Fax 028 4062 624251

Established 1957

Host & Guest Service
Central reservation service for

The Farm Holiday Bureau
For overseas visitors

**Easy and convenient method to book
your farm holiday accommodation**

Directions and maps supplied with your booking
Itineraries arranged if you require more than one location

103 Dawes Road London SW6 7DU
Tel: 020 7385 9922 Fax 020 7386 7575
E-mail: farm@host-guest.co.uk
Web: http:www.host-guest.co.uk

The British Incoming Tour Operators Association

European contacts

For information on farm holidays in various countries in Europe please contact the following:

GERMANY

Arbeitsgemeinschaft für Urlaub auf dem Bauernhof in der Bundesrepublik Deutschland e.V.
Godesberger Allee 142-148
53175 BONN
☎ [49] 228 81 98 220
Fax [49] 228 81 98 231

Deutsche Landwirtschafts gesellschaft
Eschborner Landstraße 122
60489 FRANKFURT
☎ [49] 69 247 880
Fax [49] 69 247 88 110

BELGIUM

Gîtes de Wallonie
Rue de Millénaire, 53
6941 VILLERS SAINTE GERTRUDE
☎ [32] 86 49 95 31
Fax [32] 86 49 94 07

FINLAND

Lomarengas
Malminkaari 23
00700 HELSINKI
☎ [358] 0 351 61 321
Fax [358] 0 351 61 370

FRANCE

Fédération Nationale des Gîtes de France
56, rue Saint Lazare
75009 PARIS
☎ [1] 49 70 75 75
Fax [1] 49 70 75 76

Agriculture et Tourisme
Assemblée Permanente des Chambres d'Agriculture
9, avenue George V
75008 PARIS
☎ [1] 47 23 55 40
Fax [1] 47 23 84 97

HUNGARY

Association of Village Farm Houses
Szoboszalai u. 2-4
1126 BUDAPEST
☎ [36] 1 155 533 312
Fax [36] 1 155 18 57

Hungarian Federation of Rural Tourism
Klauzal Ter 5
1072 BUDAPEST
☎/Fax [36] 1 268 05 92

ICELAND

Icelandic Farm Holidays
Hafnarstraeti 1
101 REYKJAVIK
☎ [354] 562 36 40
Fax [354] 562 36 44

IRELAND

Irish Farm Holidays
2 Michael Street
LIMERICK
☎ [353] 61 400 700
☎ [353] 61 400 707
Fax [353] 61 400 771

Irish Country Holidays
Rural Development Centre
ATHENRY CO GALWAY
☎ [353] 91 44 473
Fax [353] 91 44 296

ITALY

Agriturist
C. SO Vittorio Emmanuelle, 101
00186 ROMA
☎ [39] 66 85 23 42
Fax [39] 66 85 24 24

LUXEMBOURG

Association pour la Promotion du Tourisme
Rural au Grand-Duché du Luxembourg
c/o Centrale Paysanne
2980 LUXEMBOURG
☎ [352] 48 81 61
Fax [352] 40 03 75

PORTUGAL

Privetur
Nucleo Regional Do Minho E Litoral Norte
Largo das Pereiras
4990 PONTE DE LIMA
☎/Fax [351] 58 741 493

ROMANIA

Antrec
National Association of Rural, Ecological, Cultural, Tourism
B. P. 22-559
BUCAREST
☎/Fax [40] 1 222 83 22

Bran Imex
Bran Jud. Brasov
Str. dr. A. Stoian 395
☎ [40] 68 23 66 42
☎ [40] 1 666 59 48
Fax [40] 68 15 25 98

SLOVAKIA

Slovensky Zväz Vidieckej
Turistiky A Agroturistiky
Trencianska 55
82101 BRATISLAVA
☎ [42] 7 215 800/209
Fax [42] 7 214 903

SPAIN

Red Andaluza de Alojamientos Rurales
Apartado Correos 2035
04080 ALMERIA
☎ [34] 50 26 50 18
Fax [34] 50 27 04 31

SWEDEN

The Sweddish University of Agricultural Sciences
Ala Box 7013
75007 UPPSALA
☎ [46] 18 67 19 12
Fax [46] 18 67 19 80

SWITZERLAND

Verein "Ferien auf dem Bauernhof"
Feierlenhof
8595 ALTNAU
☎/Fax [41] 71 695 2372

Further information

These official tourist organisations will be happy to supply you with further general information on their areas.

National Tourist Organisations

English Tourism Council
Thames Tower, Black's Road, Hammersmith, London W6 9EL
☎ 020 8563 3000

Northern Ireland Tourist Board
St Anne's Court, 59 North Street, Belfast BT1 1NB
☎ 028 9023 1221

Scottish Tourist Board
23 Ravelston Terrace, Edinburgh EH4 3EU
☎ 0131 332 2433

Wales Tourist Board
Brunel House, 2 Fitzalan Road, Cardiff CF2 1UY
☎ 029 2049 9909

Regional Tourist Boards

Cumbria Tourist Board
(covering the county of Cumbria)
Ashleigh, Holly Road, Windermere, Cumbria LA23 2AQ
☎ 015394 44444

Northumbria Tourist Board
(covering Durham, Northumberland, Tees Valley and Tyne & Wear)
Aykley Heads, Durham DH1 5UX
☎ 0191 375 3000

North West Tourist Board
(covering Cheshire, Greater Manchester, High Peak District of Derbyshire, Lancashire and Merseyside)
Swan House, Swan Meadow Road, Wigan Pier, Wigan WN3 5BB
☎ 01942 821222

Yorkshire Tourist Board
(covering East Riding of Yorkshire, North Lincolnshire, North East Lincolnshire, North Yorkshire, South Yorkshire and West Yorkshire)
312 Tadcaster Road, York, North Yorkshire YO2 2HF
☎ 01904 707961

Heart of England Tourist Board
(covering Derbyshire, Gloucestershire, Herefordshire, Leicestershire, Northamptonshire, Nottinghamshire, Rutland, Shropshire, Staffordshire, Warwickshire, West Midlands and Worcestershire)
Woodside, Larkhill, Worcester WR5 2EZ
☎ 01905 763436

East of England Tourist Board
(covering Bedfordshire, Cambridgeshire, Essex, Hertfordshire, Lincolnshire, Norfolk and Suffolk)
Toppesfield Hall, Hadleigh, Suffolk IP7 5DN
☎ 01473 822922

London Tourist Board
(covering the Greater London area)
6th Floor, Glen House, Stag Place, London SW1E 5LT
Written enquiries only.

West Country Tourist Board
(covering Bath & North East Somerset, Bristol, Cornwall, Devon, North Somerset, Somerset, South Gloucestershire, Isles of Scilly, Western Dorset and Wiltshire)
60 St David's Hill, Exeter EX4 4SY
☎ 01392 425426

Southern Tourist Board
(covering Berkshire, Buckinghamshire, Eastern Dorset, Hampshire, Isle of Wight and Oxfordshire)
40 Chamberlayne Road, Eastleigh, Hampshire SO50 5JH
☎ 023 8062 0006

South East England Tourist Board
(covering Kent, East Sussex, Surrey and West Sussex)
The Old Brew House, Warwick Park, Tunbridge Wells, Kent TN2 5TU
☎ 01892 540766

Britain On-Line
Information about all aspects of holidaying in Britain can be found on the British Tourist Authority Website: www.visitbritain.com

Tourist Information Centres

 There are over 800 Tourist Information Centres (TICs) throughout the UK and they are there for you to use both before your holiday and during your holiday. Look in your local telephone directory under 'Tourist Information' to find your nearest TIC, or for details of any TIC in England call Scoot™ on 0800 192 192. TICs can provide details about local attractions, events and accommodation and many will even be able to book it for you. Look out for the information sign.

Index to farms

Key

B&B	Bed & Breakfast
SC	Self-Catering
C&C	Camping & Caravanning
B/CB	Bunkhouse/Camping Barn
(C)	Colour Advertisement

SCOTLAND Area/Farm		Page no.	Accessibility category	Caravans and/or camping	Working farm (p=participation)	Stabling/grazing for visiting horses	En suite available	Business people welcome	Meeting room (capacity)	Gift tokens accepted
Aberdeen & Grampian										
B&B	Bandora	58			✔		✔	✔		✔
	Haddoch Farm	58			✔			✔	✔(6)	✔
	Milton of Grange Farmhouse	58			✔		✔	✔		
	The Palace Farm	58			✔P		✔	✔		✔
SC	Upper Crichie	59			✔			✔		
Angus & City of Dundee										
B&B	Blibberhill Farm	68			✔P		✔	✔	✔(10)	✔
	Purgavie Farm	68		✔	✔	✔	✔	✔	✔(10)	✔
	Wemyss Farm	68			✔P	✔	✔	✔	✔(12)	✔
SC	Purgavie Farm	68	⌖	✔	✔	✔		✔	✔(10)	✔
Argyll, Isles, Loch Lomond, Stirling & Trossachs										
B&B	Drumfork Farm	61			✔		✔	✔		
	Inchie Farm	61			✔			✔		
	Lochend Farm (Carronbridge)	61			✔	✔		✔		✔
	Lochend Farm (Port of Menteith)	61			✔P		✔	✔		✔
	Lower Tarr Farm	61			✔		✔	✔	✔(10)	✔
	Mains Farm	62			✔			✔		✔
	Shantron Farm	62			✔		✔	✔		✔
	Thistle-Doo	62		✔			✔			
	The Topps Farm	62			✔	✔	✔	✔		✔
	Trean Farm	62			✔		✔	✔	✔(6)	✔
	West Auchencarrach Farm	62			✔P		✔	✔		✔
	Wester Carmuirs Farm	63			✔			✔		✔
	West Plean	63		✔	✔P	✔	✔	✔	✔(12)	✔
	Woodcockfaulds Farm	63			✔		✔	✔		
SC	Edenbrook Cottage	63			✔P					
	Shemore Farm Cottage	63			✔			✔		✔
Ayrshire & Arran										
B&B	Dunduff Farm	80			✔P		✔	✔		
	Fisherton Farm	80			✔		✔	✔		
	Muirhouse Farm	80			✔		✔	✔	✔(8)	✔
	Shotts Farm	80			✔		✔	✔	✔(6)	✔
	South Whittlieburn Farm	80			✔P	✔	✔	✔	✔(9)	✔
SC	Bothy Cottage	81		✔	✔P		✔	✔		
	Fisherton Farm	81			✔			✔		
	Mill Cottage	81			✔P			✔		
Dumfries & Galloway										
B&B	Airds Farm	83			✔	✔	✔	✔		✔
	Blair Farm	83			✔		✔	✔		✔
	Burnside	83					✔	✔		✔
	Coxhill Farm	83			✔	✔	✔	✔		
	Ericstane	83			✔		✔	✔		
	Glengennet Farm	84			✔		✔	✔		✔
	Mains of Collin	84			✔P	✔	✔	✔		
	Nether Boreland	84			✔P	✔	✔	✔	✔(8)	✔
	Rascarrel Cottage	84			✔		✔	✔		✔
SC	Aldermanseat Cottage	84			✔					✔
	Upper Barr Farm	85			✔		✔	✔		✔

SCOTLAND Area/Farm	Page no.	Accessibility category	Caravans and/or camping	Working farm (p=participation)	Stabling/grazing for visiting horses	En suite available	Business people welcome	Meeting room (capacity)	Gift tokens accepted
Perthshire									
B&B									
Blackcraigs Farm	65			✔		✔	✔		✔
Fingask Farm	65			✔	✔	✔	✔		
Letter Farm	65			✔P		✔	✔		✔
SC Laighwood Holidays	65			✔			✔		✔
Strathearn Holidays	66			✔	✔		✔		
West Cottage	66			✔			✔		
Scottish Borders									
B&B									
Birkenside Farm	87			✔		✔	✔	✔(12)	
Cockburn Mill	87			✔P		✔	✔		✔
Lyne Farm	87			✔P	✔		✔	✔(12)	✔
Over Langshaw Farm	87			✔P		✔	✔		✔
Plum Braes Barn	87			✔	✔	✔	✔	✔(10)	✔
Thirlestane	88			✔		✔	✔	✔(8)	✔
Wiltonburn Farm	88			✔P	✔	✔	✔	✔(8)	✔
SC Ashieburn Lodge	88	🚶		✔P			✔		✔
Bailey Mill	88	♿		✔P	✔		✔	✔(20)	✔
Cockburn Mill	88			✔P			✔		✔
Hutlerburn Cottage	89			✔P	✔		✔		
Plum Braes Barn	89			✔	✔		✔	✔(10)	✔
Rowan Tree Cottage	89			✔			✔		✔
Roxburgh Newtown Farm	89	🚶		✔	✔		✔		✔
Thirlestane Farm Cottages	89			✔			✔		✔

ENGLAND County/Farm		Page no.	Accessibility category	Caravans and/or camping	Working farm (p=participation)	Stabling/grazing for visiting horses	En suite available	Business people welcome	Meeting room (capacity)	Gift tokens accepted
Derbyshire										
B&B	Bank Top Farm	151		✔	✔	✔	✔	✔		
	Beechenhill Farm	151			✔		✔	✔	✔(10)	✔
	Beeches Farmhouse (C)	151				✔	✔	✔	✔(12)	
	Chevin Green Farm	151		✔			✔			✔
	Cote Bank Farm	151			✔P	✔	✔	✔		✔
	Dannah Farm Country House (C)	152			✔		✔	✔	✔(20)	✔
	Lydgate Farm	152			✔		✔	✔		✔
	Mercaston Hall	152		✔	✔	✔	✔	✔	✔(12)	✔
	Middlehills Farm	152		✔	✔P		✔	✔	✔(25)	✔
	The Old Bake & Brewhouse	152		✔	✔		✔	✔		✔
	Park View Farm	152			✔		✔	✔		✔
	Shallow Grange (C)	153		✔	✔P	✔	✔	✔	✔(15)	
	Shirley Hall	153			✔		✔	✔		✔
	Throwley Hall Farm	153			✔P	✔	✔	✔		
	Wolfscote Grange Farm	153		✔	✔	✔	✔	✔		
	Yeldersley Old Hall Farm	153			✔		✔	✔		✔
SC	Beechenhill Cottage & The Cottage by the Pond	154	♿		✔		✔	✔	✔(10)	✔
	Briar, Bluebell & Primrose Cottages	154			✔			✔		✔
	Burton Manor Farm Cottages (C)	154					✔	✔		
	Chapelgate Cottage	154			✔			✔		✔
	Chevin Green Farm	154		✔				✔		✔
	The Chop House	155			✔			✔		✔
	Cote Bank Farm Cottages	155			✔P	✔		✔		✔
	Cruck & Wolfscote Cottages	155		✔	✔	✔		✔		✔
	The Hayloft	155		✔	✔P	✔		✔		✔
	Honeysuckle & Brook Cottages	155			✔			✔		✔
	Honeysuckle, Jasmine & Clematis Cottages	155	♿	✔	✔P			✔	✔(25)	✔
	The Old House	156			✔P	✔		✔		✔
	Old House Farm Cottage	156			✔P			✔		✔
	Plattwood Farm Cottage	156			✔		✔	✔	✔(8)	✔
	Shatton Hall Farm Cottages	156			✔	✔		✔		✔
	Throwley Moor Farm & Throwley Cottage	156			✔P	✔				✔
Devon										
B&B	Beera Farm	304			✔P	✔	✔	✔	✔(8)	✔
	Berry Farm	304			✔		✔	✔		✔
	Buckyette Farm	304					✔			
	Burton Farm	304			✔P		✔	✔	✔(50)	✔
	Callisham Farm	304			✔		✔	✔		
	Catshayes Farm	305			✔P			✔	✔(10)	
	Colcharton Farm	305			✔P			✔	✔(12)	
	Combas Farm (C)	282		✔	✔		✔	✔		✔
	Combe Farm	305			✔P		✔	✔		
	Coombe Farm (Countisbury)	282			✔	✔	✔	✔	✔(20)	✔
	Coombe Farm (Kingsbridge)	305			✔P		✔			✔
	Court Barton Farmhouse	305			✔P		✔	✔	✔(25)	✔
	Crannacombe Farm	305			✔P	✔		✔		✔

ENGLAND County/Farm	Page no.	Accessibility category	Caravans and/or camping	Working farm (p=participation)	Stabling/grazing for visiting horses	En suite available	Business people welcome	Meeting room (capacity)	Gift tokens accepted
Dorset (cont)									
Old Dairy Cottage	301			✔	✔		✔		✔
Orchard End	302			✔			✔		
Park Farm	302		✔	✔p	✔		✔		
Rudge Farm Cottages	302	♿		✔					✔
Top Stall	302	♿		✔p	✔				✔
Westover Farm Cottages	302			✔			✔		
White Cottage	302			✔p			✔		
Durham									
B&B									
East Mellwaters Farm	112		✔	✔p	✔	✔	✔	✔(20)	✔
Greenwell Farm	112			✔p	✔	✔	✔	✔(35)	✔
Holywell Farm	112			✔p	✔				✔
Lands Farm	112			✔	✔	✔	✔		
Low Cornrigg Farm	112			✔p	✔	✔	✔	✔(12)	
Low Urpeth Farm	113			✔		✔	✔		✔
Rokeby Close Farm	113			✔		✔	✔	✔(10)	
Rose Hill Farm	113			✔p	✔	✔	✔		✔
Wilson House	113			✔		✔	✔		✔
SC									
Arbour House Bungalow & Cottage	113		✔	✔			✔		
Bail Hill	114			✔p			✔		✔
Brackenbury Leases Farm	114			✔			✔		
Bradley Burn Cottages	114	🚶	✔	✔			✔		✔
Browney Cottage	114			✔p			✔		✔
Buckshott Farm Cottage	114			✔p			✔		
Greenwell Hill Stables & Byre	114			✔p	✔	✔	✔	✔(35)	✔
High House Farm Cottages	115			✔p	✔		✔		✔
Katie's Cottage	115			✔		✔	✔		✔
North Wythes Hill	115			✔p			✔		✔
Romaldkirk Cottages (C)	115			✔p			✔		
Sandycarr Farm Cottage	115			✔	✔				✔
Stonecroft	115			✔p	✔		✔		✔
West Cottage	116		✔	✔p	✔	✔	✔		
Westfield Cottage	116			✔p					
East Yorkshire									
B&B									
Clematis House	130			✔	✔	✔	✔		
Eastgate Farm Cottage	131				✔	✔	✔		
High Belthorpe	132		✔	✔	✔		✔		✔
High Catton Grange	132			✔	✔	✔	✔		✔
Kelleythorpe Farm	132			✔	✔	✔	✔	✔(10)	✔
West Carlton	136		✔	✔p	✔	✔	✔	✔(12)	✔
The Wold Cottage	137		✔	✔p	✔	✔	✔	✔(14)	✔
SC									
The Cottage	138			✔			✔		✔
Field House	139			✔	✔		✔		✔
Trout Inn Cottage	140			✔		✔	✔	✔(6)	
East Sussex									
B&B									
Funnells Farm	259			✔p	✔	✔	✔	✔(6)	
Moonshill Farm	259		✔	✔	✔	✔	✔	✔	
Ousedale House	259					✔	✔	✔(25)	✔
The Stud Farm	259			✔	✔	✔	✔		✔

ENGLAND County/Farm		Page no.	Accessibility category	Caravans and/or camping	Working farm (p=participation)	Stabling/grazing for visiting horses	En suite available	Business people welcome	Meeting room (capacity)	Gift tokens accepted
Gloucestershire (cont)										
	Court Close Farm	197			✔			✔		
	Coxhorne Farm	197			✔			✔		
	Folly Farm Cottages	197		✔	✔			✔	✔(300)	
	Manor Farm Cottages	197		✔	✔P	✔	✔	✔	✔(10)	✔
	Old Mill Farm	198			✔	✔		✔		
	The Old Stables	198			✔		✔	✔		
	Warrens Gorse Cottages	198			✔					
	Westley Farm Cottages	198		✔	✔P		✔	✔		
Greater Manchester										
B&B	Boothstead Farm	143			✔			✔		✔
	Needhams Farm	143		✔	✔		✔	✔		
SC	Lake View	143			✔			✔	✔(5)	✔
	Shaw Farm	143			✔P		✔	✔		✔
Hampshire										
B&B	Brocklands Farm	247		✔	✔			✔	✔(14)	✔
	Compton Farmhouse	247			✔			✔		✔
	Hucklesbrook Farm	247		✔	✔	✔	✔	✔	✔(5)	
	Moortown Farm	247					✔	✔		
	Oakdown Farm Bungalow	247			✔			✔		✔
	Peak House Farm	248			✔		✔	✔		✔
	Pyesmead Farm	248			✔P	✔	✔	✔		✔
	Roughwood House	248				✔	✔	✔	✔(10)	
	Vine Farmhouse	248			✔		✔	✔		
SC	Beacon Hill Farm Cottages	248	♿		✔			✔		✔
	Meadow Cottage	249			✔	✔		✔		✔
	Owl Cottage	249		✔	✔P	✔		✔		✔
Herefordshire										
B&B	Amberley	179			✔		✔	✔		✔
	The Fieldhouse Farm	179			✔P	✔		✔		✔
	Garford Farm	179			✔	✔	✔	✔		
	Grafton Villa Farm	179		✔	✔P	✔	✔	✔	✔(25)	
	The Hill	179		✔	✔	✔	✔	✔		
	Hill Top Farm	180		✔	✔P		✔	✔		✔
	The Hills Farm	180			✔		✔			✔
	Home Farm	180		✔	✔			✔		
	Linton Brook Farm	180			✔		✔	✔	✔(12)	
	Moor Court Farm (C)	180			✔P		✔	✔	✔(20)	✔
	New House Farm	180			✔P	✔	✔	✔		✔
	Old Court Farm	181			✔P		✔	✔	✔(120)	✔
	Sink Green Farm	181			✔		✔	✔	✔(10)	
	Upper Gilvach Farm	181		✔	✔P		✔	✔		✔
	The Vauld House Farm	181			✔P		✔	✔		✔
	Warren Farm	181			✔	✔	✔	✔		
SC	Anvil Cottage	182	♿	✔	✔P	✔	✔	✔	✔(25)	✔
	Brooklyn	182			✔			✔		✔
	Carey Dene & Rock House	182			✔P					
	Grafton Cottage	182			✔P	✔				
	Home Farm	182			✔					
	Old Forge Cottage	183	♿		✔			✔	✔	

ENGLAND County/Farm		Page no.	Accessibility category	Caravans and/or camping	Working farm (p=participation)	Stabling/grazing for visiting horses	En suite available	Business people welcome	Meeting room (capacity)	Gift tokens accepted
North Somerset										
B&B	Icelton Farm	275			✔			✔		✔
North Yorkshire										
B&B	Ainderby Myers Farm	129			✔		✔	✔		✔
	Barn Close Farm	129			✔p	✔	✔	✔		✔
	Bay Tree Farm	122			✔		✔	✔		✔
	Beech Tree House Farm	129			✔p			✔		✔
	Bondcroft Farm	122			✔	✔	✔	✔		
	Bushey Lodge Farm	122			✔		✔	✔		
	Carr House Farm	129		✔	✔		✔	✔		✔
	Church Farm (Hubberholme)	122			✔		✔	✔		✔
	Church Farm (Scackleton)	129			✔p		✔	✔	✔	
	Crag Farm	130			✔p	✔	✔			
	Croft Farm	130			✔	✔	✔	✔		✔
	Cuckoo Nest Farm	130			✔		✔	✔	✔(6)	✔
	Dimple Wells	130					✔	✔		
	Dromonby Hall Farm	130		✔	✔	✔	✔	✔		
	Easterside Farm	131			✔	✔	✔	✔		✔
	Elmfield Country House	131					✔	✔	✔(30)	
	Fowgill Park Farm	123					✔	✔		
	Gatehouse Farm	123			✔	✔	✔	✔		✔
	Goose Farm	131			✔		✔	✔	✔(6)	✔
	The Grainary	131	♿	✔	✔p	✔	✔	✔	✔(20)	
	Graystone View Farm	123			✔p		✔	✔		✔
	Harker Hill Farm	131					✔	✔		
	High Force Farm	132			✔	✔	✔	✔		✔
	Island Farm	132			✔	✔	✔	✔	✔(10)	
	Killerby Cottage Farm	132			✔		✔	✔		✔
	Knabbs Ash	123			✔		✔	✔		✔
	Lane House Farm	123			✔		✔	✔		✔
	Laskill Farm Country House (C)	133		✔	✔p	✔	✔	✔	✔(15)	
	Lovesome Hill Farm	133	⚐	✔	✔p	✔	✔	✔		✔
	Low Gill Farm	133			✔	✔	✔	✔		✔
	Mallard Grange	124			✔		✔	✔		✔
	Manor Farm	133		✔	✔	✔	✔	✔		✔
	Manor House Farm	133			✔p	✔	✔	✔		✔
	Mill Close Farm	133			✔p	✔	✔	✔	✔(8)	
	Mount Pleasant Farm	134	⚐		✔p	✔	✔	✔	✔(12)	
	Newgate Foot Farm	134		✔	✔p		✔	✔	✔(16)	
	North Pasture Farm	124			✔p		✔	✔		
	Oldstead Grange	134			✔p		✔	✔	✔(10)	✔
	Oxnop Hall	134			✔	✔	✔	✔		
	Plane Tree Cottage Farm	134			✔		✔	✔		
	Rains Farm	134			✔		✔	✔	✔(15)	
	Redmire Farm	124			✔		✔			✔
	Rokeby Close Farm	135			✔		✔	✔	✔(10)	
	Rose Cottage Farm	135			✔		✔	✔		
	St George's Court	124			✔	✔	✔	✔	✔(10)	
	Seavy Slack	135			✔p		✔	✔		✔
	Sinnington Manor	135			✔p	✔	✔	✔	✔(8)	✔

ENGLAND County/Farm		Page no.	Accessibility category	Caravans and/or camping	Working farm (p=participation)	Stabling/grazing for visiting horses	En suite available	Business people welcome	Meeting room (capacity)	Gift tokens accepted
North Yorkshire (cont)										
	Studley House	135		✔	✔		✔	✔		✔
	Summer Lodge Farm	135			✔	✔	✔	✔		✔
	Sunley Court	136			✔	✔	✔	✔		
	Throstle Gill Farm	136			✔	✔		✔		
	Valley View Farm	136		✔	✔		✔	✔		✔
	Walburn Hall	136			✔		✔	✔		✔
	Whashton Springs Farm	136			✔		✔	✔	✔(12)	✔
SC	Bellafax Holiday Cottage	137			✔					
	Blackmires Farm	137								
	Cawder Hall Cottages	125	🚶					✔		✔
	Clematis, Well & Shepherd's Cottages	137		✔	✔P			✔		
	The Coach House	137			✔			✔		✔
	Cow Pasture Cottage	138		✔	✔			✔		
	Croft Farm Cottage	138			✔	✔		✔		✔
	Dove Cottage	138			✔			✔		✔
	Dukes Place	125		✔	✔	✔		✔		✔
	Easthill House & Gardens	138			✔P		✔	✔		
	The Farm Cottage	138			✔	✔		✔		✔
	Farsyde Farm Cottages	139		✔	✔	✔		✔		✔
	Layhead Farm Cottages	126			✔P			✔		
	Lund Farm Cottage	139		✔	✔P		✔	✔		✔
	Maypole Cottage	126			✔P			✔		✔
	Mount Pleasant Farm	139			✔P	✔		✔		✔
	Old Spring Wood Lodges	126	🚶					✔		✔
	Pasture Field House	139			✔			✔		✔
	Rains Farm	139			✔			✔	✔(15)	
	Rhuss Cottage	140			✔P			✔		
	Stanhow Farm Bungalow	140			✔	✔		✔		✔
	Street Head Farm	126			✔P	✔	✔	✔	✔(10)	
	Sunset Cottages (C)	140			✔P			✔		
	Trip's Cottage	126			✔			✔		✔
	Two Hoots Cottage	127			✔P			✔		
	Valley View Farm	140		✔	✔	✔	✔	✔		✔
	Wayside Farm	140			✔	✔	✔	✔		✔
	Wren Cottage	141			✔			✔		✔
C&C	Pond Farm	141		✔	✔					✔
	Woodhouse Farm Caravan Park	127		✔	✔P	✔				
B/CB	West End Outdoor Centre	127			✔		✔	✔	✔(30)	
Northamptonshire										
B&B	Dairy Farm	206			✔	✔	✔	✔	✔(10)	
	The Elms	206			✔			✔		✔
	Meadows Farm	206			✔		✔	✔		✔
	Pear Tree Farm	206		✔	✔P		✔	✔	✔(8)	
	Spinney Lodge Farm	206			✔		✔	✔		
	Walltree House Farm	207			✔		✔	✔	✔(14)	✔
	Wold Farm	207			✔		✔	✔	✔(10)	✔
SC	Granary Cottage	207			✔		✔			
	Rye Hill Country Cottages	207			✔P			✔	✔(20)	✔

ENGLAND County/Farm		Page no.	Accessibility category	Caravans and/or camping	Working farm (p=participation)	Stabling/grazing for visiting horses	En suite available	Business people welcome	Meeting room (capacity)	Gift tokens accepted
Northumberland (cont)										
	Outchester & Ross Farm Cottages (C)	110			✔			✔		
	Shepherd's Cottage	110			✔P	✔		✔		✔
	Titlington Hall Farm (C)	110			✔	✔		✔		
C&C	Barmoor South Moor	110		✔	✔					
Nottinghamshire										
B&B	Blue Barn Farm	158			✔		✔	✔		✔
	Far Baulker Farm	158		✔	✔	✔	✔	✔		✔
	Forest Farm	158			✔		✔	✔		✔
	Jerico Farm	158			✔		✔	✔	✔(6)	
	Manor Farm	158			✔			✔		
	Norton Grange Farm	159			✔			✔	✔(12)	
SC	Blue Barn Cottage	159			✔			✔		✔
	Foliat Cottages	159			✔			✔	✔(8)	✔
	Foxcote Cottage	159			✔			✔		
	The Granary	159			✔			✔		
	The Mews	160			✔			✔		✔
Oxfordshire										
B&B	Banbury Hill Farm	231		✔	✔	✔	✔	✔		✔
	Bould Farm	231			✔	✔	✔	✔		✔
	Bowling Green Farm	231			✔		✔	✔		✔
	Chimney Farmhouse	231			✔		✔	✔		✔
	Crown Farm	231		✔	✔	✔	✔	✔		
	Ducklington Farm	232		✔	✔		✔	✔		✔
	Fords Farm	232			✔			✔		
	Hill Grove Farm	232			✔		✔	✔		✔
	Morar	232					✔	✔		✔
	North Farm	232			✔		✔	✔		
	Oakfield	232			✔			✔		
	The Old Farmhouse	233					✔	✔	✔(8)	✔
	Potters Hill Farm	233			✔		✔	✔		✔
	Rectory Farm (C)	233			✔		✔	✔	✔(10)	✔
	Sor Brook House Farm	202		✔		✔	✔	✔	✔(12)	
	Vicarage Farm	233				✔		✔		
	Weston Farm	233			✔		✔	✔		✔
SC	Banbury Hill Farm	234		✔	✔	✔	✔	✔		
	Coxwell House	234			✔	✔	✔	✔		✔
	Hill Grove Cottage	234			✔			✔		✔
	Lower Court Cottages	234			✔	✔		✔		
	Rectory Farm Cottages (C)	234			✔			✔		✔
	Walltree House Farm	235			✔			✔	✔(14)	✔
Shropshire										
B&B	Acton Scott Farm	166			✔		✔	✔		✔
	Avenue Farm	166			✔	✔	✔	✔		
	Brereton's Farm	166			✔		✔			✔
	Broughton Farm	166		✔	✔P	✔	✔	✔		✔
	Church Farm	166					✔	✔	✔(12)	✔
	Cox's Barn	167			✔		✔	✔		
	Grove Farm	167			✔	✔	✔			✔

ENGLAND County/Farm		Page no.	Accessibility category	Caravans and/or camping	Working farm (p=participation)	Stabling/grazing for visiting horses	En suite available	Business people welcome	Meeting room (capacity)	Gift tokens accepted
Somerset (cont)										
	Orchard Farm	276			✔		✔	✔	✔(10)	✔
	Prockters Farm	276			✔		✔	✔	✔(10)	
	Springfield Farm	276			✔	✔	✔	✔		
	Temple House Farm	277			✔		✔	✔		
	Tor Farm Guesthouse	277			✔		✔	✔	✔(20)	
	Townsend Farm	277			✔		✔	✔		✔
	Wood Advent Farm (C)	277		✔	✔	✔	✔	✔	✔(30)	
SC	Cockhill Farm & Orchard Farm	277			✔		✔	✔		✔
	The Courtyard	278			✔			✔		✔
	Cutthorne Farm	278			✔			✔		✔
	Double-Gate Farm	278	♿		✔			✔		✔
	Hale Farm	278			✔			✔		
	Halsdown Farm	278			✔P			✔		
	Highercombe Farm	278			✔P	✔		✔		✔
	Hindon Farmhouse Cottage	279			✔P	✔	✔	✔	✔(12)	
	Holly Farm	279	♿		✔			✔		✔
	Leigh Holt (C)	279	♿		✔		✔	✔	✔(12)	
	Liscombe Farm	279			✔	✔	✔	✔		
	Lois Barns	279			✔P		✔	✔		
	Pear Tree Cottage	279		✔	✔			✔		
	Pigsty, Cowstall & Bullpen Cottages	280			✔			✔		✔
	The Tallet	280			✔P			✔		✔
	Westermill Farm	280	♿	✔	✔P	✔	✔	✔		✔
	Wintershead Farm	280				✔	✔	✔		
C&C	Oxenleaze Farm Caravans (C)	280		✔	✔			✔		
Staffordshire										
B&B	Brook House Farm	174			✔P		✔	✔		
	Ley Fields Farm	174			✔P		✔	✔		
	Manor House Farm	174			✔			✔	✔(8)	
	Oulton House Farm	174			✔		✔	✔		✔
	Parkside Farm	174			✔			✔	✔(10)	
	Ribden Farm	175			✔		✔	✔		
SC	Keepers Cottage	175			✔			✔	✔(8)	
	Rosewood Holiday Flats	175			✔	✔		✔		
	Swallows Nest	175			✔		✔	✔		✔
	Upper Cadlow Farm	175			✔P	✔		✔		
Suffolk										
B&B	Brighthouse Farm	219		✔	✔		✔	✔		
	Broad Oak Farm	219			✔P		✔	✔		✔
	Church Farm (Bradfield Combust)	219			✔		✔	✔		
	Church Farm (Corton)	219		✔	✔		✔	✔		
	College Farm	219			✔		✔	✔	✔(10)	✔
	Colston Hall	220			✔		✔	✔	✔(12)	✔
	Earsham Park Farm	220			✔P	✔	✔	✔	✔(20)	✔
	East Farm	220			✔	✔	✔	✔		✔
	Elmswell Hall	220			✔		✔	✔	✔(12)	✔
	Grange Farm	220		✔	✔		✔	✔		✔
	Grove Farm House	220			✔			✔		✔
	The Hall	221			✔			✔		✔

ENGLAND County/Farm	Page no.	Accessibility category	Caravans and/or camping	Working farm (p=participation)	Stabling/grazing for visiting horses	En suite available	Business people welcome	Meeting room (capacity)	Gift tokens accepted
Suffolk (cont)									
Hall Farm (C)	221			✔		✔	✔		
Laurel Farm	221			✔P		✔	✔	✔	✔
Moat Farm	221			✔P	✔		✔		
Oak Farm	221			✔	✔		✔		
Park Farm	221			✔		✔	✔	✔(20)	✔
Priory Farm	222		✔	✔	✔		✔		
Red House Farm	222		✔	✔		✔	✔		✔
Rendham Hall	222					✔	✔	✔(10)	
Rumburgh Farm	222			✔		✔	✔		
Shrublands Farm	214			✔		✔	✔		
South Elmham Hall	222			✔		✔	✔	✔(20)	✔
Uggeshall Manor Farm	222			✔	✔	✔	✔		✔
Watersmeet	223			✔			✔		✔
Woodlands Farm	223					✔	✔		
SC Baylham House Farm Annexe & Flat	223			✔P			✔		✔
Bluebell, Bonny & Buttercup	223			✔			✔	✔(20)	✔
The Bothy	223		✔	✔		✔	✔		✔
Colston Cottage	224			✔			✔	✔(6)	✔
The Cottage	224		✔	✔			✔		✔
The Court	224		✔	✔		✔	✔		
The Granary	224		✔	✔	✔		✔		
Hall Farm Cottage	224			✔			✔		✔
Old Wetherden Hall Cottage	224			✔			✔		
Rowney Cottage	225			✔			✔		
Stable Cottages & The Granary	225	♿		✔		✔	✔		✔
Tom, Dick & Harry	225			✔		✔	✔		✔
Surrey									
B&B Borderfield Farm	254		✔	✔P	✔				
Bulmer Farm	254	🚶	✔	✔	✔	✔	✔	✔(12)	✔
Sturtwood Farm	254			✔		✔	✔		
SC Badgersholt & Foxholme	254	🚶	✔	✔	✔		✔	✔(12)	✔
Warwickshire									
B&B The Byre	200			✔	✔	✔	✔		✔
Church Farm	200	🚶		✔	✔	✔	✔	✔(10)	
The Coach House	200			✔		✔	✔		
Crandon House	200			✔		✔	✔	✔(12)	
Frankton Grounds Farm	200			✔	✔	✔	✔		
Hill Farm (Priors Hardwick)	201		✔	✔P		✔	✔		✔
Hill Farm (Radford Semele)	201		✔	✔		✔	✔		✔
Holland Park Farm	201			✔P	✔	✔	✔	✔(10)	
Lawford Hill Farm	201			✔		✔	✔		✔
Lower Watchbury Farm	201			✔		✔	✔	✔(8)	
Packington Lane Farm	201		✔	✔P		✔	✔		
The Poplars	202			✔		✔	✔		✔
Shrewley Pools Farm	202			✔P	✔	✔	✔	✔(6)	✔
Sor Brook House Farm	202		✔		✔	✔	✔	✔(12)	✔
Tallet Barn	202			✔		✔			✔
Walcote Farm	202			✔		✔	✔		✔

ENGLAND County/Farm	Page no.	Accessibility category	Caravans and/or camping	Working farm (p=participation)	Stabling/grazing for visiting horses	En suite available	Business people welcome	Meeting room (capacity)	Gift tokens accepted
Warwickshire (cont)									
Whitchurch Farm	202		✔	✔		✔	✔	✔(12)	✔
SC Furzen Hill Farm Cottages	203			✔			✔		✔
The Granary	203						✔		✔
Hipsley Farm Cottages	203	♿		✔			✔		✔
Knightcote Farm Cottages	203	♿		✔P		✔	✔	✔(100)	✔
Lawford Hill Farm	203			✔			✔		
Little Biggin	204			✔			✔		✔
Piggery Cottages	204			✔		✔	✔	✔(12)	
West Sussex									
B&B Compton Farmhouse	256			✔			✔		✔
Goffsland Farm	256		✔	✔P	✔		✔	✔(10)	✔
Manor Farm	256			✔	✔	✔	✔		
New House Farm	256			✔	✔	✔	✔		✔
SC Black Cottage	257			✔			✔		✔
Byre Cottages	257			✔		✔	✔		
West Yorkshire									
B&B Brow Top Farm	122			✔P			✔		✔
Far Laithe Farm	123			✔		✔	✔		
Scaife Hall Farm	124			✔P		✔	✔		✔
SC Bottoms Farm Cottages	125			✔	✔		✔		✔
Brontë Country Cottages	125			✔P	✔		✔		✔
Heather & Bilberry Cottages	125			✔P			✔		✔
Meadow, Field & Daisy Cottages	126						✔		✔
Well Head Cottage	127								✔
Wiltshire									
B&B Ashen Copse Farm	291			✔		✔	✔	✔(6)	✔
Beeches Farmhouse	267					✔	✔		✔
Boyds Farm	291			✔		✔	✔	✔(8)	✔
Church Farm (Hartham Park)	291		✔	✔	✔	✔	✔		✔
Church Farm (Steeple Ashton)	291			✔			✔	✔(12)	✔
Fairfield Farm	267			✔		✔	✔		✔
Friday Street Farm	291			✔P		✔	✔		✔
Frying Pan Farm	292			✔		✔	✔		✔
Great Ashley Farm	292			✔	✔	✔	✔		✔
Hatt Farm	292			✔		✔	✔		✔
Higher Green Farm	292			✔P			✔		✔
Home Farm	292			✔		✔	✔		✔
Leighfield Lodge Farm	292			✔		✔	✔		✔
Lovett Farm	293			✔P		✔	✔		✔
Lower Foxhangers Farm	293		✔	✔		✔	✔	✔(12)	✔
Lower Stonehill Farm	293			✔		✔	✔		✔
Manby's Farm	194					✔	✔		✔
Manor Farm (Corston)	293			✔		✔	✔	✔(8)	✔
Manor Farm (Wadswick)	293			✔	✔	✔	✔		✔
Oakfield Farm	293			✔		✔	✔		✔
Oakwood Farm	195			✔			✔		✔
Olivemead Farm	294			✔	✔		✔		✔
Pickwick Lodge Farm	294			✔	✔	✔	✔		✔
Saltbox Farm	269			✔		✔	✔		✔

WALES Region/Farm		Page no.	Accessibility category	Caravans and/or camping	Working farm (p=participation)	Stabling/grazing for visiting horses	En suite available	Business people welcome	Meeting room (capacity)	Gift tokens accepted
North Wales										
B&B	Bach-y-Graig	349			✔P		✔	✔		✔
	Bryn Celynog Farm	337			✔		✔	✔		✔
	Bryncoch	349			✔	✔	✔	✔		✔
	Bryn Tirion Farm	337		✔	✔		✔	✔		
	Cae'r Efail Farm	337					✔	✔		
	Cwm Hwylfod	337			✔P		✔	✔		✔
	Cynfal Farm	346			✔P		✔	✔		
	Drws y Coed	335		✔	✔P		✔	✔		✔
	Erw Feurig Farm	337			✔		✔	✔		
	Frongoch Farm	338					✔			✔
	Fron-Haul	349		✔	✔P	✔	✔	✔	✔(25)	✔
	Gogarth Hall Farm	346			✔P	✔	✔	✔		✔
	Gwrach Ynys	338					✔	✔		
	Hendre Wen Farm	338			✔P		✔			
	Horseman's Green Farm	349			✔	✔		✔	✔(14)	✔
	Llainwen Ucha	349			✔					✔
	Llannerch Goch	338					✔	✔		✔
	Llwydiarth Fawr	335			✔	✔	✔	✔	✔(10)	✔
	Llwyn Goronwy	338			✔		✔	✔		
	Llwyn Mafon Isaf	338		✔	✔P		✔	✔		
	Mill House	350					✔	✔		✔
	Mynydd Mwyn Mawr	335			✔P	✔	✔	✔		✔
	Nant-y-Glyn Isaf	339			✔P		✔	✔	✔(10)	
	Pengwern	339			✔		✔	✔	✔(6)	
	Plas Tirion Farm	339			✔P	✔	✔	✔		✔
	Rhydydefaid Farm	339			✔		✔	✔		✔
	Tan-yr-Eglwys Farm	339			✔P		✔			
	Tyddyn Chambers	350			✔P	✔	✔	✔		✔
	Tyddyn Du	339			✔P	✔	✔	✔		✔
	Tyddyn Du Farm	340			✔P		✔	✔		✔
	Tyddyn Iolyn	340					✔	✔		✔
	Ty-Mawr Farm	340			✔P	✔	✔	✔	✔(10)	✔
	Ystumgwern Hall Farm	340	♿		✔		✔	✔		✔
SC	Bach-y-Graig	350			✔P		✔	✔		✔
	Bryn Beddau	340			✔	✔		✔		
	Caerwych Farmhouse	341			✔	✔				
	Cartref	341						✔		
	Cefnamwlch	344			✔					
	Chwilog Fawr	341		✔	✔P	✔		✔		✔
	Cynfal Farm Cottages	346			✔P		✔			
	Dol-Llech	341			✔P			✔		
	Dwyfach Cottages	341			✔		✔	✔		✔
	Garth-y-Foel	341		✔	✔	✔				✔
	Gogarth Hall Farm	346			✔P	✔		✔		✔
	The Granary	350						✔		✔
	Gwynfryn Farm	344	🚶	✔	✔P					✔
	Hafod & Hendre	342			✔P	✔		✔		✔
	The Old Coach House	342						✔		✔
	Penmaenbach Farm Cottages	347	♿		✔		✔	✔	✔(80)	✔

WALES Region/Farm	Page no.	Accessibility category	Caravans and/or camping	Working farm (p=participation)	Stabling/grazing for visiting horses	En suite available	Business people welcome	Meeting room (capacity)	Gift tokens accepted
North Wales (cont)									
Plas y Nant Cottages (C)	347			✔P			✔		✔
Tai Gwyliau Tyndon Holiday Cottages	344						✔		✔
Tyddyn Isaf	350			✔			✔		✔
Ynys	342	🚶	✔		✔	✔		✔	
Mid Wales									
B&B									
Beili Neuadd	358		✔	✔	✔	✔	✔		✔
Blaencar Farm	360			✔P	✔	✔	✔		✔
Broniwan	352			✔P	✔	✔	✔	✔(4)	
Broughton Farm	166		✔	✔P	✔	✔	✔		✔
Bryn y Fedwen Farm	360			✔	✔	✔	✔		✔
Cefnsuran Farm	358			✔P	✔	✔	✔		✔
Cwmcamlais Uchaf Farm	360			✔		✔	✔		✔
Cwmllwynog	355			✔P		✔	✔		✔
Dol-Llys Farm	355		✔	✔P		✔	✔		✔
The Drewin Farm	355		✔	✔	✔	✔	✔		✔
Dyffryn Farm	355			✔P		✔	✔		
Ffordd-Fawr Farmhouse	360	🚶	✔	✔		✔	✔	✔(10)	
Gaer Farm	358			✔P	✔	✔	✔		
The Hayloft	360			✔P		✔	✔		
Highgrove Farm	361			✔	✔	✔	✔		✔
Holly Farm	358			✔		✔	✔	✔(10)	
Little Brompton Farm	355		✔	✔	✔	✔	✔		✔
Llettyderyn	356	🚶		✔P	✔	✔	✔		
Llwyn yr Eos	352			✔P	✔	✔	✔		
Lodge Farm	361			✔		✔	✔		✔
Lower Gwerneirin Farm	356			✔		✔	✔		✔
Moat Farm	356			✔	✔	✔	✔		✔
Neuadd Farm	358			✔	✔	✔	✔		
Pant-Teg	352					✔	✔		
Pentre Farm	352	🚶		✔		✔	✔		✔
Trehenry Farm	361			✔P		✔	✔		✔
The Wenallt Farm	361			✔P	✔	✔	✔	✔(20)	✔
Wervil Grange Farm	352		✔	✔P	✔	✔	✔	✔(12)	✔
SC Gwydre Cottage	361			✔P			✔	✔(6)	
Pant-Teg Studio Cottage	353				✔	✔	✔		
Penmaenbach Farm Cottages	356	♿		✔		✔	✔	✔(80)	✔
Red House	356			✔P		✔	✔		
Trehenry Farm	362			✔P		✔	✔		
Upper Bettws Farm	362			✔P	✔		✔		
B/CB Broughton Bunkhouse	172		✔	✔P	✔				✔
South & West Wales									
B&B Barley Villa	364					✔	✔		
The Bower Farm	364		✔	✔P	✔	✔	✔	✔(10)	
Brunant Farm	364			✔		✔	✔		
Castell Pigyn Farm	371					✔	✔		✔
Cilpost Farm	364			✔		✔	✔		✔
Cwmgwyn Farm	371			✔		✔			✔
Dolau Isaf Farm	364		✔	✔P		✔	✔		✔

WALES Region/Farm	Page no.	Accessibility category	Caravans and/or camping	Working farm (p=participation)	Stabling/grazing for visiting horses	En suite available	Business people welcome	Meeting room (capacity)	Gift tokens accepted
South & West Wales (cont)									
East Hook Farm	365			✔p		✔	✔		
East Llanteg Farm	365			✔p	✔	✔	✔	✔(6)	
Erw-Lon Farm	365			✔p		✔			
Fron Isaf	365			✔p					
Gilfach Goch Farmhouse	365					✔	✔		✔
Hardwick Farm	373			✔p		✔	✔		✔
Knock Farm	365			✔	✔	✔	✔		
Knowles Farm	366		✔	✔	✔	✔	✔	✔(10)	✔
Lochmeyler Farm (C)	366			✔p	✔	✔	✔	✔(50)	✔
Lower End Town House	366			✔p	✔	✔	✔	✔(8)	✔
Lower Haythog	366			✔p		✔	✔		✔
Pentre-Tai Farm	373		✔	✔p	✔	✔	✔		✔
Penygraig Farm	366			✔	✔	✔	✔		✔
Penylan Farm	373			✔		✔	✔		
Plas-y-Brodyr	366			✔p		✔	✔		✔
Poyerston Farm	367			✔p		✔	✔		✔
Skerryback	367			✔	✔	✔	✔		✔
Torbant Farmhouse	367					✔	✔		✔
Trebersed Farm	371			✔p		✔	✔		✔
Trepant Farm	367			✔		✔	✔		✔
Ty-Cooke Farm	373		✔	✔			✔	✔(12)	
The Wenallt Farm	373			✔p	✔	✔	✔	✔(20)	✔
Werngochlyn Farm	374			✔p	✔	✔	✔		
SC Blackmoor Farm	367			✔			✔		
Broomy & Purkis Cottages	374			✔			✔		
Castell Pigyn Cottage	368						✔		✔
Croft Farm & Celtic Cottages	368	⟁	✔	✔p			✔	✔(15)	✔
Gilfach Goch Cottages	368						✔		✔
Granary & Coach House	374			✔p			✔		✔
Gwarmacwydd	368			✔p			✔		✔
Hopyard Farm	374				✔		✔		
PantglasCottage	371		✔	✔p	✔		✔	✔(6)	✔
Parsons Grove	374						✔		
Rogeston Cottages	368			✔p			✔		
The Stable & Coach House	368			✔			✔	✔(12)	
Ty Geifr	369			✔p	✔		✔		✔

NORTHERN IRELAND County/Farm		Page no.	Accessibility category	Caravans and/or camping	Working farm (p=participation)	Stabling/grazing for visiting horses	En suite available	Business people welcome	Meeting room (capacity)	Gift tokens accepted
Antrim										
B&B	Beechgrove	380		✔	✔p	✔	✔	✔	✔(25)	✔
	Brown's Country House	380	↟					✔	✔		
	Carnside Farm Guest House	380		✔	✔p		✔			✔
	Cullentra House	380	↟		✔		✔	✔		✔
	Neelsgrove Farm	380			✔		✔	✔		✔
	Sprucebank	381			✔		✔	✔		
	Valley View	381	♿		✔p	✔	✔	✔		
Armagh										
B&B	Ballinahinch House	387		✔	✔p	✔	✔	✔	✔(30)	✔
Down										
B&B	Beechhill Farm	389		✔	✔p			✔		✔
	Greenlea Farm	389		✔	✔p	✔		✔		
	Mourneview	389	↟		✔		✔	✔	✔(10)	
	Pheasants' Hill Country House	389			✔p	✔	✔	✔	✔(6)	✔
	Sharon Farmhouse	389	↟		✔p			✔		✔
	Trench Farm	390			✔	✔		✔		✔
	Wyncrest	390			✔		✔	✔		✔
Fermanagh										
B&B	Riverside Farm	385		✔	✔	✔	✔	✔		✔
Londonderry										
B&B	Brown's Country House	380	↟				✔	✔		
	Drumcovitt House	377			✔		✔	✔	✔(20)	✔
	Greenhill House	377					✔	✔	✔(14)	✔
	Heathfield Farm	377			✔p		✔	✔	✔(15)	
	Killeague Farm	377			✔p	✔	✔	✔	✔(10)	✔
	Killennan House	377			✔		✔	✔		✔
	Tullans Farm	378		✔	✔p		✔	✔	✔(50)	
SC	Drumcovitt Cottages	378	♿		✔		✔	✔	✔(20)	✔
Tyrone										
B&B	Greenmount Lodge	383	♿		✔	✔	✔	✔	✔(70)	✔

You don't
have to
be a farmer
to insure
with us.

NFU **Mutual**

The best in the country.